DIGITAL SOCIOLOGIES

Edited by

Jessie Daniels

Karen Gregory

Tressie McMillan Cottom

First published in Great Britain in 2017 by

Policy Press	North American office:
University of Bristol	Policy Press
1-9 Old Park Hill	c/o The University of Chicago Press
Bristol BS2 8BB	1427 East 60th Street
UK	Chicago, IL 60637, USA
t: +44 (0)117 954 5940	t: +1 773 702 7700
e: pp-info@bristol.ac.uk	f: +1 773-702-9756
www.policypress.co.uk	e: sales@press.uchicago.edu
	www.press.uchicago.edu

© Policy Press 2017

British Library Cataloguing in Publication Data
A catalogue record for this book is available from the British Library.

Library of Congress Cataloging-in-Publication Data
A catalog record for this book has been requested.

ISBN 978-1-4473-2901-5 paperback
ISBN 978-1-4473-2900-8 hardcover
ISBN 978-1-4473-2903-9 ePub
ISBN 978-1-4473-2904-6 Mobi
ISBN 978-1-4473-2902-2 ePdf

Permission to use the opening quote on p 195, Chapter 13, from Athique, A. (2013) *Digital media and society: An introduction*. Malden, MA: Polity Press, was granted by Polity Press.
Cover design by Soapbox Design
Front cover: image kindly supplied by istock
Printed and bound in Great Britain by CPI Group (UK) Ltd, Croydon, CR0 4YY
Policy Press uses environmentally responsible print partners

Contents

CONTENTS

Acknowledgements

Any book is a collaborative effort, but a large edited one such as this is several orders of magnitude more so. Thus, we have many debts that can only be repaid with acknowledgements and heartfelt thanks. We began this work together as part of the Eastern Sociological Society Annual Meeting, and are indebted to Emily Mahon who handled all the administrative logistics of our first digital sociology convening with skill and unflappable grace. In an austere environment in academic publishing, when few publishers are willing to take on an edited volume, we found a rare exception in Policy Press. We also owe many thanks to the editorial team, Victoria Pittman, Rebecca Tomlinson, and Dawn Rushen, who persevered with us over changes in department, institution, residence, and country to make this book a reality. Of course, this volume would not exist without all the authors who shared their work with us. They are part of a growing community of scholars who are producing rigorous research and intellectual fellowship for digital sociologists. We are especially grateful to Saskia Sassen for writing the Preface to this volume, and encouraging us in this work.

We also have individual debts to pay here. Karen Gregory thanks Jessie Daniels and Tressie McMillan Cottom. Not only are they tireless collaborators who are committed to public, digital scholarship, but they are also scholars who make the often-overlooked labor of coordination and editing pleasurable. Thank you for your energy and your vision for the field of digital sociology. I also thank my colleagues at the University of Edinburgh for their support as I worked on this collection, particularly Kate Orton-Johnson and Nick Prior.

Tressie McMillan Cottom acknowledges that it takes a village to raise a book. I am fortunate. My village is large. I will only be able to thank a few by name, but I am in debt to everyone who nurtured me, my ideas, and this process to fruition. First, thank you to my co-editors, Jessie Daniels and Karen Gregory. More than collaborators on this project, they have been partners-in-crime organizing the Digital Sociology mini-conference at the Eastern Sociological Society meeting. I must also thank the Sociology Department and Laney Graduate School at Emory University for their generous conference and research support. Similarly, my colleagues at the Microsoft Research Social Media Collective were great supports, even going so far as to orchestrate my first face-to-face meeting with Jessie Daniels and contributor Kishonna Gray. In particular, Nancy Baym has been a great champion. I would also like to acknowledge my research assistant Olivia Pryor for her help with logistics. And I must thank my colleagues at Virginia Commonwealth University's Sociology Department, where the entire team has embraced digital sociology as praxis, policy, and professional commitment to social justice.

Jessie Daniels would also like to thank Karen Gregory and Tressie McMillan Cottom, who are that rare combination of powerful intellectuals and good company. They have made the work on this volume a joy. I would also like to thank all my colleagues in the Department of Sociology at Hunter College. While this book was in process, I moved departments from public health to sociology, where work such as this is more legible. I am grateful to have colleagues who appreciate the contribution that digital sociology is making to the discipline.

Preface

Saskia Sassen

Across time, people and social conditions have complicated the straightforward implementation of technologies. The mix of specific materialities of daily life and people's cultures of use is not easily predictable. Such a mix can unsettle or disrupt the best technical designs – and has done so in past eras and in today's digitally driven world. This holds at many levels – from advanced complex systems to daily applications of standard technologies.

Guided by the enormous variety of sociological issues, research on the technical can function as a lens: it allows us to understand a range of diverse interactions between users (whether systems, organizations, or people) and digital technologies (more precisely, the design and implementation of these technologies). Thus, a sociological approach can, for instance, bring to the fore a feature of electronic *interactive* domains that remains insufficiently examined: it is that the technical properties of these domains deliver their utility to users through complex ecologies that include more, often much more, than the technical capacities in play. They include specific social and cultural variables. It is this intermediation that brings in the sociological, the political, the economic, the cultural, and more, into a technical space. An analysis that centers only on the technical capacity to communicate or interact in novel ways leaves out precisely that which the social sciences can add to the analysis. This brings to the fore a feature of electronic interactive domains that remains insufficiently examined: it is that the technical properties of these domains deliver their utility to users through complex ecologies that include more than the technical. Such ecologies include (a) "non-technological" variables – the social, the subjective, the political – all variables that characterize users more so than the technology; (b) the fact that these "non-technological" variables can and do shape technical developments but probably could do much more of this, especially by broadening the range of cultures and social differences present in this shaping; and they include (c) the particular cultures of use of different actors.

An example of the need to bring these variables into the picture is that of smart city development. In this case technology inputs are akin to infrastructure and are mostly run centrally; this is good for handling specific needs, mostly standardized, that concern both the buildings as such and people's needs. But it leaves users' capacities and at least some needs out of the picture. The user is reduced to choosing from pre-designed options with little if any chance to contribute to those choices (or to designs, or types of technical applications, and so on) and thereby have a sort of learning curve about the technical. In short, one key dimension of having a genuinely smart city is open-sourcing the pertinent systems.

A basic hypothesis in my work on the rise of the digital (including smart cities) has been that as we add intelligence to tools and systems, we must enable human intelligence to move as well in order to be part of it. This is not confined to programming. Critical are forms of knowledge that bring in the social, the cultural, and the political into the digital as it instantiates in diverse settings. If we do not introduce these, admittedly messy, components we delegate the making of knowledge *about* these technologies to the engineers and software designers. From the social perspective this would mean we simply fall back onto basic mechanizing, where the machine takes over and our role disappears or is routinized. Instead, we should recognize that at least some of these technologies, when used by people, can be constituted partly in social terms.

When we look at electronic interactive domains as part of larger ecologies, rather than as a purely technical condition, we make conceptual and empirical room for the broad range of social logics driving users and the diverse cultures of use through which the digital interactive space acquires meaning. Each of these logics and cultures activates an ecology. These activating features tend to be absent in much of today's technically driven analysis of digital capabilities and their implementation to address human needs (and whims). And herein lies a vast research and theorization agenda. The authors in this book contribute to fill this massive gap. They do so in both conceptual and applied ways. They introduce a variety of methods, concepts, research designs, and hypotheses that can enable social scientists to incorporate diverse types of situated knowledges, of human needs, of projects, and much more, in the analysis of digital instruments and digitized domains.

Notes on the authors

Stephen R. Barnard is an Assistant Professor of Sociology at St Lawrence University. His research interests focus on the sociology of new media, culture, and communication. His work has appeared elsewhere in *Journalism: Theory, Practice and Criticism*, *Studies in Media and Communications*, *Hybrid Pedagogy*, and *Cultural Studies and Critical Methodologies*.

Phillip Brooker is a Research Associate at the University of Bath, UK, working in social media analytics, with a particular interest in the exploration of research methodologies to support the emerging field. His background is in sociology, drawing especially on ethnomethodology and conversation analysis, science and technology studies, computer-supported cooperative work and human-computer interaction. Phillip has previously contributed to the development of Chorus (www.chorusanalytics.co.uk), a Twitter data collection and visualisation suite. He currently works on CuRAtOR (Challenging online feaR And OtheRing), an interdisciplinary project focusing on how "cultures of fear" are propagated through online "othering".

Scott Bulfin is Senior Lecturer in the Faculty of Education at Monash University, Australia, where he studies young people's use of digital media. Before coming to Monash, Scott was a secondary school English teacher. He can be found on Twitter @scottbulfin.

Adrian Cruz, PhD, is Assistant Professor of Sociology at the University of Massachusetts Lowell. He has published articles primarily on the struggle of Asian and Mexican farm workers in California. Cruz's most recent piece, published in *Social Movement Studies*, is titled "The Union within the Union: Filipinos, Mexicans, and the racial integration of the farm worker movement".

Harry T. Dyer (MRes) is a PhD candidate and Associate Tutor at the University of East Anglia, UK. He has published articles on identity presentation in social media and is currently finishing his PhD focusing on the effects of online site and app design on identity performances. Harry blogs at HarryTDyer.com and can be found on Twitter @HarryTDyer.

Jessie Daniels is Professor of Sociology and Critical Social Psychology at Hunter College and The Graduate Center, CUNY. She has published five books, including *White lies* (Routledge, 1997) and *Cyber racism* (Rowman & Littlefield, 2009), along with dozens of peer-reviewed journal articles. Some of her writing has been published in *The New York Times*. Daniels blogs at Racism Review (www.racismreview.com), and hangs out on Twitter (@JessieNYC). Around the edges of her day job, she writes memoirs.

Kishonna L. Gray is Assistant Professor in the School of Justice Studies, Eastern Kentucky University. Her work focuses on the intersecting oppressions experienced by women of color in Xbox Live, a virtual gaming community. Dr Gray's research and teaching interests incorporate an intersecting focus on marginalized identities (race, gender, class, sexuality, citizenship, etc) and new media. She has published in a variety of outlets including *Ada: A Journal of Gender, New Media, & Technology*, *New Review of Hypermedia and Multimedia*, *Crime, Media, Culture*, the *Bulletin of Science, Technology, & Society*, *Information, Communication, & Society*, and the *Journal of International and Intercultural Communication*. Her most recent book, *Race, gender, and deviance in Xbox live*, examines marginalized gamers in a virtual gaming community.

Karen Gregory, PhD, is a Lecturer in Digital Sociology at the University of Edinburgh, UK, where she directs the MA program in digital society. Her research explores the possibilities for solidarity in a digital economy and her writings have appeared in *Workplace: The Journal For Academic Labor*, *Women's Studies Quarterly*, *Women and Performance*, *Visual Studies*, *Contexts*, *The New Inquiry*, and *Dis Magazine*. You can find her on Twitter @claudiakincaid.

Yuliya Grinberg is a PhD candidate in anthropology at Columbia University. Her research investigates the historical and cultural conditions of possibility that have made meaningful work out of collecting digital data about one's life. Throughout she pays special attention to the aesthetics and language that mediate the cultural discourse on personal data, affecting the way these data sets are taken up, circulated, and debated. Yuliya is also a contributing editor to the CASTAC (Committee on the Anthropology of Science, Technology, and Computing) blog.

Benjamin Haber is a PhD candidate in sociology at The Graduate Center, CUNY and a Digital Fellow at The Center for the Humanities. He has published a number of articles on queer theory and digital media, including *The queer ontology of digital method* for WSQ's special issue on Queer Method. Haber recently organized the two-day conference, "Queer Circuits in Archival Times: Experimentation and Critique of Networked Data." Find him at benjaminhaber.net and on Twitter @benjaminhaber.

Theresa A. Hunt, PhD, is a University Lecturer in Humanities and Science, Technology and Society at New Jersey Institute of Technology in Newark. She holds an MA in English and PhD in Global Affairs, both from Rutgers University. Dr Hunt's current research investigates the use of gender, youth, and technology narratives in global activism, as well as the history of youth organizing in transnational social justice movements. Her work has appeared most recently in *Women's Studies International Forum*.

Trevor Jamerson is a PhD student at Virginia Tech currently teaching American Indian and African American Studies. His research interests include race and tourism studies, indigenous studies, and digital sociology. He is presently working on a review article for the *Sociology Compass* discussing intersections of critical race and tourism studies.

Jeffrey Alan Johnson, PhD, is a social theorist and Assistant Director of Institutional Effectiveness and Planning at Utah Valley University. He is, most recently, the author of several articles and a forthcoming monograph on information justice, and makes marginally relevant wisecracks on Twitter as @the_other_jeff.

Nicola F. Johnson, PhD, is Senior Lecturer and Deputy Head in the School of Education, Gippsland, in the Faculty of Education and Arts, Federation University, Australia. Nicola's research concerns internet over-use, the social phenomena of internet usage, technological expertise, the use of information and communication technologies within teaching and learning, and more recently, interventions with at-risk, regional students. Find her on Twitter @nfjnic.

Kazuyo Kubo, PhD, is an Assistant Professor at Lesley University. She is the author of "Desirable difference: The shadow of racial stereotypes in creating transracial families through transnational adoption" (2010) in *Sociology Compass*, and has had several articles published in *Sociology of Family*.

Deborah Lupton is a sociologist who has researched the social and cultural aspects of medicine and public health, parenting culture, the body, risk, fear of crime, digital technologies, the emotions, obesity politics, food, and HIV/AIDS. Her latest research focuses on critical digital health studies, big data cultures, the sociology of self-tracking, and digital sociology. She is the author/co-author of 14 books and over 130 articles and book chapters on these topics. Her latest books are *Medicine as culture* (3rd edn) (2012), *Fat* (2013), *Risk* (2nd edn) (2013), *The social worlds of the unborn* (2013), *The unborn human* (edited, 2013) and *Digital sociology* (2015). She blogs on sociological issues at 'This Sociological Life' and tweets as @DALupton.

Alexia Maddox, PhD, is a Research Librarian at Deakin University and research consultant at RMIT University. She is author of *Research methods and global online communities: A case study* (Routledge, 2015), and has published articles on the nexus between community, digital frontiers, and research methods. Maddox blogs at alexiamaddox.com and can be found on Twitter @alexiamadd.

Alison Mayne is an amateur textile maker and a doctoral researcher in women's crafting experiences at Sheffield Hallam University, UK. She is undertaking PhD research into experiences of wellbeing in amateur knit and crochet craftswomen who make alone but share in online yarn groups. She blogs at newbieresearcher.wordpress.com and can be found on Twitter @newbiephd.

Andrew McKinney is a PhD candidate in sociology at The Graduate Center, CUNY, a Fellow at The Graduate Center's Teaching and Learning Center, and a Community Facilitator at the City Tech OpenLab. His research centers on the digital labor of sport fandom specifically, and how digital media has changed political economy in general. You can find him on Twitter @andrewgmckinney.

Tressie McMillan Cottom, PhD, is an Assistant Professor of Sociology at Virginia Commonwealth University and Faculty Associate with Harvard University's Berkman Klein Center for Internet & Society. Her research on higher education, work, and technological change in the new economy has been supported by the Microsoft Research Network's Social Media Collective, The Kresge Foundation, the American Educational Research Association and the UC Davis Center for Poverty Research. Millions List, a leader in publishing, named her book *Lower ed: The troubling rise of for-profit colleges in the new economy* one of the most anticipated non-fiction books of 2016.

Monita H. Mungo is a sociologist who is sensitive about her sh★t. She is currently a Lecturer in the Department of Sociology and Anthropology at the University of Toledo, located in Ohio. Her research focuses on racial inequality, teaching and learning outcomes in post-secondary institutions, and the sociology of education. You can follow her on Twitter @MoMungo.

Selena Nemorin is a PhD Research Fellow in the Faculty of Education at Monash University, Australia. Her research interests include digital sociology, philosophy of technology, Maker education, surveillance and society, and brain-machine interfaces. Selena has worked previously at the University of Toronto on research projects exploring educational equity and inclusion, the experiences of internationally educated female teachers and their integration into K-12 schools, as well as human rights policies and procedures in post-secondary institutions. Follow her on Twitter @digiteracy.

Mikael Ottosson, PhD, is Associate Professor in Work Science at Lund University, Sweden. His research encompasses different topics such as craftsmanship in the Swedish glass industry, gender and nationalism, the Swedish marksman movement, and the moral economy of work. In recent years his research has focused on social norms in relation to the performance of work. He is currently conducting research on working time and the role of trust and loyalty in the Swedish labor market. His recent publications include *What the hell is a high standard?* (Time & Society, 2016) and *The construction and demonization of the lazybones* (Fast Capitalism, 2015).

Alexandrea J. Ravenelle is completing her dissertation, *Hustle: The lived experience of workers in the sharing economy* in the Sociology Department at The Graduate Center, City University of New York. Her work explores the lives of workers for Airbnb, Uber, Taskrabbit and Kitchensurfing.

Timothy Recuber, PhD, is a Visiting Assistant Professor in the Communication Department at Hamilton College. He is the author of *Consuming catastrophe: Mass culture in America's decade of disaster* (Temple University Press, 2016), and has published a variety of articles on digital culture and mass media.

Calle Rosengren, PhD, is Assistant Professor in Technology and Social Change at Lund University, Sweden. In a broad perspective his research examines working time, with a particular focus on the ongoing relations between new technologies, organizing structures, cultural norms, and work practices. He has published a variety of articles on working time in international journals, among others *Performing work: The drama of everyday working life* (2015).

Saskia Sassen is the Robert S. Lynd Professor of Sociology and Chair of the Committee on Global Thought, Columbia University (www.saskiasassen.com). She is the author of several books and the recipient of diverse awards and mentions, ranging from multiple doctor honoris causa to named lectures and being selected for various honors lists. Her latest book is *Expulsions: When complexity produces elementary brutalities* (Harvard University Press, 2014).

Neil Selwyn is a Professor in the Faculty of Education, Monash University, Australia. He previously worked at the Institute of Education, University College London, and before that, at Cardiff University's School of Social Sciences. Neil's research and teaching focuses on the place of digital media in everyday life, and the sociology of technology (non)use in educational settings. Neil has written extensively on a number of issues, including digital exclusion, education technology policy-making, and student experiences of technology-based learning. Follow him on Twitter @neil_selwyn.

Sanjay Sharma is Senior Lecturer in the Department of Social Sciences and Communications, Brunel University London, UK. He has published in the areas of race and representation, critical pedagogy, digital networks, and is the author of *Multicultural encounters* (Palgrave, 2002). His recent work explores social media, assemblages and affect, and online antagonisms. He is particularly interested in developing methodologies for exploring networked racism as an emergent phenomena. Sanjay is a founding editor of the open access journal *darkmatter*.

Miriam E. Sweeney is an Assistant Professor in the School of Library and Information Studies at the University of Alabama. Her research explores intersections of gender, race, and information technologies, particularly focusing on digital media and internet technologies. Dr Sweeney's current projects examine anthropomorphic computing interfaces, emojis, and virtual assistant technologies. She has related research interests in information ethics, digital labor, and social justice in information professions.

Francesca Tripodi is a PhD candidate in sociology at the University of Virginia researching how media interacts with society. Her dissertation focuses on how participatory media products (Wikipedia, Yik Yak, and Reality Television) shape community identity, a phenomenon she terms "integrated audiences." Updated research endeavors and publications can be found at her website, ftripodi.com

Kara van Cleaf, PhD, teaches media studies and sociology classes. Her work examines the relationship between digital media, motherhood, and feminism. She is a Visiting Lecturer at Monmouth University.

Apryl Williams is a PhD candidate and Diversity Fellow in the Sociology Department at Texas A&M University. She is the Associate Series Editor of *Emerald Studies in Media and Communications*, and has published several articles on race, selfies, and digital media.

Elizabeth Wissinger is Professor of Fashion Studies and Sociology at the Borough of Manhattan Community College (BMCC) and The Graduate Center (CUNY). Her book, *This year's model: Fashion, media, and the making of glamour* (NYU Press, 2015), examines how models and modeling popularized glamour labor, and the work on body and self to be even better and more interesting in person than one appears in one's selfies. Wissinger's current research focuses on how wearable technologies impact gender and embodiment.

Jonathan R. Wynn is an Assistant Professor of Sociology at the University of Massachusetts Amherst, and is the author of *Music/city: American festivals and placemaking in Austin, Nashville, and Newport* (University of Chicago Press, 2015) and *The tour guide: Walking and talking New York* (University of Chicago Press, 2011).

Introduction

Karen Gregory, Tressie McMillan Cottom, and Jessie Daniels

"The digital revolution is far more significant than the invention of writing or even of printing," Douglas Engelbart, an engineer and inventor of the computer mouse, speculated. While Engelbart's claim about the revolution may be up for debate, what is not in dispute is that digital media technologies are changing everyday life, social institutions, and even how we experience our embodied self. The array of digital media technologies, which often get lumped together as "the digital" or "the internet," are playing a central role in the unfolding transformation of society. Digital technologies are reshaping large-scale institutions such as government, finance, and education in ways that are still unfolding, at once embracing more openness and enacting more surveillance. Digital technologies are weaving their way into the quotidian, reconfiguring daily routines. We text "I love you" over morning coffee to someone as close as the next room, post a picture to Instagram in the morning on the way to work, type away at our laptops in the afternoon, and engage with our networks of "friends" and "followers" on platforms like Facebook and Twitter in the evening while we watch *Scandal* on broadcast television. Then, when we want to get away from it all, we explore vacation destinations on TripAdvisor and book a place to stay through Airbnb. With each mediated interaction, we leave a trail of digital debris tracked by a vast surveillance apparatus capable of generating so-called "big data" (Kitchin, 2014). The rise of ubiquitous computing, data generation, and data capture through digital media has ushered in an opportunity for reconceptualizing the working of our understanding of "the social."

The transformations and challenges of digital technologies offer a chance to reinvigorate the sociological imagination. The sociological imagination, as C. Wright Mills described it, is the task of comprehending the ways in which biography and history, the individual and society, intersect (Mills, 1959). The central task of sociologists, understanding this intersection of the individual and society, is being reconfigured just as our everyday lives, our institutions, and our sense of self is being re-worked in the digital era. A tension exists within this reconfiguration. Digital technologies simultaneously offer liberatory possibilities for destabilizing old hierarchies while at the same time they create mechanisms for retrenching well-established patterns of inequality, stratification, and domination. It is through the recognition of this tension that we have come to see the need for the critical practice of what we now call "digital sociology" (Wynn, 2009; Orton-Johnson and Prior, 2012; Carrigan, 2013; Marres, 2013; Lupton, 2014; Orton-Johnson et al, 2015). Digital sociology provides a lens through which to understand the individual and society after digitization.

Digitization is the process of converting information from analog into discrete units of data that can be more easily moved around, grouped together, and analysed. Moving, remixing, sharing, and circulating information is easier and faster when that information is digitized. Digitization is perhaps easier to understand if we consider what we mean when we use the common phrase "cut and paste." For generations of more senior scholars, "cut and paste" meant to take scissors, cut paper with paragraphs typed on them, rearrange their order, and then glue them to another sheet of paper, in analog fashion. For another generation of scholars who have come of age in a world where the internet has always existed, cut and paste has only ever meant the simple keyboard commands: ctrl+x, ctrl+v. Just as the ctrl+x, ctrl+v commands of cut and paste make it quicker and easier to move text around than typing, scissoring, re-arranging and pasting, other forms of digital activity allow for easier distribution and redistribution of text and all variety of media (Daniels and Thistlethwaite, 2016). While this example may seem trivial, the shift from analog to digital is not. The digitization of information has deep and wide implications for our ways of knowing, studying, and understanding the social world.

Digitization "makes possible new creative ways of imagining and doing sociology" (Marres, 2013). Such new and creative modes of thought and practice are currently happening across different subfields within sociology, which has tended to tuck media work into more established fields of sociological inquiry – such as the sociology of work and labor, the sociology of the family, the sociology of education, or more broadly conceived research in the sociology of race, class, and gender. In that regard, we understand that there will be no singular *digital sociology* methodology, nor a unified agenda. Critical analysis of digital media technology pervades and cuts across multiple subfields within sociology, hence, the plural you will find in the title of this volume, *Digital sociologies*. However, it is our hope that the works collected in this volume will begin to connect sociologists to each other and to a community of practice that will bear fruit in the form of fostering productive conversations between sociological theories and sociological methods that engage with digital media technologies, as well as a reconceptualization of the longstanding polarization of qualitative and quantitative theory and practice.

In practical terms, the examples of digital sociology in this volume are an illustration of "the opportunities which digital tools afford for rethinking sociological craft" (Carrigan, 2013). It is this reflexive practice that makes digital sociology an exciting pursuit, as Orton-Johnson, Prior and Gregory (2015) observe. It offers the opportunity to develop "inventive methods" (Lury and Wakeford, 2012). Digital sociology presents the opportunity to theorize the nature and shape of the social world, as we simultaneously explore and experiment with inventive approaches to craft, theory, and methods.

An (unnamed) history and now a tipping point

Digital sociology is inherently an interdisciplinary practice that draws from a long history of research done in internet studies, information and communication studies, media and cultural studies, the sociology of science and technology, surveillance studies, computer science, digital humanities, and computational social science (Orton-Johnson and Prior, 2013). And it is also a practice that continually reflects on the core concerns of sociology. Many of the social implications of the internet were articulated more than two decades ago by leading sociologists such as Castells, DiMaggio and colleagues, Sassen, Wajcman and Wellman (Wajcman, 1991, 2002; Castells, 1998; DiMaggio et al, 2001; Wellman, 2001; Sassen, 2002). Other sociologists have built digital tools to help us better understand the social world. For example, "Social Explorer," which enables users to dynamically map US Census data over specified time periods (Beveridge et al, 2008), and "NodeXL," which graphically displays people's social networks using data from their social media interactions (Hansen et al, 2010), are but two examples of digital sociology tools. Yet, the field of sociology to this point has no (sub)field of study in which to situate this work. Sociology, as Deborah Lupton observes, has only just begun to take account of the broader implications that the digital raises about the practice of sociology and social research itself (Lupton, 2014). As a discipline, sociology has been less concerned with redefining itself through its understanding of the digital, and has instead been content to cede this terrain to those working in communication, cultural and media studies, internet studies, library and information science, digital humanities, and data journalism. This period of ignoring the digital within sociology is coming to an end, particularly beyond the borders of the US.

Digital sociology is gaining traction as a field in Australia, Canada, and the UK, and to a lesser extent, in the US. As of this writing, the field of digital sociology is experiencing something of a tipping point. In 2013, the first academic book with the title "digital sociology" appeared (Orton-Johnson and Prior, 2013), then another in 2015 (Lupton, 2015). That same year, the editors of this volume organized the first-ever academic conference on digital sociology in New York, which brought together an international group of scholars from 11 countries. Two of the editors of this volume are leading the formation of sociology degree programs that focus on digital sociologies. At Virginia Commonwealth University, Tressie McMillan Cottom is faculty founder and also teaches a capstone course in critical theories of digital in the Sociology Department's Master of Science degree program. At the University of Edinburgh, Karen Gregory will lead a Master's program entitled "Digital Sociology". Such a program, while housed in a Department of Sociology, will foster interdisciplinary research and draw together work currently being done in science and technology studies, informatics and computer sciences, and the digital humanities. These courses and programs represent some of the ways that sociological inquiry of digital space, place, and problems are being institutionalized.

Throughout the volume we pay homage through citation practices to internet studies, computational social science, digital humanities, critical theory, feminist theory, and a widely interdisciplinary body of scholarship that has engaged the digital for quite some time. We also build on sociology's longstanding interest in technological change as a mechanism for social formation and conflict. This volume extends and builds on this work, opening new forms of inquiry that provide the necessary intellectual exchange for critical knowledge production that includes "not just the architecture of the internet but the social transformations that produce it and are produced by it" (McMillan Cottom, Chapter 14, this volume). These observations about a field in formation raise a set of additional questions: *Why digital sociology? Why digital sociology now?*

Why digital sociology?

Disciplines are "so last century," explains Cathy Davidson (Davidson, 2011). She foresees a future of higher education where disciplinary boundaries matter less and less. In the 21st-century university we are all interdisciplinary, she contends. Davidson is a prescient observer of the landscape of higher education and digital technologies, so she is very likely right about this. Given this trend, it is perhaps folly to set out to form an academic subfield, to, in effect, create a new discipline at a time when disciplines are *so last century*. Or perhaps this is a crucial form of intellectual activism (Collins, 2012). In our view, disciplines are here to stay for the foreseeable future because so much of our labor is organized within disciplinary boundaries. We cannot wait for an unspecified future date when we are beyond disciplines to consider how sociological insights can help us understand the digital world in which we live now. Our work of intellectual activism in forming digital sociology is also meant as an intervention in the broader discipline.

The sociology we were trained in grew out of a theoretical response to the transformations of the Industrial Revolution. If sociology is to continue to thrive as a field that is relevant to the concerns of the 21st century, it must offer a compelling theoretical understanding of the current revolution in digital media technologies (Castells, 1998; Sassen, 2002; Wajcman, 2002). If sociology expects to attract graduate students and the next generation of scholars, we have to offer some guidance on what sociological theory and research methods might have to offer in a digitally networked era. And, if we expect to engage undergraduate sociology students who have grown up immersed in digital media technologies, we would do well to offer them research that speaks to their lived experience with these technologies. And if we hope to address wider audiences beyond our peers in the academy and the students in our classrooms, we would do well to understand digital technologies (Stein and Daniels, 2017). Sociologists, beyond the desire to share their work with a wider audience, might want to engage with such tools to offer a critical understanding of what is happening in our contemporary, digitally mediated world. If sociologists do not, then those in other fields surely will.

The field of internet studies is well established and generative of a rich body of scholarship (Baym, 1999; Brock, 2005; Consalvo and Ess, 2011; Ess and Dutton, 2013). More than 10 years ago, internet studies had already experienced at least three "eras" (Wellman, 2004). A widely interdisciplinary field, internet studies is focused heavily on "the internet" as a mode of communication and related set of questions along with identity and community (Nakamura, 2002, 2009; Brock, 2005; Burgess and Green, 2013; Weller et al, 2013). In some ways, it may be useful to think of "internet studies" as similar to "area studies" in which scholars from many different disciplines focus on one geographical area. While we draw from this body of work, digital sociology is concerned first with social problems (social inequality, race, gender) and *then* with technology (Wajcman, 2002).

The digital humanities claims most of the research money and sets much of the agenda for how we think about digital media technologies in relation to teaching and digital tools for scholarship (Borgman, 2009; Gold, 2012). The traditional humanities disciplines – literature, philosophy, religion, languages, and musicology – are now often joined with history, linguistics, and semiotics as part of the digital humanities. Social sciences such as anthropology and sociology are sometimes included under the umbrella of digital humanities, as one co-editor heard a preeminent scholar exclaim at a recent talk, "we have a colonizer's view of what is included in the digital humanities – if you're doing digital work, it's digital humanities!" This joking reference suggests some of the quite serious critiques leveled at digital humanities (Koh and Risam, 2013). The cumulative effect of the colonial tendencies of the digital humanities is that it ends up with two primary contributions: the development of new tools, such as those that do the work of data mining digital archives, and the preservation of a predominantly white, male canon of literature (McPherson, 2012; Golumbia and Koh, 2013; Golumbia, 2014). Of course, not all digital humanities projects focus on tools nor valorize the work of a white male canon, and this is not an epistemological move unique to that field. Sociology has its own history of ignoring scholars of color, such as W.E.B. DuBois, in order to canonize a white male elite (Morris, 2015). Countering such erasure, digital humanities scholar Jessica Marie Johnson creates media (text/audio/visual) and curates archives relating to black history, black futures, and social justice, and does important work that speaks to the potential of digital humanities (Johnson, 2016). Johnson's work is situated within a broader effort among black feminist scholars to counter the erasure of black women from the digitized record and to expand the scope of digital humanities. Our work here takes this as a starting point throughout, most especially in pieces by Gray about the platform Twitch.com (see Part III) and McMillan Cottom about for-profit educational institutions (see Part II). By conceptualizing digital sociology as starting from a black feminist standpoint, rather than bringing it in later to transform extant work, we hope to offer a more fruitful line of inquiry.

In many ways, the early and ardent embrace of the digital by disciplines within the humanities was a response to threats (perceived or actual) to cuts in humanities programs and funding. To look at the funding infrastructure of the Office of Digital Humanities division of the National Endowment for the Humanities (NEH), this was a shrewd, strategic, and successful move on the part of forward-thinking humanities scholars of 20 years ago. The NEH Office of Digital Humanities has funded a project called "W.E.B. DuBois in cyberspace" to digitize and make available all of DuBois' papers (Sternfeld, 2015). This important work of preservation and access is at the heart of digital humanities. Work that opens up knowledge and makes it accessible to scholars anywhere is part of the profound changes affecting what it means to be a scholar today (Daniels and Feagin, 2011; Daniels and Thistlethwaite, 2016). And such tools and open access to knowledge are part of what makes digital sociology possible. But, a reader may ask, is it necessary?

Scholars in already established fields engaged in the study of the internet may fairly critique sociology for being the proverbial "Johnny come lately" to the digital party. Sometimes the late-comer to the party is the one who brings a new bottle of wine, changes the music, and gets people dancing. Our hope is that related fields will see digital sociology as just this kind of late comer, arriving with more libations and a new beat to enliven the digital party. But lateness is relative. From the perspective of internet studies and digital humanities we may be late, but within sociology, we are right on time, because the need for digital sociology is now.

Digital sociology: a field in formation

"I'm a huge fan of sociology," says Patricia Hill Collins. This is perhaps not surprising coming from a former president of the American Sociological Association (ASA). She has her reservations about the field, however:

> At the same time, I think that the field of sociology could do a better job of embracing its existing strengths. Sociology is a border discipline that touches political science, philosophy, some of the natural sciences, anthropology, and literary criticism. Yet sociologists often do not see sociology's interdisciplinary inclinations as a strength. Ironically, as the world itself becomes more interdependent and interconnected, it needs interdisciplinary analyses that can make sense of these relationships. Sociologists are well positioned for interdisciplinary collaboration.... (2013: 107)

It is this inclination toward interdisciplinarity that Collins identifies that gives rise to digital sociology. "Digital sociology is best understood as an interdisciplinary practice," writes Noortje Marres (2013). And this in line with how we think of the work collected here: making a contribution to digital sociology while drawing on an interdisciplinary practice. This collection is a response, in many ways, to Collins' observation that as we become more interdependent and more interconnected, we need an interdisciplinary sociology to make sense of the networked world. A wide array of pressing social issues, and contemporary attempts to address them, make digital sociology necessary. "One Laptop per Child" and "Apps for Good" are just two of the many non-profit organizations that have emerged that seek to use digital technologies to solve intractable social problems. To understand such endeavors and the problems they are trying to address, we need scholars who are trained to understand digital technologies and who have sociological training that is linked to a politics of liberation. This "liberation sociology" takes the perspective of those seeking liberation from oppressive conditions, and is the framework from which we need to understand what it means to be a child that receives "one laptop" from a US-based non-profit or someone who uses an "app for [their own] good" coded by someone else (Feagin et al, 2015). As we conceive it, digital sociology is rooted both in interdisciplinarity and in the politics of liberation. There are also methodological reasons that digital sociology is necessary.

There is a crisis on the horizon in sociological methods. Over the past 40 years sociologists have led the way in methodological innovations, notably the random sample survey and in-depth interviews (Savage and Burrows, 2007). These methods allowed sociologists to claim a distinctive access to understanding the "social," and both have been widely used by sociologists and adopted by scholars in other disciplines. However, these research methods are less and less useful for understanding the social world and present sociologists with something of a methodological "crisis" (Savage and Burrows, 2007). The diminishing value of these methods means that sociologists can no longer claim any special knowledge about the "social." Part of what makes these methods less compelling is the rise of "big data," which proposes radically different ways of making sense of culture, history, economy, and society. The shift data analytics from "big data" (scraped from the web and social media) is reconfiguring how research is conducted (Kitchin, 2014). It is a paradigm shift that has profound epistemological implications for sociology as a field (Burrows and Savage, 2014; Kitchin, 2014). Our work here, collecting a range of examples of digital sociological methods, is intended to address the pressing need for new methods in sociology that are suited to understanding a networked world. Throughout this volume, scholars grapple with the issues of big data in a variety of ways. For instance, Maddox offers a way to model and analyse data generated in and through an international online community (Part I, Chapter 2). Rosengren and Ottosson consider what big data means when it is collected by employers through workplace surveillance schemes (Part II, Chapter 12). Lupton calls our attention to the way that we actively participate in generating big data through our use of personal tracking devices, and offers a critical analysis of how we begin to think about how this shapes human behavior and society (Part III, Chapter 21). Grinberg offers a thoughtful contemplation about the implications of discourse about big data rendering us all "nude" (Part III, Chapter 26). And Sharma and Brooker use a data–scraping tool to analyse the vast amount of tweets using the hashtag #notracist to help us understand the mechanisms of racism denial (Chapter 29). These contributions are a starting point for a conversation about the challenges that big data presents to sociology as a field.

The work in this volume also presents a wide range of inventive digital sociological methods. Hunt's investigation of transnational feminist activists and Recuber's examination of the digital detritus of suicide notes left online both point to the need for a sociological understanding of "small data," of the intimate spaces people create as part of their everyday life (Part I, Chapters 4 and 7). Several of the pieces in this volume analyse online discussion boards as their primary data source, such as Jamerson's investigation of TripAdvisor comments about Harlem Heritage Tours (Part I, Chapter 8) and Cruz and Kubo's examination of the hate-filled comments about Philippine-born US immigration activist Jose Antonio Vargas (Part III, Chapter 27). Several contributions here combine in-person, face-to-face interviews with some form of digital media technology. For instance, McMillan Cottom interviews African-American women who have encountered for-profit educational institutions, and in some instances, the women she interviewed found her through social media and asked to be interviewed (Part II, Chapter 14). As another example of the innovative *pastiche* of methods in this volume, Wynn investigates geocaching, an outdoor activity played among strangers, using the internet and Global Positioning System (GPS) data, to share the location of "caches" hidden in public locations. To study this, Wynn interviews a small group of avid geocachers and participates in geocaching himself, which enables him to identify the key issues when mobile technology, leisure, urban spaces, and heightened concerns over terrorism intersect in urban public places (Part II, Chapter 19). These are by no means intended to be a comprehensive catalog of possible methods for digital sociology, but rather a starting point for a field in formation. Of course, sociology graduate students and early career researchers are *already* using digital sociology research methods, but this often pushes (and pulls) them out of the field.

Sociology programs are sending the best and brightest graduates to work in other disciplines. Disciplines such as communications, cultural and media studies, library and information science, and journalism have eagerly stepped in to the void left by sociology to claim many of our top job candidates. When sociology loses top job candidates to other fields, it is likely that they will publish less often in sociology journals, attend fewer of our conferences, and contribute less to knowledge that circulates within sociology. In our view, one of the crucial tasks for digital sociology is transforming the broader discipline of sociology and creating opportunities for early career scholars to stay in sociology. This is part of what Stephen Barnard addresses in his contribution to this volume when he writes about the "vocational potential" of digital sociology (Part II, Chapter 13). Forming a field also generates possibilities for connection, which is crucial for knowledge creation.

Those of us doing digital work within sociology need to connect, collaborate, and create new knowledge with others. The British Sociological Association established a digital sociology section that is growing. In the US, there are scholars within the ASA that do this sort of work, but it is often difficult for them to connect. This is made all the more difficult by the nomenclature. The sections within the ASA devoted to the study of digital media technologies call themselves "CITASA" (communications and information technologies section of the ASA). This section recently merged with one on media sociology, so now the section is called "CITAMS" (communication, information technologies and media). If one were a digital sociologist trying to find other digital sociologists, it is unclear how one might do this given such obtuse naming conventions. Thus, one of the vital functions of this field in formation is to provide an apparatus by which those doing digital sociology might connect with one another.

The moment in which we write in is one in which there are sociologists around the globe who are doing related and relevant work on different aspects of digital media technologies in ways that illuminate the intersection of the individual and society. Yet, without a disciplinary field, we can scarcely find each other's work. Put in terms of the digital media practices of creating metadata, if we effectively "tag" our work as digital sociology, it makes it easier to find the work and to find each other. We offer this volume, and the collection of works it brings together, as a way to suggest that there is a power in naming the work that we do digital sociology because it enables us to find each other.

The volume

When we were gathering papers for this volume, we wanted to open the peer review process beyond the three co-editors. We asked all the potential contributing authors to participate in the open peer review process. We did this for two reasons. First, we wanted to use the affordances of open, digital scholarship to help us think together about the ideas here. And second, we are persuaded by the growing body of evidence that suggests that traditional peer review is deeply, perhaps irretrievably, flawed (see, for example, Smith, 2006), and the converse, that open peer review is more equitable and generative (see, for example, Morey et al, 2016). To do this, we set up a Wordpress blog and uploaded the initial round of contributing papers. We invited the authors of those papers and potential contributors to the volume to review 1–2 submissions by using the "Comments" field on the Wordpress blog. This process created an opportunity for contributors to read other scholars' work as it was in formation. It also enabled a much more open, horizontal, peer-to-peer conversation and dialogue rather than reinforcing a hierarchy between editors and writers. The comment period lasted for several weeks and was quite lively. It also helped us to clarify our own thinking about which papers we thought belonged in the volume and which ones needed further development. This type of open peer review is increasingly common in other disciplines (see, for example, Lopez et al, 2015), but it is relatively rare in sociology. Given this, we chose a modified version of openness, and made the peer review site only available to those who had submitted pieces and not open to a wide, public audience of readers. We were pleased to find everyone participated in this open peer review process, and in general, reported a positive experience with it. However, one contributor voiced concern about the additional labor required in conducting such a review. This is a legitimate concern that raises some of the key issues we address in this volume, particularly around digital labor. And it is a broader issue. The fact of the uncompensated and unacknowledged labor of peer review is part of an ecosystem of scholarly publishing that many agree is broken (Daniels and Thistlethwaite, 2016). Still, we are convinced that the modestly open peer review process for this volume was a fruitful exercise for us, for the contributors, and certainly to the shape and quality of the volume.

In the volume that follows, we have organized the collected works of digital sociology into three sections: Part I: Digital sociology in everyday life, Part II: Digitized institutions, and Part III: Digital bodies. Karen Gregory introduces Part I with an exploration of the sociological imagination in the light of digitization. She suggests that the ubiquity of quotidian digital technologies and digital practices in the Western world is prompting a Janus-faced moment for the discipline of sociology – a moment that encourages us not only to look back to writers such as C. Wright Mills, but to understand how emerging terrains of data production, data capture, and data analysis may be fundamentally pressuring taken-for-granted sociological binaries. In Mills, however, Gregory also finds a necessary admonition to attend to the politics of our methods and to contextualize our work as a process of critical thinking – critical thinking in and through digital domains and digital methods. Tressie McMillan Cottom introduces Part II with an exploration of how digital sociologies will have to consider the form and function of institutions. To talk about institutions in sociology is to engage a rich history and debate about what constitutes an institution. There is, of course, the idea of social institutions like economic systems, family, education, and religion. There is also the Weberian concept of institutions as organizations and organizational relationships. Perhaps in the most precise, contemporary sense institutions refer to the formal rules that link individuals and collectivities to macro-social processes. In this volume, we conceived of institutions in their plurality. Contributors consider the political economy of digitization with particular attention to social processes such as identity formation, group boundaries, and social cohesion. We also focus on the three dominant trends in studying institutions: education, work, and culture. In keeping with the volume's interest in groups and inequalities, these chapters practice critical sociology. Critical sociology is concerned with social problems and sociology's promise for addressing them. Contributors use a variety of methods that significantly overlap with those that have become most common among those studying the digital: interviews, surveys, ethnography, and textual analysis. They practice what Lupton has called a hallmark of digital sociology: using digital data for social research (2012). These chapters also develop various aspects of social theory. They consider how technological affordances reconfigure theoretical assumptions about urban ethnographies, privacy, identity, mobility, and stratification.

Jessie Daniels introduces Part III by discussing the way embodiment is implicated in our understanding of digital inequality. While the early days of the internet had many people, from commercial advertisers to esteemed scholars, contemplating how digital technologies might allow us to escape embodiment, few believe this now. As we move into the era of the Internet of Things, the digital realm is no longer a destination, somewhere to go that is separate from us, it is in thing, in us and on our bodies (Howard, 2015; Neff and Nafus, 2016). The pieces included in this section move from a focus on the hardware of devices and digitally aware clothing to the queerness of Facebook to gendered "mommy blogs" and sexualized search engines to the virulent racism directed toward racialized bodies. Throughout this section, these scholars raise compelling questions about the sociological and political implications of bringing our embodied selves into contact with digital media technologies. Reaching beyond facile binaries that pose dichotomous questions (for example, will these technologies make us free or put us in chains?), the pieces in this section offer nuanced and thoughtfully crafted contributions to the emerging field of digital sociology and what it means for our embodied selves situated as we are within systemic inequality.

References

Baym, N.K. (1999) *Tune in, log on: Soaps, fandom, and online community*, Vol 3. London, UK: Sage Publications.

Beveridge, A.A., A. Lacevic, S. Weber, and J. Segall (2008) "Social explorer" (www.socialexplorer.com/).

Borgman, C.L. (2009) "The digital future is now: A call to action for the humanities." *Digital Humanities Quarterly* 3 (4).

Brock, A. (2005) "'A belief in humanity is a belief in colored men': Using culture to span the digital divide." *Journal of Computer-Mediated Communication* 11 (1), 357–74.

Burgess, J. and J. Green (2013) *YouTube: Online video and participatory culture*. New York: John Wiley & Sons.

Burrows, R. and M. Savage (2014) "After the crisis? Big data and the methodological challenges of empirical sociology." *Big Data & Society* 1 (1), 2053951714540280.

Carrigan, M. (2013) "What is digital sociology?" (http://markcarrigan.net/2013/01/12/what-is-digital-sociology/).

Castells, M. (1998) *The rise of the network society, the information age: Economy, society and culture*, Vol I. Oxford, UK: Blackwell.

Collins, P.H. (2012) *On intellectual activism*, Philadelphia, PA: Temple University Press.

Consalvo, M. and C. Ess (eds) (2011) *The handbook of internet studies*, Vol 14. New York: John Wiley & Sons.

Daniels, J. and J.R. Feagin (2011) "The (coming) social media revolution in the academy." *Fast capitalism* 8 (1) (www.uta.edu/huma/agger/fastcapitalism/8_2/Daniels8_2.html).

Daniels, J. and P. Thistlethwaite (2016) *Being a scholar in the digital era*. Bristol, UK: Policy Press.

Davidson, C.N. (2011) *Now you see it: How the brain science of attention will transform the way we live, work, and learn*. New York: Viking.

DiMaggio, P., E. Hargittai, W.R. Neuman, and J.P. Robinson (2001) "Social implications of the internet." *Annual Review of Sociology*, 307–36.

Ess, C.M. and W.H. Dutton (2013) "Internet Studies: Perspectives on a rapidly developing field." *New Media & Society*, 1– 11.

Feagin, J.R., H. Vera, and K. Ducey (2015) *Liberation sociology* (3rd edn). London, UK: Routledge.

Gold, M.K. (2012) *Debates in the digital humanities.* Minneapolis, MS: University of Minnesota Press.

Golumbia, D. (2014) "Death of a discipline." *Differences* 25 (1), 156–76.

Golumbia, D. and A. Koh (2013) "Postcolonial Studies, Digital Humanities, and the Politics of Language", May 31 (www.uncomputing.org/?p=241)

Hansen, D., B. Shneiderman, and M.A. Smith (2010) *Analyzing social media networks with NodeXL: Insights from a connected world,* Burlington, MA: Morgan Kaufmann.

Howard, P.N. (2015) *Pax Technica: How the Internet of Things may set us free or lock us up.* New Haven, CT: Yale University Press.

Johnson, J.M. (2016) "Diaspora in hypertext" (https://diasporahypertext. com/).

Kitchin, R. (2014) "Big data, new epistemologies and paradigm shifts." *Big Data & Society* 1 (1), 2053951714528481.

Koh, A. and R. Risam (2013) "Postcolonial digital humanities" (http:// dhpoco.org/).

Lopez, A., F. Rowland, and K. Fitzpatrick (2015) "On scholarly communication and the Digital Humanities: An interview with Kathleen Fitzpatrick." *In the Library with the Lead Pipe.*

Lupton, D. (2012) "Digital sociology: An introduction." Social Science Research Network (http://papers.ssrn.com/sol3/papers.cfm?abstract_ id=2273418).

Lupton, D. (2014) *Digital sociology.* Abingdon: Routledge.

Lury, C. and N. Wakeford (eds) (2012) *Inventive methods: The happening of the social.* London, UK: Routledge.

McPherson, T. (2012) "Why are the Digital Humanities so white? Or Thinking the histories of race and computation." In M.K. Gold (ed) *Debates in the digital humanities*, pp 139–60.

Marres, N. (2013) "What is digital sociology?" CSISP, blog of the Centre for the Study of Invention & Social Process, Goldsmiths (www.csisponline. net/2013/01/21/what-is-digital-sociology/).

Mills, C.W. (1959) *The sociological imagination.* Oxford, UK: Oxford University Press.

Morey, R.D., C.D. Chambers, P.J. Etchells, C.R. Harris, R. Hoekstra, D. Lakens, S. Lewandowsky, C.C. Morey, D.P. Newman, F.D. Schönbrodt, and W. Vanpaemel (2016) "The peer reviewers' openness initiative: Incentivizing open research practices through peer review." *Royal Society Open Science* 3 (1), 150547.

Morris, A. (2015) *The scholar denied: W.E.B. Du Bois and the birth of modern sociology.* Berkeley, CA: University of California Press.

Nakamura, L. (2002) *Cybertypes. Race, ethnicity, and identity on the internet.* London, UK: Routledge.

Nakamura, L. (2008) *Digitizing race: Visual cultures of the internet.* Minneapolis, MN: University of Minnesota Press.

Neff, G. and D. Nafus (2016) *Self-tracking.* Cambridge, MA: The MIT Press.

Orton-Johnson, K. and N. Prior (eds) (2013) *Digital sociology: Critical perspectives.* Basingstoke, UK: Palgrave Macmillan.

Orton-Johnson, K., N. Prior, and K. Gregory (2015) "Sociological imagination: Digital sociology and the future of the discipline." *The Sociological Review* December 17 (www.thesociologicalreview.com/information/blog/sociological-imagination-digital-sociology-and-the-future-of-the-discipline.html).

Sassen, S. (2002) "Towards a sociology of information technology." *Current Sociology* 50 (3), 365–88.

Savage, M. and R. Burrows (2007) "The coming crisis of empirical sociology." *Sociology* 41 (5), 885–99.

Smith, R. (2006) "Peer review: a flawed process at the heart of science and journals." *Journal of the Royal Society of Medicine* 99 (4), 178–82.

Stein, A. and J. Daniels (2017) *Going public: A guide for social scientists*, Chicago, IL: University of Chicago Press.

Sternfeld, J. (2015) "W.E.B. DuBois in cyberspace." National Endowment for the Humanities (www.neh.gov/divisions/preservation/featured-project/web-du-bois-in-cyberspace).

Wajcman, J. (1991) *Feminism confronts technology*, University Park, PA: Penn State Press.

Wajcman, J. (2002) "Addressing technological change: The challenge to social theory." *Current Sociology* 50 (3), 347–63.

Weller, K., A. Bruns, J. Burgess, M. Mahrt, and C. Puschmann (eds) (2013) *Twitter and society.* New York: Peter Lang.

Wellman, B. (2001) "Computer networks as social networks." *Science* 293 (5537), 2031–4.

Wellman, B. (2004) "The three ages of internet studies: Ten, five and zero years ago." *New Media & Society* 6 (1), 123–9.

Wynn, J.R. (2009) "Digital sociology: emergent technologies in the field and the classroom." *Sociological Forum* 24 (2), 448–56.

PART I
Digital sociology in everyday life

1

Structure and agency in a digital world

Karen Gregory

igital technologies, digital media, and mobile technologies now shape and influence the nature and experience of everyday life in the Western world. Technologies ranging from personal devices to sensors in our shared environments have brought with them an era of ubiquitous computing, data gathering, and data analysis. Such an era may even be ushering in a "new onto-logic of sociality or the social itself" (Clough et al, 2014: 147). Learning to live in and through these media, learning to both maximize their potential, as well as resist their domination of time, attention, and labor is an ongoing challenge for many individuals (Wajcman, 2015). New forms of technology and digital media are often presented by their creators as time saving or "life hacking," as expanding access to goods and resources, or increasing personal choice. They may even be presented as liberatory. Yet the reality of our entanglement with digital media is far from clearly understood.

As scholars such as Deborah Lupton (2015) have shown, new digital capacities for self-tracking and its attendant forms of self-fashioning are accompanied by questions of labor, politics, datavallience and privacy. Digital technologies have been particularly adept at collapsing easy distinctions between private and public life, and giving rise to much larger questions about the role of government in our lives, the nature and experience of work and labor, the social functions of health care and education, as well as how we understand just how "public" or civil spheres could or should be organized and maintained. As such, digital technologies, even in their most banal or quotidian forms, speak to issues of power and to the relationship between our individual biographies and the larger tides of history. As we will see in this section, through studies of the digital everyday, sociologists are beginning to do the vital work of reinvigorating the sociological imagination in light of digitization.

Looking back to Mills' classic text, we find that the promise of sociology lies within the discipline's ability to cultivate the "quality of mind" that is capable of critically reflecting on the relationship between our personal, subjective lives and larger social realities – as well as clearly articulating those findings beyond the walls of academics. For Mills, the ability to draw links between biography and history enables us to explain how and why a particular society has come into being, as well as explore and clarify mechanisms for social change. As such, the cultivation of a sociological imagination is a critical and ongoing project. It is, fundamentally, a project of learning to think in relational terms that cannot be reduced to data and method. Rather, the sociological project that Mills advocated was a call to resist what he referred to as "abstracted empiricism" or an over-wrought devotion to methodologies and the over-production of research based on the routine application of easily mastered methods. Although written in 1959, *The sociological imagination* speaks directly to the challenges and opportunities that contemporary digital sociology brings to the fore. If digital sociology is to more adroitly avoid the mental traps of such methodological devotion (as well as become relevant outside of a small circle of professional practitioners), we will have to continually engage with Mills' charge to locate thought and interpretation at the center of our project.

This is no easy feat as data science and computational social science stand to dominate the methodological field. Mills' keen observation that the "intellectual administrator" and the "research technician" would eventually compete with the scholar and professor has certainly been born out in the contemporary university. Yet digital sociology is a field that is actively drawn to and interested in the possibilities of new media, digital technologies, and digital methods, or what Lury and Wakeford (2012) have called "inventive methods." As researchers, however, we have a dual charge to experiment with and work through new digital tools, but to not take the tools so seriously that we lose sight of the very social conditions that have given rise to them. Algorithms, for example, may be both research companion for the digital sociologist, as well as their own site of analysis as performative, embodied, and material social actors (MacKenzie, 2014). In this regard, the emergence of digital sociology, as it is happening within an increasingly neoliberal university, is prompting a Janus-faced moment for the discipline of sociology: a moment to take stock of the key tenets of sociological thought in light of the challenges that emerging technologies and new forms of data are bringing about.

This section of *Digital sociologies* begins to do that work. The chapters here move between theory and method, often struggling with how to go about designing a research framework, as we see in Timothy Recuber's work on "small online spaces," or how to work ethically as a digital researcher, as we see in Alison Mayne's work with textile crafters' online communities. The chapters speak to the need to continually interrogate one's position as a researcher and sociologist, and to reflect on the process of knowledge creation. Additionally, the work gathered here encourages us to revisit sociological interests in community formation (see Alexia Maddox), the nature and possibilities of social movements (see Theresa Hunt), as well as emerging forms of work and leisure (see Alexandrea Ravenelle), yet they do so with a focus on the agency and materiality of digital technologies and platforms.

If, for Mills, the essential units of sociological analysis are the individual and the social structure (and the relationships forged therein), the works in this section update such a configuration by articulating the role that digital technologies and digital media play in modulating such a clear-cut distinction between the individual, the self, and the social. Taking up the charge that Orton-Johnson and Prior (2013: 2) have given "for sociology to conceptually move beyond the binary oppositions of virtual and real and transformation/ continuity that have characterized much of the debate" surrounding digital technology, chapters such as Alexia Maddox's "Beyond digital dualism: Modeling digital community" move us far beyond those oppositions. For Maddox, community must be rethought as spatially distributed, global, and mediated. Working with such concepts entails rethinking methods that might account for the complexities of time and temporality, as well as rethinking the status of the individual. As Maddox writes, "I would argue that the networked individual can be thought of as emitting a multi-modal digital signal that is evident in their sites of activity, leaving digital traces across the online environment." Here, we learn to work with both those traces, as well with the notion of distributed life and the question of how such an ephemeral sense of the social may show us how communities dynamically form, but not be bound by, a sense of duration.

The figure of the city and urban publics is brought up again in Trevor Jamerson's work, but this time we encounter the traveler and the tourist. In his chapter, "Positively digital orientalism: Identifying authority in online tourist reviews," Jamerson brings the often-overlooked economy of internet-based travel into direct dialogue with critical race theory and the work of Edward Said. Looking to the history of the travelogue and travelers' tales, Jamerson historicizes TripAdvisor and, as such, begins to problematize notions of access and representation in the digital realms. Jamerson's piece is vital for understanding the ways in which digital platforms are not simply neutral aggregators of information, fostering equal access to consumers, but rather that these commerce platforms may be forging hidden ecologies and economies of inequality. As much as TripAdvisor and its ilk have sought to "disrupt" the tourism industry by extending the "authorial" voice of the travelogue, it may also truck in what Jamerson calls the technology "of orientalism."

Furthering the discussion of disruption and emerging forms of work and labor, Alexandrea Ravenelle's "A return to *Gemeinschaft*: Digital impression management and the sharing economy" looks to understand how gig economy workers manage, guide, and control their digital identities in order to more fully market themselves. Ravenelle's work links us to Erving Goffman's dramaturgical sociology while paying close attention to the significance that platforms such as Airbnb, TaskRabbit, and Kitchensurfing have for workers in a shifting economy. Her attention to the production of value found in these reputation economies is timely, and provides a subtle analysis of the line between marketing one's self as a choice and being modulated towards these platforms in the wake of larger economic restructuring.

Alison Mayne's "Virtually ethical: Ethnographic challenges in researching textile crafters online" continues the investigation of digital communities, this time taking up a Facebook community of textile crafters. Here, we find that digital research affords us an ethical opportunity to think through the status of digital data. For Mayne, there is a need to locate the human actor in the research project, and she advocates for platform-specific ethical guidelines that can enable a researcher to adopt a dialogical and transparent process. Mayne argues that research participants, if given the choice in such a research project, may opt for non-anonymous data collection.

Such methodological reflectivity is the hallmark of Theresa Hunt's "The digital solidarity trap: Social movement research, online activism, and accessing the other's others." In her work with women's transnationalist feminist networks, Hunt encountered the methodological limitations of qualitative work done in digital environments, particularly for the researcher of subaltern populations. As power dynamics mask voices within the network, Hunt became increasingly aware of the possibility that the most marginalized "minority" populations in the network could be silenced by a reliance on digital methods alone. This chapter is a needed call for caution in digital method design, and is a case study for understanding how and why "analog" methods must remain firmly within the digital sociologist's toolkit. Hunt's work stands as a corrective to the notion that digital methods inherently foster greater access to individuals and communities.

In line with thinking through issues of who and what is accessed in the digital realm, Timothy Recuber's "Digital discourse analysis: Finding meaning in small online spaces" is a necessary rejoinder to the currently flurry of big data research. As Recuber writes, "if digital sociology is to be about more than just the ascent of big data, then those who traffic in qualitative, interpretive, and textual approaches to social sciences need to explain how their own methodologies can adapt to and take advantage of the digitization of social life, and in ways that big data cannot." Recuber's chapter will be a refreshing and thought-provoking work for the sociologist who has struggled with digital methods or who is considering a research project of small and overlooked digital spaces that lie beyond Facebook and Twitter, such as long forgotten blogs, Tumblrs, and abandoned digital archives. Recuber's chapter provides a step-by-step guide for getting started on such a project.

Finally, Harry T. Dyer's "Interactivity, social media, and Superman: How comic books can help us understand and conceptualize interactivity online" puts "new media" in conversation with older forms of media, specifically with comic books, to look at the complex phenomena of interactivity. Conceptually, Dyer finds that interactivity is both overlooked and under-theorized, yet it sits at the heart of all digital media. His detailed analysis of interactivity as a process broadens the scope of discussion, and draws attention to the relations between human, non-humans, and the digital.

References

Clough, P., K. Gregory, B. Haber, and J. Scannell (2014) "The datalogical turn." In P. Vannini (ed) *Nonrepresentational methodologies: Re-envisioning research* (pp 146–63). Oxford, UK: Taylor & Francis.

Lupton, D. (2015) *Digital sociology*. London, UK: Routledge.

Lury, C. and Wakeford, N. (2012) *Inventive methods: The happening of the social*. London, UK: Routledge.

MacKenzie, D. (2014) "A sociology of algorithms: High-frequency trading and the shaping of markets" (www.maxpo.eu/Downloads/Paper_DonaldMacKenzie.pdf).

Mills, C.W. (2000) *The sociological imagination* (new edn). Oxford, UK: Oxford University Press.

Orton-Johnson, K. and Prior, N. (2013) *Digital sociology: Critical perspectives*. London, UK: Palgrave Macmillan.

Wajcman, J. (2015) *Pressed for time: The acceleration of life in digital capitalism*. Chicago, IL: University of Chicago Press.

2

Beyond digital dualism: Modeling digital community

Alexia Maddox

Introduction

In response to the question of how traditional analog sociological methods become digital, this chapter proposes a digitally native methodological approach to guide the study of digital communities. Drawing on data collected from a case study of the community of people interested in reptiles and amphibians (Maddox, 2015), it presents a conceptual model that is intended to enable the research practitioner to gather data across physical and virtual social practices. This model has been derived from the case study analysis and has been developed to conceptualize how data collected at the individual level can be extrapolated to characterize a digital community. One of the most significant challenges faced by researchers when conducting community studies in contemporary societies is the imbrication of digital networked technologies with sociality. This digitally enhanced social connectivity has both opened up new spaces for the experience of community, and created a schism in research methods and theory for how to characterize the movement of social engagement across online and offline environments.

This chapter follows the critique of Nathan Jurgensen (2012) against digital dualism to use alternative socio-spatial metaphors, theories and methodological approaches to define the environment of a community rather than to separate community experience into online and offline spaces. Through resolving the online–offline dualism inherent to research that views social behaviors as either/or, the notion of an online community is shifted through an environmental lens into a discussion of digital community. In addition to this, the use of an environmental lens allows researchers to move beyond using a priori assumptions of community, place, social composition, boundaries, and mechanisms of social cohesion to define a community through its imprint in the socio-technical landscape. In this way, both digital and physical activities are blended in the experience of community, and the rigid definitions of the properties of community are made flexible and porous through their characterization within the niche environment through which the community flourishes.

The model proposed in this chapter builds on this approach to clarify relationships between individual behaviors and values and how these extrapolate out to identify a community environment. The model is based on the activities of an individual person (whom we can refer to as "ego"), and is an egocentric data profile of a networked individual (Wellman et al, 2003; Comunello, 2012). However, the data collected to illustrate the portfolio activity of the individual speaks also to collective behaviors and resources within a group, such as organizational engagement, social networks, and the communicative fabric across which these are maintained. These collective characteristics can then be analyzed through three layers that illustrate the ecological niche or environment of the community. This collective aspect is discussed further in Maddox (2015), and the focus of this chapter is on the egocentric data model and its possible applications within mixed-methods research. However, a brief description defining the community environment from the data-driven model follows.

The environmental niche of a digital community can be observed both conceptually and methodologically through three layers, the built environment of a community, its patterns of social organization, and the mediating culture. The built environment is a technological layer which refers to the digital (hardware and software), locational, and material environment of the community. This defines both its place and boundaries and speaks to aspects of its sociality. The social layer of the community is constituted by patterns of social organization that speak to the wealth of social capital, the characteristic of the social networks, and elements of social cohesion. The mediating culture of the community, through which collective identity is ascertained, is constituted by values that are overlapping rather than shared, the social context within which these values gain credibility, and a topic focus that draws people together. The quantitative and qualitative data that can be gathered on the individual and focused through their portfolio of participation, mediated sociability, and group engagement is then aggregated within each layer to articulate the environment of the community.

By drawing on a digitally native mid-range theory (cf Merton, 1948) of social action such as networked individualism and personalized communities, the approach proposed here is argued to transcend existing limitations to community conceptualization and research methodology in which boundaries and memberships are clearly defined before the conduct of the research. It aims to do this by accommodating for augmentations to community experience related to the embeddedness of the internet and information communication technologies (ICTs) in everyday life (cf Wellman and Haythornthwaite, 2002).

The digital augmentations of community tend to challenge the discrete nature of spatiality across which a community occurs, and diversify the population composition and membership of the community through networks of strong and weak ties. Rather than thinking about communities as occurring in a physical space or an online website, this chapter draws on the metaphor of an environmental niche as the holding container of community and densities in the network of social ties as the heaving and dynamic site of community (see Sassen, 2001, 2007; Latham and Sassen, 2005, for a discussion of digital formations that move across and beyond nation-state borders). Connecting the environment of a community to the notion of digital formations proposed by Latham and Sassen (2005) facilitates the incorporation of physical and digital spaces alongside mediated sociability and in-person social engagement. Consequently, thinking surrounding the episodic emergence of social structures as a defining characteristic of contemporary digital communities can be put forward in a context of open, rather than closed, social structures that thread within and across the fabric of a Network Society (Castells, 2010). In developing a model to bridge the conceptual leap of translating data into a spatial metaphor (Ekbia et al, 2015), such as an environment or ecological niche, this chapter seeks to enter the discussion of developing methods to increase the accuracy within which we can identify the episodic emergence and open social structures of digital communities.

In order to ease the reader into and through this conceptual approach, and to demonstrate the utility of the model proposed to assist other research projects, this chapter begins with a targeted discussion of the research literature drawn on to characterize the environment of a digital community. It then provides a brief description of the community that formed the case study cohort in order to illustrate the population scope and social breadth that can be studied through the application of this model. From this point, the chapter leaps into the murky details of how the data points harnessed within the model were developed from the research findings, and then extrapolated into a discussion of a collective and emergent social form defined by the imprint of its environmental niche. This discussion also considers the practical alignments that were made across the qualitative and quantitative data collected to generate the model, and then moves into a speculative finale for how a model developed through an identified community system may be reverse-engineered to direct alignments in big data streams that may identify community imprints.

Characterizing the environment of digital community

Poole and Contractor (2011) observe a chestnut within organizational studies that is also at the crux of research methodology in community studies. They identify that previous research into small groups has "operated under a restrictive model that treats groups as well-defined, clearly bounded entities with a stable set of members" (2011: 194). While this discussion may speak from the field of organizational studies, it can be equally applied to community studies that look at neighborhoods (a place-based study that focuses on in-person proximity and postal code affiliation), and single website community forums (a virtual community study that focuses on co-presence and website address). In an equally resonant manner, they observe that viewing groups as well-bounded, relatively small and stable units with a clearly defined, role-based membership makes conducting research on such groups "straightforward." From a research methods perspective, defining the population is a matter of document research. The place, membership profile, and community boundaries are mapped out for the researcher before they begin the study. For research into digital communities, characterized by open social systems, technological mediation, and global dispersion, such approaches will not provide insight into the magnitude and diversity of membership and community experience. In Poole and Contractor's (2011: 198) words, group settings are more uncontained entities, with a dynamic and variegated nature that is expressed through a complex system of groups and individuals operating as an ecosystem.

The ecosystem of digital community leaves an imprint in the socio-technical landscape, which I refer to as its "environmental niche," the actor within which is defined as the networked individual. The conceptual model of the networked individual provided in this chapter articulates the agency and activity patterns of the individual within a digital community. As I argue in the research presenting the case study findings (Maddox, 2015), this approach can be seen as continuous with existing community studies, particularly in connection with the environmental awareness developed through the work of early Chicago School scholars (Hawley, 1950; McKenzie, 1967; Park, 1915; Park and Burgess, 1921), with updates for the information age drawn from the fields of internet and networked sociability studies. These concepts are connected by the environmental approach to characterizing a community that incorporates a topological perspective and surveyable population. This approach is based on the idea of viewing a digital community as a "foci of activity group" (Feld, 1981), an idea drawn from the field of social network analysis in which the densities of social ties identify emergent groups within more loosely connected networks. This notion resonates with a networked approach to community conceptualization put forward by Wellman (Wellman, 1979; Wellman and Leighton, 1979). In particular, the "foci of activity group," which singles out a particular personalized community for study, facilitates the extrapolation of the collective from the individual through their portfolio of participation (Wellman, 2001; Wellman et al, 2003).

Through the case study analysis, I argue that the environmental approach derived from these ideas enacts the extrapolation of social data from individual to community forms that are characterized by open social structures, global distribution, and a digital backbone of mediated sociability and exchange (Maddox, 2015). This approach for translating an individual portfolio of participation into a community environment is derived from the work of Latham and Sassen (2005) in characterizing global digital formations, and Foth and collaborators in describing the communicative ecology of an urban apartment complex (Foth and Hearn, 2007; Klaebe et al, 2009). Within this conceptual framework, the place, composition, boundaries, and mechanisms of social cohesion within a community are characterized through the aggregation of individual profiles into three conceptual layers. These are constituted through the networked individual's community-specific engagement with the built environment (the technological layer); the patterns of social organization and configurations of sociality evident within their community engagement such as group engagement, social capital, and their demographics (the social layer); and the topic focus, value field, identity project, and social context they bring to and collectively manifest through the community (the mediating culture). Data speaking to each of these three layers can be drawn from quantitative measures (such as technology use, demographics, and social capital measures) and qualitative approaches to characterizing symbolic processes and the construction of collective identity. Maddox (2015) provides a further discussion on how this conceptual model acts as a lens through which to transform individual actions to a community environment within a mixed-methods approach. Foundational to this idea, however, is that each layer contributes to a derived (rather than researcher-imposed) characterization of community, place, social composition, internal and external boundaries, and mechanisms of social cohesion.

A brief description of the case study

This section offers a brief description of the case study community, and illustrates how its members can be characterized through the attributes of a networked individual. The case study of people interested in reptiles and amphibians – the Herper community – was drawn on to articulate data streams and to provide a real-world laboratory for developing concepts and methodological tools that can be used to characterize digital community in the contemporary age.

The Herper community is a unique group of people that numbers in the millions of animal lovers, adventure tourists, scientists, photographers, zoo and government employees, museum curators, entrepreneurs, school and university students, medical professionals, veterinarians, smugglers, organizations, businesses, and families that affiliate themselves with reptiles and amphibians. What is unique about these people is that a love of reptiles and amphibians is not an interest that can usually be pursued through mainstream culture in any society. This is a social world where the basic unit of exchange is the "herptile," a shorthand term used to refer to reptiles and amphibians. The animal is objectified as a symbol or value that is traded, bred, related to, documented, displayed, legislated, digitized, dissected and recombined, loved, and loathed.

The breadth of this profile of community involvement raises the question – how could a group with so many social distinctions be considered a community? It exists within a spatially distributed social system that is characterized by a unique market system, the production and consumption of knowledge, a distinct vocabulary, squabbles and rivalry, cultures of consumption, a virtual landscape of websites, forums and other digital resources, a physical landscape of deeply regulated spaces, transnational flows and a black market underbelly, dominated by personalities, informal social networks, societies, and other organizations. The question of how to conceptualize the emergent form of this group, its boundaries, its membership patterns, its spaces of social cohesion, continuity and change, and its coordinates in time and place became the challenges of the research.

The research methods for the case study included participant observation for a period of two years, an online survey, and in-person interviews. The resulting data constituted 1,498 survey respondents across 47 countries, interviews with 80 participants ranging from 30 minutes to two hours, and participant observation conducted across 12 countries. The model proposed in this chapter was used to structure and triangulate the findings from the qualitative and quantitative data analysis.

Conceptualizing data intersections

The model proposed below (see Figure 2.1) is intended to assist the triangulation of the quantitative and qualitative analyses by clarifying the relationships between sets of variables and theoretical ideas that were used to analytically describe the community under study. The underlying process of the model articulates the way that the networked individual engages in the Herper community, and how their data profile can be aggregated into an environmental understanding of community form, process, and function. I consider this diagram the first step in the triangulation of the case study results in that it acts as a visual guide to the analytical process. Figure 2.1 diagrammatically represents this model, and the subsequent discussion here considers how the findings of the case study contributed to the development and interpretation of the various components that constitute it. For the

Figure 2.1: Conceptualizing the link between egocentric data imprints to the digital community

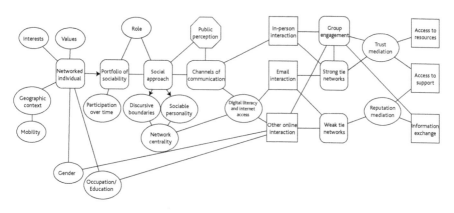

purposes of visual simplicity, complex and overlapping relationships between technology use and patterns of social engagement have been streamlined to represent the dominant pathways used by participants from the quantitative and qualitative results.

The networked individual diagrammatically represented through the model was shown by the research findings to be influenced initially by what they were interested in, their values, physical location, and mobility. In addition to these factors, their activity profile was shown within the quantitative analysis to also be influenced by their occupational skill and education levels and gender (rather than by their age). However, from both the qualitative and quantitative results we learn that it was the participants' passions, rather than their demographic affordances, that facilitated their engagement in the network. This finding leads us to the next set of influential factors that define agency within community, their enactment of portfolio participation within the community, which both the quantitative and qualitative findings suggested was linked to their role, gender, and involvement profile over time.

Within the quantitative findings, participants experiences of community engagement were largely characterized by engagement with multiple groups and loose networks of strong and weak social ties. From the qualitative findings we learned that these ties were fostered by engagement in private spaces in the home, during trips to see reptiles and amphibians in private and public collections, and in the wild and online. In addition to this, the quantitative findings suggested that the way participants engaged with the network was influenced by their network centrality, which was, in turn, related to their social approach. If we pause here, we can see that we have moved through the first third of the model, covered the influences of demographics and a general sociability profile of the individual. From this point, we consider their communication patterns, and the channels across which they do this from in-person to mediated sociability, which then leads us to an understanding of the spatiality of the network. After we develop a sense of the socio-technical space through which the individual operates, we then move into the wealth of the networks (aka social capital) that they then have access to.

The "place" of the network is located in the channels through which participants engage with other Herpers. However, public perception of this marginal interest group prompted the use of online forms of interaction for Herpers as they sought a space for social acceptance. This is illustrated in the model through the linking of a person's social approach with their choices in channels of communication, mediated by public perception. From this point in the model, we can see how face-to-face or embodied engagements go on to foster strong ties, and that sociability is mediated by the participant's internet access. Both the qualitative and quantitative findings from the Herper community case study suggested participants' experiences of the Herper community were a combination of face-to-face interaction alongside mediated interaction by email and other online platforms. Intuitively, the quantitative findings suggested that a participant's engagement with the internet-based channels is mediated by their internet access but less so by their digital literacy. In a nod to the unique nature of the mediating culture of the case study community, the research findings suggested that a participant's gender and level of education or occupation were likely to be an indicator of whether they engage in online social spaces within the community. In this way the research findings tied gender and place together, with most spaces of social engagement replicating a gender imbalance, but identified that it was the common interests and overlapping values that drew people into and across the multiplicity of spaces and places that constituted the socio-technical niche of the community environment. From the quantitative findings it was clear that the physical places of the network were mostly experienced as local to the networked individual, however regional, national, and international spaces were connected through participants' social ties. This suggested that the relational space of the community was local, global, and mobile.

In a deeply intertwined manner, the communication channels used by participants, alongside their organizational engagement, facilitated exchange, support, and reciprocity within the community (key elements of social capital). The final section of the model documents the various ways that social capital has been measured, both through social ties and organizational engagement across online and physical environments. Findings from the quantitative and qualitative data suggested that participants engaged in person with groups of Herpers mainly through societies, conferences, expos, and in the workplace. They also were evidenced to engage with groups of people through online forums and in virtual societies. This type of organizational or society-based engagement was evidenced within the quantitative findings to build strong-tie relationships, and to suggest that there were higher levels of trust among people who are organizationally involved. Resource exchange, information, access, and support are available to participants through these strong-tie relationships. However, these resources were not shown to be characteristic only of those who engage with organized groups of Herpers. Mediated interaction by email and other online channels such as instant messaging and forums were shown to maintain local and strong ties, although these forms of interaction also appeared to nurture larger numbers of weak-tie relations, and consequently provide higher levels of access to information. Within this context, the case study findings suggested that it was reputation, rather than trust levels, that mediated exchange across weak-tie relations. These findings and how they then articulated the links within the model both demonstrate the complexity of social capital within a community and the variable role of mediators to exchange such as reputation and trust.

Moving beyond the case study of the Herper community, the analysis of data collected through this rubric is argued to animate social action into a community construct, constituted methodologically through the four domains of community characterization: its place, composition, internal and external boundaries, and mechanisms of cohesion. Findings from the data collected articulate these domains through an environmental lens of the built environment, patterns of social organization and mediating culture. This process produces a four/three dance in how the data is conceptualized, gathered, and interpreted. For example, the individual actor, their interests, values, demographics, and locations are collated within the framework of their portfolio of sociability. This is the technical conduit that intersects the individual with their personal community. Aspects such as values and interests of the individual can be collated into depicting the mediating culture of the community, with the collective identity and overlapping value sets evident within the mediating culture being a key aspect of social cohesion. Other aspects, such as the geographies associated with individual actions, speak to the notion of the "place" of the community. These actions are articulated through channels of communication and locations of interaction, producing coordinates of interaction from physical space to code space (which can be collectively referred to as the built environment; cf Indergaard and McInerney, 1998).

While at this point the data is speaking to the construction of place through an environment of technology use and physical locations, it is also speaking to the external boundary construction of the community through its cultural context within wider societies. These coordinates of portfolio participation within a personalized community have been shown through the case study findings to articulate the external and internal boundaries of the community, particularly in how loci of interaction are selected in part as a reaction to public perception and divisions within the community. This shows the dual construction occurring within data interpretation that uses the same data point to articulate different aspects of community form.

Similarly, technology use through its overlay with and facilitation of networked sociability and exchange is connected to a discussion of social capital, and from this to the larger discussion of mechanisms of cohesion within the community. Speaking to the notion of social cohesion that is characteristic of a community, social capital measures embedded with notions of trust and exchange across strong and weak ties bridge and interpret individual actions into a social layer of the community environment. The movement from one set of data points on the individual's technology use patterns to how this imbricates with their social networks through trust and reputation mediation demonstrates how the links within individual activity patterns can be connected to depict the emergent form of a community. While the model proposed characterizes an individual set of actions per se, it is the conceptual layering directing aggregation, clustering, and visualization of these patterns across multiple portfolios of participation that articulates the environmental niche within which the community proliferates.

Bridging the conceptual leap within big data analysis

A key concern that arose during the case study research was the global reach of the community, which created a methodological drive to access big data analytics that operated at this level. This need for access to data sets that equate individual actions within a global context rather than nation-state jurisdictions also speaks to current methodological concerns within the social sciences that seek to identify the presence of social forms within big data. An example of this within the research literature is the identification of social movements through the analysis of connective behaviors within social media (Ackland et al, 2014; Bennett and Segerberg, 2012; McDonald, 2015). However, this approach to the identification of collective forms is often limited to a single platform, and runs counter to the multimodal nature of engagement that occurs within a digital community. It is also counter to the evolving definition of big data that is characterized by descriptors of volume, variety, velocity, veracity, and value (Hitzler and Janowicz, 2013), and alignments or agglomerations of a variety of data sources. Crawford and Schultz (2014) suggest that rather than thinking of big data as it is commonly conceptualized through these descriptors, it is a practice of data generation through the establishment of correlations across data flows. Drawing on boyd and Crawford's (2012) notion of the relational nature of big data, Leszczynski (2015) argues that big data is a process of generating more information beyond that contained within "piecemeal data" by forming linkages between data events. Given the changing role and scale of human involvement in big data analysis, the methodological concern for the interpretation of correlations in data streams becomes the conceptual leap that is made between raw data and the visualization of this information (Ekbia et al, 2015). In addition to this, when the focus of big data analysis becomes the identification of social formations, Gerbaudo and Treré (2015: 4), who focus on social movements, argue that the resulting quantitative nature of big data analysis is not well suited to revealing symbolic processes and the construction of collective identity. Within this critique of the definition and practice of big data, there remains the need for a conceptual model that allows for the correlation of "quotidian" digital behaviors across streams of data that draws on both qualitative and quantitative techniques. For me, this is an opportunity to speculate whether the model generated within the context of the Herper community case study can be reverse-engineered to identify social forms within agglomerated data streams. The following discussion considers this proposition through an analysis of components within the model and how they may connect with current thinking surrounding the construct of big data.

To begin, I would argue that the networked individual can be thought of as emitting a multi-modal digital signal that is evident in their sites of activity, leaving digital traces across the online environment. Existing research methods through which these digital traces of personalized community activities can be traced include website hyperlinking analysis (Rogers, 2009, 2012) and networks resulting from social media engagement (Ackland, 2013; Bruns, 2007). Other data profiles that can be constructed from digital trace data that move beyond the web environment include postal code-based consumption profiles that produce globally equated demographics (Burrows and Gane, 2006; Parker et al, 2007), geotagging of activities through online and interactive mapping (Elwood et al, 2011; Rodríguez-Amat and Brantner, 2014), and spatial profiles of users created through locative media (Lemos, 2010). In addition to this, the sensory scapes through which these individuals move are also digitized in terms of visual attributes (gathered through CCTV and user-generated images, for example), and there is an increasing movement to capture sound, thermal, and activity-sensing information (Nafus, 2014) gathered through the advent of the Internet of Things (IoT) and ubiquitous computing (Crang and Graham, 2007). These data attributes and generating sources are spatial, quotidian, and environmental, suggesting that imprints of social signals are reflected in digital data streams.

Through existing digital methods, the analytical vocabulary of big data may be expanded into qualitative methods. Qualitative or symbolic content within the online environment may be scooped up through digital methods such as the automated content analysis of web scrapes (Herring, 2002; Marres and Weltevred, 2013). In terms of the use of content analysis on big data, there is a parallel body of literature investigating automated content analysis that aims to capture the emotional scape of conversations as much as their topic scope through digital methods (Jockers, 2013; Neviarouskaya et al, 2007), particularly in the field of sentiment analysis as a form of public opinion (Cho et al, 2003; Li and Wu, 2010; Prabowo and Thelwall, 2009). While current approaches are usually limited to a single platform, the symbolic processes and meaning-making that occurs within the online group conversations of digital communities may become recognizable through the aggregation of this information. More generally, the aggregation of this content into an analytically useful product requires the application of a conceptual model linking the networked individual to the environment of a digital community.

In terms of the reality of translating the model proposed within this chapter into a conceptual bridge that frames the aggregation and visualizations of digital trace data into the environmental imprint of digital community, there is still a long way to go. A possible limitation to the translation of the model proposed to the clustering and interpretation of digital community imprints emerging within big data is that it is derived from egocentric data. Within the case study research, this model was generated through anonymous survey data that took a holistic view of the individual and anonymized interviews using a life history approach that provided the meaning-making and links between the data points. The implications of this for the aggregation of big data may be the promise of a more holistic and consistent view of the individual actor across their technology use, social networks, and the topics through which they engage with the community. In the current climate, such approaches are deployed by government actors to locate individuals through their digital traces or to use large data sets to create predictive indicators of "persons of interest" through their associations with people and topics (cf Leszczynski, 2015). While the environmental approach may assist in using the established model to interpret information in aggregates rather than by an individual actor, there are likely to be ethical implications for this practice within research methodology.

One of the lines of debate that has developed alongside the notion of big data are the ethical implications of its use within research practice (Ackland, 2013; boyd and Crawford, 2012; Buchanan and Ess, 2009; Crawford and Schultz, 2014; Markham and Buchanan, 2012; Soghoian, 2012). Given the definition of big data as the "establishment of correlations across data flows," this raises ethical questions surrounding privacy, consent and identification through unintended alignments of personal information. These questions for researchers are also set in the social context of increasing public concern surrounding social control, surveillance and privacy (Lyon, 2013), particularly through the Snowden revelations (Bauman et al, 2014; Gehl, 2014). The increasing state of awareness of "dataveillance" has been argued by Crawford and Schultz (2014) to have instilled a state of "surveillant anxiety," while Leszczynski (2015) argues that it is more an anxiety over the sense of being able to control one's own digital traces.

> [...] the realities of living in a (spatial) big data present are better characterized in terms of what I designate as 'anxieties of control': the desire to *discern* (be aware of) and *direct* (determine the disclosure of) flows of personal spatial big data about oneself while feeling that any attempt at exerting such control is effectively futile. (Leszczynski, 2015: 1)

The identification of the imprints of digital communities within aggregated streams of data sits within this debate as both a challenge and a promise. Our digital imprints are a quotidian archive through which we can learn more about ourselves, both individually and collectively. Because of this it is also a timely discussion for social scientists to engage with the opportunities raised by big data by contributing our critical lens, conceptual capacities, and insights into understanding humanity and its imbrications with technology. The model proposed within this chapter is a step towards this discussion, both in the possibilities it affords as an analytical lens and as a framework through which to integrate quantitative and qualitative insights into the visualization of social form.

Conclusion

This chapter has discussed how the changing format of community experience has provoked a need to develop new conceptual tools and approaches to researching digital communities. Inherent to the structure and process of these communities is their global reach and technological mediation. I have argued that these characteristics make contemporary communities partially invisible to existing research approaches. This chapter proposed a model of data alignments from individual to digital community that assists in moving beyond ascribed understandings of community characterization to providing a derived environment through which digital communities can be identified. This has been developed through a mixed-methods study of a real-world community as a way to demonstrate the application of research methods to provide an environmental imprint of digital community. Future research could validate this model within a similar network, and continue to develop and refine the model as a way to describe and characterize the emergent form and environmental imprint of contemporary community experience. At the drawing together of this discussion, I raise the possibility of this model to not only act as a mechanism through which to gather and triangulate mixed methods research, but to act as an information structure through which to aggregate flows of big data. The foundation of this possibility is based on the derived approach taken within the research methodology to defining the location, social composition, boundaries, and mechanisms of social cohesion through the environmental imprint or niche within which a digital community proliferates.

References
Ackland, R. (2013) *Web social science: Concepts, data and tools for social scientists in the digital age.* Los Angeles, CA: Sage Publications.

Ackland, R., M. O'Neil, and C.E. Pérez (2014) "Tweeting the frame: Frames and fields in the age of the networked individual." In *Social media and social movements 2014*. St Petersburg, Russia: Higher School of Economics (http://linisevents.hse.ru/data/2014/08/21/1313274458/Perez%20-%20 SMSM2014_ExtendedAbstract.pdf).

Bauman, Z., et al (2014) "After Snowden: Rethinking the impact of surveillance." *International Political Sociology* 8, 121–44.

Bennett, W.L. and A. Segerberg (2012) "The logic of connective action." *Information, Communication & Society* 15, 739–68.

boyd, d. and K. Crawford (2012) "Critical questions for big data: Provocations for a cultural, technological, and scholarly phenomenon." *Information, Communication & Society* 15, 662–79.

Bruns, A. (2007) "Methodologies for mapping the political blogosphere: An exploration using the Issue Crawler research tool." *First Monday* 12.

Buchanan, E.A. and C. Ess (2009) "Internet research ethics: The field and its critical issues." In K.E. Himma and H.T. Tavani (eds) *The handbook of information and computer ethics* (pp 273–92). New York: John Wiley & Sons, Inc.

Burrows, R. and N. Gane (2006) "Geodemographics, software and class." *Sociology* 40, 793–812.

Castells, M. (2010) *The rise of the network society*. Cambridge, UK: Wiley-Blackwell.

Cho, J. et al (2003) "Media, terrorism, and emotionality: Emotional differences in media content and public reactions to the September 11th terrorist attacks." *Journal of Broadcasting & Electronic Media* 47, 309–27.

Comunello, F. (2012) *Networked sociability and individualism: Technology for personal and professional relationships*. Hershey, PA: Information Science Reference.

Crang, M. and S. Graham (2007) "Sentient cities, ambient intelligence and the politics of urban space." *Information, Communication & Society* 10, 789–817.

Crawford, K. and J. Schultz (2014) "Big data and due process: Toward a framework to redress predictive privacy harms." *Boston College Law Review* 55, 93–128.

Ekbia, H., et al (2015) "Big data, bigger dilemmas: A critical review." *Journal of the Association for Information Science and Technology*, 66, 1523–45.

Elwood, S., M.F. Goodchild, and D.Z. Sui (2011) "Researching volunteered geographic information: Spatial data, geographic research, and new social practice." *Annals of the Association of American Geographers* 102, 571–90.

Feld, S.L. (1981) "The focused organization of social ties." *American Journal of Sociology* 86, 1015–35.

Foth, M. and G. Hearn (2007) "Networked individualism of urban residents: Discovering the communicative ecology in inner-city apartment buildings." *Information, Communication & Society* 10, 749–72.

Gehl, R.W. (2014) "Power/freedom on the dark web: A digital ethnography of the dark web social network." *New Media & Society*, October 15, 1-17.

Gerbaudo, P. and E. Treré (2015) "In search of the 'we' of social media activism: Introduction to the special issue on social media and protest identities." *Information, Communication & Society*, 1–7.

Hawley, A.H. (1950) *Human ecology: A theory of community structure.* New York: Ronald Press.

Herring, S.C. (2002) "Computer-mediated communication on the internet." *Annual Review of Information Science and Technology* 36, 109–68.

Hitzler, P. and K. Janowicz (2013) "Linked data, big data, and the 4th paradigm." *Semantic Web* 4, 233–5.

Indergaard, M.L. and P. McInerney (1998) "The embedded net: Making silicon alley, remaking cyberspace." Presentation at Annual Meeting of the American Sociological Association, San Francisco, CA.

Jockers, M.L. (2013) *Macroanalysis: Digital methods and literary history.* Champaign, IL: University of Illinois Press.

Jurgenson, N. (2012) "When atoms meet bits: Social media, the mobile web and augmented revolution." *Future Internet* 4, 83–91.

Klaebe, H.G., B.A. Adkins, M. Foth, and G.N. Hearn (2009) "Embedding an ecology notion in the social production of urban space." In M. Foth (ed) *Handbook of research on urban informatics: The practice and promise of the real-time city* (pp 179–94). Hershey, PA: Information Science Reference, IGI Global.

Latham, R. and Sassen, S. (2005) *Digital formations: IT and new architectures in the global realm.* Princeton, NJ: Princeton University Press.

Lemos, A. (2010) "Post-mass media functions, locative media, and informational territories: New ways of thinking about territory, place, and mobility in contemporary society." *Space and Culture* 13, 403–20.

Leszczynski, A. (2015) "Spatial big data and anxieties of control." *Environment and Planning D: Society & Space* 0, 1–20.

Li, N. and D.D. Wu (2010) "Using text mining and sentiment analysis for online forums hotspot detection and forecast." *Decision Support Systems* 48, 354–68.

Lyon, D. (2013) *The electronic eye: The rise of surveillance society-computers and social control in context.* New York: John Wiley & Sons.

McDonald, K. (2015) "From indymedia to anonymous: Rethinking action and identity in digital cultures." *Information, Communication & Society*, 1–15.

McKenzie, R. (1967) "The ecological approach to the study of the human community." In R.E. Park and E.W. Burgess (eds) *The city* (pp 63–79). Chicago, IL and London, UK: University of Chicago Press.

Maddox, A. (2015) *Research methods and global online communities.* Aldershot, UK: Ashgate.

Markham, A. and E. Buchanan (2012) "Ethical decision-making and internet research: Recommendations from the AoIR ethics working committee." Chicago, IL: Association of Internet Researchers.

Marres, N. and E. Weltevrede (2013) "Scraping the social?" *Journal of Cultural Economy* 6, 313–35.

Merton, R.K. (1948) "Discussion." *American Sociological Review* 13, 164–8.

Nafus, D. (2014) "Stuck data, dead data, and disloyal data: the stops and starts in making numbers into social practices." *Distinktion: Scandinavian Journal of Social Theory* 15, 208–22.

Neviarouskaya, A., H. Prendinger, and M. Ishizuka (2007) "Textual affect sensing for sociable and expressive online communication." In A.R. Paiva, R. Prada, and R. Picard (eds) *Affective computing and intelligent interaction*, vol 4738, *Lecture notes in computer science* (pp 218–29). Berlin and Heidelberg, Germany: Springer.

Park, R. (1915) "The city: Suggestions for the investigation of human behaviour in the city environment." *The American Journal of Sociology* 20, 577–612.

Park, R. and E. Burgess (1921) *Introduction to the science of sociology*. Chicago, IL: University of Chicago Press.

Parker, S., E. Uprichard, and R. Burrows (2007) "Class places and place classes: Geodemographics and the spatialization of class." *Information, Communication & Society* 10, 902–21.

Poole, M.S. and N.S. Contractor (2011) "Conceptualizing the multiteam system as an ecosystem of networked groups." In S. Zaccaro, M.A. Marks and L. DeChurch (eds) *Multiteam systems: An organizational form for dynamic and complex environments* (pp 193–224). New York and Hove, UK: Routledge.

Prabowo, R. and M. Thelwall (2009) "Sentiment analysis: A combined approach." *Journal of Informetrics* 3, 143–57.

Rodríguez-Amat, J.R. and C. Brantner (2014) "Space and place matters: A tool for the analysis of geolocated and mapped protests." *New Media & Society*.

Rogers, R. (2009) "Mapping public web space with the Issue Crawler." In C. Brossard and B. Reber (eds) *Digital cognitive technologies: Epistemology and Knowledge Society* (pp 115–26). London, UK: Wiley.

Rogers, R. (2012) "Mapping and the politics of web space." *Theory, Culture & Society* 29, 193–219.

Sassen, S. (2001) *The global city: New York, London, Tokyo*, Princeton, NJ: Princeton University Press.

Sassen, S. (2007) *Deciphering the global: Its scales, spaces and subjects*. New York: Routledge.

Soghoian, C. (2012) "Enforced community standards for research on users of the Tor anonymity network." In G. Danezis, S. Dietrich, and K. Sako (eds) *Financial cryptography and data security*, vol 7126, *Lecture notes in computer science* (pp 146–53). Berlin and Heidelberg, Germany: Springer,

Wellman, B. (1979) "The community question: The intimate networks of East Yorkers." *American Journal of Sociology* 84, 1201–31.

Wellman, B. (2001) "Physical place and cyberplace: The rise of personalized networking." *International Journal of Urban and Regional Research* 25, 227–52.

Wellman, B. and C.A. Haythornthwaite (2002) "The internet in everyday life." *The information age series*. Oxford, UK: Blackwell.

Wellman, B. and B. Leighton (1979) "Networks, neighborhoods and communities: Approaches to the study of the community question." *Urban Affairs Quarterly* 14, 363–90.

Wellman, B. et al (2003) "The social affordances of the internet for networked individualism." *Journal of Computer-Mediated Communication* 8 (3).

3

A return to *Gemeinschaft*: Digital impression management and the sharing economy

Alexandrea J. Ravenelle

The sharing economy claims to be "disrupting"[1] the world as we know it, using big data, innovation and responsiveness to change the world into "neighbors helping neighbors."[2] Suddenly an app and a smartphone is all you need to hail a cab, hire a handyperson, or find a hotel room; and in each case, you're working directly with individuals through peer-to-peer connections, as opposed to corporations. The breathless consensus is that the so-called sharing economy will return us to the idyllic days of *Gemeinschaft*, where everyone knows your name, people trust each other, and resources are used in a more efficient and environmentally-friendly-way.

Digital records are the key to working together in the sharing economy or "gig" economy. In *Gemeinschaft*, reputations could follow a family for forever, and today one's Facebook trail is everlasting. Sharing economy services often link through Facebook and LinkedIn accounts for identity verification, attempting to digitally recreate the neighborly interactions and social network linkages that defined pre-industrial society. Users are also asked to post personal photos and profiles and to communicate before each stay or task. Workers are rated on responsiveness and performance, with low scores triggering instant, unappealable termination. Meanwhile, TrustCloud is working to collect people's "online data exhaust," posts from Facebook, Twitter, and TripAdvisor that could be used to calculate reliability, consistency, and responsiveness – a "trust rating"[3] similar to the credit rating of the offline world.

Most people are familiar with the idea that first impressions matter. Employment advice handbooks are chock-full of suggestions on how to dress for the job you want, the appropriate fingernail length, even advice on which piercings are appropriate where. But whereas in *Gemeinschaft*, where reputations were formed over months and years of interactions with an individual and his or her family, in the sharing economy, impressions are formed in a millisecond as someone scrolls down a screen, viewing a dozen or more competitors. In addition to managing their first digital impression, workers must also manage themselves "on the job" to ensure that they receive positive reviews that can also make or break their sharing economy success. As a result, managing impressions is a circular reaction where successful management leads to more bookings, resulting in higher placement in site search algorithms and more work – and where negative impressions can quickly spiral into unemployment.

In this chapter I use interviews with 27 gig economy workers to explore how they present their digital selves and engage in face-to-face interactions to further support those selves, with the goal of generating positive impressions and digital reviews. I was interested in how users picked their photographs (whether of themselves, their homes, or food) and of the text descriptions they provided. What tactics do they use to market themselves? When it comes to face-to-face encounters with clients, how do they ensure that their carefully crafted online persona is deemed an authentic and accurate representation? How does the process of being actively reviewed on a daily process affect their interactions with others? In a world where one comment on Twitter can result in virtual – and sometimes actual – mob action (Ronson 2015), what does it mean to have your digital identity determine your employability?

The sharing economy

The sharing economy is a catch-all term for "'peer-to-peer' firms that connect people for the purposes of distributing, sharing, and reusing goods and services" (Mathews, 2014). The concept encompasses everything from multi-billion dollar companies such as Airbnb (room rental) and Uber (on-call taxi and delivery service) to free durable good sharing sites such as Neighborgoods. Definitions of the sharing economy vary and often seem arbitrary: Airbnb is seen as the epitome of the sharing economy, but traditional bed and breakfasts are not. Ebay, the online marketplace of essentially everything, is hailed as an early founder, but free local libraries and parks are not. Juliet Schor, a preeminent researcher in the field, notes that definitions of the sharing economy tend to be "pragmatic, rather then analytical: self-definition by the platforms and the press defines who is in and who is out" (Schor, 2014: 2). The general view is that the sharing economy "represents an innovation that is capable of re-allocating wealth across the 'value chain,' specifically away from 'middlemen' and towards small producers and consumers" (Schor and Fitzmaurice, 2014: 4).

The sharing economy, also described interchangeably as connected consumption, collaborative consumption, or the on-demand economy, is generally dated to the 1995 invention of eBay by Pierre Omidyar (Alden, 2014). Later contributory organizations included Craigslist.com and the free hospitality exchange website Couchsurfing.org, founded in 2003. The rise of the sharing economy is thought to be "fueled by the convergence of smart phone ubiquity; secure cashless payment systems, and the relatability and transparency of customer review sites," but not all of the impetus is technological (McGowan, 2014). The recession and post-recession fall-out also meant a need to monetize possessions, to make do with less, and the rampant underemployment of college graduates (McGowan, 2014). In addition, the gig economy's focus on laissez-faire capitalism and deregulation suggests strong neoliberal roots (Hill, 2014) and earlier efforts to shift risk to workers and consumers (Hacker, 2006).

Goals of the sharing economy range from reversing economic inequality to stopping ecological destruction to countering materialistic tendencies to enhancing worker rights and empowering the poor (Mathews, 2014). But as Jon Evans, *TechCrunch* writer and self-described "relatively-wealthy techie" points out, the "'sharing economy' is mostly spin. It mostly consists of people who have excess disposable income hiring those who do not.... Far more accurate to call it the 'servant economy'" (Evans, 2013). This focus on the workers as the ultimate in at-will employees – hired for a few hours or days and actively reviewed all the while – is at the forefront of my research.

Three sharing economy companies

Founded in San Francisco in 2008, Airbnb was created by two roommates who couldn't make rent that month. In an oft-repeated story, the founders of Airbnb rented out three air mattresses for $80 a night over the weekend of the Industrial Designers Society of America conference and soon had a business (Friedman, 2013). In May 2015, Airbnb's website noted that it had more than a million listings worldwide in 190 countries; by November of the same year, the number exceeded 2 million. The website allows hosts to list their home or extra space[4] online and to rent it out to guests. The company operates as a listing service and escrow account; payment for the host is held until the guest arrives and ensures that all is as expected.

Kitchensurfing is a personal chef service. The platform offers two opportunities for chef rental: a Kitchensurfing Tonight dining option[5] that costs approximately $25 per person and where diners choose from one of three pre-set menus, or Traditional Kitchensurfing, a personalized, anytime option for up to $100 each. The $25 per person is all-inclusive: a chef arrives with all of the necessary ingredients and cooking tools, cooks and serves the meal, and then cleans up afterwards. Tips and transportation are also included in the $25 price. The second, more expensive and expansive option, Traditional Kitchensurfing, allows clients to choose a chef from more than 100 different menus and to personalize the menu to their liking and guest count. Options range from $40/head cocktail parties to $100/head formal dinners for up to 16 people.[6]

TaskRabbit is a personal assistant service that allows people to "live smarter by connecting you with safe and reliable help in your neighborhood" (TaskRabbit, no date, a). Users answer a series of questions about the task that they want done (errand running, cleaning, Ikea furniture assembly, party-planning, etc) and are given an algorithm-selected listing of available Taskers[7] and their hourly rates. Taskers are interviewed and background checked by the company and receive task assignments based on their availability, or can be requested specifically by a client.

Research project

This chapter investigates, through in-depth mixed-methods research, how sharing economy workers utilize impression management to market themselves. This study is part of a larger qualitative study on the sharing economy, the changing nature of work, and how social inequity contributes to the sharing economy. Respondents for this study were recruited through messaging tools available on Airbnb and Kitchensurfing websites and through direct contact with workers. In addition, several respondents were recruited through online discussion boards such as the New York City TaskRabbit's Facebook page. I focused my research on workers who work within the five boroughs of New York City.

I interviewed 27 people: 14 Airbnb hosts, 6 TaskRabbit workers and 7 Kitchensurfing chefs between March and May 2015. Matching the heavily White demographics often found in sharing economy services, 19 of the participants were White, 4 were African American or Black, 1 was Hispanic and 3 identified as racially mixed. Sixteen were men and 11 were women. Their ages ranged from 20 to 54, with 85 percent in their 20s and 30s. Education levels also varied: 11 had a Bachelor's degree, six had a graduate degree (JD, MD, PhD, or MA), and 8 described themselves as either currently students or with some college or graduate credit hours. One international respondent described himself as having a high school diploma and one had an Associates degree. Ten were married or living with a partner; two of the single respondents mentioned definitive plans to move in with a significant other within the next few months.

All of the interviews were conducted face-to-face, and the length of the interviews ranged from just under an hour to slightly more than three hours, although most were approximately an hour and 45 minutes. I used Weiss' (1994) interview matrix to guide the interview as needed, but I generally relied on a more conversational method, which allowed interviewees to discuss additional issues that they felt were relevant and to provide stories about their experiences in the sharing economy. Each respondent was also given a short two-page survey to assist in gathering demographic information such as race, age, income, education, marital status, and the number of hours worked each week. Anonymity was assured and all names were changed.

I tape-recorded and transcribed all interviews and systematically coded categories using a standard system as utilized by Taylor and Bogdan (1984). I then analyzed the data using grounded theory (Glaser and Strauss, 1967) and an inductive approach, allowing the concepts and theories to emerge from the data.

Impression management strategies

In *The presentation of self in everyday life*, Erving Goffman (1959) examines how people guide and control the impressions that others form of them, a concept he calls "impression management." With the language of theatre, Goffman utilizes the concepts of a front region or stage, where the performance is conducted, and the back region, where one prepares for the performance, stores props, or can otherwise relax. According to Goffman, social interaction rituals reflect power dynamics among individuals as they work to create and maintain a positive image of the self. Most people want to think the best of themselves and to emphasize the positive in the online marketplace.

Impression management is often used to influence the outcome of job interviews (Ralston and Kirkwood, 1999) and in promotion decisions (Giacalone and Rosenfeld, 1991). However, in the sharing economy, where work may last only a few hours or days and "job searching" is constant, impression management takes on additional importance in hiring. In addition, sharing economy workers can become, in Goffman's (1963) terms, "discreditable" if they present too rosy a picture, generating claims of false advertising. Likewise, a sharing economy worker in particular must always be a "disciplined performer" with "self-control" who "does not give the show away" (Goffman 1959: 216).

Goffman's work is usually applied to face-to-face interactions and has been used to analyze such unrelated phenomena as how presidents utilize first ladies (Klapp, 1964), how female psychopathic killers work to diminish accountability (Perri and Terrance, 2010), how presentation of self can be used to motivate one to exercise (Martin Ginis et al, 2007), and how mothers use children's appearances to maintain their identities (Collett, 2005). Although the technical core of the internet was developed in the late 1960s, the World Wide Web wasn't established until 1989, roughly seven years after Goffman's untimely death. However, applying Goffman's work to internet interactions is hardly unprecedented. Papacharissi (2002) and Dominick (1999) applied Goffman's concept of impression management to examining personal homepages, Dwyer (2007) explored impression management on instant messaging platforms, and Pollach and Kerbler (2011) used the same concepts in their analysis of chief executive officer (CEO) profiles on corporate websites.

Respondents believe it is important to market themselves well on the various platforms through photography, text descriptions, and their general responsiveness to potential customers. To explain the front stage strategies used by sharing economy workers, I first explain the reasons behind these front stage/back stage performances, and provide a few typical points made by members of the sharing economy. I then explain how respondents interpret each strategy before focusing on status symbol crafting and utilizing external resources.

Front stage presentations

Goffman (1959: 22) defines the front as the "expressive equipment of a standard kind intentionally or unwittingly employed by the individual during his performance." This equipment includes the setting, which features furniture, décor and physical layout, and together "supply the scenery and stage props for the spate of human action" (1959: 22). The personal front is often divided into appearance and manner. Appearance can include race and sex, but also age, clothing, and facial expressions. Meanwhile, manner can be thought of as how one carries oneself, for instance, are one's interactions egalitarian or haughty?

Although the importance of worker photographs varies on Airbnb, Kitchensurfing and TaskRabbit, all three sites require workers to provide a photo, and workers repeatedly noted the importance of appearing friendly or maintaining a friendly manner in the photos they utilized.

> I made sure to smile – and smiling indicates friendliness – so I wanted people to know that I'm a friendly person. (Samantha, 23, Airbnb host)

> I want people to look at my picture and say, 'oh my goodness, that guy looks like fun and I want to hire him' and then when they meet me they think 'that's exactly the guy that I thought I was hiring.' (Robert, 28, TaskRabbit)

Smiling is important to successful impression management. Research by Peace, Miles, and Johnston (2006) suggests that genuine smiles in advertisements are more likely to lead to more positive evaluations as compared to neutral and faked smiles, and work by Scanlon and Polage (2011) showed significant preference in respondents' likelihood to purchase products when accompanied by a smiling photo. Some workers, such as Ashaki, a 35-year-old Kitchensurfing chef, mentioned being told by consumers that their smiling even landed them the job: "They're like, 'We like that you smiled on your picture and that made us feel like you are friendly. That's the reason why we went for you.'"

A photo of the individual worker is important, but depending on the service being offered, workers are often given additional tools with which to market themselves. For instance, individuals who list homes or rooms for rent on Airbnb are called "hosts" by the company. In addition to their individual profiles, hosts are also responsible for creating a listing profile. Hosts write catchy headlines, select pictures of the rental space and themselves, provide house rules, descriptions of the space and surrounding neighborhood, a personal profile, and set their availability and rates. Although Airbnb provides some suggestions of what hosts should include in each section of their listing, the content is very much in the hands of the user. Even though homes are often viewed as back stage locations where one can relax and be one's self, a home listed on Airbnb is suddenly front stage. Just like a real estate broker may stage a home, Airbnb hosts can carefully curate their listings, shaping the back stage in order to create authenticity. As a result, hosts utilize each section of their listing to convey a particular impression of themselves to prospective guests.

For Daniel, a 31-year-old branding professional, and his girlfriend, the text descriptions of their home were a deliberate effort to address topics that they felt people would be concerned about. Daniel says that their listing utilized such phrases as "a smoke-free house keeps our linen fresh" in a conscious and intentional effort to let people know that it was a clean and smoke-free apartment. He explains,

> And even just like little things, like, 'We always have avocado available in the kitchen for you guys.' Yeah, it was a very conscious effort to make it like a certain personality and like, here's who you're going to be staying with without saying it that directly. Like we definitely want to give people clues for like, you know, you're going to be with a couple, we're young professionals and we're probably not going to be out drunk all the time, but we're probably going to come home late. And it helps people who also do that to be like, 'oh cool, I can probably find a bar with them.'

Reassurance is a common theme among Airbnb users. Many are conscious of the fact that strangers are renting out space in their homes, and that Airbnb is still a relatively new service that not all people are entirely familiar – or comfortable – with. In particular, there's a perception that single women may be wary of staying with male hosts and as a result, men often listed female partners as co-hosts, referenced them in the listing or put the listing in the name of a girlfriend.

> The first time we went on, it was my boyfriend who made the profile and he used a picture of me and my name because he felt that a woman was like safer. He didn't ask me but this was his rationalization afterward, and then we packaged ourselves as a couple which was also a calculation about making ourselves appear normal. (Ramona, 28, Airbnb host)

Single men were being careful to mention female partners or to take photos that showed them with female friends in order to reassure prospective guests. This need to provide assurance that women won't be sexually assaulted in the home of a stranger also extended to gay men:

> I provide a couple of photos of myself. I don't state that I'm gay in my profile but I think some people can pick up on that which, obviously for women probably, is very ... reassuring, yeah.... There's also one of me and my best friend T–. Oh, yeah. That's right. That, I think, was probably also somewhat reassuring to women to see me with another normal-looking girl having a good time. (Andrew, 28, Airbnb host)

Given that single travelers and women make up a considerable portion of the traveling public (Rosenbloom, 2014, 2015), being successful in this reassurance can literally make or break a host's listing success.

Taskers, workers affiliated with the personal assistant service TaskRabbit, are limited to approximately 150-word descriptions of themselves and their work skills. Perhaps because of this limitation, they repeatedly mentioned that they didn't believe that people read the actual text accompanying their profile; however, they still used the text descriptions to make themselves seem like a safer hire by highlighting their education level and prestigious alma maters.

> Interviewer: Were there things that you did on your profile to make you seem more trustworthy?
> Jamal: You dropped the S word.
> Interviewer: You dropped the S word?
> Jamal: Stanford.

For Jamal, a 25-year-old African-American man with a college degree from a highly prestigious university, noting that he attended Stanford was a way to emphasize his qualifications and assure potential TaskRabbit clients of his legitimacy.

For Kitchensurfing Tonight chefs, who arrive otherwise sight-unseen at a client's home, name dropping must be done verbally. Ladu, a 39-year-old dreadlocked black man from the West Indies, explained that he deliberately mentions cooking at one of the most famous and iconic New York City restaurants when he needs to reassure people of his qualifications.

Storing the self in back regions

Examining the back region allows us to better identify the hidden work involved in the presentation of self. Airbnb hosts in particular walk a fine line in their impression management strategies. Although the home is often seen as a prime back stage region, for Airbnb hosts, their homes are transformed into front stage regions as the homes are staged, photographed, and displayed online for public perusal and renting. In addition, because guests are paying for the space, the act of purchasing brings a certain expectation of service. Hosts must provide the New York City local living experience, while protecting themselves and their belongings. They have to ensure that guests have a place for their possessions without putting personal items at risk of being used or broken. In order to maintain the impressions they cultivated through their profiles, hosts also utilize Goffman's concept of backstage. Goffman (1959: 112) defines the backstage as a place where the impression fostered by a performance is knowingly contradicted. In the back region, "stage props and items of personal front can be stored ... different types of liquor or clothes, can be hidden so that the audience will not be able to see the treatment accorded to them in comparison with the treatment that could have been accorded to them." Many hosts discuss preparing their homes in advance of renting them out. This preparation has two purposes: (1) it allows hosts to hide or protect items that are perceived to be valuable from their guests, and (2) it allows the home to mimic the clean, organized state depicted in the Airbnb listing. In accordance with Goffman's description of the backstage, a closet is often used to hide or remove items that could otherwise be used by guests.

Items that are left behind run the risk of being damaged. Amy, 36, an Airbnb host who had temporarily moved with her family out of their apartment in order to register her child in a better school, expressed dismay at leaving behind personal items and was one of the few to tell the story of a destroyed memento, a handmade airplane that she had given her child. Amy noted, "I was really torn to leave personal things but we're in a much smaller place, I couldn't move everything."

Ramona, a graduate student who rents out her apartment with her boyfriend, illustrates this backstage management of the setting perfectly. Like many hosts, she hides valuables, stores them with friends, or takes them with her:

My boyfriend has a projector, which is an $800 thing, which feels valuable [laughs] and so we put that up away in the back of a closet. We take all our booze out of the cupboard and put it in the closet and ask people not to go into the closet. The closet is never locked but it's just kind-of packed full of stuff and the booze is hidden. [laughs] Those are our priorities: booze and electronics.

But as the conversation continues, perhaps feeling uncomfortable with the impression she is creating as someone for whom "booze and electronics" are priorities, she redirects her description of hiding things to more of a focus on how she ensures that guests get the "hotel experience."

It's usually less about hiding valuables and more about like clearing space. So we clear cupboard space, we clear out the fridge, we clear out our dresser drawers, we clear out the clothes racks in the room. We kind-of make our place into a hotel so that when they get there it's less like they're living in our space.

For some, the clearing of space not only made their home but also served the goal of making it easier to clean between guests:

I did a lot of making space for people on surfaces and things, so that you could very easily arrive and settle in the place and then pack up and leave without feeling like you had to go into cabinets and all that kind of stuff. And like making space for hanging clothes, for example, and space in the fridge.... So one of the things that I adapted was that I didn't have anything on my floor. Everything had legs or was sort of light so that vacuuming can be very easy and quick. (Matthew, 36)

In this way, Matthew also takes advantage of common strategies in hotel rooms – lightweight, legged furniture and few additional items – that make it easier to clean the room between guests.

Even though Airbnb often emphasizes that guests get the authentic experience of staying with locals, the locals I interviewed made a conscious effort to reduce their physical presence and to allow guests to take the space and "make [it] their own." Samantha, a 23-year-old host, went so far as to emphasize this freedom to create in the listing photos she featured of her room: "I made sure my room was clean and clear of personal stuff because I wanted them to know, it's like a canvas, which is how I leave it."

For TaskRabbit and Kitchensurfing workers, their backstage occurs off-stage, before they arrive at the client's home. Workers with both groups mentioned using time between gigs to rest and recharge on the subway, grab a slice of pizza, or visit a Starbucks bathroom. For Kitchensurfing Today chefs, the additional backstage work of prepping that night's meal (cutting up vegetables, assembling spice packets) is done at the commissary kitchen by other cooking personnel, making it easier for them to remain within their 30-minute face-time time limit.

Impression management: a team effort

Goffman notes that the effective presentation of self requires the collaboration of a team of social actors. Two cast members that contribute to the digital performance are the product itself (that is, the space on Airbnb and the food on Kitchensurfing) and external resources via legitimizing reviews. Although it is common to think of the performance team as being actual individuals, such as the audience or co-stars, the utilization of static images or places has precedence in work by Bonsu (2007) analyzing how obituaries from the Asante people of Ghana are used to craft self-presentation strategies and Zavattaro's (2013) work on place-branding. Airbnb hosts and Kitchensurfing chefs in particular used status symbols and external resources to market themselves.

Crafting the status symbol

Goffman writes that a status symbol can "express a point of view, a style of life and the cultural values" of an individual (1951: 295). Even as work in the US becomes increasingly service-based, most workers are not located in other people's homes, or make money by renting our their own homes. As a result, Airbnb hosts and Kitchensurfing chefs must use status symbols to demonstrate to potential clients that they are "one of our kind."

Even though hosts and chefs are the ones providing the labor and often mention trying to offer a personal experience, they are given second billing in the listings compared to the product on offer. For Airbnb, the main photo is of the apartment and the image takes up approximately half of the screen vertically. By comparison, the image of the host is roughly the size of an American quarter. On Kitchensurfing, the main chef-listing page features 12 different food photos with chef thumbnails that are approximately a tenth of the size of the food images. Food remains front and center with the Kitchensurfing Tonight service. Chefs hired through the weeknight service are assigned via algorithm and only the food is featured – consumers don't know who their chef will be until that evening's assignments are made and distributed via email around 4pm. Both traditional Kitchensurfing chefs and Airbnb hosts are conscious of the power of the status symbol in their midst, and actively work to showcase it through photography, often putting more attention to the photos and description of the "product" than of themselves.

For instance, James, 36, noted that he "put very little thought into my profile." By comparison, he took "probably like 40 shots" for the apartment's listing on Airbnb and then chose the best 12 to feature. He explains,

> I was conscious with the opening shot. Everyone else has a picture of their living room. I have a picture with a view from my roof.... Because people are looking to come to New York and here's a picture of the skyline in New York versus a tiny spot. It's like tiny spots? There are plenty of those. Here's a beautiful view. Then I have a pool on my roof, I feature that too.

The status symbol of the gorgeous apartment or beautifully plated food is not only given the most attention in the performance, it's also given attention in the marketing that leads up to the in-person performance. Even though James notes that the outdoor rooftop pool is only open for approximately three months of the year, it gets much more attention on his listing and from guests than his personal information, and helps to differentiate his listing from the rest. For Ashaki, a chef who specializes in Western African food, making food the star comes with additional challenges. She explains,

> If you ever Google African food, they just slap it on the plate. I'm like, 'What is this?' If you know it, you're like, 'Wow. It's delicious,' but if you see the picture, if you've never tried, you're like, 'I will never try that.'... I try to really make sure that images are really captivating, and they make you want to basically eat it off of the page.... That way, it helps the customer ... to book me.

Even though Ashaki spends hours sourcing, prepping, transporting, and marketing her farm-to-table food and Kitchensurfing describes itself as "putting chefs in your kitchen," she is very much put second to the food in her listing. As a result, in response to this challenge of marketing Nigerian food, Ashaki took advantage of Thanksgiving to enlist her family to stage and photograph the items on her Kitchensurfing menus. She explains, "It dresses it up. It makes it more presentable, more appetizing. You want to try it. It's not just cooking. It's just the presentation of it. It's everything."

However, the sharing economy is not just about marketing. There's also a fine line between selling and over-marketing. Users who run afoul of this division are likely to experience negative reviews as a form of user policing. Too many negative reviews can result in reduced bookings in the future, or, in the case of TaskRabbit, possible deactivation from the platform. As a result, hosts emphasize the best parts of the space that they're renting, while still being careful to note any possible problems.

> When I was making the profile, it was all about the location. I
> mean, it's a good location, and it's really close to great restaurants,
> easy access to the subway, it's a clean room, it's got good windows
> and good light. So for me, it was more about, you know, making
> the room seem desirable, because it is…. I mean at the same time,
> I don't have a door, I just have a curtain that blocks my room,
> so I put that in there as a disclaimer. 'This room doesn't actually
> have a door that separates it from the living room.' (Samantha, 23)

Most people would never rent a hotel room that didn't have a lock, much less
a room that was missing an actual door and an entire wall, but in the New
York Airbnb world, such a room can be listed for $95/night. Still, Samantha
is conscious that such a room might not qualify as a room for everyone,
describing her notation as a "disclaimer" so that she can repudiate any possible
claims of misrepresentation.

Photos can also be used as visual disclaimer, to help minimize the expected
status of a product that has been reviewed favorably. Joshua, 32, who runs
a sell-described Airbnb "syndicate" of roughly 10 apartments split between
multiple user profiles had an apartment that he designated, "The Dungeon."
The tiny, box-like ground floor apartment had problems with mice, kitchen
sink drainage, and a front door lock that was constantly breaking; eventually
Joshua gave the space up. He explains, "I still had like four stars which is
actually a good lesson for anyone doing Airbnb. Just because a place has a lot
of stars, you should still look at the pictures, and say what does this look like?"

Harnessing external resources

Reviews are powerful in the sharing economy, with users alternatively
describing them as exciting and scary. There's a common perception that bad
reviews can make or break a listing. At the same time, the user reviews are
also seen as a marketing resource. Given by an outsider, positive reviews are
often seen as an endorsement and can make it possible for a user to move up
in the placement algorithm and to receive more bookings, even in unrelated
areas, as this Tasker mentions.

> It's also really great to get the reviews because that's how you get
> more clients and when clients want to hire you they see that and
> they say, 'oh well, they have great reviews.' And it may not even be
> in the task that you are doing but they see that you have reviews
> and so that's a really good thing. And especially when you have a
> review and the task that you've already done and people see that,
> that moves it forward. (Robert, 28, Tasker)

All workers studied discussed actively working to ensure that their reviews were positive. Common strategies for Airbnb hosts included making sure that the home had plenty of towels, special bath products, a well-stocked medicine cabinet, and even leaving gifts for their guests.

> I try to provide some sort of like granola or a couple of pieces of fruit. I will normally put like two or four juices in the fridge depending on how long their stay is ... it depends also who is coming. If it's like a fun couple maybe I'll think, 'oh they'll like this beer' or if I have someone coming for their honeymoon, I'm going to definitely buy them like wine or champagne, those sort of things. (Brittany, 24)

> First it was just a box of chocolates then I was like, I don't want to give chocolates to everyone, I want them to feel special. So sometimes I do wine – sometimes I'd get Broadway tickets. (Aalia, 30)

Leaving items for guests isn't perfunctory, but is a part of making it a personalized experience and is intended to make a visitor feel special. Hosts who don't provide gifts often work to make guests feel unique through personalized service.

> I try to build goodwill mostly being like an on-demand concierge because I tell them they can always reach me on the iPhone, via text message, if they have any questions.... I consider myself an expert on the city so I'm more than happy to share that, especially for people who are interested in the same things as I am. I want them to have the best experience possible so I encourage that they use me as a resource. (Andrew, 28)

The focus on the self as a resource also allows users to educate users, and, if especially successful, they may find that the user reviews assist in their marketing. Ashaki, a chef, often finds that her clients' exposure to African food is limited to Ethiopian cuisine. As a result, she must actively work to educate her clients about the food by comparing it to other items they may have tried:

> There's one particular review that had my thing. I think that was almost eight months ago when I got it. My whole thing is trying to make connection about African food for people. Kind of, 'You might have tried tamales before. We have *Moi Moi* that is Nigerian that's almost similar to tamales, but they're not the same.' The process of cooking them is the same because you put them in plantain leaf. It's black-eyed beans versus corn. You put different

seasonings. So they are from the same family, but they're just a different flavor. That customer made that connection. When she did my review, she basically did a lot of that like, 'When me and my husband tried it, it reminded us of tamales. When she cooked this, it reminded us of this.' I love that.

For Ashaki, careful management of her interactions with clients can also result in harnessing those clients to further her mission of explaining what her food is, giving additional legitimacy to her listing.

Given the risk of negative reviews, users also actively worked to transform problematic situations. Airbnb hosts who encountered unhappy guests utilized a number of strategies including offering to buy dinner; delivering wine, chocolates and presents for a child; letting ill guests stay after the customary check-out time; letting guests check in during the middle of the night; and delivering space heaters when an apartment was too cold. Sometimes their efforts result in a positive review after all, but hosts also noted that sometimes their additional efforts may have simply prevented a negative review. Joshua explains:

> Some people don't review because they forget or maybe they were dissatisfied in some way, but they don't want to ruin your profile. That's why I respond and am very friendly with people because I think it makes it harder to give someone a terrible review if you talk to them and they've been helpful.

Discussion

Gemeinschaft/Gesellschaft is often described as the city-country divide. For Tönnies (1887), *Gemeinschaft* was a community focused on primary relations organized by natural will, house, village, and town, with a focus on collective consciousness and effervescence. In a *Gesellschaft*, connections are abstract and more tenuous, bonds have to be imagined and connections organized through contracts. By this definition, when one moves to a "modern" day society – or at least a city – one loses the community connections of *Gemeinschaft*.

But the sharing economy paints itself as a solution, as a return to small town or even village life. The sharing economy is thought to make trust easier because electronic trails are supposed to make it easier to know everyone. In the small community of old, reputations could follow a family for forever, but today people are equally followed by their online personas. Yet rather than lead to a wholesale embracing of trust, every interaction is turned into a performance. In the past, home was viewed as a refuge from the workplace, a place without the pressures of performance for pay. But with Airbnb hosts renting their entire homes or "sharing" them with guests, the home is transformed from a refuge from the marketplace to an additional performance space, a place where the back stage is displayed front and center as a way to support authenticity and build trust. Likewise, the rise of TaskRabbit and Kitchensurfing also bring workers into the home and contributes to the division of labor: cooking and errand running become the activities of those for hire.

As the ultimate in temporary workers, members of the sharing economy must actively work to cultivate and maintain positive impressions among users. Through photos and text descriptions, workers focus on creating positive impressions of themselves and their sharing economy work. They utilize Goffman's concept of the backstage to literally hide the personal – whether valuable possessions or their own eating and bodily functions – in order to provide positive impressions to prospective clients. Sharing economy workers also craft stars, manage social risks, and harness reviews in their digital impression management strategies. This digital crafting of profiles may contribute to the sense of community, but is also necessary to employability.

Rather than returning to the community-focused *Gemeinschaft*, the rise of the sharing economy commodifies services, adding a paying component to things that used to be done for free and turning "neighbors helping neighbors" into a quantifiable and reviewable performance. Instead of returning to the pre-industrial village, the sharing economy extends the Industrial Revolution.

Notes

[1] Disruptive technology, according to Clayton Christensen, is when a product or service relentlessly moves up market, eventually displacing established competitors (see www.claytonchristensen.com/key-concepts/#sthash.3Ae1oMhH.dpuf). This technology does not have to be groundbreaking; it just has to start to edge out established competitors – something Airbnb and Uber are doing quite well.

[2] TaskRabbit, one of the sharing economy companies explored in this chapter, describes itself as, "an old school concept – neighbors helping neighbors – reimagined for today" (Taskrabbit.com, no date, a).

[3] Readers may note that some of the terminology in this chapter contradicts standard definitions, such as the use of "trust" to describe background checking and identity verification or "home sharing" to describe charging someone to sleep in your spare room. I argue that this expropriation is often crucial to the marketing of sharing economy (Ravenelle, under review). Likewise, in regards to the use of "disrupting," many sharing economy companies use this term to describe their services, although their use of the term is often at odds with commonly accepted definitions of disruption as "groundbreaking" or "wreaking havoc."

[4] Airbnb's definition of extra space is especially broad. Listings include everything from a spare bedroom to treehouses to castles to sleeping in the trunk of a Tesla.

[5] Although Kitchensurfing.com is available in seven cities, this new weeknight dining option is only available in Manhattan, south of 116th Street and was launched in 2015. As a result, I refer to these as Kitchensurfing Tonight and Kitchensurfing Traditional.

[6] The gig economy is constantly changing. In the fall of 2015, Kitchensurfing noted that it was disbanding the Traditional service and focusing entirely on Kitchensurfing Tonight. A future article will address the effect this sudden service change had on workers.

[7] Originally, the workers were called "TaskRabbits." In 2014, as part of an overhaul of the system, the workers were renamed the less disparaging "Taskers."

References

Airbnb.com (no date) "About us" (www.airbnb.com/about/about-us).

Alden, W. (2014) "The business tycoons of Airbnb." *The New York Times Magazine*, November 25.

Bonsu, S.K. (2007) "The presentation of dead selves in everyday life: Obituaries and impression management." *Symbolic Interaction* 30 (2), 199–219.

Collett, J. (2005) "What kind of mother am I? Impression management and the social construction of motherhood." *Symbolic Interaction* 28 (3), 327–47.

Dominick, J.R. (1999) "Who do you think you are? Personal home pages and self-presentation on the World Wide Web." *Journalism & Mass Communication Quarterly* 76, 646–58.

Dwyer, C. (2007) "Digital relationships in the 'Myspace' generation: Results from a qualitative study." 40th Annual Hawaii International Conference on System Sciences, IEEE.

Evans, J. (2013) "Meet the new serfs, same as the old serfs." *TechCrunch*, October 5.

Friedman, T.L. (2013) "Welcome to the 'sharing economy.'" *The New York Times*, July 20.

Giacalone, R.A. and P. Rosenfeld (1991) *Applied impression management: How image-making affects managerial decisions.* London, UK: Sage.

Glaser, B.G. and A.L. Strauss (1999) *The discovery of grounded theory: Strategies for qualitative research.* New York: Aldine de Gruyter.

Goffman, E. (1951) "Symbols of class status." *The British Journal of Sociology* 2 (4), 294–304.

Goffman, E. (1959) *The presentation of self in everyday life.* New York: Doubleday Books.

Goffman, E. (1963) *Stigma notes on the management of spoiled identity.* New York: Simon & Schuster.

Hacker, J.S. (2006) *The great risk shift.* New York: Oxford University Press.

Hill, S. (2015) *Raw deal: How the "Uber economy" and runaway capitalism are screwing American workers.* New York: St Martin's Press.

Klapp, O.E. (1964) *Symbolic leaders: Public dramas and public men.* New York: Minerva Press.

McGowan, H. (2014) "Underemployment and income inequality: Occupy or collaborate." *LinkedIn Pulse*, August 25 (www.linkedin.com/pulse/20140825182254-22726740-underemployment-and-income-inequality-occupy-or-collaborate).

Martin Ginis, K.A., M. Lindwall, and H. Prapavessis (2007) "Who cares what other people think? Self-presentation in exercise and sport." In R. Eklund and G. Tenenbaum (eds) *Handbook of sport psychology* (pp 136–153). Hoboken, NJ: John Wiley & Sons.

Mathews, J. (2014) "The sharing economy boom is about to bust." *Time*, June 27 (http://time.com/2924778/airbnb-uber-sharing-economy/).

Papacharissi, Z. (2002) "The presentation of self in virtual life: Characteristics of personal home pages." *Journalism & Mass Communication Quarterly* 79, 643–60.

Peace, V., L. Miles, and L. Johnston (2006) "It doesn't matter what you wear: The impact of posed and genuine expressions of happiness on product evaluation." *Social Cognition*: 24 (2), 137–68.

Perri, F.S. and T.G. Lichtenwald (2010) "The last frontier: Myths and the female psychopathic killer." *Forensic Examiner*, Summer, 50–67.

Pollach, I. and E. Kerbler (2011) "Appearing competent: A study of impression management in US and European CEO profiles." *Journal of Business Communication* 48, 355–72.

Ralston, S.R. and W.G. Kirkwood (1999) "The trouble with applicant impression management." *Journal of Business and Technical Communication* 13, 190–207.

Ravenelle, A.J. (under review) "Sharing economy workers: Selling, not sharing." *Cambridge Journal of Regions, Economy and Society*, Special Issue.

Ronson, J. (2015) "How one stupid Tweet blew up Justine Sacco's life." *The New York Times Magazine*, February 15.

Rosenbloom, S. (2014) "Zeroing in on the female traveler." *The New York Times*, July 31.

Rosenbloom, S. (2015) "Travel industry responds to rise in solo sojourners." *The New York Times*, May 15.

Schor, J.B. (2014) "Debating the sharing economy." *Great Transition Initiative*, October (http://greattransition.org/publication/debating-the-sharing-economy).

Schor, J.B. and C. Fitzmaurice (2015) "Collaborating and connecting: The emergence of a sharing economy." In L. Reisch and J. Thogersen (eds) *Handbook on research on sustainable consumption* (pp 410–25). Cheltenham, UK: Edward Elgar.

TaskRabbit.com (no date, a) "About us" (www.taskrabbit.com/about).

TaskRabbit.com (no date, b) "What does TaskRabbit offer" (https://support.taskrabbit.com/hc/en-us/articles/204411410-What-does-TaskRabbit-Offer).

Taylor, S. and R. Bogdan (1984) *Introduction to qualitative research methods: The search for meanings.* New York: John Wiley.

Scanlon, A.E. and D.C. Polage (2011) "The strength of a smile: Duchenne smiles improve advertisement and product evaluations." *Pacific Northwest Journal of Undergraduate Research and Creative Activities* 2 (3).

Tönnies, F. (1971) *Community and society: Gemeinschaft and Gesellschaft* (translated and edited by Charles P. Loomis). East Lansing, MI: Michigan State University Press.

Weiss, R.S. (1994) *Learning from strangers: The art and method of qualitative interview studies.* New York: The Free Press.

Zavattaro, S.M. (2013) "Expanding Goffman's theater metaphor to an identity-based view of place branding." *Administrative Theory & Praxis* 35 (4).

4

Digital discourse analysis: Finding meaning in small online spaces

Timothy Recuber

Digital devices and online, networked forms of communication have become so ubiquitous in social life that to mention this fact has almost become unnecessary. Yet social scientists are still coming to terms with the fact that "we now live in a digital society" (Lupton, 2015: 2), and are still figuring out how to adapt our research accordingly. For example, mobile communication technologies have posed significant challenges to traditional methods of survey research (Blumberg et al, 2006; Kempf and Remington, 2007), and online personae make the traditional anonymity of the ethnographic subject increasingly difficult for researchers to guarantee (Thomson, 2014).

On the other hand, digital sociality also offers exciting new methodological possibilities for social research. "Big data" has almost certainly been the most discussed of these. Big data refers to the continuously generated, exhaustive, and fine-grained data that is created today by things such as mobile media devices, banking and retailing transactions, and social networking sites, which is beyond the scale or scope of older ways of knowing about these aspects of the social world (Kitchin, 2014; Schroeder, 2014). Many sociologists have speculated about their discipline's ability to incorporate this new kind of data into existing research paradigms. Although Savage and Burrows worried that big data threatened to muddle "the role of sociologists in generating data" and possibly unseat the discipline's "claims to jurisdiction" (2007: 886), many sociologists have embraced these challenges. Some claim that new computational technologies "and their allied data have the potential to 'digitally re-master' classic questions about social organization, social change and the derivation of identity from collective life" in ways that might invigorate the discipline (Housley et al, 2014: 4). And important work is certainly being done using big data to map information flows across networks, to link qualitative with quantitative levels of analysis, and to apply new kinds of data visualization to large data sets (see Bail, 2014; Healy and Moody, 2014; Tinati et al, 2014; Wiedemann, 2013).

But big data is not without its critics. Writing in *The New Inquiry*, Nathan Jurgenson argued that, "The rationalist fantasy that enough data can be collected with the 'right' methodology to provide an objective and disinterested picture of reality is an old and familiar one: positivism" (2014: para 6). As he put it, "that unwieldy aspiration has been largely abandoned by sociologists in favor of reorienting the discipline toward recognizing complexities rather than pursuing universal explanations for human sociality. But the advent of Big Data has resurrected the fantasy of ... ratifying social facts with sheer algorithmic processing power" (2014: para 7). Similarly, Kate Crawford has criticized the kinds of "data fundamentalism" that support "the notion that correlation always indicates causation, and that massive data sets and predictive analytics always reflect objective truth" (2013: para 1). Crawford instead reminds us that:

> Data and data sets are not objective; they are creations of human design. We give numbers their voice, draw inferences from them, and define their meaning through our interpretations. Hidden biases in both the collection and analysis stages present considerable risks, and are as important to the big-data equation as the numbers themselves. (2013: para 2)

Of course, it is certainly possible to avoid positivist proclamations about the objective truth of even the largest data sets, and sociologists who work with big data are likely to be more attuned to such epistemological concerns than those in other disciplines, given the substantial sociological history of post-positivist or anti-positivist thought (see, for instance, Jain, 2013; Lally and Preston, 1973). But if the digital turn in sociology is to be about more than just the ascent of big data, then those who traffic in qualitative, interpretive, and textual approaches to social science need to explain how their own methodologies can adapt to and take advantage of the digitalization of social life, and in ways that big data cannot.

One way to do so is to foreground the importance of the kinds of small data produced within digital culture. In addition to the massive data sets discussed above, the internet provides access to intimate spaces, with small sample sizes, that let us see people making sense of the world on their own terms, and at a profoundly human scale. Everyday actors make available their thoughts and experiences online in a variety of ways and at a great diversity of sites. This is often at a scale far beneath the thresholds for big data, and in ways difficult to capture with the kinds of automated content and sentiment analysis tools associated with quantitative approaches to textual research. Meaning gets made online in the deep recesses of the internet, beyond Facebook and Twitter, in forgotten Tumblrs, abandoned digital archives, and other out-of-the-way digital spaces. If digital sociology is to flourish, it needs to be able to attend to this sort of data as well. But making sociological sense out of them requires different approaches.

Of course, the affordances of digital technology can enhance traditional forms of qualitative research, such as ethnography, that are more attuned to questions of meaning and working with small sample sizes (Smith, 2014). In Murthy's (2008) formulation, "digital ethnography" involves the incorporation of digital technologies such as online questionnaires, digital videos, social networking sites, and blogs into the ethnographer's traditional toolkit. Others go further, and advocate a kind of "netnography" in which online interactions constitute the entirety of the research site (see Kozinets, 2010). Yet this approach has been criticized for drawing an untenably sharp distinction between the on- and offline world, and ignoring the latter (Dumetricia, 2013).

The approach advocated in this chapter is not a form of digital ethnography, however, as it does not involve becoming a participant in an online community, either overtly or covertly. In that way, it avoids one of the thornier questions of all ethnographic work – the extent to which the researcher's presence has influenced the observed interactions – and takes advantage of the fact that most online spaces automatically record the interactions that take place in threaded posts and archives without requiring the presence of any researcher. Of course, such an approach cannot centrally address the offline connections and interactions that produce online discourse, but by thoroughly contextualizing the research site, it aims at engaging in dialogue and informing the larger scholarly debate around both on- and offline behaviors.

This chapter thus presents a guide to doing digital discourse analysis on small sets of texts in online spaces. This method seeks to deeply understand one aspect of social life online: how meaning gets made through texts. Digital discourse analysis accomplishes this by systematically collecting, reading, and analyzing what gets left behind in the small, sometimes forgotten sites of online discourse that are scattered throughout the World Wide Web. The chapter ultimately argues that digital discourse analysis can reveal much about the ways that social actors make sense out of the messiness of everyday life, and that it can reveal this with a kind of transparency and reflexivity that big data methodologies often lack.

Discourse analysis

Even the term "discourse analysis" is fraught with definitional issues. Often the sort of systematic analysis of textual material advocated here is labeled "content analysis." But beginning with Berelson's (1952) work, content analysis has been associated with a very quantitative approach to media texts, and has also been criticized for its pretense to objectivity and its lack of sensitivity to the nuances of the texts being analyzed (Denzin and Lincoln, 1998; see Kracauer, 1953). Berelson (1952) himself described content analysis as producing "objective, systematic quantitative description of the manifest content of communication" (1952: 18). Discourse analysis, by contrast, is often couched as the more reflexive research practice, more attuned to the ways that institutions and cultures are "enacted and reenacted moment-by-moment" and to the idea that "language-in-use is everywhere and always political" (Gee, 1999: 1). Discourse analysis is, then, also concerned with "the latent meaning of discourse(s) … what is suggested by them or even what is hidden in them" (Ruiz Ruiz, 2009: 8). In practice, such distinctions may be blurrier than advocates of discourse analysis suggest, but in any case, given its more explicit concern with power and reflexivity, discourse analysis appears the more appropriate term for a textual study of online spaces that can counterbalance the positivistic assumptions of big data.

Many studies have already applied the kinds of discourse analysis advocated in this chapter to a variety of relatively small samples or sensitive subject matter in online spaces. To name just a few, Hughey and Daniels (2013) analyzed racist comments at online news sites; Mudry and Strong (2013) analyzed the recovery narratives of gambling addicts; Weaver (2011, 2013) examined racist joke websites; Heinz et al (2007) compared environmentalist rhetoric at Greenpeace websites in three different national contexts; Swan and McCarthy (2003) investigated online animal rights argumentation; and Pulos (2013) studied posts at a World of Warcraft discussion forum devoted to LGBTQ players. My own work has applied these techniques to an anti-Occupy Wall Street Tumblr called "We are the 53 percent" (Recuber, 2015), and to user-submitted messages at digital archives devoted to the September 11th attacks and Hurricane Katrina (Recuber, 2012).

Research like this can say much about how social life is made meaningful online, but these research sites are not, of course, amenable to big data methodologies, or even to more traditional quantitatively oriented forms of content analysis, since they don't really lend themselves to standard kinds of sampling, and they likely wouldn't generate strong measures of statistical significance. Following Mautner (2005), Vann (2009) has argued that discourse analysis methods might be used on big data sets in order to bolster analysts' claims of generalizability, while acknowledging that to do so might hinder the ability of discourse analysis to "continue to make the kinds of close qualitative readings that are its mark of distinction" (2009: 166). Yet digital discourse analysis derives its value precisely from its ability to get at the parts of the internet that are hard to reach or hard to understand with automated text mining tools or other computer-assisted techniques. It is not necessarily important for such data to be numerically large or widely representative of all public opinion on a subject.

In that way, what digital discourse analysis ought to aim for is not capturing all the data, or even a large enough sample of the data to claim generalizability, but simply "transferability." As Lincoln and Guba (1985: 124) explained it, "the degree of transferability is a direct function of the degree of similarity between the two contexts, what we shall call 'fittingness'." Others have elaborated that "the way that the author/researcher helps to establish fittingness vis-à-vis future users of his/her research, is to describe the context of the case/situation in sufficient detail, so that the receiver has an appropriate base of information on which to make a judgment" (Hellström, 2008: 326–7). This notion of transferability is often applied to qualitative work where small and non-random samples suggest that, "local conditions make it impossible to generalize" (Lincoln and Guba, 1985: 124). In any case, the aim of digital discourse analysis ought to be to show that the meanings and norms in the digital texts under analysis are transferable – that they have relevance to other texts in other small, forgotten digital spaces, or in other online sites with similar thematic or emotional content, and to build up from there in future research.

That said, discourse analysis need not shy away from counting. Even Kracauer's (1953) qualitative challenge to the content analysis of Berelson (1952) acknowledged this possibility:

> What counts alone in qualitative analysis – if the verb is permissible in a context which defies counting – is the selection and rational organization of such categories as condense the substantive meanings of the given text, with a view to testing pertinent assumptions and hypotheses. These categories *may* or *may not* invite frequency count. (Kracauer, 1953: 637–8; original emphasis)

Indeed, discourse analyses have often involved counting, either based on the frequency of key words in the texts being analyzed or on the salience of important or ambiguous themes. In either case, "the goal is to use keywords as a heuristic for guiding a close semantic reading of a manageable set of samples" (Vann, 2009: 169). Moreover, the seemingly sharp distinction between quantitative and qualitative approaches to textual analysis may be untenable anyway, as "qualitative decisions" come into play in even very rigid, quantitative coding systems (Popping, 2012: 88). And as Roberto Franzosi (2010: 1) reminds us, "qualitative scholars often use quantitative expressions … and quantitative scholars conveniently forget that often the words are right below the surface of their numbers."

Although many varieties of discourse analysis exist, "critical discourse analysis" – as first outlined by Norman Fairclough (1989) – has been perhaps the most influential. Beginning with the assumption that language and society mutually constitute one another, critical discourse analysis moves through the description and interpretation of texts in order to determine the way other discourses, institutions, and ideologies have come to condition those texts. This view of language as a social process and texts as social products has clear connections to sociology, but discourse analysis – or really any form of textual analysis – is usually treated cursorily in sociology methods classes and textbooks (see Franzosi, 1998). Thus it bears mentioning that methods like critical discourse analysis can provide evidence for core sociological concepts such as the social construction of reality, and can hone in on classic sociological concerns like norms and values (see Grimshaw, 2001).

Some sociologists have attempted to lay out rules specifically for sociological discourse analysis, although these were not concerned with digital texts and online research sites. For instance, David Altheide's (1989, 1996) attempt to bridge the gap between traditional quantitative content analysis and sociological participant observation resulted in a method he labeled "ethnographic content analysis," which has much in common with later models of discourse analysis. And Jorge Ruiz Ruiz (2009) has laid out other methodological guidelines for a specifically sociological form of discourse analysis. In his lucid formulation, discourse analysis begins at the textual level with a mixture of content and semiotic analysis, addressing both manifest and latent meanings. It then proceeds to contextual analysis, focusing on "the space in which the discourse has emerged and in which it acquires meaning" (Ruiz Ruiz, 2009: 11). Finally, the third stage of sociological interpretation "involves making connections between the discourses analyzed and the social space in which they have emerged," focusing especially on "discourse as social information … as a reflection of the ideologies of the subjects who engage in it, and … discourse as a social product" (Ruiz Ruiz, 2009: 15). The aforementioned works have thus supplied the theoretical and methodological grounding for the method of digital discourse analysis presented here. In the remainder of this chapter I lay out this method in seven simple steps, and discuss several ethical considerations associated with this approach.

Digital discourse analysis, Steps 1–3: Research phase

1. Locate an online research site or corpus of digital texts

In selecting a body of texts to analyze, smaller is generally better. Digital discourse analysis cannot compete with the "strength in numbers" of projects that scrape Twitter's application programming interface (API), or which employ Linguistic Inquiry and Word Count software or other sentiment analysis programs to huge numbers of texts. Nor should it. Moving beyond the manifest content of a corpus of texts still requires a human reader, so research sites should be chosen in which all texts, or a manageable random sample of them, can be individually read and re-read by human researchers.

2. Allow categories/themes/keywords to emerge from an initial reading of the texts

Altheide (1996) was critical of the tendency within quantitative content analysis to pre-code categories, which were often quite numerous, and suggested that in his ethnographic content analysis method, researchers ought to instead "treat the development of your protocol as part of the research process and let it emerge over several drafts" (Altheide, 1996: 27). This is an advantage of doing digital discourse analysis on small corpora of texts, and especially texts with very sensitive subject matter. We can let the authors of these texts themselves tell us what is meaningful to them, and use that to animate our research. What's more, as sociologists we likely want to distinguish our work from the more literary or linguistic approaches to discourse analysis, so staying grounded in the meanings of the texts and their authors is important, to the extent that these can be determined. These meanings, whether emerging out of sheer frequency of expression or some other measure of the salience of particular themes, should guide the research categories. It may even be the case that the site being analyzed employs user-generated "folksonomies" (Vander Wal, 2007) in which texts are thematically tagged or ranked by their authors. Basing one's own categorization scheme on such folksonomic data would have the obvious benefit of demonstrating that one's interpretations are attuned to the meanings of the authors themselves. Of course, this approach is not a necessity, as user-generated tags and rankings may be either unavailable at one's research site, or be geared more towards organizing the site's manifest content than classifying its latent themes and discourse.

3. Keep categories to a minimum, and be flexible as you code or organize the texts

Altheide has also suggested that researchers should "keep categories to a minimum at first, but others can be added as the investigator interacts with documents and relevant theoretical issues" (1996: 27). Such flexibility is a strength of discourse analysis. Moreover, keeping categories to a minimum is especially important when one's corpus of texts is relatively small – if categories are too complex or too numerous, they won't be well populated. Also, the more fine-grained one's distinctions between categories become, the more likely that a reader will quarrel with the researcher's interpretations. In my own work I want categories to be almost self-evident, so that when I quote examples, the rationale behind my interpretations is clear and demonstrable. That is one way to convince readers about the "correctness" of one's interpretations, in the absence of inter-rater reliability statistics or big sample sizes. After all, the most important insights in discourse analysis do not come from relatively simple decisions about how to categorize content, but rather, from the way such content is contextualized and interpreted (see Ruiz Ruiz, 2009), or shown to reflect larger discourses, ideologies, and power structures (see Fairclough, 1989).

Digital discourse analysis, Steps 4–7: Writing phase

4. Thoroughly describe the context of the research site

As the earlier discussion of "transferability" suggested, the contextual information that you provide will at least partly determine the degree to which it resonates for readers, and whether or not your findings and theories get applied to other research sites by other researchers. You need to be clear about the contours and limits of the space, or the methods behind the collection of the corpus, their connection to other spaces and corpuses, and about the relevance of these texts to larger, ongoing debates in popular culture and academia alike. One way to create a particularly rich description of one's research site might be through a process of "triangulation," in which textual analysis is supplemented with interviews of site users or participant "netnography" on the site as well. However, as Norman Denzin has reminded us, "objective reality can never be captured. We only know a thing through its representation. Triangulation is not a tool or a strategy of validation," but ought simply to be considered part of "an attempt to secure an in-depth understanding of the phenomenon in question" (2012: 82). In other words, multiple research methods do not get one closer to "truth," but may be used to demonstrate a more fully developed and reflexive understanding of the sites and texts under analysis.

5. Quote liberally as you write up your results

Even if the work you're doing and the arguments you're making proceed from some comparison of categories and frequencies, one advantage of this work as opposed to large-scale content analyses and especially big data is that digital discourse analysts can show our work. We can persuade readers about the validity of our categorization schemes by putting them right there on the page, not hiding them behind statistics. For example, the infamous Facebook "emotional contagion" study (Kramer et al, 2014) angered so many by suggesting that the site had experimentally altered the moods of over 600,000 of its users, yet it did not show a single example of the sort of emotional textual expressions that resulted. Digital discourse analysis is well situated to combat the opacity in big data research by showing readers rich, meaningful examples of primary source data.

6. Be transparent and reflexive about the choices you've made

Along those lines, one key strategy ought to be anticipating counter-arguments about the choices one has made in selecting the research site and categorizing texts. Researchers ought to be able to justify these choices and, especially if one is comparing discourse in more than one site or the texts from a variety of spaces, the grounds for comparison must be clear. Essentially, one must be able to describe why these texts and not others have been analyzed, why they have been placed in these and not other contexts, and how the researcher's own positions and interests factor into these decisions. This is especially important in online discourse analysis, where a body of scholarship specifically on the effects and affordances of the internet must be addressed in concert with the literature on the specific themes one is interested in studying, such as the work on racism, environmental discourse, recovery narratives, collective memory of disasters, and grassroots political movements mentioned earlier in this chapter. Though sharp on- and offline distinctions are certainly not tenable in this day and age, researchers still need to explain the ways that online affordances are uniquely threaded into the fabric of the larger social issues under investigation.

7. Embrace the argument

Even the largest of quantitative content analyses and the biggest of big data projects are still using texts to make arguments about the social world. But the problem with big data is often that its proponents fail to recognize this fact, and imbue their claims with an aura of objectivity and truth that stifles critique and leads to misreading. This is a significant weakness of big data that digital discourse analysis ought to exploit, to the extent that the two are in any sort of methodological competition. As boyd and Crawford (2012: 668) explain:

> Interpretation is at the center of data analysis. Regardless of the size of a data, it is subject to limitation and bias. Without those biases and limitations being understood and outlined, misinterpretation is the result. Data analysis is most effective when researchers take account of the complex methodological processes that underlie the analysis of that data.

Thus, the reflexivity built into digital discourse analysis, along with the fragility of interpretation and claims-making based on small data sets, help guard against the assumption that one is capturing an objective reality, rather than persuading readers about a particular interpretation of the world. In this way, digital discourse analysis might even provide a model for future big data researchers hoping to avoid such epistemological pitfalls.

Ethics and anonymity

The research sites described earlier in this piece – things like message boards, comments sections, websites, Tumblrs, and digital archives – are all public spaces unlikely to require the approval of an Institutional Review Board (IRB). Federal regulations classify research as exempt from IRB approval when it involves "the collection or study of existing data, documents [and] records … if these sources are publicly available" (US HHS, 2009). Nonetheless, ethical guidelines for such research are still important, as the authors of the texts in these spaces likely did not expect that their words would end up as source material for an academic paper. Although hardly exhaustive, here are some sensible rules for protecting the human subjects who produced the discourse under examination.

1. If the spaces or texts being analyzed have already been in the news quite a bit, or if the users themselves clearly wrote with a public audience in mind, it may be fair to use first names of authors, rather than pseudonyms, or to use the actual usernames and handles with which these authors identify themselves. It also may be fair to provide direct links to particular posts and to quote verbatim from them. I employed these guidelines in my paper on the anti-Occupy Wall Street Tumblr (Recuber, 2015) since those users were making explicitly political statements in what they knew to be a public space, and since the site had received a substantial amount of press coverage covered before I analyzed it.
2. Researchers ought to default to conventions of anonymity in the event of uncertainty about the practical publicness of the research site. That is, just because a site is technically public, it may be frequented by such a small niche of users that the thought of larger public attention may be completely outside the users' realm of possibility. If an initial read-through of the texts or research into the site's larger context suggests as much, researchers ought to create pseudonyms and not provide direct links. Direct quotes may still be used, as these are quite important to the methods of discourse analysis, but should be done with added concern for the situation of the authors and the sensitivity of the subject matter being discussed.
3. Of course, direct quotes should be altered or removed altogether if authors of the texts being analyzed are under 18 years of age, or if you think they might be but can't tell. In other words, don't make any quotes that may be from users under the age of 18 searchable or traceable back to those original users. Protection of minors, or any other particularly vulnerable population, should be at the forefront of all social researchers' concerns, regardless of the public availability of the data under investigation.

Conclusion

This chapter has laid out steps and guidelines for the production of digital discourse analysis. It has situated such work as an extension of existing models of discourse analysis, many of which have already been applied to online research sites, although without any explicit methodological continuity between them. At the same time, it has argued that digital discourse analysis might help broaden the boundaries of the emerging field known as digital sociology, which is currently in some danger of being subsumed by big data approaches to textual analysis.

The method of digital discourse analysis outlined here is rooted in small samples of text from lesser-trafficked corners of the internet. It privileges transparency and reflexivity, concerns itself with the ways that meaning is produced by users through texts, and the ways these texts might reflect larger social and cultural forces. It aims not for objectivity or generalizability, but simply for the transferability of its findings into other similar contexts. In these ways, like all good scholarship, it aims to keep the conversation going, to further our knowledge of the social world by increments and in dialogue with other scholars. It attempts to stay grounded in the meanings of those texts it studies, while still making connections to the larger world outside those texts. This is undoubtedly messy business, as this sort of textual interpretation is always open to multiple and competing variations, especially because it does not make the kind of pretensions to objective truth associated with big data. But as Deborah Lupton (2015: 110) reminds us, "the neatness and orderliness of big data sets ... are mirages." In comparison, then, it is precisely the messy, argumentative, interpretive nature of digital discourse analysis that can provide digital sociology with an alternative to big data and, in its own way, a smaller sort of truth.

References

Altheide, D. (1987) "Ethnographic content analysis." *Qualitative Sociology* 10 (1), 65–77.

Altheide, D. (1996) *Qualitative media analysis.* Thousand Oaks, CA: Sage.

Bail, C.J. (2014) "The cultural environment: Measuring culture with big data." *Theory and Society* 43 (3–4), 465–82.

Berelson, B. (1952) *Content analysis in communication research.* Glencoe, IL: Free Press.

Blumberg, S.J., J.V. Luke, and M.L. Cynamon (2006) "Telephone coverage and health survey estimates: Evaluating concern about wireless substitution." *American Journal of Public Health* 96, 926–31.

boyd, d. and K. Crawford (2012) "Critical questions for big data." *Information, Communication & Society* 15 (5), 662–79

Crawford, K. (2013) "The hidden biases of big data." *Harvard Business Review*, April 1 (https://hbr.org/2013/04/the-hidden-biases-in-big-data).

Denzin, N.K. and Y.S. Lincoln (eds) (1998) *Collecting and interpreting qualitative materials.* Thousand Oaks, CA: Sage.

Denzin, N.K. (2012) "Triangulation 2.0." *Journal of Mixed Methods Research* 6 (2), 80–8.

Dumetricia, D.D. (2013) "Review – Netnography: Doing ethnographic research online." *Canadian Journal of Communication* 38 (1), 156–8.

Fairclough, N. (1989) *Language and power.* New York: Longman.

Franzosi, R. (1998) "Narrative analysis – or why (and how) sociologists should be interested in narrative." *Annual Review of Sociology* 24, 517–54.

Franzosi, R. (2010) *Quantitative narrative analysis.* Los Angeles, CA: Sage.

Gee, J.P. (1999) *An introduction to discourse analysis: Theory and method.* New York: Routledge.

Grimshaw, A. (2001) "Discourse and sociology: Sociology and discourse." In D. Schiffrin, D. Tannen, and H.E. Hamilton (eds) *The handbook of discourse analysis.* Malden, MA: Blackwell, pp 751–71.

Healy, K. and J. Moody (2014) "Data visualization in sociology." *Annual Review of Sociology* 40, 105–28.

Heinz, B., H.-I. Cheng, and A. Inuzuka (2007) "Greenpeace greenspeak: A transcultural discourse analysis." *Language and Intercultural Communication* 7 (1), 16–36.

Hellström, T. (2008) "Transferability and naturalistic generalization: New generalizability concepts for social science or old wine in new bottles?" *Quality and Quantity* 42, 321–7.

Housley, W., R. Procter, A. Edwards, P. Burnap, M. Williams, L. Sloan, O. Rana, J. Morgan, A. Voss and A. Greenhill (2014) "Big and broad social data and the sociological imagination: A collaborative response." *Big Data and Society*, July–December, 1–15.

Hughey, M.W. and J. Daniels (2013) "Racist comments at online news sites: A methodological dilemma for discourse analysis." *Media, Culture & Society* 35 (3), 332–47.

Jain, S. (2013) "Bourdieu's sociology: A post-positivist science." *Thesis Eleven* 117 (1), 101–16.

Jurgenson, N. (2014) "View from nowhere: On the cultural ideology of big data." *The New Inquiry*, October 4 (http://thenewinquiry.com/essays/view-from-nowhere)

Kempf, A.M. and P.L. Remington (2007) "New challenges for telephone survey research in the twenty-first century." *Annual Review of Public Health* 28, 113–26.

Kitchin, R. (2014) "Big data, new epistemologies and paradigm shifts." *Big Data & Society*, April–June, 1–12.

Kozinets, R.V. (2010) *Netnography: Doing ethnographic research online.* Thousand Oaks, CA: Sage.

Kracauer, S. (1953) "The challenge of qualitative content analysis." *The Public Opinion Quarterly* 16 (4), 631–42.

Kramer, A.D.I., J.E. Guillory, and J.T. Hancock (2014) "Experimental evidence of massive-scale emotional contagion through social networks." *Proceedings of the National Academy of Sciences* 24, 8788–90.

Lally, J. and D.L. Preston (1973) "Anti-positivist movements in contemporary sociology." *Journal of Sociology* 9 (2), 3–9.

Lincoln, Y.S. and E.G. Guba (1985) *Naturalistic inquiry.* Newbury Park, CA: Sage.

Lupton, D. (2015) *Digital sociology.* New York: Routledge.

Mautner, G. (2005) "Time to get wired: Using web-based corpora in critical discourse analysis." *Discourse & Society* 16 (6), 809–28.

Mudry, T.E. and T. Strong (2013) "Doing recovery online." *Qualitative Health Research* 23 (3), 313–25.

Murthy, D. (2008) "Digital ethnography: An examination of the use of new technologies for social research." *Sociology* 42 (5), 837–55.

Popping, R. (2012) "Qualitative decisions in quantitative text analysis research." *Sociological Methodology* 42, 88–90.

Pulos, A. (2013) "Confronting heteronormativity in online games: A critical discourse analysis of LGBTQ sexuality in World of Warcraft." *Games and Culture* 8 (2), 72–97.

Recuber, T. (2012) "The prosumption of commemoration: Disasters, digital memory banks, and online collective memory." *American Behavioral Scientist* 56 (4), 531–49.

Recuber, T. (2015) "Occupy empathy? Online politics and micro-narratives of suffering." *New Media and Society* 17 (1), 62–77.

Ruiz Ruiz, J. (2009) "Sociological discourse analysis: Methods and logic." *Forum: Qualitative Social Research* 10 (2), 1–30.

Savage, M. and R. Burrows (2007) "The coming crisis in empirical sociology." *Sociology* 41 (5), 885–9.

Schroeder, R. (2014) "Big data and the brave new world of social media research." *Big Data & Society*, July–December, 1–11.

Smith, R.J. (2014) "Missed miracles and mystical connections: Qualitative research, digital social science, and big data." In M. Hand and S. Hillyard (eds) *Big data? Qualitative approaches to digital research* (pp 181–204). Bingley, UK: Emerald.

Swan, D. and J.C. McCarthy (2003) "Contesting animal rights on the internet: Discourse analysis of the social construction of argument." *Journal of Language and Social Psychology* 22 (3), 297–320.

Thomson, P. (2014) "Anonymity – how now?" *Patter*, May 1 (http://patthomson.net/2014/05/01/anonymity-in-research-how-now/).

Tinati, R., S. Halford, L. Carr, and C. Pope (2014) "Big data: Methodological challenges and approaches for sociological analysis." *Sociology* 48 (4), 663–81.

US HHS (US Department of Health and Human Services) (2009) *Human subjects research: Code of federal regulations* (www.hhs.gov/ohrp/humansubjects/guidance/45cfr46.html).

Vander Wal, T. (2007) "Folksonomy" (vanderwal.net/folksonomy.html).

Vann, K. (2009) "Animating vernaculars, wired: Critical discourse analysis on an awkward scale." *Critical Discourse Studies* 6 (3), 165-83.

Weaver, S. (2013) "A rhetorical discourse analysis of online anti-Muslim and anti-Semitic jokes." *Ethnic and Racial Studies* 36 (3), 483–99.

Weaver, S. (2011) "Jokes, rhetoric, and embodied racism: A rhetorical discourse analysis of the logics of racist jokes on the internet." *Ethnicities* 11 (4), 413–35.

Wiedemann, G. (2013) "Opening up to big data: Computer-assisted analysis of textual data in social sciences." *Forum: Qualitative Social Research* 14 (2).

5

Virtually ethical: Ethnographic challenges in researching textile crafters online

Alison Mayne

This chapter is based on research that explored wellbeing among women who engage in knitting and crocheting while alone in physical, domestic settings and who subsequently elect to share their making online. This research is specifically focused on the ways that participants comment on and present images of their making to a digital social community on Facebook. Choosing a method that involves gathering data online brings with it a number of significant challenges. Research on the dilemmas of ethical practice in using social media for academic purposes remains relatively limited (Henderson et al, 2014), and is fraught with ambiguities and contradictions. What follows is an exploration of the ways a dialogic, transparent process can be applied to research design, in an effort to remain "virtuous" in conducting an online ethnographic study.

First, the chapter discusses some of the literature on the principles and ethical considerations of using social media, particularly focusing on the debates surrounding notions of identity, privacy, and consent in the ocean of data offered to us through modern online practices. The key tool for the early phase of research – a closed Facebook group established specifically for this study – is presented, along with an exploration of participants' engagement. Complexities generated by this experiment in digital ethnography are then unpacked, including the ways that time, place, and cultural group behave differently in this "virtual" environment – if indeed that is the right term. Next, participants' views on the ethics of the research project are shared, including their comments on information security, the opportunities offered by research through social media, and an interest in having their voices heard. The chapter closes with some reflections on what has been learned to date – and how this will have an impact on the next stages of research design.

A little background

Digital sociology is perhaps no longer "new," but still emergent in terms of academic practice. We are exploring the parameters and possibilities of what it means to apply ethical considerations to studying what we learn through participants' engagement in the online environment as it evolves (Robinson and Schulz, 2009). Discussions regarding the research validity of computer-mediated communication or the crumbling of a utopian society through a focus on banal up-date culture (Carr, 2010; Keen, 2007) are surely behind us now. However, social media research ethics are still much debated – particularly regarding the principles of informed consent – not least because of the ethical concerns arising from the Facebook "emotional contagion" study, where the mood of unwitting participants was observed and manipulated in response to status updates (Kramer et al, 2014). This study seeks to address the need for rigorous good practice as identified in the 2014 NatCen report (see Beninger et al, 2014), where participants expressed concerns that consent for online data was morally right, and that terms of privacy and confidentiality should have greater transparency.

Nevertheless, current guidelines are sparse and somewhat flexible. The British Sociological Association is currently redesigning their ethical recommendations for social media research. The Association of Internet Researchers provides guidance but admits tensions and ambiguities in suggesting that ethical consideration related to human subjects only *may* be a requirement (Markham and Buchanan, 2012). There is an extended continuum of ethical choice (James and Busher, 2015) to navigate in the effort to demonstrate academic integrity and respect for participants. Much of the contention surrounds the interpretation of the validity of online identity and what may be perceived as public as opposed to private.

A question of identity

Debating and defending social media as a valid arena for research, and particularly reframing the faceless user who creates an alternative identity in cyberspace as a holistic being, has long been the focus of digital sociology academics. It is particularly in the field of early studies of the internet that a lack of trust in the veracity of online identity can be observed. The idea that an alternative virtual identity, different from that in the physical world, could be performed online muddies the waters in considering the trustworthiness of the data we are collecting or from whom we are really gaining consent. Believing that participants make new and different personae reconstructed "on the other side of the looking glass" (Turkle, 1995: 177) or use digital space to experiment and play with an identity significantly discontinuous (Robinson and Schulz, 2009) from the offline self contributes to the binary separation of "real-life" participant versus virtual simulacrum. To seek permission to explore this range of new or false identities (Rheingold, 2000) as a basis for research has been seen by some as reckless (Fritch and Cromwell, 2001).

However, Baym expresses the view that "most social users of computer-mediated communication create online selves consistent with their offline identities" (1998: 45), and Wellman and Gulia saw participants' engagement in social media communication as "an integral part of expressing one's self-identity" (1999: 73). Capurro and Pingel perceived "a tension, not a dichotomy" (2002: 190) in the consideration of on/offline identity, as one's identity may be projected in different ways in the digital medium but will still remain connected to the embodied user. Similarly, Lüders expresses concern over the binary view of on/offline identity that focuses on searching for differences "rather than on the embodied realness of online behaviours ... as an integral part of life" (2015: 80). Ess (2013) and Nissenbaum (2011) both posit that online behavior is rooted in our physical, social lives. If we accept these nuances, conventional ethical consideration for those involved in digital research simply must be equal to that offered to participants involved in parallel physical studies.

A question of privacy

There is a deluge of information available to us in the growth of Facebook or the advent of Twitter – much of which post-dates writing on the ethics of digital or social media-based research. More than ever, we are exercised by decisions about privacy – the dilemma of interpreting the context of data as "a conversation in a public space ... or a quiet chat behind closed doors" (Dawson, 2014: 433). The contention surrounding sources deemed publically available in contrast to perceived as private (Rosenberg, 2010) is illustrated in the amendments by the International Council on Human Rights (2011) clarifying that privacy is only partly under one's own control in the world of social media communication. Participants may anticipate that posts to an open forum are public, but that a post to a personal page, or one requiring a password, are private and only accessible to identified "friends." However, all this may be moot if they are unaware of the implications of their own out-of-date security settings or the absence of security settings for those with whom they communicate. Recognition of the context in which the participant originally generated data is crucial here – whether it is perceived as "not for public consumption" and should therefore be treated as private (Henderson et al, 2013).

Publically available "big data" originates from a context that may be understood as openly accessible to all, and therefore more flexible ethical considerations of privacy could be applied. However, there is also a problematic erosion of conventional concepts of privacy and consent in contexts where the assumption of what constitutes private communication online may differ between researcher and participant:

> Although many users of social networking sites may have misplaced expectations of privacy ... this does not mean they should have a right to privacy. (Wilkinson and Thelwall, 2011: 151)

A step further from this, we have the notion of digital data being separated entirely from its human source, interpreted instead as cultural product (Wilkinson and Thelwall, 2011) or found text (Bassett and O'Riordan, 2002) and therefore available for academic consumption without consent. In other studies, participants who may otherwise be deemed as meriting consent could be perceived as simply cost-effective "units of analysis" (Langer and Beckman, 2005: 200). Such de-humanizing of participants is deeply troubling. This study seeks rather to acknowledge the complex space – neither totally public nor wholly private (Eysenbach and Till, 2001) – in which data is collected from participants who possess a justifiable expectation of how their shared communications may be presented and respected in research (Bakardijeva and Feenberg, 2000; Whiteman, 2010, 2012).

Digital data as "fair game"?

The online world provides us with a vast and messy source of data, as d'Orazio (2014) has highlighted, and it is challenging to provide regulations for something that is ever changing and growing. It appears that the sheer range and convenient accessibility of social media can tempt researchers into justifying uses of data that are somehow divorced from their source. This study reflects the view that to consider content gleaned from social media as "fair game" (Zimmer, 2010) is highly questionable – why should online participants not have an equitable experience in the treatment of their responses? Online interactions are recognized as real and of value to those involved as "(t)o do otherwise would be to treat online identities as if they did not matter to participants, whereas in many settings they do patently matter" (Hine, 2000: 219).

Capurro and Pingel (2002) suggest that online communication research should be guided by an ethics of care where respect for the interests and values of the people involved in online research provides an opportunity for participants to actively consider the implications for their cooperation. This has been echoed by Henderson et al (2013) in recommending an explicit focus on ethical processes throughout research experience that reflects the context of data source, consent, and confidentiality.

This is not the place for a wide-ranging overview of what ethics may mean in research. However, it is worth noting that the principles of Aristotlean virtue ethics, idealistically grounded in the notions of moral conduct, do provide a framework here (James and Busher, 2015; Ess, 2015). While it is entirely appropriate that researchers must deliberate on their choices and justify their accountability in the research process, ethical behavior in research is also about – and is perhaps above all – a matter of personal choice and moral integrity. Every decision made in the research process brings with it some form of compromise or challenge. The focus placed in this study on a dialogic approach to ethics is simply one created by a commitment to respect and protect participants.

Sharing craft making in a digital world

Why Facebook?

While it is acknowledged that using an internet-based study has its limitations in terms of the digital divide in less developed countries (van Dijk, 2015) or the digital skills divide (Hargittai, 2011), Facebook remains an important arena for research as the most popular social media platform. Figures from Pew Internet Research (Duggan et al, 2015) indicate that 71 percent of US citizens engage with Facebook, with a slightly higher figure of 77 percent for women. Internet World Statistics (2015) suggest that the continued popularity of Facebook remains global, with 936 million daily active users and significant growth in Africa and the Middle East between 2013 and 2014. In comparison, users of Instagram and Pinterest represent under 30 percent of US users (Duggan et al, 2015), which, along with the public nature of the data and primary focus on image over text commentary, indicated they would not be a suitable vehicle for this research. The reach of craft blogs is, by their specialist nature, more likely to be limited. For example, popular yarn craft blog "Look What I Made" has over 15,000 blog subscribers in comparison to over 27,467 Facebook followers (Strydom, Alison Mayne, email message to author, May 13, 2015); similarly, the blog "A Creative Being" has over 38,000 Facebook followers, compared to a little over 4,000 blog subscribers (Slump, Alison Mayne, email message to author, May 13, 2015). In this study, therefore, Facebook appeared to offer the greatest opportunity to reach a wide audience, particularly with its established tradition in enabling craft groups to share online, from the giant The Crochet Crowd, with over 560,000 members, to I Love Crochet & Knit at around 12,000 members and Winwick Mum Sockalong with around 750 participants.

Facebook created group settings at least partly in recognition that individuals may wish to share posts with parties other than (and hidden from) family and friends (Henderson et al, 2013):

> Facebook Groups make it easy to connect with specific sets of people.... Groups are dedicated spaces where you can share updates, photos or documents and message other group members. (Facebook, 2015)

Security settings within "closed" groups meant that the study could be found through searches and links, with a permanent post visible to all readers to provide information regarding the parameters of the research. However, only members accepted into the group are able to access content – a secure way of enabling a shared interest rather than shared geography (Wellman and Gulia, 1999) to facilitate engagement in research.

The Woolly Wellbeing Research Group

The early stage of this wider qualitative study, seeking to interpret amateur craft makers' opinions and experiences of wellbeing, isolation, and connectedness, was facilitated through the creation of a closed Facebook group designed to engage participants in sharing their views. Launched at the beginning of February 2015, this chapter reflects participants' activity, including comments and posted images, collected in just the first two months. Data was gathered from a pragmatic and purposive sample of participants who self-identify as women, initially invited through Twitter and other Facebook crafting groups. Publicity about the research also expanded through word-of-mouth, retweets, and sharing through craft bloggers and other public and "closed" Facebook pages.

That the Facebook research group has grown so swiftly to over 300 members suggests that there is a strong desire to engage with the ideas it seeks to explore, but this has brought with it some unexpected difficulties. Currently, there are 324 members of the group, 247 of whom are engaged, that is, they have liked, commented, and posted. A weekly "Wednesday Research Question" post draws on average over 60 comments, with a number of posts receiving between 150 and 250 responses. Over the first two months of the research group being online, 216 posts have been made, generating 1,403 comments and 2,419 "likes;" only 0.5 percent of posts are without a response of some kind. Dealing with this amount of data is still a learning process: group analytics software is being used to collate data into spreadsheets that can be categorized and quantified, and images are being stored and grouped.

Every researcher has to grapple with the volume of their data, but there is an added layer of complexity in this stage of the study through operating in a virtual environment.

Ethnographic challenges online

Baym (2010), Clemens (2014) and Hine (2015) each remind us that the ethnographic tropes of place, time, and cultural group operate differently in a digital world, with asynchronous exchanges, settings separated by geography or time zones, and where membership is fluid. The impact of the researcher in ethnography online, managing dominant voices, and identifying ambiguity in computer-mediated communication are all challenging, but Hine (2015) reassures us that the uncertainty in analyzing what is being represented through the virtual world remains as much a part of the ethnographer's role as it ever was. Capurro and Pingel (2002) point out that we are as capable of being misleading in the digital world as we are in the physical, and attempting to analyze the implications of a Facebook post may be as inscrutable and challenging to read online as it is offline:

> When one of our informants updates his status on Facebook, he may tell us what he meant by it, but we cannot be quite sure what his friends make of what he writes ... any more than, as Geertz (1973) reminds us, we can understand from observation of the action alone what is meant when we see someone close one eye to wink. (Hine, 2015: 3)

Place and time

The membership of the Facebook Woolly Wellbeing Research Group is global: there are over 100 participants in both the UK and US; Australia, Canada and South Africa each have around 20 participants. In all, the 324 women currently involved in the project represent 34 countries, from Albania, Egypt, the Netherlands, and Singapore to Zambia. It is a "glocalized" community, where women are coming together in a virtual place that has significance for them.

Communication mediated online has always been asynchronous, with responses being delayed in time from hours to days. The global nature of the research group means that there are waves of posts over a 24-hour period in differing time zones. While this may, in fact, mean that questions and responses are perhaps more likely to receive a timely response – there is always someone "present" – there are challenges for the researcher in monitoring and managing comments as they are posted. The key point is that, as participants move between archived posts and ephemeral, fleeting "chat" responses, they are using the group as a means to sustain social interactions across geographical place and temporality (Baym, 2010).

Cultural group

The group of research participants is also fluid – with 324 members currently, and a total of 351 participants to date – membership is affected by women who choose to engage but who then withdraw over time. Different participants engage through different kinds of activities, including posting extensive comments, answering queries or requests for advice, and providing status updates with images of their work. Some are more likely to be involved in commenting or just "liking" rather than posting independently – and significantly, active participants are a minority.

Of course, there are members who do not visibly engage at all – the "lurkers." A group constituting 26 percent of the participants appear to be inactive – they have never liked, commented, or posted to the page. Hine (2000) highlights the difficulties in managing the silent – those who are present and can see and access material, but who leave no traces to analyze. Just because some members are not observable or meaningfully present does not mean, however, that they are unimportant. Any community becomes "an elective phenomenon in which some who could participate choose not to" (Hine, 2000: 220), and so "lurkers" are acknowledged as an audience (Hine, 2000, 2015; Preece and Maloney-Krichmar, 2005).

Influence

It is also noted that the impact of the researcher here is – as always – problematic. Operating as a participant-observer, "perceived ... to be an in-group rather than an out-group member (that is, understood to be 'one of us' and hence 'like me')" (Cruwys et al, 2014: 231) is crucial in developing the ethnographic focus of the Facebook research community group. The work is clearly identified as being for PhD study; it is the identified researcher who – usually – posts research questions and responds to comments, although the perceived "power" of the researcher is being modified by group members who are beginning to post their own queries about wellbeing and yarn-making. Participant comments are also frequently crafted, extensive and occasionally edited, creating data that may be more akin to a semi-structured interview than a "naturalistic" response. That the response of participants therefore may be reactive or adjusted to create a particular representation "for research" is accepted. Examples of crafted and lengthy responses may also raise questions about in/equalities among participants of not merely digital access or skill, but education, articulation, and fluency in the use of the English language. However, it is not possible to resolve such tensions here – it is an aspect of the ethnographic research experience to be balanced regardless of digital/ physical setting.

Nevertheless, some interesting patterns emerging about clear voices contributing responses, beyond that of the researcher. In data collected over a 60-day period, some participants are more prolifically engaged with the group – those who have posted most frequently, those who are most likely to comment on others' posts, and those who are influential, that is, their interactions generate the most likes or comments from the wider community. "Gay" is highly involved in building the community through contributing 24 posts and 65 comments, with a frequency similar to the researcher, who had contributed 26 posts and 71 comments. A new figure emerges when we explore those who most frequently comment – "Wendy" rarely posts independently, but is engaged significantly in responding to the posts of 43 others, representing a participant who is key in providing information, promoting self-esteem, and responding with reciprocal support for others (Baym, 2010; Cutrona and Russell, 1990). Finally, we can observe that "Danielle," the least likely member of this group to post (with 8 contributions) or comment (38 contributions) herself, but in fact generates the most responses from the community in the form of 405 comments and likes. "Danielle" represents the figure in any community where they may not speak most frequently, but their views appear to be valued or influential.

Engaging with ethics

From the very beginning of the Facebook study, I sought to be transparent in highlighting issues around research online, through explicit discussions about ethical considerations on the Facebook group threads. In this way, consent has been negotiated as an ongoing process throughout the study, rather than as an isolated initial event. In order to become involved, participants had to respond to the information that highlighted the key differences in conducting research that would be confidential in writing, but not anonymous within the group, and that participants could be traceable (Henderson et al, 2014). Mindful of this in particular, all were offered the choice of creating a pseudonym, although fewer than five participants elected to take this option. Additional threads have also been developed to highlight both concerns and protocols regarding trolling or flaming – where negative or directly vindictive responses could derail the community.

It would appear that, in posting images of making from intimate domestic interiors or comments that reflect on topics such as mental health, participants in this research are blurring the boundaries of the public and private spheres (Habermas, 1989) through Facebook. Therefore, iterative permissions are sought for the use of images in publication or presentation, and particularly personal responses are double-checked for inclusion in the research through back channels in private messaging. This ongoing dialogic approach (Henderson et al, 2013) is both about creating trust and "an atmosphere of collaboration and mutual support" (Capurro and Pingel, 2002: 193) in addition to reflecting a broader ethical process that illustrates respect for participants perceived as equal in the research relationship (Schrijvers, 1991).

Protection online?

In discussion threads surrounding the ethics of confidentiality, participants expressed an understanding of the issues surrounding the impossibility of guaranteeing anonymity in research online. There was almost exclusively a weary cynicism that:

> Nothing is safe. (Bettina)

> Nothing is truly private anywhere on the internet. (Pat)

As such, a large number of comments were posted indicating that participants acknowledged that protecting their identity was not necessarily secure – but that accepting this problem became part of their decision process in deciding to engage in the research:

> If I didn't feel comfortable having an opinion and voicing it then I would not join. (Sandra)

> If I don't want something to be known publicly then I won't post it, including in closed groups. (Ruth)

Here, comments serve as an interesting illustration of the ways that participants appear to be balancing their expectations of privacy on Facebook with their desire to communicate – both with other knit and crochet makers, and with a channel for research into their experiences of wellbeing.

Some members explicitly focused on the importance of a strong administration of the group, which meant that they knew trolling or flaming would be blocked.

> It's really interesting and at the same time a little scary that anyone from around the world can look at these pages.... I only associate with groups and admins that will block, report and remove inappropriate content, users, and spam, making me feel mostly safe. (Taylor)

In fact, there has been no flaming to date, adding to participants' sense of the groups being a supportive and "safe place" (Michelle).

Using Facebook as a platform for research was also considered a benefit as it allowed participants to engage with research questions at their own pace, selecting the extent they wished to share personal information and to respond to one another's comments:

> I'm fine with this medium of sharing as I also feel that you explained it fully before we started. For me it is a very convenient method of sharing as I can read responses and add my own whenever it suits me.... I also like that, so far, your questions and comments have been open enough for me to choose, albeit quite carefully, how much or how little I write and share. (Paula)

The positive responses to engaging with the research through Facebook, regardless of concerns or cynicism about online safety, are illustrated usefully here:

> Facebook is a really powerful tool for collaboration ... look at us all! there are always security risks etc but we shouldn't let those risks prevent us from gaining the positive rewards from interacting with one another ... in the risk vs reward deliberation ... reward wins for me. (Cat)

The risks of security and confidentiality are debated and acknowledged in the group, with the gains of forming part of a community being seen as more valuable. The complex nature of privacy in a "closed" Facebook group is acknowledged by participants – there are concerns regarding sharing personal views and, in some cases, disclosing deeply moving experiences. However, the perceived benefits to be gained from sharing in a digital community appear to be more powerful than anxieties regarding anonymity.

Shared interests, not shared geography

For some participants, the nature of the closed group did make them feel secure in expressing ideas to a supportive community, reflecting Wellman and Gulia's (1999) statements about the importance of perceiving companionship in a group organized by shared interest rather than shared geography. A response such as this is not unusual, making clear that participants are being considered in their decisions of what to post:

> There are statements and or photos I would never post on my personal timeline but will post in a 'closed' group. Usually because

the people in the group have become closer to me than the neighbor next door, not only because we share in common our crafts but because we share our everyday struggles. (Gay)

Sometimes it's easier than on my timeline where 'friends' know me.... It's great that we are all so geographically spread yet share a common bond. (Jill)

The group fostered a sense of belonging between participants who did not have contact with each other in the physical world, but who felt they were part of a community that could provide:

A cheerleader when you complete any project. A friend when you feel lonely, and support when you have a problem. (Wendy)

A way to be heard

Perhaps parallel to a participant's right to withdraw from research and be forgotten online (European Commission, 2014; Weber, 2011) is the right to be heard in research. To some extent this is indicated by the number of participants who explicitly asked that their names were used in the research, suggesting that to be clearly linked to one's opinion is empowering, and to omit the names associated with voices in research could be disempowering rather than protective. A number of women were engaging with the investigation process and discussing ethical issues in research conducted online because it was accessible through social media. For those who self-identified as experiencing physical disability, mental health issues, or social isolation, it is a rare opportunity to feel that one's voice matters and that somebody is listening:

Being a stay at home mom I don't get my opinion out there much, I'm not 'heard' much ... so I appreciate fb & these lovely groups where I can get help or help someone else! Or at least let someone else know they were heard! (Rebecca)

Next stages

Writers on virtual ethnography and digital sociology, from Nancy Baym and Barry Wellman in the 1990s to Christine Hine in 2015, challenge us to understand the internet not as some "other" discrete place – a "cyberspace" – but as something more accepted and everyday. Hine suggests "We find ourselves being online in an extension of other embodied ways of being and acting in the world" (2015: 14). Participants have responded to the Facebook group page as a participatory space, where socially meaningful activities are supported and social relationships are developing – even thriving. The crucial point is that this originates from real people who perceive themselves to be a community, and therefore there can be no difference in the ethical approaches to managing their data simply because it was generated online.

The next stages for this research include developing online focus groups for interested "Woolly Wellbeing Research Group" participants, including an extended "eJournal" study to explore experience of wellbeing over time. There are clusters of UK-based participants who will be invited to engage in further face-to-face semi-structured interviews and workshops. Additionally, new participants who operate "in real life" retail or social "sit and stitch" groups or community arts schemes will be invited to engage in the research as responses are triangulated and compared between the physical and digital worlds.

Much of the research design for this project has been a deliberate response to calls from the UK Arts and Humanities Research Council (AHRC) to explore the "ethics and ontologies of participation and collaboration ... via digital networks" (Armstrong et al, 2014: 58) and to consider where an online creative arts community has a contribution to make in building meaningful social relationships that can support and empower. Using the Woolly Wellbeing Research Group on Facebook to engage and communicate with participants has allowed a sustained conversation about the virtues of and ethical approaches in research online to develop. In some respects, the challenge may lie in ensuring that physical participants in the research process have as much opportunity as their digital counterparts to explicitly consider the ethical implications of consent in sharing their views.

References

Armstrong, L., J. Bailey, G. Julier, and L. Kimbell (2014) *Social design futures: HEI research and the AHRC.* Brighton: University of Brighton and Victoria and Albert.

Bakardjieva, M. and A. Feenberg (2000) "Involving the virtual subject." *Ethics and Information Technology* 2, 233–40.

Bassett, E. and H. O'Riordan (2002) "Ethics of Internet research: Contesting the human subjects research model." *Ethics and Information Technology* 4 (3), 233–47.

Baym, N.K. (1998 [2013]) "The emergence of online community." In C. Hine (ed) *Virtual research methods* (pp 29–56). vol 1, Sage Benchmarks in Social Research Methods. 2013. London, UK: Sage.

Baym, N.K. (2010) *Personal connections in the digital age.* Digital Media and Society. Cambridge: Polity Press.

Beninger, K., A. Fry, N. Jago, H. Lepps, L. Nass, and H. Silvester (2014) *Research using social media: Users' views.* London, UK: NatCen (National Centre for Social Research).

Capurro, R. and C. Pingel (2002) "Ethical issues of online communication research." *Ethics and Information Technology* 4, 189–94.

Carr, N.G. (2010) *The shallows: How the internet is changing the way we think, read and remember.* London, UK: Atlantic.

Clemens, R. (2014) "Friends, lovers and social media experimentation: The need for new ethical guidelines." In K. Woodfield (ed) *Social media in social research: Blogs on blurring the boundaries.* London, UK: NatCen [eBook].

Crochet Crowd, The (no date) Facebook page (www.facebook.com/pages/ The-Crochet-Crowd/116482731742088).

Cruwys, T., S.A. Haslam, G. Dingle, C. Haslam, and J. Jetten (2014) "Depression and social identity: An integrative review." *Personality and Social Psychology Review* 18 (3), 215–38.

Cutrona, C.E. and D. Russell (1990) "Type of social support and specific stress: Toward a theory of optimal matching." In B.R. Sarason, I.G. Sarason, and G.R. Pierce (eds) *Social support: An international view* (pp 319–66). New York: Wiley.

Dawson, P. (2014) "Our anonymous online research participants are not always anonymous: Is this a problem?" *British Journal of Educational Technology* 45 (3), 428–37.

van Dijck, J. (2015) "After connectivity: The era of connectication." *Social Media & Society* 1 (1), 1–2.

d'Orazio, F. (2014) "Social media in social research." In K. Woodfield (ed) *Social media in social research: Blogs on blurring the boundaries.* London, UK: NatCen [eBook].

Duggan, M., N.B. Ellison, C. Lampe, A. Lenhart, and M. Madden (2015) "Social media update 2014." Pew Internet Research Center (www. pewinternet.org/2015/01/09/social-media-update-2014/).

Ess, C. (2013) "Trust, social identity, and computation." In R. Harper (ed) *The complexity of trust, computing, and society* (pp 199–226). Cambridge: Cambridge University Press.

Ess, C. (2015) "New selves, new research ethics?" In H. Ingierd (ed) *Internet research ethics* (pp 48–76). Oslo: Cappelen Damm Akademisk.

Eysenbach, G. and J.E. Till (2001 [2013]) "Ethical issues in qualitative research on internet communities." In C. Hine (ed) *Virtual research methods* (pp 105–12). vol 4, Sage Benchmarks in Social Research Methods. London, UK: Sage.

European Commission (2014) "Factsheet on the 'Right to be forgotten' ruling (C-131/12)" (http://ec.europa.eu/justice/data-protection/files/factsheets/ factsheet_data_protection_en.pdf).

Facebook (2015) *Facebook Help Center group basics* (www.facebook.com/ help/162866443847527).

Fritch, J.W. and R.L. Cromwell (2001) "Evaluating internet resources: Identity, affiliation, and cognitive authority in a networked world." *Journal of the American Society for Information Science and Technology* 52 (6), 499–507.

Geertz, C. (1973) "Thick description: Toward an interpretative theory of culture." In C. Geertz (ed) *The interpretation of cultures*. New York: Basic Books.

Habermas, J. (1989) *The structural transformation of the public sphere: An inquiry into a category of bourgeois society.* Cambridge, MA: The MIT Press.

Hargittai, E. (2011 [2013]) "Minding the digital gap: Why understanding digital inequality matters." In C. Hine (ed) *Virtual research methods* (pp 163–71). vol 1, Sage Benchmarks in Social Research Methods. London, UK: Sage.

Henderson, M., N.F. Johnson, and G. Auld (2013) "Silences of ethical practice: Dilemmas for researchers using social media." *Educational Research and Evaluation* 19 (6), 546–60.

Henderson, M., N.F. Johnson, G. Auld, and P. Dawson (2014) "Ethics in social media research: do we know what we are doing?" Learning with New Media (http://newmediaresearch.educ.monash.edu.au/lnmrg/blog/ethics-social-media-research-do-we-know-what-we-are-doing).

Hine, C. (2000 [2013]) "Internet as culture and cultural artefact." In C. Hine (ed) *Virtual research methods* (pp 209–42). vol 1, Sage Benchmarks in Social Research Methods. 2014. London, UK: Sage.

Hine, C. (2015) *Ethnography for the internet: Embedded, embodied and everyday.* London, UK: Bloomsbury.

International Council on Human Rights (2011) *Navigating the dataverse: Privacy, technology, human rights.* Geneva: International Council on Human Rights.

Internet World Statistics (2015) "Facebook usage and Facebook growth statistics by world geographic regions" (www.internetworldstats.com/facebook.htm).

I Love Crochet & Knit (no date) Facebook page (www.facebook.com/pages/I-love-Crochet-Knit/316946011783406?fref=ts).

James, N. and H. Busher (2015) "Ethical issues in online research." *Educational Research and Evaluation: An International Journal on Theory And Practice* 21 (2), 89–94.

Keen, A. (2007) *The cult of the amateur: How today's internet is killing our culture and assaulting our economy.* London, UK: Nicholas Brealey.

Kramer, A.D.I., J.E. Guillory, and J.T. Hancock (2014) "Experimental evidence of massive-scale emotional contagion through social networks." *Proceedings of the National Academy of Sciences* 111 (24), 8788–90.

Langer, R. and S.C. Beckman (2005) "Sensitive research topics: Netnography revisited." *Qualitative Market Research: An International Journal* 8 (2), 189–203.

Lüders, M. (2015) "Researching social media: Confidentiality, anonymity and reconstructing online practices." In H. Ingierd (ed) *Internet research ethics* (pp 77–97). Oslo: Cappelen Damm Akademisk.

Markham, A. and E. Buchanan (2012) *Ethical decision-making and internet research: Recommendations from the AOIR Ethics Committee.* Chicago, IL: Association of Internet Researchers (http://aoir.org/reports/ethics2.pdf).

Nissenbaum, H. (2011) "A contextual approach to privacy online." *Daedalus* 140 (4), 32–48.

Preece, J. and D. Maloney-Krichmar (2005) "Online communities: Design, theory, and practice." *Journal of Computer-Mediated Communication* 10 (4).

Rheingold, H. (2000) *The virtual community: Homesteading on the electronic frontier.* Cambridge, MA: The MIT Press.

Robinson, L. and J. Schulz (2009) "New avenues for sociological inquiry: Evolving forms of ethnographic practice." *Sociology* 43 (4), 685–98.

Rosenberg, A. (2010) "Virtual world research ethics and the private/public distinction." *International Journal of Internet Research Ethics* 3 (1), 23–37.

Schrijvers, J. (1991) "Dialectics of a dialogical ideal: Studying sideways and studying up" In L. Nencel and P. Pels (eds) *Constructing knowledge: Authority and critique in social science* (pp 162–79). London, UK: Sage.

Turkle, S. (1995) *Life on the screen: Identity in the age of the Internet.* London, UK: Simon & Schuster.

van Dijck, J. (2015) "After connectivity: The era of connectication." *Social Media & Society* 1 (1), 1–2.

Weber, R.H. (2011) "The right to be forgotten: More than a Pandora's box?" *Jipitec* 2, 120–30.

Wellman, B. and M. Gulia (1999 [2013]) "Net surfers don't ride alone: Virtual communities as communities." In C. Hine (ed) *Virtual research methods* (pp 57–85). vol 1. Sage Benchmarks in Social Research Methods. 2014. London, UK: Sage.

Wilkinson, D. and M. Thelwall (2011) "Researching personal information on the public web: Methods and ethics." *Social Science Computer Review* 29 (4): 387–401.

Whiteman, N. (2010) "Control and contingency: Maintaining ethical stances in research." *International Journal of Internet Research Ethics* 3 (1), 6–22.

Whiteman, N. (2012) *Undoing ethics: Rethinking practice in online research.* New York: Springer.

Winwick Mum Sockalong (no date) Facebook page (www.facebook.com/groups/642084589269882/).

Zimmer, M. (2010) "'But the data is already public': On the ethics of research in Facebook." *Ethics and Information Technology* 12 (4), 313–25.

6

Interactivity, social media, and Superman: How comic books can help us understand and conceptualize interactivity online

Harry T. Dyer

Interactivity is an important concept when considering any media form as it informs and envelops a number of further questions of how a media form works with and on us. Yet in the field of digital sociology, the concept of interactivity is sadly under-conceptualized; it is often utilized with an assumed definition and a perceived consistent relationship between all involved parties, or else it is reduced to an afterthought. Yet, as a concept, interactivity is worth accounting for, defining, and fully considering in order to understand what is unique and different about interactive media, who is interacting, what they are interacting through and with, what can affect, shape, and mediate interactions, and how interactions may affect, mediate, and shape our experiences and behaviors. Walther, Gay, and Hancock sum up the importance of interactivity for digital sociology, as well as the lack of consideration and consensus in defining and conceptualizing it, when they say:

> ... interactivity, as a loose term is alive and well on the Internet and is a dynamic that begs for theoretical and practical attention from communication researchers. As a construct, interactivity has been under-theorized, and as a variable, poorly operationalized. (Walther et al, 2005: 633)

The discussion and conceptualization of interactivity can generally be split into three areas of focus, detailed and expanded on later in this chapter, each of which offer a different approach towards understanding and defining interactivity (Ariel and Avidar, 2015; Weber et al, 2014). These approaches split their focus between attempting to understand and emphasize different aspects of interactivity, concentrating on either the human understanding and comprehension of interactivity, the role of design in informing and shaping the available interactions, or the processes through which interaction takes place.

These three approaches towards understanding interactivity all introduce useful concepts and ideas, and emphasize different important aspects of interactivity for digital sociology. However, there is currently a lack of research that attempts to account for and reconcile the various aspects raised in these different discussions of interactivity, or provide a bridge through which we can consider the many facets that shape and form interactivity online.

This chapter therefore aims to understand and conceptualize interactivity by combining these approaches and asking what a consideration of interactivity as a fluid, materially heterogeneous concept can add to the discussion of online social activity. In order to approach interactivity as an ongoing process shaped by materially heterogeneous actants (Latour, 2005), this chapter proposes and introduces the use of concepts drawn from the field of comic book studies (McCloud, 1993). Comic book studies provides a means to help better conceptualize and understand how relations between humans, non-humans, and online website design through, on, in, and with interactive media forms results in specific iterations of online interactivity.

Comic book studies provide a focus on the manner in which each individual comes to create their own stylistic narrative interpretation and experience of a media form. This process is guided by a number of factors such as the users' own sociocultural experiences, the sociocultural ideals and assumptions of the designers of the media form as understood by the user, the users' exposure to and understanding of other media texts, and the limitations, opportunities, and restrictions provided by the design and layout of the media form (McCloud, 1993). By adapting the ideas presented in comic book studies, we can account for interactivity as being guided by discursive and social expectations as well as by the needs and expectations of the audience, while still also accounting for individualistic and stylistic interpretations of the media text and importantly, paying detailed attention to the effects of design on interactions. Comic book studies therefore importantly:

- sees the relationship between user and design as bi-directional, with both design affecting our framing and actualization of social actions and interactions, and individual users understanding, contextualizing, and acting in novel manners within this space (while still being guided by their understanding of discursive and social expectations for social action and interactions) (see Foucault, 1984; Goffman, 1959);

- places the emphasis of understanding the implications of the design choices made within the social spaces that the user is interacting in, on, with, and through *on the user*, removing the researcher's interpretation of the designers' intentions in regards to design choices, and instead focusing the attention on how the user contextualizes, understands, and interacts with the design of the social spaces.

Using comic book studies we can look at the manner in which site design affects, mediates, and guides user action and interaction online as well as, crucially, also consider how site design reveals a number of assumptions about user actions and interactions, and how the users understand, engage with, and possibly flout these assumptions and expectations. Comic book studies focuses on the manner in which each user ultimately creates their own stylized reading of a media form through the concept of "closure" (McCloud, 1993; Schwartz, 1983), detailed later in this chapter, which attempts to understand how a user of a media form is guided towards certain behaviors by the media form's design, as well as how the users' life experiences and exposure to other media texts and discourses (see Foucault, 1979) guides their individual reading and use of a media text. "Closure" provides a useful consideration for the biases built into the design of websites, and how users negotiate these. It allows a consideration of how site design guides and shapes our ability to act and interact online, and how the design of online social spaces can favor certain types of actions, interactions, discourses, themes, users, and audience members.

In order to expand on these concepts, we must first critically consider how interactivity has previously been framed and discussed, before considering the implications and considerations arising from the abundance and variety of interactive media and technology today, and finally, highlighting some of the key concepts from comic book studies, and how they can help reconcile the various strands of interactivity research, as well as introduce some important and new considerations.

Defining interactive and active media

Over the past three decades since the growth of "interactive" technology and of academic interest in technology as a social tool, there has been an ongoing scholarly effort to understand, theorize, and define the concept of interactivity (see Avidar, 2013; Bucy, 2004; Heeter, 1989, 2000; McMillan, 2002; Moore, 1989; Rafaeli and Ariel, 2007; Schultz, 2000). Ariel and Avidar (2015: 21) point out that despite (or perhaps, because of) this multidisciplinary, lively discussion, "There has been general agreement that interactivity is an important element of the communication process.... Nevertheless, there is no agreement on the operational definition of interactivity."

One approach to conceptualizing interactivity has been to understand its place and importance as a characteristic of "interactive" mediums. Marshall (2004) attempts to do just this, pointing out the importance of interactivity at its broadest point, by defining what is meant by interactive media, and highlighting how it differs from the concept of what Marshall terms "active" media. Marshall suggests that the difference between "active" and "interactive" media lies in the style, manner, and moment of audience participation.

Marshall posits that audience participation in "active media" (AM) can be seen at the point of consumption or reception by the audience (Marshall, 2004), where the audience of the media form "works" on actively decoding and consuming media. As such, in "active" media the audience become involved in shaping the media narrative, but only *after* the media form has already been created and disseminated. Marshall argues that "interactive media" (IM), on the other hand, engages the user of the media form *during* the production of the media text, meaning the production of the media form becomes a collaboration between the users, the media text, and the "authors" or creators of the media form at the point of production. This allows the users, in various degrees, to take an active and participatory role in the creation, formation, and maintenance of an ongoing piece of media as opposed to merely dissecting an already created media from, as with AM. The involvement of the audience at the point of production in the media form rather than in the consumption of the media form, Marshall argues, means the creation of the media form becomes a collaborative process, and the media form can be thought of as a platform that the users can interact with, through, and on.

Other researchers have used similar concepts in order to understand what makes IM different from other media forms. Indeed, this approach is commonly used to discuss digital media, and the degrees to which it can be considered more interactive and engaging than other media forms (Ariel and Avidar, 2015). This is often done through extending the dichotomy of active to interactive into a scale, placing a media form along an axis from "low" interactivity to "high," based on "the extent to which users can participate in modifying the form and content of a mediated environment in real time" (Steuer, 1992: 84). Similarly, other researchers have defined low and high interactivity based on the level of involvement of the participants in the ongoing production of the media form, and the forms and modes available for them to interact through (Coyle and Thorson, 2001; Downes and Macmillan, 2000; Johnson et al, 2006; Liu and Shrum, 2009; Sundar et al, 2003).

Although there appears to be a general consensus in regards to IM involving the audience during the production process, there is some disagreement as to the exact temporal nature of this involvement, especially when taking into consideration the range of temporal options now available using digital media. For example, researchers such as Steuer (1992) have argued that interactivity takes place in real time, as users work to modify form and content. However, given the rise of a-synchronous forms such as email, text messaging, and social media feeds, other researchers such as Downes and Macmillan (2000) have made the case for a consideration of a range of temporalities and delayed activities when considering the audience involvement in an IM form. While in general the understanding of the temporal aspects of interactivity presented by Marshall (2004) and others works towards defining the stage in the media process at which the interaction takes place, this does not define what this interaction is, nor how it can be conceptualized as a process. The question becomes, what is happening between the media form and the user during the ongoing production of IM? While the distinction from AM is promising and indeed useful for understanding the importance of interactivity as a media tool, it fails to adequately define or explain what exactly interactivity is, who is interacting, or what is occurring between the audience and the media form during this stage.

In order to provide a functional and robust definition of what interactivity is, and how it is carried out in IM, we need to look at a variety of definitions and conceptualizations of interactivity that attempt to answer the questions of what, who, why, where, and how interaction is taking place. However, within academia there appears to be somewhat of a lack of consensus when considering and conceptualizing the notion of interactivity. When approaching the matter of interactivity, both Ariel and Avidar (2015) and Weber et al (2014) agree that the efforts to define and conceptualize interactivity roughly fit into three loose categories: (1) interactivity as *perception*, emphasizing the participants' understanding and experiences of interactions (Newhagen, 2004; Wu, 1999); (2) interactivity as a *medium characteristic*, in which interactivity is defined, discussed, and framed in terms of the technological features that make the interactions possible (Durlak, 1987; Lee et al, 2004; Markus, 1987; Rust and Varki, 1996; Sundar, 2004); and (3) interactivity as *process*, which focuses on the manners and means by which information and actions are transferred from one participant to another (Kelleher, 2009; Rafaeli and Sudweeks, 1997; Rogers, 2003; Stewart and Pavlou, 2002). In the following section, each of these branches of interactivity will be discussed in order to briefly introduce the concepts each focus brings separately, before considering how we can use and consolidate these concepts along with ideas raised from comic book studies to understand online social actions. We start by discussing the definition of interactivity as perception.

Interactivity as perception

Marshall's (2004) definition of IM highlights an important point for a definition of interactivity. The temporal differences between AM and IM, and the involvement of the audience during the production process rather than at the point of consumption, raises the question of how the audience understands and conceptualizes their role in this process, and how the audience processes and makes sense of the media forms. This emphasis on the audience and users' understandings and experiences of media forms has been the focus and approach for a number of studies that have attempted to conceptualize interaction.

Ostensibly, this branch of research places the focus and burden of interactivity onto the audience of the media form in order to understand how they make sense of the media form, and how they manage and complete their roles during the ongoing production process of IM (Day, 1998; Kiousis, 2002; McMillan and Hwang, 2002; Leiner and Quiring, 2008; Schumann et al, 2001). This understanding is built on the idea that any media form requires an audience, that media is made meaningful by the audience interpreting it. Therefore the focus is on the audience's understanding and ability to make the media form meaningful. As Reeves and Nass (1996: 253) suggest, "perceptions are far more influential than reality defined more objectively."

McMillan and Hwang (2002) highlight this focus on the audience's perception of their role in the creation on IM during their discussion of digital media as locations for interaction. They suggest that changes in site design may not necessarily automatically lead to changing how the users acted and interacted on the sites, and that the medium and the characteristics of the media forms do not define interactivity per se; they rely on the user to make them meaningful (Reeves and Nass, 1996; Wu, 2005). As such, a focus purely on the modes and design features that enable interaction was not enough. For McMillan and Hwang, the processes and features of interaction are important, but they are only made meaningful by the audience. Rather than taking a technologically deterministic stance and focusing on the effects of the modes and tools available for interaction, the focus is shifted instead to how the features were approached and understood. According to this approach, then, interactivity should be conceptualized "… not [as] a characteristic of the medium. The medium simply serves to facilitate the interaction" (Schumann et al, 2001: 41).

In order to understand how the users make both the IM form and their roles and actions as a media audience for IM meaningful, this approach suggests that there are two key stages of perception in interactivity: pre- and post-evaluation (Ariel and Avidar, 2015). During pre-evaluation, users draw on their understanding and experiences with similar interactive features and mediums, and use this understanding to approach the new interactions (Adami, 2015; Haneef, 2010; Hernández-Pérez and Rodríguez, 2014). Users make use of their previous experiences of IM forms to understand and contextualize their roles and expectations in each particular interactive experience, meaning that different users may approach, understand, and contextualize interactive mediums, and their roles within these mediums, differently (Downes and McMillan, 2000; Kiousis, 2002; Leiner and Quiring, 2008; Wilson, 2014). This leads to the second stage, post-evaluation, in which the user makes sense of the interactions that have taken place, and uses them as guides and directives for future interactions (Lee, 2000; Livingstone, 2004; Leiner and Quiring, 2008; Newhagen, 2004).

While this approach provides a useful understanding of the importance of individual users and their approach towards media forms, we should be careful not to downplay the effects of the medium in shaping and mediating our interactions and actions online (Dyer, 2015; Lee et al, 2006; van Dijck, 2013). Online, and indeed offline, our choice of actions are not limitless, but bound to, and are often choosen specifically for (Goffman, 1959), the situations in which we are acting and interacting. A focus purely on the perceptions of the user would not allow us to account for the effects that many technical and logistical factors and choices can have on the manners and means by which we are acting and interacting online (Ariel and Avidar, 2015; Kelleher, 2009; Lee et al, 2006; Sundar, 2004). Although part of interactivity is evidently shaped by the users' understandings of their past experiences and of the various maxims of interactivity, consideration needs to also be given to the role that that medium itself has in shaping interactivity. Newhagen's (2004) assertion that interactivity takes place only within the mind of the users during their work to create meaning within the interactive landscape fails to adequately explain and consider the myriad of effects that interactive environments can have on the users' actions (Dyer, 2015). As such, we now move on to look at definitions of interactivity as a medium characteristic.

Interactivity as a medium characteristic

Heading back to Marshall's (2004) definition of IM, one of the interesting aspects of interactivity is how this temporal shift and the involvement of the user in the media production process affords the user a greater agency in shaping the media. By focusing on the tools that enable the user to gain this ability to take a role in media production, we can begin to understand how the audience are afforded this agency, and how different tools and modes can shape and affect our ability to act and interact within this landscape. Rather than situating interactivity as a result of human behavior, this approach attempts to look at how our ability to act and interact with and through media is shaped and facilitated by the specific tools through which we are afforded the ability to play a role in media production (IM) rather than purely consumption (AM).

The "interactivity as a medium characteristic" approach attempts to understand the many actions that technology and tools make possible (Lee et al, 2006); the effects that technology can have on our ability to act with, through, on, and in media; and the ways in which we are guided towards certain interactions. The focus for this approach then becomes which specific tools make IM different from AM, and which are most effective at engaging the user to interact. This has been the subject of many studies in the field of business and advertising as they attempt to optimize the chances of users fulfilling their role in the creation of media online (Adami, 2015; Fotouhi-Ghazvini et al, 2011; Kim et al, 2012; Quiring, 2009; Sicilia et al, 2005; Wu, 2005; Yoo et al, 2015). Such an approach argues that certain features encourage the user to become engaged in media production and are therefore more interactive than other features. For example, Warnick et al (2005) posits that an increase in number of hyperlinks on a website will increase the website's potential for interactivity. McMillan (2002) similarly suggests that certain features such as email, registrations forms, surveys, comment forms, search engines, and games can increase the interactive potential of a platform.

This approach is similar to the idea of "low" and "high" interactivity mentioned earlier, with a focus on the specific tools that enable users to become more involved in the media production process. As such, Bucy and Tao (2007: 656) define interactivity as the "technological attributes of mediated environments that enable reciprocal communication or information exchange, which afford interaction between communication technology and users or between users through technology." In other words, this approach understands interaction as something that involves the user, but that is impossible without the technology, which can mediate and shape the ways and means available for users to act on and through. Different tools will affect the extent to which users can take actions, and the ways users can act (Hausman and Siekpe, 2009; Rogers, 2003; Teo et al, 2003).

A similar approach has been taken when considering interactive art instillations (Goodman, 2012). Researchers such as Kwastek (2013) and de Meredieu (2003) highlight that although interactivity may at times seem boundless, it is a restrictive process that is guided by the means afforded to the user to interact through. Essentially, interactive platforms do not present us with limitless options, but leave us with a ranged, but ultimately restricted, set of actions, which are guided by the design and the designers (Dyer, 2015; Massumi, 2011). Total autonomy within a platform is not given, nor should it be presumed, and arguably, no matter how many platforms we are given to interact, the platform is still bound and limited. Massumi (2011: 47) defines this as "the tyranny to interaction," the ability of interaction to present us with agency, the reality that the mechanisms that provide us with this freedom bind, restrict, and mediate our abilities to interact. The same tools that facilitate interaction and greater agency also restrict and contain possible interaction (Richards, 2006).

This approach, however, has been accused of technological determinism and of overplaying the importance of technology and the effects that it can have on the user (Bakker and Sadaba, 2008). Although these features give the potential of interaction, as the previous discussion of interactivity as a perception highlights, it is still up to the user to realize the potential of these tools; a website with a large number of interactive features is no guarantee that an audience will become involved in the production of the media form. Researchers such as Sundar (2004) have pointed out that the level at which a piece of technology can be considered interactive is dependent on the user, and is not provided solely in or through the medium alone. For example, Sundar (2004) highlights that although an extremely advanced platform can offer a large variety of tools through which the user can act and interact, it may be less interactive than a potentially more restrictive platform such as email, as it relies in part on the user's experience, knowledge, and expertise, and therefore may be less useable to fewer users than an simpler, more ubiquitous system. Similarly, Novak, Hoffman, and Yung (2000) point out that certain potentially interactive features may be less effective based on measures such as waiting and loading times. As such, restricting a definition of interactivity to purely a consideration of the medium denies "The user's ability to exert control over content" (Nash, 2012: 199). Although the focus on how design can afford greater potential for user involvement is useful, a consideration is needed that highlights and also accounts for the ability of the user to fulfill and engage with these features.

Interactivity as a process

The final definition of interactivity focuses on the process through which interaction takes place. In particular, it focuses on the roles of the audience, and how messages are transferred, understood, and received by the audience (Ariel and Avidar, 2015; Kelleher, 2009; McMillan and Hwang, 2002; Rafaeli, 1988). Drawing from a linguistic focus, this branch attempts to define interactivity by differentiating interactive communication from other forms of communication. It does so by positing three types of communications: one-directional, responsive, and interactive (Ariel and Avidar, 2015).

One-directional interactions can be thought of as declarative statements that do not demand any response from the receiver of that information. Any party can be the sender or the receiver of the message (Rafaeli, 1988), but the message is only ever sent in one direction, with the roles of sender and receiver remaining static during the communication.

Two-way communication, or responsive communication, encourages reaction from the receiver of the communication, and elicits an exchanging of roles from receiver to sender, and vice versa, in order to allow for a response. However, this type of communication only allows for response to the information given in the original message, and does not prompt continued further messages (Ariel and Avidar, 2015). It is reactive to the information that is given, and results in a call-and-response type exchange, bringing the communication to a close after the response (Rafaeli, 1998). Two-way communication does not encourage further communication after the response, but does allow for the participants to be both receivers and senders of communicative information.

Finally, interactive communication allows for an extended, continued two-way flow of information, with participants taking the role of both sender and receiver. The communication is not only responsive to the immediate message that has been received, as in two-way communication, but can refer back to "previous turns and encourages the continuation of an interaction" (Ariel and Avidar, 2015: 23). As such, interaction is an ongoing communication that encourages further and continued engagement.

As Haeckel (1998: 63) highlights, "the essence of interactivity is exchange." For interactivity as a process, interactivity is best thought of as a two-directional exchange of both information and roles, an exchange that "involves responsiveness of the displayed message to the message receiver" (Miles, 1992: 150). The defining feature of interactive communication for this approach to interactivity is the ability of participants to take dual roles, and the continued flow of information. This process does not necessarily only involve two participants, and can involve "... multidirectional communication between any number of sources and receivers" (Pavlik, 1996: 137). As such, Ha and James (1998: 461) argue for a definition of interactivity that encompasses dual roles and responsiveness, suggesting that "interactivity should be defined in terms of the extent to which the communicator and audience respond to, or are willing to facilitate, each other's communication needs." Bezjian-Avery, Calder, and Iacobucci (1998) argue that digital media technology allows and encourages this type of interactive participation, as the user gets to be in control of the interaction, taking the part of both receiver and giver of information, rather than acting as a passive receiver of one-way information.

This model allows for the consideration of the roles played by participants, and encourages a reflection on the responsive nature between users that interaction often demands online. It focuses on the exchange of roles from sender to receiver, and on the extent to which users encourage reciprocation (Kiousis, 2002). While this model is useful, and can be used to consider the roles of technology in facilitating the flow of information and the exchanging of roles (Bezjian-Avery et al, 1998), it does not adequately account for the perceptions of the participants, or the manner in which the interactions are made meaningful by the participants. This approach focuses largely on the manner in which reciprocation is encouraged by the messages sent, and not by the design and technological features, as highlighted in the discussion of interactivity as a medium characteristic, nor on how responses can differ based on each user's understanding of similar situations, as raised in the discussion of interactivity as perception.

This approach does not account for the myriad effects that the environment the communication takes place in can have on the overall flow and style of the communication (Dyer, 2015; Kress, 2004; Massey, 1994; Schwartz and Halegoua, 2014; Stedman, 2003; van Dijck, 2013). Instead, it places the burden and focus of interaction on the information itself and the manner in which it allows for reciprocation, rather than how, for example, each user may react to the same information differently based on their experiences and exposure to other media texts, as raised in the discussion of interactivity as perception. A focus on the other myriad factors that may shape, mediate, and affect the reciprocation of information and the exchanging of roles is needed. As such, we now consider how we can bring together the points raised in all three approaches, using ideas drawn from comic book studies.

Using comic books to combine a sensitivity to space, perception, and process

All three definitions explored above raise interesting points and considerations, and a number of researchers have called for a weighted consideration of all three definitions when approaching interaction (Ariel and Avidar, 2015; Coyle and Thorson, 2001; Lieb, 1998; McMillan and Hwang, 2002; Weber et al, 2014). A robust conceptualization of interactivity would need to build on these diverse and dynamic definitions to consider the myriad potential effects of the interactive landscape, how these potentials are actualized and understood by the participants in a stylized manner guided by a number of external factors and social influences, and the roles of the human and non-human participants. An approach is needed that combines all three strands of definition, one that considers how the users make sense of an interactive environment, that focuses on what this space is filled with to enable the user to become involved in ongoing media production, and that considers how the roles of the participants are shaped and defined.

Such an approach can be procured by looking further afield at other approaches to conceptualize media forms and their effects on audiences. One such useful approach is comic book studies. Although, according to Marshall's (2004) definition, comic books are AM forms that only involve the audience after the production of the media form, comic book studies holds many useful parallels, allowing for a sensitivity to both form and to personal agency that can help us unpack the many facets that shape interactivity online.

Comic book studies offers a consideration of a media form that is built through the relationship between user, form, design, and designer, and provides a useful counterpoint through which to frame the discussion of the conceptualization of interaction.

Comic book studies attempts to not only look at media forms as a human and technology-based creation, but asks how this ongoing narrative creation is shaped and guided by various aspects such as page design, style, modal arrangements, shapes, sizes, and colors, as well as considering the processes of active participation required by readers to make sense of the messages presented to them, and readers' experiences with other media and exposure to discourses (Foucault, 1984) that form guided yet personal, stylistically realized individual narratives.

This understanding of the myriad factors that create and guide the individual users' interpretation of the media text is understood and conceptualized through the concepts of "closure," "intertextuality," and "extratextuality" (McCloud, 1993). It is these concepts, expanded on below, that allow for and demand a consideration of both design and personal stylized agency. Comic book studies manages to provide a working model that combines a sensitivity to individual perception and an understanding of a media form as mentioned in the discussion of interactivity as participation, a consideration of the effect of form and design mentioned in the discussion of interactivity as a medium, and a consideration of the roles of participants mentioned in the discussion of interactivity as a process.

Closure, intertextuality, extratextuality, and gutter space

Comic book studies posits that comic books present the reader with a media form that encourages them to take an active role in creating a narrative, but suggests that process and their role as reader is guided and shaped by the author, the features of the images and texts, and the nature of the medium. Scott McCloud (1993) suggests that a key aspect that separates comics from other media forms is the degree of audience participation; comics are a highly participatory media form as the audience has to actively and consistently be engaged in creating the narrative in order to make sense of the series of juxtaposed images they are provided with. The images that are presented to the audience in comics only reveal parts of the overall story; the audience is left to decide how to make sense of these images and literally to "fill in the gaps" between each image in order to create a continuous narrative. They are presented with a series of discrete images, and have to create a continuous whole from these images. The act of creating a continuous whole image out of the series of images the audience is given is known as "closure" (McCloud, 1993; Schwartz, 1983).

Closure is a useful term when considering how a narrative whole is created, as it not only implies that the audience takes an active role in creating the story, but it also allows for a consideration of how this narrative whole is created in a personal, stylized, and individual manner. Much like the discussion of interactivity as perception, closure suggests that the narrative that is created will not be the same for each reader; it is a narrative that is effected by our own perceptions, experiences, and understandings. Closure suggests that different readers will complete the narrative differently. When presented with a series of images, different users may draw on different experiences and frames of reference in order to make sense of the gap between the two presented images, making each narrative potentially different and personable (McCloud, 1993).

This act of closure can heavily involve the audience as they dissect and compile the given information from panel to panel. The space that this closure is committed in is known as "the gutter," literally the blank space between any two panels in a comic. This is the space where human imagination comes into play; although comics themselves are mono-sensory, engaging only one sense to read them, in the gutter between the panels users are free to engage and call on all of their senses to fill in the gaps (McCloud, 1993). Each image acts as what Lessing (1984) in 1766, who was discussing the effects of physically framing pieces of art in different types of frames, described as a "pregnant moment," giving birth to a whole world that is fleshed out by the reader.

Closure is aided and achieved through utilizing and linking the images given within the text to our "intertextual" knowledge of other media texts, and our "extratextual" experience of different events in action (Bakhtin, 1981; Fairclough, 1992; Kristeva, 1980; McCloud, 1993). Here extratextuality can be understood as the audience's use of experiences and knowledge beyond solely that which is given in the text, allowing them to understand and make sense of the text. Intertextuality is the audience's ability to draw on their experiences of other texts they have consumed in order to make sense of the given media text (Bakhtin, 1981). Through these notions the meaning of a text to the audience is shaped not only by the text itself and the design features of the text, but also by their experiences with other texts, and to their wider experiences and exposure to discourses (Foucault, 1984). As such, each narrative is guided by the text, but experienced and actualized on a personal level. McCloud (1993) suggests, then, that comics can be seen as offering a jagged staccato rhythm of unconnected moments "which we then connect, via closure, to mentally construct a continuous, unified reality." This reality is impacted by our knowledge of other texts and information beyond that given in the text alone.

However, this narrative creation is by no means completely boundless; it is restricted and guided by the design and form of the comic book. Certain actions can be taken by the author and artist to restrict the amount of work needed to be done by the audience to create a narrative, and to guide to reader towards a certain understanding of events. One such method is through the use of different "transitions." The degree of involvement required by the reader to fill in these gaps between images can vary depending on how much the two images differ, or the types of "transitions" used from panel to panel. Some panel transitions will require very little information to be filled in by the reader as not much happens between the panels, while others can require the audience to be heavily involved in rendering the transitions meaningful. However, the audience is kept constantly and heavily involved in the media form from image to image.

In essence then, comic book studies highlights that the users' understanding of a media form can be guided by their own agency (closure), their sociocultural "baggage" (extratextuality), and their understanding of similar media (intertextuality), as well as by the design of the media form and the amount of space they are given to create their own understandings. Comic book studies suggests that researchers can give equal consideration to both a sensitivity to design and to user perception. This approach also highlights that media forms can be collaboration between a number of parties: authors, audiences, designers, design, and wider social discourses (Foucault, 1984). By highlighting that a realized media form can be both guided by design and by the audience's own understanding and interpretations drawn from their intertextuality and extratextuality, comic book studies presents a complex media form that accounts for a number of factors in the creation of a narrative.

Such an approach applied to interactive texts could highlight the myriad of influences that result in the creation of specific user roles during the process of media creation and in specific, individual, and stylized outcomes of media creation. In collaborative interactive text the user is afforded the ability to become not only a consumer of texts, but also a creator of texts. This allows them to not only create a media narrative through their understanding of the text, but to switch roles, shaping and creating their own texts within the confines of the designed social space, and being shaped by the texts of other users as well. Users become not only receivers of information but also active creators in an ongoing dual role and an ongoing process. When receiving information, not only are they creating their own stylized narratives, guided in varying degrees by the creators of the site and the design of the site, but they are receiving the input of other users as well, creating their narratives from this content as well. They, in turn, also get to create their own content for other users to unpack in their own stylized manner, again guided and confined by the specific design of the social spaces.

Understanding digital media through comic books

Comic book studies offers a model through which we can reconcile the divide between the effects of form and medium and the effects of personal understanding. It allows for a consideration of the manner in which the audience is able to create their own understanding of the media form, as well as the manner by which this process is guided by the design of the media form. It also reveals how a media form can be considered as a relationship between human and non-human elements, working together to create a meaningful form. It is worth considering in greater depth the degree to which social networking sites involve the audience and how the audience renders the given information meaningful. This vital area of research is often overlooked; however, comic book studies could offer a vital lens to allow consideration of how a media narrative is understood and conceptualized by the user, and how this process is shaped and guided by design. Approaching media texts from this angle could provide much needed insight into how a personalized experience is shaped and formed in digital media.

Comic book studies highlights that with any media form we see many actors coming together to create a unique and personalized media form that is a blend of different social, discursive and technical elements. It is worth noting that, with this understanding of media forms, this is more than just human-to-human interaction, but is a blend of human and non-human, of discursive, social, and technical elements. This network of different actors interact, engage, and impact on each other to create, shape, and produce the specific occurrence of media, and subsequent interactions and identities witnessed online. This shapes a unique media form which can be viewed as an actor-network (Latour, 2005), made from the interaction of many actors, human and non-human, coming together to define and shape each other, and effecting how we can act and interact online (Galloway, 2012). Not only do humans and non-humans and technology co-inhabit online spaces, they co-produce them, impacting on one another, with humans shaping the content of media, and media shaping and mediating the actions of the humans (see Whatmore, 2006; Panelli, 2010). Indeed, in 1984 Foucault noted the importance of environment in shaping and creating social actions and interaction, and the links between space and knowledge. He noted that it was "somewhat arbitrary to try to dissociate … the practice of social relations, and the spatial distributions in which they find themselves. If separated, they become impossible to understand" (Foucault, 1984: 246). We can understand social spaces, including the internet, as a blend of human and non-human, rather than being exclusively human or a pre-given structure.

Such an understanding of the link between the design of social spaces and the prevalence of specific social discourses in the use of these social spaces is also essential when considering the use of the internet to spread, facilitate, strengthen, and legitimize many existing social discourses. Much has been, and continues to be, made about the exclusion of minorities through design features of social media, such as the effect of social media on users with a variety of disabilities (Caron and Light, 2015; Davies et al, 2015; Goggin and Newell, 2003; Kent and Ellis, 2015; Pinchevski and Peters, 2015). Using an approach that highlights and asks for an examination of the discursive assumptions present in the design of online social spaces, we can also begin to consider how the design of a social media site can privilege and prioritize the use of certain discourses and certain users during the closure process, and equally how design can marginalize, and even make invisible, other discourses and other users.

Such a discussion seems increasingly necessary, especially when considering applications such as Yik Yak, which have been rife with reports of bigotry, misogyny, and racism. Some researchers have begun to suggest that Yik Yak facilitates and encourages such behavior through its design, often citing the anonymity it offers as particularly troubling feature as it affords users a lack of accountability for the use of harmful discourses (Black et al, 2016; Whittaker and Kowalski, 2015). Similarly, sites such as Twitter and Facebook are still attempting to create design features to facilitate the reporting of hate crimes, bullying, and harassment. Unfortunately, such acts of closure are still all too prevalent on many social networking sites, and such discourses of harassment are found throughout many corners of the internet. It is worth considering not only how these acts of harassment are carried out by specific groups of users, but also how design facilitates and perhaps even encourages these types of "closure," and how we could better design social media sites to minimize the likelihood of users creating these types of narrative readings and realities. It is worth considering that comic book studies posits that the design of a media form can suggest the most appropriate "closure" to be carried out by the reader, but equally, that this closure is always open to different interpretations and different individual realizations. Nonetheless, it should not be a case of either/or when tackling subjects such as the continued harassment of women on social media – both design and larger discourses need to be challenged and held accountable. As Adrienne Massanari (2015) aptly and crucially points out, both Reddit's algorithm and the toxic culture present on the site allowed and encouraged many of the misogynistic and harmful elements of events and trends, such as "the fappening" and "Gamergate."

Such an approach highlights that we must be careful not to presume that this interaction and ability to play a role in shaping the media form does not solely prioritize human actors. Agency online is negotiated, constrained, and shaped by a number of factors that shape the possible and preferred actions online (Hu et al, 2014; Nelson and Irwin, 2014; Phethean et al, 2015; Rector-Aranda and Raider-Roth, 2015; Willett, 2008). We are not entirely free to act of our own accord online but are shaped by many factors, from space and design online (boyd, 2014; Dyer, 2015; Ma and Agarwal, 2007; Merchant, 2006; Orsatti and Riemer, 2015) to pre-existing ideals and power structures offline (Bowker and Tuffin, 2002; Campbell, 2014; Christensen, 2003; Huffaker and Calvert, 2006; Nakamura, 2013). New media is highly structured, and many of the websites have made choices in regards to design aspects of the site that for one reason or another encourage certain behaviors and restrict or deny others (Dyer, 2015; Emanuel et al, 2014; Kimmons, 2014; Massanari, 2015; Sun and Hart-Davidson, 2014; van Dijck, 2013). Studies into IM should therefore not presume that the interactivity offered online necessarily means greater freedom or control, as many choices have already been made for us in advance (see Manovich, 2001).

These restrictions are not just physical or spatial, but are grounded in the offline and pre-existing social structures (Buckingham and Willett, 2013; Campbell, 2014; Christensen, 2003; Nakamura, 2013). We must also acknowledge "'the spatially specific *accumulations* of 'constraints' and 'coercions' on action that flow from human life being lived in coordination or competition with others" (Couldry, 2012: 26–27; original emphasis). These online social spaces affect not only our way of speaking, communicating, and socializing, but also potentially affect how meaning is made both online and offline. Thus different spaces and sites can have different rules and means of socializing (Foucault, 1984). A consideration of the manners in which our actions and interactions in IM are guided by design as well our own perceptions can allow for a potentially deeper understanding of both the systemic structures and logics of the particular media culture as well as the potential occurrences and quirks of individual agents.

Using comic book studies, digital media can importantly be seen as a blend of online and offline actors, spaces, and elements. By making use of extratextuality and closure, we can begin to see how the users' experiences and understandings of digital texts are affected and shaped by their pre-existing experiences with other texts and their exposure to social discourses and ideals. Digital media forms exist both online and offline through the interactions between users, technologies, designs, and interfaces. They are formed through a constant integration of online and offline elements, and impact online and offline lives at the same time. Through the notions of intertextuality and extratextuality we can view and dissect these online media forms and understand their existence in the offline and online world at the same time, and their impact on both the online and offline world. By using intertextuality we can understand how they function as interactive texts whose meaning to the audience is shaped in part by their relation to other online and offline texts. In turn, online media can impact and affect how readers understand and approach other texts, again, both online and offline. Comic book studies therefore offers yet another frame through which academics can conceptualize the breakdown of digital dualism and the merging of the online and offline world (see Bauwens et al, 2013; Jurgenson, 2011; Rice et al, 2014; Winetrobe et al, 2014). To think of the online and offline as two separate poles of existence is to deny thinking of the flow of information and action *between* them. The online and offline are not abstracted, disconnected, and detached realms, but overlapping fields that exist together and impact each other together. Using comic book studies, we can highlight how online reality impacts and is impacted by the audience's knowledge of other texts and information beyond that given text alone.

Comic book studies encourages a consideration of a "messy" reality that consists of many actors and voices (or heteroglossia, as Bakhtin, 1981, called it), creating and shaping each other into a specific media form. By moving away from a focus on media as a system, or media as an object, and moving towards an understanding of media at the level of actor and audience, we can begin to focus on how online action and interaction is shaped, and how it in turn shapes other social situations. The "social" online, and indeed in any situation, must be explained rather than merely providing the explanation (Latour, 2005).

A call to arms: embracing the human and the technological

Sociology is often understood as the study of the effects humans have on the world. Digital sociology must stand up to this, and acknowledge its role as a study of technology that highlights that this can never be a one-way relationship. With the rise of technology we cannot deny the impact that the world has on us. I strongly suggest that due to the focus on technology, it is the role of digital sociology to lead the way in the re-evaluation of the role of humans and non-humans in sociology. We should test the borders between humans and technology and ask for, if not insist on, the inclusion and acknowledgement of the impact that technology can have on us. As the increasingly popular movement in sociology towards actor-network theory (Latour, 2005) has made clear, we can no longer deny the myriad ways that the realm of the physical and technological can affect, mediate, and alter our actions and interaction; we must account for it, we must study and embrace it, and not attempt to maintain the façade of sociology as a separate sphere. It becomes harder and harder to maintain the boundary of sociology, and as digital sociologists we must embrace the mess, and account for the technology. This does not mean, however, as comic book studies makes abundantly clear, that we should ignore the role of the individual in navigating the digital landscape and creating novel, original, and stylistic understandings of the landscape. It can sometimes be too easy to slip into digital determinism, and we must be careful not to deny the many, often surprising, interventions of humans within the digital landscape.

Comic book studies allows us to embrace the impact the physical world has on the ways we act and the methods we have available to interact with, on, in and through, while still allowing and demanding the involvement of humans to make sense of the world around them. It is this understanding of the ongoing, non-fixed, multidirectional, and multifaceted relationship between the physical landscape, the discursive landscape, and the humans' own stylized individual actions, guided by intertextuality and extratextuality, that can help us move towards a comfortable understanding of how users and design can coexist, and how they can all be accounted for in our research. We cannot deny the users' ability to exert control over the content, but we cannot assume that this is a one-way relationship. Using comic book studies, we can unpack how the user will ultimately make sense of the content, but also acknowledge that their understanding of the content and their process of making sense of this content will be guided by a number of facets including wider social discourses and the content itself.

Using the sensitivity to design and the understanding of individual realizations of media as highlighted by comic book studies, along with the discussion of interactivity and the manner in which users understand, realize, and partake in interactive media, interactivity can be viewed as a personal ongoing narrative creation by a number of authors, guided and shaped by the a number of facets including design features, sociocultural contexts, designed closure, the users' intertextual and extratextual situating and interpreting of text and the "gutter spaces," and the various authors present within the interactive landscape. This understanding can help us consider the duplicity of roles present in IM, the temporal understanding of interactivity, the role of the users' interpretations and contextualizations, and the role of design to shape our actions, interactions, and understandings of the media's narrative. Through an active consideration of both design and user, we can begin the vital work of unpacking digital spaces, focusing both on how the user is understanding the landscape, and how the landscape is impacting the user's actions and understanding.

References

Adami, E. (2015) "What's in a click? A social semiotic framework for the multimodal analysis of website interactivity." *Visual Communication* 14 (2), 133–53.

Ariel, Y. and R. Avidar (2015) "Information, interactivity, and social media." *Atlantic Journal of Communication* 23 (1), 19–30.

Avidar, R. (2013) "The responsiveness pyramid: Embedding responsiveness and interactivity into public relations theory." *Public Relations Review* 39 (5), 440–50.

Bakhtin, M.M. (1981) *Dialogic imagination: Four essays.* (edited by M. Holquist, translated by C. Emerson). Austin, TX: University of Texas Press.

Bakker, P. and C. Sadaba (2008) "The impact of the internet on users." In L. Küng, R.G. Picard, and R. Towse (eds) *The internet and the mass media* (pp 86–102). London, UK: Sage.

Bauwens, J., K. Verstrynge, and the Philosophy Documentation Center (2013) "Digital technology, virtual worlds, and ethical change." *Techné: Research in Philosophy and Technology* 17 (1), 124–43.

Bezjian-Avery, A., B. Calder, and D. Iacobucci (1998) "New media interactive advertising vs traditional advertising." *Journal of Advertising Research* 38, 23–32.

Black, E.W., K. Mezzina, and L.A. Thompson (2016) "Anonymous social media – Understanding the content and context of Yik Yak." *Computers in Human Behavior* 57, 17–22.

Bowker, N. and K. Tuffin (2002) "Disability discourses for online identities." *Disability & Society* 17 (3), 327–44.

boyd, d. (2014) *It's complicated: The social lives of networked teens.* New Haven, CT: Yale University Press.

Buckingham, D. and R. Willett (2006) *Digital generations: Children, young people, and new media.* New York: Routledge.

Bucy, E.P. (2004) "Interactivity in society: Locating an elusive concept." *The Information Society* 20 (5), 373–83.

Bucy, E.P. and C.-C. Tao (2007) "The mediated moderation model of interactivity." *Media Psychology* 9 (3), 647–72.

Campbell, J.E. (2014) *Getting it on online: Cyberspace, gay male sexuality, and embodied identity.* London, UK: Harrington Park Press.

Caron, J. and J. Light (2015) "Social media has opened a world of 'open communication:' Experiences of adults with cerebral palsy who use augmentative and alternative communication and social media." *Augmentative and Alternative Communication*, 1–16.

Christensen, N.B. (2003) *Inuit in cyberspace: Embedding offline identities online.* Copenhagen, Denmark: Museum Tusculanum Press.

Couldry, N. (2012) *Media, society, world: Social theory and digital media practice.* Cambridge, UK: Polity Press.

Coyle, J.R. and E. Thorson (2001) "The effects of progressive levels of interactivity and vividness in web marketing sites." *Journal of Advertising* 30 (3), 65–77.

Davies, D.K., S.E. Stock, L.R. King, R.B. Brown, M.L. Wehmeyer, and K.A. Shogren (2015) "An interface to support independent use of Facebook by people with intellectual disability." *Intellectual and Developmental Disabilities* 53 (1), 30–41.

Day, G.S. (1998) "Organizing for interactivity." *Journal of Interactive Marketing* 12 (1), 47–53.

de Meredieu, F. (2005) *Digital and video art.* Edinburgh, UK: Chambers.

Downes, E.J. and S.J. McMillan (2000) "Defining Interactivity: A qualitative identification of key dimensions." *New Media & Society* 2 (2), 157–79.

Durlak, J.T. (1987) "A typology for interactive media." In M. McLaughlin (ed) *Communication yearbook 10* (pp 743–57). Beverly Hills, CA: Sage.

Dyer, H.T. (2015) "All the web's a stage: The effects of design and modality on youth performances of identity." *Sociological Studies of Children and Youth* 19, 213–42.

Emanuel, L., G.J. Neil, C. Bevan, D.S. Fraser, S.V. Stevenage, M.T. Whitty, and S. Jamison-Powell (2014) "Who am I? Representing the self offline and in different online contexts." *Computers in Human Behavior* 41, 146–52.

Fairclough, N. (1992) "Intertextuality in critical discourse analysis." *Linguistics and Education* 4 (3), 269–93.

Fotouhi-Ghazvini, F., R. Earnshaw, A. Moeini, D. Robison, and P. Excell (2011) "From e-Learning to m-Learning – the use of mixed reality games as a new educational paradigm." *International Journal of Interactive Mobile Technologies* 5 (2), 17–25.

Foucault, M. (1979) *Discipline and punish: The birth of the prison.* New York: Vintage Books.

Foucault, M. (1984) *The Foucault reader.* London, UK: Pantheon Books.

Galloway, A.R. (2012) *The interface effect.* Cambridge, UK: Polity Press.

Goffman, E. (1959) *The presentation of self in everyday life.* New York: Anchor Books.

Goggin, G. and C. Newell (2003) *Digital disability: The social construction of disability in new media.* Oxford, UK: Rowman & Littlefield.

Goodman, A. (2012) "Rethinking interactivity. From material to organic modelling." In ACMC Interactive Conference proceedings. Griffith University, Brisbane, Australia.

Haeckel, S.H. (1998) "About the nature and future of interactive marketing." *Journal of Interactive Marketing* 12 (1), 63–71.

Ha, L. and E.L. James (1998) "Interactivity re-examined: A baseline analysis of early business web sites." *Journal of Broadcasting & Electronic Media* 42 (4), 457–74.

Haneef, M.S.M. (2010) "Intertextuality and interactivity in hypertext reading of www.timesofindia.com." *Journal of Creative Communications* 5 (3), 189–205.

Hausman, A.V. and J.S. Siekpe (2009) "The effect of web interface features on consumer online purchase intentions." *Journal of Business Research* 62(1), 5–13.

Heeter, C. (1989) "Implications of new interactive technologies for conceptualizing communication." In J.L. Salvaggio and J. Bryant (eds) *Media use in the information age: Emerging patterns of adoption and computer use* (pp 217–35). Hillsdale, NJ: Erlbaum.

Heeter, C. (2000) "Interactivity in the context of designed experiences." *Journal of Interactive Advertising* 1 (1), 3–14.

Hernández-Pérez, M. and J.G.F. Rodríguez (2014) "Serial narrative, intertextuality, and the role of audiences in the creation of a franchise: An analysis of the Indiana Jones saga from a cross-media perspective." *Mass Communication and Society* 17 (1), 26–53.

Huffaker, D.A. and S.L. Calvert (2005) "Gender, identity, and language use in teenage blogs." *Journal of Computer-Mediated Communication* 10 (2).

Hu, J., J. Frens, M. Funk, F. Wang, and Y. Zhang (2014) "Design for social interaction in public spaces." In P.L.P. Rau (ed) *Cross-cultural design* (pp 287–98). New York: Springer International Publishing.

Johnson, G.J., G.C. Bruner II and A. Kumar (2006) "Interactivity and its facets revisited: Theory and empirical test." *Journal of Advertising* 35 (4), 35–52.

Jurgenson, N. (2011) "Digital dualism versus augmented reality." *Cyborgology: The Society Pages* 24.

Kelleher, T. (2009) "Conversational voice, communicated commitment, and public relations outcomes in interactive online communication." *Journal of Communication* 59 (1), 172–88.

Kent, M. and K. Ellis (2015) "People with disability and new disaster communications: access and the social media mash-up." *Disability & Society* 30 (3), 419–31.

Kim, J., N. Spielmann, and S.J. McMillan (2012) "Experience effects on interactivity: Functions, processes, and perceptions." *Journal of Business Research* 65 (11), 1543–50.

Kimmons, R. (2014) "Social networking sites, literacy, and the authentic identity problem." *TechTrends* 58 (2), 93–8.

Kiousis, S. (2002) "Interactivity: a concept explication." *New Media & Society* 4 (3), 355–83.

Kress, G. (2004) "Reading images: Multimodality, representation and new media." *Information Design Journal* 12 (2), 110–19.

Kristeva, J. (1980) *Desire in language: A semiotic approach to literature and art.* New York: Columbia University Press.

Kwastek, K. (2013) *Aesthetics of interaction in digital art.* Cambridge, MA: The MIT Press.

Latour, B. (2005) *Reassembling the social – An introduction to actor-network-theory.* Oxford, UK: Oxford University Press.

Lee, J.S. (2000) "Interactivity: A new approach." Paper presented at the Association for Education in Journalism and Mass Communication, August, Phoenix, AZ.

Lee, K.M., N. Park, and S.-A. Jin (2006) "Narrative and interactivity in computer games." In P. Vorderer and J. Bryant (eds) *Playing video games: Motives, responses, and consequences* (pp 259–74). Mahwah, NJ: Lawrence Erlbaum Associates Publishers.

Lee, S.-J., W.-N. Lee, H. Kim, and P.A. Stout (2004) "A comparison of objective characteristics and user perception of web sites." *Journal of Interactive Advertising* 4 (2), 61–75.

Leiner, D.J. and O. Quiring (2008) "What interactivity means to the user: Essential insights into and a scale for perceived interactivity." *Journal of Computer-Mediated Communication* 14 (1), 127–55

Lessing, P.G.E. (1984) *Laocoon: An essay on the limits of painting and poetry* (translated by P.E.A. McCormick) (new edn). Baltimore, MD: The Johns Hopkins University Press.

Lieb, T. (1998) "Inactivity on interactivity." *Journal of Electronic Publishing* 3 (3), 1–4.

Liu, Y. and L.J. Shrum (2009) "A dual-process model of interactivity effects." *Journal of Advertising* 38 (2), 53–68.

Livingstone, S. (2004) "The challenge of changing audiences: Or, what is the audience researcher to do in the age of the internet?" *European Journal of Communication* 19 (1), 75–86.

McCloud, S. (1993) *Understanding comics: The invisible art.* New York: William Morrow Paperbacks.

McMillan, S.J. (2002) "A four-part model of cyber-interactivity: Some cyber-places are more interactive than others." *New Media & Society* 4 (2), 271–91.

McMillan, S.J. and J.-S. Hwang (2002) "Measures of perceived interactivity: An exploration of the role of direction of communication, user control, and time in shaping perceptions of interactivity." *Journal of Advertising* 31 (3), 29–42.

Ma, M. and R. Agarwal (2007) "Through a glass darkly: Information technology design, identity verification, and knowledge contribution in online communities." *Information Systems Research* 18 (1), 42–67.

Manovich, L. (2001) *The language of new media.* Cambridge, MA: The MIT Press.

Markus, M.L. (1987) "Toward a 'critical mass' theory of interactive media universal access, interdependence and diffusion." *Communication Research* 14 (5), 491–511.

Marshall, P.D. (2004) *New media cultures.* Oxford, UK: Bloomsbury Academic.

Massanari, A. (2015) "#Gamergate and the Fappening: How Reddit's algorithm, governance, and culture support toxic technocultures." *New Media & Society*, (http://nms.sagepub.com/content/early/2015/10/07/1461444815608807).

Massey, D. (1994) *Space, place, and gender.* Cambridge, UK: Polity Press.

Massumi, B. (2011) *Semblance and event: Activist philosophy and the occurrent arts.* Cambridge, MA: The MIT Press.

Merchant, G. (2006) "Identity, social networks and online communication." *E-Learning and Digital Media* 3 (2), 235–44.

Miles, I. (1992) "When mediation is the message: How suppliers envisage new markets." In M. Lea (ed) *Contexts of computer-mediated communication* (pp 145–67). Michigan, MI: Harvester Wheatsheaf.

Moore, M.G. (1989) "Editorial: Three types of interaction." *American Journal of Distance Education* 3 (2), 1–7.

Nakamura, L. (2013) *Cybertypes: Race, ethnicity, and identity on the internet.* New York: Routledge.

Nash, K. (2012) "Modes of interactivity: analysing the webdoc." *Media, Culture & Society* 34 (2), 195–210.

Nelson, A.J. and J. Irwin (2014) "Defining what we do – all over again: Occupational identity, technological change, and the librarian/internet-search relationship." *Academy of Management Journal* 57 (3), 892–928.

Newhagen, J.E. (2004) "Interactivity, dynamic symbol processing, and the emergence of content in human communication." *The Information Society* 20 (5), 395–400.

Novak, T.P., D.L. Hoffman, and Y.-F. Yung (2000) "Measuring the customer experience in online environments: A structural modeling approach." *Marketing Science* 19 (1), 22–42.

Orsatti, J. and K. Riemer (2015) *Identity-making: A multimodal approach for researching identity in social media.* European Conference on Information Systems 2015, Completed Research Papers.

Panelli, R. (2010) "More-than-human social geographies: posthuman and other possibilities." *Progress in Human Geography* 34 (1), 79–87.

Pavlik, J.V. (1996) *New media technology: cultural and commercial perspectives.* London, UK: Allyn & Bacon.

Phethean, C., T. Tiropanis, and L. Harris (2015) "Engaging with charities on social media: Comparing interaction on Facebook and Twitter." In T. Tiropanis, A. Vakali, L. Sartori, and P. Burnap (eds) *Internet science: Second International Conference, INSCI 2015, Brussels, Belgium, May 27–29, 2015, Proceedings* (pp 15–29). Cham, Switzerland: Springer International Publishing.

Pinchevski, A. and J.D. Peters (2015) "Autism and new media: Disability between technology and society." *New Media & Society*, 1–17.

Quiring, O. (2009) "What do users associate with 'interactivity'? A qualitative study on user schemata." *New Media & Society* 11 (6), 899–920.

Rafaeli, S. (1988) "Interactivity: From new media to communication." In R.P. Hawkins, J.M. Wiemann and S. Pingree (eds) *Advancing communication science: Merging mass and interpersonal process* (pp 110–34). Newbury Park, CA: Sage.

Rafaeli, S. and Y. Ariel (2007) "Assessing interactivity in computer-mediated research." In A. Joinson, K. McKenna, T. Postmes, U.-D. Reips (eds) *The Oxford handbook of internet psychology* (pp 71–88). Oxford, UK: Oxford University Press.

Rafaeli, S. and F. Sudweeks (1997) "Networked interactivity." *Journal of Computer-Mediated Communication* 2 (4).

Rector-Aranda, A. and M. Raider-Roth (2015) "'I finally felt like I had power': student agency and voice in an online and classroom-based role-play simulation." *Research in Learning Technology* 23.

Reeves, B. and C. Nass (1996) *The media equation: How people treat computers, television, and new media like real people and places.* Stanford, CA and New York: Cambridge University Press.

Rice, E., J. Gibbs, H. Winetrobe, H. Rhoades, A. Plant, J. Montoya, and T. Kordic (2014) "Sexting and sexual behavior among middle school students." *Pediatrics* 134 (1), 21–8.

Richards, R. (2006) "Users, interactivity, and generation." *New Media & Society* 8 (4), 531–50.

Rogers, E.M. (2003) *Diffusion of innovations* (5th edn). New York: Free Press.

Rust, R.T. and S. Varki (1996) "Rising from the ashes of advertising." *Journal of Business Research* 37 (3), 173–81.

Schultz, T. (2000) "Mass media and the concept of interactivity: an exploratory study of online forums and reader email." *Media, Culture & Society* 22 (2), 205–21.

Schumann, D.W., A. Artis, and R. Rivera (2001) "The future of interactive advertising viewed through an IMC lens." *Journal of Interactive Advertising* 1 (2), 43–55.

Schwartz, T. (1983) *Media, the second God.* New York: Anchor Books.

Sicilia, M., S. Ruiz, and J.L. Munuera (2005) "Effects of interactivity in a web site: The moderating effect of need for cognition." *Journal of Advertising* 34 (3), 31–44.

Stedman, R.C. (2003) "Is it really just a social construction? The contribution of the physical environment to sense of place." *Society & Natural Resources* 16 (8), 671–85.

Steuer, J. (1992) "Defining virtual reality: Dimensions determining telepresence." *Journal of Communication* 42 (4), 73–93.

Stewart, D.W. and P.A. Pavlou (2002) "From consumer response to active consumer: Measuring the effectiveness of interactive media." *Journal of the Academy of Marketing Science* 30 (4), 376–96.

Sundar, S.S. (2004) "Theorizing interactivity's effects." *The Information Society* 20 (5), 385–89.

Sundar, S.S., S. Kalyanaraman, and J. Brown (2003) "Explicating web site interactivity impression formation effects in political campaign sites." *Communication Research* 30 (1), 30–59.

Sun, H. and W.F. Hart-Davidson (2014) "Binding the material and the discursive with a relational approach of affordances." In *Proceedings of the 32nd Annual ACM Conference on Human Factors in Computing Systems* (pp 3533–42). New York: ACM.

Teo, H.-H., L.-B. Oh, C. Liu, and K.-K. Wei (2003) "An empirical study of the effects of interactivity on web user attitude." *International Journal of Human-Computer Studies* 58 (3), 281–305.

van Dijck, J. (2013) "'You have one identity': performing the self on Facebook and LinkedIn." *Media, Culture & Society* 35 (2), 199–215.

Walther, J.B., G. Gay, and J.T. Hancock (2005) "How do communication and technology researchers study the internet?" *Journal of Communication* 55 (3), 632–57.

Warnick, B., M. Xenos, D. Endres, and J. Gastil (2005) "Effects of campaign-to-user and text-based interactivity in political candidate campaign web sites." *Journal of Computer-Mediated Communication* 10 (3).

Weber, R., K.-M. Behr, and C. DeMartino (2014) "Measuring interactivity in video games." *Communication Methods and Measures* 8 (2), 79–115.

Whatmore, S. (2006) "Materialist returns: practising cultural geography in and for a more-than-human world." *Cultural Geographies* 13 (4), 600–9.

Whittaker, E. and R.M. Kowalski (2015) "Cyberbullying via social media." *Journal of School Violence* 14 (1), 11–29.

Willett, R. (2008) "Consumer citizens online: Structure, agency, and gender in online participation." In D. Buckingham (ed) *Youth, identity, and digital media* (pp 49–70). Cambridge, MA: The MIT Press.

Wilson, J.A. (2014) "Cosmopolitan stars, interactive audience labor, and the digital economy of global care." *Television & New Media* 15 (2), 104–20.

Winetrobe, H., E. Rice, J. Bauermeister, R. Petering, and I.W. Holloway (2014) "Associations of unprotected anal intercourse with Grindr-met partners among Grindr-using young men who have sex with men in Los Angeles." *AIDS Care* 26 (10), 1303–8.

Wu, G. (2005) "The mediating role of perceived interactivity in the effect of actual interactivity on attitude toward the website." *Journal of Interactive Advertising* 5 (2), 29–39.

Yoo, C.W., Y.J. Kim, and G.L. Sanders (2015) "The impact of interactivity of electronic word of mouth systems and e-Quality on decision support in the context of the e-marketplace." *Information & Management* 52 (4), 496–505.

7

The digital solidarity trap: Social movement research, online activism, and accessing the other's others

Theresa A. Hunt

It has become both anecdotally and empirically true that younger generations of activists are immersed in digital environments, and have developed repertoires that draw heavily on information and communications technologies (ICTs). ICTs have become faster, cheaper, and more widely available than ever before. The International Telecommunications Union (ITU) estimates the percentage of the world population using the internet, for example, increased from 16 percent in 2005 to 39 percent in 2013.[1] Estimates have also suggested young people aged 15–24 comprise a majority of these users.[2] But it is important to retain a degree of skepticism that McLuhan's visions of "the global village" or Castell's notions of "the network society," both of which hinge on ICT connectivity, have been realized. Indeed, numerous digital divides persist, many of them the result of social and economic division as well as poor or non-existent cyber-infrastructure. Nevertheless, scholars and researchers of social movements must also confront the ways in which traditional methods are challenged by increasingly digital repertoires and mobilizations, especially those led by younger activists. For sociology researchers in general, using social media for data collection has prompted a number of debates. These include ethical and privacy concerns, but also extend to the transferability of face-to-face research methods applied to the digital world. Some, like Baltar and Brunet (2012), who conducted a study of Argentinean immigrant entrepreneurs in Spain using virtual snowball sampling via Facebook, assert digitization of traditional methods can be productive in increasing sample size and representativeness. Baltar and Brunet, like others (Brickman-Bhutta, 2012; Ramo and Prochaska, 2012), ultimately conclude that "use of social networking sites (Web 2.0) can be effective for the study of hard-to-reach populations" (2012: 57).

I offer the following discussion to challenge such findings, however. My experience in studying young women's transnational feminist networks (TFNs) populated by activists from diverse global regions and diverse socioeconomic statuses within those regions has led me to conclude it is "analog" methods that enable a more extensive and comprehensive data set to be collected. Much of the activities of the networks I was studying unfolded in digital spaces. As I explain below, many of the young women participating in my study were, in fact, more comfortable interacting with me online, and were more forthcoming in response to interview questions online than they were when we met face-to-face. I pursued and engaged with a number of digital research methods in order to better understand what motivated young women to form "youth-only" feminist networks; I was also quite interested in investigating claims that their self-created digital spaces allowed more freedom and inclusion than the traditional, conventional spaces of global feminism occupied by their older generation counterparts (that is, global conferences, public mobilizations, face-to-face meetings, and consciousness-raising groups). However, the most marginalized, "minority" populations within this group were rendered nearly invisible by the digital methods I pursued. Had I not combined digital methods of social research with those that were more traditional, which for this study included snowball sampling and in-person, semi-structured interviews, I would have reached different conclusions about my sample's motivations, repertoires, and experiences.

Young activists as others; young activists' others

When legal scholar Karima Bennoune (2010) wrote about the Muslim fundamentalist movements that pose challenges to international law, she cautioned scholars to avoid falling into simplistic dualisms that pit problematic, orientalist narratives emanating from a "war on terror" against an "othered" Muslim fundamentalism. To view the problem flatly, to be silent about the complexity of Muslim populations for fear of reproducing orientalist narratives, is to "undercut opponents of fundamentalists" within those populations. Titling her work "Remembering the other's others," Bennoune argues that we must reconceptualize these "opposing" forces and move beyond "basic binaries" to understand issues with more depth and complexity (2010).

The "othering" young activists argued they experience at the hands of older-generation activists, and the digital spaces they would create and inhabit in response, reifies generation-based (young/old) dualisms mirroring the kind Bennoune cautions us about (2010). Young activists I worked with for this study argued fervently they were quite conscious of divisions and differences among the activists populating their organization or network. They sought to clarify in interviews and in materials they self-published on the web that they understood binaries to be problematic, but nevertheless chose to coalesce around the notion of *youth*. Many argued that this was a strategy aimed at surmounting other kinds of binaries that often plague transnational feminism: political divisions based on geographic location or citizenship status, sexual orientation, race, religion, and so on. Playing on the idea that universally "youth" is a state or identity in which one experiences some form of marginalization, young women reified the binary to recruit members into their organization and to define themselves in opposition to the older generations of leadership who, as one activist from Poland put it, "refused to make room" for "new generations."

But there are certainly *others* within this "othered" population – the other's others – whom, as I note above, I came to discover through the more traditional social research methods I pursued during the study. The "othered others" had become quite hidden in the digital world, or, if they were visible to some degree, left their "othering" out of the more public conversations unfolding online. To maintain a degree of uniformity and distinction from older generations, young feminist organizations often present united public images through websites, blogs, discussion forums, and other internet spaces. They organize as "youth," foregrounding that identity marker above all others. They aim to be inclusive and collaborative when defining the term and determining what "young women's" concerns and experiences are in the world of global activism and advocacy. They aim to develop polycentric leadership structures, and often contrast these against "elitist" and "exclusionary" movements run by older generations. The websites and discussion forums they use to discuss organizational business and make group decisions are examples of deliberative democracy in action. Immersing myself into these spaces as a researcher and participant observer led me to one conclusion about young activists' processes of negotiation and the way differences were settled. But in face-to-face, in-person interviews arranged through conventional methods of drawing out hard-to-reach populations such as snowball sampling, I uncovered different kinds of discussions that clarified a gap in my digitally collected and compiled data. That gap – the stories of the other's others – helped me to approach my original research questions and findings with the kind of complexity Bennoune asserts (2010) should be a mainstay of scholarly work, especially that involving social justice, transnational movements, and globalization.

Youth activism and digital spaces

I began researching the phenomenon of youth-exclusive feminist organizations in 2009, in the midst of much buzz about the term youth.

While what constitutes youth is culturally relative, it became a focal point for numerous entities, from scholars of social movements and globalization to intergovernmental organizations. The United Nations (UN) declared 2010 the "International Year of Youth," with Secretary-General Ban Ki-Moon declaring "youth should be given a chance to take an active part in the decision-making of local, national, and global levels."[3] Demographers and geographers described with concern "youth bulges" in developing countries, particularly in Northern and Central Africa. In the wake of the 1999 World Trade Organization (WTO) protests staged in Seattle, social movement scholars began to note the significant proportion of youth comprising anti- and "alterglobalization" movements that would extend through the following decade (della Porta, 2005; Juris and Pleyers, 2009). Such literature also investigated whether and how younger-generation activists engaged in new and unique ways with transnational advocacy and activism (Juris and Pleyers, 2009; Lombardo et al, 2002; Martínez, 2007; Nilan and Feixa, 2006). Many of these studies investigated the heavy use of ICTs and later, social media within their repertoires and tactics, and terms such as "dotcause" (Clark and Themudo, 2006) and "hacktivism" (Jordan and Taylor, 2004) emerged to become linked with younger generation activists. The linking of revolutionary movements in Iran, Egypt, and Tunisia with both young people and social media exacerbated such associations even further in the second post-millennium decade.

My study concerned generation-based tension within TFNs. A straightforward empirical observation made in 2009 initiated my work, which was conducted over a 16-month consecutive period from 2010–11: young women's rights activists were organizing global networks under the self-imposed label "youth." As I contacted and arranged to interview members of young women's TFNs and participate in some of their activities, I found that these activists were using "youth" with an acute awareness that the term is problematized by both class and cultural relativism. Program coordinators within an organization called the Young Feminist Association (YFA) were eager to make clear that they did not necessarily agree with intergovernmental organizations' hegemonic definitions of youth, for example; one activist specifically cited the "limitations" of the UN's classification of ages 15–25, and, referencing her Palestinian culture by contrast, explained that "women are considered young until they are married and have children, whatever their actual age is." An Egyptian activist within both the YFA and another North African young feminist network included in the study explained that "the age at which women marry, have children, work outside the home, work *inside* the home … all of these things impact the actual experience of where one is placed in the young [or] old categories, and all of these things can be determined by factors like poverty and geography."

Nevertheless, a majority of my sample's 27 participants, who comprised five "youth-only" TFNs headquartered in Egypt, Cameroon, Poland, Hungary, and Canada, asserted that there was something "universal" to young activists' experiences in social movement organizing and feminist networking in particular: marginalization. As I have written about elsewhere (Hunt, 2013), activists creating and participating in youth-only TFNs saw a benefit in organizing strategically around the concept of *youth* as an identity that marks one for marginalization, particularly where there was a need to coalesce across difference. Study participants from each of the networks in fact articulated a desire to create what Gayatri Spivak has termed "strategic essentialism" (1991) and Rita Felski has suggested we may consider collective, "self-consciously oppositional identities" (1989). This was especially the case where such activists *left* well-established TFNs in an effort to create their own autonomous spaces, or, as was the case with the YFA, lobbied an existing TFN (the Association for Women's Rights and Development, AWID) to create youth programs that are specifically young women-led. One reproductive rights activist from Poland named Maria[4] explained that when she initiated her "youth only" feminist network, she was concerned about recruitment, and about gaining the trust and even "interest" of other activists who represented "a huge group of very different people with different priorities and … political experiences." Maria hoped one thing beyond "general goals of reproductive rights" younger activists would have in common would be an interest in "speaking out against the experience of being treated like ignorant youngsters," when in fact "most of us had already been [in the field] for at least five years." She and her network's co-founders wanted to "bring out the experiences and voices of those activists [who were] dismissed in the larger and more professional [feminist networks] in the [region]," a goal the majority of youth TFN organizers expressed during interviews.

Digital communication, digital methods?

After developing research questions about generation differences and power dynamics in transnational feminism, it became clear that searching for, contacting, and communicating with participants would involve ICTs. My study called for the construction of a sample of young women who considered themselves transnational actors in the world of global women's rights advocacy. Their self-identified "transnationalism" necessitated that I use complex methodologies allowing me to consider their multiple and perhaps simultaneous identities. I was also confronted with the reality that my participants moved not only between local and global identities, but also between virtual and non-virtual spaces for their activism with ease. Studying their work meant having to do the same as a researcher, or at least developing both theories and methods that could encompass their work holistically, rather than considering it for its "parts." My intention was to study generation-based tension and difference within TFNs, especially in the form of younger women's claims of marginalization. It was not to study distinctions between online and "offline" activism or even routes young women take when navigating global-local movements. Nevertheless, the transnationality and virtual/actual lives of my participants meant having to think carefully about the methods I would use when undertaking this study.

Perhaps more importantly, the study participants themselves, both older- and younger-generation, insisted that the digital world was such a significant part of the way young women "do activism" that I *must* engage with them in this space. Tara, a 52-year-old Polish activist and former head of a large sexual and reproductive health and rights network in Central and Eastern Europe, explained that young people she knows and works with through the movement "do [come to] street demonstrations and protests ... [and] seem interested in attending conferences and talks, but do so much more of their work through the internet. To them, this *is* the activism." Young women participating in my study asserted the virtual spaces they created, from discussion forums to social media to collaborative "e-Learning" websites, constituted more accessible and democratic spaces than those (often face-to-face) created by older-generation leaders in the movement. They articulated a number of reasons this was the case: first and foremost, it was a space away from the purview of that older generation of leadership that – so the younger activists claimed – often dominated the movement. Second, it was a way to collaborate and connect, something often impossible for young women to do physically across a transnational network. Compared to their older-generation counterparts, who, one young Hungarian activist explained, can "depend on the [financial] support of the institutions they work for, or the grants they can get, or their personal finances" to travel to conferences or mobilizations, younger women often "don't have such options" and are "the [least] financially secure and physically free to travel." Finally, for many younger women, the digital world seemed to constitute a space of greater accessibility because of the control over the environment and communication forms available. "No more hanging out in the background, giving way to older [activists] dominating the agenda, or [more experienced] and professional [activists] talking on and on," explained an activist from Canada affiliated with the YFA; "here [on the YFA's site *Young Feminist Wire*], we are familiar with this interface. It's more comfortable for people our age. We can speak right up ... we do."

Like this Canadian activist, other interview participants spoke of the internet, social media, and in particular websites built by young women for their organizations as a unifying force. Ghadeer, a program coordinator from the YFA who is Palestinian-Canadian, explains that younger women are often "isolated" in organizations led by older generations of feminists, and online spaces create opportunity to draw them out, and to facilitate their bonding and collaboration across differences. She spoke of a sort of digital solidarity emerging in the process, particularly over the kinds of issues she and many others asserted are unique to younger women activists. Ghadeer was not alone in advancing such sentiments; time and again in interviews, younger women related feelings of more or better inclusion in communications, in decision-making processes, and in "inclusiveness" through online spaces. However – and this is extremely important to note – a small degree of participants whom I did *not* meet or interview virtually had significantly dissenting claims. One, named Alena, who self-identified as Romani, felt more underrepresented by the virtual world of young women's activism than the physical one. More significant to this discussion is the fact that I happened to set up a face-to-face interview with her during fieldwork in Hungary, through actual (not virtual) snowball sampling. She was friends with an activist who agreed to speak to me both face-to-face and via Skype and Facebook about her work with older- and younger-generation led networks. Through our mutual connection, Alena and I met, spending the majority of the semi-structured interview discussing her difficulty accessing the internet to participate regularly in online meetings or discussion forums. Alena explained that even when she does gain access, she feels she does not have the capability or space to express herself and her concerns about Romani women's issues. While part of this is the result of language barriers and limited internet access, it also has to do with the culture of a more elite group of younger women activists who are immersed in digital spaces. It is "a different world," she explained, than the one she inhabits. Alena was insistent this does not mean she is less committed to supporting women's reproductive rights and health in Eastern Europe, and is especially concerned with the ways Romani women's rights are included (or excluded) from such movements. But in terms of the tactics and repertoires her peers engage with in practice, Alena feels somewhat distanced.

Similar concerns were raised by an activist named Ashia, who was part of a MENA-region (Middle East and North Africa) young feminist network headquartered in Egypt. Ashia identified as "Nubian," and acknowledged that in face-to-face meetings of her network, her peers consistently include and acknowledge the concerns of minority women like her. But physical gatherings and get-togethers are few and far between, Ashia explained, citing all the aforementioned reasons: constraints of money, time, and space needed to gather. Ashia is not restricted from internet access, in terms of either infrastructure, language, or computer literacy. She is, in fact, a software engineer, and is fluent in the three languages her network converses in online. After our initial interview, she was willing and able to communicate frequently with me online for the purposes of this study. However, "something just does not happen" online the way it does "as a group of people facing each other," she explained; "it's like [online] they forget that they need to think about those other concerns [of] minority [populations]." For Ashia, this included confronting issues of racism and discrimination against Nubian populations, as well as those related to the gender concerns widely shared by the group.

Had I only relied on digital modes of accessing study participants – especially through the use of digital interview as a tool – I would have missed this important dissenting point from Alena. Had I only relied on my participant-observation of the virtual interactions of this MENA-region young feminist network, and not spoken directly to Ashia about it, I would not have seen the challenge she posed to the "digital solidary" the group otherwise presented. These are just two voices challenging the 25 who supported the idea of digital solidarity and felt comfortable moving between physical and digital representation as they participated in my study. My concern as a researcher, however, is that they are indicators of a wider problem that scholars must be conscious of: participants can be rendered less – not more – accessible because of the digitization of communication. In terms of my study, this meant some individuals, because of structural inequalities, were masked by the more powerful and (potentially) resource-rich voices of others within their collective. It also illustrated that some had greater control over content within a supposedly shared and collaborative digital space. Researchers may be acutely aware of new, "deterritorialized conceptions of communities, kinship, and identity" (McKee and DeVoss, 2007: 21) facilitated by the internet and its increasing globalization, and even the ways in which this has had an impact on social movement organizing (see, for example, Smith, 2001). However, it is the sustained reliance on traditional, non-digital methods that allowed me to access, record, and consider the experiences of the most marginalized individuals *within* the marginalized population I was studying. While I acknowledge the circumstantial nature of this finding, I do argue it challenges the conclusions within the literature suggesting digitization of methods can enable more, not less, access and representativeness within a sample.

Digital or analog? A question of methods

In order to think carefully about and access the numerous dynamics in play here – the transnationality of the participants, the ways in which they understood generation and youth, the ways they defended their assertions about digital spaces becoming more democratic – I drew from several fields to construct my study. During an exploratory phase of the study, I started with a conventional qualitative method – semi-structured interviews with eight participants from different networks and different generations. These interviews were analyzed and coded using a conceptual framework containing categories based in part on themes in the sparse but burgeoning literature on youth and transnational activism, and on the more established literature on transnational feminist activism. Coding enabled the identification of patterns informing the later phases of the project: open-ended interviews, participant observation, and case study. I planned initially to review and interpret all study data with a combination of analytical tools: process-tracing through detailed narrative (George and Bennett, 2005) and DeVault's model of "women's standpoint" (2004). However, on the participants' insistence that I not only examine but also use digital methods to work with younger women, I sought out new methods being employed by social researchers, both to gather and analyze data. Finding Kevin DePew's discussion of "triangulating data from the digital writing situation" (2007) was a significant benefit.

Because of the nature of my study, I drew extensively from feminist methodologies when considering research design. Haraway's emphasis on "situated knowledges" (1988: 581) was influential, for example, in locating the study within the realm of a "feminist objectivity" considering "truth" to be a "particular and specific embodiment" (1988: 582). My study examined multiple, even "partial" paths and mechanisms, thus allowing for the pursuit of "truths" specific to its participants. Such an approach is legitimated by Bhavnanai's call for a "partiality of vision", which must not be equated with "partiality of theorizing" (2004: 66). Indeed, it is this "partiality" of transnational feminist networking – young women's experiences with transnational activism and advocacy work, as a collective but also as individuals – that I argued in the study can contribute to a broader understanding of global feminist praxis in contemporary contexts.

DeVault's "women's standpoint" in particular provided a framework for both collection and analysis of transcripted interview data. It is important to emphasize here the need for face-to-face interaction is essential to the methods she describes. DeVault suggests employing interview protocols that "allow the exploration of incompletely articulated aspects of women's stories" (2004: 232), as "language is often inadequate for women" (2004: 246). Examining the "halting, hesitant, tentative talk" DeVault claims typically characterize marginalized populations' "difficulties of expression" (2004: 235) was an essential analytical and interpretive process within this study. Language "can never fit perfectly with experience" (DeVault, 2004: 229), particularly for women who constitute a "socially muted group" (Ardener, 1975). It is thus the responsibility of the researcher to "represent talk completely," including close attention to details and recurring conversational features often ignored or seen as "minute:" pauses, hesitations, emphasis, "indrawn breath," "elongated vowel sounds," etc (DeVault, 2004: 241). Noticing "ambiguity" and "problems of expression" in interview data can be particularly telling: this sort of conversation and discourse analysis represent "much more completely" women's experiences, as "the words available" to women under more structured, traditional methodological strictures "often do not fit" (DeVault, 2004: 233). I wanted to thoroughly understand why the young women in my sample were feeling marginalized within TFNs, and how they articulated that marginalization – even, and especially, if that articulation was non-verbal. But this kind of data collection depended on face-to-face interaction, I presumed, and most importantly my observations as an interviewer. I planned to observe and make notations about the full context of each interview – not just the words spoken or written by the participant – to produce a detailed analysis of interview transcripts, yielding a "strategy of rich and complex description" to attend to generally "neglected features of talk" (DeVault, 2004: 241).

I pursued face-to-face interviews rigorously. While most younger participants were willing and excited to participate in my study, to my surprise many declined interviews. I was left confused by the seeming contradiction, until the first few participants responding in this way followed up by explaining their digital representation – a blog, a website, a group, or personal page on Facebook, for example – would answer all my questions. Essentially, many young women invited me in to their digital spaces and/or were giving me permission to examine and perhaps make use of their work, but did not necessarily have interest in being interviewed directly. Initially, I interpreted this hesitation to be another facet of their marginalization; as the work of Gordon (2010) and various feminist theorists (see, for example, Trigg, 2010) suggests, young women activists' age and gender position them as marginalized actors in transnational activist politics, and their status (in some cases) as developing country residents can further distance them from the "center" of activist communities. Many acknowledged they were unfamiliar with the process of being interviewed, or uncomfortable with it, either because they were uncomfortable with me as a (white, Western, "older-generation") scholar, or uncomfortable with the idea of being isolated from the group. But there was also significant insistence on the better or more complete representation of their digital presence as activists, especially as a collective. My participants, in other words, seemed to insist I would get a better picture of who they were, what motivated them and what they were building if I interacted with them through *group* online structures, including discussion forums and live interactions as well as collaborative blogs and websites. It was the collective I was focusing on, one Canadian activist explained, so why would I want to talk to her specifically when I could just interact with the group?

I was completely surprised by this reaction, and my concern grew as I came to discover it was shared within the sample. Some young women agreed to be interviewed right away, some did not; some agreed and changed their minds later, declining the interview when the date drew near. Some initially declined but later agreed to be interviewed, particularly (in some cases) after other members of their network or collective had been interviewed. But one thing remained consistent, nearly across the sample: what they presented online represented them well and thoroughly. This clashed with my methodological framework, particularly that which I drew from DeVault.

As I searched through new discussions of methodology pertaining to digital activism, social media, and social movement research, I discovered Kevin DePew's suggestion that digital writing, such as blogs and discussion forums within online communities, be interpreted through a triangulation method (2007: 49). Triangulating data gathered primarily through "online" means, DePew argues, can avoid the flat, "single-voicedness" (2007: 54) that emerges from digital writing; perhaps more importantly, it can help researchers avoid what Donna Haraway termed the "god trick" (1988: 581) – a presumed omniscience, "appropriation," and ordering of information that creates reality rather than richly contextualizing it. Research of online spaces needs to be "more cognizant of the rhetors' and audiences' contexts outside of the digital space" (DePew, 2007: 55), considering, for example, a site's content and design as potentially distinct from the "writer's authorial intentions" (DePew, 2007: 62). That there are multiple actors involved in a digital writing situation – an author, a site-designer who may not *be* the author, an audience – is essential for a researcher to be aware of. How do these aspects of the digital world interact to produce the content the researcher is observing? Researchers cannot view digital content as static, or only seek out an author to probe the situation further, without consideration of design and audience. In much of the digital content I was viewing, the audience had become part of the digital writing situation. The author of a blog, for example, would often update or even change content on a young feminist web community in response to her audience's ideas and comments. Understanding this dynamic process *as* a process meant understanding (and collecting data on) several simultaneous situations: the author's original intentions in writing, the way the site was designed to display her writing and allow for interaction, the way the audience did or could interact, and the resultant and often ongoing changes to the content given those interactions. DePew offers the studies of several researchers as examples, noting if one had simply "studied the transcripts" of an online discussion rather than triangulating her data by considering a variety of other actors or processes, she would have reached a different – perhaps more limited – conclusion (2007: 61).

Power dynamics in digital spaces

I resolved to pursue this triangulation method, although I discovered it had limitations and had to be pursued a bit differently in my research situation. By interviewing content authors and site designers, I did move beyond "just" site-content analysis. I also tried to access and interview directly (and distinctly) a site's users – the young feminists belonging to the organization and participating in the web community but not necessarily authoring content or designing and maintaining the site. As DePew advises, I sought to "position the technology" being used by the activists to consider the complicated relationships between construction, design, and the words being expressed and exchanged.

But while I had been taking steps to avoid becoming "the single voice that re-creates the space" (DePew, 2007: 55), I was not able to see that the participants themselves were creating "single voiced" digital spaces until I met with Alena. Alena was rarely in "digital space," and yet was represented by it. She had what she described as a "shadow presence;" she communicated in person to some members of her collective the ideas and concerns that she prioritized, hoping they would include and represent those when they maintained and updated the group's website. She had an online identity – including a profile and photo – on the group's website. She participated in some discussion forum activities and private email exchanges about the group's agenda, especially its attempt to win a grant from a young feminist fund called FRIDA.[5] Alena explained she felt the group was receptive to and accepting of her concerns, but that they did not remember to "be inclusive later," when interacting online. Because she had some presence online, my temptation as a researcher was to see her – to see the collective – as the product of a collaboration. Not until Alena introduced the notion of being a shadow presence in this digital space was I forced to rethink my original conclusions, which had been reached after completing online participant observation and review of digital content. This mirrored her feeling of being a "shadow presence" in real life, she explained, in being a Roma woman in a network comprised predominantly of non-Roma women. Alena didn't necessarily find the distinction disconcerting. I did, however. As a researcher determined to seek out representative and inclusive samples, I found the ways in which the digital dynamics of the group erased the differences members were otherwise experiencing and expressing to be a concern. Moreover, I also found the digital tools I used to understand the group as a whole to be, resultantly, ineffective when it came to a richly textured and contextualized sample.

Ashia made similar observations about the differences between face-to-face and online interactions in her North African young feminist network. She distinguishes herself ethnically from the "Arab women" who comprise the majority of the organizations in her network. Ashia is a software engineer by training, and so is extremely comfortable navigating online spaces and digital activism. She is one of several organizational members maintaining the network's websites, and it was my interest in data triangulation that led me to interview her directly. During the interview, she articulated a difference between online and offline behavior within the group, especially in how the processes of deliberation unfolded. There was a strategic interest in keeping disagreements between the group "private;" the most serious divisions over the network's targets, goals, priorities, resource generation and spending, and future direction were reserved for twice-monthly, face-to-face sessions. But there isn't any evidence of these deliberations and disagreements on the website, *especially* if they are left unresolved. "There is an interest in a united front," she explains of the website, "and that is not always the whole story." But, she continues, "the thinking is that we need to work together," especially since "past" movements within the region were so divided by what Ashia calls "identity politics" – disagreements, for example, between Islamic and secular feminists, disagreements over issues related to race and citizenship, and so on. Ashia explained in the interview she "respected the practice of decision by consensus," even if this meant some of her own concerns for Nubian rights were marginalized by the "politics and concerns of the majority group." The content of the website would always be determined "by the group" – Ashia called herself "the messenger" as the site's designer and administrator – but did not necessarily represent everyone's concerns equally. Ashia expressed more frustration over this situation than Alena when discussing the power dynamics within her own network, although she maintained that the physical interactions between members – she cited meetings and interactions with others personally – reassured her that the network could eventually work out their differences and continue to improve its inclusiveness and representation. "It is an ongoing process," she explained during our interview, "what good relationship isn't?"

Conclusion

Ashia and Alena's stories did not challenge the findings of my original study about generation and power dynamics in TFNs: young women gravitate toward youth-exclusive networks when they feel marginalized by the older generations, and expect a different set of experiences from those networks. The tools they use to generate those different experiences are digital, and so it was logical and even necessary for me to use digital research methods in my study. However, traditional methods of sample construction, data collection, and analysis revealed limitations to these digital methods, and let me to several conclusions and recommendations.

First, I concluded Alena's use of the term shadow and Ashia's use of the term messenger indicated the powerlessness each activist felt within her own respective network. Occupation of digital space for them – even where one was in control of creating this digital space – was not an empowering experience. Thus, the images of inclusiveness and solidarity presented by the other interview participants were challenged. More significantly for my methodological considerations, the digital content produced by their networks masked these assertions. I can recommend, therefore, that scholars develop research projects that can reach beyond a sample of young women within what Desai (2009: 34) and others have termed the "transnational activist class," especially if they are concerned with representation and thick description. I can also recommend that a combination of digital and "analog" methods be pursued to complete such studies. Young women participating in my study were not necessarily from middle- and upper-class networks of professional actors. Most were volunteers, calling themselves "grassroots" activists, and identified as working class. However, most are educated, live close to urban centers of global cities, and – importantly – have relatively easy access to some form of ICTs. They thus also recognize their position as relatively privileged in comparison to the majority of young women in their respective countries. More localized, rural, or smaller-scale young women-led organizations exist, but are not as connected as the ones I studied for this project. Some of the young women participating in my study consider themselves, as Loubna

Skalli-Hanna has suggested (2006), to be "mediators," creating connections to and for these more distanced young women. While my study participants insisted they were conscious of the problems with speaking for these other women, they nevertheless articulated ideas about solidarity, representation, and collaboration. It is essential to understand the ways some of these "othered" women articulate detractions and challenge majority findings; in my case, the only access to such data was a combination of traditional methods that avoided the digital entirely.

A second and related recommendation for researchers is to refrain from de-contextualizing young activists in global networks, particularly those who seem to be most visible online. Attention to "youth movements" and the seemingly central role digital activism played in mobilizing a variety of global protests, from those associated with the "Arab Spring" to the proliferation of Occupy Wall Street, has created particular narratives about young people and global activism. Mainstream media staples such as Thomas Friedman, for example, have taken the marriage of young people, activism, and ICTs at face value, arguing movements of youth "from Athens to Barcelona … [and] across the Arab world" are not only *interconnected* because of technology, but also exemplify a "globalization of ideas" generated by a common set of internet-based practices and cultures (2011). Numerous scholarly studies have made similar assertions; the work of Juris and Pleyers (2009) and Nilan and Feixa (2006) have examined the ways in which young people the world over share "similar" activist practices, often oriented around technology. This study's findings underscore the danger of not considering young activists behind their online presence – understanding the depth of experiences and richness of contexts young activists bring to a global movement, including the ways in which their online presence can mask their distance from power, is essential for making any steps toward constructing inclusive and representative samples.

Notes

[1] See www.itu.int/en/ITU-D/Statistics/Pages/stat/default.aspx

[2] See www.statista.com/statistics/272365/age-distribution-of-internet-users-worldwide/

[3] See http://social.un.org/youthyear/

[4] As many activists participating in this study reported feelings of a critical nature, their names have been changed in order to protect them from any professional or personal consequences. Where noted, the names of projects and organizations have also been omitted for similar reasons and at the request of the study participants.

[5] See http://youngfeministfund.org/

References

Ardener, S. (1975) *Perceiving women*. New York: Wiley & Sons.

Baltar, F. and I. Brunet (2012) "Social research 2.0: Virtual snowball sampling method using Facebook." *Internet Research* 22 (1), 57–74.

Bennoune, K. (2010) "Remembering the other's others: Theorizing the approach of international law to Muslim fundamentalism." *Columbia Human Rights Law Review* 41, 635–98.

Bhavnani, K.-K. (2004) "Tracing the contours: Feminist research and feminist objectivity." In S. Hesse-Biber and M. Yaiser (eds) *Feminist perspectives on social research*. New York: Oxford University Press.

Brickman-Bhutta, C. (2012) "Not by the book: Facebook as a Sampling Frame." *Sociological Methods and Research* 41 (1), 57–88.

Castells, M. (1996) *The rise of the network society*. Oxford: Blackwell Publishing.

Clark, J. and N. Themudo (2006) "Linking the web and the street: Internet-based 'dotcauses' and the anti-globalization movement." *World Development* 34 (1), 50–74.

della Porta, D. (2005) "Multiple belongings, tolerant identities, and the construction of 'anotherpolitics'." In D. della Porta and S. Tarrow (eds) *Transnational protest and global activism* (pp 175–202). Lanham, MD: Rowman & Littlefield.

DePew, K. (2007) "Through the eyes of researchers, rhetors and audiences: Triangulating data from the digital writing situation." In H.A. McKee and D.N. DeVoss (eds) *Digital writing research* (pp 46–69). Cresskill, NJ: Hampton Press.

Desai, M. (2009) *Gender and the politics of possibilities: Rethinking globalization*. New York: Rowman & Littlefield.

DeVault, M. (2004) "Talking and listening from women's standpoint: Feminist strategies for interviewing and analysis." In S. Hesse-Biber and M. Yaiser (eds) *Feminist perspectives on social research* (pp 227–50). New York: Oxford University Press.

Felski, R. (1989) *Beyond feminist aesthetics: Feminist literature and social change*. Cambridge, MA: Harvard University Press.

Friedman, T. (2011) "Technology, globalization fueling widespread unrest." *New York Times*, August 16.

George, A. and A. Bennett (2005) *Case studies and theory development in the social sciences*. Cambridge, MA: The MIT Press.

Gordon, H.R. (2010) *We fight to win: Inequality and the politics of youth activism*. New Brunswick, NJ: Rutgers University Press

Haraway, D. (1988) "Situated knowledges: The science question in feminism and the privilege of partial perspective." *Feminist Studies* 14 (3), 575–99.

Hunt, T.A. (2013) "Transcending polarization? Strategic identity construction in young women's transnational feminist networks." *Women's Studies International Forum* 40, 152–61.

Jordan, T. and P. Taylor (2004) *Hacktivism and cyberwars: Rebels with a cause?* New York: Psychology Press.

Juris, J. and G. Pleyers (2009) "Alter-activism: Emerging cultures of participation among young global justice activists." *Journal of Youth Studies* 12 (1), 57–75.

Lombardo C., D. Zakus, and H. Skinner (2002) "Youth social action: Building a global latticework through information and communication technologies." *Health Promotion International* 17 (4), 363–72.

McKee, H. and D. DeVoss (2007) *Digital writing research: Technologies, methodologies and ethical issues.* Cresskill, NJ: Hampton Press.

McLuhan, M. (1964) *Understanding media.* Berkeley, CA: Gingko Press.

Martínez, M. (2007) "The Squatters' Movement: Urban counter-culture and alter-globalization dynamics." *South European Society and Politics* 12 (3), 379–98.

Nilan, P. and C. Feixa (2006) *Global youth? Hybrid identities, plural worlds.* New York: Routledge.Pleyers, G. (2011) *Alter-globalization: Becoming actors in the global age.* Cambridge, UK: Polity Press.

Ramo, D.E. and J.J. Prochaska (2012) "Broad reach and targeted recruitment using Facebook for an online survey of young adult substance use." *Journal of Medical Internet Research* 14 (1), e28.

Skalli-Hanna, L. (2006) "Communicating gender in the public sphere: Women and information technologies in MENA." *Journal of Middle Eastern Women* 2 (2).

Smith, J. (2001) "Globalizing resistance: The battle of Seattle and the future of social movements." *Mobilization* 6 (1), 1–19.

Spivak, G. (1990) *The postcolonial critic: Interviews, strategies, dialogues.* New York: Routledge.

Trigg, M. (2010) *Leading the way: Young women's activism for social change.* New Brunswick, NJ: Rutgers University Press.

8

Digital Orientalism: TripAdvisor and online travelers' tales

Trevor Jamerson

Online tourist reviews have emerged as an important source of information for participants in the global tourism industry. For tourists, they serve as research resources during pre-trip planning as well as outlets for expressing opinions about their travels post-trip (Leung et al, 2013). In turn, tourist operators find them valuable because they can reveal the opinions, thoughts, desires, and motivations of potential customers as well as user-generated content that act like an advertisement, or "free" publicity (Leung et al, 2013). Review-based websites such as TripAdvisor, Yelp, and Foursquare serve as digital hubs for the tourism industry within the social logic of Web 2.0 by connecting potential tourists, former tourists, and tourist operators in a virtual space.

Using data collected from millions of user-generated product reviews, these sites employ algorithms to calculate rankings and to determine categories that sort the activities and experiences of a tourist trip – hotels, restaurants, attractions, etc – according to how popular and highly rated they are among tourists. The aggregated reviews also function as online travel "communities," and it is from this perspective that much of the scholarship on online tourist reviews is focused (Jeacle and Carter, 2011; Leung et al, 2013). Most review content features short narratives in which the reviewer tells a story about their experience (Tussyadiah et al, 2011). In this sense, it is important to remember that these reviews constitute a contemporary version of a much older narrative form, the traveler's tale, which is heavily implicated in the ways Western constructions of social, cultural, gendered, racial, and ethnic types of "Otherness" are formed (MacCannell, 2011; Said, 1978; Smith, 2012).

This chapter proposes a theoretical foundation – drawing primarily from Orientalist critique and also from digital race studies – for evaluating online tourist reviews as simultaneous examples of social media and travelers' tales. This is a crucial duality to recognize, as each of these discursive platforms are invested with different kinds of authority within the global tourism industry, which itself contributes to what critical Orientalist, tourism, and neoliberal scholars refer to as "the commodification of the Other" (Behdad, 1994; Harvey, 2005; MacCannell, 2011; Said, 1978; Smith 2012). This is the process by which social constructs imagined as outside of the boundaries of Western cultural norms – commonly, but not exclusively, manifested as social, gendered, racial, cultural, or ethnic difference – become packaged as attractions and consumer goods within the global market economy. It is argued here that online tourist reviews, due to their dual authorities, occupy an influential place – or places – within this process and the discourse that sustains it.

TripAdvisor is the world's largest travel-related social media site. It exemplifies what Henry Jenkins calls a "convergence culture" where different types of media – in this case, the traveler's tale and digital social media – converge to create a new type of media culture (2006). Nick Couldry, however, in critiquing Jenkins' argument, suggests that, while useful to discuss new media in terms of convergences, to categorize them as a new kind of "culture" masks convergent media's capacity to differentiate across political, ethnic, and social spectrums: "It may be more plausible to see 'convergence' as a resource for *differentiation* between media users [and thus] ... a medium of longer term *stratification*" (2011: 494; original emphasis). This chapter adopts the position that the convergence seen in TripAdvisor maintains – through its content, organization, popularity, and digital prominence – an Orientalist discourse that is at its core both differentiating and stratifying.

Today TripAdvisor contains over 225 million individual tourist reviews, with 139 new contributions being made every minute,[1] which involves around 340 million unique monthly visitors.[2] The website depends on a dynamic of prosumption (Ritzer and Jurgenson, 2010), where site users – both the readers and writers of reviews – are responsible for the consumption and production of site content. This dynamic combines the narrative power of the individual tourist with social media's ability to effectively categorize and classify the multitude of individual accounts. Each review represents the voice of an individual tourist, while the site's rankings system – based on individual review ratings – become representative of the collective voice of the tourist. TripAdvisor is thus able to engender discursive authority at both the individual and collective levels.

With this duality in mind, two types of authority are developed using methodological devices introduced by Edward Said to analyze the authority of the Orientalist text: strategic location and strategic formation:

> [Said's] principal methodological devices for studying authority here are what can be called *strategic location*, which is a way of describing the author's position in a text with regard to the Oriental material he writes about, and *strategic formation*, which is a way of analyzing the relationship between texts and the way in which groups of texts, types of texts, even textual genres, acquire mass density, and referential power amongst themselves, and thereafter in the culture at large. (1978: 20)

The ultimate authority of online travel reviews lies in their ability to influence economic decisions made by both tourism producers and consumers, but this authority comes from different sources. Travelers' tales are invested with positional authority by virtue of their strategic locations, meaning their authority is derived from the positionality of the author, usually from the vantage point of an "expert witness." They are the original connection between the reader, or potential tourist, and the attraction being described in the review, and thus play a role in the initial framing of the attraction for the tourist. The strategic formation of social media-based discourse is invested with informational authority, which is derived from the value social media is afforded – by virtue of its aggregative abilities and classificatory capacities – as an influential source of information in the global market. These sources of discursive authority converge within the organizational structure of a website like TripAdvisor, which is simultaneously characterized by Jeacle and Carter as a site providing potential tourists with the trusted opinions of fellow travelers, and also, as "an expert system ... governed by calculative practices" (2011: 96). The result is that online reviews, and TripAdvisor in particular, are often perceived as trustworthy, truthful, authentic, and reliable sources of information when making decisions about travel plans (Jeacle and Carter, 2011; Leung et al, 2013), and thus help structure ways the Other is experienced and consumed.

The chapter unfolds in four parts. The first provides a brief contextual background based on a prior study (Jamerson, 2014) involving discourse analysis of a small group of TripAdvisor reviews concerning a popular cultural tourism company in Harlem, New York. These reviews represent some of Harlem's most prominent digital representations. The second discusses the historical development of travelers' tales and the importance of understanding online tourist reviews as a repetition, or convergence, of different genres of traveler's tale. This section draws primarily from Orientalist critiques supplied by Said (1978) and Behdad (1994) to show how different genres of travelers' tales engender different types of authority. The third part maps the growth of TripAdvisor as both an online community numbering in the millions, and as a vast repository of touristic information and knowledge, its rise to prominence within the tourist industry, and its methods of success. It links the long history of travelers' tales to the digital world of Web 2.0, and implicates both in the cultural and intellectual practices of Orientalism through understanding the discursive authorities held by each. In short, the relative "newness" of social media and its influences needs to be considered alongside the relative "oldness" of the equally influential traveler's tale. The fourth section places an Orientalist critique of TripAdvisor in conversation with recent scholarship in digital race studies concerning dilemmas of access to – and representation within – the digital realm. This section emphasizes the ways in which TripAdvisor might represent, as McPherson puts it, "the infusion of racial organizing principles into the technological organization of knowledge" in post-Second World War America (2012: 24).

Contextual background

Perform a Google search of some combination of the words "Harlem" and "tourism," and links to TripAdvisor and Harlem Heritage Tours quickly appear near the top of the results. Within TripAdvisor, Harlem Heritage Tours is the highest ranked tour company operating primarily in Harlem. This digital prominence is a reflection of their popularity with tourists, and was the primary reason I chose a small group (n=111) of reviews about this company as the subject of a discourse analysis concerning the ways that Harlem is presented as an attraction within the online tourist domain. Findings indicate that tourists find value in the temporary cultural immersion offered through tour participation, and is oriented around themes of Black Harlem – Harlem Renaissance, gospel churches, Savoy Ballroom, Apollo Theater, Marcus Garvey, Malcolm X, Geoffrey Canada, jazz music, soul food – yet the idea of race within review content is notably absent, or not discursively singled out by reviewers. These reviews are then prominent – and therefore influential – examples of color-blind rhetoric in the service of cultural commodification, which is a well-documented phenomenon (Gotham, 2007; Harvey, 2005; Werry, 2011). But why are they popular? And how are they influential? The answers can be unraveled through understanding different ways the website engenders their discursive authority. In the case of TripAdvisor, as the next section shows, this authority is partly rooted in the long tradition of travelers' tales being afforded the ability to define the parameters of cultural Otherness.

Positive Orientalism, or the Orientalism of tourism

An Orientalist discourse can be briefly defined as a communicative field that privileges Euro-American centric ways of thinking about places or people not considered part of Europe or the US. The origins of contemporary Orientalist critique can be traced back to Edward Said, whose foundational Orientalism defines it as a Western imposition across discursive and epistemological fields which results in a discourse that, "… is produced and exists in an uneven exchange" (1978: 8–9) with other types of power, such as political, economic, or cultural power. In the case of online tourist reviews we might think of their authors and readers as exercising digital powers over tourist attractions.

For Said, the authority of an Orientalist discourse is based on its ability to generate perceptions of truthfulness and objectivity in the face of biased subjectivities, narrative forms, and historical interpretations. These biases forever position the West as the center and birthplace – and therefore its citizens as the true inheritors – of modern civilization (1978). It is important to recognize that Orientalism is a discourse trafficking not in truth or "'natural' depictions of the Orient" (1978: 21), but instead in biased and misleading *representations*. Said tends to focus on those representations which perpetuate the negative image of the Other: the Other as sneaky or dirty, or savage, dangerous and threatening, but at times he hints at – as Dean MacCannell points out – a different, or "positive" side of Orientalist discourse and imagery:

> Said was aware of … what can be called the tourist version [of Orientalism] … the ultra-touristic version of the Near East proffers an endless open air bazaar by day and the romance of men on stallions, dancing girls, hashish, and moonlit oases at night. (2011: 9)

MacCannell (1976, 2011) identifies the "Other" in very broad terms as the primary site of tourist desire, and points to tourism activity as a practice of "positive" Orientalism, where, instead of being defined as negative, dangerous, or threatening, the Other is positioned as exotic, desirable, and consumable. The tourism industry has the ability to place a price tag on experience in order to meet the desires and demands of tourists, and successfully markets the notions of "Otherness" in order to cater to those desires (MacCannell, 2011). Tourism and travel have a long history more broadly of helping to shape ideas of Western cultural and intellectual superiority over peoples and places outside the boundaries of the West (Behdad, 1994; Said, 1978; Smith, 2012). Maori scholar and activist Linda Smith devotes a chapter of *Decolonizing methodologies* to the importance of travelers' tales not just in Western science and research, but also in trade and culture, or trade in culture (2012: 81–97). She links travelers' tales to knowledge exchange value, cultural economy, and Western identity formation in a process called "Trading the Other":

> In this sense, the people and their culture, the material and the spiritual, the exotic and the fantastic became not just the stuff of dreams and imagination, or stereotypes and eroticism, but of the first truly global commercial enterprise: *Trading the Other*.… Trading the Other is a vast industry based on the positional superiority and advantages gained under imperialism. It is concerned more

with ideas, language, knowledge, images, beliefs and fantasies than any other industry. Trading the Other deeply, intimately, defines Western thinking and identity. (2012: 92–93)

According to Behdad, the commodification of Otherness as well as the establishing of cultural and intellectual superiority is rooted in the discourse of tourism, which "packages the [Other] into a commodity for Western consumption that 'homogenizes' the West ideologically as colonialist" (1994: 16). He identifies two important genres of travelers' tales – prominent at different times during the colonial era – which were especially influential in forming popular conceptions of Otherness both negative and positive while still maintaining themes of Western intellectual superiority. The travelogue, popular in earlier colonial periods, was the product of an individual writer, and usually told as a longer, first-person narrative. The travel guide, on the other hand, came to prominence during late colonialism, and was the product not of an individual writer but a series of editors and publishers, a "dispersion of a plurality of voices" (1994: 41). These influential touristic exchanges – each with similar "discursive functions" (1994: 39) to exotify the Other – are distinct in terms of where they "[situate] the speaking subject" (1994: 39). In other words, travelogues are characterized by a textual focus on the writer, while travel guides are characterized by a textual focus on the reader.

In the travelogue the textual focus on the writer and their interpretation was often legitimated through the "expert" credibility of the writer that then imbued it with discursive authority (Behdad, 1994). These narratives – exemplars include works by Volney (1959) and Chateaubriand (1968) – feature the author situated as the focal point within the text. The author becomes the source of truth, thus affording the author and his story positional authority in regards to the Oriental material he is writing about (Behdad, 1994). The professionalism and elite nature of early travelers only added to their perceived mastery over Oriental subjects, both human and academic (Smith, 2012). The mid-19th century saw the advent of more inexpensive forms of mass travel, such as trains and steamships, and it is no coincidence that this period also saw the birth of mass tourism and of amateur, as opposed to professional, travelers (Behdad, 1994).

Instead of being attributed to one single writer, travel guides – produced with the amateur traveler in mind – were often credited to the publisher and not its contributors or editors (Behdad, 1994). Textual focus in this case shifts from the writer – because they are nonexistent – to the reader, thus placing the reader in the center of the material and allowing them to temporarily "become" the traveler themselves (Behdad, 1994). Travel guides were composed of lists, categories, and descriptions presented in objective fashion, most exemplified by John Murray's *Handbooks for travellers* (1840, 1859). According to Behdad, "The new mode of information was defined by the accumulation of 'informative' statements uttered in a dispersive fashion"

(1994: 43). The dispersive, dissociative voice of the travel guide enables the reader to visualize being at the places described in the guide. Rather than presenting a singularly framed narrative, à la travelogue, it presents an all-encompassing description of the far-away destination (Behdad, 1994).

The information concerning Otherness in travel guides, and the way it is presented and organized for readers to consume, can be considered to be imbued with a kind of informational authority that is able to structure the reader's interpretation of the material and foster reader visualization. Turning our attention in this regard to TripAdvisor, Leung et al find that: "In general, the content shared in online communities and blogs are travel stories and experiences that are represented in narrative format. [Tussyadiah et al, 2011] posited that stories have the ability to encourage audiences to visualize the consumption of a product or service" (2013: 9).

Behdad adds that, although they are distinctive forms of travelers' tales, the travelogue and travel guide played similar roles in the Orientalist project, and should be recognized as coeval discourses working together to disseminate and repeat Western-centric Orientalist discourse (1994). They each are in part responsible for constructing the image of the exotic and desirable Other. But where the travelogue defines the exotic through its positional authority, the travel guide reaffirms the prior definition of the exotic through its informational authority. Behdad argues that this repetitious relationship perpetuates cycles of Orientalist discourse, maintaining Western perceptions of superiority over the Other, and ultimately – through its commodification – threatening to dissolve the Other within the consumptive logic of Western capitalism. Within TripAdvisor, however, discursive authority is derivative as much from the strategic formation of social media as it is from the strategic locations of the travelers' tales themselves.

Travelogue→travel guide→travel agent→TripAdvisor

In TripAdvisor's case, there seems to be a repetition of the logics that, according to Behdad, link different types of travelers' tales together in the consumption and dissolution of the Other (1994). Ironically – because they somewhat dismiss this possibility – netnographic research by Jeacle and Carter concerning the perceived validity of reviews on TripAdvisor suggests that the discursive dynamics that generate trust and legitimation among users are based on elements of both travelogue and the travel guide (2011). Musing as to the reasons for TripAdvisor's rapid growth and popularity, they remark:

> As a relatively recent development, [TripAdvisor] possesses neither a wellspring of longstanding goodwill to tap into, nor is it part of an established tradition. (2011: 294)

Despite the suggestion that TripAdvisor does not represent "part of an established tradition," their analysis reveals that TripAdvisor's trustworthiness results from combination of "personal trust" and "systems trust" that implicates it in the discursive traditions of the traveler's tale as well as in established methods of digital computation. Reviews themselves are considered to be, like the travelogue, "authentic", written by a singular voice, an actual tourist, or even a trusted friend, while the website itself, taken as an aggregate of reviews, rankings and categories, is – like the travel guide – a valuable "unbiased" intermediary in the online relationships between potential and former tourists, hotels, tour operators, and attractions (Jeacle and Carter, 2011).

TripAdvisor was launched in 2000 with the intention of providing internet users with "unbiased" reviews of tourist attractions by city, country, and region. According to Law, "Rather than serving as an online travel agency or an agent representing any hotels or attractions, the website aims at providing unbiased recommendations for hotels and other travel related information to users" (2008: 75). By "unbiased," Law is referring to reviews written by actual consumers, or tourists, where a "biased" review would be written or otherwise influenced by tourism operators in the hopes of boosting an online ranking. The notion of bias here is being used in a very different way – based within the logic of the tourism industry – than that critiqued by Said and Behdad, which is based on the broader plane of Euro-American cultural logic and perceived ideological centrality.

Jeacle and Carter explain that TripAdvisor has become popular within the nexus of internet-based commerce, the rise of ranking systems for sifting through the piles of data found on the internet, and the proliferation of cheap jet travel that has allowed for tourism to become one of the world's largest industries (2011). For the authors, the website is able to generate both personal trust (citing Mayer et al's 1995 model) and systems trust (citing Giddens, 1990), and is ideal for the new breed of "independent traveler," "… a traveler who spurns the services of their local travel agent in favor of a do-it-yourself approach to holiday arrangements" (Jeacle and Carter, 2011: 294). This shift away from travel agents necessitated "new ways in which to replicate the trust which was previously invested in the face-to-face interaction with the expert system of the travel agent (Giddens, 1991)" (Jeacle and Carter, 2011: 294).

TripAdvisor is able to replicate that trust through its combination of "unbiased" reviews and the categories and rankings systems that collect, sort, and re-arrange review content. The notion of review content being "unbiased" is linked to the personal trust that the website engenders among its users. According to Mayer et al, personal trust is based around three qualities: ability, benevolence, and integrity (1995). In the case of TripAdvisor, ability is inscribed within the review content, or whether the reviewer is an adept storyteller; for example, "The most obvious way a TripAdvisor reviewer can impart their ability and competence to users of the site is through the narrative content of their review" (Jeacle and Carter, 2011: 299). Ability is also marked, categorized, and ranked within TripAdvisor's "badge" system, where reviewers who contribute more reviews are labeled as "Top" or "Senior" contributors. Benevolence is maintained by the "community" atmosphere emboldened by the website, where reviewers are perceived to only want to provide friendly advice to other would-be travelers. As Jeacle and Carter put it, "The impression provided by the website is that it is contributed to by self-styled cosmopolitans, who share a habitus as to what is constitutive of a good hotel" (2011: 300). Integrity is determined by the perceived "truthfulness" and unbiased nature of the reviews. One of TripAdvisor's main concerns is the threat that biased or non-consumer-based reviews will make their way on to the site, and they claim to have developed sophisticated algorithms to detect fraudulent reviews (2011). Jeacle and Carter, citing supporting research by O'Connor (2008), endorse these claims by finding that there is "little evidence of characteristics that typify false reviews" (2011: 301).

TripAdvisor engenders systems trust through its use of symbolic tokens, expert systems, and calculative practices (Jeacle and Carter, 2011). Each individual review consists of both narrative content and a reviewer rating (1–5 stars). The individual rating is a way for each reviewer to summarize in one general measure their impression of a hotel or attraction, and also provides the raw data for TripAdvisor's influential popularity index, which ranks hotels and attractions against each other. Symbolic tokens are defined by Giddens as "media of exchange which have standard value, and thus are interchangeable across a plurality of contexts" (1991: 18). The best example of the use of a symbolic token within TripAdvisor is its popularity index, which is able to project the perceived value of an attraction across distances of time and space, "a 5 star hotel booked now for next summer will probably remain a 5 star hotel in a year's time" (Jeacle and Carter, 2011: 296). The calculative practices that lend TripAdvisor perceptions of trust are "located within the algorithm which creates the site's famed rankings.... As an expert system, the rankings convert the numerous individual ramblings on the site into hard and objective fact" (Jeacle and Carter, 2011: 301). These algorithms – the basis of TripAdvisor's calculative practices – provide the formulas through which each individual tourist voice is aggregated into a collective voice in the form of a ranking.

In their study of the trustworthiness of TripAdvisor, Jeacle and Carter show how TripAdvisor's success is based on the authority created by the interdependent relationship between the writers and readers of reviews, and the website itself (2011). The personal trust TripAdvisor engenders is a manifestation of the *positional authority* of the individual review writer – which TripAdvisor guards fiercely, in part because it depends on individual reviewer ratings for its attraction rankings. The systems trust engendered by TripAdvisor is a result of *informational authority* generated by its algorithmically deduced rankings systems – which then adds more credence and legitimacy to the individual review.

As the previous section notes, communicative logics generating positional and informational authority are long established in positive Orientalist discourse, and especially prominent in travelers' tales, which, over time, feature discursive repetition that in turn cements the status of the Other as a product. For TripAdvisor, the repetitions found in the relationship between travelogues and travel guides – and thus its Orientalist roots – are encased within the trust produced from its organizational structure, specifically, how it carefully cultivates the relationship between perceptions of trustworthiness associated with each individual review and those associated with the aggregative "calculative practices" that govern its operation.

As much as TripAdvisor reviews represent a repetition of prior types of travelers' tales, they also represent the *convergence* of these distinct but related forms. It is notable that Jeacle and Carter mention that TripAdvisor's popularity is a response to shifts in the tourist industry, particularly the move away from the "expert system" represented by the individual travel agent (2011). This shift parallels in some ways the shift Behdad (1994) describes taking place between the travelogue and travel guide, with some important differences. Much like the travelogue, the travel agent represents a singular voice illuminating the texts of Otherness for its consumer. Similarly, like the travel guide, TripAdvisor features a plurality of voices to accomplish the same task. The primary difference is that, where the shift from travelogue to travel guide represents a shift from the writer to the reader (still remaining in the realm of the "human"), the shift from travel agent to TripAdvisor represents in many ways a shift from the human to the digital, or at least the digitally mediated. So where does the Other stand in this most recent discursive shift, and how does TripAdvisor help structure its reproduction?

Digital Orientalism

The travelogue and travel guide as popular discursive genres or sources of information were products of the cultural atmospheres of their respective colonial eras. The travelogue was more prevalent during early colonialism, when the Other was still being "discovered" and defined, whereas the travel guide, prevalent during late colonialism, understands and presents the Other as an already "known" quantity (Behdad, 1994). TripAdvisor, in the spirit of convergence, is able to do both by taking the "discoveries" of each individual reviewer and *re*-presenting them – through the aggregative, algorithmic conversions of their ranking systems – as "known" commodities (Jeacle and Carter, 2011). Tara McPherson argues that there are specific ways the expert systems of a website like TripAdvisor become complicit in – at the same time they are partially the result of – the perpetuation or mirroring of the ways the Other is formed today (2012). She first points out that current versions of racial discourse and ways of understanding race and the current methods of techno–digital organization that undergird the internet and social media have their roots in the same post-Second World War cultural era that saw the simultaneous rise of the Cold War, the Civil Rights Movement, the New Left – its economic and ideological rival neoliberalism – and digital computation:

> Certain modes of racial visibility and knowing coincide or dovetail with specific ways of organizing data: if digital computing underwrites today's information economy and is the central technology of post-World War II America, these technologized ways of seeing/knowing took shape in a world also struggling with shifting knowledges about and representations of race. (2012: 24)

McPherson investigates the intersection between the development of contemporary "covert" racism, characterized by color-blind rhetoric (see Bonilla-Silva, 2001), and the development of digital computation systems, such as TripAdvisor's rankings algorithms, which have their foundations in coding programs such as UNIX. She concludes – with important implications for understanding TripAdvisor's role in today's digitally mediated tourism industry – that, similar to the organizational protocols of UNIX-based programming, current notions of both "capital" and "race" are increasingly understood as "modularized" entities increasingly tracked, measured, and ultimately defined through the functions of digital computation: "[They] operate via the algorithm and the database, via simulation and processing" (2012: 34).

McPherson (2003) introduces the concept of a lenticular image to discuss the ways in which racial difference becomes covertly constructed in the US South in the post-Civil Rights era. More recently, she maps the similarities of lenticular logic within both UNIX and post-Second World War racial formation. This type of image, or logic, "… is composed when two separate images are intertwined or combined in a special way. This combined image is then viewed via a unique type of lens, called a lenticular lens, which allows the viewer to see only one of the two views at a time" (2003: 25–26). She points to the ridged plastic (lenticular) lens which covers "3-D" post-cards to illustrate her point: "The viewer can rotate the card to see any single image, but the lens itself makes seeing the images together very difficult, even as it conjoins them at a structural level" (2012: 24). For McPherson, lenticular logic is able to both hide the underlying activities that compose the "inner workings" (2012: 25) of programming – both racial and computational (we might also add touristic) – and fragment, simplify, and diversify the information that is eventually presented as the product of the programming process. McPherson characterizes it as the shell that hides the kernel:

> UNIX's intense modularity and information-hiding capacity were reinforced by its design: that is, in the ways in which it segregated the kernel from the shell…. [Similarly,] the second half [of the 21st

century] increasingly hides its racial 'kernel,' burying it below a shell of neoliberal pluralism. (2012: 29)

Once again, in TripAdvisor we see a convergence, this time between the lenticular logics of contemporary racial understanding and digital computation within the tourism industry. Lenticular logic is apparent within TripAdvisor's content and organizational structure in multiple instances. Perhaps the best example of lenticular logic within its organizational structure – the popularity index – is found in a quote used earlier by Jeacle and Carter:

> As an expert system, the rankings convert the numerous individual ramblings on the site into hard and objective fact ... such a quantification process releases the traveler from the need to place personal trust in a travel agent, glossy brochure, or even the personal reviews within the site. Instead, trust is placed directly in the numbers. (2011: 301)

This has the effect of hiding the varied opinions and thoughts of tourists behind the "hard and objective fact" of the popularity index. Trust moves from being a property of the individual reviews to a property of the programming that re-arranges them. The popularity index also represents a modularization of the review process, where, within each review, content is being separated from the individual rating. The operational structure of TripAdvisor exhibits lenticular logic on another level concerning the specific make-up of the algorithms that calculate the website's rankings. Their exact formulas are not publicly disclosed, so the precise ways in which the popularity index takes shape are kept hidden from those who place trust within it.

In terms of content, information on the website is presented in a modular fashion. Reviews can be viewed according to rating (highest to lowest) and date (starting with the most recent). The front page for each attraction or hotel displays the total number of reviews available, as well as the ratings breakdown indicating in a quick glance how many reviews correlate with each level of the 5 star ratings system. Reviews are displayed in a scrollable column made quicker and more efficient to read because initially only the first few lines of the review are visible, while the rest of the review is hidden from the screen. The rest of the content is only accessible if the reader makes a conscious decision to click on the "more" tab in the bottom of the review. The "more" tab is just a small example of the diverse array of interactions the website facilitates between itself and its users. Some of the key aspects of the lenticular logic of digital computation – diversity, efficiency, modularity, and hidden information – are found throughout TripAdvisor's content; they also happen to be common features of the way contemporary patterns of racial understanding are structured. These also seem to be, according to Behdad, key facets of Orientalist discourse as well:

Orientalism depends for its economy on a 'principle of discontinuity' that makes possible the production of a whole series of discursive practices in various epistemological domains.... What gives Orientalism its efficient discursive power, what makes it a productive force in European colonialism ... is the all-inclusiveness of its epistemological field and its ability to adapt to and incorporate heterogeneous elements. (1994: 13)

Lenticular logic, like Orientalist discourse, tends to separate cause and effect sequences, effectively hiding the former from the latter. In addition to TripAdvisor's connection to earlier iterations of Orientalist travelers' tales, there is also evidence that TripAdvisor's content adheres to the colorblind rhetoric and neoliberal pluralism described by McPherson and many others (see Bonilla-Silva, 2001; Harvey, 2005, Goldberg, 2009) as dictating the contours of contemporary racial understanding. Within review content concerning Harlem Heritage Tours, for example, the notion of civil rights and race-based inequalities as important topics in understanding the community of Harlem is relegated to a specific historical frame coinciding with the Civil Rights Movement (Jamerson, 2014). It is not identified by reviewers as a contemporary issue, even though gentrification is – and despite evidence that tour guides link gentrification to civil rights as part of tour presentations.[3] Out of the 111 reviews I analyzed, only one contained either of the words "racist" or "segregation." They were in the same review and were both mentioned in reference to the achievements of the Civil Rights Movement. The lenticular logic of color-blind rhetoric in these reviews is the shell that hides the kernel – or the inner workings of institutional – racism in the US today, and it is also a discursive strategy complicit in the commodification of Otherness within the tourism industry (Werry, 2011).

The shift from the travel agent to TripAdvisor – or from the human to the digital – represents a shift in position of the "expert" as well. In this shift the expertise that potential travelers rely on to make decisions moves from being situated within the logic of the individual travel agent – or travelogue, or travel guide, or a trusted friend – to within the lenticular logic of digital computation. This might be the best way to successfully manage or negotiate a group of over 225 million individual travelers' tales, but it also acts to reinforce the authority that is produced from their rearrangement – or modularization. Lenticular logic within TripAdvisor seems to be an important factor in the variety of ways trust is produced from the website, and in general can be seen to parallel in many ways – or perhaps make possible – the convergence of elements of both the travelogue and travel guide within the organizational structure of the website.

Conclusion

In sum, TripAdvisor's Orientalist origins are located in the ways trust is manufactured within the website's organizational structure. This organization incorporates discursive elements of longstanding narrative forms – travelers' tales – with a digital platform governed by algorithms. The result for users is a potent mix of "expert trust" and "systems trust" that has made TripAdvisor the internet's most popular travel themed social media website (Jeacle and Carter. 2011). Reviews about Harlem Heritage Tours, for example, are by no means the only digital representations of Harlem, but they are some of the most prominent (Jamerson 2014). They therefore have more potential to reach a wider audience, and shape outsider perceptions of the community. In the case of TripAdvisor, the content of each review is just as important as the way that content is managed by the website through its ranking systems. Moreover, TripAdvisor's content as well as organization can be seen to buttress contemporary discourses about racial difference and reaffirm their legitimacy. It brackets and categorizes notions of Otherness in the service of the tourism industry as well as offers a crowdsourced standard of objectivity – mediated by algorithms – that tourists have come to rely on when making decisions about travel related purchases (Jeacle and Carter, 2011; Lueng et al, 2013). TripAdvisor represents a type of digital Orientalism because of the way it packages biased tourist representations of otherness as "unbiased" online consumer reviews.

The rhetorical divide in scholarship between representation within and access to the digital realm is also characteristic of early developments and differences in techno-Orientalist critique (see Morley and Robins, 1994; Nakamura, 2002; Chun, 2003) and the notion of digital Orientalism (see Morozov, 2011). McPherson's essay addresses a problem she identifies in the development of digital race studies that early on saw the emergence of two distinct camps dealing with intersections of race and the digital: "Early analyses of race and the digital often took two forms, a critique of representations in new media, ie, on the surface of our screens, or debates about access to media, ie, the digital divide" (2012: 23). In techno-Orientalism, the technological Other is rendered less, or not properly human, because of the high degree to which it is integrated within technological systems (Chun, 2012). Digital Orientalism is grounded in a more classic notion of primitivity where de-humanization of the Other is incurred because of a lack of access to modern technology (Morozov, 2011).

TripAdvisor represents an example of a "positive" type of digital Orientalism, but the proposed framework does not seem to fit neatly within either techno or digital Orientalism critique. McPherson (2012) and Chun (2012) suggest that the relationship between racial understanding and digital media is much more intimate and intertwined than either strand of early digital race studies initially allowed for. Chun suggests that, instead of considering race and technology as distinct, there should also be the possibility for considering race *as* technology (2012). This call for understanding race and technology as at least partially convergent is also in line with Couldry's (2012) call for a more socially conscious theory in which to engage in convergent media studies. I want to suggest that TripAdvisor, in this case, represents an Orientalist technology or a technology of Orientalism, where the Orientalist traditions of the – strategically located – traveler's tale converges with the lenticular logic of digital computation and the strategic formations of social media it enables. In an era when both tourism and digital communication are two popular and broad discursive formations that act to structure contemporary definitions of Otherness, TripAdvisor stands as both a virtual portal and trusted intermediary within and between both.

Notes

1. See www.tripadvisor.com/PressCenter-c4-Fact_Sheet.html
2. Google Analytics, average monthly users, Q1 2015.
3. As part of background research for this project, I participated in two differently themed tours six months apart from each other. On each of these tours our group (of mostly white people) was taken by two neighboring buildings – one was occupied by families receiving subsidized housing and rent control (monthly rent was about $600). The next building had recently been sold to a developer that converted the building to condominiums, with the average asking price around $600,000. Our group was posed a rhetorical question: How long did we think the families in the first building would be allowed to live there? This was presented as a literal example of gentrification, and was linked to continuing civil rights struggles for its residents.

References

Behdad, A. (1994) *Belated travelers: Orientalism in the age of colonial dissolution.* Durham, NC and London, UK: Duke University Press.

Bonilla-Silva, E. (2006) *Racism without racists: Color blind racism and the persistence of racial inequality in America.* Lanham, MD: Rowan & Littlefield Publishers.

Chateaubriand, F.R. (1968) *Itineraire de Paris a Jerusalem* (edited by Jean Mourot). Paris, France: Garnier-Flammarion.

Couldry, N. (2011) "More sociology, more culture, more politics: Or a modest proposal for 'convergence' studies." *Cultural Studies* 4–5, September, 486–501.

Couldry, N. (2012) *Media, society, world: Social theory and digital media practice.* Cambridge, UK and Malden, MA: Polity Press.

Chun, W.H.K. (2003) "Orienting Orientalism, or how to map cyberspace." In R.C. Lee and S.-L.C. Wong (eds) *AsianAmerica.Net: Ethnicity, nationalism, and cyberspace* (pp 3–36). Routledge: New York.

Chun, W.H.K. (2012) "Race and/as technology, or How to do things to race." In L. Nakamura and P. Chow-White (eds) *Race after the internet* (pp 38–60). New York: Routledge.

Giddens, A. (1990) *The consequences of modernity.* Cambridge, UK: Polity Press.

Giddens, A. (1991) *Modernity and self-identity: Self and society in the late-modern age.* Cambridge, UK: Polity Press.

Goldberg, D.T. (2009) *The threat of race: Reflections of racial neoliberalism.* Maulden, MA: Wiley-Blackwell.

Gotham, K. (2007) "(Re)branding the big easy: Tourism and rebuilding in post-Katrina New Orleans." *Urban Affairs Review* 42 (27), 823–50.

Harvey, D. (2005) *A brief history of neoliberalism.* New York: Oxford University Press.

Jamerson, W.T. (2014) "Race, discourse, and the cultural economy of neoliberal New York: An analysis of online tourist reviews of Harlem Heritage Tours." Unpublished Master's thesis, Virginia Tech.

Jeacle, I. and C. Carter (2011) "In TripAdvisor we trust: rankings, calculative regimes, and abstract systems." *Accounting, Organizations, and Society* 36, 293–309.

Jenkins, H. (2006) *Convergence culture: Where old and new media collide.* New York: New York University Press.

Law, R. (2008) "Internet and tourism-part XXI: TripAdvisor." *Journal of Travel and Tourism Marketing* 20 (1), 75–7.

Leung, D., R. Law, H. van Hoof, and D. Buhalis (2013) "Social media in tourism and hospitality: A literature review." *Journal of Travel and Tourism Marketing* 30, 3–22.

MacCannell, D. (1976) *The tourist: A new theory of the leisure class.* New York: Schocken Books Inc.

MacCannell, D. (2011) *The ethics of sightseeing.* Berkeley, CA: University of California Press.

McPherson, T. (2003) *Reconstructing Dixie: Race, gender, and nostalgia in the imagined South.* London, UK and Durham, NC: Duke University Press.

McPherson, T. (2012) "US operating systems at mid-century: The intertwining of race and UNIX." In L. Nakamura and P.A. Chow-White (eds) *Race after the internet* (pp 21–37). New York and London, UK: Routledge.

Mayer, R., J. Davis, and F. Schoorman (1995) "An integrative model of organizational trust." *Academy of Management Review* 20, 709–34.

Morozov, E. (2011) The *net delusion: The dark side of internet freedom.* New York: PublicAffairs.

Morley, D. and K. Robins (1995) "Techno-Orientalism: Japan panic." In D. Morley and K. Robins (eds) *Spaces of identity: Global Media, electronic landscapes, and cultural boundaries* (pp 147–73). Routledge: New York.

Murray, J. (1840) *A handbook for travellers in the Ionian Islands, Greece, Turkey, Asia Minor and Constantinople.* London, UK: John Murray.

Murray, J. (1859) *A handbook for travellers in India and Pakistan, Burma and Ceylon.* London, UK: John Murray.

Nakamura, L. (2002) *Cybertypes: Race, ethnicity, and identity on the internet.* Routledge: New York.

O'Connor, P. (2008) "User generated content and travel: A case study Tripadvisor.Com." In P. O'Connor, W. Hopken and U. Gretzel (eds) *Information and communications technologies in tourism* (pp 47–58). Vienna and New York: Springer.

Ritzer, G. and N. Jurgenson (2010) "Production, consumption, prosumption: The nature of capitalism in the age of the digital 'prosumer'." *Journal of Consumer Culture* 10 (1).

Said, E.M. (1978) *Orientalism*. New York: Vintage Books.

Smith, L.T. (2012) *Decolonizing methodologies: Research and indigenous people* (2nd edn). London, UK: Zed Books.

Tussyadiah, I., S. Park, and D.R. Fesenmaier (2011) "Assessing the effectiveness of consumer narratives for destination marketing." *Journal of Hospitality and Tourism Research* 35 (1), 64–78.

Volney, C.F. (1959) *Voyage en Egypte et en Syrie* (edited by Jean Gaulmier). Paris, France: Mouton.

Werry, M. (2011) *The tourist state: Performing leisure, liberalism, and race in New Zealand*. Minneapolis, MN: University of Minnesota Press.

PART II
Digitized institutions

9

Digitized institutions and inequalities

Tressie McMillan Cottom

Institutions are the realization of ideologies, the conduits through which identities are articulated in accordance with political economies, and often the sites of struggle over inclusion into the body politic. This volume proposes that digitally meditated and transformed social processes are a sociological concern. If this is true, then digital sociologies will have to consider the form and function of institutions. In this section, scholars present theoretical, review, and empirical chapters on various institutions. In keeping with sociology's tradition of examining the interconnectedness of institutions, these chapters consider digitization across schooling, work, and media. Each reinforces this volume's main premise that digital sociology's greatest challenge and promise is theorizing and measuring inequalities that produce and are produced by society's datalogical turn. As Selwyn and colleagues point out, perhaps no sociological subfield has engaged the impact of digitality and institutions more consistently than the sociology of education. And few institutions are undergoing as much visible structural change than education, much of that either a consequence of, or a problem for, digital technologies. As such, the section begins with these authors' robust overview of digitization and schooling in their "Toward a digital sociology of school."

Digitized schooling

The primary and secondary school structure in the US continues to be defined by persistent inequalities in resources and outcomes. Tracking within schools (honors and general curricula) and tracking between schools (poorer urban schools and wealthier suburban schools) remain defining characteristics for formal education. The racial divide in access to and returns from education suggests that the problem of 20th-century schools will persist in the schools of the 21st century. Black students are, on average, less likely to attend a well-resourced public school, have the resources to attend a well-resourced private school, to be identified for higher track curriculums even if they do, and to be suspended and expelled from all kinds of schools for infractions that white students are not equally punished for. These trends are present for all ethnic groups with group-based differences in intensity, kind, and frequency conditioned on social class, school composition, and geography.

Across the world's wealthy and powerful elite nations, similar trends in inequality specific to the local systems of stratification can also be seen in school systems. Research on minority ethnic groups and class mobility in the UK has experienced a resurgence in academic literature. And across the less powerful nations, the oppressive forces of globalization continue to de-stabilize attempts at universal education schemes.

These historical, socially contingent patterns and structures are the broader context of technology's impact on education. Research has considered this impact at the level of nations, states, and municipalities; in classrooms and across classroom contexts; and across the three sectors of higher education: private non-profit, public non-profit, and for-profit. The work is conducted across disciplinary fields, ranging from education research and sociology to economics, humanities, business, and cultural studies. For this reason, the research is wide, some of it deep, often producing conflicting theoretical frameworks while increasingly consuming more data than ever before possible thanks to new data collection regimes. This would be a challenge for knowledge production under any circumstances. But under the reigning neoliberal (or corporate or marketized or financialized) sociopolitical ideology that disciplines individuals and groups, the challenge is particularly important. The technology industry is ascendant in the global neoliberal economic system. Armed with capital, political power, and a legitimizing narrative, the technology industry has a clear objective to shape educational systems in the US and across the globe. Audrey Watters has documented the complex web of venture capital funding, non-governmental organization (NGO) partnerships, and market relationships that tie mostly Western technology companies to almost every major trend in education for the last 20 years (Watters, 2014). Technology billionaires create non-profit organizations to give every child in the global South a laptop. Technology companies "give away" software to cash-strapped schools in exchange for copious amounts of user data that can be mined, financialized, and commodified. Technological regimes introduce "academic analytics" to make higher education institutions more efficient. At every level of education and schooling, technology is reproducing global patterns of datafication, monitoring, pedagogy, praxis, and *homo economicus* epistemologies.

At the same time, powerful group interests have converged with technological change to resist institutional exclusion and oppression. Parents use digital archives, search tools, and inexpensive platforms to buttress school deficiencies. Students use a variety of tools to form valuable peer networks and to access information usually transmitted through informal curriculums. Feminist, anti-racist, and anti-capitalist DOCCs (distributed online collaborative courses) and POOCs (participatory open online courses) have proliferated even as MOOCs (massive open online courses) have sucked the attention and capital out of most public discussions of open and online education (Daniels et al, 2014; DeMillo and Young, 2015; Juhasz and Balsamo, 2012). Some of these platforms have been studied for their sheer size, their skill-building efficacy, deep learning development, and cost-saving potential. Almost all of this research has either ignored the structural inequalities of race, class, gender, and their intersections, or treated those inequalities in superficial, atheoretical fashion. Some of the inattention to categorical inequalities in this literature is due to the nature of the data collected about those who use these platforms. Open resources compromise their openness by using bureaucratic means of access (for example, applications) that provide data on student characteristics and background. School systems are diverse ecosystems and technology adoption can vary a great deal, hampering systematic analysis. Also, much of what scholars would consider research increasingly happens under the auspices of market research at proprietary companies who own and sell technological "solutions" to educators, municipalities, and learners.

Selwyn, Nemorin, Bulfin and Johnson propose a subfield of sociology of education technology to bring synthesis to the study of technology and schooling. This chapter provides an indispensable primer on the current subfield of education research about technology. It also goes further by summarizing the technologies most often studied in research on education. They propose a "digital sociology of school" that would "properly coordinate" the competing narratives, theories, and methods in the current political economy of technology and education. The chapter makes many contributions to digital sociology's engagement with one of the most critical institutions in society. Chief among them is a position shared by the editors of this volume, namely, that digital sociology must problematize "digitizations of schools and schooling." This includes attending to the gaps outlined above: group inequalities, power, and ideologies. The authors caution that critical sociology is not the same as being persistently critical. Instead, Selwyn and colleagues harken to Mills' imperative that the sociological imagination interrogate biography and history – individuals and structures – in such a way as to put them both in greater relief.

From this important invitation to take up the challenge of a critical digital sociology of schools, several subsequent chapters go about doing just that. Jeffrey Alan Johnson's chapter, "Representing 'inforgs' in data-driven decisions," begins right where Selwyn and colleagues ask us to begin: by bringing a critical lens to a dominant ideology. For Johnson, "data-driven" and "evidence-based" decision-making in higher education is a dominant ideology ripe for critical engagement. He goes into the heart of an institutional structure, a place that I hope more digital sociologists will venture. The chapter theorizes the technological systems that sort, identify, and ultimately hierarchically differentiate students using deceptively agnostic taxonomies based on power relations. Gender, race, parental status, student states – these categories become "translation regimes" that shape the limits of "data-driven" decision-making to create institutional spaces for direct forms of participation in the university. In this chapter, Johnson provides a theoretical framework to interrogate the institutional mechanisms of technological adoption and social reproduction of inequality. It is a generative framework with far-reaching possibilities for translating a critical site of corporatization across various educational sites.

Digitized work and media

Critically interrogating technology and education is an end unto itself, but sociological interest in education has always justified its interest for schooling's role in social stratification. We go to school to become better citizens, sure, but the sociological mind is often concerned with questions of mobility, labor market entry, capital capacity, status formation, and all the attendant consequences for health and wellbeing. Stratification is the core sociological imperative. Considering schooling and technology to what ends is yet another area ripe for digital sociologies' intervention. Two contributions in this section tackle aspects of digitality and work, often by examining connections to education or the translation regimes that have an impact both on how we go to school and how we go to work.

Stephen Barnard's chapter, "Digital sociology's vocational promise," looks at higher education and technology, turning to consider the vocational promise of its intersections. Barnard begins with a valuable overview of the various interventions that digital sociology has made, and proposes a way that digital sociologies can build on those interventions. The chapter draws on lessons from the much more defined (and arguably professionalized) digital humanities field as a point of departure. As have others, Barnard points out that technological adoption – as medium and message – is conditioned on group inequalities in labor conditions within the corporate university structure. I believe Barnard also makes one of the most fundamentally sound responses to concerns that digital sociologies poaches from other fields of study when he writes "scholarly inquiry is not a zero-sum game." More entrenched in the earlier ways of university corporatization, the humanities' foray into digital modes of inquiry has created opportunities and also reproduced institutional hierarchies. Digital humanities departments, scholars, and centers have, for example, reproduced gendered and racialized notions of teaching as inferior to quantitative textual modeling. Well-funded digital humanities centers and projects often attract white, male, able-bodied, and similarly privileged scholars into institutional systems where the actual humanities departments are being starved of rights, pay, job security, career mobility, and investment. Barnard warns us to mind the gap of formal knowledge production and pre-existing patterns of inequality in our effort to bring together digital sociologies and scholars.

Calle Rosengren and Mikael Ottosson continue the section's focus on the socially contingent nature of digital processes by focusing on workplace surveillance. In "Employee monitoring in a digital context," Rosengren and Ottosson take up the challenge set forth by Johnson and Selwyn and colleagues for a critical digital sociology of education, and extend that to the economy. Specifically, Rosengren and Ottosson bring a critical lens to surveillance in the context of labor market precarity in the 21st-century workplace. Similar to Johnson, Rosengren and Ottosson find the threads of workplace monitoring in the historical march towards "data-driven" decision-making. The workplace data collection that began as a way to measure employee (and, *ergo*, company) performance has morphed into an institutional mechanism for control. Their empirical data are from field sites at two universities. One might be tempted to think the setting too narrow to have wide-ranging applicability to work. But it is worth noting that the university workplace is part of the US labor market's shift to a knowledge-based economy. That isn't to say that the majority of US workers work in the fields associated with complex cognitive tasks. They don't. However, a disproportionate share of labor market returns in pay, security, and status have shifted to jobs in the knowledge sector. This smaller sector of "good jobs" stands across the gulf from a growing sector of "bad jobs", low-wage and low-mobility jobs concentrated in the service sector (Kalleberg, 2009). This job polarization is one of the most animated discussions in the sociology of work, with a consequent impact on how we understand race, class, gender, ability, and sexuality inequalities in the new economy. Digital surveillance practices at Rosengren and Ottosson's field sites yield important insights into a feature of the best quality jobs in a labor market defined by there being fewer and fewer of such jobs.

Barnard's message is the starting point for my contribution to this section in a chapter on intersectionality and digital sociology. In the chapter, "Black cyberfeminism: Ways forward for intersectionality and digital sociology" I draw on existing research of academic capitalism and race, class, and gender for three key frameworks critical to an intersectional digital sociology that recovers more than it reproduces. The chapter argues that to study how digitized institutional mechanisms mediate categorical inequalities, sociological theory must look anew at key principles of "the digital." For example, contemporary debates about digital privacy (also discussed in Johnson's chapter on translation regimes) coalesce around the assumption that *more* privacy is a universal good. And it is true that privacy violations tend to come first and have the harshest penalties for black, brown, and poor people. These penalties lead to digital surveillance and predicative criminality of the socially vulnerable through intersecting data translation regimes across work, education, health, and political institutions. But I contend that one consequence of categorical protections before the law has been the bureaucratic regimes of data collection and categorization. The boxes for race and gender on the forms (increasingly now digital form fields) are rooted in sociohistorical struggles to translate systematic oppression. How do black queer students argue that they are being categorically discriminated against at work or school if there isn't a box to check? I present data from my six-year study of women enrolled in online for-profit degree-granting programs in the US. Part of that study was digital ethnographic research of a support group for students who met on Facebook. I show how algorithmic stratification based on categorical inequalities made these students vulnerable to unequal access to affordable, not-for-profit colleges, but also made it possible for them to form critical online support networks to navigate the consequences of that unequal access. Other forms of algorithmic stratification are unfolding in work as data-driven hiring uses social media data, lead generators, task aggregators, and credit scoring algorithms to datatize categorical inequalities in ways difficult to observe and measure. Drawing on Kishonna Gray's black cyberfeminist approach to intersectionality in Chapter 22, I argue that research should incorporate dimensions of classification situations to interrogate how digitized institutions reproduce inequality.

Educational institutions are being transformed by digital technologies in a host of unintended ways. In an economic and political context of neoliberalism, colleges and universities now employ entire departments of marketing staff, a subset of whom are assigned to manage the institution's website. In her chapter, "Deconstructing racism on college websites," Monita H. Mungo notes that institutional websites "carefully craft their digital presence to reflect a specific view of campus life and the composition of the student body," including with images and text that suggest an unproblematic embrace of diversity. Yet, as Mungo documents, these same institutional websites often hide the systemic racism embedded in the institution from the view of visitors, students, and faculty.

Surprising to no one, students who are enrolled at colleges and universities frequently use unauthorized (sometimes explicitly forbidden) digital platforms such as Yik Yak to communicate about their institutions. What is surprising is what platforms like Yik Yak reveal about the way educational institutions are being reconfigured in the digital era. In "Yakking about college life," Francesca

Tripodi visits the intersection of social media and educational institutions with her study of Yik Yak use among college students. Her work extends discussions in this volume and elsewhere about the mutability of privacy, in this case, how anonymity functions. Using virtual ethnography, Tripodi examines how the political economy of digital platforms affects institutional arrangements. Yik Yak's platform affordances shape how communities within educational institutions conceive of norms and behaviors.

Media, especially social media, is one of the most popular sites of digital study. Media is also a critical social institution for the reproduction of identity and narratives. Apryl Williams, in her chapter "'On Thursdays we watch *Scandal*': Communal viewing and Black Twitter," observes how Black Twitter has shaped a powerful communal experience of broadcast television. In turn, this communal viewing re-shapes the institution of broadcast media. Williams uses multiple qualitative methods, including content and interview analysis, to situate these communal viewing experiences within a broader context in ways that illuminate the meaning of social processes. The analysis reveals that participants present a contested view of what constitutes membership in a racialized digital space.

In Andrew McKinney's "Disruptive labor: Bleacher Report and the monetization of mass amateurization," McKinney's case study of a sports internet website builds on the section's attention to how platforms shape digital interactions. Networked news media is constrained by affordances sensitive to profit-making activities. Here, McKinney shows how the nature of work – unpaid writers – and precarious labor arrangements shape the quality and content of the news media that produces legitimizing media narratives.

Jonathan Wynn's "Covert leisure and public spaces: Geocaching in post-9/11 New York City" draws us into the world of "geocaching" and its practitioners. In so doing, Wynn invites us to consider labor, leisure, and public urban spaces through a digital sociology lens. As Wynn writes, geocaching is "outdoor activity played among strangers, using the internet and Global Positioning System (GPS) data, to share the location of 'caches' that fellow players have hidden in public locations." Tracing the history of GPS technology through its military roots, Wynn brings a critical political economy to the fore of his analysis of geocaching. While the practice tends to be seen as a leisure activity, Wynn links the pursuit of mysterious, buried treasure with questions of public space, surveillance, and war. As Wynn elegantly writes, "geocaching, in this way, sits somewhere between *flânerie* and the *derive*, to be the product and result of its own historical moment: utilizing the tools of war for leisure activity; reflecting the countless and rapidly increasing number of place-aware technologies that make for a lively digital urbanism while at the same time fetishizing the smartphone commodity...." Here, in the shadow of 9/11 and the ongoing "War on Terror," geocaching becomes a case study for understanding linkages between macro-level institutions and the quotidian use of technology while wandering the city. Wynn contributes a methodological framework for understanding how technologies mediate concepts of privacy and publics, which is a consistent theme in this section and volume.

Together, these chapters do generative work in each of their respective domains: they yield important insights into critical features of the institutions that mediate our digitized society. Each chapter opens up further possibilities while also bringing some consensus to the existing literature on digital sociologies, institutions, and inequalities.

References

Daniels, J., M.K. Gold, K. Gregory et al (2014) "The InQ13 POOC: A participatory experiment in open, collaborative teaching and learning." *The Journal of Interactive Technology & Pedagogy*, June 9.

DeMillo, R.A. and A.J. Young (2015) *Revolution in higher education: How a small band of innovators will make college accessible and affordable*. Cambridge, MA: The MIT Press.

Juhasz, A. and Balsamo, A. (2012) "An idea whose time is here: FemTechNet – a distributed online collaborative course (DOCC)." *Ada: A Journal of Gender, New Media, and Technology* 1.

Kalleberg, A.L. (2009) "Precarious work, insecure workers: Employment relations in transition." *American sociological Review* 7, 1, 1–22.

Watters, A. (2014) *The monsters of education technology* (http://monsters.hackeducation.com/) [self-published].

10

Toward a digital sociology of school

Neil Selwyn, Selena Nemorin, Scott Bulfin,
and Nicola F. Johnson

D igital technologies are now an integral feature of schools and schooling in ways that would have been hard to imagine even a few years previously.[1] Devices such as tablets, laptops, and smartphones support a diversity of learning practices within the schoolhouse, at home, and all points in between. Classrooms and other formal learning environments are awash with digital hardware and software, and a growing amount of pedagogic work is conducted on a "virtual" basis. In addition, the day-to-day management and administration of schools is underpinned by software systems that support and structure the actions of students, teachers, administrators, leaders, and parents in a variety of ways. Notwithstanding the complexity of these sociotechnical conditions, "the digital" is now an expected and largely unremarkable feature of the contemporary school. As such, the proliferation of digital technologies into schools clearly merits renewed and sustained sociological attention. This chapter teases out some of the key ways in which digital sociology can help us make better sense of contemporary school.

The need for a digital sociology of school

This volume provides a timely call to arms for anyone interested in the critical study of schools and schooling. While critical social research on schools and technology has been conducted sporadically over the past 30 years, such work has taken place largely in a piecemeal fashion and has lacked a proper "home." The sociology of education (the obvious cognate field for such work) has proven to be surprisingly uninterested in technological matters and certainly lacking in technical know-how. Elsewhere, fields such as new media studies, communications studies and internet studies have been receptive to discussions of the technological transformations of education but ultimately lacked critical "bite" and/or "edge." Conversely, science, technology and society (STS) has often felt (from our own experiences at least) too cliquey and preoccupied as an arena to pay sustained attention to something as "applied" and prosaic as technology use in schools.

So we write this in the hope that digital sociology could be the start of something better for researchers concerned with the critical study of schools and technology – a flag of convenience that interesting people and provocative ideas might gather around. Obviously, we need to remain mindful of the past two decades of education-related work in and around cyberstudies, internet research, webology, and other precursors to the current turn toward digital sociology. Yet there are many reasons to believe that digital sociology has emerged at just the right time to deliver a sharper, more pointed focus on the political, economic, cultural, and social aspects of late-modern "digital society." This is a moment in the disciplinary development of sociology that the critical study of schools and technology needs take full advantage of.

The case for a coordinated and comprehensive sociology of schools and technology is more pressing than ever – particularly given the continued limited scope of mainstream research on schools and technology. The bulk of academic work on this topic over the past 30 years or so has been stymied by an almost pathological focus on technology and learning (more specifically, the potential of technology to "enable," "assist," "enhance," or even "transform" learning). This is work rooted in the "learning sciences," "pedagogic sciences," and "design sciences." Of course, these areas are all core elements of "Education" as an applied academic discipline. Yet the predominance of such concerns in discussions of schools and technology remains highly frustrating for anyone who is more politically conscious and/or sociologically minded.

Indeed, it could be argued that the bulk of the most significant issues around technology in school has *little or nothing* to do with "learning" or "pedagogy." For instance, the current ubiquity of "Learning Management Systems" in elementary, middle, and high schools around the world has far less to do with issues of "learning" than issues of "management." So why, then, do we not have a sustained tradition of critical scholarship that addresses schools and technology *beyond* matters of learning and pedagogy? Where is the research and writing that expands our understanding of how these are technologies of domination and control; alienation and exploitation; individualization and privatization? Where are the studies of how digital technologies are used to support and sustain the ongoing hollowing-out of compulsory education – not least trends of what has been termed "conservative modernization," "neoliberalisation," and "corporate reform" of public schooling? Where is research that explores the role of the digital in reshaping schools along individualized, market-driven lines – reinforcing conditions of accountability, performance, efficiency, commodification, competition, and so on?

The answers to these questions would surely come from a properly coordinated but appropriately combative "digital sociology of school." The remainder of this chapter sketches out some elements of what such a sociology could look like and how it might be pursued. In particular, we attempt to outline at least three specific aspects of digital sociology that can embolden the academic study of contemporary schools: (1) approaching the digital as problematic; (2) describing the everyday realities of schools and technology; and (3) expanding the methodological imagination.

Approaching the digital as problematic

First and foremost, digital sociology is a means of suitably problematizing ongoing digitizations of schools and schooling, that is, challenging what is taken for granted and exposing power differentials, injustices, and inequalities. In short, a digital sociology of school should be driven by a state of perpetual unease and dis-satisfaction with how things are. Digital sociology does *not* simply involve a cynical and/or apathetic dismissal of the digital. Instead, digital sociology involves an active and committed skepticism. The starting point for any discussion is therefore the suspicion that "everything is dangerous" … as opposed to the conviction that "everything is bad." As had been argued before, this can be a productive stance to adopt:

> My point is not that everything is bad, but that everything is dangerous, which is not exactly the same as bad. If everything is dangerous, then we always have something to do. (Michel Foucault, cited in Dreyfus and Rabinow, 1982: 231–2)

A digital sociology of school therefore points to the complexity of schools and technology rather than striving to construct over-simplified "answers" and "good news." In contrast to the hubris-driven solutionism that pervades the "Ed Tech" industry (see Watters, 2015), a digital sociology of school offers a space to raise a number of contentions and concerns that are usually *not* part of mainstream conversations about schools and digital technology. First and foremost are the competing agendas and vested interests at play within the push for increased technology use in school. Digital sociology therefore provides a powerful basis from which to problematize digital education as *ideology*. This recognizes that digital technologies in schools are not neutral but political; that they are carriers for assumptions and ideas about the future of society; that their design, promotion, and use are all sites in which struggles over power are conducted. Digital sociology allows us to frame the use of digital technology in schools against long-standing and entrenched terms of ideological struggle over the distribution of power.

A second orientation that digital sociology brings to the table is the need to see schools and technology as *human experience*. In these times of augmented reality, the Internet of Things, additive manufacturing, and so on, it can be easy to forget that digital technology use is something that is as human as it is technical. When we talk about digital technology we are often referring to the activities and practices that people do in tandem with technology, rather than the technologies themselves. Digital sociology therefore foregrounds discussions in terms of people's feelings and emotions, their (dis)pleasures and (in)sensitivities when encountering digital technologies during the course of their everyday lives. In the context of the school, then, students, teachers, administrators, leaders, and parents are not simply neutral variables in any instance of school technology use. Instead, school technology is clearly something experienced within distinct human contexts and with distinct human consequences. Any investigation of the digital school is therefore an investigation of the human experience of digital technology use, that is, people's everyday practices and perceptions.

This leads on to a third orientation that digital sociology brings to the study of schools, that is, problematizing the *social structures and contexts* of technology use. Here, our concerns move beyond simply documenting the human thoughts and actions that coalesce around digital technology within a school. Instead, it compels us to consider questions of how these thoughts and actions came to be – how they were socially shaped and socially conditioned. As such, making full sense of individuals' responses to digital technologies in school requires a good understanding of the social contexts of contemporary schooling. Take, for example, the organizational structures of schools – from the timetabling and scheduling to the enactment of various policies such as common core or standardized testing. Broader contextual influences relate to social class, race, ethnicity, and gender; the subtle (and not so subtle) ways that neighborhoods bump up against schools; the religious ethos or other philosophies that schools adopt (for example, as a "sports school" or a "caring community"). Of course, we should not see these structured social processes *wholly* in restrictive, punitive, and dominating terms. Instead, digital sociology allows us "to grasp social processes in their dialectics and dynamics (instead of representing them as a concatenation of the power pressures currently in the limelight)" (Bauman, 2014: 19).

All these different orientations toward the reconfiguration and reconstitution of schools through digital means foreground important questions. These range well beyond the usual "What works?" and "What if?" questions that dominate mainstream academic work on education and technology. Instead, digital sociology points to the following types of far more significant lines of inquiry:

- What meanings and understandings of education are being conveyed through digital technologies? How do these technologies disseminate ideas about political and economic structures? What is the language that is being associated with schools and digital technology?
- What forms of educational engagement are being promoted through digital technology use in schools, and what forms are being obscured and silenced? In whose interests does the common consensus about schools and technology work? How persuasive does this manipulation of understandings and meanings appear to be?
- What freedoms and unfreedoms are associated with digital technology use in schools? How are these being experienced by different individuals and social groups? To what extent are technologies in school situated in dominant structures of production and power? To what extent do technologies in schools disrupt dominant structures of production and power?
- How is the increased presence of digital technologies in schools altering the relationship between the individual and the commons, as well as the public and private? Are digital technologies fostering a sense of obligation and communal sense of education? Are all individuals self-responsiblized and empowered by technology use in schools?
- In what ways are digital technologies enhancing or diminishing a sense of pleasure, engagement and enchantment with schools and schooling?
- What are the continuities and discontinuities between "new" forms of digital schooling and the forms of school that preceded? In what ways are existing practices and processes altered? In what ways are existing structures and relations superseded altogether?

Describing the everyday realities of schools and technology

So where should these questions be directed? What specific school-related topics and concerns does digital sociology point us toward? As is evident throughout this book, one of the key strengths of digital sociology is an ability to properly describe and question the everyday realities of digital society in terms of what C. Wright Mills (1959) identified as private troubles *and* public issues. There are clearly a number of public and private aspects of contemporary schools and schooling that digital sociology alerts us to. Perhaps most obviously, digital technologies have an impact on many of the core elements of education – not least the generation and communication of knowledge and, it follows, the ways in which learning and understanding take place. In this sense, digital technologies support different practices, literacies and "ways of doing" within schools that previously might not have been valued and/or privileged.

Digital technologies therefore clearly mediate the social relations and hierarchies within a school. As such, digital technologies need to be seen as a key site for varied forms of identity work by young people and adults alike. Digital technologies are also a focus for ongoing struggles between institutions and individuals – replicating and reinforcing tensions between structure and agency, regulation and resistance. In terms of time and space, digital technologies blur boundaries between "school," "home," and other social institutions and settings. More prosaically, perhaps, digital technologies are associated with ever-changing materialities and "stuff" of schools – the physical environments, the material objects within them, the spatial arrangements that continue to constitute the school or the classroom as a "place."

All of these are obvious but important issues that digital sociology reminds us to foreground in any analysis of schools and the digital. That said, it is perhaps worth spending more time outlining some (perhaps less obvious) areas related to the politics of contemporary schooling that we feel are not often discussed. These are additional areas of concern that the current digital sociology turn does a good job in directing our attention toward. In a little more detail, then, these issues include the following.

The political economy of schools and technology

Digital technologies have extended the commercialization of schools into new realms. From Microsoft and Google, through to News Corporation and thousands of far smaller "Ed-Tech" start-ups, digital technologies have positioned for-profit interests at the center of how public schooling is now funded, organized, and delivered. This variety of enterprises reflects the fact that schools and technology is now a very big business, with global sales of K-12 instructional technology reaching $13 billion in 2013. There is a clear need here for investigations that seek to simply "follow the capital" associated with the increased use of digital technology in schools. As the infamous case of the $1.3 billion iPad program in LAUSD (Los Angeles Unified School District) continues to illustrate, the use of digital technologies in schools is driven by an "education–industrial complex" (Picciano and Spring, 2013) of IT industry and publishing businesses, foundations and think tanks, and other vested interests.

As such, digital sociology reminds us to constantly challenge the private sector values that underpin much of what is blithely seen as the inevitable digital reform of public schooling. Take, for example, how digital technology and the imagined imperative of "the digital" is being used as justification to redesign, reform and reorientate the nature, form, and values of public schooling. Philanthropic foundations, transnational corporations, venture capitalists, and other "edu-prenuers" continue to invest substantial amounts of time, finance, and spin in attempts to "fix" and/or "disrupt" our supposedly "broken" school systems through technology-based approaches. These include promises of technology-driven "personalization," games-based-learning, "flipped classrooms," maker culture, "21st-century skills," and so on. These also include new blueprints for schooling along the lines of Altschool, Quest-to-Learn, P-TECH, and even "Steve Jobs schools." Reversions and innovations such as these might well be desirable and beneficial, but surely require sustained scrutiny and critique. Many of the "new" forms of digital education being promoted by commercial interests are based undoubtedly around different agendas and ideologies than we are used to seeing in public education. These shifts in tone and emphasis may, or may not, be a "good thing." Yet these are issues that require more recognition, debate, and scrutiny from within the educational establishment.

The management and governance of schools

Digital technologies are also entwined with the changing governance of schools – particularly as tools through which principles of "performance," "effectiveness," and "accountability" have been enacted. Alongside the proliferation within schools of computerized systems relating to "management information" and "business intelligence" are various systems that support externally facing public scrutiny of schools. This ranking and comparison is illustrated, for example, in the circulation of data from OECD's 65 country "PISA" measurements, or the Australian government's nationwide "MySchool" website. Schools are also subject to a variety of internal regimes of technology-based governance. For example, school decision-making in a range of domains – from curriculum content to teacher hiring – is increasingly dependent on systems of algorithmic modeling, calculation, and recommendation. Much of this has been driven by the increased prominence of digital data – raising concerns over the "datafication" of schooling (Lingard et al, 2014). Thus we are warned of "schools and districts becom[ing] data farms, providing an unending supply of harvestable data" (Dean, 2014: 19). Similarly, schools are seen to have been rendered "digitally rendered as a vast surface of machine-readable data traces" (Williamson, 2016).

Of course, such uses of data can be justified as supporting active and efficient modes of governance and management. Data might well be enhancing organizational preparedness and response, informing cross-border planning, and/or whole institution management (Kitchin, 2014). Nevertheless, a range of questions needs to be leveled *against* such possible benefits. These include issues of reductionism and the privileging of an "instrumental rationality" that presumes the disaggregation of complex social and cultural situations into neatly modeled and calculable problems that can be addressed through computational means (Mattern, 2013). Further questions are also raised regarding the exacerbation of unequal social relations between powerful and non-powerful groups through data-based calculations and judgments (Selwyn, 2015). In all these terms, data-based governance needs to be subject to close critical scrutiny.

The digital labor of schools and schooling

Schools are connected to work in a number of ways. On the one hand, schools play a role in preparing future workers, responding to economic imperatives of employability, and so on. Any account of schools and digital technologies must therefore take such issues into account – updating Bowles and Gintis' (1976) account of the relations between capital and education. Indeed, the correspondence between work and school has long been seen to extend beyond knowledge and curricula into all aspects of social relations, interactions, and identity formations. One key set of issues relating to the digital school, therefore, is how these conditions and correspondences might be reinforced and/or reconfigured in an age of "immaterial labor," "cognitive capitalism," and "knowledge economies." These new modalities are likely to influence the way that "work" now takes place within schools … but in what ways, and to what ends?

On the other hand, schools must be seen as sites of work for teachers, students, and administrators alike. What, then, are the "digital labor" processes involved in the increased use of digital technologies within schools? For example, with online technologies increasingly used as a means of sharing, re-purposing and out-sourcing pedagogic content, how are digital technologies implicated in the increased division of labor and alienation of teachers from their teaching? Digital technologies are also implicated in the increased blurring of previously binary distinctions between work and leisure, school and home, productive-work and busy-work. It is also important to explore the role of digital technology as a growing site for the automation of school work – from the development of automating grading systems for tests and essays, to "teacher proof" personalized learning systems that regulate the individualized instruction of each student. While such "innovations" are often justified in official terms of increased efficiency and rationalization, digital sociology raises the possibility for alternate accounts of such technologies in sustaining schools as sites of increased exploitation, performativity, and alienation.

The surveillance of schools and schooling

A further aspect of digital technologies and schools that demands heightened attention is the surveillance processes and practices that now pervade public schools. Common forms of technology-based school surveillance include the use of CCTV (closed circuit television) throughout school campuses, online monitoring techniques, the use of smart cards, RFID (radio-frequency identification) tags, and biometric tracking. Through such technologies, modes of measurement and control of school populations have increased steadily – albeit attracting less controversy and resistance than has been the case with the implementation of surveillance technologies in society more generally.

Indeed, technology-based surveillance is increasingly being justified in terms of enhancing the pedagogic efficiencies of schools and classrooms. For example, self-generation of data by individuals has led to talk of the "sentient school" where amassed forms of personalized surveillance data can be used to direct teaching and learning on a real-time responsive basis (see Lupton, 2014). In contrast, digital sociology offers a means of exploring critically the everyday conditions of surveillance in school. In particular, it guides us to question the range of surveillance practices and processes at work within schools, and to consider how these are variously encountered and experienced by students, teachers, administrators, and other members of a "school community." It also allows us to ask questions about what is occurring within prevailing conditions of watching, sorting, and controlling. One significant concern is how surveillance in schools has shifted from a panoptic to a post-panoptic state, specifically with regards to the flattening out of power hierarchies as a result of the incorporation of vertical and horizontal modes of surveillance. Digital sociology has already spent much time analyzing how the nature and form of surveillance has changed. The key challenge here is to explore how these conditions are in evidence within schools.

Expanding the methodological imagination

In tandem with these conceptual concerns, we also need to consider the methodological directions of the digital sociology turn. In short, digital sociology offers researchers a range of digitally attuned methods and methodologies that can be used to address the questions and issues just outlined. Schools and digital technology is an area of research that would certainly benefit from a methodological refresh. Indeed, the fast-moving nature of technology use within schools demands that researchers think expansively and imaginatively about how school research in "done." Put bluntly, it is becoming increasingly apparent that any form of social research seeking to capture what could be termed "the street life" of digital technology use (Hall, 2008) needs to look well beyond the survey, interview, observation, and field note as its main tools of inquiry. These once innovative and insightful techniques now come across as decidedly tired ways of engaging with digital contexts and digital issues. If the questions and concerns just raised about schools and the digital are to be properly addressed, we are going to have to do (research) better.

Clearly, there are increasing opportunities in school research to apply the emerging methods and techniques from the *computational social sciences.*

Certainly, many of the school-based applications of technology just described result in the generation of large data sets relating to individuals, institutions, and whole-school systems. The opportunities for the modeling, simulation, and analysis of school-related phenomenon is clear, especially with school districts and cities beginning to release data on public school systems on an "open data" basis (Stodden, 2014). Initial work in this direction is evident, for example, in the data mining and modeling of municipal data sets derived from annual surveys of parent, student, and teacher perceptions of NYC (New York City) public schools (Wellington, 2015).

Such techniques also point to the focusing of empirical research on the coded elements of technology use. Indeed, with much of contemporary schooling taking place online and within systems such as learning management systems, management information systems, and so on, there is a clear need to thoroughly research the digital systems, online environments and coded spaces that now constitute "school." This is a point that has been well made by writers in the fields of software studies and platform studies. As Lev Manovich (2013: 2) puts it, "software has become our interface to the world, to others, to our memory and our imagination – a universal language through which the world speaks, and a universal engine on which the world runs." The need remains for a digital sociology of school that properly interrogates the code, data, and programmed architecture of the virtual aspects of contemporary schooling.

While digital sociology has been enthused by highly quantitative approaches to data analysis, opportunities also exist for more detailed, deliberative, qualitative approaches to exploring the lived experiences of individuals within information systems and online environments. As every local school becomes more of a distributed organization, inspiration might also be taken, for example, from the "trace ethnography" of digital data (Geiger and Ribes, 2011). This is qualitative research that focuses on the detailed trace data generated and collated by online systems, such as transaction logs, version histories, institutional records, conversation transcripts, and source code. Observation of how these various forms of data have been (re)constituted and (re)circulated within various systems can yield rich insights into the online practices, collaborations, and coordinations of contemporary schooling – from virtual forms of parental "engagement" through to the organization of pedagogic work. As Geiger and Ribes (2011: 1) observe:

> Analysis of these detailed and heterogeneous data ... can provide rich qualitative insight into the interactions of users, allowing us to retroactively reconstruct specific actions at a fine level of granularity. Once decoded, sets of such documentary traces can then be assembled into rich narratives of interaction, allowing researchers to carefully follow coordination practices, information flows, situated routines, and other social and organizational phenomena across a variety of scales.

Similarly, there is much that the study of schools and technology can take from recent advances in the area of digital ethnography (Pink et al, 2015). The participatory and highly mobile nature of digital video and audio creation, for example, offers a ready means of researching the everyday places and practices of digital schooling. In particular, digital recording devices allow school-based research work to be conducted "on the move." One means of doing this is to ask people to purposively walk around their schools – therefore representing their school environments to researchers, and collaboratively exploring how digital schooling is experienced in movements. Sarah Pink's (2009) research has made good use of such "place-making walking tours" and "collaborative video touring" where participants lead camera-wielding researchers around their intimate environments.

Digital ethnography also points to the empirical study of the sensually rich and varied nature of technology use, that is, "multi-sensory" research that captures the visual, auditory, olfactory, haptic, and tactile dimensions of any digital experience. Digital schooling is obviously experienced through all senses – from the bodily movements that take place around digital technologies; the three-dimensional shaping and textures of digital devices; the beeps, clicks, whirrs, and other noises of technology use; and the heat and smells generated by 30 computers packed into one small room. There are many ways that technology in schools can be investigated in these terms – for example, through the use of decibel meters and light readers, as well as the use of audio editing software to visualize sound. Some studies have employed fine-grained "multimodal" analysis of video and still images to capture the rhythms, moods, and textures existing in schools and classrooms. Opportunities also exist to make use of participatory GIS (Geographic Information Systems) data to map movements of people and devices, or perhaps software recording traces and trails of touch on touch-responsive technologies. All told, digital sociology reminds us that empirical research should be a multisensory practice.

With regard to another of our earlier concerns, more attention also needs to be directed toward the researching of the political economy of digital schooling. Well-established methods such as critical discourse analysis offer an ideal means of interrogating the (over)selling of technology to schools, and identifying the component actors and their relationships, as well as exploring underpinning values and agendas. Similarly, policy network analysis offers a ready means of investigating the interconnections of vested interests in policy-making, lobbying, and agenda setting (see, for example, Hogan and colleagues' [2016] analysis of Pearson's education policy activities). Increasingly, these forms of research that focus on the analysis of digital texts make good use of digital analytical tools – from semantic analysis and text matching applications through to network modeling software. In all these guises, then, the concerns of digital sociology should translate into a pragmatic, varied, and eclectic approach to our understandings of research methods and methodology.

Finally, the attention of schools researchers might also be directed toward so-called live methods approach – much of which is concerned with the imaginative empirical use of techniques. As Les Back and colleagues' recent writing has explored, the "live methods" manifesto illustrates research approaches that are creative, playful, and deliberately provocative (Back, 2012). Researchers are encouraged to be "artful and crafty" – developing empirical methods and "cultural probes" that test and reinvent relations with social settings and environments. Examples of these methods include Mike Michael's (2012) encouragement of "idiotic" methods, such as the "speculative design" of provocative objects and probes that might disrupt or misbehave in social settings. Michael suggests, for example, the programming of nonsensical automated Twitter "bots" or the mailing of disposable cameras with specific instructions to photograph the "spiritual center" of one's everyday environments (see also Wilkie et al, 2015).

So why not make use of similar "de-sign" methods that allow the people working within schools to speculate implausibly but imaginatively about digital educational futures? Why not explore the research insights that might arise from using digital technologies to engage in fiction writing, filmmaking, and other creative artistic pursuits? "Live methods" highlights the empirical opportunities that can result from engaging more fully with the digital aspects of research settings that are already *in situ*. Thus it makes sense for researchers to make use of the hundreds of smartphone-based recording devices that are present in every school context, exploring the data trails emanating from even the most inconsequential digital encounter. Such devices also offer a counter-methodology to the concerned raised earlier regarding the surveillance of students within schools. Digital sociology reminds us that researching the digital in schools does not *have* to be a sterile exercise in "assassinating" the life out of social contexts.

Conclusion

We hope that this brief overview provides some hope and inspiration for further refinements of these ideas and approaches. Digital sociology clearly lends a renewed vigor to thinking about how best to engage with schools and the digital – offering researchers a wealth of critical perspectives, probing questions, and eclectic methods of inquiry. We are confident that digital sociology can form the basis for insightful, intelligent, and suitably inventive research and writing around the topic of schools and technology. Digital sociology certainly challenges us to broaden our attentiveness to the political, moral, and aesthetic conditions of schools and technology. Digital sociology also reminds us that pursuing academic work in this manner requires an imaginative bent, that is, a creativity, reflexivity, craftiness, awareness, and mindfulness that is often lacking from education research, that we need to engage fully with all aspects of the digital both as a research topic *and* as a research resource.

Much of what has been suggested in this chapter relates to a borrowing of concepts, methods, and sensibilities from other areas of digital sociology – not least work on divisions of labor, inequalities, critical data studies, surveillance, and governance. Perhaps most cognate to the school-specific issues outlined in this chapter is the notably larger literature on digital technology and higher education. Indeed, academic writers and researchers have proven much more keen to a sociological gaze towards the digitizations of university and college settings. It is telling, for example, that our chapter in *Digital sociologies* sits alongside four chapters on the digital sociologies of higher education. These cover topics as diverse as the datafication of universities (see Chapter 11, this volume); digitized institutional assumptions of race (Chapter 15); and the entwinement of social media platforms with the cultural complexities of student life (Chapter 16). Similarly all three editors of *Digital sociologies* have written critically on various problematic aspects of digital higher education (McMillan Cottom, 2016; Daniels and Feagin, 2011; Gregory, 2013).

Such work has some resonance with studies of compulsory schooling in the digital age, not least with regard to common concerns over the neoliberal rationalization of educational process and practice; corporate reforms of public education; and the changing nature of academic labor. Yet schools are distinct from higher education in a number of important ways – particularly in terms of compulsion and control; the mandated nature of participation and presence; and the structured nature of school knowledge, communication, and subjectification. While schools are not *wholly* distinct from post-compulsory education institutions, they certainly require separate sociological scrutiny and sense-making. While it might well be easier for digital sociologists to write, research, and reflect on the educational settings that they are most familiar with, widening these concerns to compulsory schools (the only sector of education that touches the lives of the majority of the world's population) is surely necessary for the mainstreaming of digital sociology within the social sciences.

In this spirit, then, it is important to remember that digital sociology is an ideal means of offering insights into *thinking otherwise* about schools in the digital age. Lest we have given the impression, digital sociology is certainly not an exercise in defeatism. On the contrary, foundational to any sociological study should be a "yearning for further improvement" (Bauman, 2014: 26). Sociological investigations of the school therefore need to be directed toward the residual hope of change. Given the state of flux of many aspects of contemporary schools and schooling, the need for critical research to involve itself in the question of "where do we go from here?" is essential. There is little value in *only* pointing out that things are clearly not as good as they should be. A digital sociology of school is not an exercise in defending the *status quo* or denying the need for change. Of course, few sociologists would deny that schools as they currently stand are sites for numerous injustices and replicators of numerous inequalities. Yet this is no reason to give up on the idea of schools altogether, or to dismiss them as broken, anachronistic places that require complete replacement. Instead, digital sociology offers a powerful means to work with schools rather than work against them – echoing bell hooks' (1994: 207) exhortation that "the classroom, with all its limitations, remains a location of possibility."

Thus, alongside documenting the patterns of power, politics, inequality, and injustice implicated in the use of digital technologies, any digital sociology of school should also be concerned with constructing *alternative* trajectories. If we are at odds with the conditions to be found in the contemporary "digital school," what alternatives might there be? How, then, could digital technologies be used to *counter* rather than compound dominant cultures of inequality, competitive individualism, performativity, and/or exploitation? What would meaningful, respectful, and/or pleasurable forms of digital schooling look like? What forms of digital tools, techniques, and practices would be required to possibly empower otherwise sub-ordinated groups? These are all questions that educators and education researchers need to consider as the digitization of schools and schooling continues to gather momentum.

Above all, digital sociology reminds us that the critical study of schools and technology requires new ideas, new sensibilities, and new techniques. In a practical sense these are most likely to be led by the introduction of new conferences and publication outlets, as well as a renewal of research training within educational research. Yet it is important to recognize that a digital sociology of school is not simply a summation of [Digital + Sociology of Education]. Instead, this needs to be *more* than the sum of its parts. In short, a digital sociology of school must be entered into as a new set of practices, perspectives, and preoccupations. As Alexander Galloway has observed of "new" media studies in general....

> [We need] to cease adding 'new media' to existing things. Media are transformative. They affect conditions of possibility in general. Mediation does not merely add something to the existing list of topics that scholars study. *It changes the practice of study itself.* (Galloway et al, 2014: 1; original emphasis)

This chapter has *not* described approaches, questions, and methods that can be engaged with simply by "doing the same old thing" that the sociology of school has always done. On the contrary, our call to arms for a socially aware, politically conscious, theoretically driven digital sociology of school challenges sociologists to think carefully about what it is they are doing when researching the digital. Moreover, it challenges us to strive to be imaginative in our thinking. In all these ways, then, there is much to be gained from bringing digital sociology to bear on the academic study of schools. As such, it is vital to keep these conservations going.

Acknowledgements
This chapter arises from a research project funded by the Australian Research Council (award number DP140101258).

Note
1   In making these arguments we are well aware that we are discussing the concept of "school" from the privileged position of (over)developed countries such as the US and Australia. At a rudimentary level, it is important to remember that well over 50 million children are still denied the right to basic primary education and therefore classed as "out of school." Concurrently, it is important to remember that around half the world's population has no direct experience of using "the internet" at all. Issues of unequal access to schooling *and* digital technology remain major concerns around the world.

References

Back, L. (2012) "Live sociology: social research and its futures." In L. Back and N. Purwar (eds) *Live methods* (pp 18–39). London, UK: Wiley-Blackwell.

Bauman, Z. (2014) What use is sociology? [interviews with M. Jacobsen and K. Tester]. Cambridge, UK: Polity Press.

Bowles, S. and H. Gintis (1976) Schooling in capitalist America: Educational reform and the contradictions of economic life. New York: Routledge.

Daniels, J. and J. Feagin (2011) "The (coming) social media revolution in the academy." *Fast Capitalism* 8, 2 (www.uta.edu/huma/agger/fastcapitalism/8_2/Daniels8_2.html).

Dean, J. (2014) "Big data: Accumulation and enclosure" (www.academia.edu/7125387/Big_data_accumulation_and_enclosure).

Dreyfus, H. and P. Rabinow (1982) *Michel Foucault: Beyond structuralism and hermeneutics*. Brighton, UK: Harvester.

Galloway, A., E. Thacker, and M. Wark (2014) *Excommunication: Three inquiries in media and mediation*. Chicago, IL: Chicago University Press.

Geiger, S. and D. Ribes (2011) "Trace ethnography: following coordination through documentary practices." *Proceedings of the 44th Annual Hawaii International Conference on Systems Science* (www.stuartgeiger.com/trace-ethnography-hicss-geiger-ribes.pdf).

Gregory, K. (2013) "The teaching of labor and the labor of teaching: reflections on publicness and professionalism." *The Journal of Interactive Technology & Pedagogy* 3, November 12 (http://jitp.commons.gc.cuny.edu/the-teaching-of-labor-and-the-labor-of-teaching-reflections-on-publicness-and-professionalism/).

Hall, G. (2008) *Digitize this book!* Minneapolis, MN: University of Minnesota Press.

Hogan, A., S. Sellar, and R. Lingard (2016) "Commercialising comparison: Pearson puts the TLC in soft capitalism." *Journal of Education Policy* 31 (3), 243–58.

hooks, b. (1994) *Teaching to transgress*. New York: Routledge.

Kitchin, R. (2014) *The data revolution*. London: Routledge.

Lingard, R., S. Sellar, and G. Savage (2014) "Re-articulating social justice as equity in schooling policy." *British Journal of Sociology of Education* 35, 5, 710–30.

Lupton, D. (2015) "Data assemblages, sentient schools and digitised health and physical education." *Sport, Education and Society* 20, 1, 122–32.

Manovich, L. (2013) *Software takes command*. London, UK: Bloomsbury.

Mattern, S. (2013) "Methodolatry and the art of measure." *Design Observer: Places, 5* (https://placesjournal.org/article/methodolatry-and-the-art-of-measure/).

McMillan Cottom, T. (2016) *Lower ed: How for-profit colleges deepen inequality in America*. New York: New Press.

Michael, M. (2012) "Toward an idiotic methodology: de-signing the object of sociology." *Sociological Review* 60, s1, 166–83.

Mills, C. Wright (1959) *The sociological imagination*. Oxford: Oxford University Press [new edition 2000].

Picciano, A. and J. Spring (2013) *The great American education-industrial complex: Ideology, technology and profit*. New York: Routledge.

Pink, S. (2009) *Doing sensory ethnography*. London, UK: Sage.

Pink, S., H. Horst, J. Postill, L. Hiorth, T. Lewis, and J. Tacchi (2015) *Digital ethnography principles and practice*. Thousand Oaks, CA: Sage.

Selwyn, N. (2015) "Data entry: towards the critical study of digital data and education." *Learning Media & Technology* 40, 1, 64–82.

Stodden, V. (2014) "Enabling reproducibility in big data research." In J. Lane, V. Stodden, S. Bender, and H. Nissenbaum (eds) *Privacy, big data, and the public good* (pp 112–31). Cambridge: Cambridge University Press.

Watters, A. (2015) *The monsters of education technology*, http://monsters.hackeducation.com/ [self-published].

Wellington, B. (2015) "Safe hallways, successful tests." *I Quant NY*, March 22 (http://iquantny.tumblr.com).

Wilkie, A., M. Michael, and M. Plummer-Fernandez (2015) "Speculative method and Twitter: Bots, energy and three conceptual characters." *The Sociological Review* 63, 79–101.

Williamson, B. (2016) "Digital education governance: data visualization, predictive analytics, and 'real-time' policy instruments." *Journal of Education Policy* 31 (2), 123–41.

11

Representing "inforgs" in data-driven decisions

Jeffrey Alan Johnson

Introduction

Data, it seems, is to be the savior of the 21st century. Whether in business, government, or higher education, pressures toward "data-driven" or "evidence-based" decisions are ubiquitous, promising more insight, more efficiency, and better outcomes than was previously possible. Through expansive use of data (often, as below, conflated with open data, network architectures, and analytical processes),

> [G]overnments now have the opportunity to better understand the needs of their citizens and citizens may participate more fully in their government. Information becomes more valuable as it is shared, less valuable as it is hoarded. Open data promotes increased civil discourse, improved public welfare, and a more efficient use of public resources. (Open Government Working Group, 2007)

Implicit in this view, however, is a scientifically realist view of data: data can save us because it is an objective representation of observed reality that can thus transcend politics to bring organizations to the correct decision.

But if this realist view of data is incorrect, the edifice that legitimizes data becomes far less stable. Creating data requires some process that narrows the many possible representations of a given state of the world to a single data state. This process is carried out within translation regimes: systems of technical rules and social practices that establish a one-to-one correspondence between a given state of the world and a data state. The technical structures of a relational database, such as tables, functions, business rules, and queries, translate states of the world into data states based on standards established by social structures such as cultures, states, and organizations. These regimes also translate the entities about which data is collected into "inforgs," entities that exist solely as bundles of information.

Within many of the structures that guide data use and data-driven decision-making inforgs behave quite differently than people, fundamentally changing the power dynamics of representation in the decision process. In this chapter I explore two structures related to representation. First, inforgs significantly complicate the way that data-driven decision processes can be considered representative of students. While a less data-driven process emphasizes a trustee model of representation in which the decision-maker is seen as acting in the best interests of the student, a data-driven process that translates students as inforgs requires decision-makers to create constructs that ultimately represent themselves rather than students. Standard approaches to protecting student privacy are also considerably more problematic in translated data processes. Approaches to privacy typically rely on restricting the flow of information. A traditional approach views this as protection of an individual. But when the individuals exist solely as inforgs, as in a data-driven decision process, restrictions on the flow of information destroys or at least degrades the inforg itself, excluding the associated person from the process. I conclude by suggesting that mitigating practices, critical institutional research, and a justice-centered approach to information can help manage these challenges.

Data systems in higher education: a reference case

The objective of this chapter is to establish a theoretical framework for understanding the structural dimensions of a normative question, seeing data as a type of social artifact that influences the achievement of social justice. To provide an empirical referent for theorizing the nature of inforgs in translation regimes, I examine the data systems and practices commonly used by institutional research offices in US higher education, specifically those in place at Utah Valley University (UVU) while I worked as a senior research analyst in its Institutional Research & Information Office from 2009 to 2013.[1] This is supplemented by discursive analysis of the Structured Query Language (SQL) implementing the data systems and the data standards established by the federal Integrated Post-secondary Education Data System (IPEDS) and the Utah System of Higher Education (USHE) reporting processes, and occasionally by analysis of online interviews with eight UVU students regarding their own perceptions of their social identities conducted as a pilot project for a larger study.

Institutional research offices in US universities typically have responsibility for two areas: meeting mandatory government reporting requirements such as completing IPEDS surveys or reporting to regulatory agencies at the state level; and extracting, transforming, and analyzing data in institutional data systems to support data–driven decision-making throughout the university. The latter responsibility is the focus of this analysis. Typical projects might include developing data dashboards to display and analyze retention and graduation rates for student affairs programs, collecting and reporting quantitative data used to review academic programs or to meet accreditation requirements for program assessment, developing data architecture for federal and state reporting data, or implementing new data systems. Much of this work is carried out in conjunction with other campus offices, and both the internal structure of institutional research and its relations with other offices varies widely across universities.

Nonetheless, UVU's data systems are sufficiently common to be considered representative. UVU's data backbone is the Ellucian Banner relational database running on an Oracle 10g database server.[2] Banner consists of a normalized set of several thousand data tables managing student and administrative data and optimized for Online Transactional Processing (OLTP), locally referred to as "Prod" (a reference to it as the production database). The bulk of institutional data analysis is performed using the Banner Operational Data Store (ODS), which consists of a denormalized set of fewer but much larger tables optimized for Online Analytical Processing (OLAP). The data contained in the ODS is either identical to or derived from that in Prod. Both databases are extensively customized for UVU. Prod also connects to several other data systems, including the Wolverine Track advising information system, Ellucian Student Success CRM, and the Canvas learning management system.

Most government reporting comes from three customized relational tables. One table, referred to locally as STUDENT,[3] contains information that is constant about individual students across courses within a term such as demographics, contact information, or overall academic characteristics. The second table, COURSE, contains information that is constant across all students in a section for a term. The final table, STUDENT_COURSE, contains information specific to a student within a specific course such as course grade or (since some courses can award variable credit) credits attempted. Using appropriate joins, STUDENT, COURSE, and STUDENT_COURSE can provide most of the information that the institution would need to understand its students and academic offerings. For example, joining STUDENT and STUDENT_COURSE would allow the institution to determine the distribution of courses taken by major and gender. STUDENT_COURSE would identify the courses taken by each student; STUDENT would provide the major and gender information. Each table is a "live" data table, showing data as it exists currently for all terms (including any transactions that affect data for a term after the term has ended, such as retroactive withdrawals from courses). A set of "freeze tables" contains data snapshots allowing time-series analysis throughout a term, and include freezes for the official census and end-of-term reporting dates.

These frozen data from the official reporting dates is used principally for state and federal government reporting. But there is a strong expectation that data reported by the institution for non-government purposes, including that used to make and justify decisions, will be consistent with the government reporting data. For example, between 2010 and 2012, UVU created a web-based data dashboard to provide more specific information on retention and graduation rates than was reported to IPEDS. It nonetheless relied on IPEDS definitions of retention and graduation rates, demographic categories, and reporting cohorts. The cohort definition is especially important, as the IPEDS cohort includes only first-time, full-time, degree-seeking undergraduates entering in the fall, who made up only 32 percent of new UVU students in the 2012–13 academic year. Because of the expectation that the data used locally for decision-making will be consistent with government reporting data, the translation regime (defined below) in place at UVU is defined disproportionately by the rules that govern the three customized government reporting tables.

Inforgs in data-driven decision processes

In recent decades, higher education in the US has seen dramatically increasing corporatization, bureaucratization, and rationalization derived from the for-profit sector but increasingly common in the public and private non-profit sectors as well. A central feature of this has been the emergence of accountability regimes, in which:

> ... a politics of surveillance, control, and market management disguise[es] itself as the value-neutral and scientific administration of individuals and organizations (Tuchman, 2009). Related to strategic planning, this accountability regime supposedly minimizes risks for an organization (or corporation) by imposing rules about how work will be done and evaluated. (McMillan Cottom and Tuchman, 2015: 8)

The scope of such regimes goes far beyond traditional notions of legal and financial risk, reaching into the realm of operational control through data-driven decision-making processes. Accrediting bodies demand that mission fulfillment and student learning be demonstrated through "meaningful, assessable, and verifiable data – quantitative and/or qualitative, as appropriate to its indicators of achievement" (Northwest Commission on Colleges and Universities, 2010: 4.A.1) and that institutions practice "regular, systematic, participatory, self-reflective, and evidence-based assessment of its accomplishments" (Northwest Commission on Colleges and Universities, 2010: 5.A.1). The results of these data-driven analyses are "used for improvement by informing planning, decision making, and allocation of resources and capacity" (Northwest Commission on Colleges and Universities, 2010: 4.B.1). Institutions that fail to use appropriate data-driven processes to evaluate mission fulfillment and student learning risk punitive actions by accreditors. For example, in June 2013 the Middle States Commission on Higher Education, the largest of the regional accrediting bodies in the US higher education system, issued warnings that the accreditation of 10 schools was in jeopardy; nine of these institutions had failed to demonstrate compliance with standards relating to planning, effectiveness, and learning assessment (Middle States Commission on Higher Education, 2014).

The reliance on data in assessment, evaluation, and planning – arguably the most important decision processes in a university – is a paradigmatic case of the broader model of data-driven decision-making. Mandated at the primary and secondary levels in the US by the now superseded No Child Left Behind Act of 2001, data-driven decision-making compels institutions to use data "to stimulate and inform continuous improvement, providing a foundation for educators to examine multiple sources of data and align appropriate instructional strategies with the needs of individual students" (Mandinach, 2012: 72). The model is based on business management theories (especially those derived from manufacturing), including Total Quality Management and Continuous Improvement. The model organizes and interprets multiple types of data into information that is meaningful to the users. This then becomes actionable knowledge when users evaluate and synthesize the available information, ultimately using the information to either inform discussion or to choose actions. This process is cyclical and takes place within a range of varying organizational contexts (Marsh et al, 2006). The result is held to be a more rigorous and informed decision process that allows educators to teach more effectively and administrators to operate more efficiently and reliably (Mandinach, 2012).

Unexamined in this model is the nature of the data that is driving decision-making. Data is, from the perspective of data-driven decisions, seen as an objective representation of a real world. This realist view is fundamentally flawed, however. A growing body of work in critical data studies suggests that data is inherently constructed and thus subjective. Much of this work builds on arguments about the inherent value-ladenness of technology generally, such as Feenberg's (1991) arguments that the challenges of technology are a consequence of the values embedded in technologies, Kranzberg's (1986) famed formulation that "Technology is neither good nor bad; nor is it neutral," and Winner's (1980) assertion that technological facts can have political qualities. To speak only of the recent highlights of the peer-reviewed work in a literature growing faster than it can be published, let alone consumed:

algorithms used in many big data applications show that algorithms' content reflects a political economy dominated by large corporate interests (Pasquale, 2015) and the spaces of contestation in which they operate (Crawford, 2015). The problems, knowledge, and actors algorithmic actions include are mutually constitutive rather than independent, as the realist view of data would suggest (Introna, 2015). The "city of visualized facts" that comes from such a realist and instrumental view of data obscures the assemblages that constitute metrics, benchmarks, and dashboards (Kitchin et al, 2015).

A common thread in these critical perspectives is the rejection of a realist or positivist view of data in favor of constructive views. Two key elements are posited as the basis for alternatives. First, data is seen as inherently linked to practices beyond the data structures. The constitution of data is best understood, rather than from a realist perspective, as what Lupton (Chapter 21, this volume) calls digital data assemblages, "configurations of discourse, practices, data, human users and technologies" that are simultaneously material and ephemera. These structures are necessary for the interpretation of data. Data is unique to bureaucratic forms of government, rooted in the need to make its subjects legible to the apparatus of authority by transforming an underdetermined reality into standardized, aggregatable, static facts that are capable of consistent documentation (Scott, 1998: 80–1). This is, of course, a central requirement of the processes of rationalization that McMillan Cottom and Tuchman described above, and especially of accountability regimes. In order to understand what a data point means it must be understood as a representation of something within a nexus of problems, models, and interventions rather than as an abstracted object.

The process of making reality legible reflects a fundamental problem: the relationship between that which is to be represented and the data state ultimately representing it is one-to-many; therefore data systems must select a single data state from among the many possible in order to produce legible knowledge. Hence the second key element: that data is itself constructed by social processes. I have elsewhere (Johnson, 2015) called this process the *translation regime*, which one might define as the set of implicit or explicit principles, norms, rules, and decision-making procedures through which single, commensurable data states are selected to represent states of the world,[4] that provides an external source of stability for the data system and allows it to bring legibility to the represented conditions (Mitev, 2005). One could look to gender as a paradigmatic case of translation, with myriad possible gender expressions reduced to a small number of values, most commonly "male" or "female," by data standards and validation tables that reflect social norms, in particular those at work in the accountability regime of the institution.

From this perspective, data-driven decision-making takes place within an abstracted model world that resembles any reality external to it in one of many possible ways selected by the translation regime. In a data table, data exists in columns where the data has a common framework, but it also exists in rows that relate data points in different columns to each other through association with some sort of entity: data is information about some things, students and courses in the case of UVU's core institutional research data systems. These things in the database can have no more objective existence than the characteristics that the database attributes to them. The translation regime does not simply translate the characteristics of objectively existing entities into the columns of a database; those entities that make up the rows are also translations, whose existence is defined strictly by the information with which they can be associated.

These data entities are best described as what philosopher of information Luciano Floridi terms "inforgs":

> In many respects we are not stand-alone entities but rather interconnected informational organisms or *inforgs, sharing with biological agents and engineered artefacts a global environment ultimately made of information, the infosphere. This is the informational environment constituted by all informational processes, services, and entities thus including informational agents as well as their properties, interactions, and mutual relations.* (Floridi, 2010: 9; original emphasis)

An inforg is characterized as an entity that is de-physicalized, typified (represented as an instance of a class of identical objects), perfectly clonable, and existing only through its interactions with other inforgs. While the extent to which this ontology, which Floridi calls "informational structural realism," is an adequate description of being more broadly remains controversial, the sense of inforgs inhabiting an infosphere captures well the ontology of the model world in which a data-driven decision process takes place. In such a model world, data consists of signifiers of states that attach to inforgs. In a star schema, for instance, data is divided into fact tables that describe entities and dimension tables that describe conditions that those entities can take on. Each row in the fact table represents one entity, named by the data table's primary key, and that entity has no characteristics other than the facts stored in the row, that can be joined to the row, or that are stored in the related dimension tables. These inforgs are thus the only kind of entity that can exist within a data-driven decision process.

Informational representation

Decisions in higher education are political decisions in the most basic sense: they are decisions made to govern a collective entity, in this case a postsecondary educational institution. As such, those that are affected by this decision, as in all political decisions, have a legitimate claim that they ought to have meaningful input into it in some fashion. This is the origin of the problem of representation, a problem not challenged by the fact that the decision takes place in a bureaucratic rather than legislative institution. Presumably, then, decision-makers in higher education intend for their decisions to represent, in some form and among other considerations, the students about whom they are making decisions.

One might analyze different modes of representation along two dimensions. The first concerns the level of participation. Participatory models involve all those who have a claim to input in the process of making the decision; representative models vest that power in a relatively small group of individuals who act for the group as a whole. A second dimension considers the relationship between the decision-makers and the group. Promissory models view the decision-maker as an agent who acts on behalf of those they represent as principals, while autonomous models allow the decision-makers the freedom to act on their own. The most common models fall into either the autonomous/participatory or the promissory/representative quadrants. Direct democracy, in which all members of the polity participate directly in policy-making, is the standard case of the former; the trustee-delegate dichotomy, in which representatives act respectively in the best interests of the represented or as the represented themselves would, is the basis of the latter.

This is not to say that the only coherent models of representation fit into one of these two quadrants. Frameworks of representation in the two other quadrants are less commonly observed but nonetheless important. In descriptive representation, representatives act without any moral obligation toward the positions of the represented but, "in their own backgrounds mirror some of the more frequent experiences and outward manifestations of belonging to the group" (Mansbridge, 1999: 628). This correspondence of backgrounds acts as a mechanism to ensure correspondence between the interests of the representative and the represented so that a representative acting in their own self-interest is coincidentally acting in that of the represented as well, rather than acting out of an obligation to do so. Descriptive representation is an important case of representation that is both autonomous and representative, used especially to study representation in bureaucracies (see, for example, Wilkins and Keiser, 2004). Jean-Jacques Rousseau's *On the social contract* proposes a system in which citizens participate directly in government but represent not their particular individual wills but the "will that one has as a citizen," which he terms "the general will," thus directly participating in government but as an agent of the collective body of citizens that serves as principal. However, neither of these models is of practical value in higher education decision processes. In the case of descriptive representation, decisions are made by actors who cannot resemble the key characteristic of those they might be taken to represent: administrators are not students. Concepts related to the general will have never been shown to be sufficiently clear in any applied context to be of use in making a specific decision. Analysis of representation will thus focus on the direct and promissory models of representation.

In a personalized decision-making context, which we might define in contrast to a data-driven process as one in which either single or multiple decision-makers use their personal judgment to make what they consider the best decision given the available information under some degree of uncertainty, higher education tends toward a trusteeship model of representation. Even at the smallest of institutions, direct participation in all decisions is impractical because of the number of students and of decisions involved in governing the institution. But there is also a strong strain of paternalism in decision-making at colleges and universities. Students, it is frequently held, cannot be counted on to do what is best for them. Consider, for instance, Austin Peay State University's use of predictive analytics in student advising:

> [Provost Tristan] Denley points to a spate of recent books by behavioral economists, all with a common theme: When presented with many options and little information, people find it difficult to make wise choices. The same goes for college students trying to construct a schedule, he says. They know they must take a social-science class, but they don't know the implications of taking political science versus psychology versus economics. They choose on the basis of course descriptions or to avoid having to wake up for an 8 am class on Monday. Every year, students in Tennessee lose their state scholarships because they fall a hair short of the GPA cutoff, Mr Denley says, a financial swing that 'massively changes their likelihood of graduating'. (Parry, 2012)

Such students would, if they chose themselves, make choices that run counter to their true interests (presumably, in receiving a generic college degree at minimum cost); decision-makers must therefore choose not what the students would choose but what they should choose. Such a model of representation is defensible only to the extent that the decision-makers do, in fact, have an adequate view of that interest.

This model of representation breaks down when students are translated into inforgs. Initially, one is tempted to see the translation of students (or of anyone with a claim to voice in a political process) as a gain for direct participation. The promissory models both break down when applied to inforgs. The trustee and delegate approaches both require a unifying concept that acts as the wholeness of the represented (interest or will, respectively) that guides how the agent acts on behalf of the principal, one that is lacking when the principal is no more than a bundle of information: which piece of information defines that unifying concept? But while a personalized process of direct participation requires some complex structure that allows universal participation in the process of developing policy alternatives, manages extensive deliberation among those alternatives, and aggregates preferences into a decision, a data-driven process can bring the participants in as inforgs and then aggregate their informational characteristics. The capacity for participation in data-driven decision-making is apparently limited only by the power to collect and process the information that constitutes the inforgs.

Figure 11.1: Representation of students in personal decision processes

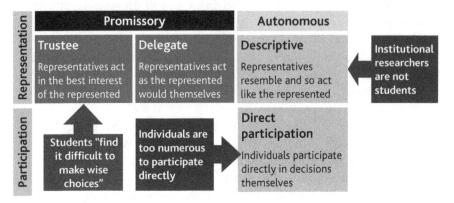

This understanding of representation assumes that inforgs have an objective or realist ontological status, existing in their own right rather than being constituted by actors outside of themselves: the data row represents a physically existing student as they are in the "real" world rather than existing as an inforg that has been created by someone other than the represented. The analysis of the data structures above shows that this is not the case. Inforgs are themselves social constructs, and both their existence and their characteristics reflect the same social pressures and structures that data fields do. As such, the idea that inforgs are capable of being independently represented in a data-driven decision process is fundamentally unsound; what is represented is the constructive activity of those creating the inforgs. There is the appearance of direct participation, although the participants are not representations of students but actants created through the translation regime. The construction of those actors defines the information that constitutes them, supplying the unifying concept of a promissory-representative model independently of the students the inforgs claim to correspond. What is represented is as much the constructors' understanding of students that is built into the data driving the decision process.

Data-driven decision processes thus present a fundamental contradiction. While they are instituted as objective processes, it is clear that no process of representing students can take place within them without the process of data creation also being a process of imposing external values and assumptions. The inforgs are created by those who create the data system, and decisions about them can only be made if decision-makers supply their own concepts of interests of will to guide the application of promissory models of representation. This is, to be sure, true of personal decision models as well, but in those models there is a clear connection to individuals against which those assumptions can be checked. In a data-driven model there is nothing to check against beyond the data; the students exist solely as data. The objectivity of the process, its supposed virtue, is thus a fiction needed to make the process work.

Figure 11.2: Representation of inforgs in data-driven decision processes

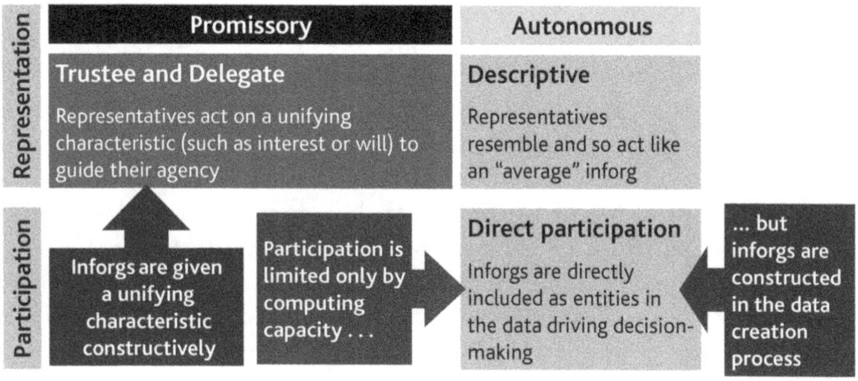

Representation	Promissory	Autonomous
	Trustee and Delegate Representatives act on a unifying characteristic (such as interest or will) to guide their agency	**Descriptive** Representatives resemble and so act like an "average" inforg

Participation	Inforgs are given a unifying characteristic constructively	Participation is limited only by computing capacity ...	**Direct participation** Inforgs are directly included as entities in the data driving decision-making	... but inforgs are constructed in the data creation process

Destructive privacy among inforgs

Representing inforgs becomes more seriously compromised when considered in relation to information privacy. In the US, students are protected first and foremost by federal laws including but not limited to the Federal Education Rights and Privacy Act (FERPA), but also by a range of state laws, institutional policies, and data handling standards. All of this is meant to ensure that students are able to maintain a sphere of personal identity and activity safe from intrusion by others, including others' knowledge about the student. Most commonly this is protected by the twin principles of consent and anonymity: personal information may only be used or transferred with the consent of the subject; all other information must be stripped of personally identifying characteristics before use or transfer (van Wel and Royakkers, 2004). Certainly these opt-in or opt-out procedures are the bedrock of most institutions' privacy policies, with the latter likely far more common than the former.

Growing pressures on personal privacy have given rise to more complex perspectives on privacy. It is increasingly common to interpret privacy as a property right in information about one's self. Subjects hold initial ownership rights in information about them, and can exchange that information contractually in information markets, receiving appropriate compensation – or they can refuse to permit the use of such information in the absence of sufficient compensation to encourage the transaction (Solove, 2004: 76–81). This approach makes sense, for example, of the willingness of so many to give access to their email to Google: in exchange for an outstanding product, consumers are willing to allow Google to use the information captured to generate profit for itself. Alternatively, Helen Nissenbaum (2010) argues for a reliance on social context to protect privacy. As technosocial systems, the context of information flows is as much a defining feature of data exchange and use as the content of that information flow. The combination of situation, actors, information attributes, and practices of transmission for accepted information exchanges constitute an existing norm of practice that may be violated in the case of new uses of information, such as a data mining practice. Changes in this context that are not supported by its underlying norms are violations of the contextual integrity of the information flows, and in the absence of separate justification violate one's privacy rights. More recently, the European Court of Justice has embraced a "right to be forgotten" under which individuals are entitled to have information about them essentially destroyed, in the instant case by having Google remove links to information about them from search results (Case C-131/12 *Google Spain SL vs AEPD [2014]*).

The common thread of each of these approaches to privacy is that they aim to restrict flows of information across parties, transactions, or both. This restriction is frequently considered the essence of data privacy. The centrality of collection (the flow of information from a subject to a data system) and dissemination (the flow of information across data systems or from a data system to subjects) in common definitions of information privacy makes restrictions on flow the sine qua non of data privacy. Such a model of privacy is at least plausibly appropriate for the governance of subjects who are persons; preventing the transfer of information will, presumably, prevent those receiving information from using it to do harm to the subjects of that information. This meets the fundamental criteria of a wide range of ethical frameworks, such as Mill's harm principle, which permits the infringement of one's liberty in order to prevent harm to others, or the more recent proposal of a Hippocratic Oath making "do no harm" the first principle in the use of information and communication technology for development (Mill, 2011: 17; Rodrik, 2012).

Restricting the flow of information fundamentally fails, however, when the subjects are constructive inforgs. The flow of information is what translates subjects (in this case, students) into inforgs in the first place. To restrict that flow is to change the inforg itself. Such restrictions might, for instance, limit the data known about an inforg in absolute terms as privacy restrictions prevent the transfer of certain types of information (when, for example, the subject opts out of sharing of internet use information). Or it might do so in relative terms as it prevents the transfer of information from one source (when the subject installs a privacy plug-in in Chrome) but allows that same transfer from another source (when the subject doesn't bother reading the 31-page terms and conditions for the latest iOS update). Since an inforg is nothing more than a typified and clonable bundle of information, a difference in the information constituting the inforg violates the principles of typification (the difference resulting in inforgs that are instances of two different types) and clonability (the difference distinguishing two instances as different rather than as clones), and is thus the creation of a different inforg.

This becomes even more problematic when a subject opts out of a data system altogether. For a constructive inforg, a complete data opt-out is not simply a withholding of information; it is a complete destruction of itself as an inforg. Prohibition of data flows prevent the inforg from being constructed in the first place. It is perhaps only slightly overdramatic to characterize complete restriction of the flow of data as information suicide for a constructive inforg, as the inforg that protects its privacy ceases to exist in the model world of the data-driven decision process. The physical entity corresponding to the inforg (in this case, the actual student) is at best reduced to context – that there are some students who are excluded by privacy protections. But context, again, exists only in relation to data, which is to say, in relation to inforgs. Students who opt to protect their privacy thus exist only as others to the inforgs' selves, defined not individually as entities in themselves, but collectively as a typified characteristic of the inforgs (that is, as a group of identical entities of which the inforgs are not members). Reduced to context that is meaningful only in relation to entities that have corresponding inforgs, those students cease to exist analytically, and instead are subsumed as information into inforgs corresponding to other students.

That further complicates the problem of representation as well. Partial restrictions change how subjects are represented; complete prohibitions exclude subjects from being represented entirely. Students are faced with a difficult choice: they can be represented (with varying levels of adequacy given the process of constructing inforgs) in the data-driven decision processes that run the institution that shapes a significant part of their lives both now and long into the future, or they can choose to minimize the extent to which that institution is allowed into the student's sphere of private activity and identity. To exactly the extent that students choose one good, they undermine the other. In personalized decision processes, the unifying concepts of principal-agent representation can moderate this, with decision-makers taking into account expressions of students' best interests and wills regardless of – and perhaps taking into consideration – the privacy status of individual students, as these are not data-dependent. In data-driven decision processes, however, with those unifying concepts absent and decisions formally constrained by the available data, representation and privacy are fundamentally irreconcilable.

Conclusion: what is to be done?

Clearly data-driven decision-making becomes much more problematic when we recognize that data is made, not collected. As decision-making increasingly takes place within model worlds created by the process of collecting, managing, and analyzing data, it increasingly transforms people into inforgs, and marginalizes considerations not rooted in data as mere context.[5] Data-driven decision-making is part of a larger ethos, one connecting managerialism, technocratic government, and neoliberal politics, that increasingly pervades higher education. The problems of representation and privacy, and especially the tension between the two, stem from the very core of this ethos.

There are thus no clear or easy solutions to these problems. Immediately, one might hope that awareness of the problem might promote decision-makers to take mitigating steps. Institutions might take efforts to broadly discuss findings before making final decisions based on them in order to identify the ways in which a particular data-driven process has not adequately represented students. Institutional researchers might also analyze generally the privacy decisions of students to better understand who is exercising their privacy options, what concerns drive those students, and what effects those privacy elections are likely to have on data once it becomes part of a data-driven decision process. Steps like this will not solve the problems, but they can at the least create additional context that can moderate the effects of representing students as inforgs rather than people.

An emerging agenda exploring "critical institutional research" might also be of use here. Such an agenda aims to explore institutional research from perspectives of critical thought about current ideas and practice, critical methods that challenge the dominance of positivist or behavioralist research, and critical theories that take seriously diverse perspectives and the places of race, class, gender, sexuality, and especially the intersections of these in institutional research. This analysis illustrates the value of critical thought about institutional research; critical methods might challenge the dominance of data-driven decision-making with methods that emphasize synthesis of research subjects rather than analytically fragmenting them into data bits, while critical theories would challenge the claims to objectivity of data and explore connections between data-driven processes and neoliberal political and economic ideology. Together, these idea would enable institutional researchers to consider our practices from the perspective philosopher Iris Marion Young takes on critical politics: rather than being the natural or obvious way of doing things, our practice "does not have to be this way, it could be otherwise" (Young, 1990: 6).

But ultimately the clear failure of existing notions of representation and privacy suggest that they might be better subsumed into a conception of information justice that broadens these specific concerns into a large framework that understands information as a social structure and evaluates it from the perspective of how it contributes to the good of individuals, groups, and society more broadly. Such a perspective would clearly challenge the authoritative claims of data-driven decision models, showing that these decisions are inherently political acts and thus that the social structure of information is itself of interest to both decision-makers and the subjects of those decisions. While the details of such a theory are quite far from developed, it would certainly encourage more inclusive decision practices, and consider both the ends for which information is to be used and the means by which information is analyzed as ethical questions in themselves. A more explicitly just framework for information might even go further to create an environment in which students and institutions cooperate in the pursuit of justice rather than conflict over who has the right to students' information. A robust framework for information justice is the long-term solution for protecting students as inforgs.

Notes

[1] The analysis presented here is strictly my own, and should not be taken as representing in any way the policy of Utah Valley University or the views of its leadership.

[2] As a full review of database structure and operation is beyond the scope of practicality in a chapter, tedious for those already familiar with them, and redundant give the many excellent sources available, this discussion presumes a basic, non-technical understanding of databases. I have aimed to provide enough background to understand the points in my argument in ways that do not overly burden those unfamiliar with databases with technical knowledge, but are still recognizable to technical specialists. I apologize to readers of both sorts to the extent that I haven't succeeded in that.

[3] Table and field names are indicated in capital letters, with TABLE_NAMES in Roman typeface and *FIELD_NAMES* in italics. Specific table names have been replaced with generic descriptive names to maintain data security. These descriptive names often correspond with similar tables and fields included in a standard Banner installation that may exist but are generally not used at UVU. Field names have also been changed where the name in the table is sufficiently obscure to make understanding difficult for the reader.

[4] This definition follows that of Krasner (1982: 186), used to define regimes in international relations.

[5] One might argue that the portrayal of data-driven decision-making presented here is something of a straw-man argument that neglects the subtleties and importance of context in the models advocated in higher education. I would argue to the contrary that those models themselves only pay lip service to context; the more context can be used to override data and the more that conflicting data points are to be considered in the decision process, the less data-driven decision-making is distinct from personalized decision-making. If there is something distinct about data-driven decision-making it is that data must take priority over context.

References

Crawford, K. (2015) "Can an algorithm be agonistic? Ten scenes from life in calculated publics." *Science, Technology & Human Values* (http://sth.sagepub.com/cgi/doi/10.1177/0162243915589635).

Feenberg, A. (1991) *Critical theory of technology*. New York: Oxford University Press.

Floridi, L. (2010) *Information: A very short introduction*. Oxford, UK and New York: Oxford University Press.

Introna, L.D. (2015) "Algorithms, governance, and governmentality: On governing academic writing." *Science, Technology & Human Values* (http://sth.sagepub.com/cgi/doi/10.1177/0162243915587360).

Johnson, J.A. (2015) "Information systems and the translation of transgender." *TSQ: Transgender Studies Quarterly* 2 (1), 160–5.

Kitchin, R., T.P. Lauriault, and G. McArdle (2015) "Knowing and governing cities through urban indicators, city benchmarking and real-time dashboards." *Regional Studies, Regional Science* 2 (1), 6–28.

Kranzberg, M. (1986) "Technology and history: 'Kranzberg's laws.'" *Technology and Culture* 27 (3), 544.

Krasner, S.D. (1982) "Structural causes and regime consequences: Regimes as intervening variables." *International Organization* 36 (2), 185–205.

McMillan Cottom, T. and G. Tuchman (2015) "Rationalization of higher education." In R.A. Scott and S.M. Kosslyn (eds) *Emerging trends in the social and behavioral sciences: An interdisciplinary, searchable, and linkable resource* (pp 1–17). Wiley Online (http://onlinelibrary.wiley.com/book/10.1002/9781118900772)

Mandinach, E.B. (2012) "A perfect time for data use: Using data-driven decision making to inform practice." *Educational Psychologist* 47 (2), 71–85.

Mansbridge, J. (1999) "Should blacks represent blacks and women represent women? A contingent 'yes.'" *The Journal of Politics* 61 (3), 628–57.

Marsh, J.A., J.F. Pane, and L.S. Hamilton (2006) *Making sense of data-driven decision making in education: Evidence from recent RAND Research*. RAND Corporation (www.rand.org/content/dam/rand/pubs/occasional_papers/2006/RAND_OP170.pdf).

Middle States Commission on Higher Education (2014) "Summary of Commission actions on institutions" (www.msche.org/institutions_recentactions_view.asp?dteStart=4/29/2014&dteEnd=6/26/2014&idCommitteeType=0&txtMeeting=Commission).

Mill, J.S. (2011) *On liberty*. Project Gutenberg eBook. London: The Walter Scott Publishing Co, Ltd (www.gutenberg.org/files/34901/34901-h/34901-h.htm).

Mitev, N.N. (2005) "Are social constructivist approaches critical? The case of IS failure." In D. Howcroft and E.M. Trauth (eds) *Handbook of critical information systems research: Theory and application, Elgar Original Reference* (pp 70–103). Northampton, MA: Edward Elgar Publishers.

Nissenbaum, H. (2010) *Privacy in context: Technology, policy, and the integrity of social life*. Stanford, CA: Stanford Law Books.

Northwest Commission on Colleges and Universities (2010) "Accreditation standards" (www.nwccu.org/Standards%20and%20Policies/Accreditation%20Standards/Accreditation%20Standards.htm).

Open Government Working Group (2007) "Annotations to the 8 principles." *OpenGovData.org* (www.opengovdata.org/home/8principles/annotations) Retrieved March 5, 2013.

Parry, M. (2012) *College degrees, Designed by the numbers* (https://chronicle.com/article/College-Degrees-Designed-by/132945/).

Pasquale, F. (2015) *The black box society: The secret algorithms that control money and information.* Cambridge, MA: Harvard University Press.

Rodrik, D. (2012) *A Hippocratic Oath for future development policy* (www.policyinnovations.org/ideas/commentary/data/000244).

Rousseau, J.-J. (1988 [1762]) *On the social contract.* Indianapolis, IN: Hackett Pub. Co.

Scott, J.C. (1998) *Seeing like a state: How certain schemes to improve the human condition have failed.* New Haven, CT: Yale University Press.

Solove, D.J. (2004) *The digital person: Technology and privacy in the Information Age.* New York: New York University Press.

Tuchman, G. (2009) *Wannabe U: Inside the corporate university.* Chicago, IL: University of Chicago Press.

van Wel, L. and L. Royakkers (2004) "Ethical issues in web data mining." *Ethics and Information Technology* 6, 2, 129–40.

Wilkins, V.M. and L.R. Keiser (2004) "Linking passive and active representation by gender: The case of child support agencies." *Journal of Public Administration Research and Theory* 16 (1), 87–102.

Winner, L. (1980) "Do artifacts have politics?" *Daedalus* 109 (1), 121–36.

Young, I.M. (1990) *Justice and the politics of difference.* Princeton, NJ: Princeton University Press.

12

Employee monitoring in a digital context

Calle Rosengren and Mikael Ottosson

W orking life is undergoing a transformation in the sense that new digital technologies are pervasively changing the nature of labor and its organizational forms, regardless of profession, and regardless of whether those affected are qualified professionals or laborers. The framework that previously regulated the content of work, as well as when, where and how it would be conducted, is being reconsidered. One aspect of new digital technologies concerns the manner in which the work process is being monitored and controlled.

Workplace monitoring has existed for a long time in different shapes and forms. Depending on the modes of production, workplace monitoring has assumed various forms, from counting and weighing output and payment by piece rate in pre-industrial society to clocking in and punching out in industrial society (Ball, 2010; Negrey, 2012). In other words: surveillance in the workplace is not a novelty (Lyon, 2013/1994). Seen from the logic of capitalism, it is not incongruous or unreasonable to expect that employers both have rights and reason to do so. However, in today's working life, many employees use company digital equipment privately as well as professionally (Table 12.2; cf Paulsen, 2014). Partly in response to this, there is an increasing availability of relatively inexpensive and easy to use technology, such as software monitoring programs, which enable employers to expand the range and scope of their control over their employees' activities (Fairweather, 1999).

This chapter aims to highlight workplace monitoring in the digital era, which includes, for example, internet and email monitoring, location tracking, biometrics, and covert surveillance. The increase in potential methods to

181

track and monitor employee behavior poses questions that concern where the borders for personal integrity are drawn. Who has the right to personal details, and at what point? How does this monitoring affect the social relations between employer and employee in terms of control, autonomy, and trust? We argue that issues of trust and integrity in a digital context are of such importance to our society that they must be afforded a distinct place in both public awareness and in political deliberations.

Workplace surveillance in the digital era

Throughout the historical process that has led to modern working life, different technological innovations have come to affect not only what is being produced but also how. Much as the steam engine released production from natural limitations and forever changed the world of work a couple of hundred years ago, the rapid development of digital information technologies has had a tremendous impact on working life, both in terms of the products and services being produced, but also on business processes and organizational structures (Ragu-Nathan et al, 2008). Unlike the 1900s large-scale technology, digital technology has been flexible. One fundamental aspect of this new technology is that it can make employees more accessible to others and allow work to be more available to the employee. Employees can communicate with each other much more efficiently through email and the internet. Easy access to functions such as email, text, and voice messages also enable employees to continue work after leaving the workplace for the day (Porter and Kakabadse, 2006), thus challenging the traditional borders between working life and personal life. This is a development that holds much promise in terms of more interesting and challenging jobs, but there is also a potentially darker side to it.

On superficial observation, it is easy to conclude that the development in working life has moved from a situation where the employer monitored and controlled the alienated worker's every move in the dirty and noisy factory, to a knowledge economy, where the employee's need for personal growth goes hand in hand with the goals of the organization – a change that makes monitoring and surveillance obsolete, since the co-worker is expected to be driven by an inner motivation. Perhaps there is some truth to this assumption concerning some individuals and in some labor market segments. But much as the factory organization enabled certain kinds of surveillance, digital technology enables others (Lyon, 2013/1994).

When one considers digital surveillance from a historical perspective, for example, when making comparisons between digital technology and the steam engine's bearing on the evolution of work, it is easy to lapse into a techno-deterministic perspective. We run the risk of claiming that the rapid development of digital information technologies has in itself caused greater control of the labor force. We also run the risk of ignoring the fact that various technological systems, the means of production, various technical applications, and so on, only create the conditions for certain behaviors, while it is the surrounding social norms that influence how this technology is used (Lyon, 2013/1994). Digital technology opens up for certain kinds of monitoring and surveillance, for example, examining the performance of employees through a variety of software and electronic equipment, and reporting it (Alder and Ambrose, 2005). However, the extent and consequences largely depend on the social fabric interwoven into the organization in terms of culture and trust.

According to a study conducted by the American Management Association (AMA), the number of companies that monitor their employees' phones and computer use is extensive. In 2007, as many as 43 percent of companies monitored their employees' email, and 73 percent of these companies did so with automatic equipment. Fully 45 percent of the companies monitored time spent and phone numbers called, and according to the survey, another 16 percent record phone conversations. The same frightening extent of surveillance applies to text messages. According to the same survey, it is not uncommon for companies to terminate their employees for abusing their internet access, email or smartphone policies (AMA, 2014). Neither this type of monitoring of employee communications activities nor the disciplinary measures are new. Monitoring is increasing, but the same pattern can be seen over a long period of years (Nord et al, 2006). The figures may vary between different studies, but are, beyond doubt, increasing. In line with the companies' increased interest in surveillance, the industry for employee monitoring software is growing rapidly. According to Gartner, one of the leading information technology research and advisory companies, the industry is growing, and the company expects that 60 percent of corporations have implemented formal programs for monitoring external social media for security breaches and incidents by 2015 (see Gartner, 2012; see also Tam et al, 2005).

Not only the extent, but above all, the target, form, and shape of surveillance has undergone changes. According to Stanton (2000), electronic monitoring has moved from performance measuring of easily quantifiable clerical work in the 1980s and 1990s to monitoring a much broader range of work-related activities not directly linked to performance, such as monitoring websites visited. The change can be partly explained by the fact that work has changed and become more complex and thus more difficult to monitor. Aside from that, the reasons for monitoring are often discussed in relation to the work morale standards of the workforce and the fears of loafing or immoral online behavior (Paulsen, 2014). According to Appelbaum et al (2005), concerns over workforce morale and the need for surveillance in relation to this is a historical continuity. In a historical perspective, wage labor has generally received a negative interpretation, and the laborer has usually been seen as a despised character (Ottosson and Rosengren, 2015a); Thompson, 1983). Work individualization and increased complexity, along with increased access to the internet, has fueled this negative approach to workforce morale (Paulsen, 2014). An example concerning a contemporary debate on this topic is to what extent, and at what cost, people spend their working day browsing the internet for porn instead of diligently performing their work. For example, there is a widespread quote traveling the internet that claims: "70 per cent of traffic on porn sites takes place during work hours" (Alder et al, 2006; Corbin, 2000; Grodzinsky and Gumbus, 2005). This is a number that easily evokes the image of hordes of libidinous office workers that discard their regular duties and instead, hunkering beneath their tables, indulge in their depraved inclinations. Even though this figure is cited in numerous scientific studies, it is rather hard to tell where it comes from. The source used for reference is SexTracker, an online service whose slogan is "Whatever your taste, SexTracker satisfies." It is possible, although not probable, that this company delivers reliable surveys. The problem is that there is no way to follow up and replicate this study, since SexTracker does not publish its criteria for inclusion or analysis. This does not, however, hinder Grodzinsky and Gumbus (2005: 251) from using the numbers to claim it as a proof of "the rampant abuse of Internet privileges." This kind of attack on employee morale seems to be fueled by the providers of employee monitoring software. According to the website of one of the largest suppliers of such software, this is a matter of productivity and high costs for businesses:

> Almost every company in the world has employees who abuse the Internet, some of whom spend hours per day surfing news, shopping, sports, gambling and sex sites.... This abuse by employees is costing their companies huge amounts of money in lost productivity alone. For example, a company with just ten employees who each waste an hour a day on the Internet is losing $50,000 per year in lost productivity. (spector.se, 2015)

The methods for monitoring employee online behavior are mainly email monitoring and/or internet monitoring and filtering. There are numerous suppliers in the market claiming that they can both improve productivity and help secure legal liability. According to the manufacturers, marketing employee monitoring software enables the mapping of: websites visited, social media sites, system activities, search terms, chat conversations, keystrokes, microphone conversations etc, and so forth. Many of the features closely resemble software that is sold to parents to monitor their children's internet use, which leads one to think that the same suppliers have found a new way to frame and market their products. Nevertheless, it would appear this business is both about marketing and dealing with mistrust.

Consequences of monitoring

How does increased monitoring affect the social relations between employer and employee in terms of control, autonomy, and trust? The social impacts of surveillance technology have been approached from several disciplines, such as psychology, organization theory, and legal studies. According to Stanton and Weiss (2000), employee monitoring and surveillance can basically affect employees in two ways: either their attitudes and feelings about work are impacted (for example, motivation, levels of trust), or their behavior is (for example, productive or unproductive behavior). However, it is not easy to assess whether monitoring always affects the employee's perception of their work negatively. The social fabric of the organization has to be taken into consideration. As monitoring and surveillance becomes embedded in organizational life and practices, it is also subjected to different meanings based in previous procedures. For example, monitoring with a clear objective in a high trust culture may be perceived as fair and within the framework of the social contract. Tabak and Smith (2005) claim that it can be seen as a more objective form of productivity assessment than traditional direct supervision by a manager. Also, if you suspect that colleagues practice social loafing, a tighter control over workplace behavior might be welcomed and appreciated. In other words, increased surveillance may, under certain circumstances, be perceived as a positive development, not only by employers, but also by those subjected to surveillance (Ball, 2010). Further, the results in a study by Stanton and Weiss (2000) indicate that employee reactions to monitoring are dependent on how the organization intends to use the collected information. Additionally, their study indicates that employee monitoring may have certain effects on employee behavior, for example, leading to a reduction in the use of company email for personal messages, and surfing the internet for other purposes than company projects.

Monitoring and surveillance is to be viewed as the opposite of management by trust and positive expectations of the employees. On the one hand, monitoring is based on mistrust, and on the other hand, trust is based in an implicit psychological contract between employer and employee (Rousseau, 1989, 1990; Ottosson and Rosengren, 2015b). Monitoring employees indicates that the employer does not trust them to behave in the appropriate manner. Frey (1993) formulates this relationship in terms of a misattribution effect, and argues that monitoring crowds out morale. More intensive monitoring and regulation does not always result in destroying excess morale. In particular, the agents do not feel that they have excess morale if monitoring and regulating clearly and exclusively serves to prevent others from "shirking" (Alchian and Demsetz, 1972: 781). Gouldner (1960) formulates this phenomenon in terms of "norms of reciprocity," which describes the equilibrium of recognition and work morale. In other words, the employees perform in accordance to moral standards as long they are entrusted with discretion and autonomy. An obvious effect of monitoring is that you only do what is monitored, and that you do not put your heart into your work, but rather "man your station" and only perform as little as possible (d'Urso, 2006). Thus the relation between trust and surveillance is a two-way street, since a lack of trust can both encourage the use of surveillance and reinforce the behavior that causes the desire to monitor. As indicated by Alder et al (2006), a lack of trust can also be the result of monitoring that is perceived as unjust or too far-reaching.

Anticipatory conformity – and self-surveillance

As mentioned above, surveillance in working life is not a unique novelty. We have probably all seen Charlie Chaplin's classic, yet even in our age, spot-on interpretation of surveillance in Fordist production in the 1936 film *Modern Times*. When the laborer (Chaplin) tries to sneak a smoking break in the bathroom, he is watched by the CEO of the factory – and the smoking break is interrupted when the TV monitor on the wall lights up: "Hey! Quit stalling! – Get back to work! Go on!" What Chaplin had noted was that industrial organization, through its far-reaching division of labor, was creating beneficial conditions for the type of surveillance that Jeremy Bentham had etched out in his panopticon surveillance system. Division of labor separated a complex situation into smaller, demarcated, and more manageable objects. To monitor something, of course, entails that there is something, some object to monitor. From that perspective, it seems logical not only to monitor production, but also the bathroom. When human existence has been divided into measurable units, even visits to the bathroom became units to be monitored. The CEO's all-seeing eyes did not leave any blank fields!

Based in capitalist production logic, it is reasonable to argue that the purpose of surveillance and control is to generate value for money when purchasing labor. The laborer not only sells his or her labor, but also his or her capacity to work during a certain, prearranged time span (Braverman, 1975; Thompson, 1983). As far as motives are concerned, surveillance is therefore not of particular research interest. Michel Foucault (in Foucault and Sheridan, 1995/1977) argued that the object of interest was, instead, the disciplinary effect that surveillance has on the laborer. What makes the panopticon especially interesting is not primarily its design, or the lack of confidence that is implicitly embedded in the purchase of labor, but that the panopticon creates the experience and consciousness of being constantly visible. In modern society and in the panopticon, power becomes invisible while the individual becomes visible (Foucault and Sheridan, 1995/1977). When our awareness of being watched increases, our behavior changes – and we become disciplined. According to a Foucauldian perspective, modernity results in a shift from external and visible constraints to internal and invisible constraints, the latter constraints being administered by the individuals themselves (Campbell and Carlson, 2010). In describing this process, Foucault expressed that "[...] it is this inversion of visibility in the functioning of the disciplines that was to assure the exercise of power even in its lowest manifestations. We are entering the age of the infinite examination and of compulsory objectification" (Foucault and Sheridan, 1995/1997: 189).

This process, Foucault argued, arose in modernity and the organizations of industrial society. But according to many succeeding scholars, the process is reinforced by digital information technology. Power is provided with new opportunities to be both everywhere and to come from everywhere (cf Campbell and Carlson, 2010; d'Urso, 2010; Lyon, 2013; Zuboff, 1989). At the same time, this technological change also changes the object, and the disintegrated and visible work effort becomes very much less visible when the abstract knowledge content in production increases (Allvin et al, 2011; Dessein and Santos, 2006; Drucker, 1999). The collection of information also changes form and pattern based on technological conditions. In relation to the monitoring that took (and is still taking) place in the traditional factories of the industrial society, it is not always clear what kind of information is being gathered. This uncertainty constitutes the ultimate conditions for the perfect panoptical tool (Büyük and Keskin, 2012).

In Bentham's ideal prison, the "panopticon" inmates could be imperceptibly observed by a prison guard, a condition that was presumed to generate self-discipline. In the same vein, covert modern surveillance technology disciplines individuals. Those subjected to surveillance adapt their behavior in order to conform to what they believe those monitoring their movements and actions will find acceptable or normal (cf Brannigan and Beier, 1985; Goffman, 2008; Westin, 1967). The private sphere shrinks: "Electronic monitoring systems are a kind of virtual simulation of the panopticon. All video recordings, electronic monitors, GPS signals, sound recordings create a prison environment in our daily lives by not allowing a single dark spot" (Büyük and Keskin, 2012: 83).

A literature review shows that the idea of the all-seeing, omnipresent eye did not end with Foucault. Rather, Bentham's panopticon has inspired a considerable number of researchers. Social science research on surveillance normally takes its starting point in Foucault's interpretation of Jeremy Bentham's prison system (cf Campbell and Carlson, 2010; d'Urso, 2006; Sewell et al, 2006). As d'Urso (2006) notes, the panopticon metaphor provides a good tool for understanding the effects of electronic surveillance in the workplace. In line with this view, the physical barriers that objectified and individualized workers in Bentham's system share striking similarities with the electronic information and communication systems of today. In most literature, the authors note that the employee's awareness of being surveilled constitutes a crucial aspect of the panoptical potential of the technology (cf Botan, 1996).

Internet behavior, for example, communication, performed by employees is both task-oriented and socially oriented, a ratio that is enhanced by weakened boundaries between work and private life. For many employees, a work day means a mixture of professional and private activities. It is reasonable to assume that this new form of work and the employer's provision of digital equipment makes issues of monitoring and surveillance explicit. In our opinion, it is therefore of interest to study employees' awareness of their employers monitoring systems and its possible "panopticon effects" in the intersection between the workplace and social media. To what extent are employees aware of the type of information their employers could gather about their internet behavior? To what extent do employees adapt what they post on social media with respect to present or potential future employers? The chapter continues with an analysis of Swedish employees' awareness of potential electronic surveillance, and to what extent this affects online activity.

Material and methods

The material was collected within two multidisciplinary research projects at Lund University: "DigiTrust – Privacy, identity and legitimacy in the digital society" and "Going home already? A study of the importance of social norms for spatial and temporal working patterns in knowledge intensive companies." The aim of these two projects is to further the understanding of (1) trust-based issues in a digital context, and (2) social norms regulating work time. In order to gain a broad perspective of how people relate to questions such as monitoring and surveillance in a digital context, traceability, what kind of information people trust online, etc, five central areas, that each in their own right represents different aspects of our daily life, were identified:

- surveillance
- banking
- healthcare
- working life
- medias.

A questionnaire was sent by email to 1,193 respondents, of which 1,118 responded, a response rate of 93.7 percent. The respondents were selected randomly from the CINT CPX (Cint Panel eXchange) that consists of around 400,000 individuals, representing the entire Swedish population. The selection was stratified to represent the population in terms of a balanced distribution among men, women, and age groups. The questionnaire was comprised of 35 questions. Most of the questions were in the form of assertions the respondents could either agree or disagree with using a five-point Likert scale.

In order to understand how employees relate to digital monitoring, and more specifically, whether it is possible to see a "panopticon effect" in their way of relating to private internet activity, five questions (worded as statements) were included in the section "Working life":

- I adapt what I publish on social media because it could be read by my present or future employer.
- The risk of being monitored affects my behavior on the internet.
- My employer uses technology that limits internet use.
- I am aware of the type of information my employer collects regarding my internet use.
- I worry that my employer will monitor my use of internet and email.

Results

According to the questionnaire, the attitudes towards surveillance in general are somewhat permissive among the respondents. A weaker interpretation would be that the results detect indifference or lack of interest. This is manifested, among other things, in that only 20 percent of the respondents agree with the assertion that camera or video surveillance (CCTV) is a potential threat towards people's privacy and personal integrity. Men seem to be generally somewhat more negative towards surveillance than women. Of the male respondents, 24 percent considered CCTV to be a potential threat towards people's privacy. This is compared with the group of women where only 15 percent considered CCTV to be a potential threat. The same pattern can be seen with regard to the surveillance of people's work and of working life in general (Larsson and Runesson, 2014).

In this study, our focus is on the response to employers' surveillance of the internet at work, and the results indicate a general awareness of surveillance in this area as well. According to the questionnaire, half of the respondents were not aware of the type of information their employers gather on their internet behavior. And conversely, only 21 percent agree with the assertion "I am aware of the type of information my employer collects regarding my internet use" (see Table 12.1).

Nor did the respondents express much concern for the type of information their employers could potentially collect. Only little more than one out of five respondents (21 percent) voiced concern for the assertion "I worry that my employer will monitor my use of internet and email." It is also of interest to note that as many as 28 percent of the respondents state that their employer uses technology that limits their internet use (see Table 12.1).

Finally, from the questionnaire one can note that the ability to screen potential employees affects the kind of information being submitted to social media. As many as 45 percent of the respondents agree with the assertion "I adapt what I publish on social media because it could be read by my present or future employer." This result indicates "anticipatory conformity", even if an overwhelming majority simultaneously claims that the risk of surveillance does not affect their behavior on the internet. Only 22 percent agree with the statement "The risk of being monitored affects my behavior on the internet" (see Table 12.1).

Table 12.1: Attitudes towards surveillance in working life among the Swedish population

Assertion	I agree	I neither agree nor disagree	I disagree	N
I adapt what I publish on social media because it could be read by my present or future employer	45%	25%	30%	1,029
The risk of being monitored affects my behavior on the internet	22%	27%	51%	1,027
My employer uses technology that limits internet use	28%	25%	47%	1023
I am aware of the kind of information my employer collects regarding my internet use	21%	27%	52%	1024
I worry that my employer will monitor my use of internet and email	21%	23%	56%	1025

Therefore, to a direct question concerning whether their behavior is influenced by the risk of being monitored, the response is no. However, in response to a more specific question on their online behavior, it becomes obvious that people tend to appropriate their behavior in relation to a potential employer. Clearly, it also seems that potential "Googling" or screening by a potential future employer seems to be more important, and affects behavior to a larger degree than the fear of being actively monitored online in their current job.

As discussed earlier, digital technology has the potential to challenge the borders between private life and (or perhaps, rather than) working public life. For example, every fourth respondent (25 percent) claims that they use their employer's equipment to carry out private errands on the internet on a weekly or daily basis, thereby making ignorance of the type of information the employer collects yet more alarming, since it potentially implies information of a private nature. On the same note, it can be said that 30 percent of the respondents claim that they use the internet to perform their work from home on a weekly or daily basis (Table 12.2).

Table 12.2: Use of employer's equipment and use of the internet to work from home

Assertion	Never	Sometimes	Weekly or daily	N
I use my employer's equipment to perform personal business on the internet	36%	39%	25%	1020
I use the internet to work from home	38%	33%	29%	1022

Discussion

In relation to working life, digitalization in general, and the changing nature of work, an increasing amount of work is carried out in an online environment. One aspect of this change is probably that there is a greater effort to monitor employees' internet behavior. A second aspect is that surveillance has changed in form and content. Overall, the amount of information has grown more extensive and has changed in nature. It seems that the goal, as well as the purpose, of the data collection becomes more vague with regards to the type of information that is to be gathered.

The information collected can be used both to improve productivity and to take action against immoral behavior such as loafing, harassment, and even activities of a pornographic nature. The extent of surveillance stands in relation to the image of the employee's character. Fear of low work morale means more surveillance. The unique novelty of online surveillance, in the context of a (post-)industrial society, is that it potentially invades the employee's life more thoroughly – this since private and public spheres are often confused. Private chores are carried out during working hours and work duties are performed at home. A situation emerges where the employee's home becomes a place of work and where the employer's equipment is used for private communication.

The development of a potentially omnipresent digital surveillance, it is argued here, has direct implications in terms of trust/distrust for the relation between employer and employee. In the long run, it can also affect behavior in other areas of life. Not knowing what kind of information is being gathered and at what time can give the impression of constantly being monitored. In line with Foucault's arguments concerning the panopticon and the self-discipline of the individual, one could say that the purpose of surveillance is not the object of interest, but rather its effects. Probably, the labor force is monitored in order to protect the company's brand and to increase production by delimiting the maneuverable space for any potential lack of work morale, but at the same time, the awareness of being monitored also creates an awareness of being visible.

The results indicate that the discomfort expressed by the respondents concerning the experiences of being monitored is relatively weak. Further, respondents report that they do not in any significant way adapt their behavior online due to the risks of being monitored. In response to a more specific question concerning whether they adapt what they write in social media with an eye on current or future employers, it appears that they do so, despite the contrary claim. Not knowing when one is being observed is/can be a powerful panoptical tool, which is why this inherent uncertainty can be favorable for the employer in the context of behavioral control. However, this is also a system that can potentially challenge trust between employee and employer; previous studies show that collecting data on employees' behavior based in undetermined and vague mandates can lead to the erosion of trust. Gouldner (1960) formulates it in terms of "norms of reciprocity": the employees perform in accordance to work morale standards as long they are entrusted with discretion and autonomy. Or, as Frey (1993) argues in terms of misattribution effect, surveillance crowds out morale. In other words, a system designed to combat immoral behavior can, in fact, contribute to creating the very same behavior it is said to annihilate. It is not monitoring itself, or its causes or technical forms, but rather the fear and uncertainty it creates. It is our uncertainty about the digital footprints we leave that is of most interest.

References

Alchian, A. and H. Demsetz (1972) "Production, information costs, and economic organization." *The American Economic Review* 62, 5, 777–95.

Alder, S. and M. Ambrose (2005) "An examination of the effect of computerized performance monitoring feedback on monitoring fairness, performance, and satisfaction." *Organizational Behavior and Human Decision Processes* 97, 2, 161–77.

Alder, S., T. Noeland, and M. Ambrose (2006) "Clarifying the effects of Internet monitoring on job attitudes: The mediating role of employee trust." *Information & Management* 43, 7, 894–903.

Allvin, M. et al (2011) *Work without boundaries: Psychological perspectives on the new working life.* Oxford. Wiley-Blackwell.

AMA (American Management Association) (2014) "The latest on workplace monitoring and surveillance" (www.amanet.org/training/articles/The-Latest-on-Workplace-Monitoring-and-Surveillance.aspx).

Appelbaum, S., K. Deguire, and M. Lay (2005) "The relationship of ethical climate to deviant workplace behaviour." *Corporate Governance: The International Journal of Business in Society* 5, 4, 43–55.

Ball, K. (2010) "Workplace surveillance: an overview." *Labor History* 51, 1, 87–106.

Botan, C.H. (1996) "Communication work and electronic surveillance: A model for predicting panoptic effects." *Communication Monographs* 63 (4), 1–21

Braverman, H. (1974) *Labor and monopoly capital: The degradation of work in the twentieth century* (2nd edn). New York: Monthly Review Press.

Brannigan, V. and B. Beier (1985) "Informational self-determination: A choice based analysis." *Datenschutzund Datensicherung*, April.

Büyük, K. and U. Keskin (2012) "Panopticon's electronic resurrection: Workplace monitoring as an ethical problem." *Turkish Journal of Business Ethics* 5, 10, 75–88.

Campbell, J. and M. Carlson (2010) "Panopticon.com: Online Surveillance and the Commodification of Privacy." *Journal of Broadcasting & Electronic Media* 46, 4, 586–606.

Corbin, D. E. (2000) "Keeping a virtual eye on employees." *Occupational Health & Safety* 69, 11, 24–6.

Dessein, W. and T. Santos (2006) "Adaptive organizations". *Journal of Political Economy* 114, 956–95.

Drucker, P. (1999) "Knowledge-worker productivity: The biggest challenge." *California Management Review* 41, 2, 79–94.

d'Urso, S. (2006) "Who's watching us at work? Toward a structural-perceptual model of electronic monitoring and surveillance in organizations." *Communication Theory* 16, 201–303.

Fairweather, B. (1999) "Surveillance in employment: The case of teleworking." *Journal of Business Ethics* 22, 1, 39–49.

Foucault, M. and A. Sheridan (1995/1977) *Discipline and punish: The birth of the prison.* New York: Vintage Books.

Frey, B. (1993) "Shirking or work morale?: The impact of regulating." *European Economic Review* 37, 8, 1523–32.

Gartner (2012) "Gartner says monitoring employee behavior in digital environments is rising" (www.gartner.com/newsroom/id/2028215).

Goffman, E. (2008) *Behavior in public places.* New York: Simon & Schuster.

Gouldner, A. (1960) "The norm of reciprocity: A preliminary statement." *American Sociological Review* 161–78.

Grodzinsky, F. and A. Gumbus (2005) "Internet and productivity: ethical perspectives on workplace behavior." *Journal of Information Communication and Ethics in Society* 3, 249–56.

Larsson, S. and P. Runesson (2014) *DigiTrust: Tillit i det digitala – Tvärvetenskapliga perspektiv från ett forskningsprojekt.* Lund: Punedorfinstitutet.

Lyon, D. (2013/1994) *The electronic eye: The rise of surveillance society – Computers and social control in context.* Oxford: Polity Press.

Negrey, C. (2012) *Work time: Conflict, control, and change.* Cambridge: Polity Press.

Nord, D., T. McCubbins, and J. Nord (2006) "E-monitoring in the workplace: privacy, legislation, and surveillance software." *Communications of the ACM* 49, 8, 72–7.

Ottosson, M. and C. Rosengren (2015a) "The construction and demonization of the lazybones." *Fastcapitalism* 11 (1).

Ottosson, M. and C. Rosengren (2015b) "The Swedish Confederation for Professional Employees (TCO) and trust-based working hours 1950–1970." *Management Revue* 26 (1), 52–68.

Paulsen, R. (2014) *Empty labor: Idleness and workplace resistance.* Cambridge, UK: Cambridge University Press.

Porter, G. and N. Kakabadse (2006) "HRM perspectives on addiction to technology and work." *Journal of Management Development,* 25, 6, 535–60.

Ragu-Nathan, T.S., T. Monideepa, B. Ragu-Nathan, and Q. Tu (2008) "The consequences of technostress for end users in organizations: Conceptual development and empirical validation." *Information Systems Research* 19, 4.

Rousseau, D. (1989) "Psychological and implied contracts in organizations." *Employee Rights and Responsibilities Journal* 2, 121–39.

Rousseau, D. (1990) "New hire perceptions of their own and their employer's obligations: A study of psychological contracts." *Journal of Organizational Behavior* 11, 389–400.

Sewell, G., J. Barker and D. Nyberg (2012) "Working under intensive surveillance: When does 'measuring everything that moves' become intolerable?" *Human Relations* 65, 2, 189–215.

spector.se (2015) "Every company has employees who abuse the internet" (http://spector.se/spector_cne.html).

Stanton, J. (2000) "Reactions to employee performance monitoring: Framework, review, and research directions." *Human Performance* 13, 1, 85–113.

Stanton, J. and E.M. Weiss (2000) "Electronic monitoring in their own words: an exploratory study of employees' experiences with new types of surveillance." *Computers in Human Behavior* 16, 4, 423–40.

Tabak, F. and W. Smith (2005) "Privacy and electronic monitoring in the workplace: A model of managerial cognition and relational trust development." *Employee Responsibilities and Rights Journal* 17, 3, 173–89.

Tam, P.-W., E. White, N. Wingfield, and K. Maher (2005) "Snooping email by software is now a workplace norm". *The Wall Street Journal.* March 9.

Thompson, P. (1983) *The nature of work: an introduction to debates on the labour process.* London: Macmillan.

Westin, A. (1967) *Privacy and freedom.* New York: Anthema Press.

Zuboff, S. (1988) *In the age of the smart machine: The future of work and power.* Oxford: Heinemann Professional.

13

Digital sociology's vocational promise

Stephen R. Barnard

In the final analysis, the problems that we identify and resolve through technological innovation will always be essentially human concerns which engender characteristically human solutions. Much the same can be said for the practice of sociology. (Athique, 2013: 263)

Introduction

In 2009 Jonathan Wynn penned the first American essay on the promises of "digital sociology" (Wynn, 2009). Around that same time, digital sociology started blossoming abroad, with a growing body of engaging work from scholars in Australia and the UK (Beer and Burrows, 2013; Lupton, 2015; Orton-Johnson and Prior, 2013; Ruppert et al, 2013). But, despite its emergent potential, digital sociology is still on the margins in the US, with relatively few academic references to the topic, and far fewer to the term "digital sociology." For example, a recent search of the Social Sciences Citation Index yielded a mere two references, one being Wynn's inaugural contribution, and another a general critique of digitally oriented research for being temporally shallow and ahistorical (Uprichard, 2012). If the top journals in American sociology are any indication, there is little support for the task of helping our discipline catch up to, and thus make better sense of, life in the digital age. At the same time, adoption of digital technology

– not just in American society, but also in many sub-disciplines as well as interdisciplinary contemporaries of sociology – has grown tremendously. This contradiction forces us to consider a difficult yet important reality: we are living in a society increasingly mediated by digital technologies, but a majority of sociologists have thus far been resistant to adopting appropriately modernized methods for addressing this transition.

This chapter seeks to make the case for a more digitally attuned sociology, and to forge a path in that direction. To accomplish this task, I begin with a brief history of digital sociology in order to lay important groundwork for the continued study of digital dynamics from sociological perspectives. Next, I examine the state of social life in the digitally networked era, including the persistence of inequality, and discuss two non-mutually exclusive approaches – "digital scholarship" and "scholarship of the digital" – in order to evaluate the breadth of opportunity for the emerging field of digital sociology. Then, I outline some lessons from the prominent and parallel field of digital humanities, and make the case for sociology's need to update its epistemological orientation to put an end to fetishisms of technology and the "real world." Finally, I outline an agenda for digital sociology, and consider how the traditions of public sociology, social justice, critical pedagogy, and community-based learning can help the field re-envision and realize its vocational promise in the digital age.

Digital sociology in context

According to Deborah Lupton, the realm of digital sociology includes four main applications: professional digital practice; analyses of digital technology; digital data analysis; and critical digital sociology (2015: 15–16). Professional digital practice includes all uses of digital technology for doing sociology in public – a form of praxis frequently championed by scholars of the digital (Daniels and Feagin, 2011; Tufekci, 2014). The latter three applications of digital sociology each highlight various aspects of scholarly uses of digital tools in the study of sociological phenomena.

On some level, sociology has always been aided by, although not necessarily attuned to, technological innovations. Most basically, sociologists have long applied computer-assisted methods for data management and analysis. The increasing digitality of social life has also created new frontiers for sociology, beginning with opportunities for data collection and analysis, and progressing into new fields of inquiry. Furthermore, the saturation of technology in society has given rise to theoretical perspectives, which highlight digitally mediated forms of agency and experience.[1] These developments have also given rise to new bodies of research that distort and overstep traditional disciplinary borders. For example, recent work on digital inequality and literacy (Hargittai, 2010; Hughey and Daniels, 2013; Schradie, 2011), digital culture and interaction (boyd, 2014; Marwick, 2012; Papacharissi, 2010; Trottier,

2013), networked society and social movements (Clark and Themudo, 2012; Earl and Kimport, 2011; Rainie and Wellman, 2012; Smith, 2002), medical sociology and the quantified self (Lupton, 2014), political sociology (Kreiss, 2014), science and technology studies (Law, 1990, 2008; Wajcman, 2002), work (Liker et al, 1999), and media sociology (Benson et al, 2012; Gillespie et al, 2014; Waisbord, 2014) are part and parcel of sociology's contribution to the study of the digital age.

Despite the strength of these studies, as well as the progress made in other related fields, the discipline of sociology as a whole has yet to fully commit to the consideration of society's increasing digitization. Given the profound impact of recent technological transformations on modern social relations, as well as the remaining gap in contemporary sociology's consideration of digitally mediated dynamics, we must redouble our collective efforts to build grounded, socially relevant knowledge. As Wynn put it, "the discipline needs to have a broad discussion on the effects of [media and technology], and how we evaluate scholarly labor" (2009: 455). In other words, we need sociological practices and values to be better attuned to the realities of the digital world. This will require significant reconsideration of our ontologies and epistemologies, our theories and methods, and even the orientation of scholarship itself.

But the task of digital sociology is not just theoretical and methodological; it is also an issue of medium and message. The growth of blogs, social media platforms, open-access journals, and other avenues all provide fruitful outlets for distributing scholarly work. Many of these spaces – most notably social media sites such as Twitter and Facebook, paper-sharing networks such as the Social Science Research Network (SSRN) and Academia.edu, as well as countless scholarly blogs and online publications – provide opportunities to build an audience, engage with readers, and receive feedback, and even to "change your mind in public" (Waldman, 2015). These networks can provide powerful affordances to networked scholars, but, as this chapter will make clear, there are many notable limitations, including the increased publicness of scholarship and the inequities of networked society.

The struggle is real: networked society, inequality, and the challenge of digital sociology

Like much of the modern world, American society is currently undergoing a technocultural revolution marked by the rise of the internet, mobile "smart" phones, and ubiquitous social networks (Rainie and Wellman, 2012). Approximately 90 percent of American adults own a cell phone (58 percent own a smartphone), and 63 percent of cell phone owners use their devices to access the internet (Pew Research Center, 2014). Furthermore, more than half of Americans (58 percent, or 71 percent of online adults) use Facebook, while use of Twitter, Instagram, LinkedIn, and Pinterest vary from 19–23 percent of all Americans (Duggan et al, 2015). This kind of penetration yields profound changes in social relations, amounting to what Rainie and Wellman (2012) term the "new social operating system" made up of "networked individuals" who are less bound by traditional conceptions of place and group association.

However, despite the clear promise of digital technologies, the persistence of structural inequalities undeniably tempers this potential. The "digital divide" between those who have access to the internet and mobile devices and those who do not remains significant (Rainie, 2015). Furthermore, internet access does not guarantee outcomes. For example, many networked individuals are unequally reliant on mobile devices (Smith, 2015), and often lack the requisite literacies to leverage these devices to their full potential (Hargittai, 2010). Even as minority access to digital technologies increases, the persistence of "production inequality," where members of traditionally underrepresented groups are disproportionately absent from participation in the public sphere, continues to "perpetuate the ... dominance of elite voices" (Schradie, 2011: 166). And while access, capital, and usage are all divided along the lines of class, race, age, and education in the US (Rainie, 2015; Smith, 2015), the digital divide is even wider when viewed on a global scale (Tharoor, 2014). Sociologists of the digital age must not overlook such persistent inequalities; indeed, they must thoroughly and critically interrogate them. Still, there are reasons to believe that the increasing adoption of digital technologies may hold promise, especially when they are used to counter hegemonic forces (Brock et al, 2010; Carr, 2012).

These inequalities are also reflected in the realities of contemporary academe, and engagement in public scholarship is not without its costs (Daniels, 2013a, 2015; Newkirk, 2015). For example, the weight of these pressures have been disproportionately levied against public scholars, especially those whose work and identities support or represent marginalized groups (Grollman, 2015). And while blogging may not yet count for tenure, it does provide a valuable service to individuals and institutions committed to digital scholarship (Daniels, 2013b; Grollman, 2014). At a time when scholarship is increasingly visible and vulnerable to the pressures of public opinion, it is important for institutions to develop robust and adaptable policies for supporting open scholarship (McMillan Cottom, 2015).

There are reasons why the field of sociology in particular, and academe in general, has lagged behind the curve in adapting to the digital age. Benson's (2014) pointed assertion that "strategy follows structure" demonstrates the impact of institutional forces on the practice of scholarly work. Given that "the nature of the relationship of scientific work and its presuppositions varies widely according to their structure" (Weber, 1958:143), there is great reason for sociologists to create and share knowledge that is bound to make a difference in public life. Thus, we must work to ensure that the promise of critical, digital sociology is honored – in our teaching and research, in our communities, and certainly by our institutional policies (Gold, 2012).

To be clear, digital sociology is not merely a catch-all term for sociologists who use digital tools, and nor is it an excuse to fall back on techno-utopian or determinist discourses about the role of technology in society. As I discuss below, concerns about fetishism – both of technology and of the "real world" – can help us avoid the pitfalls of both extremes. Digital sociology seeks to highlight the increasing digitality of social reality, and to direct our attention toward a more systematic analysis of these trends. It asserts that "the significance and usage of these technologies is expansive enough to warrant a wide-ranging discussion that correlates how 'we shape our tools and our tools shape us'" (Athique, 2013: 261). Given the ubiquity of digital technology and connectivity in contemporary society, an honest, empirically driven, and sociologically grounded discussion of these dynamics is long overdue.

From digital scholarship to scholarship of the digital

The increasing digitality and augmentation of social relations offers endless opportunity for scholars to leverage the power of networked technologies in their research and teaching. At the same time, the digital turn offers a much deeper opportunity to alter sociological paradigms. This acknowledgement requires that we distinguish between two types of digitally attuned scholarship. On the one hand, there is *digital scholarship*, a term used to describe scholarly work that leverages digital tools in the process of academic inquiry. Such applications can range from data collection (that is, content from social media platforms or other websites, online surveys, and other forms of digital data, however "big"), to methods (that is, social network analysis, digital ethnography, collaborative coding, etc), and even publication outlets (that is, blogs, social media platforms, paper-sharing sites, and open-access publications). On the other hand, *scholarship of the digital* underscores the explicit consideration and analysis of issues arising from the proliferation of digital technologies. Across the field of sociology, work on digital culture, science, technology and society (STS), and media studies, among many other sub-fields, have all made significant contributions to scholarship of the digital.

These two types of digitality are non-mutually exclusive, and both have a place in the past, present, and future of digital sociology. Nevertheless, (digital) sociology has thus far placed much greater emphasis on digital scholarship than on scholarship of the digital, and it is time we refocus our efforts to better account for the breadth of sociological implications stemming from life in a digital age. This does not mean abandoning core sociological theories, methods, and lines of inquiry. It only requires that we broaden our focus to be more mindful of the complex reality of digitality. In other words, we must take care to open, connect, and synthesize our methodologies rather than approaching digital sociology with an "add digital data and stir" mindset. Thus, in addition to our methodological tools informing our sociological orientations, changes in our social world should drive us to pose new questions and to cultivate innovative methodologies that help us to better understand our unfolding realities. Overall, the vocational promise of digital sociology is not simply to add shiny new polish on top of the discipline's well-worn lenses. Rather, the future of digital sociology will be best served by approaches that combine digital scholarship with scholarship of the digital, and make critical, reflexive, and practical contributions to the discipline's core concerns.

Lessons from the digital humanities

It would be shortsighted to envision the future of digital sociology without first engaging with the rich history of scholarship that falls under the umbrella of "digital humanities." What began with the usage of computer-based tools for archiving and analyzing historical artifacts (first labeled "humanities computing") later developed into a full-blown field of study. According to Google Ngram, the phrase "digital humanities" first appeared in book publication in 1994. Its usage remained fairly sparse until 2000, where it began a steady upsurge until tapering off somewhat in 2007 (see Figure 13.1).[2]

Figure 13.1: Google Ngram of book references to "digital humanities"

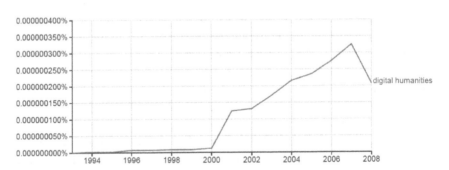

While the humanities disciplines had a deep and rich digital history prior to the meteoric rise of digital humanities at the start of the 21st century, its emergence was largely enabled by innovations in digital technologies (Jones, 2013). After years of methodological exploration and field formation, digital humanities has reached a *meta* stage, where:

> ... computing is both means and matter for the digital humanities. Besides using computers to research literature or art or history, self-identified practitioners doing DH [digital humanities] have

also ... applied the methods, insights, and research questions of the humanities to the study of computing and digital media. (Jones, 2013: 6)

In other words, digital humanities is a "big tent" that can encompass a variety of topical and methodological applications depending on how it is approached. But there are always well-positioned interlocutors who define the field's boundaries according to their own interests. Digital humanities has no shortage of such interventions (Liu, 2013). For example, the field has struggled somewhat with "who's in, who's out?" divisions, demarcated most visibly by those who "code" or "build" digital tools and those who do not (Ramsay, in Gold, 2012: x). This kind of imposition does more to perpetuate inequalities than to build a diverse and unified whole. A homogeneous field made up of only actors that strictly adhere to a single set of doxa – be they theories, methods, or topical foci – is bound for a crisis of stasis and ultimately, obsolescence. To be sure, many digital humanities scholars are aware of the pitfalls of this divisiveness, and have been quite vocal in rejecting them (Gold, 2012; Liu, 2013).

As we envision the emergence of a more digital sociology, we must resist the temptation to engage in dialectics of inclusion and exclusion because such authenticity policing is entirely counter-productive to the objectives of sociology as a vocation. To be clear, this cautioning does not require the abandonment of critique, nor of the formation of sub-fields. One research agenda need not supplant another; scholarly inquiry is not a zero-sum game. Indeed, digital sociology has much to gain from a synthesis of fields, theories, and methods, not least of which includes greater parity with other fields (Gillespie et al, 2014; Jones, 2013; Liu, 2013).

Despite the strengths of digital humanities-inspired questions and methods, there are also some undeniable drawbacks. Some have charged that digital humanities has swapped a fetishism of the material for a fetishism of the digital (see Bassett, 2012). Others resent the term "digital humanities" itself, seeing it as yet another buzzword that comes with big promises but little (unique) in terms of payoff. As Alan Liu put it,

> ... the digital humanities serve as a shadow play for a future form of the humanities that wishes to include what contemporary society values about the digital without losing its soul to other domains of knowledge work that have gone digital to stake their claim to that society. (2013: 410)

To the extent that the field of digital humanities has successfully staked such a claim in an increasingly digital world, it has done so by adapting to emergent realities. However, this adaptation is still a work in progress, as the brunt of attention remains focused on how to use digital *methods* in humanities research.

Indeed, for most of the field, digital humanities has thus far functioned primarily as a methodological intervention, rather than a theoretical or substantive project. Like digital humanities, the field of digital sociology is now tasked with the challenge of continuing its development of the ongoing methodological repertoire (that is, digital scholarship), while refocusing its aim on the development of and commitment to theories and questions of the digital age (that is, scholarship of the digital).

Digitally mediated reality: a tale of two fetishisms

Scholars have long argued that while new technologies are undeniable factors in social life, any attempt to understand their significance must avoid imposing undue power or adornment on them. In other words, we must avoid fetishism. Fetishism is "the habit humans have of endowing real or imagined objects or entities with self-contained, mysterious, and even magical powers to move and shape the world in distinctive ways" (Harvey, 2003). There are two distinct forms of fetishism surrounding the role of technology in modern social life: first, the fetishism of technology, and second, of the so-called "real world" or "real life."

When applied to technology, the concept of fetishism highlights the tendency to project undue power and agency onto objects as well as to distort or disguise the social relations that create and animate the tools themselves. Building on the work of Bruno Latour, Alf Hornborg argues that the Cartesian paradigm that "distinguishes the domain of material objects from that of social relations of exchange" renders invisible the political-economic base of technologies, therefore limiting epistemological orientations for proper critical examination of modern power relations (2014: 120). For example, one common manifestation of technology fetishism arises when researchers are inconsiderate of the limitations of so-called "big data" (Couldry, 2014: 888; Hargittai, 2015; Tufekci, 2013). Whereas the constancy and given nature of big data can lead to ahistorical applications (Lupton, 2015), the logic and power relations inherent in it commonly serve the interests of governments and corporations (Couldry, 2014; Fuchs, 2013; Tufekci, 2014). Given the data collection and construction processes that contribute to the structure and content of publicly available digital data, which are inherent but often invisible to researchers, many studies relying on big data are limited by observational biases and other matters beyond the researchers' control. Until and unless researchers are mindful of these biases, the burgeoning body of research relying on big data will be riddled with unacknowledged shortcomings.

Contrary to these concerns, there is another brand of fetishism that manifestly resists changes in culture and technology by fetishizing that which is the apparent antithesis of technology – human sociality – and by constructing a dualistic view of reality: digital versus physical. While there is great variance in how strongly an argument relies on this fallacy, cases of digital dualism – whether in academic or popular discourse – frequently dismiss digitally mediated connections as somehow inferior to, and lacking, the undefined yet magical properties of the material world (Jurgenson, 2012a, 2012b). Nathan Jurgenson refers to this refrain as the "IRL [in real life] fetish" in an attempt to call attention to those positions and dispositions that impede our ability to grasp the significance of modern social relations, which are increasingly augmented by digital media and communication technologies (Jurgenson, 2012c).

Given these competing concerns, we are faced with a dilemma over our approach to two key and conflicting instances of fetishism. On the one hand, we must not ignore the fetishism of technology (Fuchs, 2013; Hornborg, 2014). On the other hand, we cannot merely dismiss the reality of digitality by fetishizing the "real world" over augmented relations (Jurgenson, 2012a). The challenge for critical, digital sociology is to strike a balance that avoids the pitfalls of both extremes while also serving our various communities. Thus, I argue that the emergence of digital sociology provides a unique and timely opportunity for our field to reflect and recommit to our collective pursuit of public praxis.

Toward a critical, digital pedagogy for sociology

One way to address the concerns outlined above – avoiding fetishisms while bolstering critical, sociological perspectives that serve our communities – is to remain attuned to the persistence of social stratification and systemic inequalities, issues that are often overlooked in studies of the internet (Daniels, 2013a, 2015). As a discipline, sociology is uniquely and persistently concerned with issues of inequality and social justice, and is thus uniquely situated to address them. Given that the wealth gap between middle- and upper-class American families is the largest on record (Fry and Kochhar, 2014), as well as the long history of academic institutions' marginalization of critical, praxis-oriented sociology, there is a reason to bring our focus back to issues of social justice (Feagin, 2001: 7–10; Gans, 2014).

Considering the publicity and accessibility of the networked world – ranging from the research opportunities emerging from digital data and augmented reality to the dissemination of sociological knowledge through online platforms – the growth of digital sociology provides a unique opportunity to pursue such praxis and in turn, fulfill its yet-to-be-realized vocational promise. As Jessie Daniels explains, the internet "enables all of us to create knowledge in new ways, connect with those beyond the academy, and try to transform entrenched forms of inequality" (Daniels, 2013c). Thus, the networked fields may just be an ideal space for scholar-activists to serve and engage the public (Barnard and van Gerven, 2009; Daniels, 2013c). We can do this by engaging members of our communities in open dialogue about issues that concern them, by creating and sharing sociological knowledge, and even by working collaboratively to improve their conditions and social positions. In other words, sociology can be of service to the public, and in doing so we can re-establish the discipline's emphasis on serving academic and marginalized groups alike (Blouin and Perry, 2009)

While there are many possible avenues for the pursuit of this goal, I argue for a greater consideration of the benefits of critical pedagogy and community-based learning (CBL) because they provide a unique opportunity to address a broad array of needs that are currently underserved in our discipline as well as our communities. In addition to its concern with systemic inequalities, the field of sociology has a deep and rich history with public pedagogies such as community-based and service learning (Blouin and Perry, 2009; Mooney and Edwards, 2001; Treviño and McCormack, 2014). Although many disciplines can benefit from CBL approaches or other praxis-oriented pedagogies, some have argued that, "sociology and service learning were made for each other" (Fritz, 2002: 67). If sociology is an ideal site for the dialectical progression of knowledge through the interplay of teaching, research, and service, then the implementation of networked technologies and praxis-oriented pedagogies such as CBL provide unique opportunities for a synthesis of these interconnected ends. The combination of sociology with CBL and social justice pedagogies can help cultivate students' critical consciousness (Rondini, 2015), which can be put to use through increased public engagement. It is this practical application of sociology that "fulfils the duty of bringing about self-clarification and a sense of responsibility," which Weber saw as part and parcel of our field's vocational promise (Weber, 1958: 152).

Considering the affordances of digital technologies and the learning opportunities they can offer (Haythornwaite, 2012), digital sociology could be an ideal expression of publicly situated, praxis-oriented work that is *of*, *with* and *for* underserved populations. The practice of critical, digital pedagogy encourages student-teachers to be active in their own problem-posing education, which can lead to increased public engagement and community-based praxis (Freire, 2000). Because self-expression and reflection often lead to new dimensions of sociological thinking, practitioners of digital sociology should harness the potential of digital tools to teach digital literacies while also sharing sociological perspectives through public engagement. Thus, adding a digital component to our teaching and research could also provide opportunities for greater discovery and publicity.

Given the proliferation of networked technologies it is now possible to extend our discipline's reach even further – through web platforms, social media, and even massive online open courses (MOOCs) – into communities that have traditionally been underserved. And while these models have undeniable shortcomings, there are opportunities to maximize impact by fostering greater participation (Daniels, 2013c). For example, in my own sociology CBL course, "Social justice in the digital age," student-activists made several visits to a county jail to learn about criminal (in)justice, community reintegration, and to pursue praxis-oriented solutions to recidivism. Students contribute to this learning by creating personal blogs as well as a larger, collaborative project. The class project, North Country Resource (see http://northcountryresource.org/) is an online collection of local social services built in collaboration with incarcerated individuals, the professor and academic support staff. Beyond the impact this collection of resources may have on members of at-risk populations, working directly with a sizable portion of the incarcerated population allowed us to create a mutually beneficial relationship with a direct impact in the local community.[3]

Beyond the countless opportunities digital scholars have to commit public sociology in the age of the internet and social media, such digitally mediated praxis could take a variety of different forms. Digital sociology projects may even be used to inform and augment more traditional forms of sociological research. Of course, there are obvious limitations in terms of accessibility and literacy that cannot be solved by mere technological solutionism. Nevertheless, digital sociology provides a unique opportunity to recommit to the goals of public sociology and critical, reflexive pedagogy by reorienting our work *in*, *of*, and *for* the community.

Conclusion: fulfilling the promise

This chapter has explored the history and vocational promise of digital sociology, and has sought to pave the way toward its fulfillment. While digital sociology faces many challenges and even more opportunities, I propose five main objectives for the future of digital sociology. First and foremost, we must renew our analytical orientation – this includes our theories, methods, ontologies, and epistemologies – to better account for the ongoing shift toward an increasingly networked social world. Second, we must recommit to a balanced consideration of structure and agency, and reject reductionist and deterministic theories of technology. This requires avoiding fetishism, both of technology and the so-called "real world." Third, we must remain empirically and theoretically focused, while also staying committed to preserving interpretive meaning and "thick description" (Geertz, 1973), especially in the age of big data and computational social science. Fourth, we must strike a healthy balance between *digital scholarship* and *scholarship of the digital*. Last, but not least, we must broaden our definitions of teaching, scholarship, and service in order to recommit to the *public* and *praxis*-oriented roots of sociology. This will include committing sociology that is *of*, *with*, and *for* the public through greater engagement with the members of today's networked society.

Overall, the hybridity of fields and practices in the networked era present a valuable opportunity to reevaluate sociology's vocational promise. While sociology has historically been attuned to viewing the world as a commingling of agents and interactions with/in institutional contexts, it is also possible for sociological approaches to recognize the emergence of a digital, hypermediated superstructure that augments traditional social relations. Just as actors in other fields have developed networked practices and dispositions to suit changes to the media environment (Papacharissi and Easton, 2013), sociologists can (and should) adapt to living and researching in a networked society. If sociology is to remain valid and legitimate, both as a science and a vocation, we must reconsider and reinvest in the realm of the digital.

Notes

[1] See, for example, actor-network theory, mediatization, augmented reality, and networked individualism.

[2] It is important to note that this metric, like all metrics, is limited by the data on which it is based. Given that Google's Ngram database does not include data beyond 2008, the apparent decline in mentions of "digital humanities" may be misleading. In fact, the continued growth of the field in published literature suggests this is likely the case.

[3] Visits included group discussions, numerous interactive and reflexive exercises, as well as training for how to take advantage of the resources. Additionally, printed copies of the resource collection were distributed for immediate use given the jail's current restrictions on access to digital technology.

References

Athique, A. (2013) *Digital media and society: An introduction.* Malden, MA: Polity Press.

Barnard, S.R. (2016) "'Tweet or be sacked': Twitter and the new elements of journalistic practice." *Journalism* 17 (2), 190–207.

Barnard, S.R. and J.P. van Gerven (2009) "A people's method(ology): A dialogical approach." *Cultural Studies – Critical Methodologies* 9 (6), 816–31.

Bassett, C. (2012) "Canonicalism and the computational turn." In D.M. Berry (ed) *Understanding digital humanities* (pp 105–26). Basingstoke: Palgrave Macmillan.

Beer, D. and R. Burrows (2013) "Popular culture, digital archives and the new social life of data." *Theory, Culture & Society* 30 (4), 47–71.

Benson, R. (2014) "Strategy follows structure: A media sociology manifesto." In S. Waisbord (ed) *Media sociology: A reappraisal* (pp 26–44). Cambridge, UK: Polity Press.

Benson, R., M. Blach-Ørsten, M. Powers, I. Willig, and S.V. Zambrano (2012) "Media systems online and off: Comparing the form of news in the United States, Denmark, and France." *Journal of Communication* 62 (1), 21–38.

Blouin, D.D. and E.M. Perry (2009) "Whom does service learning really serve? Community-based organizations' perspectives on service learning." *Teaching Sociology* 37 (2), 120–35.

boyd, d. (2014) *It's complicated: The social lives of networked teens*. New Haven, CT: Yale University Press.

Brock, A., L. Kvasny, and K. Hales (2010) "Cultural appropriations of technical capital." *Information, Communication & Society* 13 (7), 1040–59.

Carr, J. (2012) "No laughing matter: The power of cyberspace to subvert conventional media gatekeepers." *International Journal of Communication* 6, 21.

Castells, M. (2012) *Networks of outrage and hope: Social movements in the internet age*. Malden, MA: Polity Press.

Clark, J. and N. Themudo (2012) "The age of protest: Internet-based 'dot causes' and the 'anti-globalization' movement." In J. Clark (ed) *Globalizing civic engagement: Civil society and transactional action* (pp 109–26). Sterling, VA: Earthscan.

Couldry, N. (2014) "Inaugural: A necessary disenchantment: Myth, agency and injustice in a digital world." *The Sociological Review* 62 (4), 880–97.

Daniels, J. (2013a) "Race and racism in internet studies: A review and critique." *New Media & Society* 15 (5), 695–719.

Daniels, J. (2013b) "From tweet to blog post to peer-reviewed article: How to be a scholar now." *Impact of Social Science Blog*, September 25. London, UK: London School of Economics (http://blogs.lse.ac.uk/impactofsocialsciences/2013/09/25/how-to-be-a-scholar-daniels/).

Daniels, J. (2013c) "MOOC to POOC: Moving from massive to participatory." *JustPublics@365*. February 5 (http://justpublics365.commons.gc.cuny.edu/2013/02/05/mooc-to-pooc-moving-from-massive-to-participatory/).

Daniels, J. (2015) "'My brain database doesn't see skin color': Color-blind racism in the technology industry and in theorizing the web." *American Behavioral Scientist* 59 (11), 1377–93.

Daniels, J. and J.R. Feagin (2011) "The (coming) social media revolution in the academy." *Fast Capitalism 8.2* (www.uta.edu/huma/agger/fastcapitalism/8_2/Daniels8_2.html?buffer_share=3496f).

Duggan, M., N.B. Ellison, C. Lampe, A. Lenhart, and M. Madden (2015) "Social media update 2014." Pew Research Center's Internet & American Life Project (www.pewinternet.org/2015/01/09/social-media-update-2014/).

Earl, J. and K. Kimport (2011) *Digitally enabled social change: Activism in the internet age*. Cambridge, MA: The MIT Press.

Feagin, J. (2001) "Social justice and sociology: Agendas for the 21st century." *American Sociological Review* 66, February, 1–20.

Freire, P. (2000) *Pedagogy of the oppressed: 30th anniversary edition*. London, UK: Bloomsbury Academic.

Fritz, J.M. (2002) "A little bit of sugar: Integrated service-learning courses." *Sociological Practice* 4 (1), 67–77.

Fry, R. and R. Kochhar (2014) "America's wealth gap between middle-income and upper-income families is widest on record." Pew Research Center, December 12 (www.pewresearch.org/fact-tank/2014/12/17/wealth-gap-upper-middle-income/).

Fuchs, C. (2013) *Social media: A critical introduction*. Thousand Oaks, CA: Sage Publications Ltd.

Gans, H.J. (2014) "American sociology in an era of rising inequalities." *Footnotes*, September/October (www.asanet.org/footnotes/septoct14/inequalities_0914.html).

Geertz, C. (1973) *Interpretation of cultures*. New York: Basic Books.

Gillespie, T., P.J. Boczkowski, and K.A. Foot (eds) (2014) *Media technologies: Essays on communication, materiality, and society*. Cambridge, MA: The MIT Press.

Gold, M.K. (ed) (2012) *Debates in the digital humanities*. Minneapolis, MN: University Of Minnesota Press.

Grollman, E. (2014) "Please blog responsibly." *Conditionally Accepted*, February 6 (http://conditionallyaccepted.com/2014/02/06/blog-responsibly/).

Grollman, E. (2015) "How I became an intellectual activist." *Conditionally Accepted*, October 20 (http://conditionallyaccepted.com/2015/10/20/becoming-activist/).

Hargittai, E. (2010) "Digital na(t)ives? Variation in internet skills and uses among members of the 'net generation'." *Sociological Inquiry* 80 (1), 92–113.

Hargittai, E. (2015) "Is bigger always better? Potential biases of big data derived from social network sites." *The ANNALS of the American Academy of Political and Social Science* 659 (1), 63–76.

Harvey, D. (2003) "The fetish of technology: Causes and consequences." *Macalester International* 13, 1 (http://digitalcommons.macalester.edu/macintl/vol13/iss1/7).

Haythornthwaite, C. (2012) "New media, new literacies, and new forms of learning." *International Journal of Learning and Media* 4 (3–4), 1–8.

Hornborg, A. (2014) "Technology as fetish: Marx, Latour, and the cultural foundations of capitalism." *Theory, Culture & Society* 31 (4), 119–40.

Hughey, M.W. and J. Daniels (2013) "Racist comments at online news sites: A methodological dilemma for discourse analysis." *Media, Culture & Society* 35 (3), 332–47.

Jones, S.E. (2013) *The emergence of the digital humanities*. London, UK: Routledge.

Jurgenson, N. (2012a) "When atoms meet bits: Social media, the mobile web and augmented revolution." *Future Internet* 4 (1), 83–91.

Jurgenson, N. (2012b) "Strong and mild digital dualism." *Cyborgology* (http://thesocietypages.org/cyborgology/2012/10/29/strong-and-mild-digital-dualism/).

Jurgenson, N. (2012c) "The IRL fetish." *The New Inquiry* (http://thenewinquiry.com/essays/the-irl-fetish/).

Kreiss, D. (2014) "Seizing the moment: The presidential campaign's use of Twitter during the 2012 electoral cycle." *New Media & Society* 1461444814562445.

Law, J. (1990) "Introduction: Monsters, machines and sociotechnical relations." *The Sociological Review* 38 (S1), 1–23.

Law, J. (2008) "On Sociology and STS." *The Sociological Review* 56, 4, 623–49.

Liker, J.K., C.J. Haddad, and J. Karlin (1999) "Perspectives on technology and work organization." *Annual Review of Sociology* 25 (1), 575–96.

Liu, A. (2013) "The meaning of the digital humanities." *PMLA* 128 (2), 409–23.

Lupton, D. (2014) "Critical perspectives on digital health technologies." *Sociology Compass* 8 (12), 1344–59.

Lupton, D. (2015) *Digital sociology.* London, UK: Routledge.

McMillan Cottom, T. (2015) "'Who do you think you are?' When marginality meets academic microcelebrity." *Ada: A Journal of Gender, New Media, and Technology* (http://adanewmedia.org/2015/04/issue7-mcmillancottom/).

Marwick, A. (2012) "The public domain: Surveillance in everyday life." *Surveillance & Society* 9 (4), 378–93.

Mooney, L.A. and B. Edwards (2001) "Experiential learning in sociology: Service learning and other community-based learning initiatives." *Teaching Sociology* 29 (2), 181–94.

Newkirk, P. (2015) "Academe must confront its racist past." *The Chronicle of Higher Education*, December 13 (http://chronicle.com/article/Academe-Must-Confront-Its/234534/).

Orton-Johnson, K. and N. Prior (2013) *Digital sociology: Critical perspectives.* Basingstoke, UK: Palgrave Macmillan.

Papacharissi, Z. (2010) *A networked self: Identity, community, and culture on social network sites.* London, UK: Routledge.

Papacharissi, Z. and E. Easton (2013) "In the habitus of the new: Structure, agency, and the social media habitus." In J. Hartley, J. Burgess, and A. Bruns (eds) *A companion to new media dynamics* (pp 171–84). Oxford: Wiley-Blackwell.

Pew Research Center (2014) "Mobile Technology Fact Sheet." Pew Research Internet Project (www.pewinternet.org/fact-sheets/mobile-technology-fact-sheet/).

Rainie, L. (2015) "Digital divides 2015." Pew Research Center: Internet, Science & Tech, September 22 (www.pewinternet.org/2015/09/22/digital-divides-2015/).

Rainie, L. and B. Wellman (2012) *Networked: The new social operating system.* Cambridge, MA: The MIT Press.

Rondini, A.C. (2015) "Observations of critical consciousness development in the context of service learning." *Teaching Sociology* 43 (2), 137–45.

Ruppert, E., J. Law, and M. Savage (2013) "Reassembling social science methods: The challenge of digital devices." *Theory, Culture & Society* 30 (4), 22–46.

Schradie, J. (2011) "The digital production gap: The digital divide and Web 2.0 collide." *Poetics* 39 (2), 145–68.

Smith, A. (2015) "US smartphone use in 2015." Pew Research Center: Internet, Science & Tech, April 1 (www.pewinternet.org/2015/04/01/us-smartphone-use-in-2015/).

Smith, J. (2002) "Globalizing resistance: The battle of Seattle and the future of social movements." In J. Smith and H. Johnson (eds) *Globalization and resistance: Transnational dimensions of social movements* (pp 207–22). Lanham, MD: Rowman & Littlefield.

Tharoor, I. (2014) "Map: The world without the internet." *The Washington Post*, December 15 (www.washingtonpost.com/blogs/worldviews/wp/2014/12/15/map-the-world-without-the-internet/?Post+generic=%3Ftid%3Dsm_twitter_washingtonpost).

Treviño, A.J. and K.M. McCormack (eds) (2014) *Service sociology and academic engagement in social problems*. Aldershot, UK: Ashgate Publishing, Ltd.

Tufekci, Z. (2013) *Big data: Pitfalls, methods and concepts for an emergent field*. Rochester, NY: Social Science Research Network (http://papers.ssrn.com/abstract=2229952).

Tufekci, Z. (2014) "Engineering the public: Big data, surveillance and computational politics." *First Monday* 19, 7 (http://firstmonday.org/ojs/index.php/fm/article/view/4901).

Trottier, D. (2013) *Identity problems in the Facebook era*. London, UK: Routledge.

Uprichard, E. (2012) "Being stuck in (live) time: The sticky sociological imagination." *Sociological Review Monograph* 60, 124–38.

Waisbord, S. (ed) (2014) *Media sociology: A reappraisal*. Cambridge, UK: Polity Press.

Wajcman, J. (2002) "Addressing technological change: The challenge to social theory." *Current Sociology* 50 (3), 347–63.

Waldman, S. (2015) "7 ways Andrew Sullivan changed blogging." *Columbia Journalism Review*, January 29 (www.cjr.org/the_kicker/andrew_sullivan_appreciation.php).

Weber, M. (1958) "Science as a vocation." In H.H. Gerth and C. Wright Mills (eds) *From Max Weber: Essays in sociology* (pp 129–56). Princeton, NJ: Oxford University Press.

Wynn, J.R. (2009) "Digital sociology: Emergent technologies in the field and the classroom." *Sociological Forum* 24 (2), 448–56.

14

Black cyberfeminism: Ways forward for intersectionality and digital sociology

Tressie McMillan Cottom

Millions of people use social media to navigate identities that are more complex than single analytical frames like race, class, gender, and sexuality can fully capture. Here, the potential of intersectionality as a theoretical framework for understanding the reproduction of unequal power relations has not yet been fully realized. Never just an analytical tool to describe the lived experiences, intersectionality was meant to be an account of power as much as it was an account of identities (Crenshaw, 1991). This chapter considers what intersectionality brings to digital sociology. Here, I use digital sociology to mean observing social processes at the micro, meso, and macro level that are transformed or mediated by digital logics, technologies, and platforms. The most common application of intersectionality in studies of the internet or the digital is to social media. This is especially true of macro and meso, or institutional, analyses. Drawing on my research of online and for-profit education, I argue that black cyberfeminist theory can refine digital sociology's understanding of identities, institutions, and political economies in the data age by centering intersectionality. Specifically, I examine how privacy debates benefit when intersectional analysis reveals how different groups use strategic hypervisibility and resist forced context collapse. Fourcade and Healy's theory of classification situations offers the analytical concept of algorithmic stratification, which refines black cyberfeminism's key themes. Next, I discuss intersectionality broadly, the potential of black cyberfeminism, and present case study examples of how classification situations complement this theoretical turn in digital sociology.

Intersectionality as theory, method and praxis

To discuss intersecting inequalities and digital platforms, one has to be clear about what intersectionality framework one is adopting. A full treatment of the various debates in and about intersectionality falls beyond the scope of this chapter (Cho et al, 2013; Davis, 2008; Lewis, 2009; McCall, 2005). In brief, however, intersectionality is one of those rare social theories to combine precision of theoretical mechanisms with broadness of method (Lykke, 2011). That combination has served intersectionality's diffusion through social sciences and humanities quite well. It has also created tensions about what intersectionality really means and how best to measure it (or, if it should be measured at all!). I most often study digitally mediated engagements through institutions like education and work (McMillan Cottom, 2014c; Neem et al, 2012). And I understand one dimension of power as the mobilization of capital and politics to the benefit of some at the expense of others. Through that lens, any site of cultural production exists in a hierarchy of groups and resources, with power flowing betwixt the two, like the Thames. In the black feminist tradition, examining the points of various structural processes where they most numerously manifest is a way to isolate the form and function of those processes in ways that can be obscured when we study them up the privilege hierarchy (Hill Collins, 2000). Essentially, no one knows best the motion of the ocean than the fish that must fight the current to swim upstream. I study fish that swim upstream. Given all of these attestations to my social location vis-à-vis my intellectual production, I call on a methodological practice of "contextual and comparative methodology" grounded in the theoretical imperative to center marginalized groups by examining intersectionality in a "process-centered, institutionally complex way" (Choo and Ferree, 2010: 131). For the purposes of this critical interrogation of intersectionality and digital sociology, this means that I focus on institutions as nadirs of power, the processes by which various intersecting oppressions are enacted, and the means by which groups resist and experience these inter/intra-actions. These levels of analyses are consistent with the three themes of black cyberfeminism, as Gray details them in Chapter 22. I use examples from the case of financialized higher education institutions and online credentials to explore black cyberfeminism's utility for understanding intersectionality and digital sociology.

Background and literature review

I begin this inquiry for an intersectionality of institutions and power in digital spaces close to my home turf. In my pre-academia life, I worked for a social services agency that aimed to move people from "welfare to work." One part of that initiative included employment counseling. My job was to match those on welfare with possible job opportunities. In 2000, that meant sending them out into a labor market where unemployment hovered at around 4 percent. If they could not find a job under those conditions, the next tool in the social services toolkit was to send recipients somewhere for job training. The majority of my clients were women. Over half were black or Hispanic. For them, job training often lent itself to short-term certificate programs in gendered occupations such as allied health care[1] and cosmetology. The cosmetology program would take approximately nine months to complete while allied health courses could take up to 12 months or longer. Sensitive to life-time limits on their benefits[2] and pressures to re-enter the labor market quickly to escape social stigma, most of my clients chose the cosmetology program even though it was more expensive and had lower labor market returns. Some area cosmetology schools offered federal student aid programs and others did not. Those that did not were often cheaper but required cash payment. As a result, most of my clients ended up enrolled in the more expensive cosmetology program because they could get a student loan to pay for it. Put another way, the same structural inequalities that made my clients vulnerable to labor market vicissitudes made them more likely to borrow against future earnings that, on average, would pay less than other occupational certifications. These are some of the ways in which social inequalities and intersecting oppressions manifest offline: political power; obscure language like "block grants" transform the welfare state for the most vulnerable in ways they cannot often understand; and labor markets that reproduce gender through occupational segregation also reproduce racial inequalities because black and brown women have fewer social safety nets and higher risks for falling down the mobility ladder (Alexander et al, 2014).

Consequently, I understood the notable ascension of for-profit colleges[3] as the number one producer of black bachelor's degree holders in the US (Borden and Brown, 2003; Hayes, 2010) as a digitally mediated phenomenon that reproduces intersectional inequalities. That was a marked departure for black degree holders who have, historically, been produced by historically black colleges and universities (HBCUS) and public colleges (Anderson, 1988; Cole and Omari, 2003). Data suggest that students who go to online for-profit degree-granting colleges are likely doing so for reasons manifested by intersections of state power, public policy, historical discrimination, and contemporary disparities. Despite this, there are few models to put the literature on privatization, online education, and intersecting oppressions in conversation with each other.

Digital divides literature provided one way to conceptualize how "offline" inequalities manifest in online platforms, but the relationship between digital access and social status stratification complicates its utility (Hassani, 2006; van Dijk, 2006). For example, the growth of mobile technology in the US and the diffusion rates of platform adoption challenged digital divide's focus on internet access as the primary point axis of stratification (Madden et al, 2010; Smith and Brennan, 2012). Greater access did not seem to necessarily ameliorate group differences as it relates to the internet. A way to resolve this apparent paradox of greater access and more inequality is to operationalize how status diffuses and maintains social hierarchies (Ridgeway, 2014). DiMaggio and Hargittai (2001) offer a multidimensional framework of how status, both achieved and ascribed, complicates dialectics of the haves and have-nots. Of education and technological access, they "hypothesize that, in the long run, education will be a strong predictor of the use of the Internet for the enhancement of human capital, the development of social capital, and political participation" (2001: 13). If sociology of education has contributed anything at all to how we understand stratification, it is that educational institutions reinforce and reproduce inequalities.[4] Historically, as educational access expands and populations became more heterogeneous, educational institutions in the US have differentiated. That differentiation creates stratified access to cultural and material capital. Since higher education participation in the US has reached an historical high, we have produced thousands of private sector, unranked, for-profit colleges, and exactly zero elite colleges and universities (Fry, 2010).

The difference is instructive. Access is easier to produce than equal access to high status rewards. Similarly, increased internet access (or "penetration") may be easier to produce than egalitarian access to skills, know-how, social networks, and capital. For education, greater online participation independent of macro change games access while leaving mobility untouched (if not outright reinforcing structural impediments to mobility). Another weakness of digital divide theories[5] was that they mostly theorize structural stratification at points prior to digital access. After achieving digital access, digital divide framings tend towards cultural explanations of difference (Hassani, 2006). From the perspective of online students in for-profit degree programs, structural stratification manifested at the point of access and beyond, to include group formation and status maintenance. Digital divides may not go far enough to capture the various intersections of privilege, access, and power that operate online and offline simultaneously, and which can also be mutually constitutive.[6]

By 2013 there was a growing literature about alternative credentialing like badging (Ostashewski and Reid, 2015; Schmidt-Crawford et al, 2014) and Massive Open Online Education Courses (MOOCs) (Daniel, 2012; Reich, 2012). At best, this literature spoke about heterogeneity as a proxy for numerous intersecting inequalities. At the opposite of "at best," that literature was preoccupied with what I call "roaming autodidacts." A roaming autodidact is a self-motivated, able learner, simultaneously embedded in technocratic futures and disembedded from place, culture, history, and markets. The roaming autodidact is almost always conceived as Western, white, educated, and male. As a result of designing for the roaming autodidact, we end up with a platform that understands learners as white and male, measuring learners' task efficiencies against an unarticulated norm of Western male whiteness. It is not an affirmative exclusion of poor students or bilingual learners or black students or older students, but it need not be affirmative to be effective. Looking across this literature, our imagined educational futures are a lot like science fiction movies: there's a conspicuous absence of brown people and women. Intersectionality theories or methods have not yet been fully realized in the study of digitality and education, a critical institutional axis of social stratification.[7]

Intersectional theory and methods have also not been fully realized in studying for-profit colleges, which are a case study of financialization, institutions, status groups, and technological affordances. According to the literature at the time (and still mostly true today), there was no racial or gender inequality component in for-profit college expansion (Chung, 2008a, 2008b; Hentscke et al, 2010; Kinser, 2006, 2010; Tierney and Hentschke, 2007). Even research that centered racial categories obscured systemic racism and inequalities by using human capital theories and choice models to explain black participation in for-profit colleges as rational given some un-named constraint (Iloh and Tierney, 2015). The hegemonic narrative said for-profit credentials were instead growing at a rate of over 200 percent (during the sector's highest point of expansion in the early 2000s) because they enrolled "non-traditional" students. It was difficult to square this with the empirical reality of almost three-fourths of for-profit students being women, 1 in 10 of all black college students and 1 in 15 of all Hispanic students being in a for-profit college, and lists like those from *Diverse: Issues in Higher Education*. It was, for me, a call for critical social science, as well as intersectional theories and methods. In my study of status groups (race, class, gender, and their intersections) and for-profit colleges, I faced core challenges for digital sociology (McMillan Cottom, 2017: forthcoming). First, because for-profit colleges are private businesses, they are not publicly accessible for data collection and observation. For-profit colleges are not obligated to provide access to independent researchers. The privatization of critical institutional arrangements like higher education is a serious challenge for digital sociology's focus on studying inequalities. And to keep expenditures low and profits high, faculty at for-profit colleges largely do not have a research imperative and physical campuses have few unstructured spaces for observation. Financial imperatives of privatized public goods shifts institutional responsibility from knowledge production to market penetration, privileging market competition over social inquiry. Despite these severe limitations, students enrolled in for-profit higher education are creating spaces for peer interaction and collective meaning-making (Weick et al, 2005). Some of these spaces are in online social media platforms, such as Facebook, where students exploit the group controls, permissions, and social connections to form informal learning spaces. Their social media content, comprised of posts and peer interactions, constitute digitally mediated autoethnographic narratives of their educational milieus. The digital component is not just for show; it had methodological significance. The platform affords student-users control of how and with whom they share their narrative accounts. Those narratives have been produced without an expectation of performing for the researcher's gaze or approval from important gatekeepers at their institutions.

Participation is entirely voluntary and the exchanges are unstructured, unlike surveys or interviews. Additionally, the social media context affords analysis of discourses across time and various interactions. This could reveal patterns harder to identify via survey or interview methods that offer a snapshot of memory or observation. In the tradition of intersectional theory and method, this project sought first to "give voice to the particularity of the perspectives and needs of women of color who often remained invisible"(Choo and Ferree, 2010: 132). Social media platforms afforded students who are rendered invisible in analysis because of privatization and intellectual enclosure to speak their experiences into legibility.

However, to move beyond "giving voice to" uncovers the way in which power and privilege are often unmarked in social science research (Bonnett, 1996; Zuberi, 2008). Intersectionality demands that we examine process and power relations. That is part of intersectionality's political imperative. Essentially, in studying black and Hispanic women in isolation, I could reinforce hierarchies that reify whiteness, especially middle-class whiteness on whom the higher education norms are predicated. This is a consequence of what Choo and Ferree discuss as an intellectual blindspot for unmarked categories. Take, for instance, why we think for-profit colleges are a bad choice. They are bad because rational actors choose a "real" college (that is, a not-for-profit college) as high up the institutional prestige hierarchy as one's academic record and finances will allow. Consequently, research on for-profit colleges using this model of college choice argues that the demographic characteristics of for-profit college students are evidence of poor decision-making. I did not want to buy a ticket to that party. Intersectionality theory argues that narrative methods de-center privilege in rational actor theories. Therefore, I conceptualized the social media data I collected as autoethnographies rather than content. While content can absolutely be analyzed as narratives, it is most often analyzed as a quantitative abstraction or without attention to qualitative differences in the power that frames content. In contrast, ethnographic data's imperative is to situate meaning among various relational dynamics like power, privilege, and social location (Ellis and Bochner, 2006). Autoethnographies resist hegemonic sense-making paradigms by centering self-authored texts and the co-construction of meaning. These theoretical imperatives, mechanisms, and methodological choices are consistent with black cyberfeminism's focus on intersectionality and unique characteristics of digitized social processes. Next, I discuss the robust potential of black cyberfeminism for digital sociology.

Black cyberfeminism

In Chapter 22 Kishona Gray outlines a framework for black cyberfeminism. That framework explains how categorical inequalities are translated through and in digital spaces. Black cyberfeminism builds on black feminist thought

(Crenshaw, 1991; hooks) as well as feminist technology studies (Daniels, 2009; Everett, 2004; Faulkner, 2001; Orgad, 2005). Cyberfeminism articulates a feminist theory of how gendered bodies and relations shape technologies and how we interact with them. Daniels argues that cyberfeminism is a range of theories and methods more than it is a "clearly articulated political agenda" (2009: 102). Despite this, there is a coherent logic to cyberfeminism, namely, an interest in how digital technologies "enable women to engage in new forms of contestation and in proactive endeavors in multiple different realms, from political to economic" (Sassen, 2002: 368). By explicitly theorizing those multiple different realms, black cyberfeminism offers a more cohesive intersectional project than cyberfeminism. Whereas cyberfeminism does not often articulate the relationship between specific mechanisms for the political economies of how different groups engage digital technologies in multiple different realms, black cyberfeminism pays particular attention to precisely that. In Chapter 22 in this volume, Gray offers three major themes of black cyberfeminism theory:

(1) social structural oppression of technology and virtual spaces;
(2) intersecting oppressions experienced in virtual spaces; and (3) the distinctness of virtual feminism.

When presented as postulations for a particular case – here, for-profit colleges – black cyberfeminism's potential for digital sociology become clearer.

The first theme translates a central interest of black feminist studies: how structural oppression operates along multiple planes of social location (Hill Collins, 1990). Black cyberfeminism would interrogate how social relations of dominance are translated through digitally mediated relationships with technology, the interests that produce it, and the processes that resist them. This is an inherently political imperative, more clearly articulated as an epistemological project than is currently stated in cyberfeminism studies

The second theme argues that structural oppression is translated through technologies and reproduces different individual and categorical experiences by race, class, and gender. This seems pedantic, but it is a critical contribution to how we currently discuss digitality in sociology. Digitization is not a neutral process in social relations, cannot be understood as necessarily democratizing, and should reproduce unequal social relations of the society that produces it. And digitization does not just happen at the micro level of identity or interactions or the macro level of markets. Digitization is a relationship rationalized through bureaucracies, institutional forms of work and civic participation, taken up because of the constraints produced by differential institutional access. This is a departure from sociological interest in technology as a tool, whether for markets or innovation or social change. If we accept this premise of black cyberfeminism, digital sociology should ask how and under what conditions intersecting oppressions are translated through digitization differently for different groups.

The third theme argues that there is something distinctive about virtual feminism. A way to understand this is that unmarked categories of race, class, and gender operate in specific ways. And the specificity of those categories can be marked, or revealed, theoretically, when black cyberfeminism's focus on power relations is centered on analysis. To interrogate how black middle-class women pursue credentialing is to understand, theoretically, that those categories are defined in relation to white poor men, for one example. For digital sociology, this presents a challenge that is worth taking: how can we both theorize and operationalize marked and unmarked social categories in a relational way when technology can obscure our usual methods of doing so (for example, observation, surveying, and bureaucratic records)?

I have argued that black cyberfeminism brings an intersectional theoretical framework to studying digitally mediated social processes, and that it shapes the sociological questions we ask of the internet. Black cyberfeminism's three themes are an important ideological contribution to sociology's imperative to study groups, processes, power, and relations in, on, and through digital transformations. Black cyberfeminism is more assertively political than cyberfeminism, functional theories, and neo-institutional theories of the internet. Black cyberfeminism offers a cohesive argument for interrogation and resistance. Black cyberfeminism is attentive to the mechanisms of political economy in its attention to power relations that define and constrain social mobility: race, class, gender, and sexual orientation. One challenge for black cyberfeminism is an articulation of the mechanisms by which social categories and their attendant inequalities become transformed and reconstituted in virtual spaces. And how do those virtual spaces also reconstitute non-virtual categorical inequalities? I argue that emerging work on classification situations contributes a refinement for implementing black cyberfeminism studies of social phenomena.

Classification situations

Classification situations take up social theory's interest in how economic classifications stratify group access and mobility. Rooted in classic Weberian models of occupational and social stratification, classification situations refer to the way institutions systematically "sort and slot people into new types of categories with different economic rewards or punishments attached to them" (Fourcade and Healty, 2013: 561). Their focus is on social class and the actuarial process of the new economy's digitized institutions. These means of sorting and stratifying were largely illegible to those who needed the scores to participate under the new rules of financialization, but who did not have the wealth to buffer them from its risks. Fourcade and Healy make the analogy to redlining, or the practice of excluding African Americans from living in white neighborhoods. Like redlining, algorithms do not just give us a personal internet. These algorithms also stratify group-based access to critical institutions such as markets, financial institutions, education, and work. Further, I argue that eventually capital is reorganized to correspond with algorithmic efficiencies, reinforcing structural inequalities.

Classification situations is an analytical lens through which to understand how systemic linkages between macro characteristics of markets are translated through institutions to shape the life chances of social-categorical groups. Fourcade and Healy notably give two illustrations of these trends: credit scoring and higher education. They expound on credit scoring. I expound on higher education. Algorithmic sorting of credit-worthiness has shaped how categorical groups access and benefit differently from market relationships. Classification situations offer two critical refinements worth taking up in black cyberfeminism studies in digital sociology. First, classification situations respond to the challenge presented above, where it was clear that something about being black, working class, and a woman had shaped students' institutional access to digitally mediated relationships with higher education institutions. These differences were as much about categorical power relationships as about individual identity. Classification situations propose that categorical groups matter to the study of digitality. Second, classification situations offer algorithmic stratification, or the means by which algorithms differently sort categorical groups' access to resources, as a way to understand how digitality transverses the virtual space. What we do online is, in part, about who we are categorically when we do it. And our returns to what we do online is stratified based on how we are translated by algorithms in accordance with institutional efficiency preferences. This is an important bridge that has eluded dialectical approaches to the internet (online and offline, real and virtual, space and place). It is an approach that reveals the mechanisms of digitally mediated stratification by adhering to the black feminist tradition of centering marginalized groups to reveal systemic inequalities.

Classification situations offer a mechanism to apply black cyberfeminist themes in analysis. Those themes focus on processes and relations produced by the given conditions of the political economy in which digital platforms are produced and used. Classification situations clarify one way that this happens: through categorical relationships with institutional practices rationalized and diffused in a political economy of neoliberal transformations of society. In this framework, how black women take up higher education choices using digital platforms is shaped by pre-existing categorical constraints produced by markets and states. The choices made given those constraints are conditioned on categorical differences in relationship to civic norms such as privacy as well as differentiated higher education systems, where different institutions organize differently to efficiently allocate marginalized groups to different kinds of educational life chances. Next, I provide examples of how black cyberfeminist theory and classification situations clarify current tensions in privatized, financialized higher education.

Case studies of intersectionality and the internet

A black cyberfeminist analysis refines two emerging debates about the internet. Here, I present two cases to illustrate this point. Both emerge from my ongoing research of intersectionality and for-profit credentials in the US between 1994 and the present day. This period of rapid for-profit college expansion is intertwined with the diffusion of internet access, technologies, platforms, and institutional adoption. The first example considers how privacy as commonly positioned in current scholarly and public debates obscures how marginalized communities use technological affordances to balance anonymity with oppressions stemming from ascribed categorical status groups. The second case considers how an intersectional focus on the processes by which groups interact with various institutional processes on the internet are embedded in various structural processes of inequality.

Privacy versus hypervisibility

This study of black and Hispanic women earning online PhDs in marginalized for-profit colleges problematized the utility of privacy online. There has been a rich conversation about what constitutes privacy in online spaces, with concerns about how tracking, cookies, and private data caching constitute a form of surveillance (Barnes, 2006; Daries et al, 2014). Often, the most vulnerable are centered in these discussions to draw stark emotional lines around the scope of the problem. For example, privacy debates have frequently centered on youth and teenagers, because children and young adults are especially vulnerable (Livingstone, 2008; Youn, 2005). Most of this literature assumes, if not explicitly argues, that privacy is most fragile for socially vulnerable groups. If I take as a point of departure that black women and Hispanic women constitute a group that are often marginalized by social, economic, and cultural processes, it would follow that we should err on the side of more privacy controls for these groups. However, analyses of these students, in this particular institutional context, suggest that privacy can compound students' marginality rather than ameliorate it.

Most of the students in my study found the online support group through (1) Facebook ads and (2) secondary ties with group members. Because the group is restricted to women, gendered network ties predisposed members to finding out about the group. And because three-fourths of the group members are black or Hispanic, those network ties hinged on shared ascription among group members. The group moderator, Janice, said she used Facebook profile pictures to screen potential new members. Profiles without evidence of gender were denied. From the students' perspectives, sharing members' ascribed status in the group increased social trust. That trust is very important when the group is a platform for co-creating meaning around sensitive topics like debt and academic performance. One member, Lisa, says that her online school used to require all of the students to post their real pictures and to engage in online discussion groups. After some students complained that the posting requirement was burdensome, the school dropped it. Lisa says that without the user profile images and online group requirement, she did not know how to judge her academic performance (and fears about it) relative to the other students' social location. There was little to be learned from comparing herself to a white male student, for example. She could assume that he did not share similar time constraints because of childcare arrangements. His performance in class was not meaningful for Lisa because she intuited that his social location afforded him resources that she did not have. In contrast, Lisa said that the members of the online Facebook group being all women "mattered" because "I know they know what I go through." She trusts that the group moderator has properly screened members, and Facebook profile images reinforce this trust is well placed. For the women in this group, the kind of privacy often discussed among researchers and policy-makers would blunt a tool for educational persistence. Not knowing who the group members are would make Lisa less likely to use the online support group, a group she credits for pushing her to degree completion.

This kind of complicated relationship with privacy goes beyond the institutional context of formal education. Take, for example, recent debates on Twitter about "stealing" tweets (Wong, 2014). There is a whole brand of (mostly digital) journalism that culls social media content for stories. Many users have pushed back against this practice, saying that their content is used without their express permission. There is a procedural debate about the chain of ownership given terms and conditions, private ownership, and public diffusions. That is another debate. However, there is something about the difference between privacy and hypervisibility to be learned from these tensions. Context collapse[8] offers some much needed clarity to the debate about media institutions borrowing tweets from marginalized groups who use the platform for consciousness-raising, networking, and finding community. Context collapse, broadly, is about how we switch our performance depending on who is watching. We decide how to act based on who is around because we know that not all people are created equal. And when we might need access to privileged resources like, say, jobs, we act differently around audiences we presume are comprised of people who govern access to jobs.

Context collapse has mostly been about the control tweeters can exert over how and when and where one performs the identity one thinks most appropriate for a situation. But media organizations' "tweet borrowing" strips tweeters of that autonomy. They do this through institutional power to reallocate amplification. By virtue of being media and a company, these institutions are more powerful than most of its users and content producers. They have greater amplification power and more money to spend drowning out individual resistance and more protection when they make a mistake. Because they are charged with keeping political power in check, media organizations get more benefit of the doubt than people. Because of the difference in power, media can force context collapse that may not have happened without its intervention. Thought of another way, I sign up for Twitter assuming the ability to hide in plain sight when my amplification power is roughly equal to a few million other non-descript content producers. Media amplification changes that assumption and can do so without my express permission. Effectively, power can force context collapse, or produce what Davis and Jurgenson have called "context collision" (2014), altering marginalized users' strategic deployment of hypervisibility. Like the students in my study, it appears that marginalized groups find value in hypervisibility precisely because it affords them something blanket privacy may not while preserving the aspects of privacy that work for their purposes. Hypervisibility makes one's social location legible, through images, discourse, language, and affective practices. I am part of "black Twitter" precisely because other users can encode and decode these signals to locate me in shared discursive practices on an open, private media platform. As long as the power to amplify is kept in check, hypervisibility affords me community without the burden of excessive interrogation. It is hiding in plain sight. In contrast, blunt attempts at privacy like those that happened at Lisa's for-profit online college became a hindrance. Nixing student photos and the discussion board requirement compounded Lisa's feeling of institutional isolation. The difference could impact our objective measures of inequality and mobility, that is, educational attainment, persistence, and occupational access. As one student said when friends expressed concern about using her real name in her online educational communities, because it would signal to gatekeepers that she is a black woman, "Hell, my name is LaKeisha. Changing that doesn't stop me from being black." Changing the performance of marginality online does not change the offline marginality for people who live in both simultaneously. And the context of the online use matters. Earning a credential is serious business with serious risks and rewards. For black women who bear the brunt of controlling images (Hill Collins, 1996, 2000) that circumscribe their social mobility, educational attainment is an important social signal. These controlling images, or hegemonic tropes, circulate in internet memes. The controlling image of Sapphire, a fast-talking, loud-mouthed, and angry black woman, persists in memifications of black women's images with text like "I'm a strong black woman who don't need no man." Those kinds of persistent controlling images are always a specter in the shadow for the students I interviewed.

Credentials were a way of resisting racist sexist tropes of social deviance. When the stakes are that high, the students I interviewed relied on signals of social inclusion like images, moderator screening, and discursive practices. They were trying to minimize their exposure to powerful actors, often understood as the "white gaze" (Bonnett, 1996), while navigating institutional contexts where that is impossible. At best, they could use social media platforms to erect porous boundaries to define the composition of their digital student lounges. But to build those boundaries the members had to use the very aspects of identity that many privacy controls would minimize. Facebook's architecture was most amenable to this kind of malleable hypervisibility, affording privacy while also designing the platform around social signals that made the students feel safe in the online community. What we learn from this intersectional approach to LaKeisha, Lisa and Janice's approach to online privacy is that certain types of privacy are privileges that some groups cannot pretend to have if the internet is to be useful for their purposes.

Algorithmic stratification

The study of women in online PhDs was instructive not only because of its findings, but for how the group found me: algorithmic sorting of network ties, ads, and content. I am black. I am a woman. I have been a Facebook user for 12 years. My educational affiliations are listed in my biography. Some combination of those identities and behaviors filtered me through Facebook's (proprietary) algorithms and one day listed this Facebook group in my newsfeed. I had no prior affiliations with any members of the group. None of them were Facebook friends. Interviews suggested that many in the group found it through similar algorithmic means. They were placed in each other's path by the invisible hand of internet sorting, stratifying and signaling that defines much of our internet experience without our knowing it (Pasquale, 2015).

I return to my studies of for-profit colleges for an example. As I noted previously, the hegemonic narrative about the rapid expansion of for-profit colleges attributed it to the sector's success with enrolling "non-traditional" students. They offered "flexible" online courses that appealed to busy working adults. Working adults and non-traditional students is a discursive collapse of several intersecting inequalities: gendered time gaps, racial inequalities in educational access to college preparatory curriculums, class inequalities in reliance on public sector labor markets, and a growing service economy that disproportionately impacts the life chances of the poor and working class. Students classified in the literature as "non-traditional" comprise half of all students enrolled in degree-granting institutions (Deil-Amen, 2012). Despite comprising a significant number of all college students, non-traditional students are marked as different from traditional students. The distinction has utility because of ideological, cultural distinctions about normativity, race, class, and gender. Deil-Amen says, "Our conceptions of the typical idealized college student are based on traditional notions and an imagined norm of someone who begins college immediately after high school, enrolls full-time, lives on campus, and is ready to begin college level classes" (2012: 2). Traditional notions and imagined norms are allusions to cultural ideologies about an ideal student type. Like the ideal worker type (Kelly et al, 2010), these ideologies begin as material realities. When higher education organizations were defining their institutional norms, de rigeur and de facto segregation prevented women, non-whites, and non-elite status groups from participating in higher education. The ideal student type has persisted despite sociopolitical extra-institutional changes like demography patterns. When we unpack the categorical definition of "non-traditional student," we find intersectional oppressions lurking just beyond the neologism.

To recruit status groups similarly vulnerable because of those intersecting oppressions, for-profit colleges became one of the single biggest internet advertisers in history (McMillan Cottom, 2017: forthcoming). In 2012, the Apollo Group, the largest for-profit college company and owner of the University of Phoenix brand, spent $400,000 a day in Google ads alone. For-profit colleges made the "jobs and education" sector the fourth-highest industry advertising on the major search engine and e-commerce platform (McMillan Cottom, 2014b). And of that sector, the top five advertisers also happened to be the largest national for-profit college chains. Together, they spent more than $1.1 billion in online advertising with a single search engine in 2011. For-profit colleges also kept "lead generation aggregators" in business after their other major client, the mortgage industry, took a hit during the Great Recession. Lead generation aggregators capture user content, ostensibly under the guise of providing free college information. They then sell that customer information to for-profit colleges who use it to recruit new students. Senators in 2013 wrote to the Federal Trade Commission about lead generators that they "have become a key part of the aggressive recruiting strategy for many for-profit colleges" and they "deceive consumers to obtain personal information by misrepresenting their affiliation with for-profit colleges, as well as concealing how and by whom their information will be used." Googling for "college grant money" is a practice in information democracy. Wealthier students, or those with the cultural know-how to navigate the complicated student aid process, often know about grants and loans. Students without the benefit of that cultural largesse do not. The internet makes finding that information more accessible. But lead aggregators and privatized relationships between the financial sector and educational institutions use algorithms to skew searches in favor of capital interests. When my Google is no longer everybody's Google, my structural inequalities are transposed into new kinds of ephemeral inequalities through algorithms one cannot see, touch, or easily contest.

For a thought experiment of what such an approach might look like, let us consider again a status group for the purposes of for-profit college expansion. They targeted non-traditional students. Non-traditional students are not defined just by descriptors like age or parental status. They are also defined in opposition to the ideal norm of a "traditional" student. A traditional student is not only unfettered and younger than 24 years old. She is also adequately prepared for college-level coursework. Benefiting from the vast educational industrial complex of tutors, sports leagues, essay coaches, college application consultants, and standardized test prep certainly helps one be prepared for college-level coursework (Stevens 2009). So, too, does parental income and wealth that strongly correlates with the neighborhood segregation that drives group differences in access to high-performing primary and secondary schools in the US (Massey and Denton, 1988; Massey and Fischer, 2006). All of those resources, both the material and cultural, also provide prospective students with a fairly good cognitive map of the institutional prestige that defines US higher education. Knowing what a small liberal arts college (SLAC) means in real, practical terms is an example of the kind of cognitive maps born of privilege and wealth. When an algorithm is calibrated to capture attention for non-elite, low status, controversial forms of school like a for-profit college, it would be most efficient if it targets groups without the capital to know that the University of Phoenix is not a SLAC. Targeting inequality is transformed into a technical efficiency. The same report on for-profit colleges' use of lead aggregators found that "unemployment insurance" was one of the sector's top five targeted search terms. If those targeted messages resonate across social locations, it is likely because those groups share similar levels of resources to discern types of colleges or are similarly constrained in their ability to choose among different types of colleges. An analytical focus on race, absent a consideration of the cumulative and integrated effects race with class and gender, can easily lead one to conclude, "race is not a significant predicator of enrollment" in for-profit colleges, as Chung finds in a recent study (2013). Race is not a biological construct with inherent associated abilities. There is no reason that race should predict enrollment in a higher education institution. But race *is* a social construct. It is constructed, in part, through the classification activities of institutions. These classification activities not only reproduce social class but also intersecting planes of race, class, and gender. Focusing on the process by which attention is stratified using technical affordances like lead generators and search algorithms can clarify these processes.

Conclusion

Black cyberfeminist theory bridges gaps in current theory and method in internet studies, as well as various other disciplinary modes of studying the internet. Status groups are constantly morphing, but the power relationships that define status groups are remarkably stable. Focusing on categorical descriptions to the exclusion of process conflates compositional change for structural change. In the case of for-profit colleges, they need not singularly recruit black students or poor students or female students to recruit from those groups in significant proportions. They need only to target the shared vulnerabilities among those various social locations. Once that is done – flexible online classes you take from anywhere after the kids are asleep – technology makes targeting those vulnerabilities efficient and scalable. Broadly conceived, algorithmic stratification captures the shifting landscape of intersectional groups; macro changes in economies and policy that bracket how the internet works; and the conditions under which groups use the internet for critical institutional engagements. Importantly, algorithmic stratification would attend to class, but not only class. If the aim is to understand the nature of contemporary inequality, there is value in discerning the life chances of poor white women in Western nations distinctly from those of poor second-generation Congolese immigrants in a Western nation. Algorithmic stratification would account for the intersections of history and biography that define integrative intersectionality under contemporary structural conditions. As privatization complicates datafication,[9] neoliberalism weakens social reforms, and capital further inserts its way into how we live our daily lives on the internet, intersectionality is critical to internet studies and social science. Algorithmic stratification's focus on process, both online and off, across intersecting power relations is a way to move the study of contemporary inequalities forward.

In my study of minority women in online for-profit degree programs, intersectionality complicated common prescriptions for privacy, suggesting that calibrations of an internet for everybody cannot be tuned for a typical user without exacerbating the very inequalities we hope the internet can redress. As critical institutional arrangements are increasingly mitigated by (often proprietary) digital platforms, intersectionality gives us a framework to consider how these contexts contour access differently. All evidence points towards a future where platforms and algorithms mediate everything from healthcare and education to civic participation and labor participation. If classification situations urge us to consider the role of algorithms in reproducing class inequalities, thinking more broadly about class as an intersectional social location strengthens the utility of algorithmic studies in understanding contemporary social inequalities.

Notes

[1] "Allied health care" refers to the paraprofessional medical field occupations, for example, phlebotomists, medical records clerks, and nursing assistants.

[2] Famously, Work First training requirements rarely conceded that many welfare recipients would not qualify for even minimally competitive post-secondary admissions. This delimits the pool of potential institutions greatly. Additionally, not all open-access post-secondary institutions offer qualifying short-term certificates or admissions to them as frequently as those constrained by Work First guidelines would need to stay benefits-eligible. See Shaw et al (2006) and DHHS (2013) for more.

[3] For-profit colleges are so named because their Internal Revenue Service designation permits extracting profit from tuition revenue to be distributed to owners. They are more expensive, on average, than comparable not-for-profit public college credentials at every level from certificate to graduate degrees. And they are almost as expensive as the most elite private not-for-profit colleges with few institutional or foundational subsidies like grants to reduce student tuition costs.

[4] There is so much here that oddly rarely crosses the disciplinary divide. I would start with the following key readings for the trajectory of sociology of education (Bowles and Gintis, 2002; Collins, 1979; Stevens, 2009; Stevens et al, 2008).

[5] I acknowledge the lively debate about "digital dualism", particularly among cultural studies scholars. For analytical clarity I occasionally use "online" and "offline" in the structural sense. It primarily refers to the centrality of space (online) as opposed to place (offline) as the dominant mode of interaction being addressed. These are analytical distinctions.

[6] I am also aware of a parallel and intersecting literature on "digital natives." This framing recalls linear theories of racial assimilation (see, for example, Robert Park) that disquiet me. For a history of linear racial theories one may want to read Eduardo Bonilla Silva to consider the complexity of that framing for status groups defined, in significant part, by the legal, political and social ascription of race and social enclosure (1997).

[7] If I had one wish I would think long and hard about using it to make Massey et al's *The source of the river* required reading for all conversation about technology and education.

[8] And at the aggregate level, those assumptions would match data that continue to show gendered, classed, and racialized differences in everything from parental care responsibilities, care work, extended kin support, and the experience of the "time bind". danah boyd cites Goffman as the intellectual tradition of "context collapse" (2013). Exercising a little academic iteration, I prefer to think of context collapse's intellectual tradition as DuBoisian. Not only does it call to mind DuBois' classic double-consciousness dialectic, but as I use it and think through it, double-consciousness engages the political economy of ascription in useful ways to think of context collapse as it relates to intersecting power relations and institutions.

[9] For more on the issues of privatization and datafication specific to the institutional context of formal education, I suggest Audrey Watters and Jeffrey Alan Johnson (Johnson, 2014; Watters, 2013).

References

Alexander, K., D. Entwisle, and L. Olson (2014) *The long shadow: Family background, disadvantaged urban youth, and the transition to adulthood.* New York: Russell Sage Foundation.

Anderson, J.D. (1988) *The education of blacks in the South, 1860–1935.* Chapel Hill, NC: University of North Carolina Press.

Barnes, S.B. (2006) "A privacy paradox: Social networking in the United States." *First Monday* 11, 9 (http://journals.uic.edu/ojs/index.php/fm/article/view/1394).

Bonilla-Silva, E. (1997) "Rethinking racism: Toward a structural interpretation." *American Sociological Review* 62 (3), 465.

Bonnett, A. (1996) "'White studies': The problems and projects of a new research agenda." *Theory, Culture & Society* 13 (2), 145–55.

Borden, V. and P. Brown (2003) "The top 100: Interpreting the data. Black issues in higher education." *Black Issues in Higher Education* 20 (10), 40–81.

Bowles, S. and H. Gintis (2002) "Schooling in capitalist America revisited." *Sociology of Education* 75 (1), 1–18.

boyd, d. (2013) "How 'context collapse' was coined." apophenia (www. zephoria.org/thoughts/archives/2013/12/08/coining-context-collapse. html).

Cho, S., K.W. Crenshaw, and L. McCall (2013) "Toward a field of intersectionality studies: Theory, applications, and praxis." *Signs* 38 (4), 785–810.

Choo, H.Y. and M.M. Ferree (2010) "Practicing intersectionality in sociological research: A critical analysis of inclusions, interactions, and institutions in the study of inequalities." *Sociological Theory* 28 (2), 129–49.

Chung, A. (2008a) "For-profit student heterogeneity" (http://mpra.ub.uni-muenchen.de/18967/).

Chung, A. (2008b) "The choice of for-profit college" (http://mpra.ub.uni-muenchen.de/18971/).

Chung, A.S. (2012) "Choice of for-profit college." *Economics of Education Review* 31 (6), 1084–101.

Cole, E.R. and S.R. Omari (2003) "Race, class and the dilemmas of upward mobility for African Americans." *Journal of Social Issues* 59 (4), 785–802.

Collins, R. (1979) *The credential society: An historical sociology of education and stratification.* New York: Academic Press (www.tcrecord.org.proxy.library. emory.edu/library/abstract.asp?contentid=1005).

Crenshaw, K. (1991) "Mapping the margins: Intersectionality, identity politics, and violence against women of color." *Stanford Law Review*, 1241–99.

Daniel, J. (2012) "Making sense of MOOCs: Musings in a maze of myth, paradox and possibility." *Journal of Interactive Media in Education* 3, 18.

Daniels, J. (2009) "Rethinking cyberfeminism (s): Race, gender, and embodiment." *WSQ: Women's Studies Quarterly* 37 (1), 101–24.

Daries, J.P. et al (2014) "Privacy, anonymity, and big data in the social sciences." *Communications of the ACM* 57 (9), 56–63.

Davis, J.L. and N. Jurgenson (2014) "Context collapse: theorizing context collusions and collisions." *Information, Communication & Society* 17 (4), 476–85.

Davis, K. (2008) "Intersectionality as buzzword: A sociology of science perspective on what makes a feminist theory successful." *Feminist Theory* 9 (1), 67–85.

Deil-Amen, R. (2012) "The 'traditional' college student: A smaller and smaller minority and its implications for diversity and access institutions." Mapping Broad-Access Higher Education Conference, Stanford University, Stanford, CA (http://cepa. stanford.edu/sites/default/files/2011).

DHHS (Department of Health and Human Services) (2013) *Work First – About Work First.* North Carolina Department of Health and Human Services (www.ncdhhs.gov/assistance/low-income-services/work-first-cash-assistance).

DiMaggio, P. and E. Hargittai (2001) *From the "digital divide" to "digital inequality": Studying internet use as penetration increases.* Working Paper Series 15. Princeton, NJ: Center for Arts and Cultural Policy Studies, Woodrow Wilson School, Princeton University (www.princeton.edu/~artspol/workpap/WP15%20-%20DiMaggio+Hargittai.pdf).

Ellis, C. and A. Bochner (2006) "Communication as autoethnography." In G. Shephard, J. St John, and T. Sriphas (eds) *Communication as...: Stances on theory* (pp 110–22). London, UK: Sage.

Everett, A. (2004) "On cyberfeminism and cyberwomanism: High-tech mediations of feminism's discontents." *Signs* 30 (1), 1278.

Faulkner, W. (2001) "The technology question in feminism: A view from feminist technology studies." In *Women's studies international forum* (vol 24, no 1, pp 79–95). Pergamon.

Fourcade, M. and K. Healy (2013) "Classification situations: Life-chances in the neoliberal era." *Accounting, Organizations and Society* 38 (8), 559–72.

Fry, R. (2010) *Minorities and the recession-era college enrollment boom.* Washington, DC: Pew Research Center, Social and Demographic Trends Project.

Hassani, S.N. (2006) "Locating digital divides at home, work, and everywhere else." *Poetics* 34 (4–5), 250–72.

Hayes, D. (2010) "Confronting the for-profit conundrum." *Diverse Issues in Higher Education*, August 20 (http://diverseeducation.com/article/17311/).

Hentscke, G.C., V.M. Lechuga, and W.G. Tierney (eds) (2010) *For-profit colleges and universities: Their markets, regulation, performance, and place in higher education.* Washington, DC: Stylus Books.

Hill Collins, P. (1996) "What's in a name? Womanism, black feminism, and beyond." *The Black Scholar*, 9–17.

Hill Collins, P. (2000) *Black feminist thought: Knowledge, consciousness, and the politics of empowerment* (revised 10th anniversary edn), New York: Routledge.

Iloh, C. and W.G. Tierney (2013) "A comparison of for-profit and community colleges' admissions practices." *College and University* 88 (4), 2.

Johnson, J.A. (2014) "From open data to information justice." *Ethics and Information Technology* 16 (4), 263–74.

Kelly, E.L., S.K. Ammons, K. Chermack, and P. Moen (2010) "Gendered challenge, gendered response confronting the ideal worker norm in a white-collar organization." *Gender & Society* 24 (3), 281–303.

Kinser, K. (2006) "What Phoenix doesn't teach us about for-profit higher education." *Change: The Magazine of Higher Learning* 38 (4), 24–9.

Kinser, K. (2010) *The global growth of private higher education.* Oxford: Wiley.

Lewis, G. (2009) "Celebrating intersectionality? Debates on a multi-faceted concept in gender studies: Themes from a conference." *European Journal of Women's Studies* 16 (3), 203–10.

Livingstone, S. (2008) "Taking risky opportunities in youthful content creation: Teenagers' use of social networking sites for intimacy, privacy and self-expression." *New Media & Society* 10 (3), 393–411.

Lykke, N. (2011) "Intersectional analysis: Black box or useful critical feminist thinking technology."." In H. Lutz, M.T. Herrera Viver, and L. Supik (eds) *Framing intersectionality: Debates on a multi-faceted concept in gender studies* (pp 207–20). Aldershot, UK: Ashgate.

Madden, M., A. Lenhart, S. Cortesi, and U. Gasser (2010) *Pew Internet and American Life project.* Washington, DC: Pew Research Center.

McCall, L. (2005) "The complexity of intersectionality." *Signs* 30 (3), 1771–800.

McMillan Cottom, T. (2014a) "The university and the company man." *Dissent* 61 (2), 42–4.

McMillan Cottom, T. (2014b) "Mitigating concerns and maximizing returns: Social media strategies for injury prevention non-profits." *Western Journal of Emergency Medicine* 15 (5), 582–86.

McMillan Cottom, T. (2014c) "For-profits are us." *AFT On Campus* 33 (4), 7–14.

McMillan Cottom, T. (2015) "Becoming real colleges in the financialized era of US higher education: The expansion and legitimation of for-profit colleges." Dissertation, Emory University.

McMillan Cottom, T. (2017: forthcoming) *Lower ed: The rise of for-profit colleges.* New York: The New Press.

Massey, D.S. and M.J. Fischer (2006) "The effect of childhood segregation on minority academic performance at selective colleges." *Ethnic and Racial Studies* 29 (1), 1–26.

Massey, D.S. and N.A. Denton (1988) "The dimensions of residential segregation." *Social Forces* 67 (2), 281–315.

Neem, J.N. et al (2012) "The education assembly line." *Contexts* 11 (4), 14–21.

Ostashewski, N. and D. Reid (2015) "A history and frameworks of digital badges in education." In T. Reiners and L.C. Wood (eds) *Gamification in education and business* (pp 187–200). Cham, Switzerland: Springer International Publishing.

Orgad, S. (2005) "The transformative potential of online communication: The case of breast cancer patients' Internet spaces." *Feminist Media Studies* 5 (2), 141–61.

Pasquale, F. (2015) *The black box society: The secret algorithms that control money and information.* Cambridge, MA: Harvard University Press.

Reich, J. (2012) "Summarizing all MOOCs in one slide: Market, Open and Dewey." EdTech Researcher (http://blogs.edweek.org/edweek/edtechresearcher/2012/05/all_moocs_explained_market_open_and_dewey.html).

Ridgeway, C.L. (2014) "Why status matters for inequality." *American Sociological Review* 79 (1), 1–16.

Sassen, S. (2002) "Towards a sociology of information technology." *Current Sociology* 50 (3), 365–88.

Schmidt-Crawford, D., A.D. Thompson, and D. Lindstrom (2014) "Leveling up: Modeling digital badging for preservice teachers." *Journal of Digital Learning in Teacher Education* 30 (4), 111.

Shaw, K.M., S. Goldrick-Rab, C. Mazzeo, and J.A. Jacobs (2006) *Putting poor people to work: How the work-first idea eroded college access for the poor.* New York: Russell Sage Foundation.

Smith, A. and J. Brenner (2012) "Twitter use 2012." *Pew Internet & American Life Project*, 4.

Stevens, M. (2009) *Creating a class.* Boston, MA: Harvard University Press (www.hup.harvard.edu/catalog.php?isbn=9780674034945).

Stevens, M.L., E.A. Armstrong, and R. Arum (2008) "Sieve, incubator, temple, hub: Empirical and theoretical advances in the sociology of higher education." *Annual Review of Sociology* 34, 127–51.

Tierney, W.G. and G.C. Hentschke (2007) *New players, different game: Understanding the rise of for-profit colleges and universities.* Baltimore, MD: Johns Hopkins University Press.

van Dijk, J.A.G.M. (2006) "Digital divide research, achievements and shortcomings." *Poetics* 34 (4–5), 221–35.

Watters, A. (2013) "Strata week" (www.hackeducation.com).

Weick, K.E., K.M. Sutcliffe, and D. Obstfeld (2005) "Organizing and the process of sensemaking." *Organization Science* 16 (4), 409–21.

Wong, J.C. (2014) "Tweeters of the world, unite!" *The Nation*, March 21.

Youn, S. (2005) "Teenagers' perceptions of online privacy and coping behaviors: A risk–benefit appraisal approach." *Journal of Broadcasting & Electronic Media* 49 (1), 86–110.

Zuberi, T. and E. Bonilla-Silva (2008) *White logic, white methods: Racism and methodology.* Lanham, MD: Rowman & Littlefield Publishers.

15

Deconstructing racism on college websites

Monita H. Mungo

The culture of universities and colleges sometimes creates boundaries that prevent students of color from academic achievement. Tinto's research on student retention demonstrated the ways that universities play a role in student attrition (Tinto, 1982, 2003, 2006, 2012). For example, a student must be academically and socially engaged at an institution in order to be retained (Tinto, 2012). Campus and faculty connections reinforce student attachment and feelings of belonging to educational institutions. However, it is difficult to connect to an institution when policies and practices conspire to reproduce social inequality. The legacy of racism is embedded in every social institution in America, including the education system that continues to tout ideologies of meritocracy and equal opportunity. The online presence of colleges and universities are no different than other institutions – they reflect and reproduce structural racial inequities. Digital media may be one (previously unexplored) factor in the achievement gap debate, examining disparities in retaining students of color. Critical race theory (CRT) explores and unmasks the various permutations of racism. As an analytical tool, it is useful in digital spaces because it explores the various ways racism and the assumptions of race operate in higher education, limiting academic success for marginalized students. When applied to the digital sphere, CRT provides a theoretical lens from which to interrogate an institution's policies and practices in regards to underrepresented students and how they connect with the campus environment.

Education, inequality and racism

Racism is a normative and pervasive organizing principle of society. From the opportunities to attend specific schools to the resources available to educate students, inequality in the education system is a fact. Persistent racial disparities exist in educational institutions at all levels (Carter, 2009: 333; Feagin et al, 1996; Kozol, 1991; Ladson-Billings, 2003; Merolla, 2013, 2014; Merolla and Jackson, 2014; Orfield, 2013; Roscigno and Ainsworth-Darnell, 1999: 158). Inequality in education can be observed and measured in many ways. However, the root causes of racial inequality in educational outcomes remain a matter of scholarly debate. Some researchers suggest that the unstable structure of black families is to blame (Moynihan, 1965; Wilson, 1999). Others believe that the biological make-up of blacks makes them intellectually inferior (Herrnstein and Murray, 1994). Yet other scholars consider the historical, political, economic, and moral decisions made over time as the reason for achievement disparities (Kozol, 1991; Ladson-Billings, 2003).

Social class is also a factor that contributes to racial disparities in educational outcomes. Instead of seeing the biological differences of race/ethnicity as the cause, some researchers argue that the socioeconomic status (SES) of parents affects a student's ability to do well in school. Specifically, SES differences cause achievement differences (Duncan et al, 1998; Duncan and Magnuson, 2005; Warren, 1996; White, 1982). SES and race as indicators are important because together they predict the outcomes of racial inequality, historical disadvantage, and the significance of race in structuring who gets what economic resources. It is considered normal and certainly unremarkable that black students attend worse schools; that is the normativity of white supremacy, making the marked inequalities seem normal and unproblematic for many Americans.

Researchers also attribute the achievement gap to the residential segregation that occurs in urban areas that results in school segregation; these disadvantaged communities suffer from a decrease of school funding, and fewer resources with which to educate minority children, leaving them ill-prepared for higher education (Carter, 2009: 333; Kozol, 1991; Massey and Denton, 1993; Orfield, 2013). Low-income families tend to live in impoverished neighborhoods and attend under-resourced schools that do not present children with the same educational opportunity as schools with adequate resources. In the US, primary, middle, and high schools are funded by property taxes collected from the surrounding neighborhood in which the school resides. If the surrounding neighborhood is impoverished, the resources the school receives to educate and prepare its students for post-secondary education is meager. Most poor and underperforming schools reside in neighborhoods in which subordinate groups reside. The residents are black or Latino, poor, and disproportionately single mothers. When students graduate, both groups of students, underprepared and prepared, sit in the same college classrooms as if they are on a level playing field and are assessed in the same manner.

A relatively recent explanation cited as a cause for the low achievement of minority students is called "stereotype threat." Stereotype threat refers to the threat of being viewed through the lens of a negative stereotype, or fear of doing something that would confirm that stereotype (Steele, 2003: 679). Stereotype threat occurs when groups who are negatively stereotyped in society perceive a "threat" under certain conditions. In the classroom, stereotype threat operates by decreasing academic performance of the students who perceive themselves in a threatening situation. In digital spaces, stereotypical images associated with race are used to create a specific campus environment, signaling that certain students are more valuable than others

Social reproduction can also explain the achievement gap. Social reproduction refers to the generational transmission of social inequality through social structures such as the educational system (Bourdieu and Passeron, 1977; Doob, 2013; Sullivan, 2001, 2002). Social reproduction occurs because the ideology in the US, which characterizes education as a means for social mobility available to all who want it, implies meritocracy, therefore blaming the lack of success as being the fault of the individual. This ideology ignores the reality of how underrepresented groups experience education. It also minimizes the importance of wealth, status, and power since the philosophy of schooling is based on white, middle-class culture (Harker et al, 1990; Sullivan, 2002). As a social structure, education socializes students for specific roles in society that reflect economic class inequalities. A student's success in school goes beyond mastery of the formal curriculum. It is also dependent on their ability to acquire and wield cultural and social capital. The degree to which an individual can attain cultural capital, that is, to participate as well as succeed in the dominant culture, determines their access to resources and opportunities (Lynch, 1990; Sullivan, 2002). Cultural capital refers to the systems of values of meaning, shared outlooks, beliefs, knowledge, and skills that an individual acquires from their position in society. Social capital refers to the various relationships, networks, and potential resources that are beneficial to an individual's success. Whereas what you know and how you use it are important in the acquisition and wielding of cultural capital, who you know is most significant for acquiring and wielding social capital. The connections that a student has and the opportunities for which a student can create more using social and cultural capital allows them to connect and navigate a campus environment successfully.

One of the most well-known arguments for the achievement gap is attributed to John Ogbu who used case studies and other qualitative methods to examine the social structures and historical processes that contribute to the underachievement of racialized minorities (2003). His body of work has led to the oppositional culture theory that seeks to explain the racial disparities between whites and blacks. The oppositional culture model distinguishes between how minorities came to live in the US, citing the difference as the significant factor that has an impact on an individual's chances for success. Those who migrated voluntarily tend to be more successful than those who came to the US through slavery or colonization (Ainsworth-Darnell and Downey, 1998: 536–7; Fordham and Ogbu, 1986). In regards to educational achievement, Ogbu argues that black youth develop an oppositional identity relative to whites (Ogbu, 1992). Black students do not perform well in school in order to avoid the label of "acting white," since performing well in school is associated with the behavior of whites. According to Ogbu, involuntary minorities view participation in a society that historically compelled their behavior as an act of disloyalty to the group (Ogbu, 1992). Thus, according to Ogbu, participating in dominant cultural practices such as doing well in school is seen as an act of betrayal.

As a social institution, the education system has an enormous influence on the choices and chances available to an individual. Beyond inheritance, education is arguably the single most important tool an individual can acquire in order to access better socioeconomic outcomes, including upward mobility. However, there remains a large population of individuals who are prevented from navigating the education system. The socialization process that occurs in schools is one that is structured by the dominant group with their experiences and interests in mind that reproduces social inequality in policies, practices, as well as in digital representations of a campus environment and the student experience.

Colleges and universities do not exist as independent institutions separate from economic, political, cultural, and social contexts; accordingly they cannot be insulated from the challenges that each context provides (Carter and Welner, 2013: 218). They have ethical obligations that mean they cannot remain blind to the inequalities and structural changes around them. Prejudice, discrimination, and disadvantage do not begin at university, but universities are obligated to address these issues since they conflict with the basic principles of free thought, human rights, critical dialogue, and education. Higher education as an institution must therefore be diligent to not reinforce or increase socioeconomic and educational inequality. It is imperative that post-secondary institutions challenge the very foundation they stand on in regard to its policies and procedures, especially questioning its delivery of academic functions in digital spaces.

Digital spaces and inequality

Through the use of images and text, colleges and universities carefully craft their digital presence to reflect a specific view of campus life and the composition of the student body. They present an idealized image of the campus environment – but they also contain multiple assumptions about educational opportunities, student populations, and inequality. Given that educational disparities based on skin color, ethnicity, and social class continue to characterize the US education system (Carter and Welner, 2013), the digital field has the potential to reinforce, ignore, or reduce such inequalities. Unlike more recent digital platforms that utilize computer algorithms and software to provide real-world images that reflect the users and their preferences, websites of colleges and universities rely on a human-powered labor system to deliberately and carefully craft representations of the institution. In website sections with headings such as, "What is campus about?," "What will students look like?," and "What students can expect," colleges and universities seek to shape perceptions of the institution's structure, identity, and possibility for student experience in order to influence the decision-making of prospective students. Often the carefully crafted portrayals of a student population that can be found on a university website perpetuate taken-for-granted assumptions about race, providing a visual image of who is welcome to participate in these spaces of privilege and prestige, and who is not. Marketing departments typically choose from thousands of stock photographs in order to convey an inviting campus environment since it is not confined to the limited choices of images of virtual gaming worlds and communities. Thus, the painstaking process of impression management is deliberate, as colleges and universities work to convey specific messages about student life through websites. These intentionally constructed portrayals commodify diversity in a way that is not just palatable but pleasing, and perhaps aspirational to a specific consumer.

Diversity has become increasingly commodified as a result of the admissions and accreditation process as well as through political and financial pressure to increase retention. By invoking diversity through the use of digital images, specific information is conveyed. As a result, university websites may seem colorblind because they state that their academic missions involve diversity, multicultural knowledge, and inclusive excellence; and the prominently displayed images "prove" it to be so. However, there are many problematic assumptions that guide program and policy creation for academic achievement in higher education, especially in relation to underrepresented student groups – and these assumptions can be reproduced online. Consequently, the digital representations of campus life by colleges and universities may contribute to educational disparities by race.

The most obvious examples of such disparities may be the absence of images of people of color as academic administrators, scholars, and students. But there are other, less obvious, inequalities that may also be present in university or college websites. Such inequalities include the absence of counter-narratives about the role of structural inequality and racism on the path to educational success; the failure to overtly challenge racism, including colorblind racism (Bonilla-Silva, 2010); and the unacknowledged presence of white privilege, or alternatively, deliberate steps to refrain from reinforcing white privilege. All of these forms of inequality can overlap in terms of the presence of digital images about educational institutions – presenting images of privilege or exclusion for some populations. In this context, it is essential to examine the digital realm from an intersectional perspective that includes race, class, and gender. CRT is a useful theoretical lens from which it is possible to explore the digital representation of race from college and university websites in the US.

Critical race theory

CRT is a theoretical perspective that acknowledges that racism is engrained in the fabric of American life. It focuses on the effects of race and racism, particularly emphasizing that institutional racism is pervasive in the dominant culture. White supremacy, it suggests, is hegemonic – and it is necessary to explore and challenge power structures that are based on white privilege and supremacy. CRT is an analytical tool used to expose race and racism that serves as a source of othering marginalized individuals (DeCuir and Dixson, 2004). It offers a way to rethink traditional education scholarship by challenging the traditional claims of objectivity, meritocracy, colorblindness, race neutrality, and equal opportunity, as well as the dominant discourse of race and racism, by examining how educational theory, policy, and practice have been used to subordinate racial groups (Ladson-Billings and Tate, 1995; Solorzano, 1998). There are a number of fundamental tenets of CRT that are important for this discussion, including counter-storytelling, recognizing the pervasiveness of racism, identifying and challenging white privilege, and a critique of liberal, "colorblind" ideology.

Counter-storytelling

Counter-storytelling involves the privileging of stories told by people of color who highlight their lived experiences in a highly racialized social order as a means of critiquing dialogues and challenging the privileged discourses of the majority that perpetuate racial stereotypes (DeCuir and Dixson, 2004; Delgado, 1989; Lopez, 2003). The use of counter-storytelling in a CRT framework analyzing education research has been essential to giving voice to the personal and community experiences of people of color as sources of knowledge (DeCuir and Dixson, 2004: 27; Dixson and Rousseau 2005). Delgado and Stefancic define counter-storytelling as a story that "aims to cast doubt on the validity of accepted premises or myths, especially ones held by the majority" (2001: 144). The potential for counter-storytelling on colleges and university websites is that it can "give voice" to the campus experiences of students of color through images chosen and posted by them, using their experience as a source of knowledge. Online counter-storytelling, through images and narratives, potentially allows marginalized groups to have a voice and name their own reality in university spaces, illuminating their campus experiences.

Scholars of CRT believe that there are two different accounts of reality: the dominant reality that looks ordinary and natural, neutral, and just to most individuals; and the racial reality that has been suppressed or censored (Bell, 1980; Delgado, 1995: xiv; Lopez 2003: 84). Counter-storytelling is helpful to "understand what life is like for others, and invite[s] the reader into a new and unfamiliar world" (Delgado and Stefancic, 1993: 41). Subordinated groups have experiential knowledge that is legitimate as well as appropriate to explain the meaning and consequences of the racialized experience (Brown, 2003). For example, in 2013, when the US President, Barack Obama, identified himself with Trayvon Martin, an unarmed 17-year-old black male from Miami, Florida, who was killed by a white neighborhood watch volunteer, he was heavily criticized for "injecting himself and racial division into matters best left alone" (Branch, 2013: 9). The dominant story about race in the US in the form of complaints and criticisms against President Obama was in the media everywhere. Hashtags were plentiful, and Twittersphere was abuzz. His remarks were charged with betraying "the great achievement of our society, the possibility of not talking about race" (Branch, 2013: 9). By identifying with Trayvon Martin, President Obama gave voice to and named the reality of what it means to be a black man walking down any street in the US. His comments exposed a racialized experience that is ordinary for many people of color. These lived experiences are not natural or just, yet they occur at high frequencies and are hidden behind a cloak knitted with post racial jargon. It is not a surprise that the dominant group took issue with President Obama's remarks. How could the first black president of the United States of America – a symbol of post-racism and meritocracy at its greatest – violate the neutrality and censorship that governs colorblind ideology in our great nation?

The pervasiveness of racism

Racism shapes institutions, relationships, and ways of thinking since racist hierarchical structures are a permanent, normal, ordinary, and taken-for-granted component of American life that influences all political, economic, and social spheres, including education (DeCuir and Dixson, 2004; Dixson and Rousseau, 2005; Lopez, 2003). Racial stratification is "ordinary, ubiquitous, and reproduced in mundane and extraordinary customs and experience," and affecting the quality of life's choices and chances of racial groups (Brown, 2003: 294). The concept of the pervasiveness of racism suggests that racist hierarchical structures are a permanent component of American life. And, as the internet becomes institutionalized, patterns of use, access, and opportunities will either reproduce racial inequality or work to decrease it (DiMaggio et al, 2001).

Historically, race emerged as a social structure – a racialized social system that awarded privileges to Europeans, the people who became white, over non-Europeans, the people who became non-white (Bonilla-Silva, 2010). Its existence is connected to the distribution of jobs, power, prestige, wealth, educational access, and opportunity (Crenshaw et al, 1995; Lopez 2003). According to CRT scholars, the reason why society does not see racism is because it is a normal and ordinary daily experience that is taken for granted. We fail to see how racism functions and shapes institutions and relationships, as well as ways of thinking and seeing (Lopez, 2003). In educational institutions we fail to see how policies and models that are touted as best practice work to reproduce racial stratification.

For example, it is common practice for colleges and universities to place important forms and policy information online. Efficiency replaces the person-to-person contact that students once received in the college environment. However, the practice assumes all students have access to the internet. By making the internet a rational and normal way of doing business in college, it ignores the fact that the only access to the internet, computers, and printers that some students may have is the campus library. Students of color are more likely to become a victim of this "best" practice.

Identifying and challenging white privilege

White privilege includes the presumption that whiteness does not need to be mentioned in any discussions of identity and privilege – including educational privilege as well as other forms of economic, social, and cultural capital (DeCuir and Dixson, 2004; Harris, 1993). Legal CRT scholars contend that whiteness can be considered a property interest as a result of the legal reification of race in the US (DeCuir and Dixson, 2004). The notion of whiteness as property refers to whiteness as the ultimate property that whites alone possess (DeCuir and Dixson, 2004). Property not only describes things or the rights of people with respect to a thing, it also characterizes the rights in things that may be intangible or legally defined (Harris, 1993). Thus whiteness, as defined by law, affirms who is white, what benefits are afforded to that identity, and what entitlements result (Harris, 1993).

Within a CRT framework, whiteness is valuable and is property, granting privileges, and making the American Dream a more likely and attainable reality for white citizens. Whiteness grants privileges to the owner that a renter (or a person of color) would not be afforded. Researchers of educational inequity utilize whiteness as property in a CRT framework to examine the myriad ways that school policies and practices reify whiteness as property by asserting rights to possession, use, and enjoyment, and disposition to white students, allowing for safe and well-equipped schools, high-quality rigorous curriculum, honors and gifted programs, advanced placement courses, and well-equipped computer labs, while excluding access and use to students of color (DeCuir and Dixson, 2004; Kozol, 1991; Ladson-Billings and Tate, 1995; Solorzano and Ornelas, 2002). By privileging practices that have evolved from white, middle-class values, colleges and universities devalue other cultural norms and assign labels such as "at risk" and "under-prepared" when students do not meet the expectations.

A critique of liberal, "colorblind" ideology

Through the lens of CRT, the idea that society is "colorblind" is seen as an ideology that denies both the ongoing nature of racism and the privileges that it provides to those who are white. Racism has a persistence and pervasiveness in the US that excludes, labels, marginalizes, and limits the rights of people of color in many ways. The past and current effects of racism are denied their legitimacy by those who suggest that the US is a "post-racial" or "colorblind" society (Bell, 1980, 1992, 1995; Crenshaw, 1988; DeCuir and Dixson, 2004; Harris, 1993; Lawrence, 1995; Lopez, 2003; Matsuda, 1995). The concepts of diversity (in ambiguous forms), colorblindness, and the neutrality of the law are notions of liberal ideology that fail to acknowledge racial differences. According to Nakamura, "the language of tolerance, or of disavowing racism by simply omitting all language referring to race, functioned to perpetuate digital inequality by both concrete and symbolic means" (2008: 3). The idea that the law is colorblind and neutral ignores the history of racism in the US, specifically, since rights and opportunities were given and withheld based on race. Therefore, the concept of colorblindness fails to account for the persistence and permanence of racism and the construction of people of color as other (DeCuir and Dixson, 2004; Lopez, 2003). Second, colorblind ideology, the belief that race does not matter and racism no longer exists, has been used as a justification to change race-based policies that were created to address social inequity (Gotanda, 1991). Further, diversity, as is commonly utilized in educational settings, represents a liberal perspective that CRT argues is code for the presumption of a "homogenized we celebration" as opposed to confronting racism head on (Ladson-Billings, 1998). According to Brown (2003: 294), race problems are difficult to grasp and "possibly impossible to remedy because claims of objectivity and meritocracy camouflage the self-interest, power, and privilege of whites."

Colorblind ideology positions racism at the individual level and ignores other ways in which it functions in society (Lopez, 2003). An example of a race-based policy change is the US Supreme Court upholding of Michigan's constitutional amendment banning the use of race in public university admissions' practices (Barnes, 2014b). Supreme Court Chief Justice Roberts' famous statement from his 2007 opinion on another race-based policy case regarding public school districts' use of race to determine what schools students can attend is invoked here to demonstrate the majority opinion of the court, "the way to stop discrimination on the basis of race is to stop discrimination on the basis of race" (Barnes, 2007). In her dissent of the Michigan case, Supreme Court Justice Sotomayor called Roberts' statement from 2007 "too simplistic" (Barnes, 2014a). Roberts' statement conflates racism and discrimination as well as implies a level playing field that does not account for the crystallization of racism in America's social structures. Neutral policies ignore the fact that inequity, inopportunity, and oppression are historical artifacts that will not easily be remedied by ignoring race in contemporary society (DeCuir and Dixson, 2004).

Ladson-Billings and Tate (1995) introduced the use of CRT in educational research a decade ago, and ever since it has proven to be a powerful theoretical and analytical framework (DeCuir and Dixson, 2004: 27). As such, extending its framework into the digital sphere of college and university spaces may prove beneficial to highlight the ways the internet is being used to reproduce social inequality. CRT provides an analytical tool to examine the subtlety, pervasiveness, and salience of race and racism in higher education, and how it manifests in online spaces. CRT challenges researchers to critique school practices and policies that are overtly and covertly racist, making race the center focus (DeCuir and Dixson, 2004). For this discussion, CRT provides an interpretive framework that asserts the needs of marginalized populations while critically analyzing the presumptions and reasoning that underlie educational policies and assumptions as depicted by their online presence (Teranishi, 2007).

Critical race theory and digital spaces

CRT offers not only a way to examine how educational practices utilizing digital spaces have been used to subordinate some racial groups and privilege others, but also implies strategies to offset dominate narratives about race. It seeks to discover and disrupt institutional cultures and practices that continue to marginalize students of color and limit their academic success in college. Additionally, it identifies forms of power that are implicit in seemingly "neutral" policies that actually reinforce inequality and disadvantage. Such inequalities exist throughout contemporary society, including many university websites. For instance, the presence or absence of people of color on university websites, the text that occurs alongside their images, the roles they are shown playing, and the messages about race are all important elements of a CRT analysis of digital spaces.

CRT is not simply a critique; it offers an alternative to dominant ideologies, policies, and practices. CRT emphasizes the need for counter-storytelling that gives voice to the personal and community experiences of people of color. This is one missing element of most university websites – one that digital sociology can expose and challenge. Counter-storytelling allows marginalized groups to have a voice and name their own reality since they are able to use images and narratives to illuminate their campus experiences. Acknowledging the pervasiveness of racism moves beyond the popular colorblind American ideology about race that renders racism an individual and irrational act in a world that is neutral, rational, and just, and places it at the forefront of critical inquiry by acknowledging its pervasive role in society (Crenshaw et al, 1995; Lopez, 2003). Clearly, racism in the US abounds, as evidenced by the comments section of any local and national news media website. The digital sphere grants anonymity in such a way that some feel that it increases their "e-courage" to be candid about race and other social problems (Santana, 2014). The individual – not the social structure responsible for creating and maintaining racist spaces – is attacked and labeled as racist.

Whose digital experience?

Student populations are increasingly diverse in many ways. Student bodies constitute a myriad of races, socioeconomic backgrounds, educational preparation and intellectual abilities, which demands changes in the manner in which colleges and universities craft their online image. Being omnipresent, digital media are an inherent feature of everyday life that allows documentation, observation, and creation of experiences for many students (Lupton, 2013). Capitalizing on this fact, colleges and universities digitally construct a campus environment and student experience using images that may have an impact on a student's ability to connect to campus.

Digital images presented reflect assumptions of higher education as being spaces that reproduce privilege and power and are not representative of the actual campus. For example, the main page of the website of an urban research institution located in the Midwest section of the US depicts a carefully crafted student and campus experience. The first page of the website depicts a group of individuals walking along the sidewalk of a bustling metropolitan street. This image is placed as the focus of the page among the many choices presented to navigate the website. Seemingly, this page represents the gateway of the website since it offers selections such as "explore our programs," "register for classes," and "become a student," which indicate the importance of the page for potential, new, and current students. The page is also important for the university since it is the first digital representation of itself seen on the website. The first assumption is that we know these are students as indicated by two of the three individuals wearing shirts that promote the university. The individuals wearing the college gear are white-skinned and the third person is slightly darker-skinned. Her ethnicity is difficult to determine, as she is slightly darker than the other two students, yet her physical features are similar to individuals who label themselves as white.[1] She is carrying a backpack as an indicator of being a student. The racial composition of the city in which the university resides is 87 percent African American and 11 percent White (US Census Bureau, 2010). The racial composition of the university is currently 53 percent White and 21 percent Black. The stark contrast of the racial composition of the city and the university is visually depicted on the webpage. For a black resident of the city considering enrolling in the local university, the image suggests who the university is looking for as well as the experience a student may encounter on its campus. The image also suggests what is important to the university that resides in a city where 13 percent of individuals aged 25 and older possess a college education; 39 percent of citizens are living below the poverty level; and the per capita income was $14,870 in 2013 (US Census Bureau, 2013).

Refreshing the same webpage several times offers more images that depict similar commentary. When the page is refreshed a different image is presented – one of a bustling campus event where many individuals are engaged. The individuals are of various ages, genders, and race – and not one of them is wearing college paraphernalia. If one was not familiar with the campus, the university's name on the event tents is the only indicator that the event is located on the actual campus. This is a missed opportunity to depict diversity and multiculturalism. Further, it is commentary on what the university values and what it does not. When the page is refreshed again, another image is presented of two students, one African-American male dressed in the university's colors attempting to catch a Frisbee from another male student, who is white, also clad in the university's colors with a matching hat. The background of the image depicts four females engrossed in a conversation; three are sitting around a picnic table and the other is standing. The lawn and surrounding trees and shrubbery are beautifully manicured.

CRT provides an appropriate theoretical lens for interrogating an institution's policies and practices in regards to underrepresented students and how they experience the campus environment. It also provides the tools needed to examine the realities of students of color attending universities and colleges. There is a great need to acknowledge and reflect the varied lived experiences that exist among the student body, especially online; these experiences may greatly affect how students confront college and feel a sense of attachment to their educational institution, since campus engagement is considered an important factor in increasing retention. Counter-storytelling is a social justice strategy through which experiences of people of color – faculty, administrators, and students – should be illuminated via university and college websites. Counter-storytelling could involve testimonies from people of color who are faculty, students, alumni, and community members who would convey their experience within the university context, and the importance of education in personal and community empowerment; using images of real students, staff, and faculty, including those of color, engaged in real – not staged – activities, depicting the actual campus and student life environment as the background of testimonies. Thus moving away from picture-perfect greenery in the midst of a concrete jungle toward privileging students and their experiences. Such an approach would, by definition, address the second key concern raised by CRT: recognizing the pervasiveness of racism by disrupting the normal and expected imagery on college and university websites. Using counter-storytelling in words and images of people of color challenges white privilege by confronting the notion of white as being the representative of the "normal" college student. Instead of an over-representation of white people or people of ambiguous racial identity on university websites, they should explicitly and deliberately include people of color.

Conclusion

Higher education is essential for upward mobility in society. It is a social and economic indicator of social location and status. It is both necessary and required in order to attain the socially constructed "American Dream." It is also the key to getting a good job that pays a higher salary with benefits, thus increasing one's quality of life (Weber, 2010:49). Inequality in the use of images depicted on university and college websites may promote existing racist thoughts and behaviors. The challenge, then, is to avoid patterns of inequality by crafting images that challenge racism and avoid traditional assumptions about race in higher education. The overall effect of inclusive representations of people of color on college and university websites may help students of color create connections to campus, reinforcing student attachment and feelings of belonging to educational institutions, thereby retaining, graduating, and improving opportunities for upward social mobility. There are many factors involved in the retention of students of color. Improving the connections they are able to make to the institution by transforming educational websites is one step in addressing problems of recruitment and retention of students of color.

Note

[1] Race is a social construction of rigid categories given to groups based on the hue of their skin color and physical characteristics. As a social construction, race has direct consequences for individuals who have been racialized, and it plays out in their lived experiences. It also shapes their perceptions of social life. Using only images that depict students' race as ambiguous at best, and de facto white at worst, ignores the significance of race, and prevents the university from connecting to people of color whose appearance is far more apparent.

References

Ainsworth-Darnell, J. and D.B. Downey (1998) "Assessing the oppositional culture explanation for racial/ethnic differences in school performance." *American Sociological Review* 63 (4), 536-53.

Barnes, R. (2007) "Divided court limits use of race by school districts." *The Washington Post*, June 29 (www.washingtonpost.com/wp-dyn/content/article/2007/06/28/AR2007062800896.html).

Barnes, R. (2014a) "Sotomayor accuses colleagues of trying to 'wish away' racial inequality." *The Washington Post*, April 22 (www.washingtonpost.com/politics/sotomayor-accuses-colleagues-of-trying-to-wish-away-racial-inequality/2014/04/22/e5892f90-ca49-11e3-93eb-6c0037dde2ad_story.html).

Barnes, R. (2014b) "Supreme Court upholds Michigan's ban on racial preferences in university admissions." April 22 (www.washingtonpost.com/politics/supreme-court-reverses-decision-that-tossed-out-michigans-ban-on-racial-preferences/2014/04/22/44177ad6-9d8f-11e3-9ba6-800d1192d08b_story.html).

Bell, D.A. (1980) "Brown v Board of Education and the interest convergence dilemma." *Harvard Law Review* 93, 518–33.

Bell, D.A. (1992) *Faces at the bottom of the well: The permanence of racism*. New York: Basic Books.

Bell, D.A. (1995) "Racial realism." In K. Crenshaw, N. Gotanda, G. Peller, and K. Thomas (eds) *Critical race theory: The key writings that formed the movement* (pp 302–12). New York: The New York Press.

Bonilla-Silva, E. (2010) *Racism without racists: Color-blind racism and racial inequality in contemporary America* (3rd edn). Lanham, MD: Rowman & Littlefield, Inc.

Bourdieu, P. and J.C. Passeron (1977) *Reproduction in education, society and culture* (2nd edn). London, UK: Sage Publications.

Branch, T. (2013) "Remembering the March." *USA Weekend*, August 16–18.

Brown, T.N. (2003) "Critical race theory speaks to the sociology of mental health: Mental health problems produced by racial stratification." *Journal of Health and Social Behavior* 44, 292–301.

Carter, P. (2005) *Keepin' it real: School success beyond black and white*. New York: Oxford University Press.

Carter, P. (2009) "Equity and empathy: Toward racial and educational achievement in the Obama era." *Harvard Educational Review* 79 (2), 287–97.

Carter, P.L. and K.G. Welner (2013) "Building opportunities to achieve." In P.L. Carter and K.G. Welner (eds) *Closing the opportunity gap: What America must do to give every child an even chance* (pp 217–27). New York: Oxford University Press.

Crenshaw, K.W. (1988) "Race, reform, and retrenchment: Transformation and legitimation in anti-discrimination law." *Harvard Law Review* 101, 1331–87.

Crenshaw, K.W., N. Gotanda, G. Peller, & K. Thomas (1995) *Critical race theory: The key writings that formed the movement*. New York: The New Press.

DeCuir, J. and A. Dixson (2004) "'So when it comes out, they aren't that surprised that it is there:' Using critical race theory as a tool of analysis of racism in education." *Educational Researcher* 33 (26), 26–31.

Delgado, R. (1989) "Storytelling for oppositionists and others: A plea for narrative." *Michigan Law Review* 87, 2411–41.

Delgado, R. (1995) *Critical race theory: The cutting edge*. Philadelphia, PA: Temple University Press.

Delgado, R. and J. Stefancic (1993) "Critical race theory: An annotated bibliography." *Virginia Law Review* 79 (2), 461–516.

Delgado, R. and J. Stefancic (2001) *Critical race theory: An introduction*. New York: New York University Press.

DiMaggio, P., E. Hargittai, W. Russell Neuman, and J.P. Robinson (2001) "Social implications of the internet." *The Annual Review of Sociology* 27, 307–36.

Dixson, A.D. and C.K. Rousseau (2005) "And we are still not saved: Critical race theory in education ten years later." *Race Ethnicity and Education* 8 (1), 7–27.

Doob, C.B. (2013) *Social inequality and social stratification in US society*. Upper Saddle River, NJ: Pearson Education, Inc.

Duncan, G.J. and K.A. Magnuson (2005) "Can family socioeconomic resources account for racial and ethnic test score caps." *The Future of Children* 15 (1), 35–54.

Duncan, G.J., W. Jean Yeung, J. Brookes-Gunn, and J.R. Smith (1998) "How much does childhood poverty affect the life changes of children?" *American Sociological Review* 63 (3), 406–23.

Feagin, J.R., H. Vera, and N. Imani (1996) *The agony of education: Black students at white colleges and universities*. New York: Routledge.

Fordham S. and J. Ogbu (1986) "Black students' school success: Coping with the burden of 'acting white.'" *Urban Review* 18 (3), 176–206.

Gotanda, N. (1991) "A critique of our constitution is color-bind." *Stanford Law Review* 44, 1–68.

Harker, R., C. Mahar, and C. Wilkes (eds) (1990) *An introduction to the work of Pierre Bourdieu: The practice of theory*. London, UK: Macmillan.

Harris, C. (1993) "Whiteness as property." *Harvard Law Review*, 106.

Herrnstein, R.J. and C. Murray (1994) *The Bell Curve: Intelligence and class structure in American life*. New York: Free Press.

Kozol, J. (1991) *Savage inequalities: Children in America's schools*. New York: Crown Publishers Inc.

Ladson-Billings, G. (1998) "Just what is critical race theory and what's it doing in a nice field like education?" *International Journal of Qualitative Studies in Education* 11 (1), 7–24.

Ladson-Billings, G. (2003) *Critical race theory perspectives on the social studies: The profession, policies, and curriculum*. Greenwich, CT: IAP.

Ladson-Billings, G. and W. Tate (1995) "Toward a critical race theory of education." *Teachers College Record* 97 (1), 47–68.

Lawrence, C.R. (1995) "The id, the ego, and equal protection: Reckoning with unconscious racism." In K. Crenshaw, N. Gotanda, G. Peller, and K. Thomas (eds) *Critical race theory: The key writings that formed the movement* (pp 235–57). New York: The New York Press.

Lopez, G.R. (2003) "The (racially neutral) politics of education: A critical race theory perspective." *Educational Administration Quarterly* 39 (1), 68–94.

Lupton, D. (2013) "Digital sociology: Beyond the digital to the sociological." The Australian Sociological Association 2013 Conference: "Reflections, Intersections and Aspirations, 50 Years of Australian Sociology." Melbourne, Australia.

Lynch, K. (1990) "Reproduction: The role of cultural factors and educational mediators." *British Journal of Sociology of Education* 11 (1), 3–20.

Massey, D. and N. Denton (1993) *American apartheid segregation and the making of the underclass*. Cambridge, MA: Harvard University Press.

Matsuda, M. (1995) "Whiteness as property." In K. Crenshaw, N. Gotanda, G. Peller, and K. Thomas (eds) *Critical race theory: The key writings that formed the movement* (pp 357–83). New York: The New York Press.

Merolla, D.M. (2013) "The net black advantage in educational transitions: An education careers approach." *American Educational Research Journal* 50 (5), 895–924.

Merolla, D.M. (2014) "Oppositional culture, black habitus and education: A new perspective on racial differences in student attitudes and beliefs." *Race, Gender & Class* 21 (1/2), 99–111.

Merolla, D.M. and O. Jackson (2014) "Understanding differences in college enrollment: Race, class and cultural capital." *Race and Social Problems* 6 (3), 280–92.

Moynihan, D.P. (1965) *The negro family: The case for national action*. Washington, DC: Office of Policy Planning and Research, United States Department of Labor.

Nakamura, L. (2002) *Cybertypes. Race, ethnicity, and identity on the Internet*. London, UK: Routledge.

Nakamura, L. (2008) *Digitizing race: Visual cultures of the internet*. Minneapolis, MN: University of Minnesota Press.

Ogbu, J.U. (1992) "Adaptation to minority status and impact of school success." *Theory into Practice* 31 (4), 287–95.

Ogbu, J.U. (2003) *Black American students in an affluent suburb: A study of academic disengagement*. Mahwah, NJ: Lawrence Erlbaum Associates.

Orfield, G. (2013) "Housing segregation produces unequal schools: Causes and solutions." In P. Carter and K. Welner (eds) *Closing the opportunity gap: What America must do to give every child an even chance*. New York: Oxford University Press.

Roscigno, V.J. and J.W. Ainsworth-Darnell (1999) "Race, cultural capital and educational resources: Persistent inequalities and achievement returns." *Sociology of Education* 72 (3), 158–78.

Santana, A.D. (2014) "Virtuous or vitriolic: The effect of anonymity on civility in online newspaper reader comment boards." *Journalism Practice* 8 (1), 18–33.

Solorzano, D.G. (1998) "Critical race theory, race and gender microaggressions and the experience of Chicana and Chicano scholars." *Qualitative Studies in Education* 11 (1), 121–36.

Solorzano, D.G. and A. Ornelas (2002) "A critical race analysis of advanced placement classes: A case of educational inequality." *Journal of Latinos and Education* 1 (4), 215–29.

Steele, C. (2003) "Stereotype threat and African American student achievement." In D.B. Grusky (ed) *Social stratification: Class, race, and gender in sociological perspective* (3rd edn) (pp 678–83). Boulder, CO: Westview Press.

Sullivan, A. (2001) "Cultural capital and educational attainment." *Sociology* 35 (4), 839–912.

Sullivan, A. (2002) "Bourdieu and education: How useful is Bourdieu's theory for researchers." *The Netherlands' Journal of Social Science* 38 (2), 144–66.

Teranishi, R. (2007) "Race, ethnicity, and higher education policy: The use of critical quantitative research." *New Directions for Institutional Research* 133, 37–49 (http://onlinelibrary.wiley.com.proxy.lib.wayne.edu/doi/10.1002/ir.203/pdf).

Tinto, V. (1982) "Limits of theory and practice in student attrition." *Journal of Higher Education* 53 (6), 687–700.

Tinto, V. (2003) *Leaving college: Rethinking the causes and cures of student attrition.* Chicago, IL: University of Chicago Press.

Tinto, V. (2006) "Research and practice of student retention: What next?" *Journal of College Student Retention* 8 (1), 1–19.

Tinto, V. (2012) *Completing college: Rethinking institutional action.* Chicago, IL: University of Chicago Press.

US Census Bureau (2010) "State and county quick facts." United States Census Bureau.

Warren, J.R. (1996) "Educational inequality among White and Mexican-origin adolescents in the American Southwest: 1990." *Sociology of Education* 142–58.

Weber, L. (2010) *Understanding race, class, gender and sexuality: A conceptual framework.* New York: Oxford University Press.

White, K.R. (1982) "The relation between socioeconomic status and academic achievement." *Psychological Bulletin* 91 (3), 461–81.

Wilson, W.J. (1999) "Jobless poverty: A new form of social dislocation in the inner-city ghetto." In P. Moen, D. Dempster-McClain, and H.A. Walker (eds) *A nation divided: Diversity, inequality, and community in American society* (pp 133–5, 49–50). Ithaca, NY: Cornell University.

16

Yakking about college life: Examining the role of anonymous forums on community identity formation

Francesca Tripodi

In 2006, *TIME* magazine declared that the proliferation of online media forums gave editorial power back to the people (Grossman, 2006). This perspective argued that the contributions of millions of anonymous users to various participatory media allowed individuals to engage in public dialog otherwise constrained in face-to-face interactions (Benkler, 2006; Shirky, 2008). While prominent scholars have pushed back on this utopian vision of the internet (Morozov, 2011; Mosco, 2004; Vaidhyanathan, 2011; Wu, 2010), a new discussion focused on anonymous platforms emerged. In the wake of websites such as College ACB or apps like Whisper and Yik Yak, many mainstream media reporters have coalesced around a single narrative: users should be wary of anonymous forums because people will say hurtful things under a veil of anonymity (Barbash and Moyer, 2015; Dewey, 2014; Hoffman, 2015). Armed with this ideology, many high schools have banned Yik Yak in an effort to curb cyberbullying, and opinion writers are urging college campuses do the same (Chapin Mach, 2014). On the other hand, the creators of Yik Yak argue that anonymity is essential for creating a level playing field. They believe that anonymity makes Yik Yak a more democratic social media network than an environment like Facebook or Twitter, because users do not need a large number of followers or friends to have their posts read widely. Moreover, the creators argue that since users are protected by anonymity, they can speak more freely and openly about subjects they might not normally discuss in front of their family and friends. Both of these perspectives are predicated on the idea that anonymity provides the opportunity for users to play around with their identity and push back on otherwise restrictive community norms. This chapter challenges that mantra, arguing that users do not Yak in isolation, and that even anonymous "mediated publics" (boyd, 2007) like Yik Yak are still bound by community norms.

Sociological interactionists have long argued that our actions are based on a series of interpersonal exchanges that shape group norms and constrain individual action (Eliasoph and Lichterman, 2003; Goffman, 1959; Mead, 1934; West and Zimmerman, 1987). While this body of interactional research is rich, it is analytically limiting because it focuses on face-to-face exchanges (Westbrook and Schilt, 2014). Recent work on "mediated publics" (boyd, 2007) demonstrates how our interactions in on- and offline environments are increasingly interconnected (Baym, 2010; boyd, 2007; Jenkins, 2006; Marwick, 2013). Since content we put online is persistent, searchable, replicable, and read by unintended lurkers (boyd, 2007), our online participation is often constrained by our desire to maintain offline interactions (Marwick, 2013).

Yet few media scholars have attempted to understand how the rise of more anonymous and ephemeral spaces (that is, Yik Yak or Snapchat) might provide users the option to "play around." To what extent does anonymity afford us the ability to profess concepts we might not otherwise? In what way might community norms and programmatic functionality dictate what type of content is allowed to persist? Based on a year-long virtual ethnography of the app Yik Yak, I find that despite their ability to remain anonymous, Yik Yak's use of "geofences" (a virtual perimeter for a real-world geographic area) restricts how students engage with the app. Because the geofence is attached to a physical campus, this technical affordance constrains the content of students' posts through group norms and culture. Yakkers do not post in order to aggravate simply because no one knows who they are. Rather, students who actively Yak are much more inclined to craft posts they think will garner "upvotes" from their peers or share personal information because they feel like they can trust the community of users.

While this use of Yik Yak fosters a sense of camaraderie among the students who use the app, a more nuanced understanding of the type of content users feel comfortable posting is sociologically important. By studying the interactional effects between content on Yik Yak and a college campus in which it is embedded, I am able to focus on the "local sites of cultural meaning-making" (Livingstone, 2003: 344) to see how engagement with Yik Yak influences the "actual circumstances" of college students where the app is used (Jensen and Pauly, 1997: 158). What I find is that those who already feel like they belong on the campus use Yik Yak to reaffirm their place within the university, and use their participation on Yik Yak to reinforce their sense of belonging within what they perceive as the dominant "group" on their campus. However, the same algorithmic platform that fosters belonging (that is, voting and commenting on content) ultimately constrains the kind of information that regular users feel free to post, while simultaneously regulating and removing content that deviates from the formulaic content that routinely performs well on the app.

What is Yik Yak?

Yik Yak is a social media app, described by many as an anonymous version of Twitter. It is free to download and requires no user name or login information, creating the illusion of complete anonymity.[1] Once the user opens the app, they are immediately placed into the physical community that surrounds them based on geolocative technology. Content on the app is divided into two categories, "new" and "hot," with the "new" list set as the default. Content is listed chronologically on the "new" list, but once it receives a large number of upvotes, it transitions to the hot list. Hot list content is organized by upvotes. While all content on Yik Yak is ephemeral, content on the hot list persists for longer.

Once inside the app, users can participate in a variety of ways. They can create their own Yak, comment on other people's Yaks, and upvote/downvote content. Users are also able to read Yaks without directly participating, although the app encourages user participation by keeping track of one's "Yakarma," a numerical score based on how frequently a user Yaks, replies, votes, or shares content on the app. Users are also able to "peek" into other places by using the search feature or by clicking on one of the communities randomly featured from week to week. For example, during football season, Yik Yak featured University of Southern California when they were playing a particularly contentious football game. However, the geofencing affordance only allows users to post, comment, and vote if they are within a five-mile radius of where they are physically located. As a result, you cannot post, comment, or vote on a feed that you are "peeking" into. The one exception to this is when users set a home base (titled "My Herd") that allows users to designate one location where they participate even when they are outside that physical location. This service is particularly popular for students traveling home during the holidays or summer, or studying abroad, because it allows them to stay connected to what is happening in their college community while they are away.

Yaks are limited to 200 characters, and the company recently added the ability for users to add photographs. While most content is immediately available, there are a few programmatic features designed to curb hateful or hurtful content: (1) photographs require moderation before posting; (2) text content using names is not allowed; (3) if text content contains threatening language (such as, "I want to kill..."), a pop-up will emerge requiring the user to verify that content is safe to post;[2] and (4) content that receives a score of −5 is automatically removed from the board. Yik Yak also hires campus representatives ("campus reps") who are rewarded monetarily for promoting the app on their campus. Based on interviews with a campus rep, Yik Yak periodically asks reps to "test content," and then report back to the company about how well those test posts are received. For example, in one email shared with me by a campus rep, Yik Yak requested that reps post compliments to see how well they fared, and report back on their hypothesis that users prefer positive Yaks.

As a way of promoting their product, Yik Yak regularly tours universities giving away promotional products including buttons, cups, and socks. While not explicitly stated, Yik Yak is clearly aiming for a college audience since it was originally promoted using fraternity connections, and indicates in the Terms of Service agreement that users under the age of 17 are not allowed to use the service at any time or in any manner. Unlike many other social media platforms, Yik Yak is a completely ephemeral space. Content constantly refreshes and, depending on how many users are contributing to the app, it is typically only available for a few hours.

Theoretical framework

Rather than assume a structural understanding of the self, phenomenologists conceptualize that one's role in society is processual. The process by which we find our "self" emerges out of interactions with others in our community and becomes rooted in a set of shared experiences (Husserl and Welton, 1999; Mead, 1934). Our actions, therefore, are not driven by a normative order but rather a "continuum of typifications" of how we believe others will react to our own actions (Berger and Luckmann, 1966: 33; Garfinkel, 1967). Since action is rooted in a set of expectations of how individuals and others should behave in a given situation, as members of a society we create habits to structure our everyday activities (Garfinkel, 1967: 38). We could think of these habits as our sense of reality, and in many ways we craft ourselves to fit the various types of interactions we might face in a single day. Once habits form, our actions become institutionalized around the stereotyped expectations that we have for any given role in society (West and Zimmerman, 1987). Our sense of "self" changes based on the expected behavior that has already been established for the role we are set to play (Goffman, 1959: 37). Even backstage, in our private lives, we perform a set of actions that match what is expected of us as a spouse, parent, sibling, and so on. Since our sense of self is constantly changing, what we find to be our "true" self are our habitual actions, the day-to-day interactions that become a taken-for-granted form of reality (Goffman, 1959).

Expanding out from the micro analysis, Eliasoph and Lichterman (2003) applied the theory of symbolic interaction to community. Through examining how groups use culture in their everyday life, they argue that group style, what they refer to as "the recurrent patterns of interaction that arise from a group's shared assumptions about what constitutes good or adequate participation in the group setting" (Eliasoph and Lichterman, 2003: 737), is constructed endogenously. The schemas that groups create through continuous interactions with one another allow communities (and even nations) to form a sense of belonging to a relatively unified group with clear differentiation between insiders and outsiders (Fine, 1979; Lainer-Vos, 2014). While the process of categorization through everyday interactions is well documented, it is analytically limiting because it fails to account for how virtual or "imagined interactions" might also work to create an explicit set of assumptions about how the world should exist (Westbrook and Schilt, 2014).

When interactions on the internet first began in the form of multiplayer online games (MMO or MMOG) and chat rooms, communication theorists used internet interfaces to push back on the restrictive nature of sociological interactions. Fueled by the notion that one's internet self is different from "real life," early internet scholars theorized that people use online spaces to play around with their identities. As Turkle (1995) argued, the anonymity of the internet created a space whereby people could be many selves at once. This provided the opportunity for people to play around with their online identities since who they were offline was simply another window open on our computer (Turkle, 1995). More recent scholars have sense refuted the concept of play online, arguing that social media spaces blur the boundaries between "on-" and "off"line environments (Baym, 2010; boyd, 2014; boyd and Marwick, 2011; Jenkins, 1992, 2006; Livingstone, 2003; Marwick, 2013). Given that our on-the-ground communities increasingly fuel our online interactions, scholars reason that online environments are less about play and more intimately tied to the creation of one unified persona. Since social networking sites are increasingly interconnected, they perpetuate what scholars have termed "publicity culture," whereby one's status is linked to openness and tied to authenticity (Marwick, 2013). In order to cultivate that authenticity, individuals must constantly monitor their performance, creating a "self" entertaining enough to garner followers, but simultaneously conveying continuity between their on- and offline personas (boyd and Marwick, 2011). Since content in most online forums persists, users are wary of making available content that does not match their offline identities (Baym, 2010; boyd, 2007)

While this existing literature is rich, it is primarily focused on how individuals construct identity, and fails to account for how a wider community of users might manipulate this engagement with mediated publics. Moreover, a recent increase of ephemeral, anonymous forums require more scholastic attention to the idea of whether or not users play around with identity in online environments if they are able to conceal their "real" identity. Relying on interactional theory, this chapter expands scholastic attention on identity formation in online environments by focusing specifically on a "mediated public" embedded within a pre-existing physical community (that is, a college campus) that allows users to maintain anonymity.

Community interaction

A traditional concern of sociology has been the definition, reproduction, and building of community. Yet even though media images legitimate a cultural understanding of normality, fostering an agreed-on notion of how the world truly exists (Meyrowitz, 2010; Skeggs and Wood, 2011), little sociological research has explored the connection between media representation and community identity. Given that the line between what constitutes "real" and what is "produced" is increasingly blurred, it is of utmost importance that sociologists take into account how virtual spaces are changing what it means to constitute community. Rather than focus on communities as geographic locations or spaces "bound by place" (Doheny-Farina 1996), this chapter extends Benedict Anderson's (1983 [2006]) theory of "imagined community" by connecting it to Eliasoph and Lichterman's (2003) theory of "culture in interaction" that argues that part of the "style" in which a community is "imagined" is connected to the vocabulary, symbols, and codes that structure members' ability to think and act within a group (Eliasoph and Lichterman, 2003). While Eliasoph and Lichterman focus on physical interactions, relying on Anderson's theory of an imagined community provides the opportunity to complicate the idea of "interaction" since citizens are unable to interact physically with everyone inside a community. Despite our inability to interact face-to-face, a "group style" emerges that constitutes the boundaries, bonds, and norms of membership (Eliasoph and Lichterman, 2003). As a result, it leaves open the possibility of studying how media interacts with community members, shaping what it means to belong to that community.

While the research on interactionism and mediated identity is extensive, I am unaware of any research to date that looks at how individuals' participation in an anonymous "mediated public" (boyd, 2007) collides with their "sense of place" (Couldry, 2007) in a phenomenon I term *integrated audiences*. Analyzing a community's use of Yik Yak provides a unique opportunity to combine these theoretical frameworks. Doing so allows us to understand how Yik Yak, an anonymous forum that restricts participation based on geolocation, interacts with the community in which it is embedded.

Data collection and analysis

The data consists of a virtual ethnography of a Yik Yak feed at a large, public institution in conjunction with physical ethnographic observations at the same university.[3] Observation was conducted by visiting the app for a minimum of three times a day, for approximately one hour each visit, every day, from May 2014–May 2015 (totaling over 1,000 hours of ethnographic observations). When large events took place (for example, a basketball game) I monitored Yik Yak more frequently since the number of users increased and content would quickly disappear. As a way of explicating my findings, I also conducted 45 semi-structured interviews and three focus groups with undergraduates (totaling 58 participants). All interviewees were enrolled in the university where I conducted my virtual and on-the-ground ethnography. I recruited participants using fliers around campus as well as sending out mass emails through various departmental and housing listservs. The recruitment language used was purposefully vague, asking the simple question: "Have you ever heard of Yik Yak? Want to talk more about it? If so please contact me to see about participating in an interview or focus group."

Respondents ranged from freshman to seniors, and were from a variety of majors including biology, psychology, international affairs, communication, sociology, computer science, and engineering. Twenty-three of the respondents were male and 35 were female (a ratio fairly close to the demographics at the campus where I conducted my ethnographic observations). The majority of students interviewed were white, and 20 percent identified as a racial minority including African American, East Asian, South Asian, or Multi-racial. This ratio is only slightly less than the overall percentage of minority students reported on the university website.

After collecting my audio-recorded data, I conducted my analysis in two stages. First, I did an open coding, consisting of listening to recorded interviews while reviewing my field notes and writing down emergent ideas on a series of notecards. Second, I arranged these cards in clusters, identifying which themes were the most salient. After flagging particularly salient "in vivo codes" (Charmaz, 2006), I then conducted a more focused coding, determining the accuracy of the threads identified. Comparing the trends that I identified in my observations on the app with trends found in interviews/focus groups allowed me to triangulate my findings.

Findings

Yik Yak users: a network of networks

One hundred percent of respondents who used the app found out about it through friends and started using it because it came up in conversation so frequently. As two senior females describe in a focus group:

Julia: I think it's almost more like social networks. Like I started using it cuz your whole [sorority] house is using it, and my whole [sorority]

> house uses it. It might be more like if your friends all use it, then you have it. I don't know if they would be like –
>
> Emma: (interrupts Julia) I think most of the people I know do have it. Yeah. I don't know if I'm just making that up, but I feel like people bring it up in conversation. Like, 'Oh, did you see that funny thing on Yik Yak,' or whatever.

The fact that these women heard about the app through the Greek system is not coincidental. As Max (a senior majoring in Communication) divulged, the app was first promoted through his fraternity and was almost exclusively "Greek" when it first rolled out in spring 2014:

> I first heard about Yik Yak through an email they actually sent to my fraternity ... [the founder] sent an email to fraternities and sororities nationwide, saying 'Hey, want to help some rad dudes out? We are launching this app, like an anonymous Twitter. If it takes off, we'll bring some beer by the house.'... That was like the catch to get people to download it. I didn't download it immediately but eventually I started hearing people talking about it, and then I downloaded it ... a lot of talk was like 'Hey, did you hear about what they said about that person on Yik Yak?'

While my data indicates that many students outside of the Greek system now use the app, Yik Yak's origins are significant. Fraternities and sororities are historically places of privilege, and as Armstrong and Hamilton's recent study demonstrates, these spaces are used to discriminate by appearance, wealth and race (2013). The problem with this "party pathway" is that lower-income students become further isolated from the connections necessary to succeed after college is over. Yik Yak's creators were also in a fraternity while undergraduates at Furman. As Marwick (2013) notes, this privileged position of Yik Yak's creators is important because while the creators aimed as making a space for the "disenfranchised," they ultimately embedded privilege into the app by specifically targeting the Greek system on college campuses when they first began rolling out the app.[4] Eventually those who found out about it through their fraternities eventually passed it on to those outside of the Greek system. As Bailey, a senior majoring in communication, described:

> First my friend [who was in a fraternity] had it, then he started taking screen shots and sending it to all of us in my apartment. Then more people had it and then before it knew it, it was like everyone had it.

Or as Jacob, a freshman who had yet to declare his major described, "it just seemed like everyone was talking about it. Like people would always be saying 'hey, did you see that Yak….'"

Taking into account who uses the app and why they like it is important to consider when users describe why they enjoy the app using words like "relevant" or "relatable" or "camaraderie." As Aaliyah (a junior majoring in chemistry) describes of why her Yaks are popular:

> Because people can relate…. I think when people saw it they thought it was funny because they think the same way.

In addition to being "relatable," a successful Yak is also dependent on a large group network. Since content on the new list disappears quickly during "high-traffic" times, described by many respondents as the times when people are studying/partying (between 10pm–2am) or 10 minutes before the hour (when people are walking in between classes), respondents rely on their offline networks to upvote their content during this time so it can cross over to the hot list where it will gain more visibility. One such bolstering technique was described during the focus group:

> Yeah, cuz if it doesn't catch on, it goes away in a minute, so you have to get momentum going really fast. We got everyone in our [sorority] house, which is a large house, to upvote it, seeing if it would catch on. It got 35 downvotes and went away within a minute. (Madison)

Indeed, the success of one's Yak depended on the general mood of the campus and if one was able to pull in topics of particular concern to what users described as "the university community." Not only did posting about notable events like when one of the sports teams would win ensure that one's Yak would be successful, it also created a sense of unity between those who used the app and the others around them, as Emma, a female respondent in a focus group, described:

> Yeah, there's like – during finals and stuff I feel like there's camaraderie because everyone's like, 'Oh, eff this, I'm at the library, this sucks.'

Students also mentioned that because it was so relevant it was a way of keeping up to date on information that related specifically to their campus. When events took place users looked to Yik Yak as way of staying informed on situations unfolding around them. For example, when a shooting happened on another campus, users both checked their school and peeked in to where the shooting was happening to stay informed.

You can say whatever you want

Despite the fact that students found out about the app from their friends, they also described how Yik Yak was different from Facebook because their identity was concealed. While users described how they liked Yik Yak because it could give them a read on what was going on around them, 100 percent of the respondents also said that despite it being located within their community, anonymity provided users the opportunity to post anything that came to mind. Strikingly similar to the language used by Yik Yak to promote the product, students described how they could share their thoughts with the people around them while maintaining privacy. As many users described, the draw of the app was how easy it was to begin using, since they didn't need to create an account, and that because it was anonymous, they didn't need to think about what was posted. As David, a freshman who had yet to declare a major, described:

> … you don't even need an account you can just write a post and hit enter. It's like the best part is that it's very accessible, you don't need to log in, you don't need to link it to an account like Facebook or whatever, it's completely anonymous and completely unattached you just download the app and you can post whatever.

While there was consensus regarding the fact that Yik Yak allowed people to post whatever came to mind, there was variation regarding if that anonymity was positive or negative. Some felt that the anonymity was dangerous because people would say hurtful things under a "cloak of anonymity." As Amy, a senior double-majoring in gender studies and public policy, described:

> I have a problem a with internet comments and anonymity anyway and I feel like putting that in a college culture where depression is a problem and suicide rates are so high and so prevalent.… I think a lot of people use it as away of expressing their emotions and people could be able to respond negatively.

However, Amy also mentioned that this anonymity could provide the opportunity for some to play. In her words, "it allows people to be freer in both directions." She went on to describe this tension:

> So I think people are more themselves on an anonymous forum in both people are more likely to be more open and kind and also negative and judgmental but generally more the later.… But I think it can destroy stereotypes in a lot of ways like when OPs [the original poster] will post details in the comments about themselves to get context and it will be a question about dating something

… and turns out to be a man … like once I saw a bunch of men talking about their female crushes it was interesting to me that a guy would even say crush but maybe because it's only on an anonymous source.

Amy was not alone in her opinion of Yik Yak as being both "safe" and "dangerous." While it provided a safe haven for people to express feelings they might not normally "in public," it also provided some an opportunity to spew hate. However, each of these narratives describes the option for Yik Yak users to breech societal norms and to test the boundaries of what is acceptable within the community. When I asked users about their personal posts, the sentiment changed. While users agreed that Yik Yak facilitated a space where anyone could post whatever came to mind, individuals I interviewed claimed to refrain from taking those same liberties. When I asked if they would post whatever came to mind, an overwhelming majority of users disagreed, stating that they thought carefully and critically before posting a Yak, fearing that what they posted would be rejected by their peers.

"So, do you post whatever comes to mind?"

Even though all the respondents believed that Yik Yak was a place where anyone could say anything they wanted, a glaring contradiction emerged when I asked them if they had ever posted a Yak. While every user had posted at least one Yak, none of them posted immediately after opening the app. Rather, users described how they would take their time to learn the norms of the space, and moved slowly in their participation. First, they would just read others' Yaks and occasionally vote. Then, users described how they would begin commenting on others' Yaks to, in the words of numerous interviewees, "get their confidence up" before posting any original content. When they finally did work up the courage to post their own Yak, they were nervous by how well it would be received. This feeling was expressed in detail during one of my focus groups where I asked users to describe how they felt after posting their first Yak:

Riley: I was nervous. Like my thumb and my finger was like shaking.
Emma: Because you don't want to get –
Riley: Downvoted.
Emma: Downvoted [said at the same time as Riley]. Yeah, I mean even though it's anonymous, so no one's going to know it's you.
Julia: I definitely remember, I don't even know what it was about, but I remember discussing it with Riley beforehand…. Like do you think this is funny, like will people think this is funny?

Riley: I remember texting you asking how many upvotes yours got to see how it did afterward.

Julia: It's just that fear of not being funny.

Emma: I mean, I think about a post if I ever post, I think about it for a while. I probably have a draft of it on – I think about it for a long time. I want it to be good, even if they don't know it's you.

Julia: Yeah.

The fact that this was a focus group of all women is important, as the women more frequently described Yakking with caution, or being nervous and uncertain about their posts; but fear of Yak rejection was not exclusive to women. Male respondents who did not express trepidation before posting a Yak described a different kind of rejection apprehension. Take, for example, Aiden, a freshman male majoring in computer science. He described how he didn't get nervous when he posted a Yak, but subsequently noted that he deletes any Yak that does not score at least 50 points, what he describes as "rejection." Even though the Yak itself will likely disappear in less an a hour, Aiden's desire to have his Yak upvoted by a minimum of 100 students indicates that he takes seriously how well his Yak is received by other users. He is literally ashamed – even with the anonymity Yik Yak provides – to have authored an unpopular Yak.

Max, the senior mentioned earlier, also deletes Yaks that are not received well by other users. When I asked him to elaborate on what it felt like to have a Yak do so poorly, he described his disappointment:

> It's like you want to be accepted by the community around you, and that's what's so unique about Yik Yak. It's just the people around you. I think if you feel that what you're posting is getting downvoted, it's kind of like you're getting negative attention from the community or you're not fitting in, or you're not upholding the standards of the community…. I would feel bad about myself if I had something that had negative four…. You don't want to feel like, 'Everyone hated what I said.'

As a way of ensuring that their Yaks will not get rejected, users post content that follows an almost formulaic manner. Monica, a freshman majoring in computer science, details what the recipe for success entails:

> My most popular posts are vaguely inspirational things about [the university]…. If you praise [the university] at the right time, [and] there is definitely a right time, people will upvote it. If you write oh yah [university] this is why we're super awesome [you will get upvotes].

Respondents in my focus group echoed this sentiment, describing how they even experimented with the formula, testing out different Yaks to see which type would rise to the top.

> Julia: One time me and my friend last year we were just sitting around, and we posted I think it was three different yaks to see what would happen. We posted one that we thought was super dumb ... we were like, 'Super beautiful day at the best university in the whole fucking world.' I think that's what we yakked. Then we thought it was so dumb. Then we posted one that we actually thought was funny. I can't remember what it was. It was just like – I have no idea, but it was something that was more real. Then the one that was really dumb and about [the university] got way more upvotes.
> Emma: Yeah, the school spirit thing always does well.

Or as Steve, a senior working towards his Master's in public policy, notes:

> People are just out there to make something – they're there to pick up those upvotes or whatever. They're trying to throw out a lot of jokes out there, and a lot of them are hit or miss, I think, and that's why there are really terrible jokes and sometimes, you get a good one. People are looking for that sense of approval, I think.

Similar to the sense of stigma described by Goffman (1959), users want to avoid being rejected from their group and try to avoid breeching the established norms of their imagined community (Garfinkel, 1967). As a result, they tend to post "safer" content they know will be well received, and think carefully about what they want to Yak beforehand, soliciting friends to upvote their content so that it will persist and potentially cross over to the hot list. In addition to carefully formulating content, users repost reused or recycled content from other sites. As Diane, a senior majoring in foreign affairs described:

> I found that a lot of the jokes that people were making that were supposed to be funny that were upvoted and stuff like that were really recycled, and I had seen them six times before.

Many take offense at users trying to improve their Yakarma with unoriginal content, and will call out users in the comments sections by saying things like, "I too read Reddit." Recycled content is so frequent on Yik Yak that users have developed the term "Reyak," and it is so frequent that even the term "Reyak" has been replaced by the recycle emoji. Further evidence of copied material can be seen by peeking into other universities and looking at their hot list. Typically at least one of the Yaks on the hot list can be seen on another university's hot list or has been only slightly modified for the community where the feed is located. For example, Texas Yik Yak will make the same joke about Texas A&M that the University of Southern California would make about UCLA, or the University of Virginia makes about Virginia Tech. Other frequently seen jokes are typically cross-posted on websites like Reddit or Tumblr.

As the data demonstrate, active users do not use Yik Yak to post whatever comes to mind. Instead, they are much more concerned with the feedback of what they consider their peers at the university. As one student (Amy, quoted above) described, she now prefers to Yak verse text because of the personal gratification of seeing people upvote her material. In her words:

> It's like a heightened Facebook. Like when I post something on FB you get that weird rush when someone likes it, like someone is paying attention to you, someone cares. Whereas with Yik Yak it's like someone chuckled or was like that's right … just a rush of being acknowledged.

In this way, what is deemed funny or relatable content is iterative and based on their daily interactions both on campus but through Yik Yak. Students who use the app reinforce their sense of belonging within the campus as a result. Even Amy, who was first afraid that the anonymity of Yik Yak would make people say hurtful content because they were afforded anonymity, changed her mind once she started using the app. As she described later on in the interview:

> I post things that are more emotional. Like, I need to express something but I don't want to burden friends or family with it, if that makes sense. They always get 40 or 50 upvotes which is I think really interesting…. I use it as more of an outlet of sorts.

As much as formulaic and re-used content appears on the site, there is also a space for genuine emotional disclosure and for those seeking social support. It is this sense of belonging through interactions within the physical campus and on Yik Yak that allows students to form a sense of trust in Yik Yak and share highly sensitive information, even if it won't garner upvotes. Not only did this trend of revealing information about oneself show up in my interviews, it regularly surfaced during my virtual ethnography. Sometimes the self-disclosure was not particularly concerning. For example, students often disclosed that they binge-watched Netflix instead of studying for their exams, and in my interviews students described how seeing these posts were good for their psyche. In a campus with a culture of over-work, students described the sense of solace they found in Yik Yak when they learned they were not the only ones feeling burnt out. On a more serious note, this sense of community of trust is demonstrated in the prevalence and reaction to suicide threats regularly made on Yik Yak after the hours of 11pm. In the midnight hours when many students on the campus are feeling alone or scared, their cries for help are answered in a supportive and committed way – with students sharing the numbers for university resources and even their personal email addresses as a reminder that no one is really "alone" within their community.

Time and time again, regular Yik Yak users describe how they feel more connected and attuned to what is happening at the university (for example, during the winter many students checked Yik Yak to see if classes were cancelled and trusted Yik Yak over the university website because of its ability to deliver timely content). Even though this sense of community reaffirmation sometimes came in the form of recycled content, it also provided for many a space of trust to post content they did not want to share with others around them. If a student expressed a sense of belonging within the university, they were likely to use Yik Yak as a platform for saying things they might not normally espouse in public.

However, users also see their performance on Yik Yak as a gauge concerning how well they "fit" within their community. Given that Yik Yak is so ubiquitous in their physical environments (as described earlier, many in their peer groups discuss content they've seen on Yik Yak in face-to-face situations), users describe how they take time and think before they post, trying to craft content they think will be well received by their peers. However, for those who already do not feel like they belong at the university, Yik Yak ends up further marginalizing these students from their campus community.

Yik Yak – "Not a place for me"

While users found out about Yik Yak and were subsequently inclined to download it because of the frequency with which it was discussed in conversation, non-users failed to see the appeal in the app for similar reasons. Take, for example, what Justin, a senior majoring in communication, said when I asked if he felt out of the loop because he did not use the app:

> I feel like it's kinda hard for me to answer that question because I feel like there is a difference here between what African American students here do and what white students here do.... I just know that I'm out of the loop when it comes to a lot of things ... and Yik Yak is just one of those things.... I just feel like there is a part of [the university] that I don't want to be in the loop in and I'm not in the loop in and that's kinda how I see a lot of apps, it's really trendy and fratty, it's more of a lifestyle. I feel like if you're using Yik Yak at [the university] you're also more likely to be ... you're more likely to *not* be me. I think it's something that you're just around. So people that *should* know, get on Yik Yak, and I guess

what I'm saying is that nobody that I am close to that I see everyday is talking about Yik Yak so I really didn't have any interest in it.

As we can see, in the same way that Max felt inclined to get on Yik Yak because all of his friends were going on, Justin felt inclined to stay away because his friends were not. This is not to say that those who feel marginalized from Yik Yak fail to see the content all together.

As Alicia (a junior majoring in American studies and foreign affairs) and many others who refrained from using Yik Yak described, they could stay in the loop by following other social media sites where screenshots of offensive Yaks were posted for her to read. Using other virtual communities, Alicia was able to stay up to date and connected with those who share her same viewpoints using different platforms used by her peers (that is, Facebook or Twitter), while simultaneously making the decision that, as for Justin, Yik Yak was simply not a place for her. As she described in her interview:

> I mean everyone knows that a typical [university] student is a white student, who is middle upper-class or wealthy they wear similar things, like a LongChamp bag, running sneakers, running leggings, [sorority/fraternity] attire on their backpack or shirt ... and from what I've seen from what people have posted [to Yik Yak] I get the image in my head of someone I described, wealthy, white, privileged and used to getting their way and are irritated that anyone is less than that or working towards injustice ... and it's clear that the white community and the black community have totally different issues its like while black twitter is upset about someone shooting this person, white twitter is upset that someone got their name wrong on their cup at Starbucks and they can choose not to be aware of certain issues [on Yik Yak] everyone was celebrating [an event on campus] and we were like no, you can't just pretend nothing happened.

These sentiments, as well as the others divulged in individual interviews, are important because they indicate that the marginalization Alicia and Justin feel is not isolated to Yik Yak. For them, there is a *subset* of the community using the app and, in their words, those who frequent the app are from a privileged position. While students who use Yik Yak are drawn to the space for its relevancy or support, students like Alicia and Justin become, in a way, doubly marginalized because of the way Yik Yak has become integrated into the community that surrounds but simultaneously excludes them.

What cases like Alicia and Justin tell us is that in the same way some users describe how Yik Yak reaffirms their sense of belonging to their campus, for others, Yik Yak makes them feel more isolated. Given the roots of the app, it is no surprise that those who are not drawn to the app feel that those who are hold a more privileged position in society. Not only do interviewees like Alicia and Justin refrain from using Yik Yak all together, when others try to use Yik Yak to challenge the status quo, their viewpoints are routinely silenced (Tripodi, 2015). Using the same algorithm designed to curb cyberbullying, interviewees describe how their concerns are consistently and meticulously downvoted off the board. This is important because not only does it signify to those who try to use the board that their opinions do not match those of the university, it further marginalizes those in the community who already hold a minority position.

Conclusion

In an era when on- and offline personae seem increasingly connected, this chapter demonstrates a need for more scholastic attention to spaces where people are able to retain their anonymity. Existing frames surrounding anonymity in online spaces are dichotomous, understanding the space as producing either positive or negative outcomes – but each frame hinges on the idea that individuals will express sentiments that they might not otherwise in public when they are protected by a veil of anonymity. This line of logic rests on the assumption that when one is anonymous they are "separate" from or "outside" of a community's norms. What my study finds is that people are not just necessarily saying whatever comes to mind just because they are anonymous. As is the case with so many sociological findings, the context of anonymity matters.

For those in my study who have cultivated a sense of trust within their college campus, Yik Yak reinforces these connections. Yik Yak allows students to commiserate over final exams or particularly difficult professors. It provides students the opportunity to bond over a basketball game or to rationalize their decision to watch Netflix instead of studying. For users of the app, Yik Yak provides a special place for students to realize that they are not alone during a time of need, and allows them to express grief over the passing of a relative or thoughts of suicide. While it is true that students professing bouts of depression or thoughts of suicide might not normally say these things "in public," they are sharing these thoughts because they know they are sentiments that will still be well received by the community of users on the app. In order for that sense of belonging on Yik Yak to take place, students have to feel some level of trust with peers on their campus who use the app. Part of how students cultivate that sense of belonging is by figuring out what kind of content gets upvoted, and since many users feel a sense of reaffirmation when what they post gets upvotes, these users seem to gravitate toward content that they know will fare well. Overwhelmingly my findings suggest that regular users refrain from posting content that they think might not garner the support of the majority. But what about the minority voices?

What my study indicates is that for those who already feel a sense of marginalization from their community, Yik Yak is just another way of feeling ostracized by those around them. Part of this separation comes from the content that does well on the app. While Yakkers described to me how "racist" comments are continuously downvoted, Yaks bemoaning teaching assistants who don't speak "good enough" English are routinely on the hot list described by one of my respondents as "PC racism." Moreover, users who try to go against the status quo are routinely downvoted if they are unable to cultivate a strong enough following on the ground to support their opinions when they surface on Yik Yak.

Using these findings, my future work indicates that deleting content is just one way disenfranchised voices are silenced. Expanding on Noelle-Neumann's "spiral of silence" (1984 [1993]), my forthcoming work describes a more nuanced "web of silence." Rather than simply staying silent because they feel their views are in opposition to the majority, I find that when individuals try to speak out in participatory media spaces (like Yik Yak), they are systematically silenced using one of the following mechanisms: avoidance – marginalized expression is ignored; reappropriation – marginalized expression is modified or subtly rewritten, such as the transformation from #BlackLivesMatter to #AllLivesMatter; deletion – marginalized expression is systematically erased; and harassment – resistance to marginalized expression escalates rapidly into violent responses and threats. While instances of reappropriation and harassment are more egregious, I argue that more scholastic attention to implicit forms of silencing (avoidance/deletion) is necessary as they are often far more insidious.

In an analog era studying absences would be an impossible task, but since nothing on "the cloud" ever really goes away, a future line of research could use big data analytics to study what kind of content on Yik Yak, or similar participatory media environments, is not allowed to persist. By aggregating these forms of expression Yik Yak users would still be able to retain their anonymity, yet provide a more nuanced examination of forms of cultural expression that are not part of majority opinion.

Notes

[1] Clearly the app is not completely anonymous because users connect through a series of datapoints (that is, the Apple App store or geolocative services) that identify who is Yakking. This is made explicitly clear in the Terms of Service agreement whereby it states that Yik Yak will "collect your IP address and generate or collect a unique identifier for your mobile device, which will serve as your user ID."

[2] Here is an example of the screen shot:

[3] The name of the institution has been removed, and all names used have been changed to protect the confidentiality of those who participated in this study.

[4] In a featured article in *The New York Times* written by Jonathan Mahler, Brooks Buffington is quoted as saying "When we made this app, we really made it for the disenfranchised." This article also notes that Buffington and Droll met each other through their fraternity at Furman (Mahler, 2015).

References

Anderson, B. (1983 [2006]) *Imagined communities.* New York: Verso.

Armstrong, E. and L. Hamilton (2013) *Paying for the party: How college maintains inequality.* Cambridge, MA: Harvard University Press.

Barbash, F. and J.W. Moyer (2015) "Yik Yak: A glimpse inside an often cruel, but often revealing world" *The Washington Post*, May 8 (www.washingtonpost. com/news/morning-mix/wp/2015/05/08/yik-yak-a-glimpse-inside-an-often-cruel-but-often-revealing-world/).

Baym, N. (2010) *Personal connections in a digital age.* Cambridge, UK: Polity Press.

Benkler, Y. (2006) *The wealth of networks: How social production transforms markets and freedom.* New Haven, CT: Yale University Press.

Berger, P.L. and L. Luckmann (1966) *The social construction of reality: A treatise in the sociology of knowledge.* Garden City, NY: Doubleday.

boyd, d. (2007) "Social network sites: Public, private, or what?" *Knowledge Tree*, May 13 (www.danah.org/papers/KnowledgeTree.pdf).

boyd, d. (2014) *It's complicated.* New Haven, CT: Yale University Press.

boyd, d. and A. Marwick (2011) "Social privacy in networked publics: Teens' attitudes, practices, and strategies." A Decade in Internet Time: Symposium on the Dynamics of the Internet and Society, September (http://ssrn.com/abstract=1925128).

Chapin Mach, R. October 3, (2014) "Why your college campus should ban Yik Yak." *The Huffington Post*, October 3 (www.huffingtonpost.com/ryan-chapin-mach/why-your-college-campus-should-ban-yik-yak_b_5924352.html).

Charmaz, K. (2006) *Constructing grounded theory: A practical guide through qualitative analysis*. London and Thousand Oaks, CA: Sage Publications.

Couldry, N. (2007) "On the set of *The Sopranos:* 'Inside' a fan's construction of nearness." In J. Gray, C. Sandovoss, and C.L. Harrington (eds) *Fandom: Identities and communities in a mediated world* (pp 139–48). New York: NYU Press.

Dewey, C. (2014) "How do you solve a problem like Yik Yak?" *The Washington Post*, October (www.washingtonpost.com/news/the-intersect/wp/2014/10/07/how-do-you-solve-a-problem-like-yik-yak/).

Doheny-Farina, S. (1996) *The wired neighborhood*. New Haven, CT: Yale University Press.

Eliasoph, N. and P. Lichterman (2003) "Culture in interaction." *American Journal of Sociology* 108 (4), 735–94.

Fine, G.A. (1979) "Small groups and culture creation: The idioculture of Little League baseball teams." *American Sociological Review* 44 (5), 733–45.

Fiske, J. (1992) "The cultural economy of fandom." In L.A. Lewis (ed) *The adoring audience: Fan culture and popular media* (pp 30–49). New York: Routledge.

Garfinkel, H. (1967) *Studies in ethnomethodology*. Englewood Cliffs, NJ: Prentice-Hall.

Goffman, E. (1959) *Presentation of self in everyday life*. New York: Doubleday.

Grossman, L. (2006) "You – yes, you – are TIME's person of the year." *TIME*, December.

Hoffman, L. June 1, (2015) "Yik Yak: The age of destructive anonymity." *The Huffington Post*, June 1 (www.huffingtonpost.com/lindsay-hoffman/yik-yak-the-age-of-destru_b_6979836.html).

Husserl, E., and D. Welton (1999) *The essential Husserl: Basic writings in transcendental phenomenology*. Bloomington, IN: Indiana University Press.

Jenkins, H. (1992) *Textual poachers: Television fans and participatory culture*. New York: Routledge.

Jenkins, H. (2006) *Convergence culture: Where old and new media collide*. New York: NYU Press.

Jensen, J. and J. Pauly (1997) "Imagining the audience: Losses and gains in cultural studies." In M. Ferguson and P. Golding (eds) *Cultural studies in question* (pp 52–63). Thousand Oaks, CA: Sage.

Lainer-Vos, D. (2014) "Masculinities in interaction: The construction of Israeli and American Jewish men in philanthropic fundraising events." *Men and Masculinities* 17 (1), 43–66.

Livingstone, S. (2003) "The changing nature of audiences: From the mass audience to the interactive media user." In A.N. Valdivia (ed) *A companion to media studies*. Oxford, UK: Wiley-Blackwell.

Mahler, J. (2015) "Who spewed that abuse? Anonymous Yik Yak app isn't telling." *The New York Times*, March 8 (www.nytimes.com/2015/03/09/technology/popular-yik-yak-app-confers-anonymity-and-delivers-abuse.html).

Marwick, A.E. (2013) *Status update: Celebrity, publicity, and branding in the social media age*. New Haven, CT: Yale University Press.

Mead, G.H. (1934) *Mind, self, and society*. Chicago, IL: University of Chicago Press.

Meyrowitz, J. (2010) "Media evolution and cultural change." In J.R. Hall, L. Grindstaff, and M.-C. Lo (eds) *Handbook of cultural sociology* (pp 30–49). New York: Routledge.

Morozov, E. (2011) *Net delusion: The dark side of internet freedom*. New York: PublicAffairs/Perseus Books Group.

Mosco, V. (2004) *The digital sublime: Myth, power, and cyberspace*. Boston, MA: Massachusetts Institute of Technology.

Neumann, E.N. (1984 [1993]) *The spiral of silence: Public opinion our social skin*. Chicago, IL: University of Chicago Press.

Press, A. 1996. "Towards a qualitative methodology of audience study: Using ethnography to study the popular culture audience." In J. Hay, L. Grossberg, and E. Wartella (eds) *The audience and its landscape* (pp 113–30). Boulder, CO: Westview.

Shirky, C. (2008) *Here comes everybody*. New York: Penguin Group.

Skeggs, B. and H. Wood (2011) "Turning it on is a class act: immediate object relations with television." *Media Culture Society* 33, 941–51.

Turkle, S. (1995) *Life on the screen: Identity in the age of the internet*. New York: Touchstone Press.

Tripodi, F. (2015) "What colleges might lose by banning Yik Yak." *The Chronicle of Higher Education*, November 3 (http://chronicle.com/article/What-Colleges-Might-Lose-by/234042?cid=rc_right).

Vaidhyanathan, S. (2011) *The Googlization of everything: (and why we should worry)*. Berkeley, CA: University of California Press.

West, C. and D.H. Zimmerman (1987) "Doing gender." *Gender & Society* 1, 126–47.

Westbrook, L. and K. Schilt (2014) "Doing gender, determining gender: Transgender people, gender panics, and the maintenance of the sex/gender/sexuality system." *Gender & Society* 28 (1), 32–57.

Wu, T. (2010) *The master switch: The rise and fall of information empires*. New York: Vintage Books.

17

On Thursdays we watch *Scandal*: Communal viewing and Black Twitter

Apryl Williams

Sociologists have long debated the nature of communities online. We have questioned the authenticity of communal experiences online *ad nauseam* (see Agre, 1997; Bateman and Lyon, 2000; Baym, 1995; Hampton and Wellman, 2003; Nonnecke et al, 2006). Yet there are still some who challenge the idea that community, as defined by classical social theorists, can exist in the context of digitally mediated communication. If not questioning the integral properties of human relationships, some scholars contend that technology facilitates the departure from true face-to-face interactions, suggesting that the face-to-screen-to-face interaction presents negative unforeseen consequences (Turkle, 2011).

To some extent, the presence of the screen does mitigate our interactions in that it shapes how we say things with imposed character limits, it can compound existing inequalities by marginalizing those who cannot access the internet, and the screen can intensify or obscure our view of others' lives. But with all things considered, technology – the internet in particular – still broadens our potential for building community, allowing us to access multiple networks at a time. Moreover, we can build stronger communities because we have multiple platforms from which to interact and offer support.

Social media and social networking sites, especially Twitter, disrupt traditional boundary interactions, blurring the distinction between public and private spheres, and broadening the lines of communication between the elite and the masses (Murthy, 2012). Twitter can also make the world seem smaller by minimizing both social and physical distance. Trending topics give voice to those that have otherwise been unheard while providing community for others. One of the most powerful and unified communities to emerge on social media is "Black Twitter." Empirically, we know that African Americans use Twitter in higher proportions than other racial groups. Pew's 2013 social media report found that one in four Twitter users is African American. Beyond demography, Black Twitter showcases cultural knowledge and insider access. In addition to performing racial identity, black users also use the site as an arena for class portrayal, to mitigate identity claims, and to challenge outsider groups' perceptions of blackness (Florini, 2013). Not only does Black Twitter seem to have all of the makings of a community, but it also produces meaningful discourse and organizes resistance both online and offline, much like black community organizers have done throughout black cultural history.

Thus the aim of this chapter is to contextualize Black Twitter as a community. In order to do so, I describe Black Twitter in terms of commonly accepted sociological definitions of community via Ferdinand Tönnies' (1957) concept of *Gemeinschaft* and symbolic interactionist perspectives. Tweets, hashtags, and trends associated with the television show *Scandal* will serve as a case study. Communal watching or co-viewing of shows like *Scandal*, *How to Get Away With Murder*, and *Empire* suggest that there is a sense of social cohesion that emerges from online interactions and co-viewing. In a similar study of YouTube, researchers found that co-viewing of videos encourages future "post-viewing discussion" and enhances interaction among viewers (Haridakis and Hanson, 2009: 330). Due to the intertextuality present in the online discussion of shows written and produced by a black woman, with black women and men in leading roles – specifically within the context of Black Twitter – *Scandal* provides an opportunity to explore layered levels of meaning both in the relationship that the viewers have to the show and the relationships that they have with each other.

Using a qualitative, grounded theory approach, I analyze tweets from several thousand users who have interacted with Black Twitter. Following that, I present portions of in-person interviews that were conducted in order to gain a better understanding of the way black users conceptualize Black Twitter. Drawing on this empirical investigation, I argue that as a meaningful community, Black Twitter has the capacity to cause meaningful change, both on- and offline.

Theorizing online community (again)

The concept of community, like all of our lives, is socially constructed. Our online communities reflect this socialization process, and the boundaries of that community are defined by those who identify as part of it as well as those that exist outside of the space, although the versions of those definitions may differ remarkably. Accordingly, newer communities occupy many spaces to create meaning on multiple platforms (Gatson, 2011). Concerning race, online community has become particularly salient to activism and organization both on- and offline. In this context, the fictive on-/offline binary becomes even less apparent.

Beyond engaging with communities online, individuals in communities are also continuously negotiating their own identities. One idea that both bodies of literature – "offline" and "online" identity development – suggest is that racial identity is developed in light of, or as a reflection of, communal identity. That is to say that self and community cannot exist without each other, particularly concerning racial identity. This idea is reflected in foundational scholar Charles Horton Cooley's writings on the *Looking glass self* (1956/1998), and is further supported by Erik Erikson: "True identity depends on the support which the young receive from the collective sense of identity which social groups assign to [them]: [their] class, [their] nationality, [their] culture" (Erikson, 1964: 93). Concerning community, Cooley informs:

> Fundamental in forming the social nature and ideals of the individual. The result of intimate association, psychologically, is a certain fusion of individualities in a common whole, so that one's very self, for many purposes at least, is the common life and purpose of the group. Perhaps the simplest way of describing this wholeness is by saying that it is a 'we'; it involves the sort of sympathy and mutual identification for which 'we' is the natural expression. One lives in the feeling of the whole and finds the chief aims of his will in that feeling. (Cooley 1956/1998: 23)

Moreover, Tönnies' delineation between *Gemeinschaft* (community) and *Gesellschaft* (society) posits: "in *Gemeinschaft*, we are united from the moment of our birth with our own folk, for better or for worse. We go out into *Gesellschaft* as if into a foreign land" (1887/2001: 17). Tönnies' theorization of community translates to the idea that one's ethnic or racial identity affiliation may inform their conception of community. In fact, his idea of folk closely resembles the concept of a shared cultural history among black Americans in general, online and offline: "The word 'folk' must be given still another more particular meaning. I daresay that is connotes not only the living but also the dead, and those to be born. Indeed it especially encompasses the unity of these three levels. A community wherein the dead by far outweigh the living" (Tönnies, 1967/2014: 7). Considering the cultural history of the American Slave Trade, the case can be made that black Americans share a collective sociohistorical consciousness about "folk" and kinship (Stack, 1974). That sense of kinship carries over or is reflected by black social media use.

More recently, Marwick and boyd (2010) have supported earlier theorists' ideas, and hypothesize that online identity and community operate within "context collapse," suggesting that our on- and offline lives often merge to create an inseparable space for identity negotiation. Social media allow users to project experiences to an audience that aligns with a preconceived narrative of identity being deployed. The audience consists of users' followers and the things that they experience. Marwick and boyd suggest that users also reference an imagined audience in addition to their followers and friends on Facebook, Twitter, Instagram, and other social media. They contend that users are aware of the potentially limitless audience of social media, and use cultural norms to conceptualize an audience in their mind. In the absence of these cultural cues, users gather their information from the general social media environment to imagine an idealized community, even though the imagined community may differ from the audience who is actually consuming the posts.

Community occupies a meaningful, yet somewhat imaginative space in our consciousness:

> As much as community may be about the ties between people, it is often understood to be both a grounded place, as well as a thing whose grounded experiences may be carried along in the imagination. The things we can do in a particular space make that space more or less comfortable for us, and in becoming comfortable therein, we make it a meaningful place. This connection between the material and the symbolic highlights the community as a metaphorical concept, an amorphous one often standing in for specific place and space boundaries. (Gatson and Zweerink, 2004: 97)

That is, the community is imagined, but the people that make up that community are not imaginary (Marwick and boyd, 2010). Moreover, Hampton and Wellman highlight two advantages of online communication in terms of building relationships. Individuals are not bound by time – "people do not have to be connected simultaneously to communicate effectively" (Hampton and Wellman, 2003: 285). And individuals can engage with multiple others at a time, with varying levels of intimacy. These advantages facilitate the communing process online that can, in turn, foster a shared sense of community on- and offline. Connection is fluid and impacts the construction of social networks on- and offline with little impediment. In terms of online social organization, community more closely resembles a network instead of a localized group (Hampton and Wellman, 2001). Community, defined in terms of identity, solidarity, or shared interest, is not confined by a singular place or space. Rather, it is identified by social support and social cohesion (Hampton, 2002).

Classical theorists seem to agree that social cohesion or the feeling of "we" is central to the idea of community. Contemporary scholars that study ethnic identity and community argue that the feeling of togetherness, inclusion, and "we-ness" is important in encouraging mental health and wellbeing in black individuals (Keys, 2009; Marama and Velasquez, 2012). Therefore, it is important to analyze the framing of Black Twitter as a community instead of simply an aggregate of users. The communal interactions that occur on and through Black Twitter provide social support, allowing it to function as a community that inspires real, tangible action offline. But before delving deeper into a discussion about black community online and the idea of Black Twitter, I turn to a discussion of traditional conceptualizations of black community offline.

Ethnic identity, blackness, and community

I begin with a discussion of racial and ethnic identity because a community is in part determined by the ethnic and/or racial identity of its members. I take an interdisciplinary approach to my conceptualization of race and ethnicity. But one of the barriers to an interdisciplinary study of black community is the conflation of race and ethnicity. Authors in various disciplines use different terms and frameworks to identify both racial and ethnic identity. Generally, sociologists studying identity development in African Americans tend to use the term "racial identity" instead of "ethnic identity." However, Phinney (1996) argues that ethnic identity can include both race and ethnicity for this type of analysis because of the similarities in the patterns of race and ethnic identity development. There is not enough difference in the way the two ideas are developed to be of notable difference. Those who self-identify as black or African American often conflate the two terms, unless they are identifying a multiracial or multiethnic background. Thus concerning the terms ethnic and racial identity, I treat the terms as one in the same. My choice is particularly compelled by those who participated in this study. Several participants used both terms interchangeably when asked about their racial identity. Phinney (1996) also observes that white students follow the pattern of self-identifying both race and ethnicity as simply white, in the same manner that black students might identify as black or African American. Further, to be able to consider white racial identity development in conjunction with or in opposition to minority ethnic identity development, it is important not to overstate the difference between the two.

Understanding the way ethnic identity develops over time in individuals' lives is vital to our understanding of the intersection of community and blackness. Racial identity is part of a person's social identity and self-concept that comes from their knowledge of membership in a social group (Phinney, 1992). People then attach value, meaning, or emotional significance to group inclusion. In a study on ethnic identity development among students of color at a highly selective PWI (primarily white institution), researchers found that individuals perceived ethnic identity development as central to identity development. Students believed that their understanding of their ethnic identity related positively to their "sense of belonging, interpersonal relationships and commitments" (Maramba and Velasquez, 2012: 310). Their study confirmed previous research (Hurtado et al, 1994; Oyserman et al, 2002; Tatum, 1999), and affirms the importance of ethnic identity development in relation to a sense of belonging in people of color.

Individuals must resolve issues about self in order to have a stable self-concept that Erikson (1964) describes as achieved identity. Phinney (1992) describes the main components of ethnic identity as self-identified ethnic identity, ethnic behaviors and practices, affirmation and belonging, and ethnic identity achievement. She stresses that self-identification as part of an ethnic group is separate from simply belonging to a group. Membership in the group is determined by parents' ethnic heritage. She cautions that although individuals may identify as part of a single group, ethnic identity development varies over time and is shaped by historical and social events. But Phinney and Alipuria (1990) note that race identity is not the central aspect of identity for all people. Perceptions of other groups are not a part of an individual's self-concept of identity, although ideas about others' groups may shape how people feel about their own identity. When people don't develop a clear understanding of self, the result is identity diffusion and confusion about their place in society.

Individuals make decisions about identity early in life, but need a period of moratorium wherein they choose what their identity will encompass, according to Erikson (1964). They will then use that foundation to navigate the rest of their life choices, he theorized. More than two decades later, Phinney and Tarver (1988) found that ethnic identity development follows the general trajectory of Erikson's theorized process of identity development. Adolescents search for and commit to a racial or ethnic identity in middle school and high school. Since Erikson and Phinney's work on identity we have a better understanding of identity formation, and now know that individuals' ethnic identity is always in flux, just as their general sense of identity is.

Much of the early literature on African Americans and racial identity theorized that they have low self-esteem. Kardiner and Ovessey (1951), as well as Clark and Clark (1947), found that African Americans internalize outsider perspectives about their race, thus making them feel inferior to others (Rowley et al, 1998). Presently, social scientists have found that African Americans have a healthy sense of self-esteem. A widely supported explanation for the occurrence of high self-esteem in African Americans despite negative outsider opinions about race is the *insulation hypothesis*. It argues that African Americans compare themselves with members of their own group instead of to individuals outside of their race, *because* of segregation in the US. Racial identity helps positively influence a healthy self-identity (Broman et al, 1989; Rowley et al, 1998).

Although African Americans seem to have a healthy sense of self-esteem that acts as a barrier to outside group members, they still interact with those outside of their communities. Rollock and colleagues (2011) found that African Americans intentionally construct and enact a separate identity that they use in navigating interactions with white Americans. "Middle class blacks assert public identity in order to convince others that they are legitimate members of the middle class" (Rollock et al, 2011: 1081). This understanding of constructed identities allows us to understand how black middle-class individuals express agency and resistance against discrimination while maintaining ties to black identity. Elijah Anderson (1999) observed this same idea, code switching, among inner-city black youth as they navigated different social situations, confirming that racial identity performance is influenced by social settings.

Social media, black identity, and community affiliation

Social media provide an additional social context in which racial identity can be lived and performed. But social media have added a component in that they provide an ever-present record of identity negotiation. Twitter provides a space in which black users can enact agency when interacting with white individuals while also enacting insider status with other African Americans. Unlike in cases of traditional code switching, social media platforms keep a written record of coded interactions. Although black users operate in both spheres simultaneously, these interactions are distinct and have separate implications.

On Twitter, users of color engage in the practice of "signifying" in order to mark the social boundaries of race in the context of that platform (Florini, 2013; Papacharissi, 2012). "Signifying," which "deploys figurative language, indirectness, doubleness, and wordplay as a means of conveying multiple layers of meaning, serves as a powerful resource for the performance of Black Cultural Identity on Twitter" (Florini, 2013: 2). These coded interactions are used to make sense of events that have broken the social contract or that somehow disengage implicit social norms. Users who do not understand the code are excluded from the conversation. Signifying is just one way African Americans interact on social media and social networking sites that differ from the way that white users engage in social media and social networking sites. It also acts as a type of visual code switching. Black users intentionally code their words and hashtags to convey blackness. This can exclude users who are not familiar with the rituals, language, and syntax of that community. The distinct marking of territory by black users also ensures that if one knows the code, they can participate effectively and thus feel as though they belong to the community. Brock (2012: 530) also argues that "Black hashtag signifying revealed alternate Twitter discourses to the mainstream and encourages a formulation of Black Twitter as a 'social public'; a community constructed through their use of social media by outsiders and insiders alike."

Black users were already using Twitter in mass, as demonstrated by multi-year Pew Internet Research Surveys, but the coining of the term "Black Twitter" as a cultural descriptor brought heightened attention to the use of social media by African Americans. However, we must also consider the social construction of Twitter as a public space. The notion of Twitter as a social public for black people is important because Twitter was not, in fact, created by black people, nor was it designed specifically to be used by black people. Instead, African Americans have since adopted and appropriated the platform and modified it to meet their specific needs.

Because Twitter was created by white elites for other whites, the structure of the actual application itself is limiting for those who are not part of that group. Thus, Black Twitter cannot be completely representative of blackness because it is, and always will be, bound by the social construction of Twitter itself – and that social construction is primarily white (Brock, 2012). The structuring of Twitter as white limits the way messages can be performed and also how they will be received. White users perceive Black Twitter as an aberration, thinking that Twitter is predominantly used by white people instead of the reality that Twitter is dominated by Black and Latinx use (Smith, 2011).

Brock's conceptualization of Black Twitter and the internet in general builds on the insight that race exists as a result of and within social structure and cultural representations. The internet is part of that same social structure, and therefore race is also an integral aspect of the internet (Brock, 2012: 531). In other words, race was built into Twitter. By default, as noted by cultural studies scholars such as Stuart Hall (1997), that default culture is mainstream majority white. Therefore, Black Twitter is a cultural performance that is intentionally marked as different in order to be distinct from mainstream Twitter. Thus, we have to understand Twitter from the standpoint of mediated blackness and responses to that performed blackness online, in the specific spaces that these representations are acted out in (Brock, 2012).

"Black Twitter does not reference a monolithic black voice; rather, it refers to racialized content and practices, often marked by 'ambiguous racialized humour,'" argues Vats (2015: 2). Coded texts work together to disrupt Twitter's usual perceived whiteness. For example, the hashtag "#PaulasBestDishes" emerged on Black Twitter as a response to allegations that Paula Deen specifically hired all black servers to work at her brother's wedding. Black Twitter socially sanctioned her for the racist remarks. Vats argues that #PaulasBestDishes responses such as "Massa-roni and cheese," "40 Acres and a Moscow Mule," and "Back of the Bus Biscuits" positions Black Twitter as "an assemblage describing the 'relative magnitude of Black (especially African American) activity, and in particular the creation of certain kinds of 'hashtags'" (Vats, 2015: 1).

Following the cultural studies constructionist perspective on race and Twitter use, Sharma (2013: 46–7) argues that "the Internet has always been a racially demarcated space and today the plethora of online communication platforms (instant messaging; email lists, blogs, discussion forums and social media) continue to exhibit varying degrees of identity marking and racial segregation." He suggests that these spaces replicate offline racial demarcations, for example, "the rise of social networks witnessed the 'white flight' of users from Myspace towards Facebook" when Facebook first opened to those outside of the Ivy elite (Sharma, 2013: 47). danah boyd (2012) also contends that "distinctions in social network site adoption and the perceptions of teens – and adults – have about these sites and their users reflect broader narratives of race and class in American society" (boyd, 2012: 205). Although similar, boyd's contention differs slightly from Sharma's. For Sharma, racialization mimics segregation that users likely encounter or live in offline. For boyd, internet spaces like Myspace and Facebook have a constructed racialization of their own. They do not mimic offline racial stereotypes – the sites themselves are socially created with ideas about race according to who uses which sites. Although subtle, this distinction is important because it suggests that on spaces in which multiple racial identities lay claim, the recorded racial identity negotiation becomes particularly valuable.

I see this racialization as neither bad nor good, but a tool to be used in working out identity for black users of social media, Twitter, in this case. Although individuals on the outside may misinterpret the messages that black users are broadcasting based on their understanding of race, the value here is not for the outsider. Black Twitter is of specific value to the black community because, as stated earlier, it provides a space of insolation from the otherwise hostile world, both on- and offline. In addition to providing a space of inward support and solidarity, it also provides an active catalogue of identity negotiation, a record of peers' thoughts and actions. The writings of sociologist George Herbert Mead affirm the idea that a record of identity negotiation can help sociologists understand the formation of social ideas and collective identities. He conceptualized the self as a social process. Considering Mead's perspective, the acting or performing of racial identity on Twitter by individuals helps to establish, re-establish, or challenge *group* conceptions of a certain race through continuous dialectic engagement with ideas and one's self:

> The self is not so much a substance as a process in which the conversation of gestures has been internalized within an organic form. This process does not exist for itself, but is simply a phase of the whole social organization of which the individual is a part. The organization of the social act has been imported into the organism and becomes then the mind of the individual. It still includes the attitudes of others, but now highly organized, so that they become what we call social attitudes rather than roles of separate individuals. This process of relating one's own organism to the others in the interactions that are going on, in so far as it is imported into the

conduct of the individual with the conversation of the 'I' and the 'me' constitutes the self. (Mead, 1934: 179)

Social media provides an even greater organization of the interaction between society and self than Mead could have imagined.

Methods

Shonda Rhime's *Scandal* airs every Thursday during 13-week seasons. It generates considerable discussion on Twitter. The hashtag "ScandalThursdays" was created by the network to encourage discussion by viewers. Users in Black Twitter have co-opted it and #ScandalThursdays trends regularly on Thursdays. Thus, #ScandalThursdays will serve as a case study in online community. The sample for this study is a subset of a larger sample for a study on race and social media use. For the initial random sampling, five university pages on Twitter were selected based on the location and size of the university – two in Texas, one in Maryland, and two in New York. From those five university pages, the first 100 followers displayed were followed that were not commercial accounts. Over the course of 19 months, I followed these initial 500 users as well as others in their networks. All of the Twitter handles are pseudonyms.

In an effort to provide a more comprehensive view of Black Twitter on #ScandalThursdays, I also present a larger data set collected from Twitter by the Crimson Hexagon service.[1] Crimson Hexagon is an "enterprise social listening tool [that] provides practical insights for strategic business questions, from topic research to audience analysis" (Crimson Hexagon). Crimson Hexagon sources tweets and posts from Twitter and Facebook, among other outlets, in response to queries specified by the researcher. For this study, the service provided results based on the following input: "black twitter" AND "blacktwitter" AND "scandal" AND NOT "veterans".[2] Results from Facebook and other platforms were not part of the query and are not included here.

Finally, to ascertain a more nuanced view of the way black users identify with and describe Black Twitter, I present follow-up interviews. Out of the initial 500 users that were followed, 40 agreed to an in-person interview. The sample was racially diverse, but here I only present responses from the 17 individuals who identify as black or African American. Combining these three methods yields a more comprehensive view of Black Twitter – both on a micro level, encompassing the way individual users think about Black Twitter, and on a larger scale, offering a view of the formation of community within Black Twitter.

Results

Over the course of 22 months, 7,105 tweets were generated by users that contained all three of the search characteristics "black twitter" or "blacktwitter" and "scandal". Users also use the hashtag #ScandalThursdays. While it is difficult to search for key words that hint at togetherness, belonging, and community, Black Twitter members use other words and phrases to signify these ideas. These phrases cannot be searched for by keyword, which is why real time observations are included in this study. Black users on Twitter actively assert that viewing *Scandal* while communicating with other Twitter users is part of the viewing experience. "Discussing how my favorite part of #Scandal is #BlackTwitter. It's 100x better if you watch it real-time and get on Twitter." "Feels good to watch Scandal with #BlackTwitter! #Hilarious – Been working the last 3 wks and had to watch it on Hulu with the boo lol." Further, some users explicitly describe the communal viewing experience as a family activity. "I love when #BlackTwitter comes together and watches TV as a family #scandal." "Black Twitter family about to come together for another sitcom lol #Scandal." More to the point, those who express a relationship with Black Twitter and *Scandal* seem to recognize or claim a collective power toward influencing change. "Boosie home, Annie is black, MJ got a love child AND Scandal tonight? Black Twitter, we did it!" "If you wanna act a fool, do it on Thursday night bc that's Scandal night and black twitter will be too busy #BlackTwitterWelcomeManual." Tweets like these are common interactions on #ScandalThursdays. From these tweets we can observe that some users that identify as part of Black Twitter identify it as a family that spends time together, a family that has power to cause discussion or activate observable change. Still, we can only learn so much from 140 characters. In the next section, I have reproduced several conversations with participants of the study that identified as being part of Black Twitter.

How do Black Twitter users conceptualize Black Twitter?

Q: How frequently do you use hashtags?

@crazz: everyday. I catch myself using hashtags in text messages.

Q: Ok. Do you ever use the hashtag blacktwitter?

@crazz: Oh all the time. I definitely feel like I use #blacktwitter on nights when we all watch television together.

@sidekick: Well see I don't – is black twitter – people that are black on twitter? Is that what that means?

@crazz: (to @sidekick) Yeah like – ok so black twitter, you say stuff like…. I always see like when a show's coming on, award shows that black people are gonna watch, people will tweet, 'I love black twitter when we watch TV together.' Like Black Twitter is definitely alive and well on scandal night. Definitely.

I want to note here that we had not talked about *Scandal* during the interview at all up until this point. The participant introduced the idea of talking about *Scandal* and Black Twitter without my prompting. It is also interesting that although the participant identifies as part of Black Twitter, when asked by her friend to describe it, she struggles to find the words to do so, and instead resorts to giving examples of interactions that take place on Black Twitter. The question raised by @sidekick is an important one – "Is black twitter – people that are black on twitter?" – that I return to in the discussion. But as our conversation continued, I wanted to gain a better understanding of how both participants thought about Black Twitter. I was surprised and caught off guard by the responses to my questions.

Q: So what kinds of things do you associate with Black Twitter, like when you hashtag it, what types of things do you talk about usually? (to @crazz)

@crazz: Niggas. Doing nigga shit.

@sidekick: – She cannot write that.

@crazz: Yes she can, it's a study, Niggas doin' nigga shit on Black Twitter.

At this point, the atmosphere shifted noticeably as I had been granted insider access to the participant's feelings about Black Twitter. Although I cannot state with certainty that this conversation would not have happened if I was a white woman, the literature seems to support my understanding of the interaction in that moment. In re-reading the transcript, I wondered why I did not ask what the participant meant by "nigga shit." But at that point in time, I had a shared understanding of what she meant by the phrase based on some of her previous responses. It was clear by her laughing tone that "nigga shit" was not said with malice. Still, her use of the term warrants further exploration (see later on in this chapter).

The previous discussion occurred with two black women. In the following discussion, two black men echo some of the same sentiments and attitudes.

Q: Do you ever use the hashtag black twitter?

@onthagrind: I have –

@theboss: I don't think I've ever used it. I've said some things about black twitter before because I'm definitely in black twitter

Question: Ok so what kinds of things do you say when you talk about black twitter?

@theboss: All the rachet stuff that you seein'. All the craziness that goes on. That it's so different from white twitter. 'Cause I have some white friends that I have from high school that are on white twitter and you can totally tell the difference.

@onthagrind: You can tell the difference. Black twitter is all like *Scandal* and *Real Housewives* – Real Wives of – or LHHA. It took me the longest time to figure out that that was *Love and Hip Hop Atlanta*.

Q: Ok so when you use the hashtag black twitter, what types of things do you talk about (to @theboss)?

@theboss: Mostly it's like things that everybody is talking about at the time so like the last BET awards it was like #blacktwitter and everybody was talking about the performance and we gone talk about who's performing or how bad they outfit looks. Or who almost fell on the red carpet.

@onthagrind: Who doin' hoochie stuff. Who dressed like this 'cause they know all the black people watchin' this stuff so they just put the black twitter on there.

@theboss: Football games, basketball games, any sporting event. The Super Bowl definitely. Beyoncé. Anything about Beyoncé.

Both participants demonstrate that they conceptualize Black Twitter as a space for black people. And both sets of participants as well as one from the previous conversation make a conscious and explicit differentiation between Black Twitter and White Twitter. "You can totally tell the difference." Interestingly, when white participants were asked about Black Twitter, the most common response was "Do black people use twitter?" Of course, this points to Granovetter's (1973) thesis on the strength of weak ties; however we know empirically that black people use twitter in much higher numbers than do white users (Smith, 2014). Both men think of Black Twitter as a forum for blackness, citing topics such as fashion, sports, and other forms of entertainment. And again, one participant, @onthagrind, references *Scandal*. Even if only mentioned in passing with a few other prime time television programs, it is clear that for @onthagrind, watching television together is part of participating in Black Twitter. "Black Twitter is all like *Scandal* and *Real Housewives* – Real Wives of – or LHHA."

While it seems that most of the participants who agreed to a follow-up interview can agree that Black Twitter is for black people, some expressed reservations about others' perception of Black Twitter.

Q: Are you familiar with Black Twitter?

@bfskylight: yes

Q: Well, what is your opinion of Black Twitter?

@bfskylight: Well I think I became like aware of Black Twitter.... I think it was on like CNN. I don't know they were talking about it on the news, and this had to be like last semester maybe, and there's definitely a difference between like Black Twitter and just the whole Twitter population. And I know like Twitter is mostly made up of black people so I don't think that it's negative. I don't think that it's negative. It can be negative but I don't think that it's negative. I just prefer not to, not to put a label on there, you know?

Discussion

All of these interactions provide a basic understanding of the way black users talk and think about Black Twitter. But the interactions that go on during *Scandal* can reveal a much more vivid picture of how race is negotiated on Twitter. I wanted to understand how these ideas about Black Twitter and community play out on Twitter. Further, I want to point out how the feeling and experience of community is replicated on Black Twitter. The participants represented a wide variety of sentiments, both via tweets and the interviews. A common thread that is clearly observable is the idea of togetherness or of belonging to the group. This is central to Cooley's ideas of primary group interaction in a community. The fascinating thing here, however, is that in several of the accounts given, participants use language and conversational style with me that connotes insider access. Had a white interviewer asked the same question, "What kinds of things do you associate with Black Twitter?" the respondent probably would not have responded with "niggas doin' nigga shit on Black Twitter." The respondent and their friend both laughed because we all understood that to be a joke – not of a derogatory nature. But someone from an outsider's position may have reacted differently. This was an act of signifying. When the respondent talks about Black Twitter in this manner, they are demonstrating some familiarity with the group that they are discussing. And the historical context that goes along with the word "nigga" in particular connotes insider status because blacks are the only group for which it is socially acceptable to use the term.

Many scholars have debated the use of the term "nigger" and all of its variants in the present vernacular (see, for example, Judy, 1994; Nguyen 2013; Young, 2007), but I find that Jacquelyn Rahman's (2012) summation of the term to be most fitting for the purposes of this chapter:

> Despite the general societal ban on use of forms of nigger, a variant finds continued acceptance among some members of the African American community for intra-group self-reference.... Use of this form allows a speaker to construct an identity representing awareness of the history of African Americans and practical knowledge of the nature and implications of the diaspora experience. (2012: 137)

In Rahman's nuanced analysis of the use of the term "nigga" by the African American community, she argues that a core social meaning of nigga related to survival was part of the counter-language that early Africans in America developed. The core meaning signaled Africans and Africanness in the role as survivors and participants in the diaspora experience. Members of the African slave community shared knowledge of this core meaning, which endures in present-day uses of the term (2012: 141). She also argues that the use of the word "nigga" can be used to self-identify as part of an ethnic group while also being used to ascribe or project identity onto the person with whom the term is being used. It can also be used in an exaggerative sense to add humor to the struggle of being black (2012: 154).

Perhaps most relevant to the use of the word in this context, Rahman distinguishes solidarity as a signal of a unified, common experience. "While projecting identity as an African American who is conscious of survival in the diaspora, *nigga* may add a dimension to that identity by projecting an attitudinal stance that shows solidarity with another African American or with the African American community" (2012: 155).

Considering an additional element, Neal (2013) finds that the use of "nigga" by African Americans can be used to construct and signify authenticity to others within the diasporic community (2013: 559). The scholarly community seems to reach a consensus on the use of term as a method to connote insider status, even if some would prefer the word not be used at all. The fact that the participant used the word in conversation with me, in direct connection with Black Twitter, signifies at the very least a shared cultural experience from which she positioned her responses to my questions.

Another trend that emerged in the interview data is the belief among Black Twitter users that Twitter is comprised mostly of black users. Black participants consistently stated that Twitter is a black space, whereas white users believed Twitter to be dominated by white users. Unsurprisingly, Twitter is actually dominated by black users. According to the 2009 Pew Internet study, 66 percent of Twitter users are black. Perhaps users feel a closeness or a sense of togetherness with others in Black Twitter because most of Twitter *is* Black Twitter. By this I mean that Twitter is saturated in black community. Black users indicate an absence of white users in their networks when they say that Twitter is for black people. This finding may support the insulation hypothesis in that black users are surrounding themselves with other users who look like them. Thus, when they compare themselves to the general other, they are insulated from the negative effects of discrimination because their general other is one that reflects and privileges blackness.

Beyond community, Black Twitter sees itself as an entity that can inspire change. It has demonstrated this to be true on a number of occasions. Even when discussing something as trivial as #ScandalThursdays, the data demonstrate that Black Twitter discusses social justice 6 times more and the Affordable Care Act 14 times more than non "Black Twitter". These findings suggest that although the primary purpose is the communal watching of television, other social issues (along with other cultural hot topics) are also being discussed within the confines of the community.

Black Twitter also serves another important function, both for those who participate in it and society at large. It is an excellent space for resisting racial prejudice and overall systemic racism. Because it keeps a written record, it has become invaluable in disseminating information quickly in times of protest. Black Twitter also rallies again racial ideologies that operate to normalize the interests of the dominant group. These normative over-generalizations and micro aggressions are often present in Twitter interactions. These moments are blatant and overt acts of resistance to the normative white racial frame (Feagin, 2013). At times, particularly concerning the show *Scandal*, these interactions are less obvious. In his book, the *White racial frame*, Joe Feagin argues that counter-frames replace existing systems of white dominance with new paradigms. His "critical counter-frame thus incorporates a *countersystem* analysis, one that examines the institutionalized and systemic character of white racial oppression and calls for its replacement with a new social system" (Feagin, 2013: 162). Concerning Black Twitter's discourse on *Scandal*, the new paradigm that is being actively created is one of black community.

Interestingly, two dialogues about race exist side-by-side. The integrated segregation (May, 2014) that occurs on Twitter is not new, but it is distinct in that both sides can see what the other thinks of it. One can easily observe *some* of what Goffman (1959) would term the backstage – the preparatory or private spaces of life. In this way, Twitter removes the curtain and things that people used to say in private are now laid bare. Perhaps this is why Black

Twitter uses coded language in order to maintain some social bounds of where the community begins and ends. The observation of these discussions and interactions in real time provide a window into how race is constructed for the benefit of those in power. One issue here is that Twitter is a performative space that is used in constructing one's identity (Marwick and boyd, 2010; Williams and Aldana Marquez, 2015). Individuals may tweet or post sentiments that seem to be in support of racial equality while hiding individuals' true feelings. For this reason, I included white subjects in my interview sample, but their responses have not been reproduced here, mainly because they are saying the same things, that they only use Twitter for sports or politics, or that they genuinely believe white people are the only ones using Twitter. However as Stanfield (2011) discusses, white participants are less likely to reveal racial prejudices to minority interviewers. I found this to be true with some of the participants in my study. There were numerous things that I observed online before and/or after communicating with them in person that were not always congruous with our conversations.

Conclusion

Inspired by the oral tradition of our ancestors, watching television together in conversation with each other is a way of passing down shared cultural knowledge from generation to generation. Twitter allows for this to happen on a much larger scale. Black Twitter watches television as a community, a group whose members feel a sense of belonging and togetherness. As a community, Black Twitter creates new social meaning, generates cultural and tangible capital, and inspires its members to action, both on- and offline. It is about more than consuming television together – #ScandalThursdays is about being together in a society that is at times hostile. We've already learned that social media gratifies the need to feel close to others (Chen, 2010; Zhao, 2006). As the participants in the study expressed earlier, watching *Scandal* together is being a part of Black Twitter. The communal watching experience allows Twitter users to actively negotiate the community, including who can be in it, and what ideas are allowed to exist in the space.

Notes
[1]   Access to the service was generously provided by Harmony Institute, a media research center.
[2]   AND NOT "veterans" had to be included because of a scandal involving veterans that had nothing to do with *Scandal* and/or Black Twitter.

References

Agre, P.E. (1997) "Building community networks." In P.E. Agre and D. Schuler (eds) *Reinventing technology, rediscovering community: Critical explorations of computing as a social practice* (pp 241–8). Greenwich and London, UK: Ablex Publishing Corporation.

Anderson, E. (1999) *Code of the street: Decency, violence, and the moral life of the inner city*. New York: Norton.

Bateman, R.L. and L. Lyon (2000) "Losing and finding community: The quest for territorial and psychological community from the neighborhood to cyberspace." *Research in Community Sociology* 10, 59–78.

Baym, N.K. (1995) "The emergence of community in CMC." In S.G. Jones (ed) *CyberSociety: Computer mediated communication and community* (pp 138–63). Thousand Oaks, CA: Sage Publications.

boyd, d. (2012) "White flight in networked publics: How race and class shaped American teen engagement with Myspace and Facebook." In L. Nakamura and P.A. Chow-White (eds) *Race after the internet* (pp 203–22). New York: Routledge.

Brock, A. (2012) "From the blackhand side: Twitter as a cultural conversation." *Journal of Broadcasting and Electronic Media* 56 (4), 529–49.

Broman, C.L., H.W. Neighbors, and J.S. Jackson (1989) "Sociocultural context and racial group identification among Black adults." *Revue Internationale de Psychologie Sociale* 2, 367–78.

Chen, G.M. (2010) "Tweet this: A uses and gratifications perspective on how active twitter use gratifies a need to connect with others." *Computers in Human Behavior* 27, 755–62.

Clark, K.B. and M.P. Clark (1940) "Skin color as a factor in racial identification and preference in Negroes." *Journal of Negro Education* 19, 341–58.

Clark, K.B. and M.P. Clark (1950) "Emotional factors in racial identification and preference in Negro children." *Journal of Negro Education* 19 (3), 341–58.

Cooley, C.H. (1956/1998) *On self and social organization*. Chicago, IL: University of Chicago.

Erikson, E. (1964) *Insight and responsibility*. New York: Norton.

Feagin, J. (2013) *The white racial frame: Centuries of racial framing and counter-framing*. New York: Routledge.

Florini, S. (2013) "Tweets, tweeps, and signifyin': Communication and cultural performance on 'Black Twitter'." *Television and New Media* X, 1–15.

Gatson, S. (2011) "The methods, politics, and ethics of representation in online ethnography." In N.K. Denzin and Y.S. Lincoln (eds) *Collecting and interpreting qualitative materials* (pp 245–76). Thousand Oaks, CA: Sage.

Gatson, S. and A. Zweerink (2004) *Interpersonal culture on the internet: Television, the internet, and the making of community*. New York and Ontario: The Edwin Mellen Press.

Goffman, E. (1959) *The presentation of self in everyday life*. New York: Anchor.

Granovetter, M.S. (1973) "The strength of weak ties." *American Journal of Sociology* 78 (6), 1360–80.

Hall, S. (1997) *Representation: Cultural representations and signifying practices.* Thousand Oaks, CA: Sage.

Hampton, K. (2002) "Place-based and IT mediated 'community'." *Interface.* DOI:10.1080/1464935022015009 9.

Hampton, K. and B. Wellman (2001) "Long distance community in the network society." *American Behavioral Scientist* 45 (3), 476–95

Hampton, K. and B. Wellman (2003) "Neighboring in Netville: How the internet supports community and social capital in a wired suburb". *City and Community* 2 (4), 277–311.

Haridakis, P. and G. Hanson (2009) "Social interaction and co-viewing with YouTube: Blending mass communication reception and social connection." *Journal of Broadcasting and Electronic Media* 53 (2), 317–35.

Horton Cooley, C. (1998) *On self and social organization.* Chicago, IL: University of Chicago.

Hurtado, A., R. Gonzalez, and L. Vega (1994) "Social identification and the academic achievement of Chicano students." In A. Hurtado and E. Garcia (eds) *Educational achievement of Latinos: Barriers and successes* (pp 57–73). Los Angeles, CA: University of California.

Judy, R.A.T. (1994) "On the question of nigga authenticity." *Boundary 2: An International Journal of Literature and Culture*, 221–9.

Kardiner, A. and L. Ovessey (1951) *The mark of oppression.* New York: Norton.

Keys, C.L.M. (2009) "The Black-White paradox in health: Flourishing in the face of social inequality and discrimination." *Journal of Personality* 77 (6), 1678–706.

Marama, D.C. and P. Velasquez (2012) "Influences of the campus experience on the ethnic identity development of students of color." *Education and Urban Society* 44 (3), 294–317.

May, R. (2014) *Urban nightlife: Entertaining race class and culture in public space.* New Brunswick, NJ: Rutgers University Press.

Marwick, A.E., and d. boyd (2010) "I tweet honestly, I tweet passionately: Twitter users, context collapse, and the imagined audience." *New Media and Society* 13 (1), 114–33.

Mead, G.H. (1934) *Mind, self, and society.* Chicago, IL: University of Chicago Press.

Murthy, D. (2012) "Towards a sociological understanding of social media: Theorizing Twitter." *Sociology* 46 (6), 1059–73.

Neal, M.A. (2013) "NIGGA: The 21st-century theoretical superhero." *Cultural Anthropology* 28 (3), 556–63.

Nguyen, K.H. (2013) "Hearin what we see: Censorgin 'nigga' vernaculars, and African American agentic subjects." *The Howard Journal of Communications* 24, 293–308.

Nonnecke, B., D. Andrews, and J. Preece (2006) "Non-public and public online community participation: Needs, attitudes, and behavior." *Electronic Commerce Research* 6 (1), 7–20.

Oyserman, D., K. Terry, and D. Bybee (2002) "A possible selves intervention to enhance school involvement." *Journal of Adolescence* 25, 213–326.

Papacharissi, Z. (2012) "Without you, I'm nothing: Performances of the self on Twitter." *International Journal of Communication* 6, 1989–2006.

Phinney, J.S. (1992) "The multigroup ethnic measure: a new scale for use with diverse groups." *Journal of Adolescent Research* 7 (2), 156–76.

Phinney, J.S. (1996) "Understanding ethnic diversity: the role of ethnic identity." *American Behavioral Scientist* 40 (2), 143–52.

Phinney, J. and L. Alipuria (1990) "Ethnic identity in college students from four ethnic groups." *Journal of Adolescence* I3, 171–83.

Phinney, J. and S. Tarver (1988) "Ethnic identity search and commitment in black and white eighth graders." *Journal of Early Adolescence* 8, 265–77.

Phinney, J.S., C.L. Cantu, and D.A. Kurz (1996) "Ethnic and American identity as predictors of self-esteem among African American, Latino, and white adolescents." *Journal of Youth and Adolescence* 26 (2), 165–85.

Rahman, J. (2012) "The n word: Its history and use in the African American community." *Journal of English Linguistics* 40 (2), 137–71.

Rollock, N., D. Gillborn, C. Vincent, and S. Ball (2011) "The public identities of the black middle classes: Managing race in public spaces." *Sociology* 45 (6), 1078–93.

Rowley, S.J., R.M. Sellars, T.M. Chavous, and M.A. Smith (1998) "Relationship between racial identity and self-esteem in African American college high school students." *Journal of Personality and Social Psychology* 74 (3), 715–24.

Sharma, S. (2013) "Black Twitter? Racial hashtags, networks and contagion." *New Formations* 46–64.

Smith, A. (2011) *Twitter update 2011*. Washington, DC: Internet, Science, & Tech (www.pewinternet.org/2011/06/01/twitter-update-2011/).

Smith, A. (2014) *African Americans and technology use: A demographic portrait*. Pew Research Center (www.pewinternet.org/2014/01/06/african-americans-and-technology-use/).

Stack, C. (1974) *All our kin: Strategies for survival in a black community*. New York: Harper & Row.

Stanfield, J.H. (2011) "The transformation of the role of race in the qualitative interview: Not if race matters, but how." In J.H. Stanfield (ed) *Rethinking race and ethnicity in research methods*. London, UK: Routledge.

Tatum, B. (1999) *Why are all the Black kids sitting together in the cafeteria and other conversations about race*. New York: Basic Books.

Tönnies, F. (1887/2001) *Community and society: Gemeinschaft and Gesellschaft*. Cambridge, UK: Cambridge University Press.

Tönnies, F. (1961/2014) *Custom: An essay on social codes*. New York: Free Press of Glencoe.

Turkle, S. (2011) *Alone together: Why we expect more from technology and less from each other*. New York: Basic Books.

Vats, A. (2015) "Cooking up hashtag activism: #PaulasBestDishes and Counternattatives of Southern food." *Communication and Critical/Cultural Studies*, 1–5.

Williams, A. and B. Aldana Marquez (2015) "The lonely Selfie King." *The International Journal of Communication*. 9, 1775–87.

Young, V.A. (2007) *Your average nigga: Performing race, literacy, and masculinity*. Detroit, MI: Wayne State University Press.

Zhao, S. (2006) "Cyber-gathering places and online-embedded relationships." Paper presented at the annual meeting of the Eastern Sociological Society in Boston, US.

18

Disruptive labor: Bleacher Report and the monetization of mass amateurization

Andrew McKinney

The developing world of internet news publishing has both drastically changed the political economy of traditional news organizations and created a flourishing new media ecosystem (Berkowitz, 2010; Tapscott and Williams, 2010; Shirky, 2011; Andrejevic, 2013). A major part of this new media ecosystem is sports media. Sports media companies can be found at the early stages of most major telecommunications innovations (Hutchins and Rowe, 2013). For example, ESPN was second only to HBO in the move to nationwide pay cable, and was an early adopter of the internet as a publishing platform. As of 2014, ESPN was worth $50.8 billion (Badenhausen, 2014), and still operates the #1 sports website on the web followed by the Yahoo! Sports portal. Fourth on that list is relative newcomer and Web 2.0 native, Bleacher Report (Alexa, 2015). Founded in 2006 and fully launched in 2008, Bleacher Report (shortened as B/R in this chapter and in their branding) entered at a ripe moment of sports journalism. ESPN and Yahoo! were digital pioneers, but were still primarily national networks, unable to offer the focus on local teams that newspapers provided. Most major newspapers, however, had not been able to embrace a more digital format or reliably expand their national coverage beyond Associated Press and wire reports. Bleacher Report's gambit was that providing the breadth of an ESPN with the team and region-specific coverage of local news was a viable business model that could scale exponentially. Key to succeeding at this goal was the production of a crowd-sourced workforce that could pump out content at an unprecedented clip while not being a part of a tightly funded startup's payroll. Hence, from its origins as a small San Francisco-based start-up in 2006 to its estimated $200 million acquisition by Turner Sports in 2012 to its current status as the fourth most popular sports website on the internet,[1] B/R has continued to utilize two interlocking narratives about itself. First, its founders and boosters proclaim it a "disruptive" force in sports media and media in general because it harnesses the passion of fans to unseat the incumbent, professional class of sports media producers. Second, it has sold itself as a place where aspiring writers and sports media professionals could get a foot in the door, building a resume while getting the exposure the site afforded. Major competitors, independent sports journalists, and former writers have actively challenged both of these narratives. Utilizing a close reading of B/R's promotional materials, their in-house blog, and the ever growing corpus of critiques from other outlets and former writers, the critique of these interlocking narratives is deepened to argue that they ultimately served to justify a kind of primitive accumulation of value from exuberance in desperation, wherein fans with aspirations toward making their passions their living became the digitized raw material of a content production empire. In the last analysis, what B/R has accomplished is the mobilization of what can be called "disruptive labor."

In this chapter, I first outline the digital methods I used to research the history of B/R's interaction with its writers and how it spoke publicly about its business model. Then I provide a sketch of the site's history as it evolved from a free platform for amateur writers into a multimillion dollar asset of the Turner Sports network. Last, I trace the evolution of the critiques of B/R as they moved from critiques of content and quality to critiques of its mode of production. Arguing from this historical data, both internal and external, I offer a theorization of the labor of B/R writers as indicative of deeper, more structural changes in networked sports media (Hutchins and Rowe, 2013) and media after Web 2.0.

Methods

Outside of web-based research searching for interviews with B/R principles and critiques of the site by other digital outlets, I utilized two more specific methods to help greater understand the evolution of how B/R talks about its writers and their role in its business model. First, I scraped the B/R blog (blog.bleacherreport.com) using a script written in the Python programming language. The result of the scraping was the full text of all posts from the blog (1,074 posts dating from August 17, 2007 to January 31, 2014), their authors, headlines, urls, categories, tags, and the date they were published. The script was written to also produce all the posts in separate text files and a separate JSON file that contained metadata organized by post. There is much more to do with this data, but extra measure such as data visualization and topic modeling are beyond the scope of this chapter.

Second, in order to trace the history of B/R's public relations (PR) and interface with their writers, the Internet Archive's Wayback Machine was employed. This is an archive of cached website pages that has been in existence since 1996. A building literature in the social sciences exists that uses the Wayback Machine as a digital research method to which this study attempts to contribute (Murphy et al, 2007; Weltevrede and Helmond, 2012; John, 2013). I used the Wayback Machine to trace the changes in the design and text of B/R where users interacted with content related to the prospects and procedures of writing for B/R. These webpages have changed locations and content several times since the first time Wayback Machine captured a snapshot of Bleacherreport.com on May 23, 2006, both on and between major design changes in the site. In order to track these changes, I checked the relevant urls every three months on the first of each month between June 2006 until February 2014 (to roughly coincide with the B/R blog data set).

It is important to note that these cached pages will not necessarily show a website exactly how it appeared when a snapshot was taken. Sites often block access to certain areas by disallowing the crawling robots access to certain directories. Also, sites that use JavaScript heavily will be difficult to archive, as the JavaScript elements may need to contact the originating server to function, and the originating server may not either contain those files or be in operation at all. In essence, the Wayback Machine takes a snapshot of each page, but cannot preserve all the functionalities that varying different eras of web design afforded. In the case of B/R, there were several types of directories that were blocked, most of them having to do with user account details that would appear to be only available to logged-in users in the first place. Content in the "pages" directory was blocked, but some of that content was just moved to other places on the site, and was accessible via the Wayback Machine. The JavaScript issue was more important in this case, however. In several instances, the interfaces that were used for account sign-up were based in JavaScript and were therefore inaccessible to research, limiting this study's ability to fully trace the changing ways in which B/R interacted with its new and potential writers. The majority of the content of these pages studied here, however, were primarily text with basic html formatting, so much fruitful data could still be culled. To be clear, limitations are to be expected when dealing with digital interfaces of any kind. As Matthew Fuller has theorized, interfaces "are the point of juncture between different bodies, hardware, software, users, and what they connect to or are a part of. Interfaces describe, hide, and condition the asymmetry between the elements conjoined" (in Cramer and Fuller, 2008: 149). It should be no surprise, then, that studying and researching interfaces would involve a certain data loss, no matter the method or level of effort.

History of BleacherReport.com and its in-house blog

Founded and launched in beta in 2006 and "formally" launched in 2008 by four "lifelong friends who were not satisfied by local coverage of their favorite sports teams" (Anon, 2010), B/R began its life as a bare bones publishing platform with the intent of becoming a crowd-sourced content farm. The website's "About" page (bleacherreport.com/about) and co-founders Bryan Goldberg, Dave Nemetz, Zander Freund, and Dave Finocchio, have variously stated the original vision of the site, but their business model was to attempt to solve a very specific problem: how to cover as many teams as possible with as little paid staff as possible. Their initial proposition was to produce a platform that was entirely open. In beta they referred to themselves as "the web's first Open Source Sports Network" (Anon, 2007a, b). By this they did not particularly mean what is traditionally understood by the term "open source." As it commonly applies to software and licensing, "open source" denotes a piece of software that allows for (a) access to its source code, (b) its free distribution, (c) works derived from its source code, and (d) an open license system that fights against proprietary intellectual property among other more contested traits (Anon, 2015). By "Open Source Sports Network," however, B/R meant to describe a platform that was open to submission by writers with no prior vetting or application process. The labeling of this as "open source" and later as "an open platform" will be discussed in greater detail later, but note here that access to source code and open licensing were not part of B/R's version of "open source."

Their "open platform" was framed as a means towards giving fans with undervalued expertise a voice in sports media. It is certainly true that sports media at the time (and to this day) is largely dominated by professionals whose expertise is understood by media companies to be very valuable, but by 2006, Bill Simmons, sports blogger and pioneer of the "fan" voice online (Cohan, 2013), was already working at ESPN.com and would soon become one of the dominant faces of ESPN on multiple platforms. And B/R competitor SBNation, also explicitly catering to fans and their opinions, beat B/R to launch by a solid year. However, no one argued as combatively as B/R for the importance of the fan voice. In an early version of their "About" page from late 2006, they write:

> At BleacherReport.com, we know that the real experts aren't the stiffs with the journalism degrees and the empty catch phrases ... they're the fans who've been following their teams since age four, painting their faces since age five, and holding onto their old Topps cards for longer than they care to admit. (Anon, 2006a)

This oppositional stance combined with a deep reverence for the fan is typical of this era. On a page recruiting writers from the beta version of the site, they state:

> In a marketplace dominated by corporate outlets, the site aims to provide something different, an alternative to the stifled funk of the mainstream. Too often, great editorial work never sees the light of the day, either because it's too edgy or because its creator doesn't have the right credentials. That's where we come in. (Anon, 2006b)

As displayed here, the Open Source Sports Network's openness was primarily an openness towards submissions and to the fan experience as a valid form of writing. "Openness" also functions as a kind of code word, like many contemporary terms for activity on the internet, for unpaid labor.

Bolstering the sense of openness and community was integral to B/R's strategy of encouraging their writers to continue to create content at a continuous clip. To that end, from August 2007 until the present, B/R has operated an in-house blog that is publically accessible but generally aimed inward at their writers' community. In the early era of B/R, from the 2006 launch until the June 2010 hiring of Brian Grey and early 2011 hire of former *Salon* editor King Kaufman as Manager of Writer Development, the blog focused on a kind of cheerleading for the identity of the site. Co-founder Zander Freund characterized B/R users who "live on the site" as "Bleacher Creatures" in such a rah-rah post in 2007:

> The Bleacher Creatures are the lifeblood of the Bleacher Report network. Without them, the community would collapse at the seams. The Creatures set the tone for the network at large. They spark the debates that make Bleacher Report the thriving community that it is. They engage the network's user base with their thoughts and opinions. Overall, they make Bleacher Report the place where internet users seeking fan-driven sports journalism want to be. (Freund, 2007)

This kind of incitement to act via praise is typical of the early rhetoric of the blog, as is the rather shaky writing ("collapse at the seams"). It is important to note that the primary blog authors in the pre-Brian Grey and King Kaufman era were the co-founders themselves – Freund, Goldberg, Nemetz, and Finocchio (accounting for 51 percent of all blog posts between 2007 and 2010) – as these are not individuals trained as writers but rather as entrepreneurs, so their emphasis towards building the morale of the platform and its business goals is understandable. Other posts by writers and editors from the site also did the work of morale building and positive PR for the platform by promoting new site features, showcasing particular writers, and writing more general posts meant to pump up the writer base.

Brian Grey's hire in 2010 and King Kaufman's in early 2011 marked a very important new stage for B/R, the company and site. Grey's background at Yahoo! and Fox Sports had positioned him well to take B/R into more of a money-making direction (Swisher, 2010), important because B/R had gone through two rounds of venture capital funding by mid-2010, reaching a valuation of $8 million, but was looking to raise a significantly larger sum in their series C round (Kafka, 2010). Also of particular interest was Grey's position at Silicon Valley VC firm Polaris Venture Partners. Sports media industry writer Ben Koo wrote of the hire at the time that the "Bleacher Report team is in great hands and their investors must be ecstatic that they have someone very well suited to steer the company to a lucrative exit." Koo also correctly pointed out at that this hire was nearly coterminous with a drastic change in the editorial policy of the site (Koo, 2010). Although not available on the site any longer and not available through the Wayback Machine, a summary of the policy was posted to the blog by co-founder and then VP of Content Finocchio in early June before the Grey hiring was announced. In the post Finnochio lays out the basics of the change: writers must now apply to be writers; once they become writers, they must "have a cogent writing style, provide detailed analysis, and display solid sentence structure and command of the English language;" publishing unsubstantiated rumors, not citing sources properly, and crasser forms of aggregation would not be tolerated (Finocchio, 2010). In two interviews given around the time of his hire, Grey made special care to mention the new "editorial layer" that B/R had installed (Swisher, 2010; DVorkin, 2011). After all of these changes and Grey's hire, B/R raised $10.5 million in series C funding on December 20, 2011 (Anon, nd). Also, as Grey mentions in his interview with Lewis DVorkin on *Forbes* magazine's website, 7,000 contributors were going through that "editorial layer," 1 percent of which were paid (DVorkin, 2011). Even more reason for venture capital to fund the site.

With that new money in hand, B/R made another major move by hiring Kaufman. Kaufman's introductory post on the site itself, "Bleacher Report: I don't give a damn about our bad reputation," laid out his bonafides, his goals for the site, and even poked fun at the public perception of B/R. After sharing a story about how a writer friend had asked him if there was a way he could make his browser refuse to go to B/R, he pledged to spend some time just writing like all the other writers at B/R, and ended on this note: "If you do know me, you might guess that I'm excited to be working on one of the frontiers of what a year or two ago we were calling the future of journalism, at a startup, a disruptive business that's trying to rethink how things are done. I'm hoping this is the start of great conversation" (Kaufman, 2011a). He continued that conversation on the company blog. Kaufman posted a statement of purpose for the blog: "One of the main jobs of the Bleacher

Report Blog is going to be to serve as a kind of classroom. I'm hoping it'll be the good kind. You won't have to sit still or be quiet and you can bring candy" (Kaufman, 2011b). This would inaugurate the blog as Kaufman's podium from which to lecture as writing instructor. In the sample of the blog, Kaufman's posts total 641 of the 1,074 in the sample, 59.79 percent of all posts, even though his posts come nearly four years after the inception of the blog. Kaufman's posts followed a couple of different templates. His most used form was the "Quote of the Day" posts (14.95 percent of total posts), followed by "How It's Done" (14.71 percent) that were more functional and pedagogical in nature, and "Shoutouts" (8.66 percent), which highlighted other writers on the site. That the most popular category of all posts on the blog was "Writing Tips," only appearing after Kaufman started in 2011 (32.68 percent) is generally indicative beyond any specific examples. Kaufman represented the public face of B/R's "editorial layer" and he meant to make that face a professorial, mentoring one.

By the time of their buyout by Turner Sports on August 3, 2012 (Kafka, 2012), B/R had taken major steps to revamp their reputation. These steps were rewarded with a final funding round in August of 2011 totaling $22 million (making a total of $40.5 million in venture capital raised) (Anon, nd), a year before the eventual buyout of somewhere between $175 and $200 million (Bercovici, 2012). Clearly, venture capital and Turner were assured by these steps that any content quality questions that might scare off potential advertisers had been thoroughly addressed. However, B/R's self characterization and VC's confidence did not go unchallenged. In fact, that challenge has a history almost as long as B/R itself.

Changing critiques of B/R

It is undeniable that until very recently B/R was one of the most reviled sites in the sports blogosphere. Frequent targets of other blogs like the Gawker Media sports site *Deadspin*, USA Today/MLB Advanced Media property *Sports on Earth* (run by *Deadspin* founder Will Leitch) and sports media-focused blog *Awful Announcing* (now part of the larger Bloguin network run by *Awful Announcing* founder Ben Koo), B/R was cited for its schlocky content, its over-use of the slideshow and list formats or "listicles," the search engine optimization (SEO) gaming often associated with the over-use of slideshows and listicles, the rampant misogyny of such slideshows like "The 20 most boobtastic athletes of all time" (McD, 2010), and the argumentative yet poorly argued style of many of its writers. This style, like a good deal of other "bad" internet-based opinion writing, has been generally referred to in the past few years as the "hot take" (Reeve, 2015). Much of that criticism, according to even King Kaufman and B/R's co-founders, was justified. Although it is unclear just how much the criticism pushed B/R to change and how much was the expressed concern of investors, in the start-up world, PR is of paramount importance when the goal is to announce an initial public offering of stock (IPO) or to be acquired (Crain, 2014). B/R's shifting standards over the years have often followed on the heels of continual negative coverage by other new media sports outlets.

Deadspin, whose content model includes a heavy dose of sports media criticism, has written the most consistently negative coverage of B/R. As of the writing of this chapter there are 39 articles tagged "Bleacher Report" on Deadspin.com, nearly all of them harsh critiques. *Deadspin* is known for its profane editorial stance, but some of its more brutal headlines were reserved for B/R. For instance, "Bleacher Report editors demand Bleacher Report be less retarded" details an anonymous former B/R writer's tip about the changing editorial policy. The article was published in the fall of 2010, shortly after the housekeeping of the new editorial standard and Brian Grey's hire. At the time *Deadspin* editor-in-chief A.J. Daulerio's lead is indicative of the general tone:

> If you are one of those unlucky sports fans who has to slog through Bleacher Report's Google-raping SEO 'stories' when you do a general news search for a topic about an athlete, team, or top seventeen sideline reporters the chilean coalminers should have sex with, this is great news. (Daulerio, 2010)

Daulerio hits several of the major critiques in the same sentence (SEO gaming, sexism, and listicles), and does it with a sort of gleeful disgust. After B/R's final venture funding round won them $22 million in late 2011, future editor-in-chief Tommy Craggs posted the gleefully dismissive "The 27 hottest employees of the venture capital firm that's investing $22 million in Bleacher Report: a slideshow." *Deadspin*, as a competitor, has a very clear reason for attacking B/R along content quality lines, arguing implicitly that their readers are discerning enough to never sully their days with the pabulum being spewed from B/R's writers. The concern was less for the future of sports journalism, since *Deadspin* as a competitor could hold itself up as a more shining example, and more for the state of readers and investors who would consider such a thing to be worthwhile. The mockery comes from a place of assumed superiority, specifically that of content and intellect. So, in the face of B/R's meteoric rise and continued monetary success, *Deadspin* chose to mock the people bankrolling that success.

Interestingly, the publicly available record of B/R critiques is relatively blank until 2010. Before that, most mentions of B/R in the media press are merely accounts of press releases (Koo, 2009) or hiring moves (Swisher, 2010). Other than *Deadspin*'s coverage, the public critique of B/R doesn't really take off until after the buyout. First among this wave was a long, heavily reported piece that made the cover of *San Francisco Weekly* (Eskenazi, 2012). Generally characterized as a "hit piece" by several aggregating outlets who picked up the story, the early October publishing date makes it clear that most of the reporting for the story happened before the buyout, and therefore acts as a kind of snapshot of the general displeasure with which a majority of the media world viewed B/R during its rise to prominence. However, the piece spends ample time where others had not yet, on the gamified and unpaid nature of writing for B/R. Eskenazi writes that "some [writers] earn a monthly stipend many told us was in the ballpark of $600," and further quotes a former editor that "estimates that, even with continued editorial hiring, at least 90 percent of Bleacher Report's gargantuan writing roster remains unpaid." Or course, contrast that with Brian Grey's much bleaker figure quoted at nearly the same time as 1 percent of 7,000. Eskanazi's primary concern, however, is less the low pay or total lack thereof, but the autonomy that even writers who have worked their way up the chain still lack. He quotes a featured columnist's laments about learning that "his new job largely consisted of providing copy for his editors' pre-written headlines," and points out that even the higher profile writers hired from outside the system (the first of which, baseball writer Rob Neyer, arrived shortly after King Kaufman's hire) were subject to the same issues (Eskenazi, 2012). This concern is still in the vein of the *Deadspin* critique, however. It does start to approach the issue as a problem of labor, but still from a position of assumed superiority of content, a pearl clutching at the lack of "real" writing going on.

Starting in 2013, the year after the buyout, criticism of B/R shifted further towards arguments about shady labor practices, written without the condescension of the earlier critiques. In early 2013 a writer working for the left-of-center, more literary style sports outlet *The Classical* (founded in part by the writer Bethlehem Shoals, who would briefly be one of B/R's major outside hires) wrote about his experience enrolling in Bleacher Report University, a tutorial program that was the entry point for writers going through B/R's new "editorial layer." The piece breaks down the "assignments" that each new writer has to complete in order to be allowed to start working at B/R, and the writer highlights specifically the sections of it related to planned headline, keyword focusing, and the imperative to have a "take." Bond's detailed and immersive (essentially ethnographic) approach allows for a sense of empathy with the person who actually creates the content that *Deadspin* and others so gleefully denounced (Bond, 2013).

Second, *The Bleacher Report Report*, an anonymously written blog on Gawker Media's Kinja platform (which experimented itself with the kind of gamified ranking system that B/R used) carries a mission statement to "exists solely as an answer B/R's very powerful PR machine." *The B/R Report* is written by "Bleach" who does not disclose his relationship to B/R, but structures the blog as a place to fact check and critique their PR. Bleach also highlights critical pieces from other outlets about B/R. Much of the blog is devoted to this kind of secondary reporting and analysis, although it is clear that Bleach has contacts within B/R. Again, like Bond's piece for *The Classical*, the focus is on the interior of the institution with several posts devoted to internally faced documents like 2013's e-Book *Playbook: The basics of writing for Bleacher Report* by the Bleacher Report Quality Control Team and BR's confidentiality clause (Bleach, 2013a, b). Bleach reports with a generally woeful air of disgusted resignation at B/R milestones and achievements. Bleach's angle is a critique of B/R's business model, one whose disruptive model had filtered up into the mainstream media, making millions of dollars for its founders while it continued paying a miniscule fraction of its content producers. This anger at their labor practices stems not just from a lack of payment (payment for writing on the internet in general is in a deeply degraded state), but because Bleacher Report positioned itself as a gateway to the world of sports journalism. Bleach argues for that pedagogical rhetoric to be just, in fact, rhetoric – a university brick and mortar façade over a factory of aspiring laborers.

Implications of B/R for a theory of disruptive labor

In an article published by *Deadspin* entitled "The 200 ways Bleacher Report screwed me over," former Bleacher Report featured columnist Tom Schreier explained how the featured columnists, the top tier in the gamified ranking system for B/R writers, are themselves tiered:

> You were a FCI, FCII, FCIII, or FCIV. On a page titled 'Writer Rankings,' Bleacher Report wrote that the Featured Columnist I got 'Featured placement on B/R Team pages; Eligibility for media interviews and credentials for major events.' At FCII, writers got 'a free B/R Featured Columnist hooded sweatshirt.' Level III Featured Columnists got 'an interview for a B/R staff job,' and FCIVs received 'access to a custom-built, author-specific publishing template for all articles.' (Schreier, 2014)

In this system based almost entirely on page views (not, coincidentally, the most common metric of value that websites use to sell ad space), any mention of payment is missing entirely. Schreier detailed the manner in which B/R's business model systematically worked to limit writer pay while keeping the carrot of possible full-time employment in play until the very end. Comments on the article were predictably harsh, but a comment from a fellow former BR writer, posting as "Mets31," mirrored Schreier's experience (this comment was also highlighted on *The B/R Report*). Of note was his very clear distillation of the young writer's lack of expectation for payment and the importance of attention: "I was getting big read counts. I had several articles top the 50,000 mark and a couple over 100,000. I could go tell my friends, 'Yeah 100,000 people just read what I wrote today.' That was almost, in my eyes, as good as being paid, and it would assuredly lead to me getting a job" (Mets31, 2014).

It's no wonder that companies like B/R either publicly report their writers' analytics or give them to their writers so as to fully cement the notion that the recognition that a writer receives is, in fact, "something." The quantitative nature of this "something" allows for the hope that after accumulating enough of this "something," a tipping point will be reached that leads to paying, full-time employment. The speculative nature of this labor is akin to what Gina Neff has referred to as venture labor in her ethnography of late 1990s Silicon Alley (Neff, 2012), only in the intervening 10 years of start-up culture, the stakes have changed. Crowdsourced labor, or what Trebor Scholz has evocatively referred to as "crowdmilking" (in Terranova and Scholz, 2014), combined with the declining prospects for entry-level positions in the fields best suited to crowdsourcing (journalism, publishing in general, media production in general), has created a massive surplus army of venture laborers. Bleacher Report built a structure to scoop up this labor. They benefited from a saturated labor market and squeezed it like a sponge. Young people raised on lowered expectations, both from the medium and the economic reality, were utilized in order to run a "lean" startup, meaning one with as little fixed labor costs as possible (Ries, 2011). B/R's internally and externally facing discourse normalized the radical extraction of value from workers by selling the work experience as both valuable as education and the recognition of having been published. By utilizing a pedagogical tone in its in-house blog and ranking its writers via a page view metric, they hammered home the connection of between gaining experience and gaining attention. B/R was also able to apply the model of experience and attention to sports fandom by capitalizing on the devaluation of writing about objects of fandom, and by selling itself as a platform where fans had a voice that could be noticed, where both the fan experience and fan attention could be seen as valuable (if not monetized for fans themselves). Schreier notes that he wrote for B/R initially since it positioned itself as locally focused in a way that other large sites wouldn't or couldn't. This is fitting as B/R's original stated content model aimed towards depth of localized coverage. The reward for the writer here is recognition, not just for them, but also for the relevance of their team or sport or university or city or region. In addition, BR leveraged a sense of "community" in these fandoms. This community rhetoric folded into the recognition system, allowing writers to build prominence within their own niches. All of that activity was in some way valuable to all those who participated in it, just only monetarily valuable to a scant few. Recognition does not necessarily and in fact rarely equals payment for writers at B/R.

This is a publisher scraping off the top of an excess of desiring subjects whose desire is for recognition, a recognition that works as a credit system (an IOU) for a eventual payment, a desire that makes their labor particularly easy to exploit. That the featured writer's in-house recognition does not culminate in payment is illustrative of this situation. There, in a seeming paradox, the taint of having written for B/R (of having helped build the brand) decreases your ability to be paid for writing at B/R. The B/R stigma must be overcome by both the writers and management. B/R's management strategically moved towards outside hires and a rebranding made possible by the buyout and entrance into the upper echelons of networked media sport. However, daily uniques and page views could not maintain their steady growth without a consistent influx of new content. Hence, some kind of workforce had to be retained that could cover local teams and produce the slideshow page view juggernauts. The community-centered Newsletter that beat writers like Schreier manually assembled was replaced by Teamstream, a mobile app that aggregates AP, ESPN and major newspaper beat writer content. *The Writer's Program* and B/R blog continue to exist, however, as do their rhetoric of uplift and resume building without an increase in paid positions.

B/R representatives have made numerous attempts to address the issues of payment and in-house promotion. The founders generally argue that B/R's model has been adjusted numerous times, an agile business model quick to adapt to changing conditions. Both Bryan Goldberg and Dave Finocchio have made references to the "old Bleacher Report" of 2008–09 (The Street, 2013; Klimk, 2014). Goldberg theorized one such adjustment: "At launch, it was an open platform. Today, it functions much more as a true media company, while still opening the door to some talented contributors" (2013a). This is, of course, an echo of the old tagline "The Open Source Sports Network" from the early days of the site, but following the clearer logic of "open platform" that Goldberg lays out here is worthwhile. By using the terminology of "open" and "platform," Goldberg means to describe a website and content management system (CMS) that is owned privately and funded by venture capital with the aim of monetizing the content (platform) but that takes submission from unpaid (and possibly unvetted) content producers (open). Goldberg's use of "open" is akin to what Evgeny Morozov has identified as the Trojan horse of a neoliberal regime on the internet, and what in the 1990s Langdon Winner and more recently David Golumbia have identified under the term "cyberlibertarianism" (Winner, 1997; Golumbia, 2013; Morozov, 2014). By claiming "openness" as a value, the radical accumulation of wealth from the activity of unpaid labor appears as the fostering of opportunity, the "open platform" is the space from which a career can be launched, and to curtail that openness would be akin to curtailing freedom. Tiziana Terranova's influential "free labor" argument also applies here (Terranova, 2000). As she defines it, "free labor" is "voluntarily given and unwaged, enjoyed and exploited" (2000: 33) and "a fundamental moment in the creation of value in digital communities" (2000: 36). Both exploited and given, one can also look to an earlier era's distinction between free labor and slave labor, free labor being that which had freedom of movement and opportunity but only "free" when it was set into motion by being circulated as waged labor. In that sense, Terranova's "free labor" is that labor which has the ability to be circulated, and the role of the "open platform" is to ensure the free circulation of that free and creative labor. By maintaining an emphasis on "openness," B/R linked itself to the cyberlibertarian open source labor regime that Morozov, Winner, Golumbia, and Terranova all cite as being integral to the understanding of the ideology of capital in the digital era. In more practical terms, however, beginning as an "open platform" was necessary because the funds were not available to pay writers, a point that Goldberg makes in a column ironically titled "Writers should be paid" (Goldberg, 2013b). The money that they had was spent on things like the platform itself and putting together an ad sales team, that is, on an infrastructure that allowed for the "openness" of the platform.

When he was hired, King Kaufman said he wanted to work for a "disruptive business." And he does. The "open" platform stage of B/R is the first stage of the disruptive technology model, one constantly evolving and slowing only when a stable, paid workforce emerges (Christensen, 2013). In this first, disruptive phase, B/R built a "product" that allowed for the publication of "content" without the need for the official employment of the "content producer." This element of the CMS, the product, is a very common issue in contemporary media organizations as they adjust to the dominant employment policy of precarious freelance contracts. *The New York Times*, legacy print company of all legacy print companies, has said as much about its new CMS scoop that it rolled out in mid-2014 (Vnenchak, 2014). Bleacher Report's platform, like a lot of CMSs with strong role control and user-friendly interfaces that restrict access to only the most basic of functions, can swiftly collect a mass of content that can be pushed out continuously, again and again, without having to have every author in office or have any direct contact with the editorial staff. However, one of the primary indicators of a "disruptive technology" in the literature (Bower and Christensen, 1995; McQuivey and Bernoff, 2013) is the lower quality of the technology itself. It offers fewer features or services, and is, at least at first, of far less quality than the product it seeks to disrupt. Often the technology could be described as aiming down market, at a group of consumers who do not offer enough profitability to warrant attention and research and development (R&D) outlays from the larger incumbent firms in the industry. The lower-quality, down market character that disruption theory's founding father Clayton Christensen outlines as the necessary marker of the disruptive technology in this instance is less the platform itself, but the labor and content it affords. This is what could be called "disruptive labor" or the marshaling of lower quality workers who can produce a lower quality product that will appeal to a nascent audience afforded by a digital platform. This is the monetization of mass amateurization built on a formula: enough people who produce out of "hobby" or "passionate interest" or just a desperation for recognition would be enticed by an "open platform" that the open platform itself can be the site of monetization. Once that platform is shown to be possibly profitable, venture capital continues to invest in order to recruit and train better writers and launch a PR campaign. This is indicative of the second phase of disruption in the literature, a period of swift increase in quality of the product due to the influx of capital from sales and investment. In the disruptive labor case, the new influx of capital is not spent on wages, but on the infrastructure (the training apparatus and PR). The labor is disruptive here because it does more with less, as it gets more and more popular. It stays "lean." And what is disrupted is not sports journalism or networked media sport, but sports journalists and media workers themselves.

In this way, it is my argument that this model should be distinguished from broader concepts of "digital labor" (Scholz, 2012; Fuchs, 2014) and Terranova's "free labor," which are influenced at least in part by the autonomist Marxist conception of the "social factory" (Gill and Pratt, 2008), and have been mobilized as a way to understand how the "social" of "social media" has been made to produce value. The labor of disruptive labor is certainly digitally enabled, and is itself a form of the monetization of everyday life concerns as fandom is often categorized as an aspect of the sociology of everyday life. However, what distinguishes the disruptive labor of B/R writers is the promise of recognition and the possibility of the making of passionate interest into a viable career. The pedagogical nature of the B/R writer's blog and its gamified ranking system serves to pull potential writers into the system and keep them producing with a future in mind. One of disruption theory's most important theorems is the S-curve of development (Bower and Christensen, 1995), in which the quality of the technology itself is at first poor, slowly increases, and then rapidly increases (ideally surpassing the quality of the technology or service it seeks to disrupt). In the case of B/R's disruptive labor, the pedagogical approach of the B/R writer's blog and the "editorial layer" put in place were the vehicles through which the initial incremental growth up the developmental S-curve was made. With the carrot of possible employment in front of them, unpaid content producers produced enough content properly formatted to pull in the page views necessary for the second phase of the disruptive labor of B/R: the series of outside hires that B/R made, starting in 2011 with the hiring of Rob Neyer, a former ESPN baseball columnist. With the venture capital they had secured by the end of their series C round in August of 2011 ($40.5 million), and the money from the Turner buyout in 2012 ($175-200 million), the money available for hiring more and more outside, established professional writers and for developing product that would automate content aggregation from outside the disruptive labor pool reaching the exponential growth in quality that is indicative of the second phase of the S-curve. The disruptive laborers themselves, however, are, like the technologies produced in the earlier phases of the disruptive technology S-curve, cast aside and forgotten.

In this way, instead of "free labor," the disruptive laborers of B/R are more akin to the manner in which Christian Fuchs has theorized "digital labor" (Fuchs, 2014). Fuchs argues that digital labor is more than the social factory made digital via social media, but should be thought of as a chain of labor that stretches from the tantalum miners in the Democratic Republic of Congo, to Foxconn workers in Shenzhen, to software engineers in Cupertino. Disruptive labor does not exist solely as "voluntarily given and unwaged, enjoyed and exploited," but as part of a chain of labor and its circulation that capital calls into existence and then discards when it is no longer needed.

Note

[1] And as of January of 2015, as a part of the Turner Digital Network (as Yahoo! Sports is a vertical of the Yahoo! Network), it ranked 14th in industry standard comScore's ranking of the 50 most valuable digital media properties. ESPN ranked 18th (comScore, 2015).

References

Alexa (2015) "Alexa – top sites by category: Sports" (www.alexa.com/topsites/category/Top/Sports).

Andrejevic, M. (2013) *Infoglut: How too much information is changing the way we think and know.* New York: Routledge.

Anon (2006a) "Bleacher Report – About us" (https://web.archive.org/web/20061218213001/http://www.bleacherreport.com/about-us/).

Anon (2006b) "Bleacher Report – Writing for Bleacher Report" (https://web.archive.org/web/20061218213348/http://www.bleacherreport.com/writing-for-bleacher-report/).

Anon (2007a) "Bleacher Report – Learn more" (https://web.archive.org/web/20071229163509/http://bleacherreport.com/learn_more).

Anon (2007b) "Bleacher Report talks about Open Social" (www.youtube.com/watch?v=wlhB8o-EmgM&feature=youtube_gdata_player).

Anon (2010) "About Bleacher Report" (https://web.archive.org/web/20100114024815/http://bleacherreport.com/about).

Anon (2015) "The Open Source Definition | Open Source Initiative" (http://opensource.org/osd).

Anon (nd) "Bleacher Report." *Crunchbase* (www.crunchbase.com/organization/bleacher-report).

Badenhausen, K. (2014) "The value of ESPN surpasses $50 Billion." *Forbes* (www.forbes.com/sites/kurtbadenhausen/2014/04/29/the-value-of-espn-surpasses-50-billion/).

Bercovici, J. (2012) "Turner buys Bleacher Report, Next-gen sports site, for $175m-plus." *Forbes* (www.forbes.com/sites/jeffbercovici/2012/08/06/turner-buys-bleacher-report-next-gen-sports-site-for-175m-plus/).

Berkowitz, D.A. (ed) (2010) *Cultural meanings of news: A text-reader.* Los Angeles, CA: Sage Publications, Inc.

Bleach (2013a) "Bleacher Report's confidentiality clause is a tricky one." *The Bleacher Report Report* (http://thebrreport.kinja.com/bleacher-reports-confidentiality-clause-is-a-tricky-on-607056770).

Bleach (2013b) "King Kaufman et al have independently published a 56-page e-Book on 'The basics of writing for Bleacher Report;' You can, too!" *The Bleacher Report Report* (http://thebrreport.kinja.com/king-kaufman-et-al-have-independently-published-a-56-p-1467645583).

Bond, N. (2013) "7 stages of grief at Bleacher Report University." *The Classical* (http://theclassical.org/articles/7-stages-of-grief-at-bleacher-report-university).

Bower, J.L. and C.M. Christensen (1995) "Disruptive technologies: Catching the wave." *Harvard Business Review* 73 (1), 43–53.

Christensen, C.M. (2013) *The innovator's dilemma: When new technologies cause great firms to fail* (Reprint edn). Boston, MA: Harvard Business Review Press.

Cohan, N. (2013) "Rewriting sport and self: Fan self-reflexivity and Bill Simmons's *The book of basketball*." *Popular Communication* 11 (2), 130–45.

comScore (2015) "comScore ranks the top 50 US digital media properties for January 2015." comScore Inc (www.comscore.com/Insights/Market-Rankings/comScore-Ranks-the-Top-50-US-Digital-Media-Properties-for-January-2015).

Crain, M. (2014) "Financial markets and online advertising: Reevaluating the dotcom investment bubble." *Information, Communication & Society* 17 (3), 371–84.

Cramer, F. and M. Fuller (2008) "Interface." In M. Fuller (ed) *Software studies: A lexicon* (pp 149–53). Cambridge, MA: MIT Press.

Daulerio, A.J. (2010) "Bleacher Report editors demand Bleacher Report writers be less retarded." *Deadspin* (http://deadspin.com/5669694/bleacher-report-editors-demand-bleacher-report-writers-be-less-retarded).

DVorkin, L. (2011) "Who's doing It right? Bleacher Report turns knowing fans into reporters." *Forbes* (www.forbes.com/sites/lewisdvorkin/2011/08/22/whos-doing-it-right-bleacher-report-turns-knowing-fans-into-reporters/).

Eskenazi, J. (2012) "Top 5 ways Bleacher Report rules the world!" *SF Weekly* (www.sfweekly.com/2012-10-03/news/bleacher-report-sports-journalism-internet-espn-news-technology/).

Finocchio, D. (2010) "Changes to Bleacher Report editorial policies – The writer's blog." *Bleacher Report Blog* (http://blog.bleacherreport.com/2010/06/02/changes-to-the-bleacher-report-editorial-policy/).

Freund, Z. (2007) "Bleacher creatures: Overview – The writer's blog." *Bleacher Report Blog* (http://blog.bleacherreport.com/2007/10/04/bleacher-creatures-overview/).

Fuchs, C. (2014) *Digital labour and Karl Marx*. London, UK: Routledge.

Gill, R. and A. Pratt (2008) "In the social factory? Immaterial labour, precariousness and cultural work." *Theory, Culture & Society* 25 (7–8), 1–30.

Goldberg, B. (2013a) "What Jiu Jitsu teaches us about media companies." *PandoDaily* (http://pando.com/2013/08/08/what-jiu-jitsu-teaches-us-about-media-companies/).

Goldberg, B. (2013b) "Writers should be paid." *PandoDaily* (http://pandodaily. com/2013/05/20/writers-should-be-paid/).

Golumbia, D. (2013) "Cyberlibertarianism: The extremist foundations of 'digital freedom'" (www.academia.edu/4429212/Cyberlibertarianism_The_ Extremist_Foundations_of_Digital_Freedom).

Hutchins, B. and D. Rowe (2013) *Sport beyond television: The internet, digital media and the rise of networked media sport.* London, UK: Routledge.

John, N.A. (2013) "Sharing and Web 2.0: The emergence of a keyword." *New Media & Society* 15 (2), 167–82.

Kafka, P. (2010) "Fox, Yahoo! Sports vet Brian Grey to run sports start-up Bleacher Report." *AllThingsD* (http://allthingsd.com/20100616/fox-yahoo-sports-vet-brian-grey-to-run-sports-startup-bleacher-report/).

Kafka, P. (2012) "Turner buys Bleacher Report." *AllThingsD* (http://allthingsd. com/20120806/turner-buys-bleacher-report/).

Kaufman, K. (2011a) "Bleacher Report: I don't give a damn about our bad reputation." *Bleacher Report* (http://bleacherreport.com/reputation).

Kaufman, K. (2011b) "The Bleacher Report blog as classroom – The writer's blog." *The Bleacher Report Writers Blog* (http://blog.bleacherreport. com/2011/04/07/the-bleacher-report-blog-as-classroom/).

Klimk, M. (2014) "Dave Finocchio founder of Bleacher Report" (www. usatoday.com/videos/money/business/2014/10/17/16211141/).

Koo, B. (2009) "Bleacher Report + CBS = NFL correspondent network aka dream jobs for 32 aspiring writers/bloggers." *Koo's Corner* (http://benkoo. com/articles/biz-and-tech/bleacher-report-cbs-nfl-correspondent-network-aka-dream-job-for-32-aspiring-writersbloggers.html).

Koo, B. (2010) "Big changes at Bleacher Report." *Koo's Corner* (http://benkoo. com/articles/biz-and-tech/big-changes-at-bleacher-report.html).

McD, M. (2010) "20 most boobtastic athletes of all time." *Bleacher Report* (http://bleacherreport.com/articles/386180-the-20-most-boobtastic-athletes-of-all-time).

McQuivey, J. and J. Bernoff (2013) *Digital disruption: Unleashing the next wave of innovation* (Unabridged edn). Cambridge, MA and Las Vegas, NV: Amazon Publishing.

Mets31 (2014) "The top 200 ways Bleacher Report screwed me over." *Deadspin* (http://deadspin.com/tom-commenters-i-really-enjoyed-this-piece-i-worked-f-1609261553).

Morozov, E. (2014) "The meme hustler." *The Baffler* (www.thebaffler.com/ salvos/the-meme-hustler).

Murphy, J., N. Hazarina Hashim, and P. O'Connor (2007) "Take me back: Validating the Wayback Machine." *Journal of Computer-Mediated Communication* 13 (1), 60–75.

Neff, G. (2012) *Venture labor: Work and the burden of risk in innovative industries.* Cambridge, MA: The MIT Press.

Reeve, E. (2015) "A history of the hot take." *The New Republic*, April 12 (www.newrepublic.com/article/121501/history-hot-take).

Ries, E. (2011) *The lean startup: How today's entrepreneurs use continuous innovation to create radically successful businesses.* New York: Crown Business.

Scholz, T (ed) (2012) *Digital labor: The internet as playground and factory.* New York: Routledge.

Terranova, T. and T. Scholz (2014) "Trade unionism, digital labor and the sharing economy: Tiziana Terranova interviews Trebor Scholz." *EuroNomade* (www.euronomade.info/?p=2910).

Schreier, T. (2014) "The top 200 ways Bleacher Report screwed me over." *Deadspin* (http://deadspin.com/the-top-200-ways-bleacher-report-screwed-me-over-1608499729).

Shirky, C. (2011) *Cognitive surplus: How technology makes consumers into collaborators.* New York: Penguin Books.

Swisher, K. (2010) "Bleacher Report's Brian Grey talks about new content biz, as Patrick Keane joins board." *AllThingsD* (http://allthingsd.com/20101124/bleacher-reports-brian-grey-talks-about-new-content-biz-as-patrick-keane-joins-board/).

Tapscott, D. and A.D. Williams (2010) *Wikinomics: How mass collaboration changes everything.* New York: Portfolio Penguin.

Terranova, T. (2000) "Free labor: Producing culture for the digital economy." *Social Text* 18 (263), 33–58.

The Street (2013) "Bleacher Report: The ESPN alternative that Turner Sports bought out." YouTube (www.youtube.com/watch?v=QPeocjg7NzM).

Vnenchak, L. (2014) "Scoop: A glimpse into the NYTimes CMS." *The New York Times Open Blog* (http://open.blogs.nytimes.com/2014/06/17/scoop-a-glimpse-into-the-nytimes-cms/).

Weltevrede, E. and A. Helmond (2012) "Where do bloggers blog? Platform transitions within the historical Dutch blogosphere." *First Monday* 17 (2) (www.uic.edu/htbin/cgiwrap/bin/ojs/index.php/fm/article/view/3775).

Winner, L. (1997) "Cyberlibertarian myths and the prospects for community" (http://homepages.rpi.edu/~winner/cyberlib2.html).

19

Covert leisure and public spaces: Geocaching in post-9/11 New York City

Jonathan R. Wynn

As a onetime Boy Scout, I have fond memories heading into the woods armed with little more than a map and a military compass. I was proud of my orienteering merit badge, and enjoyed finding my way from Point A to Point B to Point C. When I recently learned about geocaching, I thought of it as a kind of orienteering for the 21st century. It also worked with how I was starting to think about how smartphone technology could be used for qualitative research.

Geocaching is an outdoor activity played among strangers, using the internet and Global Positioning System (GPS) data, to share the location of "caches" that fellow players have hidden in public locations. It is somewhat similar to the 150-year-old leisure activity of "letterboxing," which similarly required offering clues and using landmarks to hide containers and trinkets. Caches today are usually small containers (possibly Tupperware or old military ammunition boxes), and hold a miscellany of items of little value (for example, notebook to write in, a pin, crayons, a coin), and players are expected to take something from the cache and leave something behind. While orienteering and letterboxing are primarily rural activities, geocaching can be rural or urban. In fact, there is a considerable amount of urban geocaching (see Figure 19.1).

GPS technology was developed by the military and made available to the public in the 1990s, although its precision was deliberately crippled to only 300 feet of accuracy to protect military operations. On May 1, 2000, President Clinton signed a bill that immediately allowed for full public access

Figure 19.1: Geocaches in New York City, New Jersey

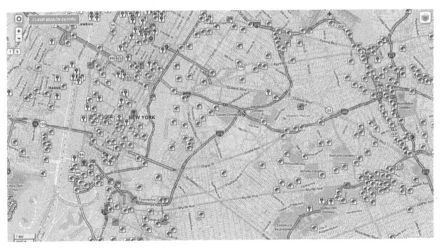

Source: Open Street Map licensed under the Open Data Commons Open Database License

to the GPS system. A man named Dave Ulmer hid the first geocache two days later, and posted its coordinates on a usenet newsgroup. The text read:

> Well, I did it, created the first stash hunt stash and here are the coordinates: N 45 17.460 W122 24.800 Lots of goodies for the finders. Look for a black plastic bucket buried most of the way in the ground. Take some stuff, leave some stuff! Record it all in the log book. Have Fun! Stash contains [sic]: Delorme Topo USA software, videos, books, food, money, and a slingshot! (Cameron and Ulmer, 2011: 7)

The stash was found five days later, and geocaching began.

An interviewee who preferred not to be named told me that most of what Ulmer did is still in "the DNA of geocaching: You hide something with some content and a logbook, you publish its location online, and the people who find it take something and leave something else." In those early days of geocaching, GPS devices were bulky and singular in purpose. As handheld mobile technology became increasingly accessible and sufficiently adaptable to these kinds of uses, the popularity of the activity grew. As of April 2015, there are over six million geocachers in the world (Lane, 2015).One of the early New York City geocachers, CacheNinja, described the activity to the *Village Voice* as:

> ... a fractured, postmodern, Internet kind of thing.... It's a community that's online, then becomes tangible in the real world. But if I met another cacher, it would just be awkward. It's about

minimal contact. We never use the phone because we all have our own personalities and characters. (Gray, 2001)

Going by the name of "FATS277," another early adopter talked about the tension between it being a "nice Boy Scout" activity and one that is for the more thrill-seeking, urban adventurer types. He said that he knows it's a "rather nerdy" activity, yet he was still irritated by the "family-friendly subpopulation," and started stashing in "not necessarily difficult to find, but dangerous places." He continued:

> One of [my caches] is out on Red Hook [Brooklyn]. Really beautiful spot. I hopped a fence and placed it on the end of the dock, near the grain silos from back when it was an active port. It's a big, old scary building. There's a huge pier that goes out behind it. I broke in and hopped the fence. And thought 'Oh, well, I'm here so I'll just place a cache here.'

This daredevil and "I-was-there!" spirit comes with a community component to it as well. Another geocacher told me:

> It's mostly for me – wanting to go somewhere and leave a mark without, you know, defacing property. But I'm starting to think about it as a grown-up graffiti thing because there's a call-and-response with it. I put a thing out there, someone finds it, there's a way for them to put something on the website for me to see that they were there. I think, 'Oh, that's cool, someone shared that experience.' There's feedback.

With interviews like this, I grew more curious to see what urban geocachers would say about their experiences as they participated in their leisure activity under the shadow of post-9/11 New York City.

Because of its military origins, global geopolitical issues have been entwined with GPS since its inception: from its early development by the US Navy in the 1950s, to President Ronald Reagan allowing all airlines to use GPS data in the aftermath of the Soviet military shooting down a civilian aircraft that had wandered into USSR airspace in 1983, to the military deliberately hobbling the accuracy of the system for fear of foreign militaries using it to their advantage in the early 1990s. But when Al Qaeda terrorists struck the World Trade Center on September 11, 2001, they created a security environment that was extremely hostile to such uses: in post-9/11 New York City, police and citizens were understandably sensitive to the idea of people hiding small, often metal boxes throughout the city, in fear of another terrorist attack.

With such a knot of issues – public space, community, safety, and technology – I was drawn to how geocaching could be linked to what I called "digital sociology" (Wynn, 2009). I grew interested in how people used smartphones to create connections in public spaces, and how sociologists could learn from these groups to augment and develop our discipline's methodologies. I saw the audio, visual, and GPS recording features utilized in geocaching as being useful tools for my ethnographic research on walking tourism in public spaces.

This chapter focuses primarily on introducing a few of the issues when thinking about how these technologies work within urban spaces, and how I learned to use these skills.

Battery Park City (40.703894, -74.017351)

We meet in Battery Park City at 8am to beat the line to the Liberty Island ferry, which leaves at 9am. I take a picture of Fritz Koenig's severely damaged sculpture, The Sphere, as it stands now: excavated from the wreckage of the World Trade Center, nine years earlier. As I put my iPhone back into my pocket, it silently and automatically geotags the image's metadata for me. I sit on a bench and finish my bagel and coffee, and Brett meets me at the agreed upon latitude and longitude. We talk logistics. It's best to get to there when there are fewer tourists.

I am following him to look for a rogue cache. There are 20 to 30 geocaching.com administrators across the US who do their best to review the appropriateness of caches as their information is uploaded on the site. One of them contacted Brett a few days ago, asking him to check out one on Liberty Island. Although geocaching is a public activity, hiding a cache in a national park is a violation of federal law, and a novice French woman stashed a key ring with a plastic seashell at the base of the Statue of Liberty. Brett invited me to join him on the rescue mission to retrieve the stash – the keyring is not a container, so he isn't calling it a "cache" – before anyone else finds it and potentially causes trouble for other geocachers. We have the string of 16 numbers comprising its GPS coordinates.

Administrators asked Brett because he is a responsible and longtime geocacher in the area. During the week he is a downtown investment trader, and he gave up a morning of work to retrieve this errant cache and introduce me to this technological leisure activity.

Brett didn't think twice about helping. He told me he wants to make sure "the game is played well," which means occasionally looking for lost caches or cleaning up a mistake like this one. Queuing for the ferry, he expresses his anxiety to me, "I think that there's always a 1/1000 chance that it all [geocaching] will be shut down."

"Why?" He sighs, and continues:

About every other week I read online that a cache somewhere caused a scare, and that a bomb squad had to come in only to find out that it was a geocache. That hasn't happened in New York yet, but we had that car bomb in Times Square a few weeks ago, and I just don't want anything to jeopardize the game.

He tells me that there are a lot of issues that arise with urban geocaching in this political climate. As compared to their more rural brethren, Brett and his ilk are concerned over triggering the police and the growing national security apparatus. As another geocacher told me: "When you're secretly placing boxes under benches, someone might call the cops, or worse. People are on high alert."

Brett cites a recent news article from Anaheim that circulated among geocachers: a dozen firetrucks, a Hazmat team, and a bomb squad were sent to the area, and three businesses were to be evacuated. "All it would take is one of those events to turn ugly," he said, "and I could see the whole thing being shut down in New York." (On the Anaheim case: witnesses called police when they saw two men pull into a parking lot and place a canister inside the base of a light pole; see Salazar and Galvin, 2010, and James, 2011.)

What Brett was saying resonated with what FATS277 told me in an interview. The heightened security awareness in the city limited his participation. He explained:

> I was really involved, but I completely stopped after 9/11. I was supposed to go out in a boat with a reporter and hide a geocache in New York harbor on a buoy, and I was like, 'that's not going to happen at all.' In this climate you don't want to go around hiding things.

Other geocachers echoed these concerns and tread lightly even if it has been years since the World Trade Center attacks, careful to not upset anyone.

As Brett and I talk about these issues we file through high levels of security for the ferry. I take off my belt, pass through a metal detector, and have my computer dusted for traces of bomb-making materials. Once we disembark Brett shows me a picture on his phone of another cache administrators had him remove from another location. It was a 1 and ½ foot long black cylinder with military-style lettering on it: "Geocache. Do Not Remove." This, Brett emphasizes, is not the type of thing that should be placed in the middle of Manhattan after September 11, 2001.

Urban + digital = achieving ubiquitous computing

To determine a location, a GPS device tracks the time it takes a signal to return from three satellites to do the task. Geocaching in cities is somewhat different from geocaching in rural areas. Conventional GPS devices have difficulty in the deep canyons of Manhattan's skyscrapers. iPhones, on the other hand, are better suited for urban geocaching because they triangulate position through a combination of satellites, nearby cellular towers, and Wi-Fi networks.

Somewhat prophetically, two decades ago Mark Weiser, who worked at the Computer Science Lab at Xerox Palo Alto Research Center, stated that "the world is not a desktop," claiming that computers would move into a third phase (the first being mainframes, the second being personal computing), wherein computers are embedded into the landscape, unperceivable, calling it "ubiquitous computing" (1994). This is most certainly the case today. The place-based aspect of smartphone technology is a new way of thinking about place.

The ability for smartphones to deliver layers of instantaneous *place-based* information on the world around us facilitates Weiser's "third phase revolution." Location-aware apps bring online content about to users based on their position. Quite simply, there is more to cities in this regard: more people, more symbolic and cultural content, more transportation information, more history, more geo-tagged content. More data.

Using all this information, smartphones marry the virtual world with the physical one. Geocaching is just one way to do so. The mobile phone is a platform for a variety of programs from music listening to social interaction to web browsing to navigation to tourism (Itō et al, 2005; Ling and Pedersen, 2005; de Silva e Souza and Sutko, 2009; Boulaire and Hervet, 2012). Mapping software, paired with a near infinite amount of data, can tell a user exactly when the subway leaves the nearest station or where the nearest Starbucks is, anytime and nearly anywhere. Location-based hardware and software, and social networking apps, provide a variety of features.

Some call it "Augmented Reality," in which smartphones use video and GPS technologies and a variety of web-based data in order to visualize a variety of otherwise invisible "environmental data" through the touchscreen. FourSquare, for example, provides personalized food and entertainment suggestions, and allows users to "check-in" and broadcast their location to others. Fieldtrip works like a virtual tour guide by providing history, landmarks, and cultural information about a place. Layar uses a smartphone's camera with the compass and GPS to layer over the screen image with links and data, from restaurant reviews to available apartment rentals. DanKam adjusts colors for the colorblind. These technologies are still nascent and ever changing: many apps, like Brightkite, GoWalla, and Dodgeball, have tried and failed.

These technologies certainly play out in that broader security and geopolitical context. Approximately 70 percent of 911 calls were made from mobile phones in 2014 (FCC, 2014). And a great deal of research has shown how mobile communication devices played critical roles in world events: in the aftermath of the World Trade Center attack New Yorkers communicated via SMS (short message service, or 'texting'); social media assisted Manilan and Iranian anti-government rioters in 2001 and 2009 and Copenhagen and Dresden's civic protesters in 2006 and 2011, and citizen journalists were reporting from their phones during the Indian Ocean tsunami in December 2004, the Sichuan earthquake in May 2008, and during the 2008 terrorist attacks in Mumbai in real time, broadcasting images and information all over the world (see Robinson and Robinson, 2006; Howard, 2010; Neumayer and Stald, 2014).

In a Foucauldian sense, the pathways that allow us to view so much information also open new lines of surveillance. Phone companies, for example, can and do actively track their subscribers – whether their phone is on or not – due to the Federal Communication Commission's move to E911, or "Enhanced 911," technologies. Through a process of "reverse geocoding," phone companies can provide police with the location of a smartphone user's 911 call within a few hundred feet. And despite a 9–0 ruling from the US Supreme Court, finding that the police need a warrant for GPS tracking of suspects (Barnes, 2012), National Security Agency (NSA) contractor Edward Snowden's release of classified security information revealed that the NSA tracks the locations of 5 billion cellphones, worldwide, every day (Gellman and Soltani, 2013a), uses powerful algorithms to collect Wi-Fi and GPS data to identify exact locations and relationships between people (Gellman and Soltani 2013b), and the US government isn't the only government to do so (Timberg, 2014).

Jack Katz notes that, "it is not obvious that publically managed public space integrates while privately managed public space segregates" (2004: 285), and it is vitally important that events and activities in public space be given careful consideration for how they bring disparate groups together, segregate others, and evince some of the key tensions and struggles in contemporary life without losing sight of the risks.

It could be argued that geocaching does, in fact, bring people together in public and in unique ways. I was very much interested in this kind of activity because, on the one hand, it developed my analysis of engagements in public spaces and re-conceptualizations of urban culture on the micro level, and at the same time it added an examination of how mobile technologies were, in a way, *emplaced*.

Here's how a particularly popular GPS app works:

42.324495, -72.629562

I download a free GPS application called MotionX-GPS onto my iPhone and head outside. The program allows me to record a path, which it calls a "track." I click "New Track" and label it "Commute." I cross the street, take a picture of my building, and log the location as a "waypoint." A waypoint is the intersection of latitude and longitude (sometimes altitude as well), and a "path" is a series of two or more waypoints. I record a brief audio clip: "This is where I live, on the second floor."

As I walk to work I watch my trajectory on the Google Map, embedded in the MotionX program.

I make another waypoint after a few blocks, at the coffee shop where I stop almost everyday on my way to work. It's hot, so I get an iced coffee and take a picture of it in the app. Meanwhile, the Elapsed Time counter ticks away the passing minutes. A few blocks later I take a picture of the Red Cross building and after five more minutes, I arrive at my office.

Alongside a map of the walk is a read-out with the details:

Elapsed Time: 14:02.9

Distance (mi): 0.69

Avg Speed (mph): 2.9

Max Speed (mph): 5.4

I export the file – which includes the map, waypoints, pictures, and the audio recording – by emailing it to myself as an .xml file (eXtensible Markup Language). Once in my office, I open my computer, download the file, and open it in Google Earth. The program zooms from a view from space onto my path, appearing as a bright red line, with a set of nodes on it, indicating where the pictures and audio files were recorded. Using a program called gCensus (developed by Stanford University) I upload Census data to see how my path passed through a series of spatial socioeconomic changes.

This brief exercise illustrates how anyone can become a neo-geographer, mapping out and analyzing place through smartphone technology: from clocking one's own jogging time and distance, to playing elaborate games, and social networking. A mash-up of location and population data takes only seconds.

Smartphones can be conceptualized as "portable microcomputers, embedded in public places" (de Silva e Souza, 2006: 262), and public places can then be embedded into a larger web of information.

Some rules of the game

The first cache in New York City was hidden by Chris Rohner on November 5, 2000 in Riverside Park. It was one of the first 200 caches in the world. It is no longer there, but the description is archived on the geocaching website:

> I have hidden a cache in New York City. I think this is the first one, and I am hoping to get more folks to hide more around NYC so we can have a kind of internal NYC geocaching game. NYC is a great place to play this game, lots of corners and hidden places to hide things. New York city also seems to provide special difficulty since tall buildings make it hard to get the needed skyview. I have hidden a small plastic box with some small toys in the northern section of Riverside Park. It is hidden in the crux of 4 medium size trees, covered in bark with two sticks forming an 'X.' I am calling this NYC Alpha cache. (Rohner, 2000)

While both the US National Park Service and the US Fish and Wildlife Service prohibit geocaching, there are other rules to the game. Caches should be no less than a 1/10th of a mile from another one to avoid mistaking one cache for another. A cache shouldn't be near a playground to prevent tampering, but also to maintain a respectful distance from other leisure activities. As Brett explained it, "despite the fact that this is a family-friendly activity, and anyone can do it with anyone else, there are still a lot of shall we say, 'nerdy' old guys – and it's almost all guys – who do this alone and it's not a great idea to have old men looking suspicious around playgrounds."

There are other concerns about the appropriateness of location. Another geocacher tells me about how someone hid a cache in the highly-manicured Strawberry Fields in Central Park, and so many people were tracking through the flowers looking for the cache that the Central Park Conservancy (the private, non-profit organization that manages Central Park) eventually found and confiscated it. They made a rule that geocachers could not hide anything in that section of the park, and all of the geocachers I spoke with were amazed that the Central Park Conservancy didn't just ban geocaching from the park entirely.

As mentioned, it is suboptimal to act suspiciously in New York City. If geocachers feel that they are making people uncomfortable, they will often try to speak with them to "cool out" the concerned onlookers (or "muggles," which is a phrase geocachers borrowed from the Harry Potter books) by bringing a business card, or some information on geocaching, just in case a security guard, police officer, or passerby gets suspicious. One tells me: "I will usually just tell people what I am doing. That it's a scavenger hunt, and that usually makes them dismiss me as a nerd and leave it at that." Nerdy types are, in his estimation, non-threatening. Finding a cache isn't as suspicious-looking as hiding one.

For most, the fun of constructing a cache is in cultivating a theme, and composing riddles or clues for the other players. Riddles and cache names often mirror the interests of the geocacher. There are, for example, a series of caches in New York City themed around the comic book superhero, Green Lantern. Many are themed with historical trivia. Brett created a puzzle cache called "The Original Colonists" that is a tour of the first 18 caches in New York City as a way to commemorate those first urban geocachers. This aspect reflects what I call in my research on walking tour guides, "urban alchemy:" the use of public spaces and public culture to craft something that is meaningful to both the city and the individual (Wynn, 2011).

Among the geocachers I spoke with, there is a tension between using public spaces and the content of their caches and the puzzles they create (Garrett, 2010; Klausen, 2014). Whose property is a cache that has been hidden on private property? Are the puzzles these folks create their intellectual property? Is it theirs or is it geocaching.com's? Brett is a little bemused over the intersection between intellectual property and technology, mostly because he knows that social media sites like Facebook use and sell social network information.

Liberty Island (40.68887, –74.044253)

Brett reached out to the French woman, who provided some clear description on how to rescue her stash: she placed it at the tip of the star-shaped base of the Statue of Liberty, under what she described as a "medium sized rock."

But we only see bricks, not rocks. We follow the base wall closely; kicking over stray candy wrappers, sticking our fingers into cracks, and checking to see if there are any loose rocks in the mortar of the wall. Reminding me of an old orienteering mission, the experience triggers a memory of the last time I was here: with my Boy Scout troop (#440), in 1985. The memory is the only thing we seem to uncover.

Brett and I think about the possibilities. Did someone see her hide her stash on one of the highest security locations in the entire United States and remove it? Did we miss it? We keep our eyes on the ground and circumnavigate about 80 percent of the base and find nothing. At a corner, I take a step back, and look up. Brett says: "Ah: That's like that cinematic moment! Where the character realized that he's been looking at a place the wrong way!" But that doesn't result in an epiphany either. We start contemplating whether or not the novice geocacher actually hid something on the *second* level of the wall, but decide against clearly violating a barrier to find out.

Brett loves movies from his childhood like *The Goonies* and *Raiders of the Lost Ark*, which stoke his interest in urban exploring. He tells me that he thinks about them when he's hiding caches. "You know, it's like that moment in the movie when the character's position allows the image of a skull or something to line up. That 'Aha!' moment. I love that." This is what geocaching does for him.

After half an hour, however, we give up. Someone must have taken it. Despite the initial enthusiasm we leave the island empty handed. Brett will report that the stash is gone, and the location will be removed from the website.

iPhone *flânerie* and digital *dérives*

While it might be easy to think of them as over-aged, technologically advanced Boy Scouts, I believe that it is useful to see geocachers as urban explorers arising within, and reflecting, the issues of their historical moment. They have important similarities and differences with two other city explorer types: the *flâneur* and the situationist.

For Charles Baudelaire and Walter Benjamin, the *flâneur* was a kind of strolling detective, almost mindlessly wandering through the streets. The *flâneur*, as a type, arose at the dawn of the modern city, an effete dandy, the consumer of urban culture. Benjamin's essay, "A Berlin chronicle," describes *flânerie*:

> Not to find one's way in a city may well be uninteresting and banal. It requires ignorance – nothing more. But to lose oneself in a city – as one loses oneself in a forest – that calls for quite a different schooling. Then, signboards and street names, passers-by, roofs, kiosks, or bars must speak to the wanderer like a cracking twig under his feet in the forest, like the startling call of a bittern in the distance. (1978: 8)

There is a tension here of an individual who is an aimless wanderer, and an individual who hunts in these spaces: a character that is particularly attuned to the city in times of political and social crisis, and in times of terror (Frisby, 1994: 91). The symbols, masses, commodities that filled the spaces of European shopping arcades were the series of clues that made up the *flâneur's* understanding of the modern city.

After the wars, Guy Debord and Constant's situationists hit the same streets under new political circumstances. While the *flâneur* takes a somewhat ambivalent saunter, the situationists – an engaged artist more than a poet, sprung from the dadaist and surrealist movements – offered "the *dérive*," or the "walk with a purpose." Their hope was to critique the capitalism and authoritarianism they saw as leading to alienation, commodity fetishism, and eventually, conflict. Through group walks, situationists would create new mental maps, new ways of understanding the city that overlaid the existing boundaries, buildings, and boulevards (Debord, 1994). Because they saw the spectacle as an important element of the urban life, situationists created occasions as a part of the *dérive* – whether conducting a play or a new art form. The situationist was keenly aware of the juxtapositions of the city, at times recording them and at other times creating them.

Surely geocaching is a 21st-century match of the leisure activity of the *flâneur* with the "walk with a purpose" of the situationist. One can only imagine what they would have thought of augmented reality apps that give detailed histories and data. The *flâneurs* of old could only dream of the city speaking such stories to them! Situationists creating little scenes tucked away in tiny public spaces! The desire to wander and drift may have always been available to city dwellers, but handheld technologies have allowed for data-saturated urbanism. The signboards and street names and gravemarkers of the digitized city speak through technology.

Geocaching, in its way, sits somewhere between *flânerie* and the *dérive*, to be the product and result of its own historical moment: utilizing the tools of war for leisure activity; reflecting the countless and rapidly increasing number of place-aware technologies that make for a lively digital urbanism, while at the same time fetishizing the smartphone commodity and succumbing to its hyperadvanced capitalism; playing at the edges of the security state, using devices that are tracked by governments and telecommunications companies in the terror age.

How to solve the puzzle cache at Trinity Church (40.708350, -74.011467)

I meet Brett at Trinity Church on Broadway in Lower Manhattan. He comes prepared. He has a "puzzle cache," which is indicated on geocaching.com with a question mark (see Figure 19.1). I thought we were going to solve one together, but he hands me the paper and invites me to crack it myself. "One learns by doing," he says with a smile.

We step off the sidewalk and into the cemetery. The pages in my hand are a printout from the website. His cache is entitled "Celebrate Life." He's proud of this new creation, which has been visited by at least 32 people since he hid it a few months ago.

A "mystery" or "puzzle cache" means that riddles play a key component to finding the actual cache. On this page there are latitude and longitude coordinates, a rating of three out of five stars on difficulty, and one-and-a-half stars out of five on the level of terrain, a long essay on the history of the church and the reasons that it is a special site, and an image of the carvings on the top of a headstone. From left to right, the engravings are an hourglass with wings, a caldron with fire, and a familiar looking square, level, and compass. "There's a Freemasonic theme here," I say to myself.

The printout also has an "Additional Hints" section with a series of letters:

Fgrc Bar – Urnqfgbar vf gur xrl gb gur obbx pvcureFgrc Gjb – "Vafpevcgvbaf va hccre-pnfr yrggref bsgra fubj gur yrggre"; 24-punenpgre nycunorg WHIRAVYR = VIIRAVYR

And a decryption key:

A | B | C | D | E | F | G | H | I | J | K | L | M
- -
N | O | P | Q | R | S | T | U | V | W | X | Y | Z

I figured that I should solve these too, and decrypted the two clues in my notebook:

Step One: Headstone is the key to the book cipher

Step Two: "Inscriptions in upper-case letters often show the letter;" 24-character alphabet JUVENILE=IVVENILE

"I guess I have to find this headstone," I say aloud. Brett's smile widens.

I stroll. I see Alexander Hamilton's grave, and Robert Fulton's. Neither of those have the symbols on them. The GPS coordinates take me to the northeast corner of the site. I find the headstone of James Leeson (d. 1794) that matches the images. The first step of the puzzle is to figure out the code on top of the headstone. It looks like a series of different brackets, some of which have dots in them. I don't have any idea what they mean. Brett offers help. "Did you ever do a pigpen cipher as a kid?" "I didn't get that merit badge," I joke.

He then tells me that a pigpen cipher is when each quadrant corresponds to a letter:

Figure 19.2: Empty symbols, from the author's notebook

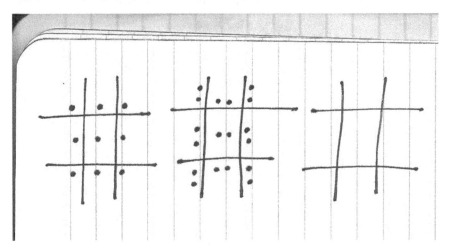

Brett pulls out a pen and draws three pound, or number signs, with dots in them. However, he points me to the second clue on the printout: at the time of this gravestone's engraving, "I's and "J" and "U's and "V's were used as the same letters.

Figure 19.3: A pigpen cipher, from the author's notebook

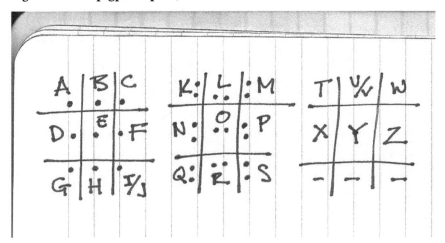

This, it turns out, is also called a "freemasons cipher," which dates back to the early 1700s. This gravestone is an early instance of this. It's meaning was unknown to most people until over a hundred years later, when the freemason's cipher was published in a newspaper.

I decode the symbols, which spell "Remember Death." Feeling some relief at solving this puzzle, I find that it is just the first piece. The printout of the puzzle has another series of symbols:

Figure 19.4: Brett's Trinity Church clue, from the author's notebook

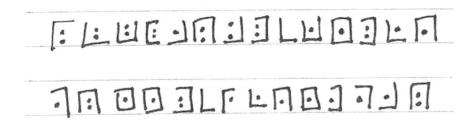

I spend some time in front of Brett, thinking through the puzzle. I slowly spell out the first line: "SMLPARKNWBENCH." I make a diagonal line to denote what I guess are the words: "SML/PARK/NW/BENCH." "*Smell* Park?" I said aloud. Brett gently corrected me: "*Small* park." "Ah, right: Small park, Northwest Bench. Cool."

I then work on the second line, "GREEN/W," but stop there. I remember that the second clue was that "I"s and "J"s were the same, so I write both like a fraction: "I/J" and continue: "CH/EDGAR." "'Greenwich' and 'Edgar.' I wonder if there is a guy named Edgar I have to find his grave.... Or Edgar Allan Poe?" "No.... I think it has to do with a location," Brett adds.

I pull out my iPhone, and realize that Greenwich Street runs somewhat parallel to Broadway, two blocks to the west. We head in that direction.

While walking we talk about the history of Trinity church and Brett tells me a bit about it – that it was the tallest building in New York City for over 50 years, and that sailors would use its spire to navigate the harbor – all of which he included on the cache's webpage. He tells me that another geocacher loaned him a historical science fiction book called *Time and again* by Jack Finney, and that he got a lot of historical information from there.

Although Edgar Street is so small that I don't easily find it on my phone, Brett leads me a bit. After three blocks we get to a small park, with only six benches and a few nice trees. I see the New York Harbor down the street. I point north, and Brett tries to correct me, but I'm right. All the benches are empty, with only a few passersby. I immediately identify the northwestern bench. I look behind it.

"I imagine it's hidden with a magnet," I say to myself as I look around and under it. After a few seconds I sit down, bend over, and reach between my legs. I pull out a small cigarette case shaped like a coffin with an iron cross on top. Pleased, I say, "Nice reference to the cemetery." Brett sits down next to me as I open the case. He's smiling.

Inside is a very small notebook. I flip through and read a few of the comments from people who found this cache too. Some seem to have written their own ciphers for visitors to solve. I write my name and the date on the first blank page, and write "NICE" in the freemason's cipher I just learned.

We talk for another ten minutes. He shows me some coins in his pocket. They are small, about the size of a nickel. On them it says, "I solved New York's Most Dastardly Puzzle Caches." He told me that they are called "pathtags," and said, "it's one of the things that geocaching.com really missed the boat on" since another company mints and sells them. He ordered them online to place them as a reward for geocachers who complete his puzzles.

"I'm amazed at how much people are into it," Brett says as he adds one to the case. "It's just a simple coin that cost me a few bucks, but it really encourages people." He has 36 puzzle caches. I just completed one of them.

Conclusion: location-aware social science

Burrows and Beers note that sociology has to become more aware and engaged with the "informatization of space" (2013: 75) and, indeed, a digital sociology should be particularly keyed into the intersection of spaces and social life. There are many connections to be made between those who study communication and information technology and urban sociology, and how citizens can play a part. Although there is a nascent field of computational social science that utilizes the "big data" possibilities of GPS and social networking information (see Spencer, 2003; Hesse-Beiber, 2011; Shah et al, 2015), I have found purchase with more qualitative, small-scale data collection as well. Ingold and Vergunst, for example, note the potential of locational data in this vein:

> No doubt the topic of walking figures often enough in the ethnographers' fieldnotes. Once they come to write up their results, however, it tends to be sidelined in favor of 'what really matters', such as the destinations towards which people were bound. (2008: 3)

While conducting research on urban walking tours I used the MotionX–GPS app to track my path, collect and tag information, and record photos of tour content (Wynn, 2011; see also Pink, 2008). For my study of music culture and cities, I conducted several *dérives* of neighborhoods, taking photos and recording audio tracks, and collecting census data of the various spaces I passed through (Wynn, 2015). By using such a ubiquitous device, I was able to inconspicuously amass a bevy of rich data for later analysis.

For the wider public, there are serious concerns that arise with these technologies. A recent Pew Research Center study, for example, found that Americans consider their location to be more sensitive data than their religious or political views, the content of their text messages, the names of friends and contacts, or the content of their text messages (Pew Research Center,

2014). These issues are compounded for social scientists who should be doubly concerned about the confidentiality and security of the data they collect.

Many location-aware apps are free, and yet, smartphones and data plans can be expensive. Their use certainly flies in the face of the image of the rogue ethnographer in the field armed with no more than a notebook, pen, and some moxie. Still, the available tools have merit. Conducting a quick study of geocachers in New York City generated new ideas and allowed me to practice using these tools for other research. It also resonated with the themes throughout my research and urban sociology in general: the tension between public spaces and private information, the role of technology and culture in changing uses of the urban landscape, and even how technology informs social science research.

References

Barnes, R. (2012) "Supreme Court limits police use of GPS tracking." *The Washington Post*.

Benjamin, W. (1978) "A Berlin chronicle." *Reflections*. New York: Schocken Books.

Boulaire, C. and G. Hervet (2012) "New itinerancy: The potential of geocaching for tourism." *International Journal of Management Cases* 14 (4).

Burrows, R. and D. Beer (2013) "Rethinking space: Urban infomatics and the sociological imagination," In K. Orton-Johnson and N. Prior (eds) *The Palgrave Macmillan digital sociology* (pp 61–78). New York: Palgrave Macmillan.

Cameron, L.S. and D. Ulmer (2011) *The geocaching handbook*, Guilford, CT: Falcon Guides (http://alltitles.ebrary.com/Doc?id=10930484).

Debord, G. (1994) *The society of the spectacle*. New York: Zone Books.

de Souza e Silva, A. (2006) "From cyber to hybrid: Mobile technologies as interfaces of hybrid spaces." *Space and Culture* 9 (3), 261–278.

de Souza e Silva, A. and D.M. Sutko (2009) *Digital cityscapes: Merging digital and urban playspaces*. New York: Peter Lang.

FCC (Federal Communications Commission) (2014) "911 wireless services" (www.fcc.gov/guides/wireless-911-services).

Frisby, D. (1994) "The flâneur in social theory." In K. Tester (ed) *The flâneur*. London, UK: Routledge, pp 81–110.

Garrett, B.L. (2010) "Urban explorers: Quests for myth, mystery and meaning." *Geography Compass* 4 (10), 1448–61.

Gellman, B. and A. Soltani (2013a) "NSA tracking cellphone locations worldwide, Snowden documents show." *The Washington Post*.

Gellman, B. and A. Soltani (2013b) "New documents show how the NSA infers relationships based on mobile location data." *The Washington Post*.

Gray, G. (2001) "Romancing the stash." *Village Voice*, February 6 (www.villagevoice.com/2001-02-06/news/romancing-the-stash/).

Hesse-Biber, S.N. (2011) *The handbook of emergent technologies in social research*. New York: Oxford University Press.

Howard, P.K. (2010) *The digital origins of dictatorship and democracy: Information technology and political Islam.* Oxford, UK: Oxford University Press.

Ingold, T. and J.L. Vergunst (2008) *Ways of walking: Ethnography and practice on foot.* Aldershot, UK: Ashgate.

Itō, M., D. Okabe, and M. Matsuda (2005) *Personal, portable, pedestrian: Mobile phones in Japanese life.* Cambridge, MA: The MIT Press.

James, E. (2011) "Geocaching device sets off Outer Banks bomb scare." *The Virginian Pilot,* September 15 (http://hamptonroads.com/2011/09/geocaching-device-sets-outer-banks-bomb-scare).

Katz, J. (2004) "On the rhetoric and politics of ethnographic methodology." *Annals of the American Academy of Political and Social Science* 595, September, 280–308.

Klausen, M. (2014) "Re-enchanting the city: Hybrid space, affect and playful performance in geocaching, a location-based mobile game." *Journal of Urban Cultural Studies* 1 (2), 193–213.

Lane, A. (2015) "Seek and you shall find: The art of geocaching in Abu Dhabi." *The National Arts & Life* (www.thenational.ae/arts-lifestyle/seek-and-you-shall-find-the-art-of-geocaching-in-abu-dhabi).

Ling, R.S. and P.E. Pedersen (2005) *Mobile communications re-negotiation of the social sphere.* London, UK: Springer.

Neumayer, C. and G. Stald (2014) "The mobile phone in street protest: Texting, tweeting, tracking, and tracing." *Mobile Media & Communication* 2 (2), 117–133.

Pew Research Center (2014) "Public perceptions of privacy and security in the post-Snowden era" (www.pewinternet.org/2014/11/12/public-privacy-perceptions/pi_2014-11-12_privacy-perceptions_03/).

Pink, S. (2008) "Mobilising visual ethnography: Making routes, making places and making images." *FQS: Forum: Qualitative Research* 9, 3.

Robinson, W. and D. Robinson (2006) "Tsunami mobilizations." In A.P. Kavoori and N. Arceneaux (eds) *The cell phone reader* (pp 85–104). New York: Peter Lang.

Rohner, C. (2000) "NYC alpha cache" (www.geocaching.com/geocache/GC9D_nyc-alpha-cache?guid=d79ac605-f3f0-450c-b363-a4ce536faa55).

Salazar, D. and A. Galvin (2010) "'Suspicious' container turns out to be part of a game." *Orange County Register,* August 21 (www.ocregister.com/articles/anaheim-244792-martinez-container.html).

Shah, D.V., J.N. Cappella Ramesh, W.R. Neuman, and W.R. Neuman (2015) "Big data, digital media, and computational social science: Possibilities and perils." *Annals of the American Academy of Political and Social Science* 659 (1), 6–13.

Spencer, J. (2003) *Global Positioning System: A field guide for the social sciences.* Malden, MA: Blackwell Publishers.

Timberg, C. (2014) "For sale: Systems that can secretly track where cellphone users go around the globe." *The Washington Post.*

Weiser, M. (1994) "The world is not a desktop." *Interactions*, January, 7–8.

Wynn, J.R. (2009) "Digital sociology: Emergent technologies in the field and the classroom". *Sociological Forum* 24 (2), 448–456.

Wynn, J.R. (2011) *The tour guide: Walking and talking New York.* Chicago, IL: University of Chicago Press.

Wynn, J.R. (2015) *Music/city: American festivals and placemaking in Austin, Nashville and Newport.* Chicago, IL: University of Chicago Press.

Part III
Digital bodies

20

Bodies in code

Jessie Daniels

In the 1990s, a television commercial asked, "Where do you want to go today?" hinting that the internet was a place. More than that, it was a destination where there was no gender, no race, no infirmity (Nakamura, 2002; Everett, 2008). In these early days of the (mostly) text-only computer-mediated communication, many people, from commercial advertisers to esteemed scholars, speculated that digital technologies would allow us to escape embodiment and its accompanying entanglements. Few of us believe this now. Indeed, our embodied selves are often the reason we are targeted for abuse and harassment online. The commonplace advice, "Don't read the comments," is in no small part about the vicious attacks on gendered and racialized bodies that are targets in the visual culture of the current iteration of the popular web. As we move into the near-future era of the Internet of Things (IoT), the digital realm is no longer separate from us, it is on and in our bodies (Howard, 2015; Neff and Nafus, 2016). The chapters in this section raise important questions about what it means to bring our embodied selves into contact with digital media technologies.

Deborah Lupton's contribution, "Personal data practices in the age of lively data," opens the section. In it, she argues that in a world of "smart objects" and "smart environments," such as smart clothes, smart cars, smart cities, smart homes, smart schools, and smart appliances, human beings have become digital data subjects. Lupton urges us to examine the affordances of so-called smart technologies as the end result of human decision-making. The people who generate the data and then use it in various ways are also making decisions about their actions within human-created third parties: insurance companies, energy companies, educational institutions, workplaces, media corporations, marketers, and government agencies. Lupton's sociomaterial approach offers a crucial development for understanding the ways bodies and code are imbricated.

In Kishonna Gray's "'They're just too urban': Black gamers streaming on Twitch," she explores the popular social video platform and gaming community, which launched in 2011. Through ethnographic participation and observation, Gray details what it is like to be a marginalized gamer, that is, one who does not to conform to the default White, male norm within the platform. She reveals a struggle over legitimacy, ideology, and economics within Twitch. The ideological constructions of what it means to be a gamer are tied closely to the bottom-line imperatives of capitalistic production, Gray contends. For corporate producers of games, and the gamers who do conform to the default norm, marginalized bodies are not valued. This is highlighted in comments about Black twitch user profiles stating "that they would be more popular if they weren't so urban," a colorblind code for Black, and a rhetorical move that emphasizes racialized and gendered embodiment.

When digital technologies were first included in fashion, the designs revealed a deep cultural ambivalence about women's bodies, what women want, and what society wants women – and their bodies – to be. In Elizabeth Wissinger's, "From 'geek' to 'chic': Wearable technology and the woman question," she examines the growing field of digital technologies embedded in clothing. Once plagued by a utilitarian look of geeks, digitally fluent fashion designers are now transforming wearables into something desirable, even chic. Her ethnographic analysis of fashion and tech designers uncovers some of these hidden biases of such designs. In doing so, Wissinger offers us a view of women's embodiment through the eyes of wearable technology designers.

While few scholars would conceptualize the internet as a place, Benjamin Haber encourages us to consider the social implications of the spatial metaphors of networked digital architectures. In his chapter, "Queer Facebook? Digital sociality and queer theory," Haber examines the social media juggernaut Facebook, which, as of March 2016, has some 1.5 billion mobile active users. He interrogates the many striking ways the history of queer sociality in public looks like the inspiration for the norms that everyone follows when they use social media. Rather than a boon for queer-identified people, such norms are deleterious, Haber argues. As the vibrant social and political life of gay and lesbian bars has declined and moved to Facebook threads, queer-identified people are exposed to increasing amounts of visibility that fosters a kind of normative self-regulation.

When Microsoft debuted an "experiential" search engine they called "Ms. Dewey" in 2006, the site featured pre-filmed clips of actress Janina Gavakar as the tool's embodied representation. Miriam Sweeney unpacks the implications of this in her chapter, "The Ms. Dewey experience: Technoculture, gender, and race." Ms. Dewey was conceived of by Microsoft software designers as a search engine that took the form of a sexy librarian or assistant, available to perform search results through conversational skits and exchanges in response to user queries. In her analysis, Sweeney finds that the "experience" in the Ms. Dewey interface is technoculturally defined by specific gendered and racialized logics that enable users the opportunity to search the interface in ways that confirm sexist and racist cultural narratives. In this way, Sweeney argues, gender and race function as crucial infrastructural elements that frame both the user's search process and the machine's performance. Sweeney offers an understanding of anthropomorphized interface design and search as technocultural processes in which cultural beliefs about technology, gender, and race are interwoven.

In a similar vein, Yuliya Grinberg invites us to look closely at the metaphors we use for digital technologies for what they can tell us about embodiment. In her chapter, "The Emperor's new data clothes: Implications of 'nudity' as a racialized and gendered metaphor in discourse on personal digital data," Grinberg takes on so-called big data, produced by an ever expanding array of computer, wearable, and sensor technology. Grinberg finds that devices are often compared to scalpels that can slice bodies open and pull back the skin to reveal the "data" lying within. These rhetorical moves suggest that data is a second skin of sorts that runs just under the body's surface that digital devices faithfully help to unveil. Grinberg contends that personal data is often presented as a material, even as a natural substance that can be abstracted from social and material entanglements. In thinking about the relationship between naked bodies and personal data, Grinberg offers us a way to understand selfhood and embodiment facilitated by expanding personal data sets in a broader sense; to ask not only about the way bodies are differently articulated through data, but about the types of bodies that mediate our relationship to data in the first place.

If digital sociology is to prove useful as a field, it must take seriously the ways that racialized and gendered bodies are attacked in and through digital media technologies. Adrian Cruz and Kazuyo Kubo take up this essential task in their chapter, "Post your comments below: A case study of immigrant bashing online." Their work is an analysis of online comments about Jose Antonio Vargas, an undocumented immigrant journalist and activist who was briefly detained and then released by US immigration. Cruz and Kubo categorize the comments along three key themes of anti-immigrant animus: (1) immigrants are innately criminal and thus a threat to an orderly society; (2) it is "third world people" who corrupt the moral fiber of the US; and (3) "illegal aliens" or undocumented people usurp jobs and benefits that should be accorded to citizens. Cruz and Kubo provide an insight into why it is that some bodies, and not others, are targets of harassment in online comments sections.

In Kara van Cleaf's chapter, "Our mothers have always been machines: The conflation of media and motherhood," she explores the way the embodied labor of motherhood has been transformed in the digital era. Through an exploration of so-called "mommy blogs," van Cleaf argues that these are mechanisms through which mothers create the cultural narratives that define what it means to mother and to be a mother. These blogs act as real-time manuals of motherhood, detailing both how to do motherhood as well as how to interpret the shifts in identity that accompany it. In other words, they attune bloggers, readers, and "lurkers" to mothering. Van Cleaf calls attention to the ordinary, unending work of motherhood as a way to highlight the ways that digital platforms and technologies move further into our bodies, our intimate lives, or our daily rituals of care. Motherhood, and the digital labor of Mommy blogs, offers a way of understanding the free labor of care work within capitalist societies after the digital turn.

In "#notracist: Exploring racism denial talk on Twitter," Sanjay Sharma and Phillip Brooker make a significant contribution to our understanding of racism expressed online and to digital sociology. As with Lupton's piece at the beginning of this section, Sharma and Brooker take a sociomaterial approach to their investigation. In their chapter, they examine the phenomenon of racism denial on the micro-blogging Twitter platform. Utilizing innovative research methods while simultaneously remaining critically reflexive of those methods, Sharma and Booker set out to offer a unique methodologically motivated study. Their goal here is to develop critical race theory vis-á-vis engaging with the technological affordances of digital media. They accomplish this by empirically analysing a relatively large data set of tweets that used the hashtag *#notracist*. Sharma and Brooker put forward a research process for examining a type of racially charged social media data that is not structured chronologically, but rather by an ambiguous "topicality."

Their findings point to online strategies of racism denial being complex and diverse, such as through the multi-hashtagging practices of "humor" and "truth" in racially charged tweets. Sharma and Brooker take an innovative and reflexive approach to the deployment of visualizations and algorithmic data processes. Rather than fetishize any tool or process, Sharma and Brooker interrogate their own process of *doing* this work as they are doing it. As they note, this kind of reflexive research process is neither "trivial nor irrelevant" to the emerging field of digital sociology. Instead, such reflexivity points the way forward to processes that may make digital sociology an essential part of any social science research.

Each of the authors in this section reaches beyond facile binaries and dichotomous questions to offer chapters with subtle and carefully argued contributions to the emerging field of digital sociology. Together, they expand our understanding of what it means to live in and through embodied selves in a deeply unequal social world.

References

Everett, A. (2008) *Learning race and ethnicity: Youth and digital media*. Cambridge, MA: The MIT Press.

Howard, P.N. (2015) *Pax technica: How the Internet of things may set us free or lock us up*. London: Yale University Press.

Nakamura, L. (2002) *Cybertypes. Race, ethnicity, and identity on the internet*. London, UK: Routledge.

Neff, G. and D. Nafus (2016) *Self-tracking*. Cambridge, MA: MIT Press.

21

Personal data practices in the age of lively data

Deborah Lupton

The lives of humans have become increasingly entangled with digital technologies due to the reactive and responsive nature of computer software and the ubiquity of the devices that people carry with them or that sense their activities as they move around in public spaces. Humans have become digital data subjects. In this world of "smart objects" and "smart environments," such as smart clothes, smart cars, smart cities, smart homes, smart schools and smart appliances, digital devices can begin to make decisions for us and generate information about us that we may not access to, and that may be used by third parties: insurance companies, energy companies, educational institutions, workplaces, media corporations, marketers, government agencies, and the like. A digital data knowledge economy has developed, in which digital data have acquired great value, viewed as configuring new forms of knowledge for commercial, managerial, educational, government, and research use.

In this chapter, I discuss the ways in which people engage with the data that are generated from their interactions with online technologies and digital sensing and communication devices. I adopt a sociomaterial approach in discussing personal data practices that acknowledges the entanglements of humans with technologies. From this perspective, both humans and the technologies with which they interact are viewed as agential actors, each influencing the other. The modes of creating and manipulating people's data are invested in such features of software as browsers, search engines, apps, and algorithms. The manner in which people interact with this software is mediated via the opportunities that are offered to them in using devices such as desktop and laptop computers and mobile and wearable devices (or what are often referred to as the "affordances" of these technologies). These affordances are the outcomes of human decision-making. The people who generate the data and then use it in various ways are also making decisions about their actions within these frameworks. These intersections of humans and non-humans form changing networks of actors (Marres, 2012; Rogers, 2013; Gillespie et al, 2014).

"Digital data assemblages" are the products of these human-technological encounters. They are configurations of discourse, practices, data, human users, and technologies. Digital data assemblages are ephemeral and motile, constantly changing as users' new encounters with digital technologies occur and as different data sets come together and interact and are taken up for a range of purposes by various actors and agencies. Each digital data assemblage represents a unique and specific moment in time – a form of "frozen data" – that then goes on to change again.

The term "big data" is now often used to describe the massive digital data sets that are generated ceaselessly from online interactions and digital devices. The generation and use of digital data involve a range of data practices on the part of individuals and organizations. Personal data practices include collecting information about oneself using self-tracking devices, contributing content on social media sites, and observing other people's interactions on these sites. Such practices are voluntary and consensual. Other personal data practices, however, involve information being collected on behalf of people by other actors. These practices include the surveillance and harvesting of people's device use, online searches and transactions by policing and security agencies, the internet empires and the data mining industry, and the development of tools and software to produce, analyse, represent, and store big data sets. While a distinction is often made between "small" data (personalized, detailed information about individuals) and "big" data (massive digital data sets), the boundaries between both are blurred. As most small data that are produced from people's interactions with digital devices and software are transmitted to cloud computing data archives, they tend to be aggregated with others' small data to become big data.

The term "data practices" describes the ways in which people collect, make sense of, and engage with digital data assemblages, including the types of "data materializations" that are generated. Data materializations are ways of representing digital data so that they may be viewed or even touched and handled: from lists of numbers, words, or terms to graphs, drawings, and other two-dimensional visualizations to 3D printed objects that are fabricated from digital data sets.

Critical digital data studies

Given the current prevalence of digital data surveillance and monitoring of people by both voluntary and involuntary activities, digital data practices and digital data assemblages have become phenomena for critical social and cultural investigations. Writing from the perspective of human–computer interaction studies, Mortier et al (2014) have suggested that a new field of research should be developed: human–data interaction. Instead of focusing on how people interact with their devices or software, human–data interaction examines the interpretations that people give to the data that these technologies generate. As outlined by Mortier et al, human–data interaction research should include researching the different forms of interaction that people may have, including their granting of access to their personal data by other actors and agencies, the ways in which people understand data, such as information about how their data are accessed by others, the inferences that may be drawn from personal data or large aggregated data sets, and the consequences of actions in making data available to others, the feedback mechanisms by which data can influence future actions or decisions, and the different actors that interact when data are generated and used.

These are all important questions. However, there are further, broader-reaching issues that also require attention. At a more critical and social level of inquiry, a body of literature in the humanities and social sciences has begun to emerge in response to digital data (see, for example, boyd and Crawford, 2012; Lyon and Bauman, 2013; Andrejevic, 2014; Kitchin, 2014; van Dijck, 2014; Boellstorff and Maurer, 2015; Clough et al, 2015; Lupton, 2016a). This research focuses on such elements as how digital data are generated and how they circulate and are purposed and repurposed, and the sociocultural and political aspects of the data practices of publics and professionals who work with digital data. From this perspective, digital data is a phenomenon that involves power relations, including struggles over ownership of or access to data sets, the meanings and interpretations that should be attributed to big data, the ways in which digital surveillance is conducted, and the exacerbation of socioeconomic disadvantage by the inferences and assumptions that are generated by big data algorithms. Digital data are viewed as highly relative, located in time, space and specific social and cultural contexts. They can only ever tell a certain narrative, and as such they offer a limited perspective. There are many other ways of telling stories using different forms of knowledges. Digital data are also partial: only some phenomena are singled out and recorded and labeled as "data," while others are ignored (see Lupton, 2015a).

Digital data may be characterized as "lively" in a number of ways (Lupton, 2016a). First, these data are about life itself. Second, they are dynamic, with their own social lives. They are constantly being configured and reconfigured as people interact with online technologies, and are circulated and repurposed by a multitude of different actors and agencies. Third, these data are a key part of the global knowledge economy, contributing to commercial, managerial, government, and research enterprises ("livelihoods"). And finally, these data have become an influential part of everyday lives, affecting beliefs and behaviors and increasingly, people's life chances via the assumptions and inferences that are developed from algorithmic analytics.Indeed, in extending the metaphor of lively data, I have drawn on the work of Haraway (2003) to argue that the digital data assemblage may be conceptualized as a companion species to the humans with which it co-evolves (Lupton, 2016b). Haraway uses the term "companion species" to describe the relationships that the human species has not only with other animal species, but also with technologies. The companion species trope recognizes the inevitability of our relationship with our digital data assemblages and the importance of learning to live together and to learn from each other. It suggests both the vitality of these assemblages and also the possibility of developing a productive relationship, recognizing our mutual dependency.

The vitality of digital data has significant implications for people's data practices. People are confronted with attempting to gain some purchase on information about themselves which is not only continually generated, but is also used by other actors and agencies in ways of which they may not be fully aware. They are also dealing with the ways in which their data are announced to themselves, such as the push notifications, "nudges" for taking action, and targeted advertising that they receive when using apps and online platforms. The commodification, motility, dynamism, and "pushiness" of digital data are aspects that are particularly characteristic of the contemporary digital data economy compared with earlier forms of collecting and using knowledges about people.

The ways in which digital data can be used for monitoring and surveillance of users are also important elements that have been addressed by some writers. The use of big data sets in surveillance activities, or what is referred to as "dataveillance" (van Dijck, 2014), has become a controversial topic. Since mid-2013 a number of highly publicized scandals concerning the monitoring of people's personal digital data have received public attention. Whistle-blower Edward Snowden's revelations about national security agencies' digital surveillance of their citizens, the Facebook and OkCupid experiments on their members, and the hacking of nude celebrity photos on iCloud and adult dating sites, for example, have publicized the ways in which people's personal (and sometimes very intimate) data may be accessed and used, often without their knowledge or consent. As the monitoring of individuals' bodies, energy use, work productivity, moods, social relationships, purchasing habits, driving practices, and so on becomes more routinized and widespread, options for avoiding becoming the subject of dataveillance are limited.

It is important to acknowledge that many forms of dataveillance are self-imposed or consensual, engaged in as part of everyday interactions with other users on social media sites, for example, or as part of personal efforts to achieve self-knowledge or self-optimization by self-tracking using digital devices. Mobile digital technologies such as the camera and audio-recording functions in smartphones and wearable self-tracking devices that are able to easily collect information about people's body functions, habits, and behaviors, and the social media platforms that facilitate the uploading and sharing of images and details about oneself and others have contributed to the practices of what has been referred to as "social surveillance" (Marwick, 2012), "participatory surveillance" (Albrechtslund and Lauritsen, 2013), or "reflexive self-monitoring" (Lupton, 2016a). These forms of watching involve the practices of sharing information about oneself with others, inviting their reactions and comments, often as part of friendships or in developing other social relationships, as well as commenting on other people or sharing information one has gathered about them (including images and audio data). They are very different forms of dataveillance from the imposed, covert, or disciplinary modes that are represented by CCTV cameras, police-worn body cameras, or the secret surveillance of online interactions by national security agencies. Nonetheless, the personal information that is generated from these modes are still part of the flows and circulations of the wider digital data economy, and as such, are subjected to potential repurposing by other actors and agencies.

Critical digital data scholars have begun to draw attention to the possible ways in which digital data sets may be used to make assumptions and inferences about individuals or social groups. Some commentators have discussed the commercialization of digital data and critiqued the ways in which people's personal data may be used for the financial benefit of others (Andrejevic, 2013, 2014; Center for Media Justice, 2013; Crawford, 2014; Lupton, 2014b, 2016a; Andrejevic and Burdon, 2015). The implications for social justice and civil rights have also been identified. Predictive algorithms that draw on personal digital data are now used in many social and economic domains to construct scores that are used to determine whether individuals should be provided with access to special offers, goods, and services, or whether they pose risks such as the possibility of engaging in criminal acts or terrorism.

Concerns have been consequently raised by privacy and ethics organizations and legal scholars about invasions of personal privacy incurred by big data practices (Polonetsky and Tene, 2013; World Privacy Forum, 2013; Crawford and Schultz, 2014; Executive Office of the President, 2014; Nuffield Council on Bioethics, 2015). For example, the predictions that are made by big data analytics can result in predictive privacy harms, in which people may be discriminated against simply because they are categorized within certain social groups based on their data. This can affect people's access to healthcare, credit, insurance, social security, educational institutions, and employment options, and render them vulnerable to unfair targeting by policing and security agencies (Crawford and Schultz, 2014; Rosenblat et al, 2014).

People may experience technical difficulties in gathering digital data, visualizing it or seeing ways of making data work for them, or they may be denied access to their own data. The affordances of the digital technologies structure the norms and expectations against which people are expected to measure their behaviors and biometrics, and limit the type of information that they collect, emphasizing some while ignoring others (Nafus, 2013; Lupton, 2014a, 2015b, 2016a). People are given access to only some of the digital data that they generate, with the vast majority unavailable to them because they are in the possession of internet companies (Nafus, 2013; Andrejevic, 2014).

In these sociomaterial conditions, how are personal digital data assemblages conceptualized? What choices do people make around collecting, interpreting, and sharing their data? How do people give meaning to their data, and how are data incorporated into everyday lives, notions of selfhood, and embodiment? I address some aspects of these questions in the remainder of this chapter. As well as referring to others' research, I draw on some of the findings from my own current projects to illustrate some points.[1] I have grouped the discussion under three themes: data valences; data communities; and data ambivalences and suspicions.

Data valences

As research by Fiore-Gartland and Neff (2015) found, different social groups give different meanings to digital data. They focused on health- and medical-related data in their research, using interviews, observations, and participation in the communities of technology designers, medical practitioners, advocates, and patients. Their research found that members of these different groups conceptualized the same digital data sets very differently, influenced by the particular social relationships and expectations within these contexts. The data are interpreted and used differently as a result: they possess different value and, in effect, become different data. Fiore-Gartland and Neff use the term "data valences" to encapsulate these shifting and contextual forms and uses of data. Healthcare workers, for example, tend to represent health and medical data in terms of actionable information for managing patients and their conditions, while self-trackers who collect data on themselves represent this information as narratives about the self.

Research on people who use digital devices for self-tracking aspects of their lives has demonstrated the emotional responses that such data practices may involve as part of the meaning and value that people give to their personal data. Ruckenstein and Pantzar's research (Ruckenstein, 2014; Pantzar and Ruckenstein, 2015) with Finns using a digital heart rate monitor found that their participants gained a great deal of pleasure from noticing how their physical activities contributed to a "good" data reading. These researchers also found that certain quotidian activities, including housework, gained new value for the participants because of their input into improved physical activity metrics as measured by the devices. Their participants enjoyed reviewing the visualizations of their personal data. When their attention was drawn to certain parts of their bodies (such as their heart, as represented by heart rate data), they began to focus more on these parts than others. The digital data that were generated from these sensors therefore came to change the ways in which these people thought about their bodies and their everyday activities. The metrics that these data generated were invested with personal significance, because they were about their own bodies. The data visualizations were viewed as more credible and accurate by the participants than the "subjective" assessments of their bodily sensations. A new kind of value was therefore given to some everyday activities and interactions and to the parts of their bodies on which these devices gathered data.

People who engage in reflexive self-monitoring of their bodily functions and activities often make reference to these devices' ability to see inside the body, uncovering "hidden" dimensions that they would otherwise be unable to perceive through their senses (Lupton, 2016a). This discourse suggests that humans require the assistance of machines to extend their capabilities and provide accuracy and enhanced interpretation and memory of information. This was evident in participants' accounts of using fitness tracking devices and software in my project with Glen Fuller. For example, one male cyclist who used self-tracking devices to monitor his rides noted the following:

> Well, like, you've got all these perceptions about how hard you're riding. What I've found is that those perceptions don't necessarily match up with what your heart rate is doing. You think they do, that's the thing. Before you have something like this, you think, 'Oh yeah, I can work out how hard I'm riding. I don't need something like that to tell me.' But the reality is actually quite different. So in a way, that's really sort of work out how to ride a bit better and harder and know when I can push myself more and that sort of thing, and when I might be a bit tired and struggling and those sorts of things, which you don't pick up on too much.

This man's words underline the ways in which digital data on people's bodies and behaviors are often conceptualized as more truthful than the perceptions that they receive from their senses. He observes that his self-tracked data can "tell" him how hard he is riding, how high his heart rate is, and how tired his is, while his bodily sensations may be misleading. He is willing to trust the numbers, which appear to offer greater accuracy.

My project addressing the use of digital media by pregnant women and the mothers of young children found that the use of digital media to provide information during pregnancy and in the early years of parenting was very common. For example, in the survey I conducted of women who were either pregnant or who had given birth in the past three years (Lupton and Pedersen, 2015), 73 percent of the respondents said that they had used at least one pregnancy app, with the majority of these respondents using between two and four apps, and using them daily or several times a week. Almost all of the women who used these apps said that they found them useful or helpful. The apps were used mostly for seeking information about fetal development and changes in their bodies related to pregnancy.

My public understandings of big data study with Mike Michael (Lupton and Michael, 2015; Michael and Lupton, 2015) also revealed a willingness on the part of the participants to exploit the possibilities of digital devices to engage in reflexive self-monitoring or the monitoring of others. For example, one of the tasks we set the focus group participants involved asking them in pairs to design data-gathering devices: one that they could use to collect any kind of data about themselves, and one for collecting data on another person (we called these "personal data machines"). Their designs demonstrated the participants' realization of the potential of digital devices to participate in ever-more intimate forms of monitoring of oneself or others that may allow others to gain greater insights into the participants' lives. One pair designed a dream-recording app that would allow them to remember their dreams the next day. They went on to describe how this could be linked to a dating app, so that prospective couples could share each other's dreams and perhaps work out how compatible they were. Another pair discussed a data machine that could monitor the social interactions of people's partners, so that the user could determine if too great a level of attention was being paid by their (possibly cheating) partners to other people. Devices that were able to closely monitor users' bodily functions were a popular choice, such as one that involved analysing the user's sweat to determine whether they were eating a nutritious diet. Devices for keeping a watchful digital eye on one's children were also frequently suggested, including features that could let parents know the location of their children, record their biometrics, and check that they were doing their homework.

My research on digitized pregnancy and parenting also revealed the desire of people to generate detailed information about themselves or intimate others. Several women were positive about using a device that tracked their infant's body metrics. The members of one focus group talked about how they would like to use such a wearable device for their infant that would convey data to their smartphone. They also suggested that they would like to use a self-tracking app during their pregnancy that would track their fetus's development, and send this information to their partner or parents so that they could also see how the fetus was developing. The participants in this research wanted digital devices such as apps and websites to be customized and tailored to their personal details: the stage of gestation they had reached in pregnancy, for example, or the age of their children or where they lived.

Data communities

Many apps and social media platforms encourage people to engage in sharing practices of their personal information as part of their engagement with these technologies. The notion that people can become closer, learn from, and even motivate and support each other by exchanging personal details is reproduced in a range of apps and platforms, from Facebook to specialized patient support platforms such as PatientsLikeMe to fitness self-tracking apps such as Strava and RunKeeper. Users are encouraged to reveal intimate details of their lives to other users as part of developing social bonds, networks, and communities. In this discourse of sharing, personal data are represented as contributing to collective knowledge stores (Lupton, 2016a).

Research has demonstrated that the pleasure of sharing personal data are inherent to the motivations of people who use social media sites such as Facebook, Instagram, and YouTube to upload photographs or videos of themselves or status updates discussing details of their lives (van Dijck, 2013; del Casino and Brooks, 2015). People who engage in self-tracking also frequently allude to the value that they gain from sharing their information with others and feeling part of a community of people engaged in similar pursuits (Barta and Neff, 2015; Lupton, 2016a).The interviewees in our fitness self-tracking study discussed the satisfaction they received from comparing the metrics from rides or runs and noting improvements, and competing with or receiving support and encouragement from other users. Several commented that they also enjoyed uploading information about their sporting pursuits to social media platforms such as Facebook, recounting the number of kilometers of their rides or runs, the time taken, or providing photographic images from the route for their friends or followers to admire. Their use of their personal data, therefore, was often performative, representing their accomplishments and exploits to others. The numbers that their devices generated allowed them to monitor, record, and display their accomplishments easily and in ways that allowed for ready comparisons.

Women who are pregnant or in the early years of motherhood are frequent users of online sites that facilitate the sharing of personal information. It has become common for pregnant women or mothers of young children to upload details of the development of the fetus or child on social media platforms or support websites, and to share ultrasound images or images of the child following their birth (Ammari et al, 2015). This personal data practice was discussed by some of the participants in my project on digitized pregnancy and parenting, as was the use of support forums on pregnancy or parenting apps, or websites or Facebook groups as a means of discussing their experiences of pregnancy and parenting. For these women, and those quoted in other research on women's use of such digital media (for a review of these studies, see Doty and Dworkin, 2014), practices of sharing information about their pregnancy, parenting experiences, and children are valuable means of representing themselves as "good mothers," feeling part of a community, dealing with feelings of isolation, and sourcing information from others in the same situation. The women in my focus groups, for example, discussed how they had gained answers to questions or concerns they had about their pregnancy or their children by asking questions on online forums or social media platforms or viewing other users' interactions. Sharing information in these contexts becomes a communal data practice, in which people's personal details become part of a crowdsourced body of knowledge that is available to other users of the sites.

Data ambivalences and suspicions

Several recent studies have suggested that the highly publicized controversies concerning dataveillance and data breaches have begun to influence people's attitudes to the ways in which digital data are routinely collected on them and used by second and third parties. Two Pew reports outlining the findings of surveys about Americans' attitudes to data privacy (Pew Research Center, 2014; Madden and Rainie, 2015) found that the respondents were aware of many aspects related to how their privacy was being challenged, and of data security breaches, including national security agencies' dataveillance of citizens and how their personal information is used by commercial companies. The first report (Pew Research Center, 2014) found that nearly all of the respondents were aware of Snowden's documents and what they revealed about the surveillance of citizens. They felt that their privacy was under threat by such surveillance and that conducted by commercial internet organizations. Nearly all of the respondents agreed that people had lost control over how their personal information is collected and used by companies. The second Pew report (Madden and Rainie, 2015) noted a significant element of personal data insecurity that had begun to affect people's attitudes towards dataveillance and data privacy. Very few respondents felt they had much control over the types of data that are collected on them and how these data are used. They expressed strong views about the importance of preserving personal data privacy and security, but had little confidence that internet companies or government agencies would achieve this. Few people in either survey said that they had taken steps to avoid dataveillance, however, suggesting a lack of knowledge on their part about how to do this.

Australian (Andrejevic, 2014) and British research (Kennedy et al, 2015) has also found that people express powerlessness in the face of the authority of the internet empires to collect, own, and harvest their personal information. This sense of powerlessness is exacerbated by socioeconomic disadvantage. Another study used participant observation and participatory action research with Americans from socially marginalized and disadvantaged backgrounds (Gangadharan, 2015). It revealed that such individuals frequently only have access to "privacy-poor, surveillance-rich" public broadband. For most of them, privacy of their personal data was viewed as a luxury rather than a right, because they had few options to protect their data and lacked the digital literacy skills to know how to do so. They expressed little concern about commercial or national security dataveillance of the type revealed by Snowden's document, but a high level of worry about government dataveillance. Such people often have a history of experiencing surveillance from government agencies, mostly stemming from their interactions with social welfare systems. Particularly when they are applying to or maintaining their eligibility in welfare programs online, they are forced to relinquish intimate details. They are therefore at risk of further marginalization, exclusion, and exploitation from the effects of dataveillance when they are using this type of internet access.

My own Australian research on public understandings of big data identified a somewhat diffuse but quite extensive understanding on the part of the participants of the ways in which data may be gathered about them and the uses to which these data may be put. We found that the participants in our focus groups tended to veer between recognizing the value of both personal data and the big aggregated data sets that their own data may be part of, particularly for their own convenience, and expressing concern or suspicion about how these data may be used by others. It was evident that although many participants were aware of these issues, they were rather uncertain about the specific details of how their personal data became part of big data sets, and for what this information was used. For example, for a female participant, the knowledge that "some people out there know as much about you as you know about yourself" was "scary." She observed that "there is a lot going on that we don't know" in terms of how other actors are accessing people's personal data. However, a male participant noted that it "depends on who's got the data." Providing the example of a person with severe depression, he commented that if others knew this information, then they might be able to provide emotional support or useful services. On the other hand, there are actors or agencies that might use this information to discriminate against a person with depression, such as potential employers.

Despite such suspicions, a remarkable degree of trust is also often evidenced in people's use of digital technologies that collect their personal information. My research on how women use digital technologies for pregnancy and parenting found that despite the very high use of pregnancy apps, very few users had sought to check where the app developers had obtained the information that they presented in the app. Nor were the women who had used pregnancy apps concerned about how their personal information may have been used by the developers of the apps. The focus group discussions that were conducted as part of this project revealed a similar lack of interest or knowledge among the participants in the ways in which their personal information were being used by second or third parties. Very few of these women were beginning to think seriously about the implications of creating an online presence for their children by posting images or comments about them on social media sites.

Discussion

Critical research into data practices, some of which I have reviewed here, has begun to suggest certain elements of the ways in which people are engaging with and interpreting their lively digital data assemblages. These include ideas about the importance of personal data for acquiring new or more detailed knowledge about oneself, the ways in which the data generated by digital devices focus attention on some aspects of the body and the self to the exclusion of others, and the emotional dimensions of digital data practices. People appear to enjoy the perceived benefits of entering personal details about themselves or intimate others to customize and personalize apps and other software to respond to their activities, social relationships and bodily functions, and using technologies that are able to monitor their own lives or others' lives in great detail.

The affordances of digital technologies for generating, storing, and manipulating personal data are valued. The quantification that many digital data assemblages adopt and promote is often considered a more neutral and accurate form of information. People often enjoy finding meaning in their personal data and applying their insights to their lives, or being the target of personalized push notifications that deliver useful information to them. They also see benefits in being able to share their personal data with others and in being able to access other people's data. These responses suggest a willingness to position oneself and others as data subjects.

On the other hand, resistances or blockages to data subjectification are also apparent. Seeking to interpret and make use of personal digital data is experienced as confusing or frustrating for some people. While collecting or using one's personal data may involve various modes of pleasure, comfort, satisfaction, playfulness, or performances of selfhood, confronting or interpreting personal data may also be experienced as disappointing, frustrating, limiting, or invasive of the user's privacy. Sometimes people feel as if they lack control over the reams of personal data that are generated about them, even those that they voluntarily produce in self-tracking efforts or by creating content for social media platforms. The data may reveal elements about the self that individuals would rather not know, or remind them of events that they would rather forget. Data practices may begin to overtake over aspects of life to the detriment of other experiences and ways of knowing. It may be difficult to make sense of data or see how various forms of data relate to each other.

The data that are available for people's use may be viewed as limited, inadequate, or as too revealing of private details. As personal digital data enter into the digital data economy, the practices of social or participatory surveillance or reflexive self-monitoring may be transformed into opportunities for more coercive, covert, or commercial dataveillance on the part of other actors and agencies. It is evident that questions of how to negotiate data privacy and security issues are beginning to be confronted by people. However, my own research and that of others suggest that they still seem mostly unaware of exactly what happens to their personal information once it is transmitted to cloud archives, or how to go about protecting their data from unwanted use or surveillance.

While most people appear to be generally accepting of or resigned to the use of their personal information by commercial bodies to target them for advertising, many still seem blind to the implications of entrusting their personal data to the developers of the devices and software that they use, including how their data may be used for profile, or for making inferences and predictions about them that may affect their life chances. While people may be aware of the more invasive or overt forms of dataveillance to which they are subjected (such as targeted marketing and advertising or CCTV cameras), there is less recognition of the more diffuse, complex, or covert technologies for monitoring, accessing, and repurposing their personal data by second and third parties.

Researching personal data practices is still a nascent field of research, particularly from a sociological perspective. Further enquiries into this topic could explore such aspects as: What are the differences in data practices that emerge between different social groups and institutions? How do other contexts shape data meanings and practices (spatial location, culture, history)? What are the power relations that support or restrict data practices?

Note

1 One Sydney-based project, with Mike Michael, investigated public understandings of big data. In late 2014 we ran six focus groups (with a total of 48 participants), in which the participants were asked to engage in various tasks together, and then to discuss the implications emerging from the tasks. The second project, with Glen Fuller, involved a series of one-to-one in-depth interviews in 2014–15 with seven people living in Canberra who were keen users of fitness tracking software and devices. The third project focused on digital technologies used by pregnant women and mothers of young children. It had two parts: four focus groups in Sydney (with a total of 36 women) and a survey that was completed by a representative sample of 410 women around Australia. Both were conducted in 2015.

References

Albrechtslund, A. and P. Lauritsen (2013) "Spaces of everyday surveillance: Unfolding an analytical concept of participation." *Geoforum* 49, 310–16.

Ammari, T., P. Kumar, C. Lampe, and S. Schoenebeck (2015) "Managing children's online identities: How parents decide what to disclose about their children online." Conference paper presented at CHI 2015.

Andrejevic, M. (2013) *Infoglut: How too much information is changing the way we think and know.* New York: Routledge.

Andrejevic, M. (2014) "The big data divide." *International Journal of Communication* 8, 1673–89.

Andrejevic, M. and M. Burdon (2015) "Defining the sensor society." *Television & New Media* 16 (1), 19–36.

Barta, K. and G. Neff (2015) "Technologies for sharing: Lessons from quantified self about the political economy of platforms." *Information, Communication & Society*, 1–14.

Boellstorff, T. and B. Maurer (2015) "Introduction." In T. Boellstorff and B. Maurer (eds) *Data, now bigger and better!* (pp 1–6). Chicago, IL: Prickly Paradigm Press.

boyd, d. and K. Crawford (2012) "Critical questions for big data: Provocations for a cultural, technological, and scholarly phenomenon." *Information, Communication & Society* 15 (5), 662–79.

Center for Media Justice (2013) *Consumers, big data, and online tracking in the retail industry: A case study of Walmart.* Center for Media Justice, ColorOfChange, Sum of Us.

Clough, P.T., K. Gregory, B. Haber, and R.J. Scannell (2015) "The datalogical turn." In P. Vannini (ed) *Non-representational methodologies: Re-envisaging research* (pp 146–64). New York: Routledge.

Crawford, K. (2014) "When big data marketing becomes stalking." *Scientific American* (www.scientificamerican.com/article/when-big-data-marketing-becomes-stalking/).

Crawford, K. and J. Schultz (2014) "Big data and due process: Toward a framework to redress predictive privacy harms." *Boston College Law Review* 55 (1), 93–128.

del Casino Jr, V.J. and C.F. Brooks (2015). Talking about bodies online: Viagra, YouTube, and the politics of public (ized) sexualities. *Gender, Place & Culture*, 22 (4), 474–493.

Doty, J.L. and J. Dworkin (2014) "Online social support for parents: A critical review." *Marriage & Family Review* 50 (2), 174–98.

Executive Office of the President (2014) *Big data: Seizing opportunities, preserving values.* Washington, DC: The White House.

Fiore-Gartland, B. and G. Neff (2015) "Communication, mediation, and the expectations of data: Data valences across health and wellness communities." *International Journal of Communication* 9, 1466–84.

Gangadharan, S.P. (2015) "The downside of digital inclusion: Expectations and experiences of privacy and surveillance among marginal internet users." *New Media & Society.* DOI: 1461444815614053.

Gillespie, T., P.J. Boczkowski, and K.A. Foot (2014) "Introduction." In T. Gillespie, P. Boczkowski, and K. Foot (eds) *Media technologies: Essays on communication, materiality, and society* (pp 1–19). Cambridge, MA: The MIT Press.

Haraway, D. (2003) *The companion species manifesto: Dogs, people, and significant otherness.* Chicago, IL: Prickly Paradigm.

Kennedy, H., D. Elgesem, and C. Miguel (2015) "On fairness: User perspectives on social media data mining." *Convergence: The International Journal of Research into New Media Technologies.* DOI: 1354856515592507.

Kitchin, R. (2014) *The data revolution: Big data, open data, data infrastructures and their consequences.* London, UK: Sage.

Lupton, D. (2014a) "Apps as artefacts: Towards a critical perspective on mobile health and medical apps." *Societies* 4 (4), 606–22.

Lupton, D. (2014b) "The commodification of patient opinion: The digital patient experience economy in the age of big data." *Sociology of Health & Illness* 36 (6), 856–69.

Lupton, D. (2015a) "The thirteen Ps of big data." *This Sociological Life* (https://simplysociology.wordpress.com/2015/05/11/the-thirteen-ps-of-big-data/).

Lupton, D. (2015b) "Quantified sex: A critical analysis of sexual and reproductive self-tracking using apps." *Culture, Health & Sexuality* 17 (4), 440–53.

Lupton, D. (2016a) *The quantified self: A sociology of self-tracking.* Cambridge, UK: Polity Press.

Lupton, D. (2016b) "Digital companion species and eating data: Implications for theorising digital data–human assemblages." *Big Data & Society* 3, (1), 2053951715619947.

Lupton, D. and M. Michael (2015) "Big data seductions and ambivalences." *Discover Society* (http://discoversociety.org/2015/07/30/big-data-seductions-and-ambivalences/).

Lupton, D. and S. Pedersen (2015) *'What is happening with your body and your baby': Australian women's use of pregnancy and parenting apps.* Canberra: News & Media Research Centre, University of Canberra.

Lyon, D. and Z. Bauman (2013) *Liquid surveillance: A conversation.* Oxford, UK: Wiley.

Madden, M. and L. Rainie (2015) "Americans' attitudes about privacy, security and surveillance", May 20 (www.pewinternet.org/files/2015/05/Privacy-and-Security-Attitudes-5.19.15_FINAL.pdf).

Marres, N. (2012) "The redistribution of methods: On intervention in digital social research, broadly conceived." *The Sociological Review* 60 (S1), 139-65.

Marwick, A. (2012) "The public domain: Social surveillance in everyday life." *Surveillance & Society* 9 (4), 378–93.

Michael, M. and D. Lupton (2015) "Toward a manifesto for the 'Public understanding of big data'." *Public Understanding of Science* [earlyview online].

Mortier, R., H. Haddadi, T. Henderson, D. McAuley, and J. Crowcroft (2014) "Human-data interaction: The human face of the data-driven society." Social Science Research Network (http://ssrn.com/abstract=2508051).

Nafus, D. (2013) "The data economy of biosensors." In M.J. McGrath and C.N. Scanaill (eds) *Sensor technologies: Healthcare, wellness and environmental applications* (pp 137–56). Berkeley, CA: Apress.

Nuffield Council on Bioethics (2015) *The collection, linking and use of data in biomedical research and health care: Ethical issues.*

Pantzar, M. and M. Ruckenstein (2015) "The heart of everyday analytics: Emotional, material and practical extensions in self-tracking market." *Consumption Markets & Culture* 18 (1), 92–109.

Pew Research Center (2014) "Public perceptions of privacy and security in the post-Snowden era." Pew Research Internet Project (www.pewinternet.org/2014/11/12/public-privacy-perceptions/#).

Polonetsky, J. and O. Tene (2013) "Privacy and big data: Making ends meet." *Stanford Law Review* (www.stanfordlawreview.org/online/privacy-and-big-data/privacy-and-big-data).

Rogers, R. (2013) *Digital methods.* Cambridge, MA: The MIT Press.

Rosenblat, A., T. Kneese, and d. boyd (2014) *Networked employment discrimination.* Data & Society Research Institute Working Paper (www.datasociety.net/pubs/fow/EmploymentDiscrimination.pdf).

Ruckenstein, M. (2014) "Visualized and interacted life: Personal analytics and engagements with data doubles." *Societies* 4 (1), 68–84.

van Dijck, J. (2013) "'You have one identity': Performing the self on Facebook and Linkedin." *Media, Culture & Society* 35 (2), 199–215.

van Dijck, J. (2014) "Datafication, dataism and dataveillance: Big data between scientific paradigm and ideology." *Surveillance & Society* 12 (2), 197–208.

World Privacy Forum (2013) *Testimony of Pam Dixon before the Senate Committee on Commerce, Science, and Transportation: What information do data brokers have on consumers, and how do they use it?*

22

"They're just too urban": Black gamers streaming on Twitch

Kishonna L. Gray

They're just too urban. I mean, if they would just be more normal, like regular gamers, then they could probably get more followers. But no one wants to hear all that. We can't relate. (message posted on a Twitch forum)

Marginalized gamers are often simultaneously active participants within gaming as well as savage critics of the hegemonic cultures in which they exist, resisting many oppressive and hostile realities within games, among gamers, and in gaming culture in general. One area in which they resist hegemonic Whiteness and masculinity specifically is through Twitch, a live streaming platform featuring players and actual gaming content. Black gamers specifically empower themselves by continuing to Twitch in the midst of so much racism and harassment by other gamers viewing and posting content while they stream. In one of the most well known quotes from Michel Foucault (1971: 96), he claims that "Where there is power, there is resistance." And as Lila Abu-Lughod (1990: 42) observes, "Where there is resistance, there is power." The mere act of existing, engaging, and producing within this hegemonic culture can be situated within the field of cultural production. While unpacking this claim, this chapter situates their actions within a framework of Black cyberfeminism as Black masculinity is punished and marginalized within Twitch as a segment of gaming culture, and this is made apparent through public comments about Black Twitchers in online forums.

Twitching as cultural production

Twitching can be examined through the lens of cultural production, as it is material generated by non-professional users (Strangelove, 2010). Twitch allows users the ability to actively engage in gaming culture by providing their own narrative and commentary while simultaneously playing. This act of actively participating within the game extends immersion of users within games; while gamers utilize Twitch differently, a primary reason is to provide in-game commentary. As de Certeau (1984) argues, audiences are not passive consumers, but instead active interpreters, and the ability for gamers to interpret games through their own lens empowers these users. This follows Stuart Hall's encoding/decoding model of communication (1997), where each person will create their own meaning from the same text, depending on their situation and unique background. As such, it is important to allow the marginalized voice to become active in hegemonic arenas such as video games (Gray, 2015).

Twitch, as a technology that allows one to be disengaged from commercial media dictating game narratives, has the capacity to produce counterhegemonic messages unarticulated by the cultural industries. Henry Jenkins (2006) believes that digital content creation is capable of operating in unauthorized ways outside of industry control. While this form of "do it yourself" labor still benefits the capitalist structure of gaming, users still feel empowered, and their labor should not be diminished. As Tiziana Terranova (2000) suggests, the internet does not truly turn users into enfranchised creators and producers, although it is in the interest of the culture industries to let them think that – to present them as wielding cultural and economic power/capital rather than as laboring as part of the culture industry's efforts to monetize culture. Additionally, Mark Andrejevic (2007) asserts that participation is not always the same thing as power sharing. But among users within Twitch, participation is viewed as contributing to gaming culture in meaningful ways. Bourdieu (1984) acknowledges that no cultural good is inherently better than another that leads to an important designation within cultural production: notions of legitimate production are contestable. Gamers of color, as Twitchers, are excluded from this area of discussion to decide what an appropriate contribution to the field is; it is decided for them by the default gamer. Their presence within Twitch exists counter to the hegemonic norm. Their bodies and mere existence runs counter to the conformist cultural practices operating not only within Twitch, but gaming culture in general.

Bourdieu and Johnson (1993) explain that no cultural product exists by itself and products are direct reflections of their producers especially within realms of power. The unequal power relations operating with virtual worlds manifest through the body: more specifically, privileged bodies. The performance of Whiteness and masculinity are accepted as legitimate and embedded in the continued cultural practices within digital technology (Gray,

2012b). Pierre Bourdieu's theory of practice reveals the material and symbolic production of cultural goods and acknowledges the mediators who contribute to the work's meaning and legitimization (Tkachev, 2006). Symbolic capital determines a specific economy of the field and is based on the speculation that what constitutes a cultural work is its social value or significant contribution to a particular culture. Within virtual communities that value privileged bodies, oftentimes the marginalized populations' contributions to the field, to innovation, to knowledge are not valued or not seen to contribute to the cultural work within the digital era.

Symbolic capital includes an authorized validation of a cultural producer and a cultural product as legitimate according to the existing standards and trends of the community or culture. What is significant in applying cultural production to virtual settings in this manner "is the definition of the limits of the field, that is, of legitimate participation in the struggles" (Bourdieu, 1990: 143). When default, privileged users within virtual settings suggest that "that's not how you Twitch" or "console gamers aren't real gamers" or "they are too urban," or any host of other disparaging comments, it means that a cultural product is denied its legitimate existence and excluded.

Cultural production and the (in)valid knowledge of Black Twitchers

The presence of women and people of color in spaces traditionally dominated by privileged bodies deems them deviant (Gray, 2012a). Sociological theories and empirical studies suggest that deviant identity is the result of being formally or informally sanctioned by social audiences. The process by which an individual develops a deviant identity is linked to the performance of some identified deviant behavior (Gray, 2012b). Although deviance is mostly a socially constructed concept, deviant behaviors in most real world settings have been agreed on by a consensus.

Deviance exists because social groups react in a condemnatory, punitive, or simply disapproving manner to any individual's behavior(s) and/or characteristic(s) that are in violation of the social standards prevailing in those groups (Clinard and Meier, 1998: 7). Stigma, on the other hand, has been defined as a sign or a mark that designates the bearer as "spoiled" and therefore as valued less than "normal" people (Goffman, 1963). An important similarity between the two is that both deviant and stigmatized individuals are perceived as individuals who failed to conform to normative standards in society. However, stigma involves perceptions of deviance that relate more to an individual's character and identity. Stigmatized individuals are not considered to be legitimate participants, but instead are considered deviants (Dovidio et al, 2000). And as researchers have suggested, deviating from the

White, heterosexual, male norm within the space designates one as deviant (Gray, 2012a).

Because people of color are not recognized as legitimate participants in virtual spaces, disparaging realities exist leading to their exclusion and full participation in the community. No matter the content, the dominant culture of video gaming still gets to decide who is valid and who is not. This is what Bourdieu calls "symbolic exclusion" or the effort to impose a definition of "legitimate practice" and "universal essence" (Bourdieu and Johnson, 1993: 14). Any practice within cultural production then becomes the symbolic site of struggle over the power to enforce the dominant definition from a hegemonic standpoint that delimits and restricts access to certain populations, defining who's entitled to take part in defining and shaping virtual spaces.

Black cyberfeminist thought

Black cyberfeminist thought can help contextualize the experiences of marginalized users existing within Twitch. Specifically, Black cyberfeminism concerns itself with three major themes: (1) social structural oppression of technology and virtual spaces; (2) intersecting oppressions experienced in virtual spaces; and (3) the distinctness of virtual feminism. While the focus of this research is mostly on Black male Twitchers and responses to these Twitchers in online forums, this framework addresses marginalized identities and Black masculinity is marginalized within this space. Black males, for failing to conform to the White male norm, are unable to take advantage of hegemonic masculinity within this space leading to an identity of marginalized masculinity.

Social structural oppression of technology and virtual spaces

Examinations of institutional racism, stereotypical imagery, sexism, and classism are routinely addressed by Black feminist thought. Incorporating the inherent masculine bias in technology and the privileging of Whiteness within virtual spaces (Gray, 2012a), this tenet within Black cyberfeminism is imperative. Kolko (2000) argued that the internet is far from liberatory, but rather is a space that continues a "cultural map of assumed whiteness." Kolko (2000) pointed out that attempts to make race and ethnicity present are met with colorblind resistance. The assumed White masculine body excludes women and people of color. As previously discussed, the mere presence of their bodies marks them as deviant in these spaces (Gray, 2012b).

Ignoring the diverse lives of virtual inhabitants also leads to the inability of marginalized bodies to define their own virtual realities. Marginalizing narratives perpetuated through the media reinforce limited conceptualizations of women. Black cyberfeminists urge the marginalized to regain control of hegemonic imagery to be able to define themselves, and internet technologies allow for this. Twitch users are able to demonstrate their knowledge of the game with some earning significant amounts of money from their followers. However, Black gamers are largely excluded from this practice as they are not deemed valid participants within the space.

Intersecting oppressions in virtual spaces

The second theme of Black cyberfeminism is that marginalized users of any technology must confront and work to dismantle the overarching and interlocking structure of domination in terms of race, class, gender, and other intersecting oppressions. Because individuals experience oppression in different ways, we must not create a one size fits all understanding of oppression. Black cyberfeminism requires an understanding of the diverse ways that oppression can manifest in the materiality of the body and how this translates into virtual spaces (Gray, 2015). Black cyberfeminism also requires recognition of the privileges that some marginalized bodies hold before we can begin dismantling these privileges and understanding the multitude of ways that intersectionality can manifest.

Black cyberfeminism encourages a privileging of marginalized perspectives and ways of knowing, because race, gender, class status, disability, sexuality, and a host of other identifiers generate knowledge about the world. Valuing these perspectives is the only way to liberate the oppressed from the confines of hegemonic notions deeming these identities unworthy (Gray, 2015).

Although all oppressed groups share a common struggle, examining the intersecting nature of their realities reveals the distinctness of their lived experiences. Women may share sexual oppression, but it is not clear how this can unite all women whose lives, work, life expectancy, and family life are also structured by the hierarchies of racism, ethnicity, colonialism, or nationalism. People of color may share racial oppression, but the gendered and classed nature of their experiences manifest in real ways. Within the current context, examining race and marginalized gender reveals a particular reality for Black men within Twitch.

Accepting the distinctness of virtual marginalization

Black cyberfeminism also addresses the distinct nature of how marginalized users employ virtual technologies. The focus of the current work is on Black males and their marginalized masculinity within gaming culture. But looking at gaming culture broadly, Blackness within gaming culture is deployed in very stereotypical ways. For instance, within video games, Black masculinity is most often stereotyped as hypermasculine, hyperphysical, and hypersexual (Gray, 2014). And while Black men still continually engage in, they resist in other ways, and that leads to their empowerment. One of major ways that Black men assert their power to resist is by constantly inserting their masculinity into spaces dominated by hegemonic masculinity. This process can be referred to as resistant masculinity. Scholars define the paradigm of resistant masculinity as an attempt by Black men to resist oppression and assert their masculinity in a society that sought to strip away any sense of manhood. There is a correlation between White southern manhood and slavery where White men established their masculinity by using slavery to make Black men inferior to them. This is apparent in men's interactions in Xbox Live. The mere presence of Blackness incites many males to lash out aggressively toward Black masculinity in the space. In turn, many Black males within Xbox Live will reassert their manhood and masculinity and attempt to reclaim the power that is trying to be usurped and diminished in the space (Gray, 2014). This is the process involved in racializing public space within virtual settings. Racialized hierarchies have manifested within these spaces situating marginalized bodies as second-class gamers. And this process becomes apparent in seeing the Twitch community's response to Black Twitchers. Many gamers have taken their concern that Black gamers just "don't have what it takes" to gaming forums.

Research method

By examining the comments posted about Black Twitchers in a public gaming forum, this study intends to investigate the online discourse surrounding Black Twitchers as well as colorblind racist attitudes expressed about these gamers within the same forum. Analysing their narratives reveals insight into the perspectives of the gatekeepers who relegate Black gamers to the margins of gaming culture.

Methodologies in the digital era must be "racially literate" to truly interrogate the presence of power inherent in constructing racialized narratives (Hughey and Daniels, 2013: 338). Just as scholars have outlined how racial code words reproduce "real-life" racial segregation and inequalities, scholars must also become acquainted with the slang and language of virtual racial invective and messaging (Hughey and Daniels, 2013: 337). As such, this study analysed online forum comments generated by Twitch users. The online forum comments were posted over a two-month period in response to a Black gamer getting banned for using racist language. The data gathered was obtained from a discussion board forum where there were 24 total users, 13 actually identifying as active Twitch users. There was no way to ascertain actual race or gender of the forum posters.

Analyzing the data

To analyze the data, I employed both thematic and critical discourse analysis. Thematic analysis was employed to establish the broader cultural norms operating inside Twitch, while critical discourse analysis formed the basis of the discourse that illuminates notions of power and the racialization of space. Thematic analysis enables the researcher to establish broad themes or patterns that highlight cultural norms. As Anzul et al suggest, "it can be thought of as the researcher's inferred statement that highlights explicit or implied attitudes toward life, behavior or understandings of a person, persons, or culture" (Anzul et al, 2003: 150).

The presence of both micro- and macro-level comments within the forum led to the inclusion of critical discourse analysis, given that several commenters normalized the behaviors and actions of the racialized discourse on Twitch and within the forum. So thematic analysis was useful to establish the discursive practices that existed within Twitch, and critical discourse analysis was used to analyse the interactions of specific discourses. Using both highlights the connections between participants' use of a particular discourse within Twitch (and online forums) and the larger discourses occurring in virtual communities and culture broadly: thematic analysis is an appropriate macro approach, which leads to the microanalysis of texts, for which I turn to the methods of critical discourse analysis.

Findings and analysis

Contextualizing Twitch culture: racializing virtual publics

The data collected for this study highlighted the racialized nature of the Twitch community. Although the data reveal a diverse range of conversations operating within the space, I describe in detail only those events that fit within the narrative schema of racialized rhetoric. For instance, the quote provided by one commenter, "They're just too urban. I mean, if they would just be more normal, like regular gamers, then they could probably get more followers," highlights the overarching theme of the entire chapter. Stuart Hall (1997) makes it clear that while language is a very important vehicle of a given discourse, imagery is also heavily involved in how people are represented, and therefore carries with it significant social repercussions. Although these are just words, the symbolic and visual nature of the creation of these words, "urban" makes it very clear that there is a particular population in mind when uttering this phrase. And as Bonilla-Silva suggests (2006), it's a method employed to mask racist practice and intent. While the study of discourse is not limited to any one particular form, format, or modality of discourse – what Foucault (1971) referred to as "orders of discourse" – the various discourses concerning "race" online take place in interactions in both public and private settings. And the anonymous spaces of the internet allow these once private conversations to be revealed publically. While discourse is fluid and constantly changing, when attached to physical bodies, any racialized discourse associated with Blackness is always immobile and unchanged.

While the comments overall are not directly hostile or negative, the assumptions inherent in them reveal extreme discontent with the presence of Blackness. These comments reveal this: "But no one wants to hear all that. We can't relate," and "What do you expect when the majority of the player base seems to be white people?" are just two examples that capture the essence of the colorblind and covertly racist commentary leading to the exclusion of Black Twitch users. This exclusion occurs through the "othering" process that refers to discursive acts that establish a binary divide between "Us" and "Them," where "They" are deviant, abnormal, and otherwise different in a negative sense, and "We" are normal and acceptable (Hall, 1997). This builds on Richard Dyer's argument that in order to understand the world, actors have to engage in organizing information into "types," or "general classification schemes" (cited in Hall, 1997: 257). Using systems of meaning, individual objects can be collapsed into groupings based on similarities to and differences from other objects, which enables actors to orient themselves accordingly as they encounter new objects. This othering is a discursive practice constructing Black users as undeserving of the full label of gamer.

Framing Black Twitchers as deviants through discursive practices

As previously explained, deviance is a term that refers to behavior that does not conform to socially accepted norms. While deviant social behavior "manifests in the materiality of the body," not all bodies are subject to the label of deviant, especially among Twitch users (Terry and Urla, 1995: 2). As researchers contend, most often, Blackness and any association with Blackness is punished the most violently within public spaces (Gray, 2012b). As Radhika Mohanram (1999: xiv) explains, "blackness is a discursive practice exercised by the confluence of history, economics, geography, and language," and these spaces continue to expand. With the diffusion of internet technologies, digital spaces (users and owners) are now reflective of this patriarchal, capitalist structured trend confirming the hegemonic domination of Whiteness (Gray, 2014). The comments posted within the Twitch forum also reflect this trend:

> I never SAY I'm black, not in game. That's almost as bad as admitting your a girl.

> They showed the black dude from The Walking Zed and everyone started dropping the N-bomb and asking 'LUCIAN IS THAT YOU?!'

> It's harmless. Damn. We said 'oh hey it's a joke guys!' Y'all are too fucking sensitive.

Discourse associated with framing Blackness as deviant dates back generations, and has very little to do with actual dangerousness and more associated with Blacks crossing cultural and racial boundaries established by Whiteness. As was stated earlier, Blackness is immobile, and when it does attempt to cross some artificial boundary or border, it is met with swift punishment. As the comments above suggest, the deviant identities of femininity and Blackness are normalized as deviant within the space and punished as such. The third comment that even attempts to diminish the seriousness of racism and sexism is part of a larger theme associated with anonymous spaces where default users will say and do things not wanting to be taken seriously.

Discourse of colorblind racism

Even though some comments may not come across as racist, they still belong under the category of colorblind racism. And the comments below may at face value appear to not be overtly racist or colorblind, they actually are on further investigation:

> 95% of popular Twitch.tv chats are filled with memes, mindless drivel, and oftentimes offensive messages. It's just part of the culture. It's not meant to be taken seriously. Anonymous people acting like idiots. It's been around forever.

> This really isn't something I think people should be getting bent out of shape about. Sure, Twitch.tv viewers can be ludicrous sometimes, but that's just how things are.

These posts urge Twitch users to just accept the reality of racism by normalizing these acts. This process of normalizing creates a racialized hierarchy where Black users and any user associated with Blackness are relegated to the periphery of the culture. This extension of othering resides directly within power relations, justifying the imbalance of power cementing members of the dominant group at the top of the social hierarchy (Hall, 1997). This racialized, social hierarchy highlights the racial privilege afforded White Twitch users.

Furthermore, other comments still hint at the lack of mal intent diminishing the serious of the textual acts of harassment and violence:

You get upset over words? grow up.

I won't tell anyone to not be offended, but I'm inclined to believe most if not all of these messages are meant to be vulgar for the sake of it without having any actual malice behind them.

Yep. Just anonymous morons. Really not worth getting worked up over.

As Bonilla-Silva articulates, and as these comments detail, many Whites continually fail to connect their racial attitudes to systemic practices of power and domination from which they participate and benefit. This echoes Blumer's (1948 [1986]) sentiments regarding racial identification – that taking on a racial identity and assigning racial identities to others is a necessary precursor to forming ideas about (one's own and others') racially marked bodies. Bonilla-Silva (2006) takes the additional step of reminding us that those racially marked bodies exist in a social system that has been and continues to be marked by power differentials, dominance, and oppression. The absence of power in these analyses results in a depiction of Whites' racial attitudes as somehow non-racial at worst, and as secondary to other structural forces (for example, social class) at best. So, in the absence of a framework that foregrounds the relations of dominance and oppression that exist between racial groups, Whites' concerns with Blacks' violations of American values and norms, for example, appear as just that – moral-cultural concerns devoid of racial sentiment (Bonilla-Silva, 2006).

Racializing (virtual) public space

"Race … [is] a worldview … a cosmological ordering system structured out of the political, economics, and social realities of people who had emerged as expansionist, conquering, dominating nations on a worldwide quest for wealth and power," Jane Hill explains (1999: 26). We have a very limited understanding of what space is; we assume it to be this fixed and permanent structure, but in reality, "space and place are not fixed or innate but rather created and re-created through the actions and meanings of people" (1999: 3). Space and place are co-produced through many dimensions: race and class, urban and suburban, gender and sexuality, public and private, bodies and buildings (Gieseking et al, 2014). While the era of public segregation may be gone, modern segregation mirrors the historical practice of designated space as Whites only. These practices come in many forms including lack of inclusion, toxic environments, and outright hostility, harassment, and violence in many contexts. Virtual spaces are direct mirrors of historical segregation as overt racism permeates (Gray, 2012b).

In society we "think of space in three interactive, interconnected ways. There is psychological; space, political space, and physical space. They are all interactive, and they are all highly racialized ... for example ... once you say 'Occupy the Hood' everyone knows you're talking about people of color. The reason that this is true is how we've racialized physical space through housing policies, land use planning, and many other public and private actions" (Wiley and Shiffman, 2012: 113). This affects how we treat each other in a public space and how we decide who to include and who to exclude is ultimately driven by political space and misplaced fear.

Contemporary examples reveal just how engrained into the public psyche word association is with racialized places. For instance, when media reports use the term "thug," it is mostly in reference to a Black or Brown body. So when the term "ghetto," "inner city," or "urban" are used, they are mostly referencing Black spaces to situate the reader into something "other." The ideological framing of these words are rooted in colorblind racism. As Bonilla-Silva (2006: 2) states, colorblind racism is a new ideology that "explains contemporary racial inequality as [being the] outcome of non-racial dynamics." This type of racism is subtle and institutional, and strives to be non-racial (colorblind) in order to maintain structures of White privilege (Bonilla-Silva, 2006). Doane and Bonilla-Silva (2003: 272) write that colorblind racism "is as effective as slavery and Jim Crow in maintaining the racial status quo." Additionally, "the beauty of this ideology is that it aids in the maintenance of white privilege without fanfare, without naming those who it subjects and those who it rewards." Bonilla-Silva (2006) effectively contrasts today's colorblindness with overt racism that permeated society during Jim Crow, by describing it as "now you see it, now you don't" (Doane and Bonilla-Silva, 2003: 272). The elements to "new racism" include the (1) increasingly subversive nature of racial discourse and practices; (2) avoidance of racial terminology and a dependence by Whites on their experience of "reverse racism;" (3) invisibility of mechanisms that reproduce racial inequality; and (4) incorporation of "safe" or model minorities. This terminology is directly rooted in this new racism. It's a way to talk about racial minorities without sounding like a racist.

As Hughey and Daniels (2013) explain, coded racial language is used to convey subtle racial meanings in ways that appear normal and reasoned. Yet this discourse is discriminatory and contributes to the reproduction of racism. Racialized discourse is the focal point of this chapter. As Gildersleeve and Hernandez (2012) discuss, discourse is the talk (or language) and action of a text. In relation to hegemony and colorblindness, racially coded language allows racist views to be expressed without seeming "racist" and this, in turn, creates a climate where "non-racist," "neutral," and common-sense language reproduce Whiteness and the status quo (Bonilla-Silva, 2006). Toni Morrison adds depth to this argument by stating that language constitutes violence and needs to be exposed:

> Oppressive language does more than represent violence; it is violence; does more than represent the limits of knowledge; it limits knowledge. Whether it is obscuring state language or the faux-language of mindless media; whether it is the proud but calcified language of the academy or the commodity driven language of science; whether it is the malign language of law-without-ethics, or language designed for the estrangement of minorities, hiding its racist plunder in its literary cheek – it must be rejected, altered and exposed. (Morrison and Denard, 2008: 201)

Twitching, as a form of cultural production, creates the opportunity to blur the boundaries of restricted production within this community. Black Twitchers may not be allowed access to the spaces and industries controlled by their White counterparts, but they are not silent, nor are they passive bystanders consuming White, hegemonic masculine ideology. Black Twitchers act as agents of social change regardless of their intent. The mere presence of their marginalized bodies disrupts the norm of the space designated for privileged bodies. They participate as social agents that engage in a dynamic and ongoing process of producing and reshaping the discourse about what it means to be a true gamer. Although they participate as cultural producers who produce meanings and values, the authority of their discourse is partly determined by the default user within virtual settings, leading to the invalidation of their knowledge. Black Twitchers lack the symbolic capital needed to be seen a full participants within this culture. And dominant culture interpretations of "Blackness" as a site of negative visibility often complicate the ability of African Americans to inhabit public spaces.

References

Abu-Lughod, L. (1990) "The romance of resistance: Tracing transformations of power through Bedouin women." *American Ethnologist* 17 (1), 41–55.

Andrejevic, M. (2007) *iSpy: Surveillance and power in the interactive era*. Lawrence, KS: University of Kansas Press.

Anzul, M., M. Ely, T. Freidman, D. Garner, and A. McCormack-Steinmetz (2003) *Doing qualitative research: Circles within circles*. London, UK: Routledge.

Blumer, H. (1948 [1986]) "Public opinion and public opinion polling." In *Symbolic interactionism*. Berkeley, CA: University of California Press.

Bonilla-Silva, E. (2006) *Racism without racists: Color-blind racism and racial inequality in contemporary America* (3rd edn). Lanham, MD: Rowman & Littlefield.

Bourdieu, P. (1984) *Distinction: A social critique of the judgement of taste*. Cambridge, MA: Harvard University Press.

Bourdieu, P. (1990) *In other words: Essays towards a reflexive sociology*. Stanford, CA: Stanford University Press.

Bourdieu, P. and R. Johnson (1993) *The field of cultural production: Essays on art and literature*. Cambridge, UK: Polity Press.

Clinard, M.B. and R.F. Meier (1995) *Sociology of deviant behavior*. San Diego, CA: Harcourt, Brace, Jovanovic Publishers.

de Certeau, M. (1984) *The practice of everyday life* (translated by Steven Rendall). Berkeley, CA University of California Press.

Doane, A.W. and E. Bonilla-Silva (2003) *White out: The continuing significance of racism*. Abingdon: Psychology Press.

Dovidio, J.F., B. Major, and J. Crocker (2000) "Stigma: introduction and overview." In T.F. Heatherton, R.E. Kleck, M.R. Hebl, and J.G. Hull (eds) *The social psychology of stigma* (pp 1–29). New York: Guilford Press.

Foucault, M. (1971) "Orders of discourse: Inaugural lecture delivered at the College de France, translated by Rupert Swyers." *Social Science Information* 10 (2), 28.

Gieseking, J.J., W. Mangold, C. Katz, S. Low, and S. Saegert (eds) (2014) *The people, place, & space reader*. London, UK: Routledge.

Gildersleeve, R.E. and S. Hernandez (2012) "Producing (im) possible peoples: Policy discourse analysis, in-state resident tuition, and undocumented students in American higher education." *International Journal of Multicultural Education* 14 (2).

Goffman, E. (1963) *Stigma: Notes on the management of spoiled identity*. New York: Simon & Schuster.

Gray, K.L. (2012a) "Intersecting oppressions and online communities: Examining the experiences of women of color in Xbox Live." *Information, Communication & Society* 15(3), 411–428.

Gray, K.L. (2012b) "Deviant bodies, stigmatized identities, and racist acts: examining the experiences of African-American gamers in Xbox Live." *New Review of Hypermedia and Multimedia* 18 (4), 261–276.

Gray, K.L. (2014) *Race, gender, and deviance in Xbox Live: Theoretical perspectives from the virtual margins*. Maryland Heights, MI: Elsevier.

Gray, K.L. (2015) "Cultural production and digital resilience." *Fan Girls and the Media: Creating Characters, Consuming Culture* 85.

Hall, S. (1997) "The spectacle of the 'Other.'" In S. Hall (ed) *Representation: Cultural representations and signifying practices* (pp 223–90). Milton Keynes: The Open University.

Hill, J. (1999) "Language, race, and white public space" *American Anthropologist* 100 (3), 680–9.

Hughey, M.W. and J. Daniels (2013) "Racist comments at online news sites: A methodological dilemma for discourse analysis." *Media, Culture & Society* 35 (3), 332–47.

Jenkins, H. (2006) *Fans, bloggers, and gamers: Exploring participatory culture*. New York: NYU Press.

Kolko, B.E. (2000) "Erasing@ race: Going white in the (inter) face." *Race in Cyberspace*, 213–32.

Mohanram, R. (1999) *Black body: Women, colonialism, and space* (vol 6). Minneapolis, MN: University of Minnesota Press.

Morrison, T. and C.C. Denard (2008) *What moves at the margin: Selected nonfiction*. Jackson, MS: University Press of Mississippi.

Terranova, T. (2000) "Producing culture for the digital economy." *Social Text* 63 (1), 33–58.

Terry, J. and J. L. Urla (eds) (1995) *Deviant bodies: Critical perspectives on difference in science and popular culture*. Bloomington, IN: Indiana University Press.

Tkachev, N. (2006) "The work of art in the field of cultural production: The principle of legitimization in the digital era." Doctoral dissertation, School of Communication, Simon Fraser University.

Wiley, M. and R. Shiffman (2012) "Racialized public space." *Race, poverty & the Environment* 19, (2), 21–3.

23

From "geek" to "chic:" Wearable technology and the woman question

Elizabeth Wissinger

A dress that responds to breathing patterns to detect threats and defend the wearer's personal space (see Svakja, 2014). A ring that signals only those incoming calls you *want* to take (see http://ringly.com). An "intimacy dress" that becomes transparent when the wearer becomes sexually aroused (see Campbell, 2013). A pin that wards off would-be attackers with loud noises and flashing lights. Welcome to the world of wearable tech fashion.[1] While some claim the phrase is still an oxymoron, fashion is on the brink of bringing wearables to the mass market, with internet-enabled and sensor-equipped clothing, jewelry, or e-textiles, poised to become a mainstream phenomenon. With worldwide sales predicted to reach $53.2 billion in 2019 (see Datamation, 2014), the hype has been fierce. High-profile collaborations between fashion houses and high-tech companies made headlines,[2] while in the resulting do or die market, some saw wearables as fatally "gimmicky" (Gilbert, 2014). Wearable technology is not going away, however.

Consumer-oriented, mass-marketed wearable technology has the potential to advance social technology and mobile computing in ways that trouble basic assumptions about bodies, technology, and gender, opening up new possibilities for how bodies are gendered. As wearables are normalized by fashion, the transition from "geek" tech to "chic" tech raises important questions regarding how the technologically enmeshed and gendered body is imagined. Will gendered assumptions about technology and the body impoverish this imagination, or can these new technologies realize their disruptive promise to upend entrenched stereotypes?

Wearable tech's potential to change our social world is immense. Its ethical deployment depends on research aimed at highlighting how cultural attitudes might potentially be smuggled into wearable products, in the name of what the market "wants."[3] The present moment begs for insight and analysis to guide the development of devices away from sexist assumptions that are damaging to women, and to encourage more ways to use these new technologies to enhance as many lives as possible.

What is wearable technology?

Arguably, wearable technology is nothing new. From the pince-nez to eyeglasses, prosthetic devices and wristwatches, technology has been worn in many forms. Some scholars date the origins of fashionable wearable tech back to the 18th century chatelaine, a waist-worn device aimed at keeping tools handy (sewing needles and smelling salts for the ladies, scissors and thermometers for a nurse). Originating in utility, the chatelaine evolved into a fashion statement in the 1700s, before falling out of favor as the handbag grew in both size and popularity (Oatman-Stanford, 2013). The current crop of wearables builds on this history, but their networked, bio-sensing, code-emitting nature is entirely new, as is their ability to make the human body a node in the Internet of Things (IoT), allowing machines to "see" and network with the wearer in novel ways.

Consumer-oriented wearable tech takes many forms, which fit roughly into the following categories: biometric, revealing/externalizing, and connectivity in biometrics. The most common fitness and wellness applications include activity trackers, which gather data such as heartbeat, steps taken, and length and quality of sleep. Less common but emerging externalizing technologies sell themselves as tools for becoming a better version of you. The NeuroSky mindwave headband (see http://neurosky.com), for example, purportedly measures brainwaves to help you track and engage your brain to boost attention and focus. The Lumo Lift zaps you when you slouch, to promote better posture, kind of like having your mother in the device, reminding you to "stand up straight, dear" (see www.lumobodytech.com/lumo-lift). Wellbe, a wristband that senses and matches heart rate levels to specific moments, claims to help wearers pin-point stress triggers, and elevates mindfulness (Basile, 2015). While all of these devices are designed to be worn, being fashion forward is not particularly high on their list of qualities, tending more toward the "geek" than the "chic" in appearance and use.

Fashionable or "chic" techs currently on the market tend toward revealing and externalizing emotion and augmenting or controlling connection. CuteCircuit, one of the pioneers of wearable tech fashion, had one of the first haute couture runway shows during New York City's Autumn/Winter 2014/15 Fashion Week. Their creations emphasize sensitivity to the environment, such as the Twitter Dress, which displayed fans' tweets as the model walked the runway, and the "first ever iPhone controlled Haute-Couture dress," that changed color according to the volume of audience tweets (#makeitpink or #makeitblack).[4] Dutch fashion has been a hotbed of development, where designers are focusing on building electronics, microprocessors, solar panels, LEDs, and other interactive interfaces into garments.[5] Designer Anouk Wipprecht's spider dress, for instance, uses biosensors and microcontrollers to move the arms of the dress to mimic a spider's defensive or receptive stance. The response reflects the speed of approach, and the wearer's breathing rate (see Svakja, 2014). Another externalizing wearable tech is the somewhat cutesy Necomimi head band. Fuzzy cat ears read your brain waves and move up or down according to whether you are "focused," "in the zone," or "relaxed," making it a technology that allows you to literally prick up your ears.[6]

While externalizing emotions or tracking the whims of a crowd are popular in very specific settings, augmenting and controlling connectivity is fashion's favorite playground and space for innovation. The Google Glass may have been a fashion flop, but the connectivity and data retrieval it afforded is now being packaged into sleek jewelry, rings, necklaces, and bracelets. This connected jewelry subtly alerts the wearer to incoming messages or social media alerts, or affords online access in unobtrusive formats.[7] These devices aim at filling a perceived need for women to be constantly connected while being available for quality face-to-face interaction. Whether aimed at revealing one's inner state, or connecting the wearer to the outer world, wearable tech aimed at women explains a lot about the way they are seen by the fashion and tech worlds.

Le Geek, c'est chic

Unlike "geek"-oriented medical or fitness devices, which tend to be marketed as unisex devices, "chic" tech is aimed at the fashion consumer, who is presumably female, healthy, and lives well within the norms of current conceptions of femininity. The push to make these data-driven gizmos fashionable and "chic," however, raises the "woman" question, famously asked by psychologist Sigmund Freud, "what does a woman want?" Interrogating how wearable devices shape and are shaped by gendered ideas is of critical importance to navigating the social transitions bringing wearables to the mainstream. Cultural assumptions about gender are crucial to examining the emergence of new technologies and social practices they prohibit or allow. For years, research has shown that technologies can be explicitly or implicitly gendered. As feminist writer Anne Balsamo has observed, "myths about identity, nature, and body" rearticulate new technologies to socially and technologically reproduce gendered bodies in the course of their adoption (Balsamo, 1996: 15). Donna Haraway and others have famously noted the cultural anxieties raised by mixing the clean, masculine, rationality of technology with the messy, unruly, materiality of the female-associated body in the form of the cyborg (Haraway, 1990). Research has clearly documented how social media and information technologies are rife with the masculinist cultures from which they were born.[8] Since technology is unisex until you put it on a body, in what ways will wearable tech reinforce or disrupt assumptions about the gendered body? Scholarship in fashion studies speaks to this question, as it investigates the interplay between bodies, gender, and clothing technologies that serve to produce the gendered body both within and against traditional assumptions of what a man or a woman can or should be (see, for instance, Entwistle, 2015; or Steele and Katz, 2013).

As fashion normalizes wearable tech, the transition of masculine-identified technology into the feminine domain of fashion sharply highlights the question of how the implementation of these new technologies interprets and shapes gendered bodies. The way fashion brings gender to the realm of wearables remains under-studied, however. Research at the intersection of wearable technology and fashion has tended toward an uncritical cataloguing of practitioners' use of – and predictions for – new technologies, rather than examining the larger gendered consequences of their widespread penetration into the fabric of everyday lives (see, for instance, Quinn, 2010; or McCann and Bryson, 2009). Even Susan Elizabeth Ryan, in her thorough-going consideration of fashion with a capital F's influence on wearable tech, noted her analysis leaves "specific feminist theoretical analysis" of this important but under researched area "to future scholarship" (Ryan, 2014: 4). Scholarship is needed to critically interrogate how cultural understandings of the gendered body are influencing access to the inherent potentials of wearable tech. The enhancement potential in wearable tech is considerable. It can only be realized if the opportunity for this enhancement is not squandered by importing limiting and tradition-based cultural assumptions about gendered bodies into its design.

Innovators within the fashion/data/body space are a key resource for analysing how gendered bodies are being interpreted and shaped by these new technologies. To access this resource, I sought out early adopters, hackers, technophiles, fashionistas, and design freaks, employing both interview and participant observation to map how wearable tech is emerging as an everyday practice. Within this mapping and analysis of the field, I sought to "read" its artifacts, to uncover the latent cultural values they express. The research explores these questions: What are the cultural assumptions inherent in the design of wearable tech for the fashion market? How do these assumptions play out in the devices and their purpose? Are there notable exceptions? What can be done to foster a more inclusive climate, less governed by knee-jerk assumptions about what women want? My findings identified several themes regarding women and technology that thread through the field, highlighting some underlying metaphors used to establish relevance and meaning for these devices. These themes emerged through focusing on the tacit assumptions about women and their needs made by the design community, and evidenced by the designs of the devices themselves.

Overall, I found three prevalent assumptions about women in the tech/fashion field. First, women are potential victims. Second, women want to achieve difficult-to-attain physical ideals of health and optimum fitness. Third, women need to be constantly available and connected virtually, while also paying close attention to achieving high-level face-to-face interaction with those they are with, thus staying fully connected and totally present, at the same time.

Who is "Woman 2.0"?

At an expo showcasing fashion as wearable tech, a panelist enthused, "we want to know who the amazing, incredible, Woman 2.0 is!"[9] The woman question is bedeviling many who seek to unlock fashion tech's enormous potential especially considering the historic construction of women as primary consumers. The "killer app" of fashionable wearable tech remains elusive, as initial forays into marrying fashion with tech have demonstrated a deep-seated cultural ambivalence about women and their needs, in both private and public space.

An apparent culture of fear, for instance, permeates many of the devices in development or now on the market. While accelerometers and email or phone message filters are a given, devices using body sensors and alarms stand out as an example of the cultural assumption that women need protection both from themselves, and from others. Fear of the uncontrollable female body and its urges were clearly in evidence in a well-publicized flop, when researchers at Microsoft developed a bra that would alert the wearer when she is in danger of overeating. In the ensuing media mayhem, Katy Waldman at Slate.com snarked, "What a sign of progress that technology now recognizes the holy trinity of womanhood, emotional instability, and concern for food and weight" (Wakeman, 2013).

It seems that if Woman 2.0 is potentially a victim of her urges to overeat in private, when she goes to work off those calories in public, she is also in danger. The assumption underlying the design of many devices is that she is always one step away from being a damsel in distress. Protection is central to many fashion device innovators, including Smart Siren Technology, Inc., whose SIREN ring offers a wearable tech solution for the independent woman. Billed as a "new brand of jewelry that offers women immediate protection when their personal safety is at risk," it emits a "shockingly loud alarm" that might "change the dynamic between attacker and target" (Yahoo! Finance, 2014). More subtle than the SIREN, but still aimed at the same goal, is a recent dress prototype that expands several inches when someone stands too close (Bischof, 2014). Many other fashionable wearable devices coming on the market have a "safety" feature built in. One device boasts a button that, once pushed, sound alarms, flashes lights, and dials 911 – all while texting the wearer's friends to geo-locate her so that they might come to her rescue.[10] Whether susceptible to a snack attack, or a literal attack, the assumed potential victimhood of bodies gendered female is a telling illustration of broader cultural anxieties being reproduced within these new technologies, anxieties that feed into the identities these technologies are helping to construct.

Taming the unruly female body

In addition to the marked ambivalence about women in public spaces, wearables are raising important questions about women and "model" bodies. The "unholy trinity" of womanhood, emotional instability, and concern about food and weight sits squarely in the realm of negative body image. As personal electronic devices become ever more personal, worn on the skin, for instance, how will they feed into the drama of living the body within contested normative metrics? Will ubiquitous step counting become the new technology of shame, the role formerly held by the scale for scolding fat people, regardless of individual physiology (Nafus and Sherman, 2014)? If you have direct access to the biometric data tracking that jelly donut's effects, will you be any less likely to put it in your mouth? And if you do, will your body be even more out of fashion when the discipline to achieve a fashionably managed body has been built into algorithms that supposedly can whip anybody into shape?

Anthropologists Dawn Nafus and Jamie Sherman's work within the "quantified self" or QS movement, focused on people who wear devices that track and graph sleep, steps, mood, and intake to promote self-awareness and altered behavior. Their work highlighted the need for "soft resistance" to hard-edged algorithms producing the self as data, within the oceans of so-called "big data" becoming so prevalent in contemporary developed societies (Nafus and Sherman, 2014). While this idea of "soft resistance" stems from culturally mandated feelings of body unworthiness in the QS movement, how will the average woman navigate the algorithmic creep of the fashionably fit ideal embodied by the growing ubiquity of step counters, accelerometers, and biometric sensors commonly found in fashionable wearable devices? This algorithmic creep is already hard at work in the workplace. Bodily data is becoming valuable enough to prompt some to employ coercion to get at it. Sociologist of technology Deborah Lupton has documented an uneasy compact between employees giving up health data in exchange for needed insurance to corporations, employee-tracking enables them to reduce their healthcare costs (Lupton, 2014). Just as other forms of workplace governance have gone "freelance," so to speak, will this type of self-monitoring follow the path of branding – from commercial tool to self-imposed personal requirement for success? The current transition to valuing the body *as* data seems to be driving much of the consumer electronics that are deemed "wearable" today, thereby laying the groundwork for just such a transition.

As wearables become the norm, they feed into the current cultural shift in emphasis from the tech functioning to bring a world of data *to* you, to *you* becoming a world of data. This question becomes particularly important as the popularization of wearable tech by fashion intensifies the datafication of the body, or the availability of the body as data. However wearables attract us to putting them on our bodies, they will have us awash in stats. At its inception, this notion seemed empowering. Early pioneers of wearable technology, such as the MIT Borg group, for instance, proudly wore their computers and used them to bring themselves immediately up to speed in conversations about research, helped themselves remember people's birthdays, and kept expert data organized and under their control. In the wake of the internet's shift from a tool for you to use to a tool for using *you*, however, scholars in the fields of media studies, sociology, anthropology, and communication are investigating how wearable technologies have the potential to turn us into data selves, a transition with broad implications regarding privacy, social connection, and bodily integrity (Horning, 2012; see also Crawford, 2014; Nissenbaum, 2014).

With bodily representations becoming more "datalogical" (Clough et al, 2015), fashion *does* have the opportunity to move away from disciplining the uncontrolled flesh of bodies to make them meet a standard. As one designer said of 3D printing and body scanning,

> You can't even think about factories in the same way again. Holding an inventory has shaped fashion in certain ways, artificially segmenting the market. Now you no longer have to design for the Chanel woman. You no longer make 10,000 shirts and then have to use an aspirational model or idea to get people to buy them. (Designer Francis Bitonti at the Decoded Fashion New York Summit, November 2014)

How will the new availability of granular data play into debates about acceptable body size, or "model" bodies? Will new levels of customization to fit clothing disrupt old assumptions about women's bodies and the fashionable ideal more generally?

As wearable tech feeds create a world permeated by data, mediations between the "represented" and "enacted" body take on a new tone.[11] As Brittany Fiore-Silfvast and Gina Neff have noted, data are not self-evident, but rather take on valences. In their formulation, "data valences" contain an "anticipation of value or expectation of performance within a particular ecology or system" (Fiore-Silfvast and Neff, 2013, 2015). How will the data valence of the fashionable body, currently made valuable within the economics of the selfie society, Instagram, and other phone-based imaging technologies, morph and shift within the possibilities wearables afford? If one can be the star of one's own show 24/7, how might realtime life-streaming technologies, such as a camera you wear on your head and leave "on" all the time, exacerbate already existing issues associated with the pains and pleasures of micro-celebrity communication documented by Alice Marwick and danah boyd?[12] How will putting these tracking and recording techs onto our bodies intensify these demands?

In this respect, wearable technology could readily exacerbate what I've called "glamour labor" (Wissinger, 2015). Glamour labor is the work on body and self to produce a fashionable self, both online and in person. The notion of glamour labor raises the question of how the fashionable body, made valuable within the economics of social media, will morph and shift within the possibilities that wearables afford. As fashion and tech meet in the space of chic wearables, what does the future portend for the technologically enmeshed body, especially when it is gendered female by male designed tech? Why does it raise such deep-seated anxieties about women and control?

Geeks are guys?

In the "well trodden" issue of the masculinity of technology,[13] the simplistic version of the logic goes like this: If fashion = feminine, and tech = masculine, then fashion + tech = tech for women designed by men. In the emergence of the internet, feminist researchers found that despite the new technology's possibilities (after all, "on the internet, nobody knows you're a dog"),[14] it nonetheless became a site where "social practices are embedded, which express and extend the social construction of two asymmetrical genders" (Rakow, 1988: 57). Will fashionable wearable technology fall prey to the same problems? How are "myths about identity, nature, and body" getting rearticulated into these new designs (Balsamo, 1996: 15)? Is there a way to influence the design community away from these assumptions? As tech researcher Natasha Dow Schüll has observed, it is

> Not just the behavior, not just the person – but the design, the configuration, and the way that can constrain and direct and guide behavior in certain directions, and why it might be a good idea to regulate it. There is no equivalent to the FDA for technology. There should be researchers and policymakers in conversation about the intimate and even physiological ways that these things affect people. (quoted in Annechino, 2015)

The way technologies are designed contain implicit assumptions. Anthropologist Jamie Sherman observes that intimate data gathering implies an ideal body that is no longer explicit but rather imagined or performed "within and through a body whose outputs are being quantified" (interview data). Can this body be "envisioned outside of cultural ideals? The visuals are implied but not articulated, as in, 'I want to run faster and stronger.' Does this mean you want a runner's body?" In an interesting twist, Sherman suggests that rather than "glue tech and fashion together," the aim should be to create something "where observers might say, 'what the hell is that for?'" (interview data), allowing more space for a design not aimed specifically at doing something pragmatic and thereby allowing more flexible constraints on behavior. Similarly, in my interview with tech fashion designer Alison Lewis, she argued that while "tech [is used] as a tool of creative self expression … personal expression is not considered a value in my experience of the wearable tech world." She conceded that the perception of value is changing but there is a "big struggle going on over it – in terms of the values the tech itself expresses."

Can the values that tech expresses be attributed to the male oriented "geek" aspect of the tech design field? Functional utility does not exactly conjure up visions of a fashionable ideal. According to the female tech/fashion designers I spoke with, the well-worn issue of the masculinity of technology seems alive and well. One up-and-coming designer observed, "the tech field is dominated by 'brogrammers,'" or, as another pointed out, "Silicon Valley is a 'boy culture.'" One technologically accomplished jewelry designer noted, "People have 'questioned my ability'" with regard to the "technological aspects of my smart jewelry." A young fashion designer who'd won a competition to be a fellow at Eyebeam, a foundation dedicated to fostering experimentation in wearable tech, mused, "the programmers seemed to be wondering what this 'pretty little fashion girl' might want to do with these complex programming languages."

As fashion normalizes wearable tech, the transition of masculine-identified technology into the feminine domain of fashion sharply highlights the question of how the implementation of these new technologies interprets and shapes gendered bodies. As digital sociology researcher Deborah Lupton acerbically observed, the male-dominated nature of digital technology culture translates into "a certain blindness to the needs of women" (Lupton, 2015). A clear example of this problem noted by Lupton and others about the Apple watch was neatly summed up by a newspiece aptly titled "When will we get wearable tech for women right?" For all of its health monitoring prowess, the ability to track menstrual cycles was "suspiciously missing from Apple's health app" when it was first released (Bolluyt, 2015).

The idea that the tech world does not value women's needs translates into the look and feel of devices as well. According to a tech designer who works on the guts that run many devices, "People are trying stuff – they are going to market really quickly without much planning." The result? "There have been a few cases of just wrapping some plastic around some nerdy stuff" (interview data). For many, "fashionable tech" has been so nerdy up to this point, it is not even an option. As one wearables newsletter declared, "Silicon Valley has always been the stomping grounds for tech's biggest thinkers, but fashion? Girl, please" (Mangalindan, 2015). Another observed: "today's elegant women will not be caught dead putting on a clunky wearable; the industry needs to rethink its function-first approach." Their tagline? "Because function needs fashion."[15] One pundit sourced the problem to the male as end user model, where the "look, size, and choice of materials seem to first consider men, and then get cosmetically tweaked for the ladies" (Taraska, 2015).

Some trace these problems more broadly to the difference between fashion and tech cultures. One fashion/tech designer saw the value of function over form, rather than a bias toward male needs or desires, as a detriment to the full development of fashion/tech's potential:

> Fashion and tech are very different cultures. Is one masculine? Not necessarily, but the idea that the tech has to DO something is firmly entrenched. (interview data)

A male tech designer, who works on providing the means for enhancing wearable device functionality, also noted this cultural divide: "If they are coming from a fashion house, you will have a different perspective than if you come from an electronics design house." Yet, he went on to describe the problem in starkly gendered terms, citing the paucity of women on the tech side as the root of these problems with wearable technology. In his view,

> The companies focusing on the fashionable aspect of wearables need to get the right people involved in the design – not just some 'women sitting in a room,' not just paying for some research – if they are designing for women then you might want to have them involved and get their feedback. You need women on the team not just one but several. Sometimes they see things differently.

Leaving the well documented lack of gender diversity in the tech community aside, even when women are in charge of tech design, sometimes the need to make products meaningful draws on cultural categories that can easily veer into stereotypical territory.

Design dilemmas

Wearable technology has the potential to shape identities, in the intimate relation of wearing it on one's body. This intimacy calls out for questioning the tacit assumptions about women's bodies and needs, as made by the design community, and as evidenced by the designs of the devices themselves. In my research, I ask about designers' design philosophy, their intended customer, and the goals of their devices, to look for signs of cultural ambivalence, and to pinpoint whether and how the gendered aspect of fashion is affecting how these technologies are deployed. I found that within the entrepreneurial sector of the fashion domain, there is a prevalence of stereotypes, including, for example, the information overloaded, hyper-connected "busy mom," or "millennial fashionista." This over-simplified view seems to characterize the imagined woman many say is their potential customer. Are these two the only options for Woman 2.0? What is limiting fashion world's interpretation of her needs?

The use of "types" is common in the fashion industry. They serve as a shorthand organizing device to speed workflow, and assume a good deal of tacit knowledge. In the modeling industry, for instance, types are used to organize casting calls. Agents will get requests for a "Bollywood" or "black black black" type of model, and will use these notions to organize who they send out for calls (Wissinger, 2015: 240, quoting from Sadre-Orafai, 2008: 150). Types perform a similar kind of work in fashion design. The type is used to help promote understanding of the brand. Asked about their target customer, one young fashion designer told me:

> Everyone has their kind of identity. Is she an uptown Eastside woman, is she like super chic, is she kind of earthy and lives in Williamsburg; different companies out there zero in on who their actual customer is. You are trying to get a loyalty and try to brand yourself and get these women who are loyal to you.

For this designer, the type makes the brand meaningful to customers. Similarly, a young woman who worked at a haute couture design house said that each designer has their "girl."

> We have a specific girl, we call her our 'girl.' It could be an idea of a woman, when you are designing something. It's a good starting off point. The designer I work for's 'girl' is like the 'cool' girl. She maybe dated a musician, or like, she skateboarded – she's super stylish. Both the designers had really cool girlfriends and they wanted to dress their friends so it starts off sort of simply in that way. (interview data)

The designer's type then gets fed through a mythos that informs the design on many levels. It does not pay to stray far from stereotypes, or gendered assumptions about what a woman wants or considers feminine.

The stereotypes of the "busy mom" or "millennial fashionista" tap into cultural assumptions about femininity, availability, and the emotional labor of human connection. Viawear's ad campaign for the "Tyia" model of their connected bracelets, plucks at working mothers' heartstrings:

Tyia is named for a busy therapist who, one day in 2012, silenced her smartphone, only to later learn she'd missed several calls and texts telling her that her 5-year-old had broken his arm. As a mother and a professional, balancing both work and home, this was a painful experience. (viawear.com)

Not only does the text resonate with the structural difficulties of being a good mother and a paid professional, the ad copy highlights the dilemma of living in a networked world – how to be "connected and available when we need to be," but also "fully present and in the moment." According to another ad campaign for a wearable designed to provide alerts to phone calls and incoming messages, their device protects against being "a slave to technology" (see http://kovertdesigns.com). The "millennial fashionista" type, chained to her device, is a common image. Kovert Designs' champion of "digital detoxification," designer Kate Unsworth, promotes the catch line "Forgoet FOMO [the Fear of Missing Out] and embrace JOMO [the Joy of Missing Out]" (vinaya.com). While the fashionista is not usually depicted as a mother, her desire to stay on her "communications game" highlights another uniquely feminine problem: women's apparel is frequently designed without pockets, an issue Ringly, a ring that vibrates alerts about texts and phone calls, handily addresses. Their video advert shows just how you can "escape from your phone," as a hands-free woman happily twirling in a pocket-less skirt nimbly responds to her vibrating jewelry by pulling her phone from her purse. Customer testimonials on the site report that Ringly helps them avoid "being rude," by letting them "keep the phone away without missing anything."

Discreet, seamless, subtle, and private are buzzwords employed to combat the perceived rudeness of the face-in-the phone problem from which so many "millennials" and "busy moms" seem to suffer. The need to return to face-to-face contact resonates with assumptions about femininity regarding emotional availability. Both women and men are suffering from technologically induced reductions in eye contact; attentiveness and availability to others' needs, however, are behaviors traditionally coded feminine (Gregoire, 2013). When the technological need for connection interferes with the human one, these devices purport to right the balance, and put a woman's focus where it should be, on family, friends, and work, not necessarily in that order, but with attention to herself significantly missing from that list. These devices allow the user to navigate the conflicting demands of a connected world, while satisfying cultural mandates to be polite, attentive, and available.

Is the male-dominated "geek" aspect of the tech design field solely to blame for these skewed views of women as end users of fashionable tech? Is the desire to return to face-to-face contact and emotional connection a gendered value or a human one? Is the desire to feel safe in the street gendered as well? Those trying to straddle the divide between wearable tech and fashion have thus far felt the need to tap broad cultural expectations of gender that shape usefulness and value. Value is a recurrent theme mentioned by designers, and to understand this theme, Brittany Fiore-Silfvast and Gina Neff's notion of "data valences" is useful here. They explain that valences contain an "anticipation of value or expectation of performance within particular ecology or system" (2013: 1470). Arguably, these anticipations of value feed through the ecology or system of gendered notions of what a body is for, and what it can do. As wearables intensify processes of becoming "datalogical," value is found in maintaining a "liquidity of capacity" through practices of "self-appreciation," as social theorist Patricia Clough et al have observed (2015: 2). This "liquidity of capacity" is the goal of the kinds of glamour labor I documented in my previous research. Glamour labor is the work to augment one's glamour across social media platforms, while striving to embody this glamorous image in the flesh, in an effort to extract as much value from one's virtual connectivity and physical embodiment as possible. Arguably it is a from of gendered labor, and the onset of wearable tech is poised to intensify the demand for women's glamour labor – to be fully up to the minute on fashion trends, friends' updates, work demands, all while being fully present to whomever you may be with, and looking gorgeous and fit while doing it.

It is the push for "liquidity" that can either hem in or free the body via wearable technologies. What if the potential of wearable tech were not shaped by gendered assumptions? Could we get our bodies out from under cookie cutter assumptions of what a body is or should be for? Could we produce our bodies in some other way than in the hustle to be "seen," or "matter," to be connected yet available face-to-face, in the kind of social media and body control-on-steroids fashionable wearables portend? As tech innovator Billie Whitehouse observed on a panel at Pratt Institute's Brooklyn Fashion and Design Accelerator (BF + DA), "wearable tech's true potential lies not just in its ability to control us, as in 'here's your data from your day – *enjoy* – but in its ability to augment our experiences," for example, to extend our reach, connect us in new ways, and perhaps break down gender binaries, rather than cement them further.

Researchers raising questions about the profound effects of wearable technology on sociality and subjectivity have called for the need to examine "moral and economic reasoning, cultural assumptions, and institutional contexts constituting enhancements" (Hogle, 2005: 685). Pursuing this line of inquiry, can help digital sociology bridge gaps between traditional sociology and STS (science and technology studies), as well fashion, media, and women's studies, to help both designers and publics better prepare for understanding and managing issues raised by wearable tech. Investigations into these intersecting fields is becoming crucially important as advances in mobile computing and social technology deeply trouble basic assumptions about bodies, technology, and gender. Just like the internet before it, wearable tech has the potential to radically enhance many lives. It would be a shame to squander this potential on short sighted devices that extend existing anxieties in ways that limit or control human potential, gendered or otherwise.

Notes

1 Wearable technology is any kind of device that can be worn on the body and interact with it. Common forms of interaction include lighting up, sensing body motion, reading sweat content, or physical prompts such as remote touch, shocks, or vibration. Wearable tech fashion implicitly assumes that the wearer is healthy and wants to look stylish. The huge range of wearable medical and fitness devices are not aimed at the fashion-conscious market, and therefore fall outside the scope of this discussion.

2 In the past year, fashion has become keenly aware of wearables. Intel's high-profile collaboration with Opening Ceremony and Barneys, resulting in the MICA bracelet, Tory Burch's chic take on the Fitbit, and the up-and-coming Cuff connective "smart" jewelry, are making managing one's personal data streams ever more fashionable, positioning the internet and social media-connected wearables for widespread adoption.

3 Please note that although the term "women" is used throughout, it is for stylistic purposes. The binary formation of "women's" versus "men's" fashion contains a problematic set of gender normative assumptions, assumptions this research is in part aimed at ferreting out, to interrogate how these binaries discipline bodies to reaffirm what is "normal" or expected. Although I am discussing the marketing of "women's" fashion, I seek to question the underlying gender normative assumption affecting a variety of bodies, queer and heterosexual, trans and cis, which thus far have not fitted into the established markets.

4 "Using the 'Q by CuteCircuit' iPhone app fans' tweets are tallied to change the color of the dress instantly while the dress is being worn on the red carpet," as noted on the CuteCircuit website (http://cutecircuit.com/pink-black-collection).

5 See www.craftingwearables.com/about.html, with thanks to Lianne Toussaint and Anneke Smelik.

6 "Your mental state is translated into ear movements," according to the website: www. necomimi.com/.

7 Such as Ringly (https://ringly.com/?utm_source=AdWords&utm_medium=CPC); Intel Opening Ceremony Barneys MICA (My Intelligent Communication Accessory) bracelet (www.intel.com/content/www/us/en/wearables/mica-smart-bracelet.html); Tory Burch for Fitbit (www.fitbit.com/toryburch); and Cuff jewelry (https://cuff.io/#), built entirely around the idea of safety, since, as their promotional video points out, "you never know what's around the next corner."

8 The recent kerfuffle about Gamergate is a prime example – see Hathaway (2014).

9 Decoded Fashion New York Summit (DFNY14), November 2014, New York.

10 https://cuff.io/ alerts a loved one with a distress call and the wearer's location. ROAR for Good provides similar functionality, but also emits a loud alarm when triggered (see www. roarforgood.com/).

11 When your interaction with the machine puts you into a "cybernetic circuit that splices your will, desire, and perception into a distributed cognitive system in which represented bodies are joined with enacted bodies through mutating and flexible machine interfaces" (Hayles, 1999).

12 It is called "Lifelogger" and it does exist, billed as a GoPro for everyday life. "Could this Small Stock be the Next GoPro?" (www.nasdaq.com/article/could-this-small-stock-be-the-next-gopro-cm413858); regarding microcelebrity, see Marwick and boyd (2011); see also Marwick (2013); boyd (2014).

13 As pointed out by Susan Elizabeth Ryan in her book *Garments of paradise* (2014).

14 An adage that began as a cartoon caption by Peter Steiner and published by *The New Yorker* on July 5, 1993.

15 "Richline, a leader in fine jewelry and the emerging category of Fine Wear Technology, announces the arrival of a new and robust blog, Wearable Style News" (see www.businesswire. com/news/home/20150812005333/en/Richline-Group-Introduces-Wearable-Style-News-Website#.VdIiks6fvdl).

References

Annechino, R. (2015) "The addiction algorithm: An interview with Natasha Dow Schüll." *Ethnography Matters*, February 9 (http://ethnographymatters. net/blog/2015/02/09/the-addiction-algorithm/).

Balsamo, A.M. (1996) *Technologies of the gendered body: Reading cyborg women.* Durham, NC: Duke University Press.

Basile, D. (2015) "5 pieces of wearable tech for meditation & mindfulness." *The Next Web* (http://thenextweb.com/lifehacks/2015/10/10/5-pieces-of-wearable-tech-for-meditation-mindfulness/#gref).

Bischof, J. (2014) "This dress makes people stand back, really." *The Wall Street Journal*, 27 May (www.wsj.com/articles/this-dress-makes-people-stand-back-really-1401237062).

Bolluyt, J. (2015) "When will we get wearable tech for women right?" *Cheat Sheet*, March 26 (www.cheatsheet.com/technology/when-will-we-get-wearable-tech-for-women-right.html/).

boyd, d. (2014) *It's complicated: The social lives of networked teens.* New Haven, CT: Yale University Press.

Campbell, A. (2014) "'Intimacy 2.0' dress turns transparent when you get sexually aroused (NSFW)." *The Huffington Post*, April 10 (www. huffingtonpost.com/2013/02/05/intimacy-20-dress-transparent-sexually-aroused_n_2622920.html).

Clough, P., K. Gregory, B. Haber, and J. Scannell (2015) "The datalogical turn." *Non-Representational Methodologies: Re-Envisioning Research* 12, 146.

Crawford, K. (2014) "When Fitbit is the expert witness." *The Atlantic*, Technology, November 19 (www.theatlantic.com/technology/archive/2014/11/when-fitbit-is-the-expert-witness/382936/).

Datamation (2014) "Will wearable technology benefit your workplace?" (www.datamation.com/print/http://www.datamation.com/mobile-wireless/will-wearable-technology-benefit-your-workplace.html).

Entwistle, J. (2015) *The fashioned body.* London, UK: Polity Press.

Fiore-Silfvast, B. and G. Neff (2013) "What we talk about when we talk data: Valences and the social performance of multiple metrics in digital health." *Ethnographic Praxis in Industry Conference Proceedings* 1, 74–87.

Fiore-Silfvast, B. and G. Neff (2015) "Communication, mediation, and the expectations of data: Data valences across health and wellness communities." *International Journal of Communication* 9, 1466–84.

Gilbert, D. (2014) "Wearable technology is still very much a gimmick." *International Business Times*, March 19 (www.ibtimes.co.uk/wearable-technology-still-very-much-gimmick-1440998).

Gregoire, C. (2013) "How technology is killing eye contact." *The Huffington Post*, September 28 (www.huffingtonpost.com/2013/09/28/why-youre-not-making-eye-_n_4002494.html).

Haraway, D. (1990) *Simians, cyborgs, and women: The reinvention of nature.* New York: Routledge.

Hathaway, J. (2014) "What is Gamergate, and why? An explainer for non-geeks." *Gawker*, October 10 (http://gawker.com/what-is-gamergate-and-why-an-explainer-for-non-geeks-1642909080).

Hayles, N.K. (1999) *How we became posthuman: Virtual bodies in cybernetics, literature, and informatics.* Chicago, IL: University of Chicago Press.

Hogle, L. (2005) "Enhancement and the body technologies." *Annual Review of Anthropology* 34, 695–716.

Horning, R. (2012) "The rise of the data self." *PopMatters*, January 25 (www.popmatters.com/post/153721-/).

Lupton, D. (2014) "Self-tracking modes: reflexive self-monitoring and data practices." SSM (http://ssm.com/abstract=2483549).

Lupton, D. (2015) "The cultural specificity of digital health technologies." *This Sociological Life*, January 25 (https://simplysociology.wordpress.com/2015/01/25/the-cultural-specificity-of-digital-health-technologies/).

McCann, J. and D. Bryson (eds) (2009) *Smart clothes and wearable technology.* Cambridge, UK: Elsevier.

Mangalindan, J.P. (2015) "Does Silicon Valley need its own fashion week?" Mashable.com (http://mashable.com/2015/05/12/silicon-valley-fashion-week/#e2AKUhqhAEqT).

Marwick, A. (2013) *Status update: Celebrity, publicity, and branding in the social media age.* New Haven, CT: Yale University Press.

Marwick, A. and d. boyd (2011) "To see and be seen: Celebrity practice on Twitter." *Convergence,* 17 (2), 139–58.

Nafus, D. and J. Sherman (2014) "Big data, big questions| This one does not go up to 11: the quantified self movement as an alternative big data practice." *International Journal of Communication* 16 June (8), 1784–94.

Nissenbaum, H. (2004) "Privacy as contextual integrity." *Washington Law Review* 79, 119.

Oatman-Stanford, H. (2013) "The killer mobile device for Victorian women." *Collectors Weekly*, May 23 (www.collectorsweekly.com/articles/the-killer-mobile-device-for-victorian-women/).

Quinn, B. (2010) *Textile futures: Fashion, design, technology.* London, UK: Berg Publishers.

Rakow, L.F. (1988) "Gendered technology, gendered practice." *Critical Studies in Mass Communication* (5) 1, 57–70.

Ryan, S.E. (2014) *Garments of paradise: Wearable discourse in the digital age.* Cambridge, MA: The MIT Press.

Sadre-Orafai, S. (2008) "Developing images: Race, language, and perception in fashion model casting." In E. Shinkle (ed) *Fashion as photograph: Viewing and reviewing fashion images* (pp 141–53). London, UK and New York: I.B. Tauris.

Steele, V. and J.D. Katz (2013) *A queer history of fashion: From the closet to the catwalk.* New Haven, CT: Yale University Press.

Svakja, H. (2014) "Anouk's new creation: Intel Edison based spider dress 2.0." *Make Magazine*, December 19 (http://makezine.com/2014/12/19/anouks-new-creation-the-spider-dress).

Taraska, J. (2015) "Smart bras aren't as stupid as they sound." *FastCoDesign*, May 22 (www.fastcodesign.com/3046580/wears/smart-bras-arent-as-stupid-as-they-sound).

Yahoo! Finance (2014) "Introducing SIREN: New technology transforms jewelry into a unique class of safety device – no smartphone required." *Market Wired*, September 11 (http://finance.yahoo.com/news/introducing-siren-technology-transforms-jewelry-181853618.html).

Wakeman, J. (2013) "Dear Microsoft: There are better ways to help women eat less than 'smart bras'." *The Guardian*, December 11 (www.theguardian.com/commentisfree/2013/dec/11/microsoft-smart-bra-emotional-overeating-ekg).

Wissinger, E. (2015) *This year's model: Fashion, media, and the making of glamour.* New York: NYU Press.

24

Queer Facebook? Digital sociality and queer theory

Benjamin Haber

I f Facebook were a person, he would be a liberal, well-intentioned, but often misguided straight ally. After attending some sensitivity seminars from GLAAD (Gay & Lesbian Alliance Against Defamation), he can now proudly recite 58 different ways of identifying one's gender. And although he still doesn't understand why the queers get so upset that he insists on using their legal names, he is promising to put some serious thought into how to make them feel more comfortable, because everyone knows that if queers don't come to your party, no one will.

In an era of "corporate personhood," this is not an outlandish metaphor. Contemporaneous with the Supreme Court's recognition of corporate religious belief,[1] companies are increasingly expected to have a distinctive "voice" and style and to be interpersonally accountable to consumers via the internet. Facebook has a public face[2] with a recognizable aesthetic, a particular affect, and a rather pushy philosophy. And while there is a blandly gay-friendly atmosphere that pervades his house, most people don't find Facebook particularly queer, in any sense of that word.[3] More commonly Facebook is seen as a rather straight-laced social network, a well-ordered, family-friendly, advertising machine, particularly in contrast with the unruly adolescent wilds of Myspace (RIP).

So why would I want to talk about Facebook specifically, and the architectures of digital sociality more generally as in some ways *queer*, a term and theory that I personally find deeply resonant, and one that has long been characterized by an epistemological queasiness towards incorporation? It is not because I particularly like Facebook – frankly, despite finding myself more or less[4] compulsively drawn to it, I would characterize my feelings as ambivalent at best. And while I find the recent proliferation of options for gender self-identification both intriguing and personally useful,[5] I don't share the fairly widespread enthusiasm by progressive journalists (McDonough, 2014) and LGBT activists (Ferraro, 2014) that saw this as a queer turn for Facebook. If nothing else, the pairing of the expansive array of boxes to check with a crackdown on the "real name policy" directed at drag queens, trans folks, and others (Rivas, 2015) should give pause to anyone suggesting that Facebook is promoting a queer political agenda. That said, I keep feeling a rather odd sense of recognition at some core queer ideas embedded in its technical logics that many scholars of social media have not sufficiently addressed.

In other words, behind the well-manicured "face" are surprisingly queer notions of social life and connection. The vast processes of algorithmic aggregating and disaggregating of words, movements, and images into potential desires and fragmented identities to be packaged and sold needs the breakdown of the nuclear family, a flexible notion of identity, and a more promiscuous sociality. Queer notions of relationality are built into the core of Facebook's central product: the mutability of identity[6] through the event and over time, the importance of non-familial community, a celebration of recognition and visibility as core strategies of political engagement, and a commitment to the non-textual, performative and indeterminate are all technically embedded in the platform.[7] I look at Facebook as a queered media particularly ripe for queer theoretical analysis.

In order to both develop a queer genealogy of social media and to demonstrate the utility of queer thought for reframing critical epistemologies of digital sociality I look to queer theory focusing on temporality and spatiality. Time and space have long been concepts through which the digital have been framed – that silicon networks reconfigure our relationship to time and space is banal to the point of cliché. Search Google Images for "internet" and ethereal lights still move around blue globes, semiotically demonstrating the ease by which media and capital move untethered to the temporal rhythms of the 20th century. To ground us in these fast-moving currents, we visualize our own digital engagements through both the language and graphics of space – homepages and the visual simplicity of our walled-off castles of apps allow us to feel in control of increasingly complex and distributed digital lives.

The queer literature on time and space has been particularly robust, and therefore my engagement here must remain introductory and suggestive. But in beginning to repurpose this literature for a new context, I hope to provoke in two ways. One, by connecting digital media to a longer social queer genealogy, I intend to unsettle the notion that digital sociality is either unprecedented or revolutionary. But just as important, I look to shake up queer orientations to digital media that remain at a comfortable critical distance. In the spirit of literature that argues that the politics of public space and urban development reveal larger insights into the conflicts and practices of queer people (Warner, 2002; Schulman, 2012; Hanhardt, 2013), I suggest that digital media has emerged as the central landscape for conflicts over queer politics and philosophy.

Queer media

My interest in queerness and the architecture of social media requires me to hold uncomfortable recognition in tension with critical inquiry. The roots of this recognition are manifold: LGBT-identified folks were enthusiastic early adopters of the social "community-minded" internet (Shaw, 1997: 136), and played critical roles in the early history of computing (Gaboury, 2013). Here, however, I'm more interested in the pre-digital legacy of queer thought and action, the many striking ways the history of queer sociality in public looks like the inspiration for the norms of social media. I reflect on that history through interdisciplinary scholarship highlighting, for example, the legacy of queer performance art that continues to inspire reflection on the importance of the affective and the ephemeral, as well as the unique relationship to public space that is the legacy of queer politics and sociality.

In terms of critical inquiry, I seek to continue the work of broadening queer theory's analytical usefulness beyond questions specifically related to sexual or gender identity. While the critical deconstruction of sexuality and gender remains an important part of the queer theoretical project, just as vital are interventions into relational form, political struggle, identity stability, and ontological interconnection. Indeed, the project of queer critique has broadened considerably in the last 20 years, to centralize the complex ways that marginality and violence assemble over time and in the event (Puar, 2007), to move away from the human subject (Giffney and Hird, 2008; Mortimer-Sandilands and Erickson, 2010) and to take up the weird ontologies and materialities of large-scale biological and technological systems.

For scholars working in the intersections of digital media and queer theory, Kara Keeling's "Queer OS" (2014) serves as sort of a rallying cry. Drawing from lineages that trace between technical and cultural logics, in particular Tara McPherson's work on the racial logics of Unix (2011), Keeling calls for a queering of the operating system, an interjection of queer "malfunction" and illegibility into the smoothly heteronormative predictability of interface. While Keeling's vision of:

> ... forging and facilitating uncommon, irrational, imaginative, and/ or unpredictable relationships between and among what currently are perceptible as living beings and the environment in the interest of creating value(s) that facilitate just relations (2014: 154)

is an imaginative and expansive vision of queer utopian world-building, my task with this chapter is smaller, and grounded in the queer interventions that might not look as uncommon or irrational as they once did.

For queer theory to maintain its critical usefulness, it can't get too comfortable in the verb form, moving around queering this and that, avoiding the uncomfortable housing of noun or even adjective stability. In allowing queerness the free reign to do the work of indeterminate critique, to always already slip away from incorporation, we miss recognizing the partial and problematic ways that queer ideas have ossified into form, have begun to resonate with ideologies and systems that continue to deny life and impose marginality on (some) queers.

To recognize that queerness can never be just a critique, a *read*, but an ethics of life and a patterned sociality, does not diminish its analytical value. Indeed, if the technical logics of digital social media have become somewhat queer, than the value of queer theory in undoing and remaking networked media is only heightened.

Space

Networked digital architectures have long been conceived through the language of physical, and particularly urban, space. From chatrooms to Myspace, spatial metaphors have felt natural and intuitive for many reasons; from user interface graphic designs that mimic the physical world to the ways the internet evokes travel by allowing us to extend ourselves as media throughout the world. The social qualities that Iris Marion Young argues are the "normative ideal" of city life – social differentiation without exclusion, variety, eroticism, and publicity (1990) – are arguably just as applicable to life on the internet (and are no doubt why both cities and the internet have long been LGBT havens). Unsurprisingly the metaphors of urban sociology have often been extended to virtual spaces.

One of the most prominent researchers writing about social media, danah boyd, regularly evokes the language and epistemological frameworks of urban sociology. We can see this most strikingly in danah boyd's essay titled "White flight in networked publics? How race and class shaped American teen engagement with Myspace and Facebook" (boyd, 2012). One of the rare works of social scientific analysis to receive widespread attention both on the internet and mainstream media, boyd's essay puts forth a theory to explain the mass defection of teen users from Myspace to Facebook.

Much of the popular sociological analysis of why Facebook overtook Myspace focused on the aesthetically cleaner look and reputedly safer atmosphere being provided. Indeed, boyd's use of urban sociological language of "white flight" is surely a provocative example of this kind of analysis. In short, boyd argues that the downfall of Myspace and the rise of Facebook can, at least in part, be explained by the perception of Myspace as a digital ghetto, with the attendant racial and class undertones that the term "ghetto" implies (boyd, 2012). Surely, by simply looking at the origins of Facebook as a "gated community," an exclusive network for Harvard, followed by other ivories and prestigious colleges, one can see the appeal of this metaphor. However, I believe it obscures more than it illuminates.

I should mention that boyd grants that borrowing the discourse of white flight "may appear to be a problematic overstatement," and cautions that her intention is not to "dismiss or devalue the historic tragedy that white racism brought to many cities" (2012: 218). Unfortunately, however, boyd's appropriation of the discourse of white flight is a framework that implicitly justifies the securitization of both cities and digital spaces. While boyd notes the fear that is central to the fleeing of Myspace (2012: 219), she allows this fear to haunt her essay untroubled, leaving its genealogy unexplored. For example, consider the following description of Myspace:

> Those teens whose family and friends were deeply enmeshed in the city of Myspace were less inclined to leave for the suburbs. Those who left the city often left their profiles unattended and they often fell into disrepair, covered in spam, a form of digital graffiti. This contributed to a sense of eeriness, but also hastened the departure of their neighbors. As Myspace failed to address these issues, spammers took over like street gangs. What resulted can be understood as a digital ghetto. (2012: 218–19)

While the point of this metaphor is to draw parallels between the failure of city governments and Myspace as a company to police its boundaries, it does this by tying the mechanized, commodity-shilling practice of companies and individuals trying to trick people into buying things with the often artistic and resistant practice of graffiti artists. More problematic, however, is what this move elides – we might ask, for example, why did cities fail to confront so-called "quality-of-life" crimes like graffiti? To compare the practices of a for-profit company like News Corporation (the one-time owner of Myspace) to the workings of city government implies both that cities can and should be run like a business, and more troublingly, that the struggles of urban centers was and is primarily a problem of management rather than a problem of resources. The notion that urban problems stem from mismanagement rather than the systematic denial of resources is a common tactic to obscure the racist and neoliberal logics that have shifted federal and state money away from cities, and indeed away from investments in the welfare state more generally. I could make a quite similar argument that problematizes the conflation of street gangs and spammers, but in the interest of space I will just mention how that, too, is a metaphor that "works" by erasing complicated political economies.

For me, Facebook is less like the suburbs than the historically gay Greenwich Village in New York City after its gentrification – still "urban," but aesthetically cleaner and selectively policed to make sure a straight tourist is not scandalized when they visit. Facebook, like New York City, sees gays as essential to their business model. Facebook's tool to add a rainbow hue to your profile picture is perhaps analogous to the advertising cities use to compete for select gay residents and tourists (Rushbrook, 2001) – a cheap, uncomplicated way to attract capital and liberal goodwill without fundamentally altering any power dynamics. Facebook/New York City markets queer social forms, but sanitized for heterosexual consumption. Stripped of sex and mutual aid, these forms are repackaged as fun, safe areas of consumption. Politicking is allowed, but few will notice unless you have the money, because visibility isn't free. The social and political life of gay bars, moved to Facebook threads, opens queers up to increasing amounts of heterosexual visibility, encouraging queer people to self-regulate their behavior and creating "something of a new and slightly more liberal panopticon" (Ingram, 1997: 50).

Like the classed and racialized specter of the riot that bubbles underneath the phenomenon of white flight from the city, boyd's analysis is haunted by the classed, raced, gendered, and queered specter of the child molester and the pervert, the affective backdrop of the idea of white flight from Myspace. This specter may have moved from public bathrooms (the famous tearoom trade of Laud Humphreys [1970]) and Jane Jacob's "pervert parks" (Ingram, 1997) to the social internet, but in both cases we see safety uncritically defined through unexplored heteronormativity. The problematic history in urban sociological literature that defines urban ideals through morally straight notions of publicness and safety have had an outsized effect on marginalized queers. And like the racialized and classed threats of urban violence that gave political cover to "slum clearance," urban renewal, and the "war on drugs," the new digital threats have pushed us all to the "safer," heavily policed streets of Facebook City, where Mayor Zuckerberg has moved far beyond broken-windows policing of "digital graffiti" and "spammer street gangs" to active collaboration with local police departments and the FBI. Without interrogating the complex political economies that entangle both spatial and digital histories of violence and exclusion, the language of white flight over-determines an under-developed phenomenon.

Queer theory might also help explain what for many commentators is the new and troubling phenomenon of over-sharing on social media. In sociology, social media has perhaps most frequently been talked about in terms of privacy, either the loss of it to companies or the loss of it among a public. The latter context often focuses on young people by porting Ervin Goffman's (1959) notion of "audience segregation" to the digital age in order to fret about what danah boyd calls "context collapse" – the inability to use different discourses in different social contexts. While boyd and Marwick (2011) highlight the conflict as a generational one between parents who worry about their kids posting too much in public and teenagers who value the freedom of social media, boyd also highlights what I would call a queer subtext to this anxiety:

> When adults think about privacy or private places, they often imagine the home as a private space. Yet, many of the teens that we interviewed rejected this, highlighting the ways in which home is not private for them. (2011: 3)

This notion of the private space of the home and the public space of the street has long been troubled by both feminist and queer theorists; as Michael Warner notes, "not all sexualities are public or private in the same way" (2002: 24). For LGBT folks, especially the young and otherwise marginalized, the opposition between the private space of the domestic and the public sphere is quite problematic. Public space is both more and less public for queer people, while the home can be both too private and not private enough. Warner, writing in the early days of the internet, argues that being in public had special relevance for queer identity formation and politics (2002). When private spaces were routinely raided, public sex and sociality broke heteronormative rules of public decorum. The recognition made possible through public "mutual witnessing and display" (Warner, 2002: 13) and "the making of a collective scene of disclosure" (2002: 63) has always been more essential to queers who have historically lacked access to both representational and affective mirrors in media.

Maybe people who post uncommon or irrational things on Facebook are not always just blissfully unaware of the potential consequences of a wider public? Maybe the thrill of that mutual witness and display – the cruisey, dangerous play of imagined and real engagement, of finding solidarity and reflection that one experiences when you post online – is actually worth the risk? In any case, it is notable that this queer desire for witness, display, and disclosure in public has arguably become a larger cultural phenomenon in the digital age. And doubtlessly this new digital access to the thrill of larger publics outside of the nuclear family already has and will continue to have profound effects on the nature of association, community, and identity.

Temporality

Facebook can have a confounding temporal rhythm, where hours feel like minutes, and a jumble of pasts and futures flatten themselves in a glowing row. While Facebook has provided a powerful aesthetic order and algorithmic definition to what and how we see what we see (driven no doubt in large part by monetization goals), company executives must also understand that the indeterminate and serendipitous affective and thematic messiness of the Newsfeed is a key reason we might scroll and flick out of time and out of mind.

When Facebook introduced the feature called Timeline, the latest version of the profile page, it appeared at least in part to be a further reassertion of clean narrative and linear time, a cleanly scrolling contrast to the messy heterogeneity of clicks and clicks (à la Myspace) that used to reign. The shift in metaphor – from wall to timeline – is like Facebook graduating from college. No longer is your profile page a dorm room wall for your friends to post media on; it is a living breathing archive of your life. José van Dijck argues that the Timeline is a shift in visual site aesthetics, from database to narrative, cajoling us to give up more data in the interest of self-promotion:

> You are asked to emphasize some events by inserting streamers and pictures, thus adding 'highlights' in retrospect. The month-by-month and later year-by-year ordering gives profiles the look and feel of a magazine. Your former profile suddenly becomes the center of a slick publication, with yourself as the protagonist. (van Dijck, 2013: 205)

And surely this analysis is right, as far as being a canny strategy for getting us to part with our media. We are doubtlessly in the age of the personal brand, and narrative is comforting and assuaging, making even unpleasant things seem fun (Massumi, 2008).

But while the magazine vision of Facebook might be the end of the year videos that Facebook algorithmically produces – media-heavy and scored with uplifting music evoking an insurance commercial – it's unlikely that many or even most users engage with the revamped profiles as if they were reading a slick publication. More likely, many users engage with the revamped profiles in a way that more closely resembles the attention-deficit, psychedelic time-scrambling experience of the Newsfeed, which remains the primary point of engagement on Facebook. Even with the slick veneer of Facebook blue, the Newsfeed has a queer sense of temporality, where untimely likes from a friend can unearth strange and serendipitous ghostly media at any moment. Of course, Facebook doesn't necessarily disrupt straight futurity and its "paradigmatic markers of life experience – namely, birth, marriage, reproduction, and death" (Halberstam, 2005: 2). But in flattening those markers on a plane of friend-curated media they are deemphasized and desacralized.

The decidedly non-linear collaging of styles, affects, media, and people is something unique perhaps to algorithmically organized social media. Even a site like Buzzfeed, which has become emblematic of a certain type of media styled and tailored to be "shared," and which is quite promiscuous in subject, is still affectively and stylistically quite homogeneous (typified perhaps by their trademarked round yellow interactive buttons that accompany each post: LOL, win, omg, cute, trashy, fail, wtf). While these queer juxtapositions can be motivating and exciting, they frequently agitate in less pleasant ways. We might think of the "people you may know" algorithm as the monstrous flip-side to the often delightful serendipity of that "like" that performatively unearths affective media. Here we might find dead relatives, bad hook-ups, high school "friends" – some people we certainly do *know* but would be better off not seeing or feeling, especially not randomly through a non-contextual experience of their media.

And indeed these time glitches can trigger not just personal traumas but misguided political movements. Tavia Nyong'o (2012) has suggested that the atemporal scrambling of social media deeply troubles queer online activism, allowing people to feel affectively involved while out of time and out of step with political action. Facebook frequently presents us with situations of "absolute minimum of knowledge provided with a sort of maximum of participation urged" (Nyong'o, 2012: 47), which leads Nyong'o to ask if "unreliability and affective intensity can enter into a negative feedback loop, such that the less reliable information we can glean, the more we attach ourselves to intensities that seem plausible insofar as they conform to imaginary structures" (2012: 49).

The atemporal mix of urgencies from now and then are an exhortation to join the fun, to post. Don't overthink it, Facebook whispers, tell me "What's on your mind?" Inserting ads of various modalities between the ephemera of user-created or curated content has become incredibly profitable for Facebook. Since their growth and continued profitability depends in large part on making us see more and more of those ads, Facebook would like you to have more friends, more intimacy, and for you to increasingly feel compelled to understand yourself through these non-familial attachments. Rob Horning has made similar arguments about the dating site OkCupid: since getting married and/or being monogamous takes you out of circulation on the site, it is in OkCupid's best interest to encourage a queerer orientation to dating and relationality (Horning, 2013).

The queer attachment to the ephemeral, to marginalia, and performance is in part the way these forms have tended to resist easy incorporation into the violence of capitalism and the military state. In discussing an image by Tony Just of a tearoom, Jose Muñoz describes it as lacking in epistemological framing, "performatively polyvalent," and carrying a "fundamental indeterminacy" (1996: 5–6). This image introduces his vision of performance studies:

> Central to performance scholarship is a queer impulse that intends to discuss an object whose ontology, in its inability to 'count' as a proper 'proof,' is profoundly queer. (1996: 6)

The tension at the heart of this queer vision of performance studies – to call attention to and discuss the ephemeral, that which typically would not be counted – is also a tension at the heart of data-hungry social media. Facebook's valuation is not based simply on that information that has typically "counted" in social science as empirically solid and methodologically grounded, but rather also on all those fleeting movements and moments that might get deleted or forgotten or seen by only one or a few but have likely already been aggregated and disaggregated into value.

Conclusion

Capitalism's metabolism for queer difference (Braidotti, 2007) has only proliferated in the digital age, where value accumulates in the thin slices of nimbly identified micro-populations. This digital surplus value is harvested through the steady creep of labor to ubiquity, where digital companies increasingly outsource their infrastructural building to the unpaid user in exchange for "free" access to a product designed to be compulsive (Terranova, 2000). The widespread adoption of the language of community has a dual function of making this labor seem non-exploitative and of creating new micro-populations, constantly in flux across space and time for maximum affective resonance and surplus potential.

Facebook's multi-billion dollar valuation stems from the company's ability to deeply integrate their architectures into over a billion people's everyday lives. Less a website or even a sprawling social authentication network,[8] the outsized attention and capital flowing to Facebook make it more akin to Fredric Jameson's notion of a cultural dominant (1991); a technology, an aesthetic, and a business model whose influence creeps into many aspects of everyday life. Facebook could be both a mascot and sieve for what Nigel Thrift has called "knowing capitalism", which he describes as when "capitalism began to intervene in, and make a business out of, thinking the everyday" (2005: 1).

If Facebook has algorithmically monetized some key queer insights about sociality, what does this mean for critique? While the queer political attachments to indeterminacy, ephemera, and a sort of promiscuous public sociability are certainly not the entirety of queer theorists' analytical and political contributions, the gradual folding in of these logics to strategies of capital should inspire reflection on how queer utopian and contrarian thought might need to once again be reimagined.

There is a too often untheorized sense that the social insights of queer theory are somehow always already deconstructive of their the potential for incorporation. If capitalism has historically needed the stable subject, then surely the queer critique of immutable identity is in conflict with the exploitations of capitalism? But what if Facebook doesn't need the uniform narrative of the timeline to serve you ads? What if the queer contingency is actually more profitable than uniform linearity? Jasbir Puar has already showed how queer narratives of transgression can be smoothly resonant with a biopolitical project of US/Western exceptionalism (2007: 21–4), so the incorporation of queer ideas into the logics of digital capitalism should come as no surprise.

In John d'Emilio's classic essay "Capitalism and gay identity" he argues that free labor capitalism was a prerequisite for sexual identity to flourish outside the traditional family form:

> Capitalism has created the material conditions for homosexual desire to express itself as a central component of some individuals lives; now, our political movements are changing consciousness, creating the ideological conditions that make it easier for people to make that choice. (1993: 474)

If gay identity is at least in part the result of capitalism needing to move production outside of the family, then perhaps there is a similar relationship between queerness and the need for capitalism to now move beyond the individual subject.

While I have focused on queer traditions of thinking sociality through space and time, contemporary queer thought on affect and the body also opens up fruitful avenues of inquiry, especially as Facebook moves beyond the stationary computer screen to more multimodal "hopes for a continuous body-machine attachment" (Clough, 2000: 70). How will sociology respond to a sociality that is measured through affective aggregates, messy locational tracings, and even the cursor hovers that Facebook logs (Rosenbush, 2013)? As digital capitalism grows weirder and more insidious, perhaps queer thought offers new avenues for critique and reflection.

Notes

[1] Famously in the 2014 *Burwell vs Hobby Lobby Stores, Inc.* decision.

[2] Notable perhaps is that in the early years of Facebook the logo was a man's face.

[3] The *Oxford English Dictionary* offers a variety of resonant definitions including, "conspicuously odd or peculiar," "to disconcert, perturb, unsettle," "to put out of order; to spoil," and of course, combined with theory, "an approach to social and cultural study which seeks to challenge or deconstruct traditional ideas of sexuality and gender."

[4] The "more or less" being critical, compulsion can not sustain itself with a consistent rhythm.

[5] The "gender questioning" option really spoke to me.

[6] Although not name. While I recognize that some have argued that Facebook, in contrast to my point here, makes you accountable to an identity, I see it as a platform where identity play not only happens but is in fact encouraged. Facebook's algorithms depend on moments of identity flux – call me this now, I'm engaged, I'm going back to school, I've stopped drinking, etc.

[7] While Facebook looks to speculatively reinvent itself as a company through acquisitions and research, in this chapter I focus on Facebook the social platform, rather than Facebook the corporate entity that includes WhatsApp, Oculus Rift and Instagram

[8] That is, "real name" login system for a vast variety of sites with social elements.

References

boyd, d. (2012) "White flight in networked publics? How race and class shaped American teen engagement with Myspace and Facebook." In L. Nakamura (ed) *Race after the internet* (pp 203–22). London, UK: Routledge.

boyd, d. and A.E. Marwick (2011) "Social privacy in networked publics: Teens' attitudes, practices, and strategies." In *"A Decade in Internet Time: Symposium on the Dynamics of the Internet and Society"*, September 22 (http://ssrn.com/abstract=1925128).

Braidotti, R. (2007) "Feminist epistemology after postmodernism: Critiquing science, technology and globalisation." *Interdisciplinary Science Reviews* 32 (1), 65–74.

Clough, P.T. (2000) *Autoaffection: Unconscious thought in the age of technology.* Minneapolis, MN: University of Minnesota Press.

d'Emilio, J. (1993) "Capitalism and gay identity." In H. Abelove, M.A. Barale, and D.M. Halperin (eds) *The lesbian and gay studies reader* (pp 467–76). New York: Routledge.

Ferraro, R. (2014) "Facebook introduces custom gender field to allow users to more accurately reflect who they are." *GLAAD*. February 13 (www.glaad.org/blog/facebook-introduces-custom-gender-field-allow-users-more-accurately-reflect-who-they-are).

Gaboury, J. (2013) "A queer history of computing." *Rhizome.org*, February 19 (http://rhizome.org/editorial/2013/feb/19/queer-computing-1/).

Giffney, N. and M.J. Hird (2008) *Queering the non/human.* Aldershot, UK: Ashgate Publishing, Ltd.

Goffman, E. (1959) *The presentation of self in everyday life* (www.worldcat.org/title/presentation-of-self-in-everyday-life/oclc/256298).

Halberstam, J. (2005) *In a queer time and place: Transgender bodies, subcultural lives.* New York: NYU Press.

Hanhardt, C.B. (2013) *Safe space: Gay neighborhood history and the politics of violence.* Durham, NC: Duke University Press Books.

Horning, R. (2013) "Single servings." *The New Inquiry*, February 12 (http://thenewinquiry.com/essays/single-servings/).

Humphreys, L. (1970) *Tearoom trade: A study of homosexual encounters in public places.* London: Duckworth.

Ingram, G.B. (1997) "Marginality and the landscapes of erotic alien(n)ations." In G.B. Ingram, A.-M. Bouthillette, and Y. Retter (eds) *Queers in space: Communities, public places, sites of resistance* (pp 22–54). Seattle, WA: Bay Press.

Jameson, F. (1991) *Postmodernism, or, The cultural logic of late capitalism.* Durham, NC: Duke University Press.

Keeling, K. (2014) "Queer OS." *Cinema Journal* 53 (2), 152–57.

Kramer, A.D.I., J.E. Guillory, and J.T. Hancock (2014) "Experimental evidence of massive-scale emotional contagion through social networks." *Proceedings of the National Academy of Sciences* 111 (24), 8788–90.

McDonough, K. (2016) "Facebook introduces LGBTQ-inclusive gender identity options for users." *Salon*, February 13 (www.salon.com/2014/02/13/facebook_introduces_lgbtq_inclusive_gender_identity_options_for_users/).

McPherson, T. (2011) "US operating systems at mid-century." In L. Nakamura and P. Chow-White (eds) *Race after the internet* (pp 21–37). London, UK: Routledge.

Massumi, B. (2008) "The thinking-feeling of what happens." *INFLeXions* 1, May.

Mortimer-Sandilands, C. and B. Erickson (2010) *Queer ecologies: Sex, nature, politics, desire.* Bloomington, IN: Indiana University Press.

Muñoz, J.E. (1996) "Ephemera as evidence: Introductory notes to queer acts." *Women & Performance: A Journal of Feminist Theory* 8 (2), 5–16.

Nash, C.J. and K. Browne (2012) *Queer methods and methodologies: Intersecting queer theories and social science research.* Aldershot, UK: Ashgate Publishing, Ltd.

Nyong'o, T. (2012) "Queer Africa and the fantasy of virtual participation." *WSQ: Women's Studies Quarterly* 40 (1–2), 40–63.

Puar, J.K. (2007) *Terrorist assemblages: Homonationalism in queer times.* Durham, NC: Duke University Press.

Rivas, J. (2015) "The drag queen revolt against Facebook has reached a new level." *Fusion*, June 1 (http://fusion.net/story/142529/the-drag-queen-revolt-against-facebook-has-reached-a-new-level/).

Rosenbush, S. (2013) "Facebook tests software to track your cursor on screen." *The Wall Street Journal*, October 30 (http://blogs.wsj.com/cio/2013/10/30/facebook-considers-vast-increase-in-data-collection/).

Rushbrook, D. (2001) "Cities, queer space, and the cosmopolitan tourist." *GLQ: A Journal of Lesbian and Gay Studies* 8 (1–2), 183–206.

Schulman, S. (2012) *The gentrification of the mind: Witness to a lost imagination.* Berkeley, CA: University of California Press.

Shaw, D.F. (1997) "Gay men and computer communication: A discourse of sex and identity in cyberspace." *Virtual Culture: Identity and Communication in Cybersociety*, 133–45.

Terranova, T. (2000) "Free labor: Producing culture for the digital economy." *Social Text* 18 (2), 33–58.

Thrift, N. (2005) *Knowing capitalism.* London, UK: Sage.

van Dijck, J. (2013) "'You have one identity': Performing the self on Facebook and LinkedIn." *Media, Culture & Society* 35 (2), 199–215.

Warner, M. (2002) *Publics and counterpublics.* New York, Cambridge, MA: Zone Books.

Young, I.M. (1990) *Justice and the politics of difference.* Princeton, NJ: Princeton University Press.

25

The Ms. Dewey "experience:" Technoculture, gender, and race

Miriam E. Sweeney

> Hey, if you can get inside of your computer, you can do whatever you want to me. (Ms. Dewey, Microsoft "Ms. Dewey" search engine)

A decade ago, in 2006, Microsoft debuted what they termed an "experiential" search engine called "Ms. Dewey." Ms. Dewey was a sleek Flash-based,[1] interactive interface overlaid onto Microsoft's Windows Live Search platform (the predecessor to Microsoft's Bing search product). A functioning search engine from its launch in 2006 through January 2009, the site featured pre-filmed clips of actress Janina Gavankar as the titular character, represented in the interface as a sexy librarian/corporate assistant. Gavankar as Ms. Dewey performs search results by offering wisecracks and commentary in response to users' search queries, sometimes incorporating elaborate skits with props. The multimedia performance of search results is foregrounded in the interface, while a secondary (more standard) listing of page-ranked search results appears in a transparent box overlaid over the right third of the screen (see Figure 25.1).

Ms. Dewey was created as one prong of a $500 million dollar multimedia marketing campaign that Microsoft launched in 2006 (Lohr, 2006). Advertising agency McCann Erickson collaborated with the digital content marketing firm Evolution Bureau San Francisco on the online advertising for the Windows Live Search product. As part of the campaign's "introductory phase to build awareness" they designed an edgy, tongue-in-cheek viral marketing campaign featuring a sexy librarian to "sex up search" (Natividad, 2006). Ms. Dewey's design marked a departure from previous minimalist search interface design conventions (typified by Google), merging search with immersive and interactive digital media features popularly used in gaming and advertising. Ms. Dewey was not overtly branded and advertised as a Microsoft product; its mysterious origin and over-the-top interactive experiences were tactics for creating excitement and viral sharing through users' social networks.

Figure 25.1: Ms. Dewey with search term "information architecture" entered

Source: http://findability.org/archives/000157.php

The (then) senior vice president of Central Marketing for Microsoft, Mich Mathews, described the vision of Ms. Dewey at the Microsoft Strategic Account Summit in 2007 in terms of *experience*:

> Another area that we've been experimenting with is sites [sic] where exposure and experience are the very same thing. Now, Ms. Dewey is an interesting example of this, because it's an experiential site that features a very chatty and very attractive interactive search assistant. As you can see here, you get the search results, but you also get it with a little attitude. (Mathews, 2007)

Mathews' framing of experience in the interface draws on well-established gendered and racialized scripts attributed to the Ms. Dewey character, namely being "chatty," "very attractive," and having "attitude." These comments suggest that gender and race were designed as central features of the interface, rather than as bugs in the system. This raises interesting questions about how gender and race are encoded in the interface, and how ideologies about gender, race, and technology shape the search process. This study explores these questions by conducting an interface analysis on the semiotic (representational) and material (technical) aspects of the interface.

This study applies what I term a "critical feminist informatics" approach to examine the intersection of identity, ideology, and interaction between people and information and communication technologies (ICTs). This approach enables an investigation of intersectional gendered and racialized ideologies in technology artifacts and their associated practices, in this case Ms. Dewey and information search. The findings reveal that "experience" in the Ms. Dewey interface is technoculturally defined by specific gendered and racial logics that afford users the opportunity to search the interface in ways that validate specific sexist and racist cultural narratives.

Data

The data for this study consists of user conversations about Ms. Dewey on blogs, forums, tech sites, and message boards, as well fan-archived audio and video clips of Ms. Dewey with associated comment threads. The unit of analysis is the topical content of the webpage in the form of a post, article, comment, or uploaded media object, generated by a given author. Websites in this study were collected on October 12, 2012 using the meta-search engine DevonAgent to aggregate crawling power of major search engines. The search term "Ms. Dewey" returned 105 results that were evaluated individually against inclusion criteria for the data set. In total, the data set consists of 85 distinct webpages, which included a total of 20 archived media objects (audio and video files of Ms. Dewey in action) and countless user comments. From this data, 100 out of the approximately 600 total scripted responses performed by the Ms. Dewey character were documented, and 88 accounts of discrete search terms linked to associated Ms. Dewey responses. There is not a strict one-to-one linkage of search terms to Ms. Dewey responses; rather some search queries are shown to generate multiple, consistent, responses from the Ms. Dewey character.

Interface analysis method

The approach to interface analysis in this study is critical in orientation, focused on the complex relationships between technological artifacts and the social/cultural contexts through which they are produced and attain meaning. This positions both the material aspects of technology, as well as the interpretive (semiotic) elements, as socially constructed. Hardware, software, content, representations, user practices, and interpretation are all the outcome of complex social processes shaped by cultural values and ideologies. I performed a "close reading" on both the material and semiotic aspects of the interface. For the purposes of this study, the semiotic aspects of the interface refer to the visual themes, web design, and representation of the Ms. Dewey character, while the material aspects of the interface refer to the search mechanics and discursive interaction between linked search queries and scripted responses. Drawing from a hybrid toolkit of techniques from visual studies, critical discourse analysis, this project explores what I term the "technological pragmatics," or the affordances, of the interface. Hutchby argues that affordances constrain the writing and reading of texts to a range of possible interpretations, allowing researchers to empirically analyse constraints and effects in different technological formations (2001: 447). This suggests that while users of Ms. Dewey may have a range of interpretations and functions available to them when they are engaging with the interface, that range is not unlimited. They could not, for instance, make the Ms. Dewey character do anything that had not already been scripted and filmed. This approach is useful because it makes clear that human intervention, and thus value sets, are present both in shaping the design and constraining the use and interpretation of technologies.

This articulation of interface analysis is influenced by Brock's (2009) critical technocultural discourse analysis (CTDA), a bifurcated approach that "combines insight into the cultural biases encoded within technologies alongside insights into the technological biases encoded within the culture of the users" (Brock, 2011: 2). CTDA, in turn, is influenced by critical discourse analysis in its focus on making connections between "texts" to larger social systems of power and domination (van Dijk, 1993; Wodak, 2001; Fairclough, 2004). CTDA borrows heavily from Wodak's (2001) "discourse-historical approach" that uses the hermeneutic circle to interrogate the interplay of texts and sociocultural contexts in historical analysis (Sweeney and Brock, 2015). CTDA similarly explores the "technocultural mediation of discursive actions embodied as online discourse and digital interfaces" (Sweeney and Brock, 2015: 3). Thus, CTDA may be understood as the combination of interface analysis with user discourse analysis, using critical cultural frameworks. For example, Brock's (2011) study of Resident Evil 5 employs CTDA to perform an interface analysis of the video game using critical race theory as a framework through which to explore gameplay, world construction, and representation in the game alongside a discourse analysis of comments from gamers about the game on a gaming website. Similarly, this project uses critical race and feminist theory frameworks to inform an interface analysis of Ms. Dewey in conjunction with a discourse analysis of user commentary about their experiences using the search engine. This enables a richer, more holistic investigation of the ways in which cultural ideologies are embedded in technologies and associated user practices.

Using CTDA as an approach, Ms. Dewey is situated as a textual object, locating the search engine as a site of power where both dominant and resistive discourses about gender, race, and technology circulate and are integral in shaping user experience with the interface and the search process. Ms. Dewey's search responses were analysed thematically using critical discourse analysis techniques (van Dijk, 1993; Wodak, 2001; Fairclough, 2004), with race and gender serving as the sensitizing frameworks. From this iterative process, seven major thematic categories of content and performance in the search results emerged: (1) overtly sexual, (2) sexually suggestive, (3) refusal or rebuke of undesired sexual attention, (4) disparaging (directed at user), (5) racialized, (6) pop culture, (7) miscellaneous (filler). In this chapter, I primarily discuss the implications of the construction of the first five thematic categories as they most explicitly factor in the construction of gendered and racialized discourses within the interface.

CTDA, an approach for highlighting the cultural mediation of ICTs, has clear applications for visual media and visual sociology scholars who are working with digital media artifacts and ICTs as their objects of study. As Pauwels (2010) notes, visual research methods are often not fully adapted for the complexity of multimodal constructions present on internet websites, mobile applications, and other forms of new media technologies. An integrated toolkit for studying internet artifacts that accounts for aesthetic, materials, and technical aspects may offer a foothold for visual researchers in mapping multimodal visual artifacts.

Ms. Dewey as technoculture

Ms. Dewey is a technocultural site where ideologies of gender, race, and technology are fused, shaping all aspects of the design, use, and meaning of the search engine. Borrowing from Pacey's (1983) tripartite definition of technology, Ms. Dewey is comprised of technical, social, and cultural aspects. The technical aspects include the search algorithm that ranks results, the Flash platform for handling multimedia applications, the database that links search terms to the performative Ms. Dewey responses, and various internet protocols. Social aspects of Ms. Dewey include user discourse about Ms. Dewey in the form of reviews, blogs, fan sites, and the practice of archiving and sharing favorite Ms. Dewey clips on YouTube and message boards. Social dimensions also include the people and politics involved with designing Ms. Dewey; its provenance as a Microsoft product, concerns with Microsoft's brand image, and the use of viral marketing to disseminate the product. Finally, cultural aspects of Ms. Dewey include beliefs about technology, gender, and race that shape the design of the search engine.

Table 25.1: The seven major thematic categories for Ms. Dewey's search responses

Categories	Description	Examples
Overtly sexual	Involving explicit reference to a sexual act (eg, sex, kissing) or being naked, performing erotically (eg, pretending to striptease), or the use of a prop that is itself explicitly sexual in nature (eg, condoms)	"Personally, I like nothing better than to curl up next to a fire with a good book." *Pulls out a copy of the Kama Sutra and pretends to read* "Safety first." *Holds a motorcycle helmet and pack of condoms*
Sexually suggestive	Flirtatious in demeanor (eg, blowing kisses, being coy with the camera), often involving innuendo in either spoken or visual content (eg, posing with props in suggestive ways)	"Girls, don't let him fool you, sometimes it IS the size of the gun." *Posing with gun prop* "I'd help you out, but I'm all tied up!" *She turns around revealing her wrists bound with rope*
Refusal or rebuke of undesired sexual attention	Responses directed at the user framed in a way that exhibit disgust, refusal, and rebukes of unwanted sexual attention	"There aren't even farm animals that would do that thing, what makes you think I would?" "Something tells me this isn't the first time you tried to sway a computer screen with this 'vocabulary.' Take off the clothes, yes, all of them. Yes, your socks too." *Presses button.* "Now you're screwed"
Disparaging (directed at user)	Ad hominem attacks directed at the user including berating the choice of search terms entered and jokes cracked at the user's expense. Ranges from playful to acerbic in tone	"For God's sake search something interesting" "You know, it's searches like that that just scream 'beat me up and take my lunch money'" "It's not easy to find someone who will love you for you. And I did mean specifically you."
Racialized	Responses that draw on racially coded linguistic patterns, words, and physical gestures to enact stereotypical performances of (particularly) urban Blackness	*In default Dewey voice.* "Ah yes, hip hop. A culture defined as by rapping, dj-ing, graffiti and breakdancing. Or, as I like to say," *Switches to racially coded performance (ie, leans back, neck rolling)* "Spittin', scratchin', spraying, and spinnin'." *Resumes default Dewey posture in a ready-to-assist stance, hands folded in front of her*
Pop culture	References to pop culture results including plot lines, characters, catch phrases from movies, song lyrics, sports figures, video games, and other Microsoft products	"Shine on you crazy diamond." [Pink Floyd] *Puts the One Ring on and off her finger until she gets bored and throws it away.* [Lord of the Rings] "Of course I took the blue pill..." [The Matrix]
Miscellaneous (filler)	Responses that are generic in content, low context, and are highly interchangeable with potential application for filler dialogue	"Now that is a fascinating topic. Frankly, I don't think people spend enough time talking about it." "Been there done that."

The tripartite aspects overlap and shape each other in complicated ways, but there is benefit in trying to tease them apart. Particularly the cultural, or ideological, aspects of technology often remain invisible, although arguably it is our beliefs about technology that need the most examining since they are foundational in constructing the mythos of systems of power and privilege. Ideologies of gender and race are bound up with beliefs about technology, creating what Dinerstein (2006) refers to as the technocultural matrix. Dinerstein (2006) identifies six key characteristics of the technocultural matrix as: progress, religion, whiteness, modernity, masculinity, and the future. Thus, technoculture incorporates a set of interrelated narratives that create a paradigm for understanding the past as well as a potential future, centered on a kind of technological religiosity that Dinerstein claims is deeply rooted in the American cultural imagination. The benefit of technoculture as a lens is that it exposes how ideologies of gender and race are inherent in the conditions of modernity, capitalism, and technoscience. Viewing Ms. Dewey through the technocultural matrix brings seemingly disparate narratives of gender, race, and technology into alignment in service of viewing search as a deeply ideological process and site of social power.

Postmodern interface design

A close read of the design of the interface reveals that Ms. Dewey breaks with the modernist design tradition that remains "one of the dominant discourses within taste in our present times" (Thorlacious, 2007: 71), and drives a great deal of web design conventions. Modernist web design conventions are typified by Google's now ubiquitous single search box on a blank, white page. The modernist mottos "form follows function,"[2] "less is more," and "truth to materials" have been widely appropriated by web designers and information architects, giving way to the veneration of minimalist, "clean" design tactics. Ms. Dewey deviates drastically from these conventions by offering up a visually saturated, interactive, multimedia interface that more closely embodies postmodern design aesthetics. Postmodern aesthetics incorporate "experiential" design, functioning as a taste discourse with "aesthetic values that favor the eclectic, multi-sensory, experience-oriented design" (Thorlacious, 2007: 72). This break in design convention is important for how it disrupts assumptions about the search process for users, making explicit ideologies about gender, race, and technology that are otherwise obscured, literally, by design.

Design aesthetics are laden with ideologies that shape interpretation of the form. For instance, the minimalism of Google can be read as an affordance that frames the search process as informational, unbiased, and scientific. The simple, sparse design works to obscure the complexity of the interface, making the results appear purely scientific and data-driven, rather than intermediated through complex social, economic, and cultural processes (Vaidhyanathan 2011).[3] Research shows that the majority of searching (80 percent) is informational in nature (Jansen et al, 2007), and as such, users do not expect to be surprised or confronted by their search experience. They approach information search expecting neutral, accurate, trustworthy, authoritative, and objective information. Minimalism is a design feature that actively shapes and reinforces these expectations about both the search process and the search results.

As in other search engines, the algorithmic mechanics of search in Ms. Dewey are hidden from the user. The genre conventions of search posit search as a one-way process where the user plugs in a query and the technology spits back an answer. Technically speaking, Ms. Dewey and Google work on the same mechanisms. However, the postmodern aesthetics of Ms. Dewey make the ideological aspects of the search experience obvious while they remain purposefully hidden in Google's design. As such users are encouraged to view Ms. Dewey's results as a discursive, rather than informational, interaction. Whereas Google actively tries to hide the human (ideological) intermediation of their results, Ms. Dewey acts the part of intermediary flamboyantly and unapologetically. Further, Ms. Dewey is not represented as even attempting to proffer unbiased search results. The Ms. Dewey character makes judgments about the user's tastes and abilities in her responses, for instance, a search for a band returns the response, "I've checked out your MP3 collection. Let's just say you have a lot to answer for. Either you tell your friends or I will." These discursive search results actively disrupt the user expectations for neutral, scientific presentation of search results that are usually part of the information search experience.

Visual themes in the interface

Although the web design of Ms. Dewey is representative of a postmodern tradition, the visual themes depicted in the interface draw heavily on modern architectural and design features. Ms. Dewey is positioned standing behind a black, reflective desk in an interior high-rise office space. Behind her, high-rise buildings and a curving monorail-like transportation infrastructure are visible through the windows. The color palette is neutral, consisting of black and gray tones with concrete and brushed metal textures. The background scene shifts, sometimes depicting the city at night, and at other times during the day.

Modernism refers to a set of cultural practices and their associated ideologies and institutions, while modernity denotes a "socio-historical moment" defined by the economic, technological, sociological, and experiential consequences of the rise of Western industrial capitalism (Wolff, 2000: 36). Barker (2005: 444) describes modernity as marked by urbanization, rationalization, institutionalization, and forms of surveillance. Characteristics of modernist architecture include minimalism, strong horizontal and vertical lines, a neutral color palette, use of industrial-produced materials (steel, concrete, etc), and the exposure of infrastructural features. The cityscape depicted in the interface, the exposed transportation infrastructure, the neutral color scheme, and the industrial materials used throughout the scene are in alignment with the tradition of architectural modernism.

Kaika and Swyngedouw describe urban architecture and networks as "materially and culturally supporting and enacting an ideology of progress" (2000: 122). Progress, a key characteristic of technoculture, is often formulated as moving in a linear, upward trajectory towards a goal of maximum social and economic efficiency. The narrative of progress, through its techno–utopian formations, is linked to white ideologies of control and power, and "the Western tendency to universalize its own perspective" (Dinerstein, 2006: 571). Dinerstein links whiteness with progress through the technocultural matrix, noting that "technology as an abstract concept functions as a white mythology" (2006: 570).

Part of the utopian vision of progress is its post–racial imagination that envisions a future free of hierarchy, social injustice, poverty, and war, usually as a result of technological interventions. Technology is key in this formulation, often centered as the key to unlocking this man-made utopia. The visual themes of the setting of the interface mirror these desires through modern architecture and common symbols of modernity.

Modernism, like modernity, is gendered male (Wolff, 2000: 37). Leslie and Reimer describe how the characteristics of modernism are constructed "in opposition to sets of binary 'Others' – ornamentation, decoration, craft, and ephemerality – which typically are further mapped onto a masculine/feminine distinction" (2003: 295). (Or, as Braham [1999] observes, perhaps they are deemed scientific and objective because they are masculine.) The binary that modernism is oppositional to casts ornamentation, embellishment, and applied colors as feminine qualities replete with irrationality, subjectivity, and intuition (Braham, 1999: 13). These qualities are aligned with artificiality (culture), bound up in "taste" instead of the ostensibly "naturally" occurring scientific "truth" of modern aesthetics.

Similarly, modernism is racialized, encoding whiteness as both a default and ideal. Whiteness encompasses a set of ideologies, beliefs, and structures that position those who have white privilege as superior, rational, and innately deserving of power (Dyer, 1997). Like masculinity, whiteness functions hegemonically as a ubiquitous, invisible status quo, the "norm" that positions anything or anyone outside of whiteness as "Other," and therefore strange. The gendered binary that Leslie and Reimer (2003) describe maps neatly onto the racialized binary as well. Thus whiteness is also manifest in the values of functionality and simplicity, rendering ornamentation, a vibrant color palette, and flashy imagery as "exotic" and Other.

By this reading, Ms. Dewey is visually surrounded by the symbolic apparatus of white, Western, masculine power powerfully symbolized by the urban scene, modernist architecture, and the corporatized setting. By this logic, we might assume that the search character would more closely represent hegemonic depictions of scientific rationality, namely a white male figure. Yet, Ms. Dewey is represented as a woman of color, albeit light-skinned, and of ambiguous ethnic and racial identity. Ostensibly, her position in the center of the interface places Ms. Dewey in the seat of authority. She is, after all, the embodiment of search, performing information retrieval as if she is accessing her own memory. On the surface, this seems like a position of empowerment. Certainly at first blush this representation can be read as a counter-narrative that position women and people of color as inherently technological instead of at the margins or deficit. However, a deeper read suggests that placing a brown woman at the center of the interface should be read as consistent with the symbolic technocultural logic we have been considering, rather than aberrant to it. Ms. Dewey's representation as a brown woman can be read as an affordance that facilitates accessibility to the interface through a technique of manageability that rests on cultural assumptions of brown womanhood.

Winner (1996: 68) notes that a common strategy to promote usability of technology involves obscuring complexity in design:

> A commonly chosen design strategy was to conceal the complexity of devices, systems, and social arrangements and to make them appear simple and manageable. Thus, for example, streamlining and other varieties of shiny metal styling were adopted to complex, technical mechanisms within soothing, attractive surfaces.

Here, the Ms. Dewey character is purposefully designed as the "soothing, attractive" surface that obscures the complexity of the search engine. While Google conceals complexity and promotes manageability through minimal features and an appeal to science, the Ms. Dewey interface achieves the same goals by placing a brown woman at the center of a space otherwise coded by whiteness and masculinity. This positioning creates a panoptic level of surveillance on Ms. Dewey that is telematic from the user perspective, reinforced by the glass windows behind her. This invokes the cultural position of brown women's bodies as sites of control and domination under white supremacy. Ms. Dewey is positioned visually and symbolically in the interface is ways consistent with white Western culture's desire to control brown bodies using technology as an extension and mechanism of domination. Simply put, Ms. Dewey is represented in a way that makes controlling her seem desirable and familiar. Gender and race in the design of the Ms. Dewey character function as affordances that shape interaction with the interface in terms of manageability.

Interaction in the interface

Interaction in the interface is shaped through the discursive interplay of the search term and search result. A single search box provides the imperative prompt "Ms. Dewey, Tell Me How." The search box changed over time, rewording the prompt to "Ms. Dewey, Just Tell Me," and adding a button besides "Search" called "Best of Dewey" that called up selected popular (often funny or provocative) scripted results. This later version of the interface also included an option below the search bar to "Share this SEARCH with a FRIEND," a feature that supports the viral sharing of the interface as part of the marketing imperative.

The Ms. Dewey character directly engages users arriving at the website, usually through an introductory sequence where she "talks to" the user. The introductory sequences rotate so that different clips are featured at random, ranging from simple vignettes of Ms. Dewey standing, ready to assist, to other more elaborate sequences involving props and sets. For example, one introductory vignette depicts Ms. Dewey fixing a motorcycle with a wrench (see Figure 25.2). She turns, noticing the searcher, and says:

> Oh – sorry! I thought I had more time. She's a beauty isn't she. Laughs. This kind of power and control, it's ... it's intoxicating. I think that's the word I was looking for, but perhaps not. But enough about my 32nd love – what are you passionate about?

This interaction is representative of how Ms. Dewey addresses the user. She looks into the camera, addressing the searcher directly using the pronoun "you" and occasionally leans forward to tap on the glass as if to get the user's attention. Ms. Dewey has an assertive demeanor, speaking in an authoritative (and sometimes pejorative) manner (that is, "For God's sake, search something interesting").

All of Ms. Dewey's search results are linked to sets of search terms and criteria. The coding of search results and search terms revealed that Ms. Dewey provides *culturally relevant*, rather than informationally relevant, results. That is, Ms. Dewey's responses serve more as cultural referents *about* the search, rather than an informational answer to the query. Some of these results are extremely specific to the user's search terms, while other responses are more generic serving as filler to handle search queries that are unique, unpredictable, or simply not suited to a more specific response. For instance, based on user reports of their search experience, it seems that math and science-oriented search terms comprise a criteria set that consistently retrieve a clip of Ms. Dewey in a lab coat with a beaker of colored liquid.

However, searches for *The Matrix* (the 1999 movie by the Wachowski siblings) retrieved Ms. Dewey saying, "Of course I took the blue pill," a specific reference to a line from the movie. An example of a filler response is Ms.

Dewey saying, "There is nothing more exciting to me" which is non-specific and plays frequently. Another specific response for the search term "Kama Sutra" retrieves Ms. Dewey pulling out a copy of the book and pretending to read it with an interested look on her face. Slightly more subtly, a search for "blow jobs" retrieves Ms. Dewey peeling and eating a banana while looking at the camera, which can be taken in context as innuendo for the sexual act. While it is not possible to determine the specific search criteria surrounding the results, it seems clear that many of the responses are keyed closely to the search terms they appear with.

Figure 25.2: Ms. Dewey introductory sequence with motorcycle

Source: www.mydigitallife.info/sexy-ms-dewey-search-engine-assistant/

The sexy search engine

The discursive framing of search performed as interactions with the Ms. Dewey character shapes the search process in a number of explicitly gendered ways, particularly in the hyper-sexualization of the interface. Both sexual and sexually suggestive search results are linked to both overtly sexual search terms and also to non-sexual search terms. For instance, Ms. Dewey's search result "safety first" (see Figure 25.3), which depicts her holding a motorcycle helmet and a pack of condoms, is generated both by the search term "sex toy" as well as the search term "terrorism."[4] When sexual terms return culturally relevant sexual results, this has the effect of reinforcing the discursive interaction and interface as inherently sexualized. In the case where the search term was not overtly sexual, Ms. Dewey's generation of a sexual response serves to reframe the interaction as sexual when it may not have initially been the user's intent. The user is encouraged in both cases to sexualize the interaction.

Figure 25.3: Ms. Dewey holding condoms and a helmet

Source: URL: http://www.podcastingnews.com/content/2006/12/microsoft-bob-just-got-kinky/

This is an experience that happens in standard search engines like Google as well. Most people have had the experience of searching for what they thought to be an innocent term only to accidently hit upon a minefield of pornography. Noble's (2012) research on the pornification of Black women and girls' identity in Google is an excellent demonstration of the ways different identities become commodified in search in exactly this way. In her work, searching for the term "Black girls" retrieves pornography of Black women instead of resources about and for Black girls' identity and cultural community. Noble's research highlights a cognitive dissonance in search, revealing a cultural clash in the interface between a user searching for positive portrayals of Black girls and women, and an algorithmic structure that prioritizes what Feagin (2010) terms a "white racial frame."

In Ms. Dewey this kind of dissonance may be lessened due to the foregrounding of the intermediary. Google's presentation of (ostensibly) neutral and scientific search results obscures these cultural failures, with the result that the user is led to believe the fault is with them and their searching skills rather than with the underlying cultural logic of the technological system. This individuation of fault is consistent with neoliberal logics that veil structural features of power and privilege. Ms. Dewey's presentation of search results as embodied performance intermediated by brown womanhood foregrounds the cultural aspects of the interface, making it clear that there are ideological mechanisms at play that the user can exploit for their pleasure.

Ms. Dewey was designed according to sexual logics that fundamentally define her as an object of sexual desire and require her to respond to requests for sexual attention. Coding for the study revealed that Ms. Dewey has search results that are sexually responsive (positive) to queries for sexual attention/actions, indulging them, as well as sexually dismissive (negative) responses. For instance, the search query term "you strip" generates both indulgent and dismissive responses:

> "OK, Just this once," as she dances a little, lifting her shirt as if simulating the start of a striptease.
> "I'm sorry, did you think it was girldoeswhateveryouwant.com?"

Whether or not the response she gives welcomes or rejects sexual attention, it is clear that Ms. Dewey is designed to respond to sexually explicit search terms as if they are requests for her to *do* something related to the topic rather than requests for her to retrieve information *about* an aspect of the topic.

Whereas users may enter search terms seeking pornography in Google, the Ms. Dewey interface encourages users to view her as the pornographic object instead.

The explicit search term "fellatio," for instance, returns Ms. Dewey saying, "I tried that with three close friends once, let's just say my memoirs will fetch a million." Her response automatically translates the request for information into a request for her to take action. Most problematic is that Ms. Dewey, on giving a sexually dismissive result to a search term, may, on another round of searching, give a sexually responsive result. The striptease result for "you strip" above was reportedly given after the user searched "you strip" three times previously and returned sexually dismissive results. This pattern of rebuffing advances, then capitulating after several persistent rounds of searches, is a pattern reported by users in regards to other search responses as well. The design parameters that have Ms. Dewey change a sexual rebuff into sexual obedience creates a crisis of consent in the interface, reinforcing the no–really–means–yes mentality that is characteristic of rape culture under patriarchy.

The design parameters that value randomness over reliability are strategic. This design makes use of the variable rewards schedule, a behavior reinforcement model described by B.F. Skinner in the 1950s. The same search term entered in Ms. Dewey does not reliably generate the same results, creating a search experience that remains novel for the user. Random rewards structures are the basis of many games and marketing designs because they hold attention of the user/player so well. The effect of randomly generated rewards is an intensifying of desire in the user who becomes more compulsive in their pursuit of the reward, in this case, hitting upon culturally specific responses. Ms. Dewey's sexualized and racialized responses hold the ultimate reward: the promise of titillation and pleasure. Analysis of user's online comments verified that a large part of Ms. Dewey fandom is based on sharing tips and tricks for generating culturally based results. The theme of these conversations was overwhelmingly sexual, hoping to find the magic query that will make Ms. Dewey behave pornographically.

Both interface designs included a "mute" option that turned the sound of Ms. Dewey's dialogue off. Not only is Ms. Dewey designed to provide novel experiences for the user so they remain constantly engaged, she demands constant attention so long as the web browser remains open. If the user takes too long to enter a search term, Ms. Dewey demonstrates that she is annoyed or bored by tapping on the glass, chiding them, "Hellooooo ... type something here!" If the website is idle in the user's browser, even hidden in a tab, Ms. Dewey displays agitation through impatient postures and facial expressions, feigning exasperation that intensifies as time passes. The message is clear, Microsoft intends the interface to be constantly engaged with and not hidden, unused in a tab in the browser window. The effects of this create a gendered dynamic of "nagging" the user to constantly pay attention to them.

Besides demanding attention from the user, Ms. Dewey at times makes insulting or disparaging comments specifically aimed at the user's searching skills ("Are you just letting your dog type now?"), or their sexual desirability ("It's not easy to find someone who will love you for you. And I did mean specifically you"). In user descriptions, these provocations inspired users to resort to gendered name calling (that is, "whore") as retaliation in the interface. Another option is to make use of the "mute" feature in the interface, which turns off the audio in the interface so that the user can continue searching without hearing Ms. Dewey speak. This does not stop the Ms. Dewey character from performing search results, however. The effect of using this feature in the interface is that Ms. Dewey becomes further objectified as a silent, performing woman on the screen. Thus Ms. Dewey somewhat represents an idealized virtual girlfriend, one that is available as a site of sexual pleasure, controllable, and mutable when the novelty wears thin.

Ms. Dewey's racialized discourses

The American actress Janina Gavankar who portrays Ms. Dewey has South Asian heritage and is outspoken in her self-identification as an Indian woman. In an interview with *Nirali* magazine in 2006, right at the time of Ms. Dewey's debut, Gavankar stated that she enjoyed playing Ms. Dewey as an "ethnically ambiguous" character (Nguyen, 2006). Gavankar's light skin and mixed features create the "ambiguity" that arguably gives the Ms. Dewey character more space for racial identity shifting than another actress would have had in this role. Racial identity shifting was used purposefully as a design affordance in the interface, enabling a range of racialized discourses to take place.

The Ms. Dewey character is theatrical in her performance of search results. She tries on different personas, sometimes affecting accents to support her character (for example, a cowboy accent in a Western gunfight scene), donning costumes (a lab coat), and wielding any number of props. Two scenes in the data set involve Ms. Dewey switching into racially coded personas that are characterized in this study as stereotypical performances of urban blackness. For these responses, Ms. Dewey switches her default style of speech, which is characterized by formal wording and professional cadences. Instead, she moves into highly stylized performances that linguistically invoke culturally black, urban vernacular accompanied by finger wagging gestures, neck rolling, and posturing:

> *In default Dewey voice.* "I only have one thing to say to that."
> *Switches to racially coded performance (that is, finger wagging, neck rolling, posturing)* "No, goldtooth, ghetto-fabulous mutha–fucker *BEEP* steps to this piece of [ass] *BEEP*, just because you pickin' some *BEEP* video, you gotta be out of yo' muthaf*ckin' mind to think yo' rental bling *BEEP*, and your big booty ass [whore] *BEEP* crumping to your [bullshit] *BEEP* track is going to turn me out, [shit] *BEEP* no, uh-uh, you can't [fuck] *BEEP* with me dawg!" *Resumes default Dewey posture in a ready-to-assist stance, hands folded in front of her.*

The content of this performance features an angry Ms. Dewey confronting the user through a barrage of expletives partially bleeped out (but still audible). She uses racially coded words, referring to herself as "ghetto-fabulous," referring to another woman as a "big booty ass [whore]." This performance draws heavily on the negative Sapphire caricature of black women as angry, emasculating, combative, and confrontational.[5] Tellingly, the search terms that generate this result include: "whore," "booty," "ghetto," and "yo mama" – all search terms that signify derogatory terms for women, racialized sexual objectifications, and racialized insults. This response is the most circulated Ms. Dewey search result in terms of fan-archived media, and was the most referenced result in user internet conversations.

The second racially coded response has Ms. Dewey defining "hip-hop":

> *In default Dewey voice.* "Ah yes, hip hop. A culture defined as by rapping, dj-ing, graffiti and breakdancing. Or, as I like to say," *Switches to racially coded performance (that is, leans back, neck rolling.)* "Spittin', scratchin', spraying', and spinnin'." *Resumes default Dewey posture in a ready-to-assist stance, hands folded in front of her.*

The search term "hardcore" is linked to this response in addition to the more obvious "hip hop." While this example does not have the blatant Sapphire quality to it, it does stand out as a linguistic performance invoking stereotypical blackness, paired with a description of hip hop, a black cultural form.

These results suggest that one "experience" to be had in the interface is the consumption of Otherness through stereotyping. Users are rewarded for searching on negatively racially coded search terms with a stereotyped portrayal of blackness, validating racist cultural narratives. hooks describes this commodification of the Other as successful because "it is offered as a new delight, more intense, more satisfying than normal ways of doing and feeling" (hooks, 1992: 21). This exploration is an affirmation of the power and privilege of whiteness and rests on a post-racial (colorblind) ideology that Gallagher (2003: 25) explains,

> ... acknowledges race while disregarding racial hierarchy by taking racially coded styles and products and reducing these symbols to commodities or experiences that whites and racial minorities can purchase and share.

Race, in the colorblind paradigm, features as a cultural symbol that can be sold and worn, instead of as a structural system of entrenched inequality. In terms of Ms. Dewey, this means that users can transform themselves through the "experience" of "consuming" the Other through search, transforming search explicitly into a site of domination.

Ms. Dewey's performances of blackness may otherwise be interpreted as an affordance that enables a discourse of urban coolness as a means to lend buzz and "street cred" to the otherwise corporatized image of the Microsoft brand. hooks (1992) describes how the commoditized white fantasy projection of blackness circulates with cash value in the global marketplace. Ms. Dewey's "ambiguous ethnicity" acts as an affordance that allows her to move in and out of identities that validate different stereotypes for the searcher. Eglash (2002) traces the ways that primitivist and Orientialist racism shapes cultural narratives about innate technological ability, mapping the Asian nerd stereotype as the counterpart to the anti-nerd black hipster, with "whiteness" occupying a position of idealized balance between the two. Both stereotypes are rooted in the cultural ideology of white supremacy and masculinity that attributes hyper-intellectualism to Asians and hyper-sexualization to Africans.

Gavankar's casting as Ms. Dewey can be read as a design choice that allows her to move along this continuum, shifting her racial identity performance to more closely align with the perceived ideological requirements encoded in the search terms. However, Ms. Dewey complicates Eglash's continuum by performing a racialized femininity, a subject position that frames all her movements in the interface as inherently sexualized. Through this lens, the interplay of user search terms and Ms. Dewey's responses create a discourse that affirms cultural expectations of masculinity and white privilege.

Conclusion

All search engines are shaped by ideologies of gender and race, although the aesthetic conventions of modernist web design effectively obscure the intermediation of cultural values in search results, leveraging the "scientific" presentation of results in minimalistic interfaces. Ms. Dewey's post-modern design foregrounds ideologies of gender and race in the interface by embodying search as a brown woman.

This study has shown that gender and race act as affordances for using the interface, framing the kinds of "experiences" that users are able to have in terms of hegemonic masculinity and whiteness. Instead of framing search as an instrumental process of neutral information retrieval, the search process becomes an ideological experiment where the user is encouraged to search in ways that validate their beliefs about the sexual availability of brown womanhood, asserting and reaffirming notions of masculinity and white privilege. According to this logic, Ms. Dewey's representation as a brown woman constitutes a technique of manageability that renders her controllable, unthreatening, and sexually available. Her light skin and features construct her as "ethnically ambiguous", enabling her to shift her racial identity performance to satisfy racist stereotypes for users.

In these ways, the interface is fashioned as a site of control and domination, where pleasure is tied to the telematic abjection of the Ms. Dewey character. This suggests that not only are gender and race are important infrastructural features of Ms. Dewey, but that ideologies of gender and race are integral for users in interpreting the technology, informing their use and practice.

Notes

[1] Flash is a multimedia and software platform frequently used to embed and stream video and audio and interactive media content to websites. Formerly a Macromedia product, currently Flash is owned, developed, and distributed by Adobe.

[2] Coined by Sullivan (1896).

[3] For further discussion on how search is intermediated through social, cultural, and economic process, see Introna and Nissenbaum (2000); Inside Google (2010); Noble (2013), and Sweeney (2013).

[4] "Terrorism" is arguably a sexualized term, loaded with imagery of penetration, rape, as well as full of racialized connotations. For the purposes of this analysis, "terrorism" was not coded as an *overtly* sexual term.

[5] Sapphire is a negative stereotype that serves as a social control mechanism to mock and silence black women who dare to vocalize dissent or dissatisfaction with their social condition. See the Sapphire stereotype definition provided by the Jim Crow Museum of Racist Memorabilia, available at www.ferris.edu/jimcrow/sapphire/

References

Barker, C. (2005) *Cultural studies: Theory and practice*. London, UK: Sage.

Braham, W.W. (1999) "A wall of books: The gender of natural colors in modern architecture." *Journal of Architectural Education* 53 (1), 4–14.

Brock, A. (2009) "Life on the wire: Deconstructing race on the internet." *Information, Communication & Society* 12 (3), 344–63.

Brock, A. (2011) "Beyond the pale: The Blackbird web browser's critical reception." *New Media & Society* 13, 1–19.

Dinerstein, J. (2006) "Technology and its discontents: On the verge of the posthuman." *American Quarterly* 58 (3), 569–95.

Dyer, R. (1997) *White*. London, UK: Routledge.

Eglash, R. (2002) "Race, sex, and nerds: From Black geeks to Asian American hipsters." *Social Text* 71 20 (2), 49–64.

Fairclough, N. (2004) "Critical discourse analysis." In M.S. Lewis-Beck, A. Bryman, and T.F. Liao (eds) *The Sage encyclopedia of social science research methods* (pp 215–17). Thousand Oaks, CA: Sage.

Feagin, J.R. (2010) *The white racial frame: Centuries of racial framing and counter-framing*. New York: Routledge.

Gallagher, C.A. (2003) "Color-blind privilege: The social and political functions of erasing the color line in post race America." *Race Gender and Class* 10 (4), 22–37.

hooks, b. (1992) *Black looks: Race and representation*. Boston, MA: South End Press.

Hutchby, I. (2001) "Technologies, texts and affordances." *Sociology* 35 (2), 441–56.

Inside Google (2010) "Traffic report: How Google is squeezing out competitors and muscling into new markets." June 2 (www.consumerwatchdog.org/resources/TrafficStudy-Google.pdf).

Introna, L.D. and H. Nissenbaum (2000) "Shaping the web: Why the politics of search engines matters." *The Information Society* 16 (3), 169–85.

Jansen, B.J., D.L. Booth, and A. Spink (2007) "Determining the user intent of web search engine queries." In *Proceedings of the 16th International Conference on World Wide Web*, pp 1149–50.

Kaika, M. and E. Swyngedouw (2000) "Fetishizing the modern city: The phantasmagoria of urban technological networks." *International Journal of Urban and Regional Research* 24 (1), 120–38.

Leslie, D. and S. Reimer (2003) "Gender, modern design, and home consumption." *Environment and Planning D: Society and Space* 21 (3), 293–16.

Lohr, S. (2006) "Microsoft reveals plan to take business from IBM." *The New York Times*, March 17 (www.nytimes.com/2006/03/17/technology/17soft.html).

Mathews, M. (2007) "Transcript of remarks by Mich Mathews, Senior Vice President, Central Marketing, Microsoft Corporation." Presented at the Microsoft Strategic Account Summit, May 9, Seattle, WA (http://news.microsoft.com/speeches/mich-mathews-microsoft-strategic-account-summit-2007/).

Natividad, A. (2006) "Ms. Dewey sexes up search." *Adrants.com*, October 18 (www.adrants.com/2006/10/ms-dewey-sexes-up-search.php).

Nguyen, B. (2006) "Ask Janina." *Nirali*, November 6 (http://niralimagazine. com/2006/11/ask-janina/).

Noble, S.U. (2012) "Searching for Black girls: Old traditions in new media." PhD dissertation. Graduate School of Library and Information Science, University of Illinois, Urbana-Champaign.

Noble, S.U. (2013) "Google search: Hyper-visibility as a means of rendering black women and girls invisible." *InVisible Culture: An Electronic Journal for Visual Culture* 19 (http://ivc.lib.rochester.edu/google-search-hyper-visibility-as-a-means-of-rendering-black-women-and-girls-invisible/)

Pacey, A. (1983) *The culture of technology.* Cambridge, MA: The MIT Press.

Sullivan, L.H. (1896) "The tall office building artistically considered." *Lippincott's Magazine*, March (http://ocw.mit.edu/courses/civil-and-environmental-engineering/1-012-introduction-to-civil-engineering-design-spring-2002/readings/the-tall-office-building-artistically-considered/).

Sweeney, M. (2013) "Not just a pretty (inter)face: A critical analysis of Microsoft's 'Ms. Dewey'." Doctoral dissertation (http://hdl.handle. net/2142/46617).

Sweeney, M.E. and A. Brock (2014) "Critical informatics: New methods and practices." *Proceedings of the American Society for Information Science and Technology* 51 (1), 1–8.

Pauwels, L. (2010) "Visual sociology reframed: An analytical synthesis and discussion of visual methods in social and cultural research." *Sociological Methods & Research* 38 (4), 545–81.

Thorlacius, L. (2007) "The role of aesthetics in web design." *Nordicom Review* 28 (1), 63–76.

Vaidhyanathan, S. (2011) *The Googlization of everything: (And why we should worry).* Berkeley, CA: University of California Press.

van Dijk, T.A. (1993) "Principles of critical discourse analysis." *Discourse & Society* 4 (2), 249–83.

Winner, L. (1996) "Who will we be in cyberspace?" *The Information Society* 12 (1), 63–72.

Wodak, R. (2001) "The discourse-historical approach." In R. Wodak and M. Meyer (eds) *Methods of critical discourse analysis* (pp 63–93). London, UK: Sage.

Wolff, J. (2000) "The feminine in modern art: Benjamin, Simmel and the gender of modernity." *Theory, Culture & Society* 17 (6), 33–53.

26

The Emperor's new data clothes: Implications of "nudity" as a racialized and gendered metaphor in discourse on personal digital data

Yuliya Grinberg

> Everyone said, loud enough for the others to hear: 'Look at the Emperor's new clothes. They're beautiful!' What a marvelous train! And the colors! The colors of that beautiful fabric! I have never seen anything like it in my life! (*The Emperor's new clothes* by Hans Christian Andersen)

Naked truths

Hans Christian Andersen's classic tale, *The Emperor's new clothes*, has long allegorized "truth" as a scene of unveiling (Robbins, 2003). In the story, the king, convinced by two swindlers that they had actually weaved him marvelous clothes, sets out before his kingdom naked. When the moment of truth arrives the courtiers recognize the king's nudity, but dare not acknowledge it. The royal suspects his indecent exposure, but pretends not to notice. The charade would continue indefinitely were it not for a young boy who bursts the bubble of illusion, declaring, "But the king is naked!"

This rhetorical convention has traveled well, and the figure of nudity as the dominant trope of discovery is now frequently marshalled to frame our relationship with digital data. For example, speaking on the value of digital record keeping, Susannah Fox (2014), a researcher at the Pew Research Center, had recently compared collecting data about the self to standing "naked in front of the mirror." Mirroring the commonplace assertion about digital data's revelatory capacity, she observes: "that's the beauty and the peril of data isn't it? To see ourselves as we really are" (Fox, 2014). While this speech was delivered at a private, invite-only event – in fact, a Public Health Symposium convened by the organizers of the Quantified Self to discuss ways in which publicly collected personal information could become a platform for scientific discovery – Fox had later transcribed the speech for readers of her blog and posted it under a telling title: "Secret questions, naked truths."

Fox's statements are hardly unique. At every turn we are saturated in a technical and visual vocabulary that repeatedly conflates computerized tracking with the state of undress. A ballooning consumer market is increasingly trained at capturing what we are often told is the "raw" output of our life experiences. And promotional images featuring fit and scantily clad models from companies that design wearable technology – rings, armbands, watches, and sensors that are worn on the body – condition contemporary sensibilities to appraise digital data as the premier technology of exposure. The feeling of transparency is further heightened when device makers frame their functionality in relationship to boundary-breaking devices such as the X-ray or CT scan. Meanwhile, the proponents of "open" science, education, government, as well as advocates of privacy compound the sense of exposure facilitated by this new technology by regularly announcing the impending delivery of a transparent society, one in which every gesture, movement, and affect will be available for transcription and transmission along digital lines. Popular author Patrick Tucker (2014) therefore warns us to expect *The naked future* while the online campaign, *NakedCitizens*, collaboratively developed by European privacy groups, similarly teaches its followers to understand one's vulnerability in a digital climate in corporeal terms. Summarizing the voyeuristic digital gaze, one commentator at a recent technology function I attended observed: "It used to be [said] that everything that could be digital will be digital. Now it is 'everything that can be known will be known.'" This cultural discourse regularly sensationalizes digital data's revelatory capacity while maintaining nudity as the master metaphor of truth.

Second skin, social skin

This chapter examines the way the trope of nudity has been used in recent popular culture to frame the operation of digital data produced by an expanding range of computer, wearable, and sensor technology. At times these devices are compared to scalpels that can slice bodies open and pull back the skin to reveal the "data" lying within. At other times they are equated with X-ray technology that effectively render the body and the self translucent. These tropes persistently suggest that we see data as a *second skin* of sorts that runs just under the body's surface, which digital devices faithfully help to unveil. As a result, personal data is too often presented as a material, even as a natural, substance that can be abstracted from social and material entanglements and seen to offer a more accurate and unobstructed view of any one person. Difference exists, but only in the sense that data is generated by different people.

A growing body of work has begun to make the opposite argument, however, suggesting that digital technology does not exist outside of what we do or how we act as people (Crawford and boyd, 2012; Jurgenson, 2014). Leveraging the broader critique of technology by the social sciences, scholars increasingly contend that digital technology, too, has to be seen as contributing to social life and as socially constituted. Here, I extend this analytical position to consider the social stakes and entanglements of personal data increasingly produced by a range of web applications and digital devices. In particular, by considering the trope of nudity as it relates to digital data generated about the self, this chapter hopes to offer a more nuanced understanding of the way data shapes an understanding of our lives and bodies, and vise versa, the way a particular view of bodies affects our perception of personal data sets. Nudity therefore is not simply a rhetorical device. Claims about the forms of nudity produced by digital data have important social purchase on the way data is socialized and interpreted. Meanwhile, the history that has forged nudity as a significant emblem of discovery continues to tacitly impact the way we make sense of digital data sets. I retrace some of this history to think about the way people are unevenly exposed and made vulnerable through data's association with nudity.

In thinking about the relationship between naked bodies and personal data, this chapter offers a way to understand selfhood and embodiment facilitated by expanding personal data sets in a broader sense; to ask not only about the way bodies are differently articulated through data, but about the types of bodies that mediate our relationship to data in the first place. By examining the biases that are recuperated and re-inscribed when digital data is interpreting as a technology of disrobing, the goal of this analysis is to contribute to a more socially sensitive view of the work of digital data sets. Rather than as *second skin*, I suggest that we think of data as "*social skin*" (Turner, 1980/2012), that is, as something that never fully bares but always already bears the imprint of social forces.

The transparent machine

Decades of post-modern and post-colonial critique have already offered important ways to problematize nudity as a sign of discovery. It is in this spirit that Derrida (1975) had suggested that we see the disrobing of the king in

Andersen's tale as a fantasy rather than as an allegory of truth. Like the dream function in Freudian psychoanalytics, the naked body for Derrida is a fetish object. It acts both as a substitute and as an index of the desire for a salacious and satisfying reveal. In *The Emperor's new clothes*, the nakedness of the king can therefore be understood as an impotent symbol: it exposes both the longing and the inability to satisfy desire.

We could likewise see the trope of nudity mobilized by Andersen as a specific historical artifact. Published in 1837 at the height of the Industrial Revolution, *The Emperor's new clothes* gained prominence in the same period as a new regime of truth – what Lorrain Daston and Peter Galison (2010) have called "mechanical objectivity"– coalesced on the heels of technological innovations like the X-ray, the lithograph, and ultimately, the photo camera. Mechanical objectivity rendered the observer an imperfect and a hopelessly flawed witness, while it endowed technology with the capacity to strip away convention or bias so as to cut through personal prejudice and directly access brute, naked facts. It is here that the figure of the nude body as a symbol of truth can be said to have acquired its contemporary salience. The nude body, cleared of obstacles and open for discovery, emerged as a sign of knowledge made transparent by technology.

In Andersen's folktale, the forthcoming child operates as the central trope of this mechanized form of discovery. Indeed, the boy's inopportune and inappropriate outburst only testifies to his own innocence before the facts. Given his age, he is assumed to be blissfully unaware of the social pressure that may have otherwise clouded his judgment. Like the machine, he appears unencumbered by social conventions and is thus able to see without obstacles. At the story's end, the king's indecent exposure reflects the boy's own youthful frankness. In folktales of the period, this is also the role occupied by the court jester or the town simpleton whose supposed social or cognitive limitations become compensated by reciprocal prophetic qualities. Critics are already beginning to note that the contemporary discourse on digital data – particularly the popular conceptualizations of "big data" – as that which is nostalgically understood to offer a photographic negative of reality, stages a marked return to this former positivism where digital data is seen to increasingly embody the ideal of the neutral by-stander, the disinterested observer able to see things plainly, for what they really are (Crawford and boyd, 2012; Jurgenson, 2014).

The nature of nakedness

The appeal to nudity goes beyond the rhetoric of technosocial positivism and objectivity, however. That it is specifically the nude body that can stand in as the master metaphor of truth and discovery itself demands to be unpacked. The nude, of course, is not simply an organic or universal property, but also a cultural and political category,[1] and it is essential to think critically about the "naked" truths produced by digital data. The relationship between truth as nature exposed and the naked body is particularly important to trace in a Western context that had historically romanticized female and native bodies as sites of pre-social authenticity, purity, and nature.

It is well documented, for instance, that the era of Western colonialism brought about an expanded understanding of worldly difference. Along with an intensified encounter with non-Western cultures, the period had also triggered a crisis of the "other" as Europe struggled to make sense of the cultural plurality it encountered. Evolutionary anthropology, arriving on the heels of Darwinian theories of evolution, helped to resolve this cognitive dissonance. Placing humanity on a continuum of development, it sought to rationalize and organize social difference. Locating Western culture at the apex of this map of progress, people of other places and spaces became variously scattered along the timeline's linear axis, distributed based on an imagined transition from the state of nature to the Westernized state of culture.[2] The conceptualization of "race" as a natural distinguishing mark between people belongs to this history (Luxemberg, 1913/2004).

In the same period, physiognomy and anthropometry were thought to contain essential truths, leading scientists like Jules Etienne Marey (1895) and Eadweard Muybridge (1887/1955) to turn to photography as a confessional medium through which the body could bare testimony to itself. In these late 19th-century experiments, the native body was often fetishized as a site of uncorrupted purity and authenticity. At the same time, the bewildered encounter between "primitive" man and machine became a favorite thematic of early cinematography (Rony, 1996: 104). The nude body of native populations was stripped of culture or history so as to be consumed and objectified as a reified time capsule from the past. In essentializing the native body *as* a naked one that is not marked by culture or history, a new relationship between nakedness and truth had become forged. The naked body as a symbol of truth continues to exert its influence today, but one must consider the colonial history from which such associations were sourced. Today, when we continue to naturalize data as a technology of disrobing, it is this history that becomes both activated and masked.

Gendered perspectives

In official marketing materials male models frequently demonstrate the denuding work of data. Muscular male bodies help endorse the message of data collection as a form of self-empowerment. More broadly, this gendered presentation often reflects an understanding of whom digital tracking devices are imagined to be for. One of the reasons this still remains so, I'm often told, is that despite the availability of increasingly more compact sensors, electronics are still not small enough to fit onto devices that can accommodate the dimensions of a woman's body. The reason that the male body is seen as the minimal requirement to meet, however, also reflects a sexist belief that to design for a man is to design for the general type, whereas to design for a woman is to design for her specific needs, say, by developing a device to keep track of periods. Much like the cockpit in early airplanes (Johnson, 2009), or the first airbags installed in automobiles (Allison, 2001), which were initially designed with the male body in mind, the cultural expectation of the "typical" wearable or sensor user shapes the way these technologies are taken up and by whom.

Female bodies nevertheless figure prominently in the more informal discourse on personal data, although less as agentive subjects of data collection and more as emblems of data and the labor of tracking itself. For instance, the naked female body often trades as an especially salient and salacious symbol of data's capacity to reveal. Consider, for instance, the moral panic that was set off in late 2014 by a spate of celebrity nude photo leaks. Private photos were released online when hackers accessed iCloud accounts of nearly 100 women including those of well-known celebrities like Jennifer Lawrence and Kate Uptown. The leak triggered a wave of anxiety around data privacy. The unwittingly exposed bodies of female actresses, however, also scandalized, sexualized, and made literal digital data's imputed power to disrobe. Arguments for privacy were made by pointing to these naked bodies as if to say that greater security was required because of the intimate ways in which data exposes us. In other words, pictures of women in the nude have come to allegorize the danger of personal data itself.

It is significant that gender mediated this public discourse on data and vulnerability. The average user was, in effect, placed in the position of the unsuspecting woman at risk of exposing her most private parts. Indeed, such rhetoric needs to be seen in context of its cultural other: pictures of the male phallus that, on the contrary, are seen to be willfully manufactured and consciously distributed that have recently become a pop culture meme.

Commenting on digital data and privacy, an art project – *X-pose* – unintentionally made a similar connection between female bodies and data. The project centered on a bodice that goes from opaque to translucent with every message that the wearer sends online. Although intended as a broader commentary on digital privacy, Whitney Erin Boesel (2014) draws attention to the critical role gender plays in this work. It sources its effectiveness, she suggests, precisely from an affiliation with female nudity: "If viewed in a cultural vacuum, the response is, 'So what. Her data is showing', and so her breasts are showing," Boesel writes. "If we exist the hypothetical cultural vacuum and re-enter contemporary US society (both artists live in New York), it becomes intelligible. We know that showing data is 'bad' because showing breasts is 'bad'" (Boesel, 2014). As Boesel points out, that the female body so fluidly telegraphs the possibilities and dangers of digital disrobing has a lot to do with a patriarchal view that treats female nudity as obscene and even dangerous.

Data and female bodies are linked in other ways as well. In particular, data is naturalized as "raw" in connection with women's bodies. In the context of the celebrity photo leaks as well as the art project *X-pose*, data's ability to expose one's self is taken as a matter of fact, without calling into question its effectiveness as an instrument of disclosure. Exemplified by the female nude, data is in fact fetishized as one's very nature exposed. What is framed as obscene is then precisely the acuity with which data is seen to cut to the quick. This equivalence is not surprising if we consider the long history where female biology has been essentialized as bearing metonymic proximity to nature. Sherry Ortner (1974) had famously articulated, for example, the social bifurcation of the sexes that both maintains the male/female binary as the normative type, and aligns men with culture and women with an unruly and undisciplined nature. Anne Balsamo (1995: 9) likewise noted that "coded as the cultural sign of the 'natural', the 'sexual,' and the 'reproductive' ... the womb ... continues to signify female gender in a way that reinforces and essentialist identity for the female body as the maternal body." In other words, it is not simply "breasts" that connect data and women, but the cultural role female bodies and female biology occupy more broadly. In our cultural imaginary, data is like a woman.

That data is interpreted in terms of women's bodies is also made evident through the language of liquidity. Flows, leaks, streams, oceans, rivers, after all, form the popular vocabulary of data. There are many ways, of course, to parse this metaphor. But it is also important to pay attention to the suggestively gendered tonality of this vocabulary. These terms speak of data as a proto-natural substance that fills objects and bodies, and, like menstruation, is always leaking out of bounds. A promotional video recently made by IBM expresses the colloquial understanding of the productive capacities of bodies (human and otherwise), for which IBM proposes a means of collection and capture: "The planet itself, natural systems, human systems, physical objects," IBM announces "have always generated an enormous amount of data but we didn't used to be able to hear it, to see it, to capture it. Now we can" (IBM, 2010). Here data is not simply something that people create, but is treated as a natural emission that never stays in place. That is part of the danger and the threat of data as conceived both by the nude celebrity photo leaks and *X-pose*. As symbolic bodily excretion, data is seen as matter out of place giving rise, not unlike menstruation, to anxieties over its proper purification and containment (Douglas, 2002). This is a notion further given voice when data scientists frame their work in terms of waste management by comparing data processing and "cleaning" to janitorial labor.

More broadly, digital data gathering is gendered when the work of keeping track of intimate lives is itself conceived as feminized[3] or maternal labor. Witness the rise of female assistants that have become a common fixture on many digital devices. In addition to the more gender ambiguous *Siri*, today we also have overtly feminized tools like *Alexa*, the new artificial intelligence program from Amazon, *Amy Ingram*, an electronic secretary, and the numerous navigation software platforms that suggest a female voice as a default setting. This is an association that partly inspired the popular Hollywood movie *Her*. In the film, the main character somewhat incredulously enters into a romantic relationship with his female digital aid, played by Scarlett Johansen.

Male proper names are not absent. IBM's *Watson*, so-called after the IBM visionary Thomas Watson – information circulating around the globe and radiating spears that look like short spiky hair – is in itself worth paying attention to for the gravitas it implies. Watson, a male proper name, connotes a different type of labor. Whereas female proper names characterize clerical work, *Watson*, a name that redoubles with Sherlock Holmes' associations, implies intellect and rationality, meant to highlight the program's critical thinking abilities. In marketing materials IBM cultivates this connections, frequently presenting Watson as an executive or a scientist's right hand, even suggesting at times that Watson's superior intelligence supersedes the capabilities of any one human. A widely publicized event even featured Watson engaged in a modern version of the Turing test when the computer competed (and won) a round of Jeopardy. The technology used for both *Watson* and *Alexa* is not distinct. Both are based on machine learning and natural language processing. They are differentiated simply at the level of gendered names. While *Watson* conveys executive decision-making, *Alexa* and *Amy* are names of technology that dominate the back office and the home.

Compounding the effect is the common conceptualization of contemporary digital tracking as maternal. In the press and casual talk one often comes across sly comments about this type of technology as simply automating "mom guilt." In marketing sessions and conference rooms device makers cultivate these associations and openly talk of digital tracking as an extension of the type of vigilance already deemed as natural to women *qua* mothers. The figure of the mother is even sometimes expressed as the benevolent other of the patriarchal Big Brother. The French home surveillance system *Mother* does double duty in this regard by packaging its sensors in a structure that takes inspiration from the Russian *matryoshka* doll, the traditional symbol of maternity and fecundity. When I asked an executive about this device, he told me people find comfort in knowing that "mother" is always watching, referring to the device by name. Mirroring the soft lines of *Mother*, another home tracking device, *Jibo*, that is billed moreover as the first social robot for the *home*, actively invites a parallel connotation. In a promotional video on the crowdsourcing platform *Kickstarter*, the female founder – an MIT engineer – somewhat unconventionally is featured prominently alongside the device in a domestic setting – in a dining room, no less – as though to better stress the equivalence between the female inventor *qua* mother and *Jibo*. The video firmly establishes *Jibo* not only as mom's assistant in the home, for instance, dictating recipes in the kitchen, but as a device that facilitates her multiplication, allowing "mom" to be present where she can't always be. One shot shows mom setting *Jibo* up to take a family portrait, *Jibo* finally freeing her up to be included in the picture.

In these instances, the female body is adopted as a mnemonic for personal tracking and data collection, surfacing broader history of women in technology, a history that has often linked female technical work with domesticity and administrative labor while connecting male labor with executive decision-making (Abbate, 2012). The former is labor that is often seen not only as less skilled, but also understood in line with other forms of feminized work such as housework and childcare, as that which is perceived as more natural and intuitive to women.

In many ways the figure of the laboring and nurturing mother exists as the cultural foil to the figure of the *femme fatale* – the image of attraction and taboo – that mediates the social discourse on data's productivity and fluidity. Ironically and subtly, as female bodies have become all but synonymous with data, women continue to be excluded from the technical work of data, struggling for recognition and legitimacy (Anchalee, 2015). And so the woman/mother is often cast in the role of the digital naïf that is awe-struck and paralysed with fear at the very sight of technology,[4] acting as the cultural other of the custodial class of data scientists and engineers that organize and sanitize data for insights, a field that remains both symbolically and practically a domain of masculine and masculinized "hard" knowledge. The feminization of technology in contemporary society reads as an unsettling extension and perhaps even endorsement of gender tropes often believed to have been overcome.

The data that becomes us

If "nudity" has thus far shaped our relationship with digital data in subtle and overt ways, I'd like to conclude with some thoughts on ways to reframe that connection. Speculatively, I suggest that we may need to theorize digital data not only as that which strips us bare, but rather that it may be productive to think of our engagement with digital data through the idiom of dress. If we think of data as that which we put on rather than take off, might we ask different questions of the data that we produce?

The notion of "dress" already haunts the cultural imaginary of digital nudity produced by data through the language of "fitness," even as we variously frame digital data as participating in a figurative striptease. If the persistent inquiries into the accuracy of information are any indication, concerns around digital data often seem to be around the degree to which data fit or does not fit us, truly the way it becomes us. This view marks a complete reversal in how we think about digital technology. Whereas several decades ago the cyborg imaginary contended that digital space was escapist and other-wordly – existing in a space apart (see Haraway, 1991) – digitally archived personal data is now popularly reframed as a parallel universe that neatly transcribes and archives the everyday, creating a virtual replica of the material world. Thus assumed to double the self and the body, digital data is increasingly conceptualized as a second skin of sorts that contains the "true" self.

To compare data to a form of dress, then, is not to imply that data functions as a disguise, with the Goffmanian "backstage" in reserve. Rather, echoing theorists of subjectivation like Michel Foucault (1994), it is to suggest that digital data generated by wearable and sensor technology is at once about the self, and in the very act of being generated already sets conditions of possibility for becoming. Therefore if data can be said to disclose and represent the self, it is only in the way it also thereby creates, that is interpolates, its subjects – as athletes, as those who care about their bodies, as technological aficionados, as geeks, as digital naïfs, as representatives of populations, as members of a given socioeconomic class.

In a recently published historical analysis of wearable technology, Susan E. Ryan (2014) proposes the term "dress acts" to understand the interpolative power of clothing. The notion of the "dress act" speaks to an expanded, almost figurative idea of garments where clothing functions not only as a disciplinary technology that still holds out the possibility of an organic or an authentic body and the self beneath, but as the very material that allows one's body to become visible in the first place. Indeed, Ryan challenges the reader to understand wearable technology in a broader sense, encompassing as well the larger history of clothing, so as to grapple with what it might even mean to appear naked and "do without dress" (Ryan, 2014: 3).

Ryan's analysis evokes Terence Turner's earlier theorization of nudity. In his 1980 article, "The social skin," Turner suggested seeing even exposed skin as already always cloaked in social forces. The flesh, he writes, is not a boundary experience between the social and the natural, but is itself always already a "symbolic stage upon which the drama of socialization is enacted" (Turner, 1980/2012: 486). Writing against a Eurocentric logic that equated the nudity of native people with a lack of material culture or social sophistication, Turner offers a way to see the naked body as replete with social significance rather than as a blank canvas. In Hans Christian Andersen's tale one may similarly note that the nudity of the Emperor is already always mediated by his authority. He in fact remains dressed, symbolically cloaked in a mantle of power.

The words we employ matter. As Tim Hwang and Karen Levy (2015) contend, the metaphors we choose to describe our experience of digital data carry important social, political, and legal consequences. It matters if digital data is described as exhaust or as oil, as waste or as a utility. Likewise, while the language of nudity aims to make the work of digital data transparent, my aim here is to trouble this efficient transmission. And if the trope of nudity shapes the expectations we have of digital data and the questions we ask of it, it does so by resonating with the multiple connotations and expectations the figure of the nude imparts.

Notes

1 Derrida has written extensively on the figure of the nude, which is part of his broader philosophical commitment to destabilize and politicize the search of origins. See, for instance, *The purveyor of truth* (1975) or *The animal that therefore I am* (1997). The latter work in particular aims to displace nudity from the category of nature, and instead places it squarely into the domain of culture. Derrida treats nudity as a threshold experience; it marks the animal from the human, and in so doing also creates the distinctions that organize the scale in the first place. Nakedness, he argues, is not natural; indeed, it is highly social and political. The theorization of nudity as the boundary experience that constitutes the categories of human and animal also echoes Georgio Agamben's well-known distinctions between *zoe* and *bios* and his own notion of the threshold – the Homo Sacer. In the book of the same name, the oppositions *zoe* and *bios* correspond broadly speaking to the categories of the human and the animal that Derrida is negotiating. Mediating this relationship is another naked body – the Homo Sacer – what Agamben himself calls *"bare life."* And much like Derrida's thoughts on the naked body, bare life must be understood as "part not outside of the political order" (Agamben, 1998: 8). Mediated by the figure of the Homo Sacer, *zoe* and *bios* emerge as fluid categories; they are relational, shifting, and politically charged. In thus rethinking the origins and nature of nudity, Derrida and Agamben encourage us to ask about the social *work* of nudity that proposes to organize humanity on a temporal and hierarchical scale.

2 In the 19th century, the Museum of Natural History had emerged as a prime site where supposed differences between culture and nature could be staged and observed. For instance, writing of this type of ideological work performed by the Museum of Natural History in New York and London, Griffith notes:

> ... merely by traversing the ethnographic exhibition halls of such grandiose public buildings, museum spectators entered into an ideologically loaded space that elaborated the metanarratives of Western cultural superiority via multisensory accounts of the primitivism of other cultures.... The grand evolutionary narrative of scientific progress was inscribed in the very architectural design of the British Museum, where visitors enacted an evolutionary logic as they moved through the highly structured sequence of spaces. (Griffiths 2002: 11)

However, such displays were not confined to the reified walls of the museum. Cinematic projects as well as *live* life groups displaying native peoples, often scandalously underdressed, in zoos and world exhibits were common fixtures of 19th and early 20th-century entertainment. These programs, operating under the rubric of salvage anthropology, sought to document as well as to preserve what they believed to be the decaying signs of man's origins (Rony, 1996).

3 An artist in New York had recently made an explicit connection between feminized labor like housework and the work of generating digital data. Adopting the 1972 feminist manifesto written by Silvia Federici "Wages Against Housework," she had replaced all of the instances of "housework" with the word "Facebook" to discover that this updated manifesto resonated strongly in the digital age. See Ptak (2014).

4 See www.linkedin.com/pulse/please-stop-designing-your-mother-jeff-weir

References

Abbate, J. (2012) *Recoding gender: Women's changing participation in computing.* Cambridge, MA: The MIT Press.

Agamben, G. (1998) *Homo Sacer: Sovereign power and bare life. Meridian: Crossing aesthetics*. Stanford, CA: Stanford University Press.

Allison, A. (2001) "Cyborg violence: Bursting borders and bodies with queer machines." *Cultural Anthropology* 16, 237–65.

Anchalee, I. (2015) "You may have seen my face on BART." *Medium*, 1 August (https://medium.com/the-coffeelicious/you-may-have-seen-my-face-on-bart-8b9561003e0f#.thgmjxto6).Balsamo, A. (1995) *Technologies of the gendered body: Reading cyborg women*. Durham, NC: Duke University Press.

Boesel, E.W. (2014) "Indecent exposure: Breasts as data, data as breasts." *Cyborgology, The Society Pages*, June 19 (http://thesocietypages.org/cyborgology/2014/06/19/indecent-exposure-breasts-as-data-data-as-breasts/).

Crawford, K. and d. boyd (2012) "Critical questions for big data." *Information, Communication & Society*, 662–77.

Daston, J.L. and P. Galison (2010) *Objectivity*. New York: Zone Books.

Derrida, J. (1975) *The purveyor of truth*. Yale French Studies, No 52, Graphesis: Perspecties in Literature and Philosophy, pp 31–113.

Derrida, J. (1997/2008) *The animal that therefore I am*. New York: Fordham University Press.

Douglas, M. (2002) *Purity and danger: An analysis of concepts of pollution and taboo*. London, UK: Routledge.

Foucault, M. (1994) *The order of things: An archaeology of the human sciences*. New York: Vintage (Reissue).

Fox, S. (2014) "Secret questions, naked truths", April 6 (http://susannahfox.com/2014/04/06/secret-questions-naked-truths/).

Griffiths, A. (2002) *Wondrous difference*. New York: Columbia University Press.

Haraway, D.J. (1991) "A cyborg manifesto: Science, technology, and socialist-feminism in the late twentieth century." In D.J. Haraway (ed) *Simians, cyborgs and women: The reinvention of nature* (pp 149–81). New York: Routledge.

Hwang, T. and K. Levy (2015) "'The cloud' and other dangerous metaphors." *The Atlantic*, January 20.

IBM (2010) "The Internet of Things" (www.youtube.com/watch?v=sfEbMV295Kk).

Johnson, D. (2010) "Sorting out the question of feminist technology." In Linda Layne, Sharra Vostral and Kate Boyer (eds) *Feminist technology* (pp 36–54). Champaign, IL: University of Illinois Press.

Jurgenson, N. (2014) "View from nowhere." *The New Inquiry*, October 9 (http://thenewinquiry.com/essays/view-from-nowhere/).

Luxemberg, R. (1913/2004) *The accumulation of capital, Section III*. London, UK: Routledge.

Marey, E.-J. (1895) "Chronophotography in moving plates." *Movement*.

Martin, E. (2001) *The woman in the body: A cultural analysis of reproduction*. Boston, MA: Beacon Press.

Muybridge, E. (1887/1955) *The human figure in motion.* New York: Dover Publications

Ortner, B.S. (1974) "Is female to male as nature is to culture?" *Woman, Culture, and Society,* 66–87.

Ptak, L. (2014) "Wages for Facebook" (http://wagesforfacebook.com/).

Robbins, H. (2003) "The Emperor's new critique." *New Literary History* 34 (4), *Multicultural Essays,* 659–75.

Rony, T.F. (1996) *The third eye: Race, cinema and ethnoraphic spectacle.* Durham, NC and London, UK: Duke University Press.

Ryan, S.E. (2014) *Garments of paradise: Wearable discourse in the digital age.* Cambridge, MA: The MIT Press.

Tucker, P. (2014) *The naked future: What happens in a world that anticipated your every move?* Westbrook, ME: Current.

Turner, S.T. (1980/2012) "The social skin." *Journal of Ethnographic Theory* 2, 486–504.

27

Post your comments below: A case study of immigrant bashing online

Adrian Cruz and Kazuyo Kubo

Given the current debate around immigration reform, sociological literature requires more research that hones in on the characterization of immigrants as ineligible for full inclusion in society. The need for this type of scholarship is especially necessary as the "racist racial project" (Omi and Winant, 1994: 71) of immigrant bashing takes hold in the world of online media. This chapter utilizes the compelling case of Filipino American journalist Jose Antonio Vargas, who entered the US as a child, and is presently an undocumented resident of the country. We are specifically concerned with the online responses to newspaper articles written about Mr Vargas' struggle for documented status. Mr Vargas entered the US through no choice of his own, and it is telling to observe the amount of vitriol leveled against his case. We analyse the online postings to draw out the myriad ways undocumented and documented workers in the US constitute a central target of anti-immigrant and racist rhetoric. Additionally, we add to the growing literature that theorizes the internet discourses around race.

To offer precise study of immigrant bashing online requires a linking between theories on the social platform that is the internet and theories of race and racial inequality. Daniels' (2013) overview of literature on race and internet studies deduces that the online social world reflects the racialized and unequal social structure of the US. She explains how this burgeoning set of literature uncovers how individuals and groups assert power and racial identity in virtual social spheres. In what follows, the assertion of power is apparent within the discourse employed by anti-immigrant online postings. Critical discourse analysis is helpful in making sense of how we should analyse *text within the social context* in which any discourse occurs (van Dijk, 2008). Indeed, as van Dijk writes (2008: 822), our contribution to this volume seeks to understand "the discursive reproduction of illegitimate domination" of immigrants and people of color as it occurs in a seemingly harmless space such as a news website.

In the past two decades the US has witnessed the passage of laws aimed at undocumented immigrants; these laws provide some indication of where many in the US stand on the issue of not only undocumented workers but also legally admitted entrants to the country as well. We find that the line is frequently blurred between documented and undocumented immigrants; this observation is particularly true for Latinos. California laid down the pathway in the 1990s for much of this recent anti-immigrant legislation. Californian voters passed a litany of propositions, which have incurred damage on all immigrant groups, especially undocumented immigrants: 187 (limits on education and medical services), 21 (youth crimes), 227 (bilingual education), and 209 (affirmative action). Regardless of whether or not these propositions were held up after judicial review in courts of law, their passage reflects a deep anti-immigrant sentiment.

However, California is not the only part of the US in which such anti-immigrant animus is expressed. The momentum behind such vehemently anti-immigrant legislation is threaded throughout the country. Arizona's House Bill 1070 – euphemistically labeled "Support Our Law Enforcement and Safe Neighborhoods Act" – is the most notorious example of efforts to harass and intimidate immigrants, particularly Latinos. Other states such as Utah (House Bill 497), Alabama (House Bill 56), and Georgia (House Bill 87) endeavored to implement legal statutes that would seek to detect and eliminate undocumented immigrants from their premises. And in the latter part of 2015, the presidential candidacy of Donald Trump and his ability to gain traction with voters is disturbing. Trump's rhetoric offers incessant bashing of Mexicans, calls to build a border wall, and recommends the establishment of a special police force that will locate and deport undocumented immigrants nationwide. While unsettling, this study demonstrates that Trump's appeal to a segment of voters should be of little surprise to any of us.

Sociologists of immigration offer that the "context of reception" (Gleeson and Gonzales, 2012: 2) is directly related to the forms of treatment and kinds of characterizations that immigrants will experience. In the US, the context for undocumented immigrants (who are widely perceived as Latinos) is one in which, increasingly, they are not only violators of immigration law, but are also served up as scapegoats for perceived and real increases in crime, and thus a dangerous threat and primary cause of perceived societal decay.

Stewart, Pitts, and Osborne (2011) argue that the term "illegal immigrant" has transformed into a "metonym" for Latino immigrants. In their study on newspaper coverage of undocumented immigration, they explain how the dehumanizing discourse on illegal immigrants frames Latinos as what Chavez

(2008) terms "virtual characters." Chavez (2008: 5) points to the media's recurrent pejorative presentation of Latinos, and writes about how "media spectacles are productive acts that construct knowledge about subjects in our world." Chavez (2008: 5) proffers that Latinos occupy a peculiar hyphenated status as "alien–citizens" in which citizenship held by Latinos is devalued as compared to other racial and ethnic groups in the country. Latinos are often subjected to immediate assessment as perpetually foreign, even when holding the status of native-born citizens.

Indeed, although our study's predominant focus is on the rhetoric and discourse around undocumented immigrants, we offer that the assailing of undocumented immigrants online is a "representational strategy" (Cisneros, 2008: 570) that actively denigrates all immigrants. The undocumented are simply the most vulnerable group of immigrants. To move against those immigrants "with papers" and those who hold citizenship is a racist tactic that devalues the legal status held by people of color. Frankenfeld's (1992) work on risk studies may seem far removed from our study on anti-immigrant racism and the internet. However, his concept of "technological citizenship" can be applied to our present discussion. Frankenfeld contends that social actors and groups move within "technological polities;" some groups access more power than others within those polities. Consequently, less powerful groups are boxed out from access to the central constitutive elements of citizenship: autonomy, dignity, and assimilation (1992: 462).

This chapter presents ways in which online social actors chip away at the humanity and dignity of immigrants by working hard to exclude them from the US polity and further along immigrant disempowerment. It is built on analysis of readers' comments to the case of Jose Antonio Vargas, because his story stirred up opinions on immigration among general spectators in the online world. The following confirms, as Hughey and Daniels (2013) have previously demonstrated, that the social space of the internet – which was initially evaluated as a democratic venue in which any voice could speak – is actually a forum that mirrors the entrenched social inequities of society.

Racial attitudes, the internet, and immigrant bashing

Michael Omi and Howard Winant (1994: 56) coin the term "racial formation" to "facilitate understanding of a whole range of contemporary controversies and dilemmas involving race, including the nature of racism ... and oppression such as sexism and nationalism." We find it necessary to widen the racial formation approach to include addressing issues of immigrant oppression and the assertion of nationalist white identity. White supremacist groups are understandably designated as extreme groups, who do not represent the majority of white opinions on people of color and immigrants. To this matter of whites' dispositions in regards to racial minorities, Bobo and Charles (2009) parse out white attitudinal contradictions in the US. On the one hand, whites, since the Second World War, increasingly support the idea and sociopolitical goal of racial equality. Thus, the vast majority of whites can hardly be framed as hardcore racists. On the other hand, whites persistently subscribe to negative stereotypes in regards to groups of color. Most significantly, while endorsing principles of racial equality, whites resist and oppose programmatic efforts that address the socially unequal lives, which people of color lead. In specific regard to attitudes on immigrants, Elizabeth Fussell (2014) delineates how native-born Americans' attitudes about immigrants are directly linked to the type of reception that immigrants receive on entering the US. Moreover, Fussell concludes that native-born attitudes on immigrants may be improving as Americans open their arms a bit wider for newcomers to the country. We aim to provide analysis that takes into account how immigrants are racialized online, and how that process of racialization affects the ways in which immigrants are perceived. That is, we suspect that arms are not necessarily held wide open for Latino immigrants.

Lisa Nakamura's studies (2002, 2007) demonstrate the multiple ways in which race and ethnic identities are built and presented online. People of color utilize websites to shape their identity and to steer the ship, so to speak, of how they are perceived in the virtual and non-virtual world. Displays of agency by groups of color indicate their longstanding demand for social equality and respect. Still, as in the non-virtual world, they encounter the virulent force of white supremacy. Jessie Daniels (2009) argues that the goal of racial equality is frequently decimated on the World Wide Web. In her study of white supremacy online, Daniels explains how white supremacist websites provide a virtual forum on which biologically racist opinions are skillfully molded into facts and gain traction as bona fide arguments. Daniels concludes that white supremacy online does not so much move us backward as much as convincingly demonstrate that the US has failed to uproot institutionalized racist ways of thinking. To counter this type of racism, we assert that anti-racist scholarship and activism remains necessary to the struggle for people of color. Further, the struggle to confront racism cannot be terminated with passage of legislation or simply noting that more tolerant attitudes are emergent; anti-racist activity must be an ongoing and vigorously pursued objective.

Recently, the US has entered into a national discussion, often contentiously, on the issue of immigration reform. Furthermore, efforts to achieve reform – legalizing undocumented workers, protecting children who did not make the decision to enter the country, or simply allowing undocumented university students to pay in-state tuition – have been stalled within the political manufacturing process. US citizens and legal residents may be opening the national door, so to speak, a bit more to immigrants, but persistent presence of immigrant bashing is disconcerting and in need of sociological study.

Methods and data

The sociology of beliefs and attitudes on immigration methodologically relies, for the most part, on survey research data (see Ceobanu and Escandell, 2010, for a multinational overview). Additionally, the sociological scholarship on racial attitudes and beliefs is also mostly drawn from social survey data sets (for prominent examples, see Bobo and Kluegel, 1997, and Bobo, 2001). These innovative pieces of research have proven invaluable to our comprehension of the range of perceptions in effect around issues of race, ethnicity, and immigration. To investigate the link between attitudes on race and attitudes on immigrants/immigration policy, we carry out the task via inspection and interpretation of online postings by social actors in response to articles on immigration. Specifically, we showcase reader reactions to the plight of journalist and activist Jose Antonio Vargas, an undocumented Filipino immigrant.

We employ discourse analysis using Nvivo 10, a qualitative research analysis software. We conducted discourse analysis of online newspaper postings extracted from the websites of the *USA Today* and *The New York Times*. The citations for these articles are listed in the References section at the end of this chapter. These online newspaper articles detail Mr Vargas' life and experience as an undocumented immigrant. Mr Vargas is the author of one of the pieces (Vargas, 2011). The articles also cover the 2014 detention of Mr Vargas by US immigration officials at an airport in McAllen, Texas, from which he was eventually released and escaped deportation proceedings. We coded and categorized readers' comments to the articles on Mr Vargas under 57 themes. After categorizing the data into the various categories, three main discourse frames emerged and are presented in this chapter.

Recurrently, online respondents to the articles commented on immigrants and immigration policy in general. They expressed concerns and points of view on national security, patriotism, the US–Mexico border, and American identity. Negative comments on immigrants were widespread as they were frequently framed as: innately criminal, third world people, and illegal aliens. Many of the comments were stand-alone, but several comments drew other online posters into a conversation on the issue of Mr Vargas' case and quickly left his case behind. We cannot completely explain why the case of a Filipino American journalist's struggle for documented status led many of the postings to move toward a focus on Latinos. Online readers may have seen the surname "Vargas" and assumed he was Latino. Alternatively – and we lean toward this explanation – people may immediately link any discussion about undocumented immigrants with Latinos.

To probe online postings, authored by readers of online news websites, unpacks the "race talk" (Alegria, 2012) that is apparent on the internet when social actors post about immigration policy and immigrants. As Daniels' (2009) previously cited study demonstrated, white supremacists assembled websites to express and promote racist rhetoric and exert white power. The online postings offered in this chapter demonstrate the nationalist and, we would argue, racist language that social actors wield to discredit and malign immigrants, who are overwhelmingly caricatured as undeserving lawbreakers. The portrayals of the undocumented are most certainly laden with racial overtones, and the picture being painted is most decidedly *not* of white people – that is, an attack on undocumented immigrants is an attack on people of color.

Indeed, immigrants in the US are *othered* by racist and nativist language that constructs them as unfit to be fully fledged members of a society in which they are deeply embedded. Gray and Raza (2012) note the long historical trail of othering by the US' "racialized immigration policy." In their work on Arizona's Senate Bill 1070, they draw out how the historical practice of othering immigrants has mutated into a racial "common sense." Consequently, anti-immigrant racism is able to avoid being labeled as racist by shrouding its rhetoric in the assertion that, "I am not racist if they are illegal" (2012: 18). Undocumented immigrants are relegated to lie outside of the realm of being people with bona fide rights. They work, pay taxes, and build communities in the US, but the onslaught of violent rhetoric proves to be effective in either its disregard of contributions from immigrants or acts to delegitimize those contributions.

We recognize that the data and conclusions offered here do not comport with a study that seeks generalizability of findings such as the studies cited above drawn from survey data. However, generalizable results are not the goal of this chapter. Our objective is exploration and ascertainment of specific discourse frames through which immigrants – both documented and undocumented – are perceived. Disturbingly, we find, as Aviva Chomsky (2014) has suggested, that the US has moved into an era that subjects immigrants to immediate categorization and perception as illegal entrants to the country.

The case of Jose Antonio Vargas

Jose Antonio Vargas is a journalist who was born and then raised by his mother in the Philippines until the age of 12. In 1993, Mr Vargas was placed on an international flight to California where his grandparents resided; he has lived in the US since then. Today Mr Vargas is a university-educated writer and activist on the issue of immigration, and advocates for the legalization of undocumented people. He "came out," a phrase Mr Vargas deliberately utilizes, as an undocumented resident of the US in a well-known, widely publicized editorial essay published by *The New York Times* magazine in 2011. In the essay, Mr Vargas detailed the struggle of an undocumented immigrant in the US, particularly the case of an undocumented individual, who entered the country as a child and had no say in the decision to migrate. In his advocacy work for the undocumented, Mr Vargas employs the term, "undocumented

American" to describe the condition of people such as himself. In many respects, these individuals are deeply integrated into US society – they work jobs, attend schools, pay taxes – yet they are denied full access to the full range of opportunities in the country. We rely on three newspaper articles and one magazine article (Mr Vargas' autobiographical editorial), and analyse reader responses to the articles as they were posted online. The readers' postings move beyond Mr Vargas' individual situation and riff on wider issues of immigration policy, national identity, and immigrants – both the documented and undocumented.

Expressing white privilege and innately criminal immigrants

Some readers railed against what they deemed Mr Vargas' argument that individuals such as himself should be allowed to attain fully documented status. To some readers, the granting of legal status to these people violated the rules of fair play and the notion that all people need to wait their turn in the queue. Furthermore, to legalize the undocumented is interpreted as tantamount to some of form of affirmative action, which offers unfair advantages to groups of color based on nothing more than being non-white. One reader exhibits these sentiments with the following:

> All I am interested in is a level playing field for everyone. That means everyone has to pass the SAME tests, meet the SAME requirements, and have the SAME qualifications to succeed. No one should get a special status because of the color of their skin, where they were born, or who their parents are. Everyone gets a clean plate, and they can choose to fill it with what they will.

The comment provides a view into a type of "laissez-faire racism" (Bobo et al, 1997) that delineates groups of color as inherently inferior and consistently failing to measure up in a social world that offers equal opportunity to all. Laissez-faire racism avoids personal, overt attacks on racial and ethnic minorities by simply stating that the responsibility of success is solely on the individual. Legalization of undocumented immigrants is therefore further evidence that racial minority groups lack the capacity to fend for themselves – they have to receive something for nothing. Implicitly, whites are presented as a capable group that can stand on their own.

While laissez-faire racism operates in a "kinder and gentler" (Bobo et al, 1997) manner, additional postings did not shy away from vicious racist language on immigrants. One online respondent caricatured undocumented immigrants as usurpers of the national wealth by stating, "… since they breed like flies and allow rampant corruption and crime, these Latinos think

they can live off the backs of American taxpayers until they outbreed us."
Latinos are relegated to the realm of hideous creatures, and represent a form
of infestation that corrupts the state of the nation since they are innately
criminal. Furthermore, the post author utilizes the term "Latinos," which
is a frequently used term of self-description by American citizens of variant
Latin American heritage. Thus, the rhetoric takes a widely accepted term of
ethnic identification for many Americans, and attempts to present the term
as a way in which to refer to foreigners.

Postings commonly offered both implicit and explicit comparisons
between the previous generations of desirable and supposedly orderly European
immigrants vis-à-vis immigrants from Latin America. The following entry
author argued that their family line emanated from finer stock, and persisted
in the framing of immigrants as immanently criminal people, that many
immigrants' very existence in the US was not only illegal, but they also
engaged in illegal activity.

> My country wanted my ancestors to come here unlike the diseased-
> ridden, parasitic, bottom feeders from Mexico and Central America
> yearning to grab all the freebies they can rob from the American
> taxpayer and send most of it home. You open door immigration
> 'tards are mad because Latinos won't control the US. Ever.

Finally, this statement poses progressive viewpoints on immigration policy as
being held by groups who desire some form of Latino domination of the US.

Immigrants as third world people

Postings also commonly expressed a clear prejudiced notion of "third
worldism" in which people and nations other than the US are depicted as
undesirable and corrupt simply on the basis that they are poorer people and
poorer countries. Neighboring countries, it is argued, to the south of the
US pose a real threat of deterioration if immigrants from Latin America are
permitted entry:

> Mexico and the rest of Central America is the disgusting cesspool
> it is because they let Spanish speaking parasites into their country.
> They created these conditions in their own countries and, rather
> than face the problem head on and solve it they run for the nearest
> safe haven whenever things get difficult. Imagine a world where
> no one would stand up to tyrants or criminals, where everyone
> just takes the path of least resistance and greatest personal safety.

Obviously, the author of this post doesn't know that current Spanish-speaking residents were not "let into" Mexico and Central America, but that Spanish is the primary language spoken in the region since European colonization nearly five centuries ago. More importantly, the racist caricature of Latin American immigrants as parasitic and usurpers persists with this online respondent. Moreover, we witness the refrain of implied superiority of white Americans, who have established an orderly nation-state, and whose primary threat is in the form of Latin American immigrants.

Further comments worked to reify the characterization of Latino immigrants as disease carriers, who import substandard and inferior practices, although postings are consistently vague as to precisely which types of practices and behaviors are being referenced. One posting argued that Mr Vargas was "advocating" for a group of people, who "will turn the US into a disease ridden, 3d world cesspool. The Central American hoards will be nothing but a drain on our resources." In accordance with this line of thought, another individual offered their disgust with immigrants from south of the US border and employed a racist ideology in regards to Latin America with the assertion that Latin Americans are less valuable people: "THAT [a corrupt environment] is the world that these people live in. Now, since they breed like flies and allow rampant corruption and crime, these Latinos think they can live off the backs of American taxpayers until they outbreed us." The language draws once again from the trove of rhetoric that argues immigrants and even American born Latinos are oversexed people, who have large families.

Furthermore, Latinos are presented on the comment lines as disease carriers. The deployment of Latinos as contagions of disease is nothing new among the rhetorical techniques that Americans have used when discussing, in particular, Mexicans. Historical analysis (McKiernan-González, 2012) presents case studies of US health officials' efforts to quarantine and separate out Mexicans in Texas as they were deemed threats to the public welfare. In her widely regarded study, Molina (2006) points to how health and racial identity were linked in 20th-century Los Angeles. Indeed, groups of color seen as inferior, unhealthy and unhygienic were categorized as ineligible for citizenship.

Immigrants as legal impossibilities

The emergence of illegal aliens as a group of people in the US offers a fascinating case study of the fault lines that run deeply and rupture between race, ethnicity, nationality, and citizenship status. Historian Mae Ngai (2004: 4) argues that "immigration restriction produced the illegal alien as a new political and legal subject whose inclusion within the nation was both a social reality and a legal impossibility." We observe this tension in the readers' comments sections that we studied. Posting authors consistently express frustration and rage toward undocumented immigrants as violators of national sovereignty.

Postings, in reference to the decision by US immigration officials to release Mr Vargas from detention in McAllen, Texas, closed in on the issue of undocumented workers and implicitly argue that no rights should be in place for such immigrants. One commenter rhetorically queried: "Do I understand correctly they let go [an] illegal alien who is in [the] US illegally breaking our laws?" Postings often draw a conclusion that because an immigrant is without legal documents, their literal presence in the country is a violation of the law. Furthermore, Mr Vargas' origins as a child immigrant, who had no say in the decision to venture to the US, is accorded absolutely no role in the assessment of his situation. Sociologist Roberto Gonzales (2011) studies the difficult process undocumented immigrants undergo, and the painful experience of "learning to be illegal." Often they view themselves as legitimate members of society but they encounter a devastating set of structural barriers and an antagonistic citizenry, as the online comments in this section demonstrate.

Additional comments hinged the release of Mr Vargas to perceived deterioration of the country: "Moving America forward to become lawless banana republic eh?" Treatment of Mr Vargas, with some semblance of human rights, rather than being framed as an act that engenders equality is interpreted as emblematic of moral decline. Moreover, the comment furthers along the othering of nations external to the US. Thus, lawlessness exists external to the US and immigrants face accusations they import it from poorer countries, which, in actuality, the US economy is actually quite interdependent on. Massey, Durand and Malone (2003) argue that North American countries are experiencing economic and structural integration with each other. Resultantly, they argue that increasing restrictive immigration measures constitute misdirected policy. Their analysis addresses the ways in which policy-makers and the US state should shift away from walling up the country toward more inclusiveness of foreign laborers, particularly Mexican workers. Discouragingly, our study illuminates how much work is to be done on the ground in combating the racist attitudes that immigrants encounter. In fact, postings viewed any move toward progressive immigration policy as a dangerous move to the political left:

> Why was this illegal alien freed? The Obama administration bowed to public pressure from other illegal aliens, and their friends on the left. All of these illegals will eventually ruin this country financially, but they will vote Democratic. And more of them will follow, and this country will look like Guatemala and the rest of the 3rd world.

The passage's final sentence invokes race in decrying the forecast that the US will "look like" brown-skinned people. We contend that this posting reveals an inability to fully accept Latinos as co-nationals, even when they have entered the country legally or, as is more commonly the case, they were born in the country.

Conclusion

Although this study relies on a small sample of postings from newspaper websites, we believe this chapter represents a necessary piece of research that puts to good use an emergent set of data. Additionally, we aim to merge studies on attitudes in regards to race, immigration, and the internet. We suggest that our study is both sociologically necessary for academic research and politically necessary to promote equal rights for immigrants and people of color. We identified recurrent frames that online commenters utilized to denigrate and disempower particular groups of marginalized people. Equally significant, we present their racist race talk as a mode by which they assert their own power as US citizens or legal residents. Indeed, as concluded by Hughey and Daniels (2013), we confirm that online social forums are no socially equal space for groups of color.

One final post alleged that all undocumented immigrants were criminals "whatever their age or excuse." In drawing such a hard line around who can belong and who cannot in the United States of America, anti-immigrant racism works oppressively hard to promote exclusivity over any sense of inclusivity. Such a sentiment also runs contrary to the numerous proclamations we hear from everyday Americans and politicians that the country is a nation of immigrants. Adoration is in place and fully expressed for the history of European origin immigrants and their descendants, but little love is lost for hardworking immigrants from Latin America.

Social actors can operate quite adroitly with their rhetoric, particularly when they aim to be discriminatory without appearing to be discriminatory. Sociologist Eduardo Bonilla-Silva's (2006) concept of "rhetorical devices" sheds light on how members of more powerful groups can engage in a manipulation of language in order to make racist comments but simultaneously avoid being labeled as racist. In the online world, social actors can secure some level of anonymity, post bigoted comments, and figuratively walk away from any culpability.

Hana E. Brown (2013) proffers that two frames of "legality" and "race" conflate to create and employ anti-Latino immigrant rhetoric. The frames engage in a process of comparison that engenders inequality. The legality frame depicts legal immigrants as law abiders, who entered the US in an honorable fashion. Failure to measure up to such a standard is to fall short of full-fledged belongingness in the country. The racial frame assesses whites as socially superior vis-à-vis Latinos. The rhetoric produced by these frames is ingeniously coded and is indicative of an era of non-racist sounding racism. A conclusion, like that from Brown, should compel sociologists of race,

445

immigration, and inequality to excavate social terrain and discourse that, on the face of it, seem harmless or even progressive. The online social world is one of those terrains and manufacturing sites of discourse in need of such analysis.

We conclude that online postings, in response to the case of Jose Antonio Vargas, freely employ abusive language in regards to immigrants for two reasons. First, the immigrants originate from Latin America and are perceived as comparatively not up to par with European immigrants. Second, undocumented workers have violated immigration law. Therefore, any defense of undocumented immigrants would most likely be met with a statement that they have violated the law. To state it in vernacular terms: they broke the law and that's that.

Once immigrants are viewed as inherently illegal social beings, they are caricatured as a group deemed unworthy to labor and live in a country as legitimate people deserving of humane treatment. Furthermore, they are lower than scapegoats – not only are they blamed for a variety of social ills, it is considered wrong to even come to their defense. As Mae Ngai writes on undocumented immigrants, the frames we offer in this study portray all immigrants as "impossible subjects." Many of these immigrants, documented and undocumented, are wholly indispensable to the US as laborers. They are also indispensable to those individuals, groups, and politicians who desire exclusive ownership of US citizenship and its accompanying rights.

References

Alegria, S. (2012) "Constructing racial difference through group talk: An analysis of white focus groups' discussion of racial profiling." *Ethnic and Racial Studies* 37, 241–60.

Bobo, L.D. (2001) "Racial attitudes and relations at the close of the twentieth century." In N. Smelser, W.J. Wilson, and F. Mitchell (eds) *America becoming: Racial trends and their consequences* (pp 262–99). Washington, DC: National Academy Press.

Bobo, L.D. and C.Z. Charles (2009) "Race in the American mind: From the Moynihan Report to the Obama candidacy." *Annals of the American Academy of Political and Social Science* 621, 243–59.

Bobo, L.D. and J.R. Kluegel (1997) "Status, ideology and dimensions of whites' racial beliefs and attitudes: Progess and stagnation." In S.A. Tuch and J.K. Martin (eds) *Racial attitudes in the 1990s: Continuity and change* (pp 93–120). Greenwood, CT: Praeger.

Bobo, L.D., J.R. Kluegel, and R.A. Smith (1997) "Laissez-faire racism: The crystallization of a kinder, gentler antiblack ideology." In S.A. Tuch and J.K. Martin (eds) *Racial attitudes in the 1990s: Continuity and change* (pp 15–44). Westport, CT: Praeger.

Bonilla-Silva, E. (2006) *Racism without racists: Color-blind racism and the persistence of racial inequality in the United States.* Lanham, MD: Rowman & Littlefield.

Brown, H. (2013) "Race, legality and the social policy consequences of anti-immigrant mobilization" *American Sociological Review* 78, 290–314.

Ceobanu, A.M. and X. Escandell (2010) "Comparative analyses of public attitudes toward immigrants and immigration using multinational survey data: A review of theories and research." *Annual Review of Sociology* 36, 309–28.

Chavez, L. (2008) *The Latino threat: Constructing immigrants, citizens and the nation.* Stanford, CA: Stanford University Press.

Chomsky, A. (2014) *Undocumented: How immigration became illegal.* Boston, MA: Beacon Press.

Cisneros, J.D. (2008) "Contaminated communities: The metaphor of 'immigrant as pollutant' in media representations of immigration." *Rhetoric & Public Affairs* 11, 569–601.

Daniels, J. (2009) *Cyber racism: White supremacy online and the new attack on civil rights.* Lanham, MD: Rowman & Littlefield Publishers, Inc.

Daniels, J. (2013) "Race and racism in internet studies: A review and critique." *New Media & Society* 15, 695–719.

Frankenfeld, P.J. (1992) "Technological citizenship: A normative framework for risk studies." *Science, Technology, & Human Values* 4, 459–84.

Fussell, E. (2014) "Warmth of the welcome: Attitudes toward immigrants and immigration policy in the United States." *Annual Review of Sociology* 40, 479–98.

Gleeson, S. and R.G. Gonzales (2012) "When do papers matter? An institutional analysis of undocumented life in the United States." *International Migration* 50, 1–19.

Gonzales, R.G. (2011) "Learning to be illegal: Undocumented youth and shifting legal contexts in the transition to adulthood." *American Sociological Review* 76, 602–19.

Gray, K.L. and A.E. Raza (2012) "Racism in the colorblind era: Examining mediated responses to Arizona SB1070." *Border-Lines: Journal of Latino Research Center at the University of Nevada, Reno* 6, 7–27.

Hughey, M.W. and J. Daniels (2013) "Racist comments at online news sites: A methodological dilemma for discourse analysis." *Media, Culture & Society* 35, 332–47.

Massey, D.J., J. Durand, and N.J. Malone (2003) *Beyond smoke and mirrors: Mexican immigration in an era of economic integration.* New York: Russell Sage.

Mckiernan-Gonzáles, J. (2012) *Fevered measures: Public health and race at the Texas-Mexico border. 1848–1942.* Durham, NC and London: Duke University Press.

Molina, N. (2006) *Fit to be citizens? Public health and race in Los Angeles.* Berkeley, CA: University of California Press.

Nakamura, L. (2002) *Cybertypes: Race, ethnicity, and identity on the internet.* New York and London, UK: Routledge.

Nakamura, L. (2007) *Digitizing race: Visual cultures of the internet.* Minneapolis, MN: University of Minnesota Press.

New York Times, The (2014) "Immigration advocate, detained on Texas border, is released in visa case", July 15.

Ngai, M. (2004) *Impossible subjects: Illegal aliens and the making of modern America.* Princeton, NJ: Princeton University Press.

Omi, M. and H. Winant (1994) *Racial formation in the United States: From the 1960s to the 1990s.* Philadelphia, PA: Temple University Press.

Stewart, C.O., M.J. Pitts, and H. Osborne (2011) "Mediated intergroup conflict: The discursive construction of 'illegal immigrants' in a regional US newspaper." *Journal of Language and Social Psychology* 30, 8–27.

Vargas, J.A. (2011) "My life as an undocumented immigrant." *The New York Times Magazine.*

USA Today (2014) "Immigration activist Vargas freed at US border", July 15.

USA Today (2014) "Vargas arrest at border distracts from cause: Column", July 16.

van Dijk, T.A. (2008) "Critical discourse analysis and nominalization: Problem or pseudo-problem?" *Discourse & Society* 19, 821–8.

28

Our mothers have always been machines: The conflation of media and motherhood

Kara van Cleaf

My study of "mommy blogs" began with the exact same reflex as did my pregnancy (and most of my early days as a new mother): with a Google search. This turn towards the internet, and all the social media platforms therein, occurs at increasingly intimate levels of our lives, especially for mothers. Recent research finds evidence for the "momification of the internet" (Dewey, 2015), which refers to the massive incorporation of digital media into mothers' daily lives. Initially, in researching mommy blogs, I set out to consider how digital networks influence the work and experience of motherhood. My inquiry started with the assumption that motherhood and technology are separate endeavors that often cross paths but then continue on along their distinct routes. I quickly found, however, that the work of maternity and that of blogging (as one form of participation[1] with digital media) share a similar logic and labor process best described as "attunement."

Attunement, or bringing things into harmony, here refers to the unending work of reading a situation (or baby, blog, reader, follower), and anticipating or altering responses to make sense of things. Kathleen Stewart describes attunement as the "alerted sense that something is happening and an attachment to sensing out whatever it is" (2010: 4). The attachment to "sensing" things out, whether a baby's cry or a comment on a post, requires the labor or "tuning up to something" (2010: 5). Mommy blogs provide a unique social location not only to observe women tune into the work and identity of motherhood, but also to study how bloggers attune to the labor of digital sociality. Just as mothers attune to their children, bloggers attune to their readers. Further, attunement is the distinctive feature of social media as these digital platforms algorithmically attune users to feelings, products, people, and pages. In this matrix of writing and reading, commenting and "liking," a shared practice of unending, and often behind the scenes, labor emerges.

The labor of motherhood is the original form of unending labor (Frederici, 2004); or, as many bloggers in my sample put it, there are no vacation days for mothers. Yet this ceaseless caretaking is not only toil: mothers, and, as I explain in this chapter, bloggers, claim they find social connection, emotional fulfillment, and purpose from such labor. The shared sense of purpose mommy bloggers experience in both motherhood and blogging leads to the argument of this chapter: digital labor operates through a similar practice of attunement, as does the labor of motherhood. Attunement, in fact, is built into the functionality of various social platforms. Digital platforms increasingly attach to our bodies, measure our states of being, and record the intimate moments of our lives. Instead of thinking of motherhood and media separately, as things that add to, or even influence, the other, focusing on the labor of attunement shows just how much motherhood and digital media share. Illuminating this shared logic highlights the labor embedded within digital media participation. Additionally, this labor is itself becoming part of the story: as digital media measure finer and finer-grained moments of life, our cultural narratives of motherhood shift from sentimentalism towards labor. Using the notion of "ordinary devotion," a term coined by Donald Winnicott and advanced by Maggie Nelson (2015: 21), I show that mommy blogs, en masse, highlight everyday work of care labor, or "the labor of living out whatever's happening" (Stewart, 2010: 2). Motherhood, as told in the digital culture of mommy blogs, reads as an episodic attuning to fleeting moments, moods, and affects that accompany the work of care.

Method

I base my argument – that maternity and digital technologies operate according to a similar logic and labor – on an analysis (of both narrative and content) of 47 blogs I followed from April 2010 to November 2013. During this period of time, I also analysed other online works that utilized digital and/or social media to work on and through the topic of motherhood, including works by artists, poets, and academic writers. In this analysis, I included among "mommy blogs" any online platform that discusses motherhood from the perspective of the mother herself. I found that blogs in this genre discuss the work of motherhood in stark, provocative, and authentic terms; through humor or memoir, mothers write about the struggles they face caring for children, negotiating careers, and dealing with partners, as well as their feelings on how maternity has altered their everyday lives. The marketing research firm Scarborough (2012) defines a mommy blogger as any woman with "at least one child in their household [who has] read or contributed to a blog in the past 30 days." According to their definition, 14 percent of all American mothers (or 23 million women) participate in blogs and 3.9 million North American mothers self-identify as bloggers. Based on my sample, Scarborough's definition may be too narrow, as I often read comments from women who stated they did not have children and from women who had adult children. The definition, however, does highlight that passive activities such as reading blogs contribute to the overall (market) activity within the genre.

Mothers' online behaviors stand out compared to other internet users. For example, recent research finds that mothers use social media more often than non-mothers. As mentioned, the phrase "the momification of the internet" refers to mothers' patterns of sharing photos, commenting on posts, and generally being more active on social media platforms compared to non-mothers and men (Dewey, 2015). According to a Pew Research Center (2015) report, mothers are more likely (45 percent) than fathers (22 percent) to "strongly agree" that they get support from their social networks. Mothers use Facebook more than other internet users, and give and receive support to friends and family members online. The headline from the *Wall Street Journal*, "Facebook's peace offering to Telcos: Data on mothers," alludes to the economic value created by mothers' online participation. The article explains how telecommunication companies are frustrated that Facebook is not governed by the same legal regulations as they are, despite the fact that Facebook provides real-time communication services. Further, Facebook has more sophisticated data on its users than telecommunication companies, that have "not had the ability to correlate the life-events of consumers with their buying behavior on such a massive scale" (Mizroch, 2015). In other words, because of mothers' active participation online, Facebook has a wealth of "moment-based, people-centric" data that has value to companies selling services and goods. The notion of "moment-based" activity parallels the concept of attunement – through tracking sentiment, photos, status updates, and clicks, digital platforms have a window into users', and especially mothers', lives.

The dynamism of the internet in general, and mommy blogs in particular, combined with the proprietary nature of social media platforms makes the entirety of the genre difficult to measure. While a set of themes may serve as parameters of the genre, my aim is less to definitively document the genre and more to think through how this online niche works – both at the interpretive level and through a consideration of the labor blogging requires and the value it produces. I now turn to specific online writings and projects describing the labor of attunement that accompanies motherhood, and then illustrate how this labor parallels mothers' digital participation (and especially their rhetorical choices). I argue that the labor of blogging reads like the labor of motherhood, and ask: What are the implications of the work digital media calls forth from its users, and of the finer measures of mothering such technology provides?

Maternal work

The philosopher Sarah Ruddick (1995: 17) argues that motherhood is first and foremost labor that "preserves the lives of children." Ruddick does not sentimentalize mothers or refer to abstractions, but instead grounds the identity in the labor it requires. Working with D.W. Winnicott's idea that mothering requires "ordinary devotion," Maggie Nelson (2015: 20) describes the work of motherhood in the following: "You, reader, are alive today, reading this, because someone once adequately policed your mouth exploring." By stressing such ordinary work as policing the objects a baby puts in its mouth, Nelson sidesteps the more dramatic and sentimental narratives found in popular culture.

Amelia Abreu (2014) suggests that the labor of motherhood is the original work of data collection and surveillance. Keeping an eye, paying attention, and counting each sleep cycle and diaper change are the devotional labors of motherhood. Care work in general involves the collection and computation of multiple sources of data throughout the day. In an online essay, Abreu explains:

> After all, as a caregiver you have a responsibility to perform as a human data tracker. Whether you are taking care of a child, an elderly or sick or disabled person, or just a professionally busy person, you track their movements, their diet, their routines and schedules, their needs and wants.... How often is what gets branded 'nagging', either maternal or spousal, just a ritual in data gathering?

In this way, the work of motherhood is the unending practice of attuning, of making sense of repetitive, if incommensurate, activities.

The artist Lenka Clayton also explores the daily, unremarkable labors of motherhood in her "Artist in Residency: Motherhood." By taking up a "residency" in her motherhood, Clayton puts both the labor of art and that of mothering into sharp relief. Her artist's statement on this residency, published on the project's website (see residencyinmotherhood.com), directly engages the devaluation of care work by framing "motherhood as a valuable site, rather than an invisible labor, for exploration and artistic production" (2014a). Clayton's project suggests that the ideal artist is one who is free of the obligations of caregiving, able to spend time and pursue her art in a semi-transient life, traveling from one residency to the next.

Some of Clayton's works during this residency include works that are performative as well as visual. In the installation titled "Maternity leave," (2014e) she connected a baby monitor from her baby's room to one in a museum for four months. The monitor was always on so that visitors at the museum could listen to the noises from her baby's room. In "Dangerous objects made safer" Clayton selected household tools that – once one becomes a parent and must engage in the policing of "mouth exploring" – stand out as alarmingly dangerous objects, and covered them in felt (2014d). In a work titled "Objects taken from my son's mouth," she placed objects she "harvested" from her son's mouth, between his eighth and fifteenth month, on a plinth, elevating Nelson's "mouth policing" to high art (2014b). For "The distance I can be from my son," she created an experiment in four settings – a park, a back alley, a supermarket, and a cloud of fog – where she recorded her son running away from her (2014c). The videos mark, with a time and distance stamp, when she begins to run after him. Together, these pieces explore Ruddick's "preservation" practices or Winnicott's "ordinary devotions" that make up the work of motherhood. Clayton's art measures a mother's attunement to both the environment and her child: everyday objects are made safe, distances are created and then closed. We see her son look back at her, then begin to run; Clayton takes off, dropping the recording device to catch him.

Clayton's works break down the technicity of motherhood. The structural forces of discrimination, such as wage inequality or subordinate social identity, operate within these infinitesimal, incommensurate, unending monitoring questions that attend motherhood: Are the scissors within reach? Which aisle of the grocery store did the child run down? What was that sound? Why is it so quiet? While Clayton's artistic renditions of maternal labor implicate the environment and our tools – baby monitors, video recorders – at a certain point, the work returns to the mother's body. The museum installation "Maternity leave" illuminates the limit of technology: someone must be able to get the baby when it cries, even if technology allows more people to listen, watch, or measure

As Abreu, Clayton, and Nelson show, mothers remain, in the parlance of the digital tech industry, a highly efficient platform for attuning to the work of preservation. Part of the efficiency results from mothers incorporating their bodies into the work of ordinary devotion. Anne Boyer (2011) describes the work of the mother's body in the preservation of the child:

> Looking cannot always help a mother distinguish between a sleeping child and a dead one, and no watch, no matter how passionate, can keep the dying alive. For a person who is a mother to an infant, the watch is the work. Rather, it is a work that is a kind of extension of the mother herself, her own body in the state of attention as she scrutinizes the child's body, inspects it for health, keeps watch at its side if it suffers, takes notice of when it requires comfort.

"No matter how passionate" the work of motherhood, it is still the unending work of watching, surveying, and collecting vital statistics – a labor of attunement that requires and extends from the mother's body. Just as Clayton had to drop her camera and run to catch her child, bloggers often describe physical aspects of their labors. Blogger Phyllis Grant (2012) responds to her son's question, "Mama, why do you always lose your keys?" on her blog with the following: "because I worry about the important things like keeping you alive and there's no more room in my brain." Winnicott's ordinary devotion is not necessarily sentimental but it is labor intensive. Following Abreu and Grant's metaphors, a mother must devote her brain-bandwith to care work. I now turn to the ways that digital media colludes with the labor of mothering.

Digital work

Mommy blogs are one of the more recent locations where mothers create the cultural narratives and spaces of attunement that define what it means to mother and to be a mother. These blogs act as real-time manuals of motherhood, detailing both how to do motherhood as well as how to interpret the shifts in identity that accompany it. In other words, they attune bloggers, readers, and "lurkers" to mothering. Lauren Berlant (2008: 152) describes the manual as "a pragmatic pedagogic genre, an opportunity for retraining a reader into something different yet more herself." Mommy blogs provide "pedagogic" "retraining," on both motherhood and digital sociality, to millions of readers. The more popular blogs in this genre share a normative figure, the white middle-class heterosexual woman, but, with little searching, one can find blogs dedicated to diverse experiences and social positions (queer, non-white, disabled, chronically depressed, single mothers). The diversity of blogs supports their pedagogic function of "retraining a reader" into a "something different" identity (Berlant, 2008: 152). Mommy blogs act as operating manuals for attuning to both the structural and subjective shifts women encounter as they become mothers, as well as the daily labors required. Framing blogs as manuals highlights the cultural, and now increasingly technical, work that motherhood demands. As an example of such technical work, mothers "are especially likely to try to respond to the good news others post, answer others' questions or receive support via online networks" (Pew Research Center, 2015: 2). Mothers, that is to say, keep an eye on their networks as part of their caregiving work.

Despite cultural ideologies that motherhood is (as close to) instinctual as humans get (see Hayes, 1996), the reality is that maternity, especially within capitalism, is always entangled with contemporary technologies. Ruth Schwarz Cowan (1983), in her study of household technologies from the Industrial Revolution until the 1980s, shows the work of family – cooking, caring, housework – is as much a part of an era's technology system as the manufacture, production, or distribution of goods. Changes in technological and economic systems occur inside the house as much as outside of it. She writes, "The history of housework cannot properly be understood without the history of the implements with which it is done" (1983: 11). As mothers' rates of online participation suggest, the latest implements in care and housework include the screen, network, and social medial platform.

Picking up where Cowan left off, I now consider how digital technology insinuates itself into the work of mothering by focusing on blogs as a digital medium that "support the creativity ... and promote exchanges" of users (van Dijck, 2013: 8). Taking Cowan's argument that every technology brings new forms of social and emotional entanglements, and that technologies occur inside the home as well as outside, I pull apart the overlapping aspects of maternity and blogging and show what draws them together.

Catherine Connors (2006), author of the blog *Her Bad Mother*, captures one such overlap of maternal and digital labor in the following passage:

> One day, during a [G]oogle search on 'extreme baby gas help,' I noticed a <u>link to a page </u>that I hadn't seen before.... Intrigued, I followed that link, and in doing so, tumbled down a virtual rabbit hole, and arrived in the mommy blogosphere. And my life changed.
>
> The page that I had arrived at was <u>Jezer's blog</u>. And the first words of hers that I read, referring to the challenge of a new baby, were, '<u>this gig is hard, dudes</u>.'
>
> I may have gasped audibly. Somebody else knows. SOMEBODY ELSE KNOWS.
>
> In an instant, I realized that I was not alone. I spent the next hour – hours – reading through her wonderful blog, laughing and wincing and nodding and goggling at the pictures of <u>her adorable baby boy.</u> (<u>Go look</u>! You will hyperventilate from the adorableness!) Then I started following her links.... And then I linked to <u>another blog</u>, and <u>another</u>, and <u>another</u>.
>
> I was totally sucked in.

Connors describes a common scene of mothering today: a Google search, clicking on hyperlinks, scrolling, viewing pictures, and, often, finding some sort of social connection ("I realized I was not alone"). This passage illustrates how blogs work as modern-day manuals on how to do motherhood ("Googling"), and how to interpret such work. Today, internet searching and blog reading are possible ways that a mother "meets the demand" of caring for children (Ruddick, 1995: 17). Blogs capture, and then expand, the "alerted sense" (Stewart, 2010: 4) found in childrearing: through blogs we get a bird's-eye view of what it looks and feels like (or, in Connors' words, "somebody else knows") to mother.

Maternal networks

While the work of motherhood is discussed in a realistic manner online ("this gig is hard, dudes"), the work of blogging is conveyed through sentimental rhetoric of the "labor of love." Commenting on posts; liking, sharing, and favorite-ing updates and images; and following certain bloggers or people who post on Twitter or Instagram or other platforms, these are all forms of digital labor and, often, care. And, like feminized labor, such work is mostly unpaid, although it may often be pleasurable (Terranova, 2004, 2012). Through such digital labor, users attune to others and the varied social contexts in which they participate (and in which they are sorted by algorithms). Of course, algorithms most often attune users in pursuit of profit – showing advertisments that are tailored to one's online activity – while mothers, according to the blogs, attune to each other to gain social connections and emotional support (and, although it would be taboo to state explicitly, to gain economic value too).

Terranova (2012: 13) points out, however, that digital media eases the conflation of economic and emotional value production. The "how-to" blog post within the mommy blog genre illustrates this conflation as it ties advice on how to become a blogger to self-help language. By explaining how she got started and why she keeps blogging, bloggers use this theme to also justify their presence online. These posts do not explain the technical details – setting up WordPress categories, creating menus, writing custom code, installing a photo slider – the nuts and bolts of blogging – but instead operate as a vague manual on femininity and feminized labor in digital economies and cultures.

These "how to blog" posts follow a certain trajectory, describing how blogging moved the writer out of stagnant work or emotional conditions and into something more fulfilling. Without fail, such posts warn against harboring fantasies of becoming the next *"dooce"*[2] because, as writers always remind readers, blogging takes an undefined amount and type of work. Success cannot be expected overnight. Such warnings are swiftly canceled out by the "ah shucks" tone of such posts – the blogger claims she innocently, accidentally, became internet famous by being authentic, honest, and true to herself.

Exemplifying the "how-to" theme, Julianna Miner, co-author of the *Rants from Mommyland* blog, wrote a four-part "how-to-blog" series for *Babble* (a parenting website). All four of Miner's posts begin with the self-deprecating disclaimer that she is no expert: "I'm not an expert. I'm a highly distractible, over-wrought moron who has written a blog for a couple of years" (Miner, 2013b); "I have no idea what I'm doing. Take everything I say with a grain of salt" (Miner, 2013a). But the notable success of *Rants from Mommyland* should serve as an indicator that Miner does have an idea what she's doing. While perhaps disingenuous, the "ah-shucks" tone so prevalent in the mommy blogging world serves an important purpose because it extends constructs of feminine non-competitiveness and non-technicality, and it reduces the distance between author and reader, both of which are critical to creating the frame of intimacy necessary for a successful mommy blog. As Lauren Berlant (2008) details, mass-produced feminine culture is marked by appeals to intimacy, especially the intimacy born from shared social subordination. Miner (2013a) utilizes this tone of friendship when describing the positive effects blogging has had on her life:

> So I'm going to be very, very honest and offer some thoughts the way I would if we were friends in real life. Because blogging has been an amazing thing for me. It helped me feel better when I was really unhappy. It helped me build relationships, to rebuild my battered self esteem, and to slowly figure out who I was as a parent and an adult. It forced me to take an honest look at myself. It even gave me a really great part-time job here at Babble.

Not only does blogging remedy Miner's "battered self-esteem," it also provides a "really great part-time job," which, for the majority of American mothers, is the ultimate coup de grâce to the structural challenges facing working parents, and mothers in particular.

Circulating throughout such how-to posts are the following scenarios: The blogger works from home, blogging, tweeting, and posting beautiful images and honest reflections, and is able to pick her kids up from school (if not homeschool them herself). She also has a community of real, online friends (the intimate friendship touted on mommy blogs is an important aspect of the fantasy). The blogger James Kiciniski McCoy (2012) exemplifies this fantasy. In her post titled "Some thoughts on blogging" she justifies her work:

> I have found a way to do two things that i love, stay home and raise my four children and to make money doing something that i love.... i chose this life, to homeschool, to raise a big family and I absolutely love it ... this is my business.

This fantasy of blogging for a living is, to quote Min-Ha T. Pham (2011: 16): "highly compatible with the lifestyle politics of neoliberalism, which emphasizes privatized modes of self-care and self-management, and the optimization of individuals' health, wealth, and happiness through the unregulated digital and global marketplace." Digital platforms such as blogs promise control over one's labor, time, self-esteem, and the home, all vaunted forms of power in societies that, as Berlant (2011: 261) writes, have been forced "to adjust emotionally to the process of living with the political depression produced by brutal relations of ownership, control, security, and their fantasmatic justifications." Part of the work visible on mommy blogs is the attunement necessitated by the confrontation between motherhood and the "brutal" economic realities it faces. Often the reader and blogger attune to such conditions together.

As an example of this shared work of attuning to the inequalities mothers face is a supportive comment left by a reader of the mommy blog titled *But I Do Have a Law Degree...* In the main post, the blogger gives her perspective on why only 4 percent of the top 200 US law firms have "female, firm-wide managing partners" (butidohavealawdegree.com, 2014). The commenter, a former attorney, backs up the blogger's interpretation and shares her reasons for leaving her own career in law:

> After 10 years of practice and a set of twins, I will be a full time mom. And for many of the reasons you discussed, I can't keep pulling myself in two trying to meet the needs of the firm and the needs of my family.
>
> So I'm leaving. And doing what seems to be the trend, starting a blog to talk about why I left and what on earth I'm going to do now. (www.butidohavealawdegree.com/2014/03/why-cant-law-firms-retain-women.html#.VpaPzpMrKRt)

By following the "trend" (starting a blog), the commenter acknowledges her need to adjust to her new condition ("full time mom"). The commenter is creating a place to figure out her next moves. By leaving her URL in the comment field, the commenter invites others over to her blog to discuss.

Mommy bloggers pride themselves on helping out one another online. They practice and emphasize non-competitiveness: a regular feature of the mommy blog is to direct readers to other mommy blogs, which drives up other blogs' "traffic" or page views. In her blog, Katie Allison Granju (2011) describes this practice of linking to other blogs as "how it works" for mommy bloggers: "We depend on one another, and we like it that way." At the very least, bloggers within this genre have, in spades, the skills of the "thank-you economy," creating a system where, as Pham (2013: 252) writes "success will come through outcaring everyone." Through hyperlinks, blog rolls, "like" buttons, retweets, and "h/t" (hat tips), blogging motherhood is a digital network of thank you notes and care work. Terranova (2012: 13) argues that participation online "can become a practice that will be able to produce different forms of subjectivity and different models of what an economy of social cooperation could be like." The proprietary nature of digital platforms, however, creates an obstacle to such economies of cooperation.

Conclusion

In our cultural imagination, mothers' work is imagined as completely opposite of our cultural ideas of technical work. This chapter offers a correction and considers how our cultural understanding of motherhood and the labor it requires parallels our conceptions of digital media and participation therein.

The producers of digital technologies increasingly seek to embed these platforms in all aspects of our lives by incorporating a model of constant attunement into their design and functionality. In other words, digital technologies are rushing to mother us: they attach to our bodies, track our physical activity, calibrate our moods and moments to various products and services, and maintain a basic level of sociality for us. Laura Portwood-Stacer (2014) finds that participation through social media platforms like Facebook run on the "genuine expressions of care" friends provide one another. Despite these digital forms of care and attunement, digital technologies are not turning out to be labor-saving devices. As Cowan found, throughout history new technologies have often created more work and new emotional entanglements. Karen Gregory (2014) notes this increased workload in the form of emails, check-ins, and general digital work; digital media re-distributes this work and, in the process, she argues, creates more "housework and maintenance for our daily lives."

As an artifact of starting with a Google search, this chapter focuses on relatively privileged mothers and bloggers – those who are more able to control their "data," write their own narratives, and freely express the ambivalences of attuning to motherhood. Not every mother has such privilege, digital or otherwise, and more research is needed to address the ways motherhood, data, and digital media constitute each other for less privileged populations. Research investigating how – across different class, racial, ethnic, and sexual populations – digital technologies operate at the household level would further expand our understanding of technology, gender, race, class, and daily life. For example, researchers could consider how digital technologies allow for greater surveillance of social benefits such as food purchases or doctor visits, and how such data is used to determine the so-called good mothers from the bad, justifying further controls and sanctions. Further, the concept of ordinary devotion, or Ruddick's work of preserving the child, remain unavailable to some mothers. As police brutality, racist incarceration systems, and gun-related terror take the lives of children, many mothers and caregivers are unable to engage in the ordinary devotions or daily labors necessary to preserve their children's lives.

Motherhood, as told on the blogs, is embedded in histories of inequalities based on race, class, ethnicity, and geography. My aim, however, is to call attention to the ordinary, unending work of motherhood as a way to highlight the ways that digital platforms and technologies similarly engage users in the work of never-ending attunement. As digital media moves further into our bodies, our intimate lives, or our daily rituals of care, the mother's work of attunement provides a useful model to understand the free labor of care work within capitalist societies.

Notes

[1] In this chapter, I use "digital participation" and "digital labor" interchangeably to refer to the ways users create content for digital media platforms. Digital labor includes such activities as setting up a blog, writing a post, sharing websites, photos, tweets or even just "liking" another person's status. Digital labor also refers to the work of self-presentation (taking, editing, posting selfies, curating links, writing brief bios) on various social media platforms. This chapter is not using digital labor in reference to paid jobs within the technology sector such as programmers, graphic designers, comment moderators, or various behind-the-scene task workers. However, digital media is of interest precisely because it is produced out of both paid labor and the free participation of its users.

[2] Heather Armstrong created the blog "dooce" (dooce.com), which became one of the first mommy blogs as she chronicled her experiences as a mother of two. *The New York Times* referred to her as the "Queen of the mommy bloggers" due to her financial success blogging (see Belkin, 2011).

References

Abreu, A. (2014) "Quantify everything: A dream of a feminist data future." *Model View Culture* (http://modelviewculture.com/pieces/quantify-everything-a-dream-of-a-feminist-data-future).

Belkin, L. (2011) "Queen of the Mommy Bloggers." *The New York Times*, February 23 (www.nytimes.com/2011/02/27/magazine/27armstrong-t.html).

Berlant, L. (2008) *The female complaint: The unfinished business of sentimentality in women's culture.* Durham, NC: Duke University Press.

Berlant, L. (2011) *Cruel optimism.* Durham, NC: Duke University Press.

Boyer, A. (2011) "Anne Boyer on Julia Margaret Cameron's photograph of her grandchild, Archie Cameron, aged two years, three months." *Open Space* (http://openspace.sfmoma.org/2011/09/one-on-one-anne-boyer/).

Clayton, L. (2014a) "About the Artist residency in motherhood" (http://residencyinmotherhood.com/about-the-artist-residency/).

Clayton, L. (2014b) "Objects take out of my son's mouth, 2011–2012" (http://residencyinmotherhood.com/portfolio-item/objects-taken-out-of-my-sons-mouth-2011-2012/).

Clayton, L. (2014c) "The distance I can be from my son" (http://residencyinmotherhood.com/portfolio-item/the-distance-i-can-be-from-my-son/).

Clayton, L. (2014d) "Dangerous objects made safer" (http://residencyinmotherhood.com/portfolio-item/dangerous-objects-made-safe/).

Clayton, L. (2014e) "Maternity leave" (http://residencyinmotherhood.com/portfolio-item/maternity-leave/).

Connors, C. (2009) "Meter Politikon: On the 'politics' of Mommyblogging." In M. Friedman and S. Calixte (eds) *Mothering and blogging: The radical act of the mommyblog* (pp 91–111). Toronto: Demeter Press.

Cowan, R.S. (1983) *More work for mother: The ironies of household technologies from the open hearth to the microwave.* New York: Basic Books.

Dewey, C. (2015) "How moms won the Internet – and what that means for the rest of us." *The Washington Post*, July 16 (www.washingtonpost.com/news/the-intersect/wp/2015/07/16/how-moms-won-the-internet-and-what-that-means-for-the-rest-of-us/).

Frederici, S. (2004) *The Caliban and the witch: Women, the body, and primitive accumulation.* Brooklyn, NY: Autonomedia.

Granju, K.A. (2011) "How much do top "mommy bloggers" earn from their blogs, and is it enough?" *Babble*, March 31 (www.babble.com/mom/how-much-do-top-mommybloggers-earn-from-their-blogs-and-is-it-enough/)

Grant, P. (2012) "Mama, why do you always lose your keys?" *Dash and Bella*, April 19 (http://dashandbella.blogspot.com/2012/04/mama-why-do-you-always-lose-your-keys.html).

Gregory, K. (2013) "Hyperemployment or feminized labor." *Digital Labor Working Group* (https://digitallabor.commons.gc.cuny.edu/2013/11/17/hyperemployed-or-feminized-labor/).

Hayes, S. (1996) The cultural contradictions of motherhood. New Haven: CY. Yale University Press.

McCoy, J.K. (2012) "Some thoughts on blogging." *Bleubird*, December 20 (http://bleubirdblog.com/?s=some+thoughts+on+blogging).

Miner, J. (2013a) "Sorta helpful advice for would be bloggers." *Babble*, March 12 (www.babble.com/babble-voices/rants-in-my-pants-julie-miner/sort-of-helpful-advice-for-would-be-bloggers/).

Miner, J. (2013b) "5 mistakes I made as a new blogger." *Babble*, March 29 (www.babble.com/babble-voices/rants-in-my-pants-julie-miner/5-mistakes-i-made-as-a-new-blogger/).

Mizroch, A. (2015) "Facebook's peace offering to Telcos: Data on mothers." *The Wall Street Journal*, March 16 (http://blogs.wsj.com/digits/2015/03/16/facebooks-peace-offering-to-telcos-data-on-mothers/).

Nelson, M. (2015) *The Argonauts.* Minneapolis, MN: Graywolf Press.

Pew Research Center (2015) with M. Duggan, A. Lenhart, C. Lampe, and N.B. Ellison. "Parents and social media: Mothers are especially likely to give and receive support on social media", July 16, Washington, DC (www.pewinternet.org/2015/07/16/parents-and-social-media/).

Pham, M.-H.T. (2011) "Blog ambition: Fashion, feelings, and the political economy of the digital raced body." *Camera Obscura* 26 (1 76), 1–37.

Pham, M.-H.T. (2013) "'Susie Bubble is a sign of the times.'" *Feminist Media Studies* 13 (2), 245–67.

Portwood-Stacer, L. (2014) "Care work and the stakes of social media refusal" (www.newcriticals.com/care-work-and-the-stakes-of-social-media-refusal).

Ruddick, S. (1995) *Maternal thinking: Toward a politics of peace.* Boston, MA: Beacon Press.

Scarborough (2012) "Blogging moms' influential voice", February 7 (http://dialog.scarborough.com/index.php/blogging-moms-influential-voice/).

Stewart, K. (2010) "Atmospheric attunements." *Rubric* 1, 1–14.

Terranova, T. (2004) *Network culture: Politics for an information age.* London, UK: Pluto Press.

Terranova, T. (2012) "Attention, economy and the brain." *Culture Machine* 13, 1–19 (www.culturemachine.net/index.php/cm/article/view/465/484).

van Dijck, J. (2013) *The culture of connectivity: A critical history of social media.* New York: Oxford University Press.

29

#notracist: Exploring racism denial talk on Twitter

Sanjay Sharma and Phillip Brooker

The study of race online points towards not only extant forms of racism enduring on the internet, but the emergence of new and unique practices (Daniels, 2009; Nakamura and Chow-White, 2012). The development of "Web 2.0" social media and networking platforms such as Twitter, Facebook, Instagram, and YouTube, have expanded user participation and intensified online interactions. The rapid rise of social media *appears* to be proliferating racism and racialized expression (in addition to forms of misogyny and homophobia). While it is difficult to ascertain if social media is responsible for escalating practices of racism (see, for example, Roversi, 2008; Meddaugh and Kay, 2009), it has been central to increasing the visibility and publicness of expressions of racialized discourse.

How may digital sociology approach the study of racism in ever-changing mediated spaces? Les Back and Nirmal Puwar (2013) advance the discussion of a "Live Sociology" by making the important claim that innovations in research methods and developing new, critically reflexive sociological devices, are essential for grasping a digital landscape. Furthermore, Lisa Adkins and Celia Lury (2009) contend that the digitization of everyday life is reconfiguring notions of stability and social structure, meaning and signification, and the changing relations of representation, experience, and understanding. They contend that sociological research is compelled to "break with representational models of the empirical ... and ... confront a newly coordinated reality, one that is open, processual, non-linear and constantly on the move" (2009: 16).

Our contribution to this volume offers an investigation of the phenomenon of racism denial on the micro-blogging Twitter platform in the form of a funded case study, which has a distinctive socio-materialist methodological focus. Twitter has established itself as an influential online communication medium for the dissemination of news and information sharing. Its "real-timeness" and virality of information diffusion have drawn attention to its capacity to intervene in the social world, such as a means of coordinating emergency relief or influencing global political events (Murthy, 2012). Breaking news stories and controversies dominate how Twitter is perceived to operate, leading to issues propagating through its network and beyond, with the capacity to acquire mainstream media status. While a burgeoning body of "Twitter studies" research is emerging, there has been limited research work studying racialized discourse (Bartlett et al, 2014). Little is known about the how modalities of everyday racial expression play out on the Twitter platform, and particularly practices of racism denial.

Our account of Twitter race talk aims to offer a unique intervention, by presenting a methodologically motivated study. Its ambition is to highlight the significance of developing critical race theory vis-à-vis engaging with the technological affordances of digital media. We elaborate an instance of doing digital sociology from an approach that deploys the concept of the *assemblage* (Langlois, 2011; Lupton, 2014) for understanding the constitutive relations between the human (social media users), social phenomena (race and racism), and the non-human (digital technologies and devices). More specifically, the study explores the technocultural practices of Twitter by focusing on use of *hashtag* operators in creating the conditions for the production of racialized meaning.

Hashtags are notable for conveying more than linguistic meaning, as they shape how users interact with the Twitter platform (Zapavigna, 2011; Sharma, 2013). We empirically examine and analyse a relatively large corpus of tweets featuring the #notracist hashtag that formulates one rivulet of the overall Twitter stream of racialized discourse. This hashtag was selected on the basis that it makes apparent expressions of racism denial. Moreover, the affiliative function of the hashtag is considered as means of exploring the "imagined audience" (Marwick and boyd, 2011; Zapavigna, 2015) of users propagating expressions of racism denial.

The first section of the chapter briefly explores the significance of racism denial talk in relation to the shifting nature of the private and public sphere. In a post-civil rights era, the public expression of racism has become increasingly regulated and sanctioned, yet it has given rise to covert forms of racialized expression that seek to deny racist intent (Picca and Feagin, 2007; Bonilla-Silva, 2010). The current understanding of racism denial is limited to "offline" spaces, and it remains an ongoing task to explore distinctive online practices.

The case study research process has not been linear, involving flitting between theory, the filtering and refinement of empirical data, and undertaking a grounded analysis. The second section of the chapter outlines our methodology, focusing on the significance of Twitter hashtags and the Chorus software tool used to undertake the data collection and analyses. A dataset of approximately 25,000 individual Twitter messages (tweets) that included the hashtag #notracist was harvested over a period of time, which formed the basis for analyses. We offer a discussion of how working with Chorus – as a "methodological device" (Lupton, 2014) – formulates a component of a socio-material assemblage in the production of visual analytics of Twitter race talk.

The third section presents a discussion of the data set via Chorus analytics, by highlighting that #notracist is not *about* any specific event or issue as such. Rather, it is characterized by a steady, relatively low-volume of tweet activity, around a wide array of different sub-topics that bubble away on Twitter without ever trending or becoming visible.

In contrast to the majority of event-based Twitter studies, we contend that an alternative approach is required for investigating everyday types of racialized "micro-aggressions," which are not necessarily explicitly visible on social media. Furthermore, our analyses indicate that for the #notracist dataset, *multi*-hashtagging is a key practice in the differentiation of types of Twitter race talk; and distinguishing between modes of racism denial can be achieved praxiologically rather than focusing exclusively on semantic meaning. Our approach seeks to grasp the digital materiality of hashtags, beyond text-based or linguistic-oriented accounts of Twitter talk that ostensibly dominate the emerging field of social media analytics.

The findings and analyses presented here are not exhaustive, and nor do they fully attend to the complexities of racialized expression on social media. Rather, our aim is to offer a modest example of a how a digital sociology of racism can develop an approach that brings together an analyses of technology, language, race, and power (cf Brock, 2012).

Racism denial

An important body of academic research examining internet racism has become established focusing on extreme right-wing/neo-Nazi websites and discourses (Daniels, 2009; Meddaugh and Kay, 2009; Roversi, 2008). While the field of internet research has diversified by exploring other forms and spaces of online racism, in relation to social media and particularly Twitter, there are currently a paucity of relevant studies. The majority of this work has been directed towards investigating forms of racist "hate speech," that includes abuse and insults towards minority groups.

Notably, Twitter is singled out to be the most popular platform for propagating forms of hate speech. For example, a recent study (Kick It Out, 2015), exploring online discourses concerning UK Football, discovered that 88 percent of "discriminatory language" (targeted at football players and clubs) specifically circulates on Twitter, in comparison to other social media platforms. The large-scale study, conducted by Bartlett et al (2014) entitled

"Anti-Social Media" investigated the presence of "hate speech" (in the form of ethnic slurs) on the Twitter platform. It found that that approximately 10,000 English language tweets per day include a slur.[1]

The Demos study also points to challenges of identifying whether changes in modes of communication are responsible for the apparent increase in hate speech. And it highlights that the explosion of online communication enables the researcher to more readily access and examine "public" forms of racism:

> [H]ate speech online ... does appear to be increasing dramatically. This might reflect a change in the way we communicate rather than an increase in the amount of hateful speech taking place: communicating online makes it easier to find and capture instances of hate speech, because the data is often widely available and stored. (Bartlett et al, 2014: 11)

Researching online hate speech is important for gauging visible and public expressions of overt forms of racism. Nonetheless, it does not directly address how phatic, everyday, and more indirect modes of racism are present, and which kinds of (rhetorical) strategies are employed to negotiate the boundaries of acceptable public speech.

The fields of critical discourse analysis, linguistics, and social psychology have developed a body of work that explicates racialized discriminatory language in everyday and institutional public talk (Potter and Wetherell, 1987; Billig, 1988; Augoustinos and Every, 2007). Martha Augoustinos and Danielle Every identify how these types of racialized discourse are invoked:

> ... patterns of talk around race ... can be seen to reflect not only interpretative repertoires, that is, a set of descriptions, arguments, and accounts that are recurrently used in people's race talk to construct versions of the world ... but also discursive resources that perform social actions such as blaming, justifying, rationalising, and constructing particular social identities for speakers and those who are positioned as other. (2007: 125)

Discourse and language analysts have acknowledged the ambiguous and contradictory nature of race talk. The unsettled and shifting meanings of racism have resulted in some analysts refraining from making explicit categorizations and judgments "as to what counts as racist but instead examine whether speakers themselves treat the talk as such and analyse how it is managed and attended to in social interaction" (Augoustinos and Every, 2007: 124–5).

However, rather than merely acknowledging ambiguity and contradiction in race talk, we can consider this kind of linguistic "indeterminacy" as *symptomatic* of contemporary forms of racism in a post-civil rights/"political correctness" era: expressions and practices of racism can be more covert and obfuscated. Moreover, from a sociological standpoint, it is crucial to maintain that racism is not simply a question of individual prejudice or pathology. Expressions of racism – whether overt, covert or contradictory – continue to reinforce racialized hierarchies and power structures in society (Picca and Feagin, 2007).

A post–civil rights era has resulted in the rise of legislation and social regulation against certain forms of racist expression and "hate speech." Direct and explicit racist discourse is less publicly and morally acceptable due to stronger anti-discriminatory social norms. There is an increased public sensitivity towards avoiding inappropriate use of racist language (Goldberg, 2009).

Critical race scholars such as Eduardo Bonilla-Silva (2010) and Leslie Picca and Joe Feagin (2007) maintain that the apparent decline in publicly (that is, offline) overt racist discourse has been substituted with subtler, covert, and coded racialized expressions. This has resulted in more *strategic* forms of public race talk, particularly in relation to practices in the "denial of prejudice" that can pervade everyday racist talk (van Dijk, 1992). Strategies of *denial* can commonly take the form of a *disclaimer*.

> Analysis of post–civil rights racial speech suggests whites rely on 'semantic moves,' or 'strategically managed ... propositions' ... to safely state their views. For instance, most whites use apparent denials ... or other moves in the process of stating their racial views. The moves act as rhetorical shields to save face because whites can always go back to the safety of the disclaimers.... Phrases such as 'I am not a racist' ... have become standard fare.... They act as discursive buffers before or after someone states something that is or could be interpreted as racist. (Bonilla-Silva, 2010: 105)

Picca and Feagin (2007) develop a Goffman-inspired analysis of contemporary racialized expression in terms of identifying differing "frontstage" and "backstage" racial performativity. Rather than overt racist discourse disappearing, its articulation has been mostly consigned to the "private" backstage, generally hidden from public scrutiny. In contrast, the frontstage performativity of covert racist expression can involve "saving face" via public disclaimers. These authors, alongside other scholars such as Nina Eliasoph (1998) and Raúl Pérez (2013), also highlight the defensive role of joke-telling and comedic performances, as a means to continue to express more overt forms of racism in public spaces.

To date, no specific studies examining the practices of *online* racism denial on social media platforms have been conducted. While there is research examining explicit modes of internet racism (see Daniels, 2012), the more coded practices of expressing racist comments, while simultaneously denying racist intent, is far less understood in terms of its online manifestations.

What is of interest is whether offline racism denial strategies are being reproduced on social media, and/or if new online practices are emerging. Do the technological affordances of Twitter facilitate unique modalities of racism denial? Moreover, online communicative practices, to varying degrees, can blur the boundaries between public/private spaces and front/backstage performances (Baym, 2010; Daniels, 2012).

The existing Twitter studies exploring hate speech indicate that some of its users breach normative boundaries of acceptable speech. Somewhat in contrast, as we shall discover in our analyses section, users in our study appear to acknowledge the existence of these boundaries through their use of the "disclaimer" hashtag #notracist. In this respect, it may be the case that different sets of Twitter users hold differing notions of their "imagined audience":

> Given the various ways people can consume and spread tweets, it is virtually impossible for Twitter users to account for their potential audience, let alone actual readers.... Without knowing the audience, [users] imagine it. (Marwick and boyd, 2010: 4)

Before turning to the analyses of our study, we discuss the methodological approach deployed, as this is central to developing a digital sociology that is presented here.

Notes on methodology

Identifying racialized talk (including racism denial) on social media is a challenging task, because there exists a huge array of linguistic terms and repertoires signifying variegated racist expression. These can range from: extreme racist abuse; insults and micro-aggressions; and obfuscated talk in which racism is covert, indirect, or coded. As expressions become less explicitly racist, they become increasingly difficult to identify and interpret by the social researcher. This is particularly the case for expressions of racism denial, because of the deployment of rhetorical and covert language in the act of refuting racist intent (van Dijk, 1992; Picca and Feagin, 2007).

Our initial foray into identifying forms of racism denial on social media resulted in identifying a handful of "anti-racist" sites or accounts which *exposed* individual users' refutation of racism (see Facebook public posts www. notracistbut.com/ and the tumblr site http://imnotaracistbut.tumblr.com/). These indicated the popularity of permutations of the phrase "I'm not racist but" on social media. Variations of this phrase were tested on the Twitter search API, which led to locating the account @yesyoureracist. This account included making visible tweets that denied any racist intent. Examining these collated tweets indicated the sporadic use of the hashtag #notracist within some messages.

Concatenated in the form of the hashtag, it appears that #notracist being included in Twitter messages echoed the "I'm not racist…" strategy of racism denial. Investigating racism denial on Twitter via a hashtag such as #notracist will exclude a whole range of potentially relevant Twitter data that does not include this hashtag. However, our intention was not to undertake an exhaustive study, but rather to focus our efforts by privileging the hashtag as a means to investigate particular practices of racism denial that actively engage with the architecture of the Twitter platform.

Hashtags are a noteworthy phenomenon, because they have multiple uses on Twitter (Zapavigna, 2015). The practice of users attaching a label or "tag" to online content such as a message, document, image, or video has become a central feature of "Web 2.0" social sites. User-based freeform tagging on social media platforms has been principally used for information retrieval and recall, and in this respect, is *a posteriori*. In contrast, tagging within Twitter is primarily *a priori*, as it is commonly used for filtering and promoting messages in real time (Huang et al, 2010).

The hashtag – a single or concatenated term prefixed by the # symbol, for example, #obama or #firstworldproblems – has become publicly synonymous with Twitter, although they feature in less than 15 percent of messages of the whole Twitter stream (Liu et al, 2014). The Twitter platform adopted this user-based "folksonomy" practice by including it in its interface and rendering hashtags as searchable hyperlinks. In particular, popular or trending hashtags are made visible as part of the main Twitter interface (both web and mobile), and can collate hundreds of thousands of disparate tweets, forming a networked sociality and enabling users to participate in collective "conversations." Many studies have focused on hashtags "amplifying" the significance and findability of tweets, and generating "ad hoc publics," often with temporary or shifting boundaries (Bruns and Burgess, 2011; Murthy, 2012).

While the function of hashtags is variegated, they are significant in Twitter as "a form of 'inline' metadata, that is, 'data about data' that is actually integrated into the linguistic structure of the tweets" (Zapavigna, 2011: 791). Hashtags can be deployed to categorize the content of a message as "topic-markers;" and as hashtags are user-created, this "bottom-up" practice of tagging can lead to both redundancy (many hashtags have the same meaning), and ambiguity (a single hashtag has different meanings) (Garcia Esparza et al, 2010). Nevertheless, as discussed by Thomas Vander Wal (2005), (hash-)tagging can be characterized by a "power law" distribution that describes the phenomenon that a few tags are frequently used by many people and in contrast, the majority of the remaining "long tail" of hashtags are infrequently deployed.

Social researchers need to be careful not to circumscribe Twitter hashtags to principally acting as online linguistic operators. One of the limits of privileging language-oriented analyses is that "… text-focused methodologies deal with content in its linguistic and social aspects rather than with the technological or material context that enables the production and circulation of signs" (Langlois, 2011: 9). What is of interest in our study is how the *technocultural* affordances of Twitter are generative of race talk in relation to the use of racialized hashtags. In this respect, it is productive to deploy an alternative account of racialization, which doesn't only dwell on semiotic meaning or the problem of representation.

Conceiving race as a "digital assemblage" – which identifies processes of heterogeneous elements brought into sets of relations with one another – facilitates an understanding of the emergence of racialization in online spaces by exploring how it works and what relations it generates, rather than only the meanings it produces (see Sharma, 2013). This materialist approach of conceiving race (cf Saldanha, 2007) considers the specificities of racism and how it is manifested in online spaces. Thus, specific forms of racism denial can be grasped in terms of how it is formed in relation to a Twitter technocultural assemblage, constituted by the informational logics of hashtags, software interfaces and algorithms, networked relations, racial dis/ordering, and meanings and affects.[2]

The dataset for our study was generated by collecting usages of the #notracist hashtag, searched via Twitter's Search API between March–November 2013. This resulted in harvesting 24,853 tweets over the eight-month time period.[3] The period was determined by the constraints of the length of the funded research project, and based on monitoring whether further harvesting led to data redundancy for the purposes of our analyses.

The empirical analyses of the dataset were developed through a visual analytic approach (Card et al, 1999). This methodology has its origins in the fields of information and computer science and has informed the development of Chorus,[4] a software suite capable of collecting and visually parsing Twitter data. Chorus was deployed for generating the #notracist dataset and assisting in its analysis. The primary tenet of visual analytics is that visualizations should serve some functional purpose; as opposed to being merely images and outputs, visual analytic representations are dynamic and interactive research tools. In our case, Chorus was initially used to identify the frequency of the appearance of the #notracist hashtag over the specified time period, and subsequently, to visualize the relationship between terms (that is, other related hashtags) in the #notracist data set.

We are aware of the technological affordances of Chorus – it is not merely a method or tool for analysing a large corpus of Twitter data, because it governs what we perceive is possible to do with this type of analytic approach. Chorus is a "methodological device" (Lupton, 2014) that connects together both method (as technique) and the research object (hashtags). The data visualizations produced by Chorus is a key step in studying the #notracist dataset. Moreover, understanding *how* the software produces these visualizations is crucial towards developing a meaningful analysis. Thus, Chorus constitutes an element involved in the production of a Twitter assemblage that activates an analysis of racialized hashtags. While the technical work of processing this type of

Twitter data is accomplished by Chorus, a methodological understanding of the workings of those processes and algorithms is necessary for explicating what is observed in that data, and how it may be interpreted (see Brooker et al, 2015).

#notracist: hashtagging racism denial

An initial exploration of the #notracist data set via the timeline graph (see Figure 29.1) generated by the Chorus software, indicated that the most useful reading of the data would not come from considering it as having a meaningful temporal dimension as a basis for analyses – little within this data is found to change across time. Figure 29.1 presents a sporadic and diverse data set with few (if any) distinguishing features in terms of how the volume of usages of *#notracist* fluctuates over time.[5]

Figure 29.1: Timeline graph of the #notracist data set

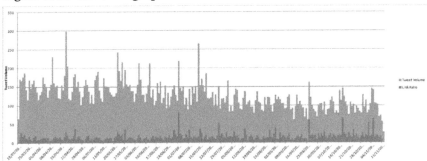

Note: The grey bar chart shows tweet frequency in daily intervals (with the dark gray bar showing proportion of tweets containing an URL link)

To give a sense of how voluminous the #notracist talk is on a day-by-day basis, it averaged out at slightly over 100 tweets per day, with the least populated day in our data consisting of 36 tweets and the most populated day featuring 239 tweets. There is little in the data set indicating that #notracist captures a *topic* in a conventional sense, that is, a visible issue or one that inspires significant discussion between Twitter users around some focal event (such as the publication of a news report or the broadcast of a TV show).

The content of the tweets in the data set exhibit a wide variety of everyday commentary that appears difficult to organize into a meaningful schema. Nonetheless, they share a commonality in the use of the #notracist hashtag as a disclaimer that has a "distancing function" (van Dijk, 1992) from accusations of racism. The inclusion of the hashtag exhibits practices of "interpersonal punctuation", which is declarative of a user's "stance" (Zapavigna, 2011).

Individual users deliberately punctuate their tweet indicating their supposed "non-racist" disposition. For example:[6]

> *MikepFennyy*: finally got a new boss today. Hes under 50 good guy has social skills totally white with zero accent. I am so pleased #notracist

> *rellavent*: I Hate Basketball and Rap Music. #notracist

> *Brodyrey22*: If its not white its not right #notracist

These tweets are exemplary for highlighting the diversity of banal racialized "content" of the data set. It is interesting to observe that in the #notracist dataset the majority of users do not have large numbers of followers, and rarely are messages with the hashtag re-tweeted.

It is difficult to ascertain the "imagined audience" of these users when deploying #notracist. Nonetheless, in addition to expressing a defensive stance, the inclusion of the hashtag suggests an *affiliative* mode of communication. The interpersonal function of the #notracist hashtag may invoke "... the notion that there are people who feel the same way as the microblogger ... regardless of the fact that it is unlikely that anyone would ever use the tag as a search term" (Zapavigna, 2015: 18). While the #notracist hashtag does not appear to beget direct interactions between users, its deployment intimates a shared predilection of racism denial.

In contrast to explicit racist tweeting that can gain social media visibility via high frequency re-tweeting and/or @mention conversations,[7] the #notracist data set lacks such traction; #notracist tweeting generally occurs in isolation without any noteworthy presence. We can speculate that the #notracist hashtag is indicative of a social media racism that follows a power law distribution, that is, a racism of the "long tail." What are usually witnessed as social media racism are those events that have gained significant traction and visibility.

Arguably, there also exist many more racist micro-events that are ostensibly inconsequential due to their "invisibility" – for example, as background chatter – yet are symptomatic of forms of everyday online racialized micro-aggressions (cf Sue, 2010). Conceptualizing a racism of the "long tail" via the hashtag highlights #notracist as an element of a Twitter-racialized assemblage: aggregating (connecting) what appears to be spontaneously occurring individual race talk that materializes seemingly coherent yet diverse practices of the denial of racist expression.

The significance of the hashtag in relation to a Twitter assemblage can be further elaborated in terms of how it functions alongside other (non-racialized) multiple hashtags in the #notracist data set, which is where our attention turns in the discussion below.

Visualising multi-hashtags: "truth" and "humor"

The timeline visualization points to a data set that is not significantly event-based. As such, our analytic efforts were directed towards the exploration of "topics" consisting of aggregations of terms that are more commonly used together. Thus, an alternative line of inquiry was pursued using Chorus' *Cluster Explorer* modeling, which builds sets of visualizations to represent and facilitate navigation around "topical" clusters. These models plot the relationships of terms (which can be words or other fields such as hashtags) as they are used together in tweets, where a relationship signifies the commonality, that is, the *co-occurrence* of the usage of one term with another in a tweet (cf Callon, 1983; Danowski, 2009; Marres and Gerlitz, 2015). A cluster map is built up from direct and indirect relations of terms that allows a spatial mapping algorithm to plot the relationship of one term to another as a function of distance (where the closer a term is to another term, the more strongly it is related).

In clustering together strongly related sets of terms – for example, the likelihood that two hashtags are co-occurring within a tweet – Chorus provides a method of identifying and mapping distinct topics and their interrelations (without relying on *a priori* categories defined by the researcher).[8] This kind of visual parsing of the #notracist dataset by the software is only one step towards an analysis. Chorus is not able to discern the sociological significance and meanings of the relations between terms it visualizes. Nevertheless, it is important to grasp how a cluster map is produced, as it influences the trajectory of a deeper exploration of the data set.

For the #notracist data set, aside from the original #notracist term there were a further 7,717 hashtags in use. That is, approximately 30 percent of the entire data set consisted of more than one hashtag being included (along with #notracist), which is remarkable as multiple-hashtagging is not a common practice in Twitter (Liu et al, 2014). The following examples of tweets illustrate practices of multi-hashtagging in #notracist data set:

> *helen_louise_*: I literally cant stop eating watermelon. and Im not even black. #notracist #JustSaying

> *PaneKilla*: How to say the alphabet in vietnamese #funny #notracist #accent #alphabet #vietnamese #peace #lol http://instagram.com/p/**********/

Given our original search query, which aimed to find usages of a specific hashtag, we plotted a model that used hashtags as "nodes" in the *Cluster Explorer* map (see Figure 29.2).

Figure 29.2: Cluster map showing the topical relationships between all hashtags within the #notracist dataset (not including #notracist)

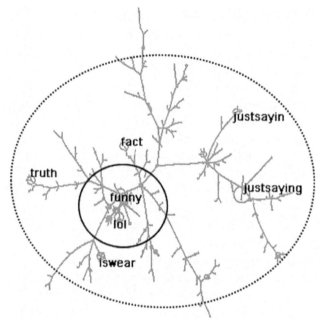

Note: Labels are given to hashtags that feature in >1% of tweets.

This visualization indicates a topical cluster map of multi-hashtags occurring with #notracist (each node being a different hashtag). Immediately observable in Figure 29.2 is a tight central cluster of hashtags (including #funny and #lol), which are closely related to each other and demarcated in the inner (solid line) radial. There are also a number of significantly populated nodes that feature on the outer branches extending from this central cluster (including #truth, #iswear, #fact, #justsayin/g), often appearing on the end of branches – located in the outer (dotted line) radial.[9]

The difference between the two radials is significant in as much they illustrate different tweeting practices. The operational tendency of the Chorus clustering algorithm is to plot all the highly populated nodes towards the center of the map so as to make room for less connected outliers around the edge of the map; we do not see this occurring.

Picking through the most frequently populated nodes in either radial, we find a thematic difference between the radials as identified by two distinct "categories," which supplements and coincides with their algorithmic difference. First, the inner radial consists largely of "humor" hashtags that are intended by tweeters to mark tweet content as containing jokes or other comedic material. Second, the most frequently occurring hashtags in the outer radial form a category of "truth" hashtags, which tweeters use to clarify or qualify their tweet statements by referring to them as so-called observations and facts. The "humor" and "truth" categories are inductively derived from the cluster map of Figure 29.2, which the radials reveal more clearly.

Table 29.1: "Humor" and "truth" categories of hashtags and the frequencies of co-occurrence with #notracist

"Humor" tags (inner radial)		"Truth" tags (outer radial)	
Hashtag	Frequency	Hashtag	Frequency
#funny	191	#justsaying	304
#lol	182	#truth	168
#justfunny	96	#fact	162
#comedy	85	#justsayin	129
#loop	77	#justtrue	46
#joke	50	#justhonest	42
#howto	39	#justfacts	35
#justajoke	39	#justafact	31
#justkidding	34	#thetruth	30
#haha	32	#itstrue	30
#lmao	31	#truestory	28
#remake	31	#observation	27
#hilarious	29	#facts	24
#maybealittle	29	#honest	23
#jokes	27	#justthetruth	23
#awkward	22	#realtalk	22
#vine	21	#justfact	20

Table 29.1 offers a means of continuing the analysis and drilling down towards further insights about hashtagged racialized talk in relation to a more nuanced grasp of what each of the two categories ("humor" and "truth" hashtags) consist of. Table 29.1 identifies other hashtags co-occurring with #notracist, which are judged as significant in the formation of the "humor" and "truth" categories throughout the dataset.[10] At this stage of the analyses, it is productive to briefly turn our attention to the word content of tweets (rather than only hashtags as visualized in Figure 29.2).

Table 29.2: Top "humor" terms within the #notracist data set

"Humor" top terms (1,131 tweets, 1,884 terms)	
Term	Frequency
Black	285
People	144
White	138
Like	75
Just	48
Guy	47
Don't	44
Asian	37
Lol	36
Racist	36

Table 29.3: Top "truth" terms within the #notracist dataset

"Truth" top terms (1,347 tweets, 2,417 terms)	
Term	Frequency
Black	474
People	280
White	241
Like	129
Just	95
Asian	72
Know	57
Guy	55
Think	51
Asians	47

Tables 29.2 and 29.3 reveal that the two categories "humor" and "truth" share (loosely) a "dictionary" – a palette of seemingly common terms used in tweets as a way of doing racism-denial Twitter talk. There are a number of key terms (words) which frequently appear in *both* "humor" and "truth" tweets, such as: "black," "white," "people," "like," and "just."[11] It seems improbable that there will be a linguistic or semantic means of consistently distinguishing between either category, for example:

> Tegan_Molly001: Black girls vs white girls in the club #lol #comedy #notracist #funny https://t.co/★★★★★★★★★

> LENNYSGUY: THE HARLEM SHAKE IS A BLACK THING. THAT WHITE GIRL ASIAN GIRL HARLEM SHAKE BULLSHIT IS WEAK. #JUSTSAYING #notracist

Both of the tweets above, despite being located in different categories, use the key terms "black" and "white," and are substantively about comparable topics – differentiating between black and white people based on stereotypes of how they dance. Hence, it is difficult to see how words alone – without *multi*-hashtags as "topic-markers" (Zapavigna, 2015) – may provide a way of distinguishing which tweets are intended as "jokes" and which are intended as "factual" statements.

A key question at this point is: what do these mappings say about the way people communicate race-denial content with hashtags on Twitter, given that both "humor" and "truth" categories draw on a broadly similar set of words? Arguably, analyses so far indicate that both categories are generated by user hashtag tweeting *practices* rather than only the literal content of their tweeting. It is useful to explore these practices more qualitatively by using Chorus to reduce the data set – via filtering relevant tweets – to continue the investigation.

A distinguishing feature between the "humor" and "truth" categories is in the usage of hashtags to achieve different purposes. To demonstrate how this is visible in the data, we note that the majority of tweets featuring a "humor" multi-hashtag *also* feature an URL link that has an additional function of embellishing the message, for example:

KokoBugz: RT @AlanCaravaggio: How white people react to black athletes #funny #revine #loop #notracist #VineStar https://t.co/WG★★★★★★

KoryBoolet: #whitepeopleproblems #howto #remake #notracist #comedy #funny #cute #magic #loop #unPOP #see #drivingvine https://t.co/ZX★★★★★★★★

It appears that "humor" hashtag usage promotes or *shares* an internet object of some kind – typically a Vine video or Instagram picture[12] – and the utilization of multiple hashtags seemingly maximizes the visibility of the link. The linking (or inclusion) of visual media is a common practice among internet users in the sharing of online humor (Shifman and Blondheim, 2010). Moreover, the juxtaposition of these kinds of humor hashtags alongside #notracist can potentially mutate both sets of hashtags: the "humor" hashtags become racially charged, and the #notracist hashtag acquires greater *affiliative* characteristics to construct an "imagined audience."

The "humor" category is remarkable for the sheer number of multiple hashtags included in a tweet, and the hashtags themselves (alongside possible links) can become the primary "meaning" (content) of the message. While the content of some of these tweets is difficult to interpret due to both a lack of meaning- and content-carrying words and an abundance of hashtags, Shawna Ross (no date: 5) intimates: "as a tweet asymptotically approaches contentlessness, the resultant tendency toward abstraction denotes increasing (not decreasing) sophistication."

Notably, there are a small set of "humor" multi-hashtags such as #lol, #haha and #loop[13] that are frequently used together (thus producing the central cluster observable in the hashtag map of Figure 29.2). The significance of these "humor" multi-hashtags can be further explored in relation to their co-occurrence. As indicated in Table 29.4 below, there is a high degree of coherence with which certain key "humor" hashtags co-occur, such as #loop and #comedy. For example, #loop features in slightly over 50 percent of tweets that also feature #funny.[14] Additionally, these types of tweets pertain

Table 29.4: Top hashtag co-occurrences with #funny, showing the strength of relationship between #funny and hashtags to which it is most related

Hashtag co-occurrences with *#funny*	
Multi-hashtag	**Co-occurrence value**
#loop	0.506
#comedy	0.456
#howto	0.282
#magic	0.257
#joke	0.217
#lol	0.207

to objects not residing within Twitter such as Vine videos.

"Humor" as a type of racialized talk relies on an implicitly-agreed-on – seemingly *a priori* – set of general classificatory hashtags that users recognize and draw on in order to situate their tweets as embodying racialized humor (and not, they may hope, actual racist intent). This practice of humor-based multi-hashtagging does not necessarily seek to explain the meaning of the tweet, because the hashtags themselves – as dense, self-referential meta-data (Ross, no date) – *are* the tweet.[15]

The circulation of humor on the web has become a "ritualized social practice" (cf Pérez, 2013), and users of social media are well versed in its discursive conventions. The use of a relatively narrow set of multi-hashtags and inclusion of links suggest that the circulation of racist texts (tweets, images, videos etc) is an *intensely* collective enterprise. The invoked "imagined audience" *shares* the joke and participates in a racialized online culture that breaches social norms. While the distancing function of the disclaimer #notracist is present, its imbrication with humor complicates and legitimizes strategies of racism denial, and makes them more resistant to critique because of the collectivizing function of jokes via their public sharing.

In comparison, in the "truth" subset of the data we discover a tendency to use multi-hashtags much more sparingly, although from a much wider range of hashtag terms, and in ways that are intended to clarify or qualify the semantic content of tweets, for example:

J3N5TT3R: Asian guys only have two volumes, quiet and shout. The ones on the next table are stuck on shout #notracist #fact

christophe1435: This economics tutorial is like 95% Asian. #notracist #truth

Here, the usage of hashtags reflects a more semantic orientation to the convention, where hashtags indicate how the tweeter intends the tweet to be interpreted – their "stance," for example – as not representing any racist intent (for example, #notracist), and *justifying* this disaffiliation with racism because the tweeter is stating what they argue is a defensible or observable everyday truth (for example, #justsayin/g). Unlike the small set of general hashtags that are frequently used in "humor" tweets alongside other multi-hashtags, "truth" tweets rely on a broad range of multi-hashtags that *do not co-occur* with other multi-hashtags for at least two reasons. First, these multi-hashtags tend not to be used with other hashtags, and second, each tag tends to be used relatively few times. This gives the "truth" cluster map (Figure 29.2) its distinctive outer-density pattern – the wide variety of largely non-associated terms appears almost entirely disconnected (and unrelated) from each other.

It is fruitful to question why "truth" as a mode of online racialized talk of denial relies on a diverse array of largely single-use hashtags, in comparison to "humor" that draws on a relatively narrow set of hashtags that are used multiple times in tweets. The shared culture of online humor suggests that the circulation of racist texts need not require an explicit justification (for example, #justjoking), and because for the user, the "imagined audience" can be a "real" one that shares the joke.

In contrast, "truth"-based statements include hashtags that attempt to make explicit their semantic intentions (however misplaced or ignorant). These hashtags are largely devoid of a shared online culture (apart from the possibility of #justsayin/g). As Zapavigna notes, "The inline nature of #tag usage opens up the possibility of play with users creating tags that are unlikely to be used as search terms and which instead seem to function to intensify the evaluation made in the tweet" (2011: 800). This strategy of intensifying a user's stance via adding another truth-type hashtag seeks to contain the ambiguity of racialized meanings, and legitimize the possible breaching of the backstage of privatized racism (cf Picca and Feagin, 2007; Bonilla-Silva 2010). Yet, as indicated by the creation of many singular truth-type hashtags, this practice is a fraught activity. The proliferation of different "truth"-based justificatory hashtags is symptomatic of the dissonant registers of how race denial is mobilized in everyday online discourse, in which the "imagined audience" in the final instance remains largely unknown.

In summary, although the two categories, "humor" and "truth" share a lexicon – which is remarkable given how little people appear to communicate with each other in the data set – the variations observed in the visualizations lie in the markedly different hashtagging practices that tweets in each category display. Where "humor" tweets use many multi-hashtags for propagation and dissemination of tweet (and often URL link) content, "truth" tweets use singular multi-hashtags (that is, #notracist plus one other hashtag) in order to rhetorically clarify a potentially or purposefully ambiguous statement. Both types of tweeting practices are modulated by a racialized digital assemblage.

The "master"-hashtag #notracist organizes and racially charges other hashtags in so far as activating differential modes of racialization. In this respect, race is not simply inscribed in Twitter messages, nor can it readily de-code their meanings. Rather, modes of racialization emerge within and across tweets through the aberrant connections elicited by multi-hashtagging practices. It is the variation of these different hashtagging practices that may distinguish between the type of racialized talk being published to Twitter, such that although the tweets themselves can broadly consist of similar terms and semantic meanings, the adoption of hashtagging practices from one category or another can change the affective meaning sufficiently to situate that tweet as joke-telling and/or truth-telling. Hence, we find that racialized hashtagging on Twitter is, as a phenomenon, not solely located in the words used by individuals, but in the evaluation of words by way of hashtagging – a technocultural practice within Twitter that is influenced by societal modes of racism denial.

Discussion

In this chapter we have advanced a research process for examining an intriguing type of racially charged social media data that is not structured temporally, but rather by an ambiguous "topicality." We explored the potential of "non-event based" modes of analysis for investigating racialized hashtagging as a practice, working to exploit the affiliative aspects of social media data, and offering sociological insights into one of society's fundamental concerns: race and racism.

The empirical findings of this study point to online strategies of racism denial being complex and diverse. In this respect, they resonate with the offline world – after all, racism is a social phenomena that has existed long before the advent of the internet – although from the methodological standpoint of our approach, can only be adequately grasped by taking into account the technological affordances of the medium they circulate in. Otherwise, we are liable to simply import existing understanding of racism denial and fail to comprehend that online modes of communication are mutating practices of racism.

The project has relied on Chorus, a software suite for collecting and producing a range of visualizations of Twitter data. Our methodological approach has avoided fetishizing visualizations or treating them as the end point of analysis. The endeavor has been to *think with* visualizations as part of an analytic process – *deploying* visualizations rather than merely viewing them. Furthermore, we have grounded our analyses in our acknowledgement of the limitations and constraints of the software. Our socio-materialist approach has been a creative process involving intuitive insight and critical reflexivity, in addition to acquiring knowledge of the workings of visualization and co-occurrence algorithms.

We have treated this research dually as a methodological enterprise and as an empirical project that informs conceptual ideas about online racism, beyond existing linguistic and text-based approaches. Our study responds to the question "What kind of technocultural assemblage is put into motion when we express ourselves online?" (Langlois, 2011) by exploring how modes of racialization modulate and are modulated by the Twitter social media platform. We discovered that variegated informational logics and multi-hashtagging practices materialize online racialized discourse.

The study aimed to develop an original account of Twitter race talk that demonstrates how hashtags work for users. This has been achieved by analysing multi-hashtagging by focusing on what purposes the practice of deploying more than one hashtag (that is, #notracist plus one or more hashtag) might hold for those doing it. The resulting data visualizations and analyses suggest two principal modes of multi-hashtag usage. These modes are distinguished by their different methods of doing hashtagging. Moreover, the two multi-hashtagging practices of "humor" and "truth" closely correlate to a complex, racially charged "topical" distinction.

Deploying visualizations and interrogating algorithmic data processes – and our consequent depiction of the process of *doing* this work – is not trivial or irrelevant to sociology's program. Rather, it reveals how such processes may come to make digital sociology a feasible and fruitful task for social research.

Acknowledgements

We thank the British Academy/Leverhulme Small Grant Research (2012–13) for funding this research project. Chorus development was supported in part through the MATCH Programme (UK EPSRC grants GR/S29874/01, EP/F063822/1 and EP/G012393/1).

Notes

[1] Although the Demos study discovered that some slurs are used in a non-derogatory manner aimed at a sender's own community.

[2] It is beyond the scope of this chapter to explore the how radicalized hashtags are produced within Twitter in relation to its *range* of technocultural assemblages (that is, as part of a wider

sphere of internet activity involving other social media services, online video, or audio clips web browsers and URLs, and so on, all of which may feature).

[3] We do not claim to have captured a *complete* data set of all tweets containing the #notracist hashtag during the time period, because collecting data from the Twitter Search API is rate-limited (number of search requests per 15 minute interval). Nonetheless, as the frequency of #notracist tweets were relatively low, it is likely we captured a comprehensive set of tweets.

[4] See the Chorus project website for further details and to download the software: www. chorusanalytics.co.uk

[5] Our intention in introducing the timeline graph is to demonstrate how this visualization facilitated the decision to pursue other modes of analysis.

[6] All tweets have been anonymized, both in terms of their user names and the tweet content itself. Where URLs feature in tweets, key identifying characters are changed to "★".

[7] The single significant display of communication – where the @mention convention (boyd et al, 2010) is used to directly address other Twitter users – is visible in some Twitter users re-tweeting messages considered as containing racist content to the account @YesYoureRacist. This account publishes tweets that claim to be not racist yet appear to feature a racist statement of some kind.

[8] Noortje Marres and Caroline Gerlitz (2015: 9) offer an important discussion of how digital sociology methodologies are innovating forms of co-occurrence/word analyses that render "text amenable to network analysis, whereby empirically occurring associations among words in a given data set provide an immanent criterion of relevance." See also the work of Roberto Franzosi (2010) for developing inductively orientated quantitative textual analyses of large data sets.

[9] As an aid to analyse the cluster map of Figure 29.2, the two radials have been added to the Chorus visualization by the researchers.

[10] Table 29.1 explores each radial in turn, noting key hashtags down to a minimum frequency of 20 usages.

[11] Common usage terms such as "like" and "just" have been included in the data set to indicate their relative frequency in relation other more charged terms such as "black" and "white." As the research focus was not on analysing the content of tweets, only a limited "stop-list" of common words was used in the analysis (that exclude terms such as "a," "the," "and" etc).

[12] It is interesting to note the multimodality of social media and internet usage for Twitter users, which features as part of the creation of their own internet assemblages as part of a broader field of activity: Twitter users do not *just* use Twitter to do their tweeting. It was not within the scope of the research project investigate the content of URL (links) within tweets.

[13] #loop refers specifically to videos posted on Vine, which are six seconds long and indefinitely looped such that they repeat until the viewer moves on to the next one or closes the browser/app.

[14] Chorus computes collocations of terms, with co-occurrence values from 0 to 1 based on the relative frequency with which those words occur together in single tweets. The co-occurrence value is the probability, local to the dataset, of finding two terms occurring together in a tweet (where 0 equates to zero probability and 1 signifies absolute certainty).

[15] To make such a claim does not beget an analysis exploring the meaning of humor-based tweets. Rather, it points to "meaning" being located in the hashtags, and only exploring these operators semantically is a limited mode of analysis of a Twitter racialized assemblage.

References

Adkins, L. and C. Lury (2009) "Introduction: What Is the empirical?" *European Journal of Social Theory* 12 (1), 5–20.

Augoustinos, M. and D. Every (2007) "The language of 'race' and prejudice: A discourse of denial, reason, and liberal-practical politics." *Journal of Language and Social Psychology* 26 (2), 123–41.

Back, L. and N. Puwar (2013) "A manifesto for live methods: provocations and capacities." In L. Back and N. Puwar (eds) *Live methods.* Oxford, UK: Wiley-Blackwell.

Bartlett, J., Reffin, J., Rumball, N. and Williamson, S. (2014) *Anti-social media.* London, UK: Demos (www.demos.co.uk/files/DEMOS_Anti-social_Media.pdf?1391774638).

Baym, N.K. (2010) *Personal connections in the digital age.* Oxford, UK: Polity.

Billig, M. (1988) "The notion of 'prejudice': Some rhetorical and ideological aspects." *Text* 8, 91–110.

Bonilla-Silva, E. (2010) *Racism without racists: Color-blind racism and the persistence of racial inequality in the United States.* Lanham, MD: Rowman & Littlefield.

boyd, d. S. Golder, and G. Lotan (2010) "Tweet, tweet, retweet: Conversational aspects of retweeting on Twitter." *System Sciences (HICSS), 2010 43rd Hawaii International Conference,* pp 1–10.

Brock, A. (2012) "From the blackhand side: Twitter as a cultural conversation." *Journal of Broadcasting and Electronic Media* 56 (4), 529–49.

Brooker, P., J. Barnett, T. Cribbin, and S. Sharma (2015) "Have we even solved the first 'big data challenge'? Practical issues concerning data collection and visual representation for social media analytics." In H. Snee, C. Hine, Y. Morey, S. Roberts, and H. Watson (eds) *Digital methods for social sciences: An interdisciplinary guide to research innovation.* Basingstoke, UK: Palgrave Macmillan.

Bruns, A. and J.E. Burgess (2011) "The use of Twitter hashtags in the formation of ad hoc publics" (http://eprints.qut.edu.au/46515).

Card, S., J. Mackinlay, and B. Shneiderman (1999) *Readings in information visualisation: Using vision to think.* London, UK: Morgan Kaufmann.

Callon, M., J.P. Courtial, W.A. Turner, and S. Bauin (1983) "From translations to problematic networks: An introduction to co-word analysis." *Social Science Information* 22 (2), 191–235.

Daniels, J. (2009) Cyber *racism: White supremacy online and the new attack on civil rights.* Lanham, MD: Rowman & Littlefield.

Daniels, J. (2012) "Race and racism in Internet Studies: A review and critique." *New Media and Society,* 15 (5), 695–719.

Danowski, J.A. (2009) "Inferences from word networks in messages." In K. Krippendorff and M.A. Bock (eds) *The content analysis reader* (pp 421-9). London, UK: Sage.

Eliasoph, N. (1998) *Avoiding politics: How Americans produce apathy in everyday life.* Cambridge, UK: Cambridge University Press.

Franzosi, R. (2010) *Quantitative narrative analysis.* London, UK: Sage.

Garcia Esparza, S., M.P. O'Mahony, and B. Smyth (2010) "Towards tagging and categorization for micro-blogs" (http://irserver.ucd.ie/handle/10197/2517).

Goldberg, D.T. (2009) *The threat of race: Reflections on neoliberalism*. Oxford, UK: Wiley-Blackwell.

Huang, Y., C. Basu, and M.K. Hsu (2010) "Exploring motivations of travel knowledge sharing on social network sites: An empirical investigation of US college students." *Journal of Hospitality Marketing and Management* 19 (7), 717–34.

Kick It Out (2015) *Case study: Kick It Out*, April (www.kickitout.org/kick-it-out-unveils-findings-of-research-into-football-related-hate-crime-on-social-media/).

Langlois, G. (2011) "Meaning, semiotechnologies and participatory media." *Culture Machine* 12, 1–27 (www.culturemachine.net/index.php/cm/article/viewDownloadInterstitial/437/467).

Liu, Y., C. Kliman-Silver, and A. Mislove (2014) *The Tweets they are a-changin': Evolution of Twitter users and behavior*. AAAI Publications, Eighth International AAAI Conference on Weblogs and Social Media (www.aaai.org/ocs/index.php/ICWSM/ICWSM14/paper/view/8043/8131).

Lupton, D. (2014) *Digital sociology*. London, UK: Routledge.

Marres, N. and C. Gerlitz (2015) "Interface methods: renegotiating relations between digital social research, STS and sociology." *The Sociological Review* (http://dx.doi.org/10.1111/1467-954X.12314).

Marwick, A.E. and d. boyd (2010) "I Tweet honestly, I Tweet passionately: Twitter users, context collapse, and the imagined audience." *New Media and Society* 13 (1), 114–33.

Meddaugh, P.M. and J. Kay (2009) "Hate speech or 'reasonable racism?' The Other in Stormfront." *Journal of Mass Media Ethics: Exploring Questions of Media Morality*, 24, 4.

Murthy, D. (2012) *Twitter: Social communication in the Twitter age*. Cambridge, UK: Polity.

Nakamura, L. and P. Chow-White (eds) (2012) *Race after the internet*. London, UK: Routledge.

Pérez, R. (2013) "Learning to make racism funny in the 'color-blind' era: Stand-up comedy students, performance strategies, and the (re)production of racist jokes in public." *Discourse Society* 24, 478–503.

Potter, J. and M. Wetherell (1987) *Discourse and social psychology: Beyond attitudes and behaviour*. Newbury Park, CA: Sage.

Roversi, A. (2008) *Hate on the net – Extremist sites, neo-fascism online, electronic Jihad*. Aldershot, UK: Ashgate.

Ross, S. (no date) "Hashtags, algorithmic compression, and Henry James's late style (Draft)" (www.academia.edu/attachments/30315675/download_file).

Picca, L.H. and J.R. Feagin (2007) *Two-faced racism: Whites in the backstage and frontstage*. London, UK: Routledge.

Saldanha, A. (2007) *Psychedelic white: Goa trance and the viscosity of race*. London, UK: University of Minnesota Press.

Shifman, L. and M. Blondheim (2010) "The medium is the joke: Online humor about and by networked computers." *New Media and Society* 12(8), 1348–67.

Sue, D.W. (2010) *Microaggressions in everyday life: Race, gender, and sexual orientation.* New Jersey: John Wiley & Sons.

Vander Wal, T. (2005) "Explaining and showing broad and narrow folksonomies" (www.vanderwal.net/random/entrysel.php?blog=1635).

van Dijk, T.A. (1992) "Discourse and the denial of racism." *Discourse and Society* 3 (1), 87–118.

Zapavigna, M. (2011) "Ambient affiliation: A linguistic perspective on Twitter." *New Media and Society* 13 (5), 788–806.

Zappavigna, M. (2015) "Searchable talk: the linguistic functions of hashtags." *Social Semiotics* 25 (3), 274–91

Index

Note: page numbers followed by 'n' refer to notes.